Ethics and Politics
Cases and Comments

Third Edition

Ethics and Politics
Cases and Comments

Third Edition

Edited by

Amy Gutmann

PRINCETON UNIVERSITY

and

Dennis Thompson

HARVARD UNIVERSITY

WADSWORTH

™

THOMSON LEARNING

Australia • Canada • Mexico • Singapore • Spain • United Kingdom • United States

Project Editor: Dorothy Anderson
Typesetter: Precision Typographers

Wadsworth Group/Thomson Learning
10 Davis Drive
Belmont CA 94002-3098
USA

For information about our products, contact us:
Thomson Learning Academic Resource Center
1-800-423-0563
http://www.wadsworth.com

For permission to use material from this text, contact us by
Web: http://www.thomsonrights.com
Fax: 1-800-730-2215
Phone: 1-800-730-2214

Printed in the United States of America
10 9 8 7 6 5 4

Library of Congress Cataloging-in-Publication Data

Ethics and politics : cases and comments / edited by Amy Gutmann and
    Dennis Thompson. — 3rd ed.
        p.   cm.
    Includes bibliographical references.
    ISBN 0-8304-1477-0
    1. Political ethics—Case studies.   I. Gutmann, Amy.
II. Thompson, Dennis F. (Dennis Frank), 1940–
JA79.E823   1997
172—dc21   97-2273
                                                        CIP

Contents

Part Two: The Ethics of Policy

Acknowledgments

This book grew out of courses we have taught at Princeton and Harvard. We are grateful to our students who helped us recognize the importance of cases in understanding political ethics and who helped us choose (and in some instances write) the cases we present here. For able and creative research assistance, we are indebted to Mike Comiskey, Ted Aaberg, and Michael McNally. Donald E. Stokes, then Dean of the Woodrow Wilson School at Princeton, encouraged this project from the beginning, and we are grateful to him and to the School for their support. We also appreciate the contributions of Peter Zimmerman, Howard Husock and the staff of the Case Program at the Kennedy School of Government at Harvard. Simone Sandy skillfully managed the process of the revision for the third edition.

Introduction

Dean Acheson, secretary of state under President Truman, described the place of morality in making foreign policy in this way: "Our discussions centered on the appraisal of dangers and risks, the weighing of the need for decisive and effective action against considerations of prudence. . . . Moral talk did not bear on the issue." When one of his colleagues objected that a proposed course was morally wrong, Acheson's reply reflected the conventional wisdom of American policymakers at the time. He told his colleague that on the Day of Judgment his view might be confirmed and that he was free to go forth and preach the necessity of salvation, but that "it was not, however, a view which I would entertain as a public servant."

The public servants whose views are revealed in the Pentagon Papers and the Watergate Transcripts apparently accepted—with a vengeance—Acheson's view that ethics has no place in politics. One has to look long and hard to find any hint of "moral talk" in these or similar documents of government of the period. Ethics was most often seen as merely a tool of public relations. To preserve national honor or to keep a president in office seemed to be the noblest aims to which these officials aspired. They were, at best, closet moralists.

Partly because of public reaction to Vietnam and Watergate, the climate is now more favorable for ethics, or at least for talk about ethics. Public officials are less hesitant to raise ethical questions and are less reluctant to accept ethical constraints on at least some of their conduct. In 1977, Congress passed the toughest code of ethics in its history. And in 1978, it imposed a strict code on the executive branch, setting up an Office of Government Ethics to enforce it. Ethics became a salient issue in the 1988 presidential campaign, and "values" have been a persistent theme in political debate ever since. Several presidents and executive agencies have appointed commissions, councils, and aides to advise them on questions of ethics. These developments have hardly brought an end to official misconduct: it remains at least as frequent and no less flagrant (as the Iran-Contra Affair and the case of the Keating Five illustrate). But public officials no longer find it so easy to avoid answering for their questionable conduct. Even more significantly, questions of undeniable moral content have captured a prominent place on the political agenda. Officials cannot escape talking about ethics when they address, for example, issues of military intervention, environmental risk, affirmative action, welfare reform, AIDS-testing, and abortion.

One reason for some of these changes is, no doubt, that politicians have discovered that moral talk, and sometimes even moral action, help them win or stay in office. But there are also, as there have always been, good moral reasons for public officials to be guided by ethical considerations in making policy. The reasons are now even more compelling, because the scope and stakes of American politics are greater than ever.

Public officials use means—such as violence and the threat of violence—that affect the fate of all of us and future generations as well. And the goods that public institutions distribute or provide the means to obtain—such as health care and employment opportunities—are among those that people value most. Because officials and institutions act in ways that seriously affect the well-being of many other people and other societies, we should want their actions to be guided by rules that prevent them from unfairly subordinating some people's interests to those of others. Because in a democracy officials and institutions are supposed to act in the name of citizens and only on their authority, we want our officials' actions to conform to the moral principles that we share.

Moral principles express the rights and obligations that individuals should respect when they act in ways that seriously affect the well-being of others and the standards that collective practices and policies should satisfy when these similarly affect well-being. What distinguishes ethical principles from the purely prudential principles common in politics is their disinterested perspective. Prudence asks whether an action or policy serves the interests of some particular individual group or nation. Ethics asks whether an action or policy could be accepted by anyone without regard to his or her particular circumstances such as social class, race, or nationality.

But prudence and ethics are not necessarily opposed in politics. A satisfactory political ethics must take into account the exigencies of political life, and effective political prudence recognizes the potency of moral criticism. If the conflict is between expedience and principle, few politicians would want to stand with the former. To be sure, some may argue that the free pursuit of self-interest will contribute to the public interest—if social and political institutions are designed correctly. But this claim does not fundamentally challenge the relevance of morality to politics. It simply proposes a supposedly more effective means of achieving moral ends in politics. If there is any dispute here, it is over the devices of moralists, not their desires.

Should we try to change the principles that motivate public officials, or should we try to restructure political institutions to elicit ethical behavior from those who are self-interested? Presumably we have to attempt both. More broadly, we may seek to change the structures of power in government and society so that citizens and officials can live together in a genuinely moral community. Whatever ways we choose to realize morality in politics, we must understand the meaning, justification, and application of moral principles and values in political life. This is the subject of political ethics.

Discussions of political ethics are in short supply in the literature on American politics and even in moral philosophy. Texts in American government tend to concentrate on the mechanics of power and the efficacy of policies. If they do not banish ethics from politics, they keep it safely segregated in a realm of ideals that rarely intrude into the real world of politics. The literature of moral philosophy often takes the opposite, but no less mistaken, approach. Philosophers tend to bring their principles of morality to the study of politics without change. They rarely attend to the special features of political life—the necessities of politics in general and the imperatives of democratic politics in particular. The moral values of the political process itself, so important in a democracy, usually meet with benign neglect.

Although political ethics must be consistent with a more general theory of ethics, it does not have exactly the same content as ordinary ethics because political life differs in morally significant ways from ordinary life. More than most citizens, public officials assume responsibility for protecting the rights and interests of all of us. They act in our name and on our behalf. And the environment in which they act is largely impersonal and intractable. It is often populated by powerful people and formidable institutions that are hostile to the purposes of public-spirited officials. These and other differences between public and private life do not make ethics irrelevant to politics. If anything they make it all the more important. But they do require us to take account of the special characteristics of politics as we frame our moral judgments.

We make moral judgments about two different aspects of politics—the ethics of the process and the ethics of policy. The first part of this book considers the moral problems of the methods used to achieve political goals, and the second part examines problems of the content of the goals themselves. The cases focus on problems of public policy and the officials who make it. Public policy is not necessarily the most important part of politics, but it plays an increasingly important role in the modern state. Knowing how to think ethically about the means and ends of public policy is essential not only for officials but for all citizens who participate in the democratic process.

The moral problem of process is that politics often requires public officials to use bad means to achieve good ends—means, such as violence, that private citizens may not use except under the most extraordinary circumstances. The moral demands of ordinary politics may include a willingness to threaten and to use violence, to deceive and manipulate, to peddle influence, and disobey orders—in short, to harm some people for the sake of helping more people or protecting the same people from even greater harm.

If we recognize that public officials cannot avoid using bad means to achieve good ends, we must seek moral limits on the use of these means. Machiavelli's advice to the Prince is inadequate: ''He should not depart from the good if he can hold to it, but he should be ready to enter on evil if he has to.'' Political necessity is at best a vague and at worst a misleading standard. We want to prevent public officials not only from pursuing their self-interest with impunity but also from unfairly sacrificing the interests of some people or societies for the sake of advancing the interests of others. To admit that politicians must get their hands dirty, therefore, is not to agree with Machiavelli that ''when the effect is good . . . it always justifies the action.'' Even utilitarians who give great weight to good consequences would not permit politicians so easily to justify using morally bad methods to achieve good ends. Utilitarians insist on a strict calculation of the costs and benefits that would rarely license the use of methods that common morality condemns. And leading critics of utilitarianism argue that some means, such as torturing innocent persons, are not justified, even when the gain in social benefits outweighs the costs.

The cases in the first three chapters of Part One invite you to examine the morally questionable means that are most commonly used in the political process: violence, deception, secrecy, and influence-peddling. Less common but no less important is the method illustrated in chapter 4 by the protests of Daniel Ellsberg, Otto Otepka, and the sixty-five lawyers who worked for the Justice Department in the late 1960s. The occasion for civil disobedience by public officials is generally a governmental policy that they believe to be seriously unjust. But their decision to disobey is itself an instance of the problem of dirty hands. We (and they) must decide whether they are justified in doing wrong in order to do good. Faced with what they reasonably believe to be a morally wrong policy, should they disobey while remaining in office, leave office (silently or in protest), threaten to resign (as did Secretary of State Shultz over the president's proposal to give lie detector tests to government employees), or comply with the policy for the sake of furthering better policies in the future (as did several of the engineers who opposed the decision to launch the space shuttle *Challenger*)?

The cases in Part Two illustrate the ethical problems of determining the goals of public policy. In everyday life we must choose among the many things that we ideally would like to accomplish. But our choices generally do not raise the same difficult moral questions as in politics, because in private life we are not responsible for acting in the interests of so many other people and reconciling their conflicts over such a wide range of values. Competing preferences, scarce resources, and stakes as high as life and death combine with the duties of office to make the choices among policy goals morally hard.

Utilitarianism is attractive as a theory for guiding hard choices in politics because it offers a seemingly simple, single principle for reconciling conflicts—maximize social welfare. The first case in Part Two shows utilitarianism in action in its technical form, policy analysis, in a controversy over use of the Tuolumne Canyon in California. Although it has often been assumed that policy analysis favors economic development over environmental protection, this case brings out the strengths (and weaknesses) of policy analysis when used to defend environmental values. The complexity of the analysis, as well as the nature of some of the criticisms of it, suggest that the utilitarian hope of theoretical simplicity may be illusory. The second case in chapter 5 features a public official who acknowledges the limitations of policy analysis. As the head of the Environmental Protection Agency, William Ruckelshaus was charged with setting standards to regulate emissions from the American Smelting and Refining Company (Asarco), which were polluting the air in and around Tacoma, Washington. "For me to sit here in Washington and tell the people of Tacoma what is an acceptable risk," he said, "would be at best arrogant and at worst inexcusable." Ruckelshaus held public workshops to inform concerned citizens and to help the EPA decide upon pollution standards. Yet the political process could not fully answer the questions that policy analysis had failed to answer, and Ruckelshaus had to combine the results of both to make his decision. The case calls into question not whether policy analysis should be used at all, but what place it should have in the broader process of policy making.

Many critics of policy analysis question whether the utilitarian principle is a desirable standard for choosing among policy options even in theory. They take issue with two assumptions of policy analysis as it is commonly practiced: that all competing goods can be reduced to a common measure (generally money) and that justice entails maximizing social welfare rather than distributing goods in a fair way among individuals. But utilitarians, in turn, challenge their critics to supply a better principle or set of principles by which public officials can make hard choices among competing goods.

This challenge was taken up by Arizona legislators who, as portrayed in chapter 6, faced a hard choice in calculating the costs and benefits of alternative uses of scarce social resources. Should state tax monies be used to fund expensive organ transplants, basic health care for the poor, or both? The Arizona legislature decided to expand basic health care for poor, pregnant women and for children, rather than to fund organ transplants for a smaller number of citizens in need of more expensive, catastrophic health care. When an Arizona resident died after being denied a liver transplant, public controversy ensued. Many of the critics of the legislature implicitly appealed to the egalitarian principle of distribution according to need. Opponents of AIDS-testing by insurance companies, the subject of the second case in chapter 6, explicitly invoke an egalitarian principle prohibiting discrimination. The insurance companies deny that setting higher rates for applicants who test positive for AIDS constitutes unfair discrimination; they argue that doing so is no different than denying coverage to applicants who have cancer, heart disease, or diabetes. "California Welfare Reform" raises similar issues of distributive justice, as well as questions of moral responsibility, and anticipates many of the disputes in the current controversies over welfare reform in other states. To decide who is right in these cases and why, we must not only evaluate but also give more content to the egalitarian moral principles that figure in the debates.

The egalitarian principle that is commonly applied to employment policy is equal opportunity. But in a society where past discrimination has prevented some minorities and women from developing their talents and obtaining the same jobs as equally talented white men, it is not obvious whether equal opportunity in employment requires nondiscrimination or preferential treatment. The cases in chapter 7 ask you to choose between competing views of what constitutes fair employment practices in industry and in government.

No choice is harder to justify in a liberal democracy than the choice between saving life and protecting liberty. Several of the cases in chapters 8 and 9 illustrate significant variations of this conflict. "Legalizing Laetrile" poses a problem of legislative paternalism: Should government restrict the liberty of some citizens for the sake of prolonging or saving their lives? The Food and Drug Administration's prohibition on marketing a "do-it-yourself kit for AIDS testing" poses the parallel problem of bureaucratic paternalism. Should the FDA, authorized by Congress to set standards for marketing health care products, restrict liberty for the sake of protecting citizens from false information or psychic trauma?

The curious practice of dwarf-tossing is intended as a challenge to strict liberals who believe that morality should never be enforced. Everyone who participates in the practice consents, and no one else is at risk; yet many citizens believe, as did the New York State legislature, that the practice should be restricted. Liberty and morality come into dramatic conflict in disputes about religion and citizenship education in the public schools. The "Controversial Curriculum" describes the form that such a conflict took in a district in Tennessee.

Abortion raises the no less difficult problem of choosing between life and liberty when citizens disagree over what constitutes a human life. Joseph Califano's account of his own struggle with this dilemma while secretary of health, education and welfare exemplifies a problem of hard choices. His story also brings us back to the problem of dirty hands with a new twist: should citizens accept a public office that requires them to pursue policies contrary to their own moral principles? In "Abortion in South Dakota," State Senator Scott Heidepriem confronts the dilemma in a slightly different form: to what extent should he act on his pro-choice views in the light of his largely pro-life constituency? For legislators, the issue is not only whether abortion should be legal but also whether it should be funded. In the 1988 congressional debate over Medicaid funding of abortions in cases of rape or incest, members of Congress faced the difficult problem of determining the government's policy on funding abortion. Excerpts from that debate bring out the complexity of the political conflict between life and liberty. If we assume that the legalization of abortion is morally justified, we must ask whether the government should give poor women the financial means to exercise their freedom to obtain an abortion. The question becomes especially difficult when we recognize that citizens reasonably disagree over the morality of legalized abortion and therefore over the value of the liberty that is at stake in the funding policy.

Recent controversies over the commercial practice of surrogate parenting present another variation on the conflict between life and liberty. Proponents defend the practice as an exercise of the fundamental freedoms of procreation and contract, while critics argue that it degrades human life by exploiting women and treating children as commodities. Two sets of proposals before the New York State legislature, one recommending and the other opposing the legal enforcement of surrogate parenting contracts, reveal the most important moral and political dimensions of the conflict.

This case, like most of the cases in the book, is full of details, ranging from scientific and legal technicalities to biographical facts about the officials who are featured. The cases are designed to represent, as far as possible, actual decisions and policies rather than hypothetical ones. One purpose of using real cases is to appreciate better the complexity that confronts officials who make policy and citizens who assess it. One of the most difficult but least examined steps in political ethics is to identify and frame the ethical issues themselves. Issues do not usually announce themselves as moral dilemmas; they often lie buried in a mass of facts and a welter of claims and counterclaims. Nearly all of the cases here call for some moral detective work to discover the ethical suspects among the many leads the facts may suggest.

The complexity of the cases also serves a second purpose. Moral principles in their pristine form often seem to have little critical force in politics. Either they are so general that everyone readily accepts them, or they are so extreme that almost no one takes them seriously. By trying to apply the principles to particular cases, we can begin to see exactly what difference which principles make in our political judgments. Finally, the complexity should remind us that context matters in political ethics. The cases, of course, cannot give a full account of the history of the events and institutions or the structures of social and economic power. But they should provide enough information to prompt you to ask what more must be known about the context to reach ethical conclusions. After reading each case, you should always ask what further information is necessary to arrive at an adequately informed conclusion. The information provided in the case is intended to be as much an invitation to further research as an account of the facts relevant to the case.

The subjects of some of the cases are officials at the highest levels of government, making decisions of great historical significance—as in the decision to use the atomic bomb against Japan. And some are statements of policies with far-reaching implications for society now and in the future—as in the national debates on abortion. We have included such cases because they raise important issues in themselves and because they illustrate principles that have wider application. But equally important are the cases that describe less famous and less momentous events in which lower level officials make decisions that directly affect relatively few people, such as the dispute about corruption in Santa Clara or education in Hawkins County. We have deliberately presented a substantial number of cases that take place in cities, counties, and states. Such cases represent the more typical moral world of politics. It is a world that both citizens and officials can more often influence because the scale of its problems is more manageable and because the patterns of its problems are more predictable. Though less dramatic than the once-in-a-lifetime dilemmas more often heard about, these decisions of normal politics cumulatively affect at least as many people.

The range of cases is intended to indicate that ethical problems may appear almost anyplace in political life. Behind the seemingly tedious and technical dispute over the "option values" in the Tuolumne case are large questions of human value and the meaning of nature. In Califano's story of the abortion battles, the seemingly petty disputes over legislative language (for example, whether rape must be reported within thirty, sixty, or ninety days) actually affect the welfare of many citizens and reveal disagreements of fundamental principle. Ethical issues do not arrive only at great moments in history; they also dwell in the routine of everyday politics.

However valuable cases may be, they cannot stand alone. All of the selections in this book are meant to be read in conjunction with works in moral philosophy and political theory. Such works provide principles to help assess the cases, and the cases may sometimes suggest revisions in the principles to take account of the special features of politics. Recommended readings accompany each set of cases. The recommendations are neither exclusive nor exhaustive, and other works not mentioned may be equally appropriate. But without some substantial basis in theory, any analysis of the cases is likely to be superficial.

At the end of each set of cases are comments and questions designed to encourage discussions of the ethical issues that the cases raise. Since ethical analysis should be viewed as a process of deliberation, it is best conducted at least in part through discussion with other people. This is especially true for political ethics. In a democracy, it is only through persuading other citizens of the moral worth of our causes that we can legitimately win their support in the making of public policies.

Recommended Reading

The best brief introduction to moral philosophy is still William K. Frankena, *Ethics*, 2d ed. (Englewood Cliffs, N.J.: Prentice Hall, 1973). Also see J.L. Mackie, *Ethics* (New York: Penguin, 1977), and Bernard Williams, *Morality* (New York: Harper and Row, 1972). Useful collections sensitive to practical ethics include: Brenda Almond (ed.), *Introducing Applied Ethics* (Oxford, England and Cambridge, Mass.: Blackwell, 1995), Tom L. Beauchamp (ed.), *Philosophical Ethics* (New York: McGraw-Hill, 1982), Peter Singer (ed.), *Applied Ethics* (New York: Oxford University Press, 1986), and Peter Singer (ed.), *Ethics* (New York: Oxford University Press, 1994). For political ethics in general, see Joel Fleishman et al. (eds.), *Public Duties: The Moral Obligations of Government Officials* (Cambridge, Mass.: Harvard University Press, 1981), and Dennis F. Thompson, *Political Ethics and Public Office* (Cambridge, Mass.: Harvard University Press, 1987). Some interesting applications of moral theory to a wide range of topics relevant to public policy are offered by Jonathan Glover, *Causing Death and Saving Lives* (New York: Penguin, 1978).

For a statement of a democratic theory that discusses most of the issues raised by the cases as well as many of the cases themselves, see Amy Gutmann and Dennis Thompson, *Democracy and Disagreement* (Cambridge, Mass.: Harvard University Press, 1996).

A general framework for questions about the ethics of process should be informed by the literature on the problem of dirty hands. The classic sources are Machiavelli, *The Prince* (New York: Random House, 1950), and Max Weber, "Politics as a Vocation," in H.H. Gerth and C.W. Mills (eds.), *From Max Weber* (New York: Oxford University Press, 1958). If you read only one modern work on the subject, it should be Michael Walzer, "Political Action: The Problem of Dirty Hands," *Philosophy & Public Affairs* 1 (Winter 1972), pp. 160–80, reprinted in Marshall Cohen et al. (eds.), *War and Moral Responsibility* (Princeton, N.J.: Princeton University Press, 1974). Some other contemporary discussions are the articles by Stuart Hampshire, Bernard Williams, and Thomas Nagel in Hampshire et al. (eds.), *Public and Private Morality* (New York: Cambridge University Press,

1978), and Dennis F. Thompson, "Democratic Dirty Hands," in *Political Ethics and Public Office*, pp. 11–39.

The ethics of policy has generated a large literature in recent years, in part stimulated by the revival of moral and political philosophy. A general approach is presented by Brian Barry and Douglas W. Rae, "Political Evaluation," in F.I. Greenstein and N.W. Polsby (eds.), *Handbook of Political Science* (Reading, Mass.: Addison Wesley, 1975), vol. 1, pp. 337–401. For a provocative view, see Robert E. Goodin, *Political Theory and Public Policy* (Chicago: University of Chicago Press, 1982). On the strengths and weaknesses of utilitarianism, the foundation of the dominant approach to policy analysis, see Jonathan Glover (ed.), *Utilitarianism and Its Critics* (New York: Macmillan, 1990), and Robert Goodin, *Utilitarianism as a Public Philosophy* (New York and Cambridge, England: Cambridge University Press, 1995).

The philosophical work that has been most influential in the study of the ethics of policy is John Rawls, *A Theory of Justice* (Cambridge, Mass: Harvard University Press, 1971). For commentaries on Rawls, see Norman Daniels (ed.), *Reading Rawls* (New York: Basic Books, 1976). Also see John Rawls, *Political Liberalism* (New York: Columbia University Press, 1993).

A selection of philosophical writing on particular policies appears in the readers compiled by the editors of *Philosophy & Public Affairs* and published by Princeton University Press. See Marshall Cohen et al. (eds.), *Equality and Preferential Treatment* (1978); *Medicine and Moral Philosophy* (1982); *Rights and Wrongs of Abortion* (1974); *War and Moral Responsibility* (1974); and Charles R. Beitz et al. (eds.), *International Ethics* (1985).

Students can keep up with current work on this subject by regularly reading the journals *Ethics* (University of Chicago Press) and *Philosophy & Public Affairs* (Princeton University Press).

Part One

The Ethics of Process

1 Violence

Introduction

Violence violates the fundamental moral prohibition against harming persons, yet governments must sometimes use violent means to defend that same fundamental principle. The most dramatic instance of the use of violence is war, and the most terrifying instruments of war are the bombs that kill civilians and destroy cities. The cases in this chapter raise questions about the morality of war—the means used to fight wars and the ends for which they are fought.

"War is cruel and you cannot refine it," General Sherman told the citizens of Atlanta who protested against the brutality of his invasion of their city during the Civil War. Many other military and political leaders as well as moral philosophers have agreed with Sherman. If your cause is just in a war, you should use any means necessary to win it. To place moral constraints on the fighting of a war, the argument goes, would simply prolong it and could increase the chances of war in the future by making war more morally respectable.

In most wars most nations nevertheless have accepted some moral constraints on their conduct (such as not torturing prisoners), and the philosophical writing on just war has long distinguished the justice of a war from the justice of the means used to fight it. The former does not necessarily determine the latter. Even in the war against Nazis, we should condemn some methods—for example, the practice of the Free French forces who enlisted Moroccan mercenaries by promising that they could, with impunity, rape Italian women. And we also distinguish moral from immoral actions of men fighting on the side of the aggressor nation: we praise General Rommel for ignoring Hitler's order to shoot all prisoners captured behind the lines.

The basic principles underlying most rules of war is that it is morally wrong to attack noncombatants. Noncombatants are defined as those who are not fighting or not supplying the means of fighting the war. Farmers and nurses are noncombatants, while munitions workers and soldiers are combatants. Different moral traditions give different reasons for this prohibition, but all regard it as important.

At the same time, most theories of just wars recognize that noncombatants will inevitably be killed in modern warfare—sometimes justifiably so. The theories then take one of two approaches: they either (1) formulate the prohibition so as to justify some deaths of noncombatants or (2) specify the conditions under which the prohibition may be suspended. The most prominent example of the first alternative is the doctrine of double-effect, which holds that the death of noncombatants is permissible if it is an unintended (though foreseen) side effect of a morally legitimate end. The doctrine would permit, for example, an air strike against an enemy missile site even

3

if civilians lived nearby. The second alternative would allow civilians to be killed directly only if necessary to stop the imminent destruction of a nation. On this view, British bombing of German cities may have been justified until 1942 but not thereafter.

Nuclear weapons, some have argued, make obsolete all these fine distinctions and the rules of war that depend on them. With the possible exception of tactical weapons, nuclear forces strike directly at civilian populations. The destruction of Hiroshima and Nagasaki could hardly be described as an unintended side effect. Nor was the bombing necessary to prevent the defeat of the United States. But others argue that the destructiveness of the new technology increases the need to take the old rules of war seriously.

Even some of those who favored the bombing of Hiroshima and Nagasaki recognized that it called for moral justification and believed they could provide it. Writing only a few months before President Harry S. Truman accepted his advice to use the bomb against Japan, Secretary of State Henry Stimson insisted that the "rule sparing the civilian population should be applied as far as possible to the use of any new weapon." Stimson's own defense of the use of that weapon, reprinted as the first selection in this chapter, shows how he came to terms with that moral rule. The selection that follows provides a broader account drawing on more recent historical sources of the considerations that led to the decision and its consequences.

From the beginning, there were critics of the decision. General Dwight Eisenhower says that he told Stimson in 1945 that he was "against it on two counts. First, the Japanese were ready to surrender and it wasn't necessary to hit them with that awful thing. Second, I hated to see our country be the first to use such a weapon." As Eisenhower's comment reveals, the controversy about the bomb usually seems at first to turn mainly on the question of military necessity (would the Japanese have surrendered soon anyhow?). But that question is so contentious because it is not independent of the question of the morality of using "that awful thing."

The controversy continues to the present day, not only among academic historians but also among politicians and citizens. In 1995 the Smithsonian's National Air and Space Museum planned an exhibition featuring the *Enola Gay* (the plane from which the bomb was dropped) along with an explanatory script that raised some questions about whether the bombing was necessary. Although the rather bland script took no position on the question, the public outcry forced the curators to abandon the script and exhibit the plane alone. The controversy thus remains significant not only as a dispute about a historical event but also as a question about the moral stance that we believe our nation should take in the use of instruments of violence.

Although the United States has not used nuclear weapons again, it has sent conventional bombers on campaigns that killed civilians, often in large numbers. The most sustained and destructive missions took place during the Vietnam War, but in more recent years more isolated and smaller scale incidents are more typical, now that the military finds itself in an era of what is called "low-intensity conflict." (The navy, more poetic in its classifications, calls it "violent peace.") "Bombing the Bunker in Baghdad'' describes one such incident. During the Gulf War, the United States ordered an air strike against a command center near which civilians lived and in which, as it turned out, civilians had taken shelter. The moral question is whether the rules of war require the United States to take more care than it did to avoid civilian casualties.

It is possible to discuss the morality of the means used in a war without considering the ends when the war is clearly just. Few people now doubt the justice of the Allies' cause in World War II, and most would accept that the U.S.-led forces in the Gulf were justified in resisting Iraq's attack against Kuwait (though the motivation was probably more economic than moral). But the question of the justice of the war is itself often more difficult than these cases suggest. The decisions to intervene that U.S. officials face now are more likely to involve murky and uncertain claims and confused boundaries than clear cases in which an aggressor nation crosses the border to impose its will on another sovereign power. And the aims of the war are not usually so simple as stopping aggression or even restoring peace. "Intervention in Somalia" provides an account of a forceful intervention that was justified on humanitarian grounds but in which the goals shifted, and the moral and logistical problems multiplied during the intervention itself.

The Decision to Use the Atomic Bomb
Henry L. Stimson

In recent months there has been much comment about the decision to use atomic bombs in attacks on the Japanese cities of Hiroshima and Nagasaki. This decision was one of the gravest made by our government in recent years, and it is entirely proper that it should be widely discussed. I have therefore decided to record for all who may be interested my understanding of the events which led up to the attack on Hiroshima on August 6, 1945, on Nagasaki on August 9, and the Japanese decision to surrender on August 10. No single individual can hope to know exactly what took place in the minds of all of those who had a share in these events, but what follows is an exact description of our thoughts and actions as I fir 1em in

the records and in my clearest recollection.

It was in the fall of 1941 that the question of atomic energy was first brought directly to my attention. At that time President Roosevelt appointed a committee consisting of Vice President Wallace, General Marshall, Dr. Vannevar Bush, Dr. James B. Conant, and myself. The function of this committee was to advise the President on questions of policy relating to the study of nuclear fission which was then proceeding both in this country and in Great Britain. For nearly four years thereafter I was directly connected with all major decisions of policy on the development and use of atomic energy, and from May 1, 1943, until my resignation as Secretary of War on September 21, 1945, I was directly responsible to the President for the administration of the entire undertaking; my chief advisers in this period were General Marshall, Dr. Bush, Dr. Conant, and Major General Leslie R. Groves, the officer in charge of the project. At the same time I was the President's adviser on the military employment of atomic energy.

The policy adopted and steadily pursued by President Roosevelt and his advisers was a simple one. It was to spare no effort in securing the earliest possible successful development of an atomic weapon. The reasons for this policy were equally simple. The original experimental achievement of atomic fission had occurred in Germany in 1938, and it was known that the Germans had continued their experiments. In 1941 and 1942 they were believed to be ahead of us, and it was vital that they should not be the first to bring atomic weapons into the field of battle. Furthermore, if we should be the first to develop the weapon, we should have a great new instrument for shortening the war and minimizing destruction. At no time from 1941 to 1945 did I ever hear it suggested by the President, or by any other responsible member of the government, that atomic energy should not be used in the war. All of us of course understood the terrible responsibility involved in our attempt to unlock the doors to such a devastating weapon; President Roosevelt particularly spoke to me many times of his own awareness of the catastrophic potentialities of our work. But we were at war, and the work must be done. I therefore emphasize that it was our common objective throughout the war to be the first to produce an atomic weapon and use it. The possible atomic weapon was considered to be a new and tremendously powerful explosive, as legitimate as any other of the deadly explosive weapons of modern war. The entire purpose was the production of a military weapon; on no other ground could the wartime expenditure of so much time and money have been justified. The exact circumstances in which that weapon might be used were unknown to any of us until the middle of 1945, and when that time came, as we shall presently see, the military use of atomic energy was connected with larger questions of national policy.

The extraordinary story of the successful development of the atomic bomb has been well told elsewhere. As time went on it became clear that the weapon would not be available in time for use in the European theater, and the war against Germany was successfully ended by the use of what are now called conventional means. But in the spring of 1945 it became evident that the climax of our prolonged atomic effort was at hand. By the nature of atomic chain reactions, it was impossible to state with certainty that we had succeeded until a bomb had actually exploded in a full-scale experiment; nevertheless it was considered exceedingly probable that we should by midsummer have successfully detonated the first atomic bomb. This was to be done at the Alamogordo Reservation in New Mexico. It was thus time for detailed consideration of our future plans. What had begun as a well-founded hope was now developing into a reality.

On March 15, 1945, I had my last talk with President Roosevelt. My diary record of this conversation gives a fairly clear picture of the state of our thinking at that time. I have removed the name of the distinguished public servant who was fearful lest the Manhattan (atomic) project be "a lemon"; it was an opinion common among those not fully informed.

"The President . . . had suggested that I come over to lunch today . . . First I took up with him a memorandum which he sent to me from _____, who had been alarmed at the rumors of extravagance in the Manhattan project. _____ suggested that it might become disastrous and he suggested that we get a body of 'outside' scientists to pass upon the project because rumors are going around that Vannevar Bush and Jim Conant have sold the President a lemon on the subject and ought to be checked up on. It was rather a jittery and nervous memorandum and rather silly, and I was prepared for it and I gave the President a list of the scientists who were actually engaged on it to show the very high standing of them and it comprised four Nobel Prize men, and also how practically every physicist of standing was engaged with us in the project. Then I outlined to him the future of it and when it was likely to come off and told him how important it was to get ready. I went over with him the two schools of thought that exist in respect to the future control after the war of this project, in case it is successful, one of them being the secret close-in attempted control of the project by those who control it now, and the other being the international control based upon freedom both of science and of access. I told him that those things must be settled before the first projectile is used and that he must be ready with a statement to come out to the people on it just as soon as that is done. He agreed to that. . . ."

This conversation covered the three aspects of the question which were then uppermost in our minds. First, it was always necessary to suppress a lingering doubt that any such titanic undertaking could be successful. Second, we must consider the implications of success in terms of its long-range postwar effect. Third, we must face the problem that would be presented at the time of our first use of the weapon, for with that first use there must be some public statement.

I did not see Franklin Roosevelt again. The next time I went to the White House to discuss atomic energy was April 25, 1945, and I went to explain the nature of the problem to a man whose only previous knowledge of our activities was that of a Senator who had loyally accepted our assurance that the matter must be kept a secret from him. Now he was President and Commander-in-Chief, and the final responsibility in this as in so many other matters must be his. President Truman accepted this responsibility with the same fine spirit that

Senator Truman had shown before in accepting our refusal to inform him.

I discussed with him the whole history of the project. We had with us General Groves, who explained in detail the progress which had been made and the probable future course of the work. I also discussed with President Truman the broader aspects of the subject, and the memorandum which I used in this discussion is again a fair sample of the state of our thinking at the time.

Memorandum discussed with President Truman April 25, 1945:

"1. Within four months we shall in all probability have completed the most terrible weapon ever known in human history, one bomb of which could destroy a whole city.

"2. Although we have shared its development with the U.K., physically the U.S. is at present in the position of controlling the resources with which to construct and use it and no other nation could reach this position for some years.

"3. Nevertheless it is practically certain that we could not remain in this position indefinitely.

"a. Various segments of its discovery and production are widely known among many scientists in many countries, although few scientists are now acquainted with the whole process which we have developed.

"b. Although its construction under present methods requires great scientific and industrial effort and raw materials, which are temporarily mainly within the possession and knowledge of U.S. and U.K., it is extremely probable that much easier and cheaper methods of production will be discovered by scientists in the future, together with the use of materials of much wider distribution. As a result, it is extremely probable that the future will make it possible for atomic bombs to be constructed by smaller nations or even groups, or at least by a larger nation in a much shorter time.

"4. As a result, it is indicated that the future may see a time when such a weapon may be constructed in secret and used suddenly and effectively with devastating power by a willful nation or group against an unsuspecting nation or group of much greater size and material power. With its aid even a very powerful unsuspecting nation might be conquered within a very few days by a very much smaller one. [A brief reference to the estimated capabilities of other nations is here omitted; it in no way affects the course of the argument.]

"5. The world in its present state of moral advancement compared with its technical development would be eventually at the mercy of such a weapon. In other words, modern civilization might be completely destroyed.

"6. To approach any world peace organization of any pattern now likely to be considered, without an appreciation by the leaders of our country of the power of this new weapon, would seem to be unrealistic. No system of control heretofore considered would be adequate to control this menace. Both inside any particular country and between the nations of the world, the control of this weapon will undoubtedly be a matter of the greatest difficulty and would involve such thoroughgoing rights of inspection and internal controls as we have never heretofore contemplated.

"7. Furthermore, in the light of our present position with reference to this weapon, the question of sharing it with other nations and, if so shared, upon what terms, becomes a primary question of our foreign relations. Also our leadership in the war and in the development of this weapon has placed a certain moral responsibility upon us which we cannot shirk without very serious responsibility for any disaster to civilization which it would further.

"8. On the other hand, if the problem of the proper use of this weapon can be solved, we would have the opportunity to bring the world into a pattern in which the peace of the world and our civilization can be saved.

"9. As stated in General Groves' report, steps are under way looking towards the establishment of a select committee of particular qualifications for recommending action to the executive and legislative branches of our government when secrecy is no longer in full effect. The committee would also recommend the actions to be taken by the War Department prior to that time in anticipation of the postwar problems. All recommendations would of course be first submitted to the President."

The next step in our preparations was the appointment of the committee referred to in paragraph 9 above. This committee, which was known as the Interim Committee, was charged with the function of advising the President on the various questions raised by our apparently imminent success in developing the atomic weapon. I was its chairman, but the principal labor of guiding its extended deliberations fell to George L. Harrison, who acted as chairman in my absence. It will be useful to consider the work of the committee in some detail. Its members were the following, in addition to Mr. Harrison and myself:

James F. Byrnes (then a private citizen) as personal representative of the President.

Ralph A. Byrd, Under Secretary of the Navy.

William L. Clayton, Assistant Secretary of State.

Dr. Vannevar Bush, Director, Office of Scientific Research and Development, and president of the Carnegie Institution of Washington.

Dr. Karl Compton, Chief of the Office of Field Service in the Office of Scientific Research and Development, and president of the Massachusetts Institute of Technology.

Dr. James B. Conant, Chairman of the National Defense Research Committee, and president of Harvard University.

The discussions of the committee ranged over the whole field of atomic energy, in its political, military, and scientific aspects. That part of its work which particularly concerns us here relates to its recommendations for the use of atomic energy against Japan, but it should be borne in mind that these recommendations were not made in a vacuum. The committees's work included the drafting of the statements which were published immediately after the first bombs were dropped, the drafting of a bill for the domestic control of atomic energy, and recommendations looking toward the international control of atomic energy. The Interim Committee was assisted in its work by a Scientific Panel whose members were the following: Dr. A. H. Compton, Dr. Enrico Fermi, Dr. E. O. Lawrence, and Dr. J. R. Oppenheimer. All four were nuclear physicists of the first rank; all four had held positions of great importance in the atomic project from its inception. At a meeting with the Interim Committees and the Scientific Panel on May 31, 1945, I urged all those present to feel free to express themselves on any phase of the subject, scientific or political. Both General Marshall and I at this meeting expressed the view that atomic energy could not be considered simply in terms of military weapons but must also be considered in terms of a new relationship of man to the universe.

On June 1, after its discussions with the Scientific Panel, the Interim Committee unanimously adopted the following recommendations:

1. The bomb should be used against Japan as soon as possible.

2. It should be used on a dual target—that is, a military installation or war plant surrounded by or adjacent to houses and other buildings most susceptible to damage, and

3. It should be used without prior warning [of the nature of the weapon]. (One member of the committee, Mr. Bard, later changed his view and dissented from the third recommendation.)

In reaching these conclusions the Interim Committee carefully considered such alternatives as a detailed advance warning or a demonstration in some uninhabited area.

Both of these suggestions were discarded as impractical. They were not regarded as likely to be effective in compelling a surrender of Japan and both of them involved serious risks. Even the New Mexico test would not give final proof that any given bomb was certain to explode when dropped from an airplane. Quite apart from the generally unfamiliar nature of atomic explosives, there was the whole problem of exploding a bomb at a predetermined height in the air by a complicated mechanism which could not be tested in the static test of New Mexico. Nothing would have been more damaging to our effort to obtain surrender than a warning or a demonstration followed by a dud—and this was a real possibility. Furthermore, we had no bombs to waste. It was vital that a sufficient effect be quickly obtained with the few we had.

The Interim Committee and the Scientific Panel also served as a channel through which suggestions from other scientists working on the atomic project were forwarded to me and to the President. Among the suggestions thus forwarded was one memorandum which questioned using the bomb at all against the enemy. On June 16, 1945, after consideration of that memorandum, the Scientific Panel made a report, from which I quote the following paragraphs:

"The opinions of our scientific colleagues on the initial use of these weapons are not unanimous: they range from the proposal of a purely technical demonstration to that of the military application best designed to induce surrender. Those who advocate a purely technical demonstration would wish to outlaw the use of atomic weapons, and have feared that if we use the weapons now our position in future negotiations will be prejudiced. Others emphasize the opportunity of saving American lives by immediate military use, and believe that such use will improve the international prospects, in that they are more concerned with the prevention of war than with the elimination of this special weapon. We find ourselves closer to these latter views: *we can propose no technical demonstration likely to bring an end to the war; we see no acceptable alternative to direct military use.* [Italics mine.]

"With regard to these general aspects of the use of atomic energy, it is clear that we, as scientific men, have no proprietary rights. It is true that we are among the few citizens who have had occasion to give thoughtful consideration to these problems during the past few years. We have, however, no claim to special competence in solving the political, social, and military problems which are presented by the advent of atomic power."

The foregoing discussion presents the reasoning of the Interim Committee and its advisers. I have discussed the work of these gentlemen at length in order to make it clear that we sought the best advice that we could find. The committee's function was, of course, entirely advisory. The ultimate responsibility for the recommendation to the President rested upon me, and I have no desire to veil it. The conclusions of the committees were similar to my own, although I reached mine independently. I felt that to extract a genuine surrender from the Emperor and his military advisers, they must be administered a tremendous shock which would carry convincing proof of our power to destroy the Empire. Such an effective shock would save many times the number of lives, both American and Japanese, that it would cost.

The facts upon which my reasoning was based and steps taken to carry it out now follow.

The principal political, social, and military objective of the United States in the summer of 1945 was the prompt and complete surrender of Japan. Only the complete destruction of her military power could open the way to lasting peace.

Japan, in July 1945, had been seriously weakened by our increasingly violent attacks. It was known to us that she had gone so far as to make tentative proposals to the Soviet government, hoping to use the Russians as mediators in a negotiated peace. These vague proposals contemplated the retention by Japan of important conquered areas and were therefore not considered seriously. There was as yet no indication of any weakening in the Japanese determination to fight rather than accept unconditional surrender. If she should persist in her fight to the end, she had still a great military force.

In the middle of July 1945, the intelligence section of the War Department General Staff estimated Japanese military strength as follows: in the home islands, slightly under two million; in Korea, Manchuria, China proper, and Formosa, slightly over two million; in French Indo-China, Thailand, and Burma, over 200,000; in the East Indies area, including the Philippines, over 500,000; in the by-passed Pacific islands, over 100,000. The total strength of the Japanese Army was estimated at about five million men. These estimates later proved to be in very close agreement with official Japanese figures.

The Japanese Army was in much better condition than the Japanese Navy and Air Force. The Navy had practically ceased to exist except as a harrying force against an invasion fleet. The Air Force had been reduced mainly to reliance upon Kamikaze, or suicide, attacks. These latter, however, had already inflicted serious damage on our seagoing forces, and their possible effectiveness in a last ditch fight was a matter of real concern to our naval leaders.

As we understood it in July, there was a very strong possibility that the Japanese government might determine upon resistance to the end, in all the areas of the Far East under its control. In such an event the Allies would be faced with the enormous task of destroying an armed force of five million men and five thousand suicide aircraft, belonging to a race which had already demonstrated its ability to fight literally to the death.

The strategic plans of our armed forces for the defeat of Japan as they stood in July had been prepared without reliance upon the atomic bomb, which had not yet been tested in New Mexico. We were planning an intensified sea and air blockade and greatly intensified strategic air bombing through the summer and early fall, to be followed on November 1 by an invasion of the southern island of Kyushu. This would be followed in turn by an invasion of the main island of Honshu in the spring of 1946. The total U.S. military and naval force involved in this grand design was of the order of five million men; if all those indirectly concerned are included, it was larger still.

We estimated that if we should be forced to carry this plan to its conclusion, the major fighting force would not end until the latter part of 1946, at the earliest. I was informed that such operations might be expected to cost over a million casualties, to American forces alone. Additional large losses might be expected among our allies, and, of course, if our campaign were successful and if we could judge by previous experience, enemy casualties would be much larger than our own.

It was already clear in July that even before the invasion, we should be able to inflict enormously severe damage on the Japanese homeland by the combined application of ''conventional'' sea and air power. The critical question was whether this kind of action would induce surrender. It therefore became necessary to consider very carefully the probable state of mind of the enemy, and to assess with accuracy the line of conduct which might end his will to resist.

With these considerations in mind, I wrote a memorandum for the President, on July 2, which I believe fairly represents the thinking of the American government as it finally took shape in action. This memorandum was prepared after discussion and general agreement with Joseph C. Grew, Acting Secretary of State, and Secretary of the Navy Forrestal, and when I discussed it

with the President, he expressed his general approval.

Memorandum for the President, July 2, 1945, on proposed program for Japan:

''1. The plans of operation up to and including the first landing have been authorized and the preparations for the operation are now actually going on. This situation was accepted by all members of your conference on Monday, June 18.

''2. There is reason to believe that the operation for occupation of Japan following the landing may be a very long, costly, and arduous struggle on our part. The terrain, much of which I have visited several times, has left the impression on my memory of being one which would be susceptible to a last ditch defense such as has been made on Iwo Jima and Okinawa and which of course is very much larger than either of those two areas. According to my recollection it will be much more unfavorable with regard to tank maneuvering than either the Philippines or Germany.

''3. If we once land on one of the main islands and begin a forceful occupation of Japan, we shall probably have cast the die of last ditch resistance. The Japanese are highly patriotic and certainly susceptible to calls for fanatical resistance to repel an invasion. Once started in actual invasion, we shall in my opinion have to go through with an even more bitter finish fight than in Germany. We shall incur the losses incident to such a war and we shall have to leave the Japanese islands even more thoroughly destroyed than was the case with Germany. This would be due both to the difference in the Japanese and German personal character and the differences in the size and character of the terrain through which the operations will take place.

''4. A question then comes: Is there any alternative to such a forceful occupation of Japan which will secure for us the equivalent of an unconditional surrender of her forces and a permanent destruction of her power again to strike an aggressive blow at the 'peace of the Pacific'? I am inclined to think that there is enough such chance to make it well worthwhile our giving them a warning of what is to come and a definite opportunity to capitulate. As above suggested, it should be tried before the actual forceful occupation of the homeland islands is begun and furthermore the warning should be given in ample time to permit a national reaction to set in.

"We have the following enormously favorable factors on our side—factors much weightier than those we had against Germany:

"Japan has no allies.

"Her navy is nearly destroyed and she is vulnerable to a surface and underwater blockade which can deprive her of sufficient food and supplies for her population.

"She is terribly vulnerable to our concentrated air attack upon her crowded cities, industrial and food resources.

"She has against her not only the Anglo-American forces but the rising forces of China and the ominous threat of Russia.

"We have inexhaustible and untouched industrial resources to bring to bear against her diminishing potential.

"We have great moral superiority through being the victim of her first sneak attack.

"The problem is to translate these advantages into prompt and economical achievement of our objectives. I believe Japan is susceptible to reason in such a crisis to a much greater extent than is indicated by our current press and other current comment. Japan is not a nation composed wholly of mad fanatics of an entirely different mentality from ours. On the contrary, she has within the past century shown herself to possess extremely intelligent people, capable in an unprecedentedly short time of adopting not only the complicated technique of Occidental civilization but to a substantial extent their culture and their political and social ideas. Her advance in all these respects during the short period of sixty or

seventy years has been one of the most astounding feats of national progress in history—a leap from the isolated feudalism of centuries into the position of one of the six or seven great powers of the world. She has not only built up powerful armies and navies. She has maintained an honest and effective national finance and respected position in many of the sciences in which we pride ourselves. Prior to the forcible seizure of power over her government by the fanatical military group in 1931, she had for ten years lived a reasonably responsible and respectable international life.

"My own opinion is in her favor on the two points involved in this question:

"a. I think the Japanese nation has the mental intelligence and versatile capacity in such a crisis to recognize the folly of a fight to the finish and to accept the proffer of what will amount to an unconditional surrender; and

"b. I think she has within her population enough liberal leaders (although now submerged by the terrorists) to be depended upon for her reconstruction as a responsible member of the family of nations. I think she is better in this respect than Germany was. Her liberals yielded only at the point of the pistol and, so far as I am aware, their liberal attitude has not been personally subverted in the way which was so general in Germany.

"On the other hand, I think that the attempt to exterminate her armies and her population by gunfire or other means will tend to produce a fusion of race solidity and antipathy which has no analogy in the case of Germany. We have a national interest in creating, if possible, a condition wherein the Japanese nation may live as a peaceful and useful member of the future Pacific community.

"5. It is therefore my conclusion that a carefully timed warning be given to Japan by the chief representatives of the United States, Great Britain, China, and, if then a belligerent, Russia by calling upon Japan to surrender and permit the occupation of her country in order to insure its complete demilitarization for the sake of the future peace.

"This warning should contain the following elements:

"The varied and overwhelming character of the force we are about to bring to bear on the islands.

"The inevitability and completeness of the destruction which the full application of this force will entail.

"The determination of the Allies to destroy permanently all authority and influence of those who have deceived and misled the country into embarking on world conquest.

"The determination of the Allies to limit Japanese sovereignty to her main islands and to render them powerless to mount and support another war.

"The disavowal of any attempt to extirpate the Japanese as a race or to destroy them as a nation.

"A statement of our readiness, once her economy is purged of its militaristic influence, to permit the Japanese to maintain such industries, particularly of a light consumer character, as offer no threat of aggression against their neighbors, but which can produce a sustaining economy, and provide a reasonable standard of living. The statement should indicate our willingness, for this purpose, to give Japan trade access to external raw materials, but no longer any control over the sources of supply outside her main islands. It should also indicate our willingness, in accordance with our now established foreign policy, in due course to enter into mutually advantageous trade relations with her.

"The withdrawal from their country as soon as the above objectives of the Allies are accomplished, and as soon as there has been established a peacefully inclined government, of a character representative of the masses of the Japanese people. I personally think that if in saying this we should add that we do not exclude a constitutional monarchy

under her present dynasty, it would substantially add to the chances of acceptance.

"6. Success of course will depend on the potency of the warning which we give her. She has an extremely sensitive national pride and, as we are now seeing every day, when actually locked with the enemy will fight to the very death. For that reason the warning must be tendered before the actual invasion has occurred and while the impending destruction, though clear beyond peradventure, has not yet reduced her to fanatical despair. If Russia is part of the threat, the Russian attack, if actual, must not have progressed too far. Our own bombing should be confined to military objectives as far as possible."

It is important to emphasize the double character of the suggested warning. It was designed to promise destruction if Japan resisted, and hope, if she surrendered.

It will be noted that the atomic bomb is not mentioned in this memorandum. On grounds of secrecy the bomb was never mentioned except when absolutely necessary and furthermore, it had not yet been tested. It was of course well forward in our minds as the memorandum was written and discussed that the bomb would be the best possible sanction if our warning were rejected.

The adoption of the policy outlined in the memorandum of July 2 was a decision of high politics; once it was accepted by the President, the position of the atomic bomb in our planning became quite clear. I find that I stated in my diary, as early as June 19, that "the last chance warning . . . must be given before an actual landing of the ground forces in Japan, and fortunately the plans provide for enough time to bring in the sanctions to our warning in the shape of heavy ordinary bombing attack and an attack of S-1." S-1 was a code name for the atomic bomb.

There was much discussion in Washington about the timing of the warning to Japan. The controlling factor in the end was the date already set for the Potsdam meeting of the Big Three. It was President Truman's decision that such a warning should be solemnly issued by the U.S. and the U.K. from this meeting, with the concurrence of the head of the Chinese government, so that it would be plain that *all* of Japan's principal enemies were in entire unity. This was done in the Potsdam ultimatum of July 26, which very closely followed the above memorandum of July 2 with the exception that it made no mention of the Japanese Emperor.

On July 28 the Premier of Japan, Suzuki, rejected the Potsdam ultimatum by announcing that it was "unworthy of public notice." In the face of this rejection we could only proceed to demonstrate that the ultimatum had meant exactly what it said when it stated that if the Japanese continued the war, "the full application of our military power, backed by our resolve, will mean the inevitable and complete destruction of the Japanese armed forces and just as inevitably the utter devastation of the Japanese homeland."

For such a purpose the atomic bomb was an entirely suitable weapon. The New Mexico test occurred while we were at Potsdam, on July 16. It was immediately clear that the power of the bomb measured up to our highest estimates. We had developed a weapon of such a revolutionary character that its use against the enemy might well be expected to produce exactly the kind of shock on the Japanese ruling oligarchy which we desired, strengthening the position of those who wished peace, and weakening that of the military party.

Because of the importance of the atomic mission against Japan, the detailed plans were brought to me by the military staff for approval. With President Truman's warm support I struck off the list of suggested targets the city of Kyoto. Although it was a target of considerable military importance, it had been the ancient capital of Japan and was a shrine of Japanese art and culture. We determined that it should be spared. I

approved four other targets including the cities of Hiroshima and Nagasaki.

Hiroshima was bombed on August 6, and Nagasaki on August 9. These two cities were active working parts of the Japanese war effort. One was an army center; the other was naval and industrial. Hiroshima was the headquarters of the Japanese Army defending southern Japan and was a major military storage and assembly point. Nagasaki was a major seaport and it contained several large industrial plants of great wartime importance. We believed that our attacks had struck cities which must certainly be important to the Japanese military leaders, both Army and Navy, and we waited for a result. We waited one day.

Many accounts have been written about the Japanese surrender. After a prolonged Japanese cabinet session in which the deadlock was broken by the Emperor himself, the offer to surrender was made on August 10. It was based on the Potsdam terms, with a reservation concerning the sovereignty of the Emperor. While the Allied reply made no promises other than those already given, it implicitly recognized the Emperor's position by prescribing that his power must be subject to the orders of the Allied Supreme Commander. These terms were accepted on August 14 by the Japanese, and the instrument of surrender was formally signed on September 2, in Tokyo Bay. Our great objective was thus achieved, and all the evidence I have seen indicates that the controlling factor in the final Japanese decision to accept our terms of surrender was the atomic bomb.

The two atomic bombs which we had dropped were the only ones we had ready, and our rate of production at the time was very small. Had the war continued until the projected invasion on November 1, additional fire raids of B-29s would have been more destructive of life and property than the very limited number of atomic raids which we could have executed in the same period. But the atomic bomb was more than a weapon of terrible destruction; it was a psychological weapon. In March 1945, our Air Force had launched its first great incendiary raid on the Tokyo area. In this raid more damage was done and more casualties were inflicted than was the case at Hiroshima. Hundreds of bombers took part and hundreds of tons of incendiaries were dropped. Similar successive raids burned out a great part of the urban area of Japan, but the Japanese fought on. On August 6 one B-29 dropped a single atomic weapon on Hiroshima. Three days later a second bomb was dropped on Nagasaki and the war was over. So far as the Japanese could know, our ability to execute atomic attacks, if necessary by many planes at a time, was unlimited. As Dr. Karl Compton has said, "it was not one atomic bomb, or two, which brought surrender; it was the experience of what an atomic bomb will actually do to a community, *plus the dread of many more*, that was effective."

The bomb thus served exactly the purpose we intended. The peace part was able to take the path of surrender, and the whole weight of the Emperor's prestige was exerted in favor of peace. When the Emperor ordered surrender, and the small but dangerous group of fanatics who opposed him were brought under control, the Japanese became so subdued that the great undertaking of occupation and disarmament was completed with unprecedented ease.

In the foregoing pages I have tried to give an accurate account of my own personal observations of the circumstances which led up to the use of the atomic bomb and the reasons which underlay our use of it. To me they have always seemed compelling and clear, and I cannot see how any person vested with such responsibilities as mine could have taken any other course or given any other advice to his chiefs.

Two great nations were approaching contact in a fight to a finish which would begin on November 1, 1945. Our enemy, Japan, commanded forces of somewhat over 5 million armed men. Men of these armies had already inflicted upon us, in our breakthrough of the outer perimeter of their defenses, over 300,000 battle casualties. Enemy armies still unbeaten had the strength to cost us a million more. *As long as the Japanese government refused to surrender*, we should be forced to take and hold the ground, and smash the Japanese ground armies, by close-in fighting of the same desperate and costly kind that we had faced in the Pacific islands for nearly four years.

In the light of the formidable problem which thus confronted us, I felt that every possible step should be taken to compel a surrender of the homelands, and a withdrawal of all Japanese troops from the Asiatic mainland and from other positions, before we had commenced an invasion. We held two cards to assist us in such an effort. One was the traditional veneration in which the Japanese Emperor was held by his subjects and the power which was thus vested in him over his loyal troops. It was for this reason that I suggested in my memorandum of July 2 that his dynasty should be continued. The second card was the use of the atomic bomb in the manner best calculated to persuade that Emperor and the counselors about him to submit to our demand for what was essentially unconditional surrender, placing his immense power over his people and his troops subject to our orders.

In order to end the war in the shortest possible time and to avoid the enormous losses of life which otherwise confronted us, I felt that we must use the Emperor as our instrument to command and compel his people to cease fighting and subject themselves to our authority through him, and that to accomplish this we must give him and his controlling advisers a compelling reason to accede to our demands. This reason furthermore must be of such a nature that his people could understand his decision. The bomb seemed to me to furnish a unique instrument for that purpose.

My chief purpose was to end the war in

victory with the least possible cost in the lives of the men in the armies which I had helped to raise. In the light of the alternatives which, on a fair estimate, were open to us, I believe that no man, in our position and subject to our responsibilities, holding in his hands a weapon of such possibilities for accomplishing this purpose and saving those lives, could have failed to use it and afterwards looked his countrymen in the face.

As I read over what I have written, I am aware that much of it, in this year of peace, may have a harsh and unfeeling sound. It would perhaps be possible to say the same things and say them more gently. But I do not think it would be wise. As I look back over the five years of my service as Secretary of War, I see too many stern and heartrending decisions to be willing to pretend that war is anything else than what it is. The face of war is the face of death; death is an inevitable part of every order that a wartime leader gives. The decision to use the atomic bomb was a decision that brought death to over a hundred thousand Japanese. No explanation can change that fact, and I do not wish to gloss it over. But this deliberate, premeditated destruction was our least abhorrent choice. The destruction of Hiroshima and Nagasaki put an end to the Japanese war. It stopped the fire raids, and the strangling blockade; it ended the ghastly specter of a clash of great land armies.

In this last great action of the Second World War we were given final proof that war is death. War in the twentieth century has grown steadily more barbarous, more destructive, more debased in all its aspects. Now, with the release of atomic energy, man's ability to destroy himself is very nearly complete. The bombs dropped on Hiroshima and Nagasaki ended a war. They also made it wholly clear that we must never have another war. This is the lesson men and leaders everywhere must learn, and I believe that when they learn it they will find a way to lasting peace. There is no other choice.

Alternatives to the Bomb
Colin Dueck

On August 6, 1945, the *Enola Gay* B-29 bomber dropped a four-ton atomic bomb—the "Little Boy"—on the Japanese city of Hiroshima, resulting in the death of up to 130,000 people. In a public statement that same day, President Harry Truman declared that if the leaders of Japan failed to surrender unconditionally to the Allied powers, they could "expect a rain of ruin from the air, the likes of which has never been seen on earth." On August 9, a second atomic bomb was dropped on the port city of Nagasaki, and five days later, Emperor Hirohito addressed the Japanese people over the radio to tell them that their country had surrendered.

By the end of June 1945, Japan had undoubtedly lost the war. Its navy had been destroyed, its lifeline to food and raw materials was being strangled by a naval blockade, its cities were subject to a massively destructive strategic bombing campaign. The conquest of Okinawa by American forces had opened up the home islands to invasion. Aware of their declining ability to wage war successfully, and with tentative support from Emperor Hirohito, Japanese cabinet members sent Prince Konoye on an exploratory diplomatic mission to the USSR, in the hopes of persuading Moscow to mediate a negotiated peace between Japan and the Western Allies.[1] The Japanese seemed to be showing some interest in a peace settlement, but they feared that accepting the longstanding Allied condition of "unconditional surrender" would mean the deposition of their Emperor—an unacceptable condition. American policymakers were aware of this fear; earlier success at cracking Japanese diplomatic codes allowed the United States to intercept messages from Tokyo to the Japanese embassy in Moscow. Secretary of the Navy James Forrestal noted in his diary on July 13 that Japan's foreign minister, Shigenori Togo, had instructed his ambassador in Moscow to tell the Soviets that "the unconditional surrender terms of the Allies were about the only thing in the way of [the] termination of the war and he said that if this were insisted upon, of course the Japanese would have to fight."[2] Secretary of War Henry Stimson had suggested to Truman on July 2 that Japan might very well surrender upon being offered a guarantee of the emperor's position.[3] General MacArthur had noted that a peaceful postwar transition within a defeated, occupied Japan would be impossible without the emperor's stabilizing influence. And as early as May, acting Secretary of State Joseph Grew—formerly, ambassador to Tokyo—had argued that:

> the greatest obstacle to unconditional surrender by the Japanese is their belief that this would entail the destruction or permanent removal of the Emperor and the institution of the Throne. If some indicator can now be given the Japanese that they themselves . . . will be permitted to determine their own political structure, they will be afforded a method of saving face without which surrender will be highly unlikely.[4]

The president had remarked casually to Stimson that it sounded like a good idea. American planners were inclined to agree with MacArthur that it would be best to keep the emperor, and Stimson had drafted an early version of the Potsdam declaration in which Hirohito's position was guaranteed. Yet Secretary of State James Byrnes, sup-

ported by President Truman, vetoed Stimson's draft, and the final declaration from Potsdam on July 26 gave no indication that the emperor's status was secure—this in spite of the fact that when Japan did surrender, less than three weeks later, the United States accepted the emperor's continued reign.[5] In 1948, Stimson himself admitted that on the question of guaranteeing the emperor's position, he had come to "believe that history might find that the United States, by its delay in stating its position, had prolonged the war."[6]

It is far from certain that the Japanese would have surrendered before Hiroshima if only they had been offered a guarantee of the emperor's position. It had cost American forces three months and almost 50,000 casualties to root out Japanese forces from the small island of Okinawa. The Japanese still held on to much of their conquests in China, Manchuria, and southeast Asia, and a large army—together with a fleet of kamikaze planes—stood ready to defend the home islands from invasion.[7] Japan had lost the war, but the military situation was not so discouraging as to require virtually unconditional surrender. A negotiated peace was a possibility; the question was, On what terms? At minimum, Japan's leaders wanted to preserve not only the emperor, but the entire imperial social, economic, and political system, or "*kokutai*," which was bound up with their own status. Before August 6, the most dovish civilian leaders in the Cabinet wanted to preserve some degree of self-rule for Japan.[8] As Foreign Minister Togo told his ambassador to Moscow on July 17, "We are not asking the Russians' mediation in anything like unconditional surrender." Such demands were incompatible with American plans for postwar occupation, disarmament, reform, and democratization of Japan, regardless of the emperor's status. More to the point, the Cabinet was divided and diplomacy incapacitated by the army's demand that Japan fight on to win a more favorable peace.

Army leaders insisted upon a continuation of the Showa regime, free from American occupation; they also hoped to keep some of the territorial gains they had made through war. Indeed, army planners expected to be able to inflict such heavy losses upon American forces, in case of an invasion, that the United States would be obliged to sign a compromise peace. As General Shoichi Miyazaki put it:

> If we could defeat the enemy in Kyushu or inflict tremendous losses, forcing him to realize the strong fighting spirit of the Japanese Army and people, it would be possible, we hoped, to bring about the termination of hostilities on comparatively favorable terms.[9]

Since the army was immensely influential, with a formal veto in the Cabinet, and since civilian leaders that acted in defiance of the army risked assassination or coup d'etat, any serious efforts at peace were ruled out.[10] No diplomatic feelers were sent to the United States. Even the famous "peace mission" to Moscow in July did not have either the support of the army or formal government backing; consequently, its proposals were vague, ambiguous, and lacking in concrete specifics.[11] As the Japanese ambassador to Moscow told Togo on July 15, "Your successive telegrams have not clarified the situation. The interests of the government and the military were not clear regarding the termination of the war."[12] In any case, by this point Stalin was uninterested in mediating any peace in the Pacific, since he had more to gain by entering the war against Japan, and Prince Konoye was not allowed into Moscow.

Even *after* the bombing of Hiroshima, military leaders in the Cabinet continued to resist the prospect of American occupation, disarmament, and war crimes tribunals. They argued that Japan still had the "ability to deal a smashing blow to the enemy" and that "it would be inexcusable to surrender unconditionally." Only after a late-night Cabinet meeting on August 9 and 10, with the direct and partisan intervention of the emperor—highly unusual in itself—did they agree to surrender to the terms laid out at Potsdam, "with the understanding that the said declaration does not comprise any demand which prejudices the prerogatives of His Majesty as a Sovereign Ruler."

A July 8 report by the Anglo-American Combined Intelligence Committee to the Chiefs of Staff informed U.S. policymakers that the Japanese Army was not yet prepared to surrender. They judged that the peace feelers to the United States through Moscow were not to be taken seriously; indeed, they feared that Japan might try to make some sort of separate arrangement with the USSR. Even Joseph Grew, a champion of guaranteeing the emperor's position, believed that the July overtures were "familiar weapons of psychological warfare" designed to "divide the Allies." Truman believed there to be little reason to offer any diplomatic concessions, given the lack of any clear indication from the other side that such concessions would bring peace. Moreover, to negotiate with Tokyo before a Soviet entry had occurred risked alienating the USSR, a powerful ally. The policy of unconditional surrender was a legacy of Franklin Roosevelt's wartime leadership, and it had strong support both in Congress and with public opinion. The memory of Pearl Harbor, and reports of war atrocities and of mistreated American prisoners of war, fed the desire for retribution.[13] Leading congressional figures were calling for Hirohito to be tried and executed as a war criminal—a view with broad public support. Consequently, even after receiving the Japanese offer of near-unconditional surrender on August 10, the American Cabinet was divided over how to respond. While Admiral Leahy advocated its acceptance, Secretary Byrnes feared "the crucifixion of the president" if Hirohito went unpunished. The reply eventually sent by the United States—and accepted by the Japanese, a few days later—was ambiguous, giving no explicit guarantee of the emperor's position; rather, it stuck to the letter of the Potsdam declaration, reiterated that the "ultimate form of government of Japan shall . . . be established by the freely expressed will of the Japanese people," and concluded that:

> from the moment of surrender the authority of the Emperor and the Japanese government to rule the state shall be subject to the Supreme Commander of the Allied Powers who will take such steps as he deems proper to effectuate the surrender terms.

State Department planners like Archibald MacLeish had said all along that the Meiji imperial system was authoritarian and feudal, a source of hypernationalism. They wanted to reform and democratize Japanese institutions under United States tutelage, and the American occupation gave them the chance to do just that. Such considerations weighed against any explicit or early guarantee of the emperor. A peace settlement based upon such a guarantee might have resulted in a less democratic postwar Japan. But had American policymakers been willing to abandon the policy of unconditional surrender in the summer of 1945—had they allowed for the continuation of both self-rule and the imperial system—there is evidence to suggest that Japan's civilian leaders might have welcomed a negotiated peace.

A second alternative to the atomic bomb, without resorting to an invasion, was to rely upon a naval blockade and conventional strategic bombing to wear down Japanese resistance—an alternative known as the "siege strategy." Up until May 1945, the United States had relied upon such a strategy. First, American submarines had destroyed Japan's merchant marine and cut off supplies of food and raw materials destined for the home islands. With most such supplies located overseas, Japan was highly vulnerable to naval interdiction; by summer, as a result, the Japanese were suffering from severe shortages of food, clothing, and raw materials vital to the war effort.[14] Second, a strategic bombing campaign was launched against Japan—beginning with

precision bombing and moving to mass fire-bombing early in 1945. The bombing campaign was immensely destructive, resulting in hundreds of thousands of Japanese civilian casualties. In later years, a number of Truman's key advisors, including Admiral Leahy, Truman's chief of staff and head of the joint chiefs of staff, General Henry Arnold, commanding general of the Army Air Force in 1945, and Admiral King, chief of staff for the navy, estimated that this strategy of bomb-and-blockade would have forced the Japanese to surrender without the necessity of either an invasion or the atomic bomb.[15] King wrote that "had we been willing to wait, the effective naval blockade would, in the course of time, have starved the Japanese into submission."[16] And in a 1946 United States Strategic Bombing Survey, air force authorities concluded that due to the effects of conventional bombing, "certainly prior to 31 December 1945, and in all probability prior to 1 November 1945, Japan would have surrendered even if the atomic bomb had not been dropped, and even if no invasion had been planned or contemplated."[17]

There is little or no evidence to suggest that United States military leaders made these arguments in the summer of 1945 with Truman or any other policymakers. Such postwar recollections and evaluations cannot be assumed to reflect what historical actors thought and did at the time. In looking back at the reasons for Japan's surrender, leaders from the navy emphasized the role of the blockade, just as leaders from the air force emphasized the role of strategic bombing. But the Strategic Bombing Survey of 1946 has since been shown to have doctored the evidence from interviews with Japanese authorities in favor of its conclusion.[18] King, Leahy, and Arnold may have come genuinely to believe, after the war, that neither an invasion nor the atomic bombs had been necessary. But at a critical June 18 meeting at the White House, all three of them agreed with General Marshall, chief of staff for the army, that the time had come to supplement the "siege strategy" with definite plans for an invasion.[19] Truman also agreed. The blockade had been very effective, but Japan still had food supplies to last until the end of 1945 and was capable of fighting on. The U.S. joint chiefs "doubted whether the general economic deterioration had yet reached, or would reach for some time, the point at which it would affect the ability of the nation to fight or repel an invasion." And as for the strategic bombing campaign, it appeared to have hardly influenced the morale or policy of the Japanese leadership. As Marshall put it, in reference to the March firebombing of the Japanese capital, "We had 100,000 people killed in Tokyo in one night, and it had seemingly no effect whatsoever." There was simply no guarantee that continuing the siege strategy without an invasion would bring Japan's unconditional surrender anytime soon.[20]

The third alternative strategy was to wait for the USSR to enter the war against Japan and to rely upon the Red Army to deal the final blow to Japanese forces. The Soviet declaration of war and rapid advance against the Japanese army in Manchuria was clearly critical in bringing about a Japanese surrender. For three days after Hiroshima, Japan's military leaders refused even to attend Cabinet meetings designed to discuss terms of surrender. Then, on August 8 and 9, the Soviet attack, and immediate collapse of Japanese forces in Manchuria, stunned Japan's military leaders and changed the strategic situation literally overnight. Upon learning of the defeat, Prime Minister Suzuki remarked, "Is the Kwantung [Manchurian] Army that weak? Then the game is up."[21]

American decision-makers were aware that Soviet entry might end the war without the necessity of an invasion. The Anglo-American Joint Intelligence Committee reported on April 29, 1945, that "the entry of the USSR into the war would . . . convince most Japanese at once of the inevitability

of complete defeat." The same advice was offered by the committee later that summer. And on June 18, General Marshall told President Truman that "the impact of Russian entry on the already hopeless Japanese may well be the decisive action levering them into capitulation." It was for this reason that Truman went to Potsdam eager to win Stalin's promise of an early entrance into the war against Japan. As the president put it, "If the test [of the atomic bomb] should fail, then it would be even more important to us to bring about a surrender before we had to make a physical conquest of Japan."[22] Stalin's promise of entry within a month left Truman reassured. He noted in his diary for July 17 that "he'll [Stalin] be in the Jap War on August 15. Fini Japs when that comes about."[23] Truman knew that a Soviet intervention against Japan would contribute significantly to ending the war and could possibly render an invasion unnecessary. Up until July 17, he encouraged such intervention by the USSR.

On that day, however, Truman learned that the first testing of an atomic bomb had taken place in the desert of New Mexico and that it had been an astonishing success. The new weapon held out the possibility of winning the war and averting an invasion without the necessity of a Soviet intervention. Stimson wrote on July 23 that General Marshall "felt as I felt sure he would, that now with our new weapon we would not need the assistance of the Russians to conquer Japan."[24] Truman noted in his diary that the "Japs will fold before Russia comes in. I am sure they will when Manhattan [the atomic bomb] appears over their homeland."[25] Some historians now argue that Truman and his close advisor Secretary Byrnes not only viewed the use of the bomb against Japan as the quickest route to victory, but that they: (i) hoped to win the war against Japan without Soviet aid, (ii) switched to a strategy of actively *delaying* Soviet entry into the Pacific war, in order to be able to drop the bomb first, (iii) abandoned any chance of modifying the policy of unconditional surrender at Potsdam, knowing that the Japanese would refuse, for the same reason, and (iv) dropped the atomic bomb on Japan primarily for "anti-Soviet," political reasons—not only to shut the USSR out of Japan, but to impress Stalin with American power and render him more compliant on European matters.[26]

Truman excluded any guarantee of the emperor's status in the Potsdam declaration because he expected to gain nothing from such a guarantee, and in any case had no desire to make such an offer, for reasons that had nothing to do with hostility towards the USSR. But American policy towards the bomb was influenced by policy toward the USSR, and vice versa. American decision-makers had high hopes that their control over this revolutionary new weapon would, as Truman told his reparations advisor Edwin Pauley, "keep the Russians straight." Stimson did advise Truman to delay any resolution of outstanding Soviet-American disputes over Manchuria, Poland, Rumania, and Yugoslavia until the atomic bomb had been tested successfully: "it seems a terrible thing to gamble with such big stakes in diplomacy without having your master card in your hand."[27] The possession of the bomb did in fact embolden Truman to take a harder line on Eastern Europe. American decision-makers probably did, in the words of Stimson's special assistant Harvey Bundy, see "large advantage to winning the Japanese war without the aid of Russia."[28] At Potsdam, on July 23, Winston Churchill observed that "the United States do not at the present time desire Russian participation in the war against Japan." Secretary Byrnes, at the least, was anxious to end the war before Soviet forces had a chance to advance far into or past Manchuria. When asked in a 1960 interview whether there had been a special urgency to end the war out of fear of a Soviet advance, Byrnes replied:

There certainly was on my part, and I'm sure that, whatever views President Truman may

have had of it earlier in that year, that in the days immediately preceding the dropping of the bomb his views were the same as mine—we wanted to get through the Japanese phase of the war before the Russians came in.[29]

There is no direct evidence, however, to show that the United States dropped the bomb on Hiroshima in order to intimidate Moscow.[30] Although Truman and his advisors spoke of gaining diplomatic leverage with Stalin through possession of the bomb, there is no reason to believe that the primary reason for dropping the bomb on Japan was anything other than what Truman said it was—to end the war as soon as possible and save American lives. Many historians agree that concern about the Soviet Union at best "confirmed" rather than "determined" the use of the new weapon against Japan—in other words, it gave one more reason not to cancel the *Enola Gay's* mission.[31] As with the siege strategy, U.S. decision-makers could not be *certain* that a soviet attack would be sufficient to defeat Japan or that it would be coming anytime soon. Indeed, it was the news of the bombing of Hiroshima—and the fear of being left out of the picture in northeast Asia—that led Stalin to move up the Soviet declaration of war from August 15 to August 8. Despite their undeniably cooling enthusiasm for such intervention by the USSR, American leaders did not actively discourage Soviet entrance into the war after mid-July.

There is evidence, however, that Truman and his advisors were eager to conclude the war against Japan as soon as possible, before any Soviet entry, most likely out of a desire both to save American lives and to prevent the USSR from gaining a foothold in Japan and its environs. The goal of keeping Soviet forces at bay seems to have provided an added reason, particularly in the case of Secretary Byrnes, to drop the atomic bomb on Japan. Stalin aimed at recovering Russia's East Asian losses from 1905, together with influence for the USSR in Manchuria, Korea, and possibly even Japan. On August

16 he asked Truman for coequal status in the occupation of Japan. Two days later Soviet troops attacked the Kurile Islands and began to move south towards Hokkaido, the northernmost of Japan's four home islands. American naval supremacy in the area probably ruled out any Soviet occupation of Japan; but the prospect of a more advanced position in the region for the USSR was of real concern to the president. The evidence suggests that had Truman and his advisors been less worried about Soviet expansion and less determined to end the war at the earliest possible moment, they might very well have been able to rely upon Moscow's declaration of war to bring about a Japanese capitulation without an invasion of the home islands and without the atomic bomb—particularly if such an approach had been supplemented by a modification in the terms of surrender.

A fourth alternative was either to stage a demonstration of the bomb for Japan in some uninhabited area or to warn Japanese leaders about the bomb beforehand in order to give them a chance to surrender. The possibility of such a warning had been raised intermittently by leading policy-makers: first at the May 31 meeting of the Interim Committee on postwar nuclear policy, attended by Stimson and Byrnes; then by Assistant Secretary of War John McCloy at the June 18 White House meeting to discuss invasion plans; and finally, by Joseph Bard, undersecretary of the navy, throughout the summer.[32] On July 25, Truman wrote in his diary that "we will issue a warning statement asking the Japs to surrender and save lives. I'm sure that they will not do that, but we will have given them the chance."[33] But despite the warning in the Potsdam proclamation of "prompt and utter destruction," no direct mention was made of the new weapon. To begin with, no one knew whether such a warning or demonstration would work. The Interim Committee concluded at its May 31 meeting that to warn the Japanese of an upcoming bombing might

allow them to shoot down the bomber or move Allied POWs to the target site. A demonstration seemed equally problematic to the committee: apart from the practical difficulties of arranging such a viewing with the leaders of a wartime adversary, the United States had a limited number of atomic bombs available, and if it turned out to be a dud or failed to impress the Japanese, the demonstration would have been for nothing.[34] Robert Oppenhemier, the leading scientist on the Manhattan Project, said that he could think of no demonstration "sufficiently spectacular" to bring about a surrender.

Still, American policymakers knew that a demonstration or warning would not cost the United States very much. Some scientists who worked on the Manhattan Project have suggested that there was enough plutonium available for several bombs like the one dropped on Nagasaki ("Fat Man") and that in any case the effectiveness of the uranium bomb ("Little Boy") was already assured well before July 16. A group of such scientists based in Chicago, led by Hungarian emigré Leo Szilard, proposed warning the Japanese about the bomb, but their efforts were resisted by Byrnes and Oppenheimer, and their petition never reached the president. American policymakers, on the whole, were simply not interested in a warning or demonstration of the bomb. They wanted not to minimize but to maximize the element of fear, shock, and surprise that would attend the first use of this terrible new weapon. Consequently, the alternative of a demonstration or warning received very little consideration. At the May 31 Interim Committee meeting, Stimson expressed the general consensus by concluding that "we could not give the Japanese any warning, that we could not concentrate on a civilian area; but that we should seek to make a profound psychological impression on as many inhabitants as possible."[35]

In the final event, even this modest admonition not to "concentrate on a civilian area'' was largely ignored in the final targeting decisions. The principle of noncombatant immunity counted for little once it came into conflict with the committee's own stated and contradictory impulse to make a "profound impression" on the Japanese. The possibility of using the bomb against a strictly military target, so as to avoid civilian casualties, received scant attention. In May, General Marshall made the case for such limited use of atomic weaponry, but was quickly overruled.[36] Stimson seems to have been troubled occasionally by considerations of noncombatant immunity, and he vetoed the atomic bombing of the ancient city of Kyoto, but this seems to have been in large part out of the desire to prevent permanent Japanese hostility towards the United States, rather than by considerations of discrimination as such.[37] Mass firebombing by *conventional* weapons had already killed hundreds of thousands of civilians—in the case of the Tokyo bombing of March 9 and 10, almost 100,000 in one night—without causing any significant controversy or meeting any opposition from American policymakers. Inured to the practice of "area" bombing, Truman and his advisors did not consider using this new weapon against a strictly military target.[38]

A fifth alternative was to drop the atomic bomb on Hiroshima but to delay the bombing of Nagasaki by a few more days, in order to give the Japanese time to surrender. The bombing of Nagasaki was made virtually automatic; Carl Spaatz, commander of the Army Strategic Air Force, was directed on July 25 to drop atomic bombs on designated targets "as made ready."[39] This meant that the Japanese Cabinet had barely seventy-two hours to let the news of Hiroshima sink in before deciding on their response. According to one historian, Truman's mistake "was signing an initial order that gave release of the go-ahead of both bombs at once." Commander Spaatz recalled in later years that he had no idea why Nagasaki had been bombed. At the time, however, American policymakers feared that a single atomic bomb might not be enough to convince Japan to surrender. To demonstrate that the United States had a number of such weapons and that Hiroshima had not been a freak occurrence, Truman and his advisors were prepared to drop two or more bombs on Japan.

Japan's military leaders in fact downplayed the importance of the atomic bomb for the first three days after Hiroshima.[40] Minister of War Anawi denied that Hiroshima had been struck at all. At the critical late-night Cabinet meeting on August 9–10, army leaders continued to resist surrender until early in the morning. News of Nagasaki arrived *during* the meeting and may have been a factor in demoralizing the military and allowing the emperor to intervene in favor of surrender.[41] As Anawi put it upon hearing of Nagasaki, "the Americans appear to have a hundred atomic bombs . . . they could drop three per day. The next target might well be Tokyo." On the other hand, there is evidence to suggest that the Soviet declaration of war earlier that day had been sufficient to demoralize Japan's military leaders, in which case the bombing of Nagasaki was extraneous.[42] Since Truman received no response from Japan in the three days after Hiroshima, he saw no reason to cancel the second bombing; but even sympathetic observers have suggested that Truman could have waited a few days longer after Hiroshima in order to give the Japanese time to respond with surrender terms.[43]

Had all five of these options failed, the sixth alternative was to go forward with the planned invasion of the Japanese home islands. Truman later claimed that an invasion would have cost anywhere from half a million to a million American lives lost, but no such estimates were made by responsible military figures at the time. The harrowing experience of exceptionally bitter fighting on Iwo Jima and Okinawa, together with being subject to kamikaze attacks, had given the Americans reason to fear heavy casualties. The planned American invasion of Japan was to have been the largest amphibious assault in military history, beginning with the November 1 landing of 767,000 soldiers and marines on the island of Kyushu (Operation Olympic) and ending with the landing of one and a half million men on the Tokyo plain some four months later (Operation Coronet). High casualties could be expected. But by the fall of 1945, the United States had clear superiority over Japan in terms of firepower, air power, and naval power. The Japanese home army, although large, was badly equipped, and production of the most basic wartime necessities had ground to a halt. Japanese capacity to resist an invasion was diminishing.[44] In a June 18 meeting with Truman at the White House, General Marshall estimated that Operation Olympic would cost the United States about 63,000 dead and wounded.[45] These numbers are roughly comparable with a June 15 report by the Joint War Plans Committee, which predicted that the entire two-stage operation would cost between 132,000 and 220,000 casualties, of which about 20 percent would have been deaths.[46] In sum, according to the best estimates of contemporary U.S. military authorities, an invasion of Japan—while costly—would not have resulted in anything like a million American lives lost.

Japan offered terms of near-unconditional surrender on August 10. Allied peace terms had not changed in the days and weeks leading up to that point. Immediately prior to the surrender, the USSR entered the Pacific war, and two atomic bombs were dropped on Japan. The role of the atomic bomb seems to have been that its sheer novelty and destructive force shocked and demoralized the Japanese Cabinet. As Kawabe Torashima, vice chief of general staff, put it, "A surprise attack with this new weapon was beyond our wildest dreams." Military leaders were given something like an honorable excuse to accept an unwelcome peace,

without having to resign or attempt a coup; they could not be expected to fight against such a weapon.[47] Civilian leaders were persuaded of the necessity of surrender. And the emperor—hitherto silent in Cabinet meetings—was convinced that the time had come to make peace on Allied terms.[48] As Hirohito said to Foreign Minister Togo upon hearing of Hiroshima, "Under these circumstances, we must bow to the inevitable. No matter what happens to my safety, we must put an end to this war as speedily as possible so that this tragedy will not be repeated." The intervention of the emperor in the August 9–10 Cabinet debate allowed the civilians to win out over the more hard-line military leaders and to send near-unconditional terms of surrender to the United States. As Kido Koichi, chancellor to the emperor, said afterwards:

> The psychological moment we had long waited for had finally arrived to resolutely carry out the termination of the war. . . . There is no doubt that the military leaders were overwhelmed by the enemy's scientific prowess. We felt that if we took the occasion and utilized the psychological shock of the bomb to carry through, we might perhaps succeed in ending the war. . . . It might be said that we of the peace party were assisted by the atomic bomb in our endeavour to end the war.

As late as August 9, Cabinet officials such as Stimson and Forrestal feared that the war might drag on for weeks or even months; Japan's offer of surrender the next day came as something of a surprise.[49] It had hardly even occurred to them to abjure the use of any weapon—including the atomic bomb—that might save American lives by contributing to the war's rapid and successful conclusion. As Stimson put it, "At no time, from 1941 to 1945 did I even hear it suggested by the President, or any other responsible member of the government, that atomic energy should not be used in the war."[50] The assumption seems to have been inherited from the Roosevelt administration that the bomb would be used.[51] Certainly, the Interim Committee never really considered any other possibility. Members of the committee worked under the widely shared assumption that the bomb would help significantly in the war effort. The need for postwar cooperation with the USSR over atomic energy was in the back of their minds as they worked under intense constraints of time and information. A victorious ending to the war in the shortest possible time was of the highest priority not only to American decision-makers but also to the general public. Moreover, the Manhattan Project had been immensely expensive. As Byrnes told Leo Szilard in May of 1945, "How would you get Congress to appropriate money for atomic energy research if you did not show results for the money which has been spent already?" In such a wartime environment, neither the Interim Committee nor President Truman ever seriously considered the possibility of *not* using the bomb against Japan. Indeed, Truman appears to have believed that the "decision" to drop it was a foregone conclusion. The final order to bomb both cities actually went out on July 25 not from Truman but from General Thomas Handy, acting army chief of staff. As General Groves, the military director of the Manhattan Project, said of the president: "As far as I was concerned, his decision was one of noninterference—basically a decision not to upset existing plans." It would have taken clear evidence of Japan's imminent defeat to convince Truman that the bombings were no longer necessary—evidence that he did not have until August 10, at which point he "interfered" to call off a third atomic bomb, adding that he "didn't like the idea of killing . . . all those kids."[52]

NOTES

1. Akira Iriye, *Power and Culture* (Cambridge, Mass.: Harvard University Press, 1981), pp. 257–60.

2. Walter Millis, *The Forrestal Diaries* (New York, Viking Press, 1951), pp. 74, 76.

3. Stimson Diary, July 2, 1945, Yale University Library, New Haven, Conn.

4. Joseph Grew, *Turbulent Era*, vol. 2 (Boston: Houghton, 1952), pp. 1446–73.

5. John Ray Skates, *The Invasion of Japan: Alternative to the Bomb* (Columbia: University of South Carolina Press, 1994), p. 249.

6. Henry Stimson and Harvey Bundy, *On Active Service* (Boston: Harper, 1948), p. 629.

7. The curators of the National Air and Space Museum, "The Crossroads: The End of World War II, the Atomic Bomb, and the Origins of the Cold War," in *Judgment at the Smithsonian* (New York: Marlowe and Co., 1995), pp. 4–5.

8. Robert Butow, *Japan's Decision to Surrender* (Stanford, Calif.: Stanford University Press, 1954), p. 161.

9. Leon Sigal, *Fighting to a Finish: The Politics of War Termination in the United States and Japan, 1945* (Ithaca, N.Y.: Cornell University Press, 1988), p. 228.

10. Ibid., p. 279.

11. Barton Bernstein, "Understanding the Atomic Bomb and the Japanese Surrender: Missed Opportunities, Little-Known Near Disasters, and Modern Memory," *Diplomatic History* (Spring 1995), pp. 263–66.

12. McGeorge Bundy, *Danger and Survival* (New York: Random House, 1988), p. 87.

13. John Dower, *War Without Mercy* (New York: Pantheon Books, 1986), p. 205.

14. Robert Pape, "Why Japan Surrendered," *International Security* 18:2 (Fall 1993): 157.

15. Henry Arnold, *Global Mission* (New York: Harper, 1949), pp. 596–98; Leahy, *I Was There* (New York: Whittlerey House, 1950), p. 441.

16. Ernest J. King and Walter M. Whitehall, *Fleet Admiral King* (New York: Norton, 1952), p. 621.

17. U.S. Strategic Bombing Survey, *Japan's Struggle to End the War* (Washington, D.C.: U.S. Government Printing Office, 1946), p. 13.

18. See, for example, interrogation with Prince Konoye, November 9, 1945, Records of the U.S. Strategic Bombing Survey, RG 243, National Archives.

19. Bernstein, "Understanding the Atomic Bomb," pp. 252–55.

20. Pape, "Why Japan Surrendered," pp. 194–95.

21. Sigal, *Fighting to a Finish*, pp. 226, 237.

22. Harry Truman, *Memoirs*, vol. I (Garden City, N.Y.: Doubleday, 1955), p. 417.

23. Truman, "Potsdam Diary," July 17, 1945, Truman Papers.

24. Stimson Diary, July 23, 1945, Yale University Library, New Haven, Conn.

25. Truman, "Potsdam Diary," July 18, 1945, Truman Papers.

26. Gar Alperovitz, *The Decision to Use the Atomic Bomb* (New York: Knopf, 1995), pp. 312–17.

27. Stimson Diary, May 15, 1945.

28. "Notes of the Use by the United States of the Atomic Bomb," September 1946, marked as draft 3, with the initials of HHB (presumably Harvey Bundy) in the upper right, and located in Top Secret Documents of Interest to General Groves #20, MED Records.

29. Byrnes, in "Was A-Bomb a Mistake?" *US News and World Report* (August 15, 1960), pp. 65–66.

30. Alperovitz, *Decision to Use the Atomic Bomb*, p. 306.

31. Barton Bernstein, "The Struggle over History: Defining the Hiroshima Narrative," in *Judgment at the Smithsonian* (New York: Marlowe and Co., 1995), p. 193.

32. John McCloy, *The Challenge to American Foreign Policy* (Cambridge, Mass.: Harvard University Press, 1953), pp. 41–43.

33. Truman, "Potsdam Diary," July 25, 1945.

34. National Air and Space Museum, "Crossroads," p. 47.

35. Ibid., p. 43.

36. John McCloy, memorandum of meeting, May 29, 1945, Records of the Secretary of War, May 29, 1945, RG 107, National Archives.

37. National Air and Space Museum, "Crossroads," p. 42.

38. Bundy, *Danger and Survival*, p. 64.

39. General Thomas Hardy to Carl Spaatz, July 25, 1945, in Truman's *Memoirs*, vol. 1, pp. 420–21.

40. Pape, "Why Japan Surrendered," p. 191.

41. Butow, *Japan's Decision*, pp. 151–52.

42. Pape, "Why Japan Surrendered," p. 192.

43. Bundy, *Danger and Survival*, p. 97.

44. Skates, *Invasion of Japan*, p. 256.

45. Minutes of June 18, 1945, meeting, U.S. Department of State, *Foreign Relations of the United States: Conference of Berlin (Potsdam)* (Washington, D.C.: U.S. Government Printing Office, 1960), I, pp. 907–8.

46. Joint War Plans Committee (JWPC), "Details of the Campaign against Japan," JWPC 369/1, June 15, 1945, file 384 Japan (5-3-44), Records of the Army Staff, RG 319, National Archives.

47. Herbert Bix, "Japan's Delayed Surrender: A Reinterpretation," *Diplomatic History* (Spring 1995), p. 218.

48. Hidenari Terasaki, *Showa Tenno Dokuhakuroku* (Tokyo, Bungei Shunju, 1991), p. 121.

49. Stimson Diary, August 9, 1945; Forrestal to Truman, August 8, 1945, Forrestal Diary.

50. National Air and Space Museum, "Crossroads," p. 29.

51. Bernstein, "The Struggle over History," p. 164.

52. Henry Wallace Diary, August 10, 1945, Wallace Papers, University of Iowa, Iowa City, Iowa.

Comment

The damage and loss of lives that the atomic bomb caused in Hiroshima and Nagasaki were no greater than the destruction caused by some conventional attacks such as the firebombing of Tokyo or Dresden. What (if any) features of nuclear weapons make their use more morally questionable than the use of conventional weapons?

Compare Stimson's argument for the bombing with this defense given by Truman:

> We have used [the bomb] against those who attacked us without warning at Pearl Harbor, against those who have starved and beaten and executed American prisoners of war, against those who have abandoned all pretense of obeying international laws of warfare. We have used it in order to shorten the agony of the war.

Documents now available suggest that Stimson's recollection of the estimates of probable casualties from an invasion (over a million Americans and even more Japanese) was much higher than the estimates that Truman actually received from high military officials at the time. The joint war planners of the Joint Chiefs of

Staff, for example, estimated that the number of casualties from the entire two-stage invasion would range between 132,000 and 220,000 (including about 20 percent deaths). Other military officials argued that even these estimates were too high. Should these differences in estimates make any difference in our moral assessment of Truman's decision?

Evaluate the alternative courses of action that Truman considered or should have considered: (1) bombing only one city; (2) bombing an exclusively military target; (3) detonating one or two bombs over the ocean as a "demonstration"; (4) intensifying the naval and air blockade; (5) waiting until the Russians entered the war; or (6) abandoning the demand for unconditional surrender (guaranteeing the preservation of the emperor's status, the imperial system, and self-rule).

Assume that dropping the bombs actually saved more Americans and Allied lives than any other option open to Truman. Would that justify his decision? What if the decision reduced the total number of lives lost (including Japanese lives)? Some historians argue that one reason Truman decided to use the bomb was to end the war quickly before Russia could enter and gain influence in the region after the war. Would this have been a morally acceptable motive?

James Conant, then president of Harvard and an influential science adviser to President Truman, argued that the bomb "must be used." It was "the only way to awaken the world to the necessity of abolishing war altogether." Given what was known at the time, how should officials have assessed the effect of the bombing on postwar efforts to prevent nuclear war? Should such effects have been a morally relevant factor in Truman's decision?

Bombing the Bunker in Baghdad

Simone Sandy

On August 2, 1990, Iraqi armed forces invaded Kuwait and subsequently occupied and annexed it. Thirty-seven nations formed an alliance to evict Iraq from Kuwait, while the United Nations responded by adopting a series of resolutions imposing sanctions.[1] Despite all diplomatic efforts and economic

sanctions, Iraq refused to retreat from Kuwait. On November 29, 1990, the United Nations' Security Council resolved that if Iraq would not withdraw from Kuwait by January 15, 1991, the Member States were commissioned to use "all necessary means . . . to restore international peace and security in the area."[2] Conforming to this authorization (but not under UN command), the United States and other allied forces began air attacks on Iraq on January 17.

On Wednesday, February 13, 1991, 4:00 A.M. Iraqi time, coalition forces dropped two 2,000-pound laser-guided bombs on a building located in Amariya, a suburb west of

Baghdad. Iraqi officials reported that bodies of 197 adults and 91 children had been removed from the structure by Thursday evening. According to the Information Ministry, at least 400 people were killed and "many would never be identified, either because they were so badly mutilated or charred or because entire families had been killed."[3] Only 8 people were reported to have survived the blast.

Iraqi authorities maintained that the facility destroyed in the air raid was a civilian bomb shelter, no military personnel were inside, and allied forces had attacked it in a calculated attempt to weaken morale. American and British journalists who visited the site of the raid reported that it did appear that the structure was being used as a civilian shelter, and that they saw no evidence that it served any military function. British, Saudi, and American briefing officers, however, insisted that the building was a confirmed military site and that Iraqi officials should have realized it would be a target.

The structure was originally built as a bomb shelter in 1985, during the Iran-Iraq War. However, according the U.S. officials, in the late 1980s the facility was "hardened to enable electronics gear to withstand the electromagnetic pulse of a nuclear blast."[4] It was also "equipped with special air filtration systems, communications gear, electronic equipment, and special wiring."[5] The facility had a steel-reinforced 10-foot-thick concrete roof, which was painted with three black circles apparently intended to resemble bomb holes.

Brigadier General Richard I. Neal (deputy chief of staff at the U.S. command in Saudi Arabia) suggested that while camouflage is typically used to hide a military post, it is unusual on a civilian air raid shelter, which, on the contrary, should have clear civil defense markings.[6] William E. Odom, a retired army general and the former head of the National Security Agency, doubted

that a facility that many people might need to enter rapidly would be surrounded by chain-link and barbed-wire fencing.[7] Lieutenant General Thomas Kelly, director of operations for the Joint Chiefs of Staff, asserted the building "stopped being a bomb shelter . . . when they went back and did a whole bunch of stuff to it to turn it into a military command-and-control facility. At that point . . . it began to be a military target."[8]

Nevertheless, according to Neal and others, the building was not a high priority on the target list until approximately a week before the bombing. At that point, officials said, military trucks began to arrive at the facility with communications equipment. Then, military messages, including orders for Iraqi troops deployed inside Kuwaiti territory, were transmitted from the site. By monitoring communications to and from the site all responsible U.S. officers assured themselves the building had a military purpose. "Signal intelligence [analysis] can confirm and therefore determine the emitter location . . . so we do have all the confidence," said Saudi Colonel Ahmed Robayan.[9]

Despite the conviction of the key briefing officers, several American newspapers reported that other officials (none identified by name) and independent analysts suggested that allied forces had bombed a dual-purpose building while it was functioning in a civilian capacity. U.S. officials, it was said, should have known there were civilians in the bunker. According to *New York Times* reporter R.W. Apple, Jr., "The nagging fear, acknowledged privately by a small number of officials, was that the building served two functions and that the allies had failed to discern it. No one seemed able to give a convincing answer to one question: If photographs taken by reconnaissance planes confirmed that people in military uniforms had been in and out of the building . . . why were there no photographs showing that civilians had been in and out as well? . . . [A] senior officer said the civilians could have entered the bunker after dark . . . when the allies were not conducting reconnaissance, whereas Iraqi military people entered it in the daytime, when the reconnaissance had resumed. But that, as he conceded, raised the question of why close nighttime observation was so lacking."[10]

However, other reports suggested that the intelligence technologies used simply were not capable of adequate nighttime observation: "Intelligence officials said normal U.S. photoreconnaisance satellites are capable of observing key military targets in Iraq more than once each day, but cannot produce images of objects shrouded in darkness. Even special satellites equipped with thermal imaging sensors cannot distinguish several hundred civilians entering or leaving a building at night, they added."[11]

Target planners said that they made no particular attempt to discover any nighttime use of the Amariya building. Rather, based on monitoring its daytime activities during the weeks preceding the raid, they concluded that the site was primarily a military command post.[12] Yet, according to several senior U.S. officials, the building was first placed on the target list because "intelligence experts concluded it was a bunker designed to shelter senior Iraqi government officials from air attack."[13] Several sources (none named) said that such a bunker would be considered by U.S. military officials to be susceptible to attack.

American officials said the day after the raid that among the civilians who died may have been officials of the ruling Baath Party and their families.[14] Asked to justify continued coalition bombings in Baghdad (as opposed to raids on troops and supply lines closer to the Kuwaiti battlefield), White House Press Secretary Marlin Fitzwater said: "Their command-and-control center is there. Their military is there, just like our military is in Washington. It's as simple as that. . . . Baghdad is where this war is orig-

inated from. It's where Saddam Hussein is. It's where the military is. It's where the leadership is."[15]

Spokesmen at the White House and Pentagon maintained that there would be neither a retrospective examination of the Amariya incident specifically nor a more general inquiry into military targeting strategies.[16] Fitzwater said, "The military has looked into this. They have considered it. They discussed it publicly; announced their conclusion. We are satisfied that we've looked into it and did the right thing for the right reasons, and we will continue to attack command-and-control centers."[17]

White House and Pentagon officials also refused to disclose surveillance photos or other evidence from intelligence sources in order to prove their case to the public. "We specifically do not talk about our ability to intercept Iraqi military communications because that would then allow them to change the way they're doing it," said Lieutenant General Kelly. Still, some intelligence experts believed that Pentagon officials had taken great risk by revealing what they already had.[18]

"[T]he openness of American society, with reporters permitted and indeed expected to challenge official versions of events, puts the United States at some disadvantage in the image war with controlled societies like Iraq," Apple suggested. "The bombing represented a significant public-relations failure, augmented by the presence of Western television reporters in Baghdad who transmitted graphic pictures of survivors and mangled bodies . . . [which implied] that the United States was merciless in using force to attain its objectives."[19]

In a letter to UN Secretary General Javier Perez de Cuellar, King Hussein of Jordan urged him to send a delegation to Baghdad to guarantee that allied military operations would not violate humanitarian norms. "The bombing of the shelter is another reminder that Security Council Resolution 678, which some see as the license to launch an organized war of devastation against Iraq, is . . . devoid of legitimate basis," Hussein wrote.[20]

In contrast, Apple pointed out, "American commanders have foresworn the use of many weapons that they have readily available for their use against cities, were their aim to try to force Iraq out of the war by demoralizing the civil population. They have used no ballistic missiles, which are relatively inaccurate, nor have they used B-52s in carpet-bombing patterns."[21] Nevertheless, Lieutenant General Kelly promised that coalition forces would try harder not to harm civilians: "We'll redouble our efforts. We're looking at every resource available to us, whatever methods we can develop to minimize civilian casualties."[22]

General Schwarzkopf charged that "the very actions of the Iraqis themselves demonstrate that they know . . . we're not attacking civilian targets," mentioning that Iraq had placed military headquarters, tanks and artillery, and warplanes in schools and residential areas.[23] Some reporters and U.S. officers suggested that Iraqi authorities had strategically put civilians in the Amariya facility, believing it would draw fire, as a "macabre publicity stunt" to gain points in a propaganda war.[24]

Neal stated that the United States Central Command policy was not to go after targets such as antiaircraft weaponry and military vehicles if placed in residential areas, because commanders did not want to "bring up the civilian casualties." However, Neal said that officials may be forced to rethink this policy if the Iraqis "started putting civilians [as human shields] into these [command and control facilities]. . . [as a] . . . war fighting strategy."[25]

According to Kelly and Herrington, in circumstances where hundreds of civilians might die as a result of a hit on a military target, U.S. commanders would have to decide whether to attack on a "case by case" basis. The United States would try to avoid civilian casualties but at the same time had a responsibility to "successfully prosecute [the] war."[26]

NOTES

1. *The U.S. Army in Operation Desert Storm: An Overview* (Arlington, Va.: Association of the United States Army, 1991), 1.

2. *United Nations Security Council Resolutions Relating to the Situation Between Iraq and Kuwait* (U.N. Dept. of Public Information, Dec. 1991), Resolution 678.

3. Nora Boustany, "Iraqi Says 288 Bodies Removed from Bombed Structure," *Washington Post*, Feb. 15, 1991.

4. Doyle McManus and James Gerstenzang, "Structure Built to Shelter Iraqi Elite, U.S. Says," *Los Angeles Times*, Feb. 15, 1991.

5. Ibid.

6. Interview with Lt. Col. Mike Gallagher and Brig. Gen. Richard Neal, Feb. 13, 1991, Dept. of Defense, USCENTCOM daily briefing, Riyadh, Saudi Arabia.

7. McManus and Gerstenzang, "Structure Built."

8. Ibid.

9. R. Jeffrey Smith, "Building Was Targeted Months Ago as Shelter for Leaders," *Washington Post*, Feb. 14, 1991.

10. "Commanders Deny Error on Target," *New York Times*, Feb. 14, 1991.

11. Smith, "Building Was Targeted."

12. Ibid.

13. Ibid.

14. McManus and Gerstenzang, "Structure Built."

15. Ibid.

16. Patrick E. Tyler, "U.S. Stands Firm on Bomb Attack and Says Investigation Is Closed," *New York Times*, Feb. 15, 1991.

17. McManus and Gerstenzang, "Structure Built."

18. Ibid.

19. "Commanders Deny Error."

20. Boustany, "Iraqi Says 288 Bodies Removed."

21. R.W. Apple, Jr., "Allies Study New Steps to Avoid Civilians in Bombing," *New York Times*, Feb. 15, 1991.

22. Tyler, "U.S. Stands Firm."

23. Apple, "Allies Study New Steps."

24. Interview with Gallagher and Neal.

25. Ibid.

26. Interview with Lt. Gen. Thomas Kelly and Capt. David Herrington, Feb. 13, 1991, Defense Dept. regular briefing, Washington, D.C.

Comment

Did U.S. officials have sufficient evidence for believing that (a) the building they bombed was a military target and (b) civilians were not using it as a shelter? In war, the answers to such questions are usually uncertain, and the answers turn not only on matters of fact but also on matters of morality. Specifically, the degree of risk that officials should accept depends on what values are at stake. Identify the values that you think were at stake in this decision, and try to specify what kind of uncertainty should be tolerated in deciding to order the bombing.

U.S. Central Command policy prohibits attacks on military targets located in residential areas. This policy is stricter than the principle of double effect, which would permit attacks on military targets even if a foreseeable (but unintended) effect is the death of civilians. Does a nation that adopts such a policy put itself (and its soldiers) at an unfair disadvantage in a war with an adversary who rejects the policy? General Neal implied that the United States might abandon the policy if the Iraqis started using civilians as "shields" as part of their war fighting strategy. If the Iraqis had deliberately placed civilians in the bunker to try to protect their command center, should that have changed the moral calculus of U.S. decision-makers?

Some U.S. officials believed that most of the civilians who died in the attack were officials of the ruling Baath Party. If the bunker were being used as a shelter for government officials, would the U.S. be justified in bombing it? In September 1990 before the war began, the air force chief of staff, General Michael J. Dugan, said publicly that the U.S. military has plans to "decapitate" the Iraqi leadership by targeting President Saddam Hussein, his family, his senior commanders, his palace guard, and even his mistress. As Dugan was relieved of his command for making these comments, Secretary of Defense Richard Cheney stated, "We never discuss operational matters, such as selection of specific targets for potential air strikes. We never talk about the targeting of specific individuals who are officials in other governments." Would the United States have been morally justified in directly attacking Saddam Hussein? Under what circumstances (if any) may a nation engage in or encourage political assassination?

Intervention in Somalia
Neal Higgins

On October 3, 1993, an American Black-hawk helicopter was shot down by small-arms fire as it attempted to withdraw from the Olympia Hotel in downtown Mogad-

ishu, the war-ravaged capital of Somalia. Eighteen U.S. Army Rangers were killed and seventy-eight wounded in the bloody firefight that ensued, with casualties on the Somali side somewhere between five hundred and one thousand. One American was captured, and the corpse of another dragged through the streets for camera crews to broadcast to a shocked television audience. The incident quickly spelled the end of American involvement in the United Nations' attempt to bring peace and stability to the Horn of Africa.

In the wake of the tragedy, many Americans indignantly asked why Somalis had turned so viciously on American troops who had come to Mogadishu on a mission of charity. The answer: what began as an effort to relieve human suffering and restore peace and stability had become, in the eyes of many Somalis, an effort to intervene in a civil war and impose a government upon a sovereign people. Had the UN and the United States wrongly taken sides in an internal dispute, had they overstepped their legal and moral authority, or was this a necessary albeit painful part of legitimate post–Cold War intervention in the affairs of an impoverished and increasingly unstable state?

SOMALIA'S DECLINE AND THE DECISION TO INTERVENE

Like many post–Cold War conflicts, the civil war in Somalia began with the fall of a dictator who had long profited from the superpower rivalry. General Mohammed Siad Barre had been in power since the 1969 coup which overthrew Somalia's Western-style democracy, a system plagued by the persistence of clan loyalties and tribal divisions.[1] Siad's corrupt and oppressive regime eventually spawned active, armed opposition groups—most with a strong tribal foundation—that engaged the government in a low-level civil war. The dictatorship's brutality towards those opposition groups eventually enraged both Somali clans and Siad's foreign benefactors. Chief among these was the United States, which chose to disassociate itself from Siad by eliminating funding to the Somali government. Cut adrift from American support, Siad was left unable to control the country-

side or maintain basic state institutions. With the government bereft of foreign aid and internationally isolated, rebel groups from the southern and central regions of Somalia began to challenge the dictatorship for control of Mogadishu.[2]

Chief among these rebel groups was the United Somali Congress (USC), jointly led by General Mohamed Farah Aideed and Mohamed Ali Mahdi. In January 1991 the USC captured Mogadishu and ousted Siad from power. Within weeks of seizing control the group suffered an internal split, with Aideed refusing to accept Ali Mahdi as the interim president. Mogadishu soon turned into a battlefield as followers of the two rival leaders fought for control of the capital. Between November 1991 and February 1992, fighting in Mogadishu alone caused an estimated 14,000 deaths and 27,000 injuries. But the destruction wasn't limited to the capital. As Siad's forces fled Mogadishu they pursued a scorched earth policy, killing livestock, burning crops, and occasionally tangling with USC forces. With Somalia already suffering from a crippling drought, the fighting quickened the spread of famine. By mid-1992 nearly 300,000 had died and close to 700,000 more had sought refuge in Kenya and Ethiopia. Only in the northwest, where independent rebel troops had already claimed victory over weak government forces, did stability prevail.

Although the international community had not directly responded to the turmoil in Somalia, it was well aware of the country's troubles. United Nations Security Council resolutions and international conferences had expressed concern over the situation, most nations had closed their embassies in Mogadishu, and the UN High Commissioner for Refugees, the United Nations Children's Fund, and the World Food Program had all evacuated their personnel to Kenya. Only nongovernmental organizations (NGOs) remained in Somalia, among them the International Committee of the Red

Cross, Save the Children UK and Médecins sans Frontières.

Despite substantial assistance from the United States and its European allies, even those NGOs still operating in Somalia experienced a range of difficulties. With gangs of armed thugs controlling both the Mogadishu ports and many of the supply routes leading to feeding centers outside the capital, looting and extortion significantly reduced the amount of food actually reaching the neediest Somalis. Furthermore, by drawing thousands of sustenance farmers who were otherwise widely dispersed into small, densely populated areas, the feeding centers often seemed to perpetuate the drought and contribute to the spread of disease. Without protection to ensure the safe delivery of food, efforts to aid the Somali people were often doing more harm than good.

Fearing an impending humanitarian disaster and succumbing to mounting public pressure, the Security Council decided to act. On January 23, 1992, in resolution 733, the Council called on the secretary-general to send an envoy to Mogadishu, imposed an arms embargo on all of Somalia, requested the delivery of aid from member states, and established a special coordinator to oversee the delivery of humanitarian assistance. The UN quickly encountered difficulty performing all four tasks. Despite efforts to stem their flow, arms continued to seep into Somalia from Kenya and Ethiopia, adding to the caches left from Cold War patronage. Meanwhile, officials from the Secretariat, apparently unaware of the USC's infighting, angered Aideed by initiating a dialogue with Ali Mahdi. Finally, after restoring good relations with the NGOs—many of whom felt that the UN had abandoned them when it withdrew personnel to Kenya—the new special coordinator for humanitarian assistance encountered the same difficulties that had plagued earlier attempts to deliver food and medicine.

With few of its efforts succeeding, in April the Security Council concluded that the best way to assist the Somali people would be to deploy military observers to monitor a tenuous cease-fire that had taken hold in Mogadishu and peacekeepers to guarantee the delivery of food and medicine. Cautiously leading the way was President George Bush, who authorized the use of fourteen C-130 cargo planes to airlift humanitarian supplies and transport the proposed peacekeeping force. Over the next six months the operation would successfully deliver more than 28,000 metric tons of food, but the peacekeepers—a Pakistani brigade deployed with the begrudging consent of the warring parties—did not arrive until September.[3] By that time the Security Council had already infuriated Aideed by authorizing the eventual deployment of three thousand more peacekeepers without first consulting any of the Somali factions.

Even before the UN Secretariat secured troop contributions for the expanded force, it was clear that simply sending more peacekeepers wouldn't solve the problem. The question was less how many troops the UN could muster than how well prepared those troops were for the situation on the ground. The plight of the Pakistani peacekeepers already in Mogadishu clearly illustrated the difficulties any UN force would face:

> While all of the Pakistani peacekeepers had arrived by late September 1992, the force's terms of reference, based on traditional notions of what constituted peacekeeping, proved to be totally inadequate to the Somali challenge. There was no durable cease-fire to preserve and cooperation with the warring parties was either non-existent or unreliable and inconsistent. Far from fulfilling their mission to secure the airport, seaport, and lines of communication in and around Mogadishu, the lightly-armed Pakistanis struggled to protect themselves from repeated militia attacks and were pinned down in their barracks near Mogadishu airport for the first two months after arrival.[4]

With Mogadishu warehouses filling with food waiting for safe delivery and the few peacekeepers in Somalia confined to their barracks, the only solution to the mounting crisis seemed to be a more forceful approach.

AUTHORIZING UNILATERAL ACTION

With the situation in Somalia worsening by the week, Congress, the media, and the NGO community all pressured the Bush administration to take action. With looting and extortion still plaguing efforts to airlift food into Somalia, in October 1992 the White House and the Pentagon concluded that 12,000 to 15,000 troops—triple the number already authorized by the Security Council—would be needed to provide adequate protection to ensure the safe delivery of humanitarian assistance. Although those proposing such an intervention had assumed that the troops in question would be primarily Canadian or Belgian, the developing crisis soon made the deployment of American forces appear ever more likely—and ever more necessary. According to the Office of Foreign Disaster Assistance at the U.S. Agency for International Development, one-quarter of southern Somali children under the age of five had already died. The U.S. Centers for Disease Control and Prevention estimated that the southern city of Baidoa had lost 40 percent of its population and 70 percent of its children under five to hunger or disease.[5] Although some critics pointed out that death rates were beginning to decline, aid workers retorted that it was only because there were fewer people left to die. Either way, deliveries of food and medicine were still unable to safely reach those who needed them most.

Facing the possibility of even greater starvation, many in the Bush administration began to sense the need for American leadership. As U.S. special envoy to Somalia Robert B. Oakley and political adviser John L. Hirsch explain:

> Somalia had emerged as such an overwhelming humanitarian crisis that there was no longer a question of inaction. Moreover, a definable mission had emerged, one which no other nation was likely to undertake. And the goodwill to be gained for helping out in Somalia might help offset the widespread criticism that the United States was dilatory in responding to aggression in Bosnia. Such action would also help mute criticism of the United States in the Arab world for not helping their Muslim coreligionists in Bosnia.[6]

With Chairman of the Joint Chiefs of Staff General Colin Powell pushing for the strongest possible option—a multinational force with the United States at its fore—the decision went to the White House. On November 25, 1992, President George Bush decided that if the Security Council concurred and other nations volunteered assistance, the United States would lead a new operation to provide full protection for humanitarian relief operations in southern Somalia. Named the United Task Force (UNITAF), the operation would function under Chapter VII of the UN Charter, which allows member states both to act without the consent of the warring parties and, when necessary, to use force in pursuit of their objectives. Although the White House and the Pentagon viewed the threat of force as necessary to restore civil order, both hoped UNITAF would could avoid hostilities. Once the operation had established a secure environment for the delivery of humanitarian assistance, UNITAF was to relinquish control to UNOSOM II, the UN's successor to its original operation.

Even with the support of the Joint Chiefs of Staff and the president's closest advisers, the decision to deploy American troops to Somalia was nevertheless controversial. Although images of starving Somali children had stirred overwhelming public support for a humanitarian intervention—producing "a moral clarity for people like few issues in recent years"—there remained troubling questions as to what role American forces should play.[7] A poll by the *New York Times* and CBS News reported that 81 percent of those surveyed believed that the United

States was "doing the right thing" by sending troops to Somalia, with 70 percent agreeing that the operation was worth both the financial and political costs and the possible loss of American lives. But the poll also revealed that the public was sharply divided as to how long the United States should remain in Somalia: while 48 percent of those surveyed thought U.S. troops should stay "only as long as it takes to set up supply lines and make sure people don't starve," 44 percent said that American troops should remain "as long as it takes to make sure Somalia will remain peaceful." Whatever their thoughts on the intervention's limits or objectives, most had already concluded that American troops and leadership were required. As the *New York Times* reported on December 13:

> There are already signs the operation may become more complicated than people expect, and the moral certainty of December could easily become the political quagmire of February. But for many people Somalia has become a Christmas-season parable, making it difficult to look at the commercial iconography of plenty—golden arches, all-you-can-eat steak joints and manic Big Boys bearing overstuffed burgers—without thinking twice.[8]

Stopping only briefly to consider the implications of such an operation, most Americans had apparently decided that in cases like Somalia "action is appropriate if only because inaction is unthinkable."[9]

Much as they too may have been moved by the images of starving Somalia, critics in both Congress and the media were far slower to endorse the deployment of American troops. While some warned that the United States must "avoid getting trapped in a moral domino theory in which intervention in one place automatically seems to compel intervention in another," others called for specific details as to what American troops would be doing in Somalia and how and when they would withdraw.[10] Among the latter was Congressman David Obey, then chairman of the House Appropriations Sub-

committee on Foreign Operations, who called on the Republican administration to clarify that "the primary message is not to pacify the entire country, but to secure limited territorial zones where those who seek it can receive critically needed UN assistance."[11] Fearing that the intervention could result in a political quagmire but nevertheless supportive of intervention, Obey and others wanted assurances that UNITAF would not be a repetition of America's failed efforts in Beirut and Vietnam.

Well aware of the widespread concerns about the intervention, President Bush quickly emphasized that the operation would be limited to ensuring the safe delivery of humanitarian supplies and would not be expanded to include a wider role in rebuilding the Somali state. Administration officials also reaffirmed that UNITAF's ultimate goal would be to hand control back to the UN. As one State Department official put it, the objective was "to make the UN a more credible actor," adding that the UN "wasn't a credible military actor before, now it will be. By not being a credible military actor, it wasn't a credible political actor."[12] Confirming that the Pentagon approved of the operation, Secretary of Defense Dick Cheney and General Colin Powell publicly cited four factors that had convinced them to propose and support an intervention by American troops; first, the mission was fully justifiable as an act of humanitarian intervention; second, UNITAF was considered to be eminently "doable"; third, it was a limited operation with a set date for withdrawal; and finally, UNITAF wouldn't run the risk of an unacceptably high casualty rate.[13]

While the operation seemed to have won the support of the White House, the Pentagon, and the American public, it had yet to receive the approval of the United Nations. Although the secretary-general and his top advisors in the Department of Peacekeeping Operations welcomed the U.S. offer to lead an operation in Somalia, they expressed deep concerns about both the high degree of American involvement and the use of force. Those two aspects of the operation, they feared, could corrupt the traditional practice of peacekeeping and taint the UN's future role in the Horn of Africa. Their concerns reflected a traditional view of UN peacekeeping, one shaped by the tensions and politics of the Cold War. Developed in an era when each superpower was wary of the other's efforts to use the UN to make geostrategic gains, peacekeeping had long been bound by a certain set of rules and restrictions. To reflect the multinational nature of the United Nations—and thus ensure that the UN was enforcing the will of the international community, not that of a given superpower—peacekeeping operations had long relied on troop contributions from every corner of the globe. Even with such contributions in place, the Security Council would only deploy an operation once it was clear that the UN had won the consent of the warring parties, that the operation could remain impartial, and that peacekeepers could refrain from the use of force.

While such restrictions all helped to appease the superpowers' many concerns, they also ensured the safety of the peacekeepers themselves. As Andrei Raevsky explains:

> The consensus on "traditional" peacekeeping was that peacekeepers should not have the obligation, the soldiers or the equipment to engage violators in hostilities. International peacekeeping forces expressed and facilitated the erstwhile belligerents' will to live in peace; they could not supervise peace in conditions of war. Turning them into a fighting force erodes international consensus on their function, encourages withdrawals by contributing contingents, converts them into a factional participant in the internal power struggle and turns them into targets of attack from rival internal factions . . . the UN tries to ensure that it is maintaining a neutral stance between the disputants, not serving the political interest of any one faction in the conflict or at the UN, and not imposing the will of a UN majority upon any party.[14]

Although the end of the Cold War had led many to speculate as to whether the UN could use force to pursue impartial humanitarian goals without first winning the consent of the warring parties, few in the Secretariat were yet willing to take that chance.

Nor were they prepared to agree that UNITAF, even as an independent American effort, should be followed by a UN peacekeeping operation. Secretary-General Boutros Boutros-Ghali even expressed doubts about UNITAF itself, arguing that the American proposal did too little to disarm the Somali warlords.[15] Although most member states of the Security Council agreed with the secretary-general, they also understood the need for immediate and effective action. On December 3, unwilling to allow the situation in Somalia to deteriorate further, the Council passed resolution 794, granting the United States permission to lead a multinational force sanctioned by the UN but not designated as a UN peacekeeping operation. Within a week U.S. forces were ready to land in Somalia and begin Operation Restore Hope.

Armed with a peak force of 36,000 troops—27,000 of them American—and a mandate to "get the food through," UNITAF was soon active across the southern half of Somalia.[16] With the authority to use force in an impartial manner and the begrudging consent of the warring parties, the operation rapidly became "a laboratory for new theories of UN peacekeeping."[17] The U.S.-led operation represented "the first time that the Security Council sanctioned an enforcement action under Chapter VII of the UN Charter in a theoretically sovereign state."[18] Neither the operation's size nor its historical significance was lost on the warring parties. Within a week the United States had convinced Aideed and Ali Mahdi to meet in person for the first time since the civil war began. Although the secretary-general's special representative in Somalia was present at the meeting, the number of American troops and the need for efficient

American command and control had put the United States firmly in charge. By the end of the meeting the two faction leaders had agreed to both a cease-fire and a conference on national reconciliation.

Promising as the agreements seemed, both the United States and the UN realized that they meant little without monitored implementation. Hoping to avoid confrontation with UNITAF forces and curry favor with the United States, Aideed and Ali Mahdi would stop at little to appear cooperative. Well aware of the warlords' motivations, UNITAF forces nevertheless took advantage of the diplomatic opening to begin delivering humanitarian aid and developing the foundation for a lasting settlement. Although the U.S. military until then had little experience with UN operations, it was clearly capable of the type of muscular peacekeeping required to keep the food flowing into the regions under its control. By using the threat of force effectively and impartially, UNITAF accomplished a number of the objectives that had eluded the original UNOSOM effort. As former Assistant Secretary of State for African Affairs Chester Crocker surmises:

> Establishing safety for relief workers while keeping the warlords somewhat placated and off balance; maintaining and demonstrating military primacy without making a permanent adversary or national hero of any local actor; pushing the military factions toward a locally led political process while opening up that process to civilian elites and eschewing precise formulas; removing heavy weapons from areas of conflict while fostering the restoration of police and government functions—these were undertakings of the highest order of delicacy in a militarized and fragmented society like Somalia's. UNITAF's accomplishments far exceeded the simple, publicly discussed goal of creating a "secure environment for humanitarian relief." They required strong leadership and a well-oiled quick-response military-civilian bureaucracy.[19]

UNITAF's greatest asset was the commitment of the United States and the many advantages that that commitment entailed. Unlike most ad hoc UN peacekeeping forces, UNITAF had well-established command, control, and communication structures and full access to the proper equipment, armament, and personnel. Well-equipped and well-prepared, the operation made steady progress towards its defined objectives.

But despite its many accomplishments, UNITAF unapologetically failed to address several fundamental concerns raised by the UN. First, American commanders chose not to confront the political crisis directly, instead recognizing both Aideed and Ali Mahdi as legitimate political actors—and considerably narrowing the possibility for an alternate political solution. As the *Washington Post* reported:

> U.S. military and diplomatic representatives missed no opportunity to treat Aideed and Ali Mahdi with public respect. The two warlords, whose struggle for power and extortion of relief supplies are blamed by outside observers for starving 300,000 of their countrymen to death, were cloaked by their American interlocutors in the mantle of legitimate power.[20]

Ignoring pleas from the UN Secretariat to assume control of all of Somalia, UNITAF's leadership next decided to limit the operation's efforts exclusively to the southern half of the country. Finally, and most importantly, Washington specifically refused to forcibly disarm the Somali warlords. The Pentagon suggested that disarmament would unnecessarily antagonize the warring parties and endanger the humanitarian effort, insisting that "the creation of a benign security environment pertained only to providing security for UNITAF forces, the relief convoys and the humanitarian relief personnel." Boutros-Ghali, on the other hand, insisted "that the UNITAF mission should be much more extensive than that the United States envisioned, with an ambitious disarmament program, broader geographic extent, and longer duration."[21]

As the deadline for the withdrawal of

American forces grew nearer, the disagreement over disarmament quickly evolved into a heated debate over the goals and limits of the intervention. Both the Pentagon and the newly elected Clinton administration viewed the operation's objectives as being strictly defined and clearly limited. Their goal was not to resolve the civil war, nor to end the drought, but rather to facilitate efforts to alleviate the short-term humanitarian crisis. While diplomats at the United States Liaison Office in Mogadishu were willing to encourage the emergence of grass-roots solutions to Somalia's more fundamental problems, they were not willing to plan the reconstruction of the Somali state. Although the decision to avoid more extensive engagement in Somalia may have had more to do with politics than principle, it nevertheless reflected a belief that it was neither the right nor the responsibility of the United States to take an active role in Somalia's domestic affairs beyond what was necessary to alleviate starvation and restore order. Provided with that level of assistance, the Somalis would be expected to develop their own solutions to the nation's other woes.

Faced with the imminent withdrawal of American forces, Boutros-Ghali saw the situation quite differently. While the American approach to the crisis had temporarily alleviated starvation and restored order, it had done little to provide for a lasting peace. By striving only for local disarmament and limited attempts at political reconciliation, UNITAF had succeeded in getting the food through but not in creating long-term stability. Moreover, with the warlords still armed and hungry for power, there was good reason to believe that Somali could quickly return to anarchy. As Boutros-Ghali saw it, unless the international community provided a lasting presence to cement UNITAF's gains and address Somalia's most pressing needs, the process of national reconciliation would collapse, the civil war would most likely reignite, and the drought

would undoubtedly continue. Fully aware that no UN force could match the military might of the United States, the secretary-general thus insisted that the United States at least complete the demanding task of disarmament, the most important precursor to Somalia's reconstruction.

THE RETURN TO UN CONTROL

The split between the United States and the UN could not have come at a worse time. In the first three months of 1993 the warring factions were to agree to a formal cease-fire and disarmament program, then travel to the Ethiopian capital of Addis Ababa to attend conferences on both humanitarian questions and the issue of national reconciliation. Instrumental to the success of these initiatives was the continuing cooperation of the warring parties. While UNITAF had managed to maintain that cooperation through the threat of force and the promise of American assistance, the UN was to have little such luck. Problems began as early as January, when a protest coordinated by Aideed prevented the secretary-general from visiting UNOSOM staff in Mogadishu. Claiming that the UN would enslave Somalia in a trusteeship arrangement tantamount to colonization, the protesters forced Boutros-Ghali to return to the airport, cutting his visit short.[22] Although Ambassador Oakley afterwards convinced Aideed that he needed to enter into discussions with the secretary-general, the warlord's respect for the UN was doubtful at best.

Difficulties began anew at the two conferences in Addis Ababa. Although the meetings resulted in agreements on the cantonment of forces, political reconciliation, and infrastructure redevelopment, they failed to resolve the question of disarmament. Yet disarmament remained the cornerstone upon which the accords depended; if the warlords suspected that their enemies were still armed for combat, they would hardly be compelled to begin the process of national reconciliation. As Hirsch and Oakley explain:

> The most significant gap in carrying out the Addis Ababa Accords pertained to disarmament. Operation Restore Hope's strategy for maintaining a stable security environment during the transition counted heavily on effective and timely follow-up. The accords were clearly far from self-enforcing: UNITAF's mandate did not cover nationwide enforcement, the UN was unwilling and unable to accept the responsibility, and the NGOs had neither the cohesion nor the resources required to do so. The factions, each watching and waiting for the other to disarm, were either too suspicious and frightened to do so or, in some cases, had no real intention of doing so. They feared both serious attacks from their enemies and the loss of future power and position, and Aideed's SNA prepared to challenge the UN peacekeepers as soon as U.S. forces had departed.[23]

Even with Washington's refusal to pursue disarmament, a seamless transition from a strong American force to a strong UN force might have convinced Aideed to stand down. But the transition to UN control was far from seamless.

The key obstacle to a smooth transition was miscommunication between the White House and the UN Secretariat. Although the United States was actually willing to offer support for a UN disarmament program, Boutros-Ghali assumed that the Clinton administration was unprepared to assist with any disarmament whatsoever. Because he himself was unwilling to assign the task to a weaker UN force, the secretary-general insisted that disarmament must be completed before the withdrawal of American troops. To demonstrate his resolve, Boutros-Ghali refused to begin planning for the deployment of UNOSOM II until disarmament had begun. Unfazed by the secretary-general's refusal and still unwilling to disarm the warlords, the United States flatly declared that it would begin its withdrawal as planned, in January 1993.

When the time finally came for the first departure of American troops, it was clear that the UN was unprepared to assume control. Even after the Clinton administration had unequivocally stated that UNITAF would neither expand operations to the north nor pursue a comprehensive program for disarmament, the secretary-general continued to insist that both were vital to a long-term settlement. Following his advice, the Security Council assigned the duties to UNOSOM II. As a result:

> The new UNOSOM II force, which consisted of 20,000 troops and 8,000 logical support staff from thirty-three different countries, was supposed to do what UNITAF had been unable to do with 17,000 troops more: disarm the warlord militias and take charge of the remaining sixty percent of Somalia's territory.[24]

But the Security Council's vision for UNOSOM II extended far beyond nationwide disarmament. The UN operation was also ordered to undertake the most ambitious postconflict peace-building program ever attempted, one which U.S. Ambassador to the UN Madeleine Albright would dub "an unprecedented enterprise aimed at nothing less that the restoration of a country."[25]

In Resolution 794 the Security Council outlined just what that enterprise would entail. First, the secretary-general was to solicit from member states contributions "to assist in financing the rehabilitation of the political institutions and economy of Somalia."[26] Then, to begin Somalia's "rehabilitation," UNOSOM II was to assist in the repatriation of refugees and displaced persons; to help establish local, regional, and national law enforcement agencies; to begin de-mining the Somali countryside; and, finally, "to create conditions under which Somali civil society may have a role, at every level, in the process of political reconciliation and in the formulation and realization of rehabilitation and reconstruction programs."[27] Although the system of regional and national councils agreed to in the Addis Ababa Accords would remain the foundation for national reconciliation, the UN's plan to revive Somalia went far beyond anything discussed by the warlords. The Security Council had chosen to undertake the reconstruction of a failed state.

Comprehensive as the UN's vision for Somalia may have been, it was soon to encounter a host of difficulties. UNITAF had succeeded in a less challenging mission by breaking down barriers between the military, humanitarian, and political elements of its presence and maintaining the threat of force as an incentive for the Somalis to develop their own solutions. UNOSOM II, on the other hand, operated in a slow, compartmentalized, bureaucratic fashion. Hardly as strong as its American predecessors, its troops seemed ill-organized, poorly managed, and clearly unprepared for the task at hand. Between the UN's bureaucratic approach to solving Somalia's problems and the sheer inadequacy of the operation's military capabilities, a sense of insecurity began to pervade UNOSOM II. That insecurity soon distanced UN personnel in Somalia from the Somalis they were there to help. Nowhere was the growing alienation more obvious than in the UN barracks in central Mogadishu. While American troops participating in UNITAF had remained in makeshift accommodations throughout their stay in Somalia, UNOSOM II arrived with prefabricated housing and proceeded to build what eventually appeared to be a fort guarding UN personnel from the Somalis outside.[28]

Acutely aware of the UN's shortcomings, Aideed soon began to challenge UNOSOM II. By far the most powerful of the remaining warlords, Aideed knew that the UN would be loathe to confront him. On a more personal level, tensions had emerged between Aideed and the secretary-general; while Boutros-Ghali still bore a grudge from Aideed's January protest, Aideed suspected that Bourtros-Ghali, as Egypt's former foreign minister, had been an ally to former Somali dictator Siad Barre. Sensing Aideed's hostility, UN officials in Mogadishu quickly concluded—as did their American counterparts—that Aideed was likely to test the new UN presence.[29] As the *New York Times* reported in November 1993, "in early summer, the Central Intelligence Agency endorsed the view, held by the United Nations and publicly supported by President Clinton at the time, that General Aideed was a disruptive force who would interfere with the rebuilding of Somalia."[30] Most analysts suspected that the warlord had little interest in sharing power and was only biding his time until the peacekeepers departed. Few, however, had any concrete suggestions as to how to handle him.

With UN officials still deciding how to deal with Aideed, relations with the warlord began to deteriorate. The tensions came to a flashpoint in mid-May, when the UN renounced an upcoming Mogadishu peace conference sponsored by Aideed as a clear ploy to seize power. As if to emphasize their point, UN officials in Somalia quickly announced that they would sponsor a competing conference, even providing free transportation to Aideed's rivals. Although SNA representatives attended the parallel peace conferences, their behavior convinced the UN that Aideed could not be included in the plans for a new nation:

> When, as a means of political pressure, some of the participants from other clans were detained by SNA militia in the Olympia Hotel, UNOSOM concluded that Aideed's ambitions could never be satisfied by genuine power-sharing and compromise. They concluded that he should be politically marginalized rather than included in continued high-level dialogue.[31]

Had UNOSOM II had the military strength of its American-led predecessor, the UN might have ultimately succeeded in marginalizing Aideed. As it was, however, the UN would succeed only in engaging him as a foe.

THE END OF UNOSOM II

Nowhere were the disparities between the UN peacekeepers and their American predecessors clearer than in south Mogadishu, where American marines were replaced by Pakistani peacekeepers who had different training, less firepower, and clear doubts about the level of tactical support they would receive from UNOSOM II headquarters.[32] It was here that Aideed would launch his first offensive against the UN. Realizing that his success would in part depend on the support of the city's population, the warlord first attacked UNOSOM II not on the ground but on Radio Mogadishu, at the time controlled by Aideed's Somali National Army. Decrying foreign interference in domestic problems, praising the SNA, and calling for a Somali solution to Somali problems, Aideed made it clear that he was not about to bend to UN pressure. Soon after the broadcast the SNA's heavy weaponry reappeared on the streets of south Mogadishu.

As the UN decided how to respond to this latest affront, rumors abounded that UNOSOM II intended to force Radio Mogadishu off the air.[33] On June 4, 1993, UN headquarters warned Aideed that on the following day Pakistani peacekeepers would be coming to the compound that housed the station as part of a routine weapons inspection.[34] Fearing that the UN was attempting to marginalize him, Aideed took action. On the morning of June 5, as they began patrols throughout south Mogadishu, Pakistani peacekeepers were ambushed by SNA forces hiding in crowds of women and children. Pinned down, the Pakistanis called for support from the U.S. Quick Reaction Force (QRF)—a remnant of UNITAF still under U.S. command—and Italian armored units stationed in Mogadishu.[35] By the end of the day twenty-four Pakistanis and scores of Somalis lay dead. The Security Council quickly convened an emergency session to denounce the violence and authorize the use of "all necessary measures" leading to the detention or arrest of those responsible for the attacks. Although Aideed was not mentioned by name, he was clearly the target. By authorizing the use of force, the Security Council had thus taken its first steps towards engaging the warlord.

While many observers had long considered Aideed to be the prime obstacle to rebuilding Somalia, the decision to use force in pursuit of his arrest represented a major turning point in the intervention. Although the intention was to bring to justice those responsible for the murder of the Pakistani peacekeepers, singling out Aideed in effect meant taking sides in a civil war. Although later painted as a rash decision on the behalf of the secretary-general and his top military adviser in Somalia, at the time the change in policy had the qualified support of the United States. As the *New York Times* later reported:

> The premise of the United Nations policy—to neutralize General Aideed's power—was shared by top Administration officials throughout most of the summer, though some were uneasy that the strategy relied too heavily on military force. The United States military at first also supported the policy of confronting Aideed with force, but later came to doubt that it would be possible to capture him.[36]

Despite their reservations, administration officials publicly supported the Security Council resolution authorizing Aideed's capture. Only days after the attack on Pakistani peacekeepers, American gunships and attack helicopters pounded Aideed's headquarters in an attack broadcast across the globe. Although President Clinton lauded the strike, claiming "the military back of Aideed has been broken" and adding that "a warrant has been issued for his arrest," it had in fact only stirred Aideed's anger.[37] With the clear impression that he was being marginalized and persecuted in a ploy orchestrated by the United States and its allies in the UN, Aideed chose retaliation over surrender. As it became clear that Aideed would refuse to yield—and would instead take every opportunity to embarrass the foreign interlocutors and disrupt the process of national reconciliation—the United States and the UN steeled their resolve and announced a manhunt for the renegade warlord.

As forces under UN and American command began the search for Aideed, the purpose of the continuing international presence in Somalia became increasingly blurred. Rather than building the framework for a lasting settlement, UNOSOM II forces—along with the American QRF—began to focus more and more on pursuing Aideed. As they did so, engaging the SNA on a regular basis, the foreign peacekeepers began to resemble belligerents themselves. In Aideed's eyes they were certainly fair targets, even for offensive attacks. Although clearly illegal, Aideed's offensive against the peacekeepers soon began to receive greater acceptance among the Somali people. In some quarters the warlord even began to resemble a homegrown hero resisting the will of imperialist intruders.

Mobilized by the broadcasts over Radio Mogadishu, popular support for Aideed was further enhanced by the tactics used to fight the warlord. According to one force commander, when pursuing Aideed it was often "hard to avoid civilian casualties" and "very difficult to tell what the casualty numbers are on the other side."[38] The confusion over casualty figures reflected the more fundamental difficulty of defining the rules of engagement for a manhunt in the midst of a humanitarian operation. As one correspondent put it, "In the murky business of fighting war as peacekeepers, understanding the rules is half the battle."[39] Unfortunately for the peacekeepers, it was a battle they were almost destined to lose. Unlike the UN and U.S. troops, General Aideed's renegade forces were bound by no rules of engagement. Fighting an unconventional war, they often launched attacks from crowds of civilians, even using women and

children as human shields. When peacekeepers accidentally killed or wounded those civilians, even in the course of defending themselves against attacks, the result was greater resentment towards the intervention. As one Somali student explained after a battle between Aideed's troops and UN peacekeepers, "If the dead men were gunmen, it is good for Somalia. But if they were not gunmen, this is an evil foreign action."[40]

Beginning in July 1993 and continuing over the next four months, the SNA and UNOSOM II forces would clash regularly, with the UN accusing the SNA of launching ambushes from crowds of women and children and the SNA retorting that the UN had fired on innocent civilians. Although UNOSOM II staged several successful raids on SNA weapons depots, the operation was ultimately unsuccessful in stopping the rebels from attacking UN personnel. Unhappy with the escalating violence and displeased with the United States's decision to have its remaining troops report to Washington rather than UN headquarters in New York, French and Italian commanders refused to use force, eventually withdrawing their units from the UN command structure.[41] Even aid agencies expressed their disenchantment over the use of force, claiming that it was making it more difficult to distribute humanitarian assistance. But the SNA continued to press UNOSOM II forces, killing four Americans with a remote controlled device that exploded under their vehicle and injuring six more with a landmine planted along a patrol route.[42] In response,

> President Clinton ordered Delta Force commandos, Army Rangers, and a helicopter detachment airlifted to Mogadishu. Though acting in support of the UNOSOM II mandate, they operated under separate U.S. command. . . . Their orders were to capture Aideed and senior SNA officials whenever the opportunity arose. . . . In effect, the Rangers and Delta Force became a posse with standing authority to go after Aideed and his outlaw band.[43]

As operations became more and more focused on fighting the SNA, life in Mogadishu began to change. With the desire to capture Aideed almost an obsession, less and less attention was paid to humanitarian operations, and the situation on the streets began to deteriorate. When not on patrol, peacekeepers took shelter in the makeshift fortress in central Mogadishu. Both the media and employees of nongovernmental organizations were increasingly evacuated to Nairobi. Those who remained often had to travel with armed escorts, even on humanitarian missions.[44]

The turning point came on October 3, 1993. After a string of firefights during the first half of September had left hundreds of Somalis and dozens of Nigerian, Pakistani, and Italian peacekeepers dead or wounded, the U.S. Rangers and Delta Force commandos stepped up their raids and patrols, arresting uninvolved Somalis and even foreign relief workers as they searched—with some success—for top SNA officials.[45] Although the new Clinton administration had privately shown signs that it might seek a political solution, the events of October 3 dashed any hopes for such an outcome. Acting on reliable intelligence, U.S. Rangers descended on the Olympia Hotel in downtown Mogadishu to search for SNA officials suspected of planning attacks on UN forces. Although the Rangers successfully captured twenty-four suspects—including several of Aideed's top aides—two of their helicopters were forced down as they attempted to withdraw. The nightmarish incident that followed spelled the end of American involvement in Somalia and sent UNOSOM II on a downward spiral from which the operation would never recover. Although UNOSOM, UNITAF, and UNOSOM II had between them saved countless lives, the UN intervention in Somalia was widely deemed a failure.

Reeling from the fallout of UNOSOM II, both the United States and the United Nations would quickly denounce the premise that force could be used to pressure warring parties to consent to a foreign humanitarian presence. The Pentagon and White House came to quick agreement that U.S. forces should engage only in traditional UN operations, ones which enjoy the full consent of the warring parties. Without the assistance of American forces or forthright American leadership on the Security Council, the UN would also shy away from using force, a decision that clearly affected the troubled operation in the former Yugoslavia. The debate continues as to how the international community can and should respond to humanitarian emergencies where intervention has not won, and perhaps could never win, the consent of the internally warring parties.

NOTES

1. Robert G. Putnam, "The UN Operation in Somalia," in Ramesh Thakur and Carlyle A. Thayer, eds., *A Crisis of Expectations: UN Peacekeeping in the 1990s* (Boulder, Colo.: Westview Press, 1995), p. 86.

2. Unless otherwise noted, background information for this section is drawn from Putnam, "The UN Operation in Somalia," pp. 86–89.

3. John L. Hirsch and Robert Oakley, *Somalia and Operation Restore Hope* (Washington, D.C.: United States Institute of Peace, 1995), p. 24.

4. Ibid., p. 91.

5. Ibid., pp. 32–33.

6. Ibid., p. 42.

7. Peter Applebome, "Seared by Faces of Need, Americans Say 'How Could We Not Do This?'" *New York Times*, Dec. 13, 1992, p. A16.

8. Ibid.

9. Ibid.

10. Thomas L. Friedman, "Clinton Inherits Conflicts That Don't Follow Rules," *New York Times*, Dec. 13, 1992, p. D3.

11. "Somalia in Brief," *The Atlanta Constitution*, Dec. 4, 1992, p. A13.

12. Don Oberdorfer, "Envoy to Somalia Follows Own Script," *Washington Post*, Dec. 11, 1992, p. A47.

13. Dick Cheney and Colin Powell, "U.S. Mission to Somalia Is Clear and Necessary," USIA, *East Asia/Pacific Wireless File*, Dec. 4, 1992, pp. 11–12.

14. Andrei Raevsky, "Peacekeeping Operations: Command and Control," in Ramesh Thakur and Carlyle A. Thayer, eds., *A Crisis of Expectations: UN*

Peacekeeping in the 1990s (Boulder, Colo.: Westview Press, 1995), p. 12.

15. Hirsch and Oakley, *Somalia*, p. 46.

16. Ibid., p. 93.

17. Chester Crocker, "The Lessons of Somalia: Not Everything Went Wrong," *Foreign Affairs* 74, 3, (May/June 1995): 4.

18. Putnam, "UN Operation in Somalia," p. 93.

19. Crocker, "The Lessons of Somalia," p. 4.

20. William Claiborne and Barton Gellman, "Rival Warlords Sign Peace Pact in Somalia," *The Washington Post*, Dec. 11, 1992, p. A1.

21. Hirsch and Oakley, *Somalia*, pp. 102–3.

22. Ibid., p. 101.

23. Ibid., p. 99.

24. Putnam, "UN Operation in Somalia," p. 96.

25. U.S.U.N. Press Release 37–(93), United States Permanent Mission to the United Nations, March 26, 1993.

26. UN Security Council Resolution 814, March 26, 1993.

27. Ibid.

28. See Michael Maren's reports from Mogadishu published in the *Village Voice* in early 1993.

29. Hirsch and Oakley, *Somalia*, p. 116.

30. Michael R. Gordon and John H. Cushman, Jr., "U.S. Supported Hunt for Aideed; Now Calls UN Policy Skewed," *New York Times*, Oct. 18, 1993, p. A8.

31. Hirsch and Oakley, *Somalia*, p. 116.

32. Ibid., p. 116.

33. Ibid., p. 117.

34. Putnam, "UN Operation in Somalia," p. 97.

35. Hirsch and Oakley, *Somalia*, p. 118.

36. Gordon and Cushman, "U.S. Supported Hunt for Aideed," p. A8.

37. Ibid., p. A8.

38. Hirsch and Oakley, *Somalia*, p. 126.

39. Bruce B. Auster, "Fighting a New Kind of War," *U.S. News and World Report*, Nov. 8, 1993, p. 60.

40. Eric Schmitt, "2 Somalis Killed in Clash," *New York Times*, Dec. 11, 1992, p. A1.

41. Putnam, "UN Operation in Somalia," p. 97.

42. Hirsch and Oakley, *Somalia*, p. 122.

43. Ibid., p. 122.

44. Ibid., p. 123.

45. Ibid., p. 125.

Comment

Evaluate the justifications for the initial intervention. Consider the reasons that officials actually gave and the reasons that they could have given. Under what circumstances and to what extent is the use of force in international politics justified for humanitarian ends?

Some critics made a point of noting that suffering and bloodshed was just as great in many other countries in the world. If so, to what extent should this count as a moral argument against intervention? Should our assessment of the intervention be affected if the nations that intervened were motivated by their own national interest (in addition to or instead of humanitarian concerns)?

Analyze the way the goals of the intervention changed as the mission proceeded. Should the military force have been limited to establishing security for distributing aid, or should it have provided support for nation-building? Did the military adequately observe rules of engagement that would minimize the risks to civilians?

Unlike the simple cases of intervention, in which one nation responds to an attack by an aggressor, this intervention involved many nations acting collectively under the auspices of the UN and in a country embroiled in a civil war. To what extent do these factors—the sponsorship of the UN and the breakdown of civil authority—strengthen the moral case for intervention? Should officials have tried to gain the consent of leaders in Somalia (for example, by convening a peace conference)?

Recommended Reading

The best contemporary discussion of the morality of war is still Michael Walzer, *Just and Unjust Wars* (New York: Basic Books, 1977). Two other general discussions worth consulting are: Douglas Lackey, *The Ethics of War and Peace* (Englewood Cliffs, N.J.: Prentice-Hall, 1989), and Richard Norman, *Ethics, Killing and War* (New York: Cambridge University Press, 1995). A wide variety of views on this topic may be found in any of these collections: Charles Beitz et al. (eds.), *International Ethics* (Princeton, N.J.: Princeton University Press, 1985), especially parts 2 and 3; Marshall Cohen et al. (eds.), *War and Moral Responsibility* (Princeton, N.J.: Princeton University Press, 1974); Jean Bethke Elshtain (ed.), *Just War Theory* (Oxford: Blackwell, 1992); Terry Nardin (ed.), *The Ethics of War and Peace* (Princeton, N.J.: Princeton University Press, 1996); and Terry Nardin and David R. Mapel, *Traditions of International Ethics* (New York: Cambridge University Press, 1992). A selection of articles and a useful bibliography on the ethics of nuclear deterrence is in James P. Sterba (ed.), *The Ethics of War and Nuclear Deterrence* (Belmont, Calif.: Wadsworth, 1985).

For historical background and the continuing controversy over the decision to drop the bomb, see Philip Nobile (ed.), *Judgment at the Smithsonian: The Uncensored Script of the Smithsonian's 50th Anniversary Exhibit of the Enola Gay* (New York: Marlowe and Co., 1995). The most recent "revisionist" interpretation is Gar Alperovitz, *The Decision to Use the Atomic Bomb and the Architecture of an American Myth* (New York: Knopf, 1995). An account sympathetic to the decision makers is McGeorge Bundy, *Danger and Survival: Choices about the Bomb in the First Fifty Years* (New York: Random House, 1988), ch. 2. A philosopher's criticism of Truman is Elisabeth Anscombe, "Mr. Truman's Degree," in Anscombe, *Ethics, Religion and Politics* (Minneapolis: University of Minnesota Press, 1981), pp. 62–71. On the ethics of the Gulf War, see Jean Bethke Elshtain et al., *But Was It Just? Reflections on the Morality of the Persian Gulf War* (New York: Doubleday, 1992).

2　Deception and Disclosure

Introduction

The successful ruler, Machiavelli teaches, must be "a great liar and hypocrite." Politicians have to appear to be moral even though they are not, because politics requires methods that citizens would find morally objectionable if they knew about them. We do not know how many politicians follow Machiavelli's advice today (those who do so most successfully may seem to be the least Machiavellian). We do know that many public officials have tried to justify deception, and so have some political commentators and political theorists.

Deception involves intentionally (or negligently) causing someone to believe something that the deceiver knows (or should know) to be false. Political deception is not always easy to recognize, because it seldom comes in the form of an outright lie. More often, officials give us half-truths, which they hope we will not see are half-lies. Or they offer us silence, which they hope will cause us to ignore inconvenient truths. Sometimes officials provide so much information that the truth is deliberately obscured, lost in a plethora of facts and figures. Thus the first task in analyzing a case of alleged deception is to decide whether deception actually occurred and precisely in what ways.

Those who want to justify political deception usually grant what ordinary morality maintains—that lying is generally wrong. But they go on to argue that no one (except perhaps Kant) believes that deception is always wrong. The general presumption against it can therefore be rebutted in certain circumstances, such as those that politicians often confront. Politics is supposed to make deception more often justifiable for several reasons: (1) political issues are complex and difficult to understand, especially when they must be presented in the mass media or in a short time; (2) the harmful effects of some political truths can be severe and irreversible; (3) the political effects result as much from what people believe as from what is actually true; and (4) organizing coalitions and other kinds of political action requires leaders to emphasize one part of the truth to some people and another part to others (telling the whole truth and nothing but the truth could make compromise impossible).

But, at least in a democracy, these reasons cannot give political leaders a general license to deceive whenever and wherever they think it necessary. Unless we can find out what officials have actually done—not just what they appear to have done— we cannot hold them accountable. At most, the special features of politics may justify exceptions to the general presumption against deception that should hold in a democracy.

If we conclude that deception may sometimes be necessary, our task should be to define carefully the conditions under which citizens should permit public officials to engage in deception. The main factors we should consider are: (1) the importance of the goal of the deception; (2) the availability of alternative means for achieving the goal; (3) the identity of the victims of the deception (other officials, other governments, all citizens); (4) the accountability of the deceivers (the possibility of approving the deception in advance or discovering it later); and (5) the containment of the deception (its effects on other actions by officials).

The first selection in this section consists of a group of minicases. They are simplified versions of actual episodes in American politics, and they provide an indication of the variety of the kinds of deception and circumstances in which politicians try to justify it. "Disinformation for Qaddafi" and "The Iran-Contra Affair" describe two foreign policy ventures in which deception was a key element; the first was formally approved by the president and key administration officials within the administration. The two episodes also differ with respect to their goals, the victims of the deception, the possibilities of holding the deceivers accountable, and chances of containing the deception.

The problem of deception is closely related to various forms of nondisclosure, especially secrecy and confidentiality. Secrecy is often the means that politicians use to deceive citizens and each other, and it can also itself constitute deception— for example, when the president's national security adviser failed to tell Congress and even some of his colleagues about some critical facts that would have shown a connection between the U.S. support of the Contras and the arms for hostages negotiations with Iran.

But there is an important moral difference between deception and secrecy. In private life, there is no presumption against secrecy as there is against deception: keeping confidences and respecting privacy are more often virtues than vices. Even in public life, where there is a presumption against secrecy, secrecy still has some positive value. The values of privacy and confidentiality provide strong reasons to keep secrets, and therefore the presumption against secrecy is more easily rebutted than the presumption against deception. This means that our moral analysis may have to be more complex in the case of secrecy. "The Senate Confirmation of Justice Clarence Thomas" brings out some of these complexities by presenting a conflict between the claims of privacy of Justice Thomas and his accuser, Anita Hill, and the demands of publicity in the democratic process. (This case also raises issues of sexual harassment and racial discrimination that are relevant to the problem of equal opportunity presented in chapter 7.)

Lying in Office
Graham T. Allison and Lance M. Liebman

1. JFK, THE "DEAL," AND THE DENIAL

On Saturday, October 27, 1962, at the height of the Cuban Missile Crisis, President John F. Kennedy receives a letter from the Soviet government proposing to strike a deal. The Soviet Union, the letter offers, will dismantle and remove its missiles from Cuba if the United States agrees to a similar withdrawal of its nuclear-armed missiles stationed in Turkey. In fact, Kennedy twice ordered the removal of these obsolescent and vulnerable missiles in the months prior to the October crisis. But each time the Turkish government had objected, and so the missiles remained—an easy target for Soviet retaliation should the United States be forced to take military action against the missiles in Cuba.

Kennedy believes, along with virtually all of his advisers, that the Soviet offer is unacceptable. To back down under fire, he reasons, would be to demonstrate that the United States was willing to trade off European security for its own. It would undermine the credibility of America's pledge to defend Europe against Soviet attack, and would invite the Soviets to stage another missile crisis elsewhere—only this time in a situation where the military deck was not so heavily stacked in America's favor. But he also knows that tens of millions of Russians and Americans might soon be dead if he cannot find some other way to resolve the crisis.

Kennedy decides to ignore the Soviet proposal and to respond favorably to an earlier, private letter from Premier Khrushchev to himself, in which the Soviet leader had of-fered to withdraw the missiles in Cuba in return only for an American pledge not to invade the island. But to sweeten the deal, guessing that Khrushchev's colleagues may have subsequently raised the price of Soviet withdrawal, Kennedy has his brother Robert inform Soviet Ambassador Anatoly Dobrynin privately that, while there can be no Cuba-for-Turkey exchange made under pressure, the President had already ordered the removal of the American missiles in Turkey and would make sure the order was carried out speedily.

At a press conference on November 20, after the crisis had passed and after the congressional elections that were on Kennedy's mind during October 1962, the following exchange occurred:

> Q. Mr. President, in the various exchanges of the past three weeks, either between yourself and Chairman Khrushchev or at the United Nations, have any issues been touched on besides that of Cuba, and could you say how the events of these past three weeks might affect such an issue as Berlin or disarmament or nuclear testing?
>
> THE PRESIDENT: No. I instructed the negotiators to confine themselves to the matter of Cuba completely, and therefore no other matters were discussed. Disarmament, any matters affecting Western Europe, relations between the Warsaw pact countries and NATO, all the rest—none of these matters was to be in any way referred to or negotiated about until we had made progress and come to some sort of a solution on Cuba. So that has been all we have done diplomatically with the Soviet Union the last month.
>
> Now if we're successful in Cuba, as I said, we would be hopeful that some of the other areas of tension could be relaxed. Obviously when you make progress in any area, then you have hopes that you can continue it. But up till now we have confined ourselves to Cuba, and we'll continue to do so until we feel the situation has reached a satisfactory state.

2. THE ELECTION DEBATE

It is November 1969. John Lindsay is running for reelection as mayor of New York. His principal opponent is Mario Procaccino, a conservative Democrat. In a TV debate the Sunday before election day, Procaccino charges that Lindsay has "made a deal with the landlords." More specifically, he claims that (1) Lindsay has a secret report on housing in New York City, (2) the report states that rent control is at the heart of the city's housing problem, and recommends revisions of the rent control law which will result in massive rent increases, and (3) the report is being suppressed until after the election.

In fact, Lindsay knows that two city consultants (RAND and McKinsey) have done such a study for the Housing and Development Administration. He has not seen their report, but has seen a preliminary summary of their findings, which do find that rent control is aggravating the city's housing shortage, and do recommend substantial revision of the rent control law in such a way that many rents will be significantly increased. At the recommendation of the Housing and Development Administrator, the reports have been labeled "highly confidential" and publication is being withheld until after the election. On the basis of the report's findings and the recommendations of other analysts in the city government, Lindsay believes that the report's analyses are essentially correct, and plans to seek substantial changes in rent control—after the election.

Lindsay knows that to announce his intention prior to the election would cost many votes. He suspects that to acknowledge the existence of the report will raise serious doubts in many voters' minds about his support for rent control. He believes that Procaccino would be a disastrous mayor for New York City. He replies:

I haven't seen this so-called report; there could well be such a report. The mayor sees thousands of reports from various persons, and it's the mayor's decision that counts in this whole matter of governing New York City, and my decisions have been constant, not only to be firm on rent control, which I am. I believe in it. I think we must have it.

Two hours after the debate, Lindsay and his staff are at campaign headquarters. A young aide says, "The Mayor's answer to the rent control question was ambiguous. We'd better put out a firmer denial. How about this?" He then proposes the following press release:

Mayor Lindsay today branded as ridiculous the charge that he is soft on rent control. He said the city is not studying the watering down of controls, and if any recommendation for higher rents is made, he will reject it out of hand.

3. MILLER AND FURLOUGHS

It is early 1970. Jerome Miller has just taken office as head of Massachusetts' Department of Youth Services, the agency responsible for managing the state's programs for juvenile offenders. After fifteen years of child-treatment experience, Miller—like many other progressives in his field—has come to believe that institutionalization is a disastrous policy, and that almost any environment outside the large state detention centers is better for the child and cheaper for the state. He believes the old, prison-like "reform schools" are brutal, oppressive institutions that teach little more than the finer points of crime; his ultimate goal is to shut them down entirely and replace them with a network of smaller scale, community-based halfway houses. But first he must prove to the legislature and the communities in which the houses will be located that the kids can be trusted.

Miller's first step toward deinstitutionalization is a program of weekend furloughs for confined teenage offenders. One hundred boys and girls go home on Friday afternoon, and ninety-one come back Monday morning. Miller is not alarmed, since this result conforms to his expectations, based on similar programs elsewhere, in which virtually all of the wanderers have returned within a week. But the press wants to know what the "count" was immediately, and Miller fears that published reports of a 9% AWOL rate will kill any chances for deinstitutionalization. He tells the press on Monday afternoon that all the furlough children were back on time. By Friday, the nine missing offenders have all returned.

4. FIDDLING THE RULES COMMITTEE CHAIRMAN

Elizabeth Jackson is a private citizen, head of an ad hoc lobbying group formed to support the Equal Rights Amendment in her state. It is December 1975. Her state has not yet ratified the ERA, but ratification is closer than it has ever been in the three years since Congress sent the amendment to the states.

(Background note: The ERA was passed by both houses of Congress in 1972. The Congressional resolution provided that the amendment would become effective if ratified by the required three-fourths of the states, thirty-eight, within seven years. By the end of 1973, thirty-four states had ratified the ERA. After a flurry of ratifications in the first two years, the battle for the ERA has come down to a grinding effort to win the few more states needed. Time seems to be on the side of the opponents. The women's movement no longer enjoys the media attention which helped win the initial passage of the ERA by projecting the image of a potent new political force. The ERA opponents seem to be getting stronger, and are able to use delaying tactics to their advantage as the 1979 deadline approaches.)

In Jackson's state, the ERA forces have had little success until this year. Although most legislators are unwilling to be recorded against the ERA, its opponents have bottled it up in committee in both houses, preventing any floor votes. Last election, the key opponent in the House retired, perhaps because he was unwilling to face the vigorous campaign of an opponent whom Jackson helped recruit. With him gone, and with the help of the Majority Leader, Jackson's group forced the bill out of committee, and the full House approved it. Now the end of the session is a day away, and the ERA languishes in the Senate Rules Committee.

The chairman of the Rules Committee, Senator Henderson, is a progressive force in the generally conservative Senate. Although he is personally ambivalent about the ERA, he has indicated to Jackson that it will reach the Senate floor. His cordiality and cooperative attitude have encouraged Jackson to be optimistic, but the end of the session is near, and the ERA still sits in Rules. Jackson now suspects that Henderson is holding the bill as a favor to his colleagues who would rather not vote on it.

Jackson is desperate to get the ERA approved this year. She knows that the national campaign against the ERA, led by Phyllis Schafly, is raising funds to support a more intensive lobbying effort next year. Moreover, her key supporter in the House, the Majority Leader, is leaving to run for Governor next year, and the Judiciary Committee chairman is running for Congress. Both of them helped to line up the necessary votes in the House, and without them next year, the prospects for the ERA look bleak. It looks to Jackson as if it's now or never.

She decides to change her tactics. She challenges Senator Henderson in his office. He's deliberately deceiving her, she charges, and she will make sure that he pays for it. He tells her that it is the Rules Committee members who are blocking the ERA, but she refuses to believe him. She tells him that her group is prepared to back Chris Carter, a young attorney active in local politics, who has agreed to run against Senator Henderson if he has sufficient funds and volunteers. She tells Senator Henderson that her group will contribute heavily to Carter unless ERA reaches the Senate floor.

In fact, she knows that her threat is pure fiction. While Carter has been rumored to be considering the race, she has not talked with him. The reason she has not is that she can see that her organization is running out of steam. They have no funds left, and fund-raising lately has been hardly worth the effort. Volunteers are tiring of the struggle, and will probably disappear if they are not successful this time. Furthermore, she herself would find it difficult to oppose Senator Henderson because of his critical role in the passage of a wide variety of progressive legislation.

5. HERMAN FIDDLES FINNEGAN

Suppose that the Acting Director of the Bureau of Consular and Security Affairs in the Department of State, Philip Herman, is trying to substitute a permanent visa for foreign visitors to the United States in place of the existing renewable visa. Only the United States, among its major allies and trading partners, maintains such a restrictive policy, a legacy of McCarthyist fear of Communist infiltration and subversion, and Herman is attempting to eliminate this imbalance. To do so, he needs Congressional approval. But the man he must convince is Representative Michael Finnegan, a fierce anti-Communist who heads the House Appropriations Subcommittee for the State Department. Finnegan is virulently opposed to any change in visa requirements that would make it possible for a single additional Communist to enter the country, no matter what benefits the United States might derive from increased foreign visitation. In fact, he has blocked such efforts before. Without Finnegan's approval, there can be no change in the visa. Thus, Herman falsely tells Finnegan that the State Department is under heavy foreign pressure to abolish visas entirely, that unless the U.S. liberalizes its visa regulations, other countries might retaliate by making it increasingly difficult for Americans to travel abroad, and that the best way to beat this pressure would be to adopt a permanent visa system, which

would at least permit an initial check on suspect foreigners. Finnegan buys the story.

6. COVERT ACTION IN CHILE

It is early 1973. CIA Director Richard Helms has just been nominated by President Richard Nixon to be U.S. Ambassador to Iran, but before he can take the post, he must be approved by the Senate. During his confirmation hearings before the Foreign Relations Committee, he is asked questions about alleged CIA covert activity in Chile.

In 1970, the CIA had spent over $8 million to prevent the election of Dr. Salvador Allende Gossens, a Marxist, as Chile's President. Despite the CIA money, Allende won the election by a small plurality. But since no candidate won a majority of the vote, the Chilean Congress was required to choose between the top two vote-getters in the general election. In the past, the Congress had always selected the leading candidate, and 1970 appeared to be no exception.

Shortly after the election, President Nixon informed Director Helms that an Allende regime would not be acceptable to the United States and instructed him to organize a military coup d'etat in Chile to prevent Allende's accession to the presidency. The CIA was to take this highly sensitive action without coordination with the Departments of State or Defense and without informing the U.S. Ambassador to Chile. Instead, the Agency was to report, both for informational and approval purposes, only to the President's Assistant for National Security Affairs, Dr. Henry Kissinger, or his deputy.

Despite Helms' belief, expressed later, that the Agency was "being asked to almost do the impossible," he attempted to carry out the President's order. In a flurry of activity immediately prior to the scheduled meeting of the Chilean Congress, the CIA made twenty-one contacts with key military and police officials in Chile. Those Chileans who were inclined to stage a coup were given assurances of strong support at the highest levels of the U.S. government, both before and after a coup. Yet the coup never took place, and Dr. Allende took office. After the death in an abortive kidnap attempt of Chilean Army Commander-in-Chief General Rene Schneider, who opposed the coup, the plot was uncovered. CIA support for the conspirators was rumored, but the allegations were unconfirmed.

Now, in early 1973, with Allende still in power but facing increasing domestic opposition, Helms is asked about the CIA's alleged role in the 1970 coup attempt:

SENATOR SYMINGTON: Did you try in the Central Intelligence Agency to overthrow the government in Chile?

MR. HELMS: No, sir.

SENATOR SYMINGTON: Did you have any money passed to the opponents of Allende?

MR. HELMS: No. sir.

SENATOR SYMINGTON: So the stories you were involved in that war are wrong?

MR. HELMS: Yes, sir. I said to Senator Fulbright many months ago that if the Agency had really gotten in behind the other candidates and spent a lot of money and so forth the election might have come out differently.

Comment

Denial is often the first response of public officials accused of deception. Richard Helms (Case 6) claimed that he literally told the truth: the CIA did not attempt to overthrow the government of Chile but tried only to dissuade the Chilean Congress from confirming Allende's electoral victory; and the CIA did not give any money directly to the candidates, only to groups that supported or opposed candidates. On what grounds should we decide that technically true statements count as deception? When should failure to disclose be considered deceptive?

In most of the cases, justifications for the deception typically mention its beneficial consequences. But we should distinguish appeals to one's own reelection (Lindsay in Case 2), the success of a public cause (the ERA in Case 4), and the avoidance of nuclear war (Kennedy in Case 1). On what basis should we make such distinctions? Another kind of justification refers to features of the act of deception itself—such as the relation of the deceiver to the deceived. Perhaps enemies do not deserve the truth, but if so, does this include political enemies as in Case 5? Politicians, like poker players, may know that the rules of the game allow some bluffing, as in Case 4, but if so, have citizens agreed to play the game too?

In each case, consider whether there were any reasonable alternatives to the deception. Perhaps Kennedy could not have given a more accurate answer or could not even have declined to comment without undermining the "deal" that resolved the crisis. Can the same be said about Lindsay, Miller, and Helms? No doubt these officials felt themselves in a bind: to reply "no comment" would bring about the same result as if they fully disclosed what they wished to conceal. Also look at the context in which such dilemmas arise. Could the officials have taken steps earlier that would have prevented the dilemma from ever arising? If so, how should that affect our evaluation of their later deception?

Disinformation for Qaddafi

Christine Huang

By spring of 1986, the Reagan administration had evidence that Libya's leader Colonel Muammar el-Qaddafi had supported and encouraged terrorist acts against U.S. citizens and U.S. installations abroad. Fearing a resurgence of terrorist activity and wishing to capitalize on the deterrent value of the April 14 U.S. air raid on Libya, the administration seized on the opportunity provided by a new intelligence report in July questioning Qaddafi's mental stability. The report triggered an inter-agency review of U.S.-Libyan policy. The State and Defense Departments, the Central Intelligence Agency, and the White House began to consider what steps might be taken to maintain the National Security Council, launching a new phase of the administration policy; first adopted in 1985, to undermine the Qaddafi regime.

On August 6, the State Department's Office of Intelligence and Research distributed a seven-page memorandum to senior mid-level officials in advance of an upcoming interagency meeting. The memo called for a "disinformation" and "deception" campaign to bring attention to Qaddafi's continuing terrorist activities, to exaggerate his vulnerability to internal opposition, and to play up the possibility of new American military action against him. Under the heading of Qaddafi's vulnerability to internal opposition, the State Department memorandum explicitly stated as its goal: "to continue Qaddafi's paranoia so that he remains pre-

occupied, off balance." If, according to the memo, Qaddafi believed that the army and other elements in Libya may be plotting against him, he might increase the pressure on the Libyan army thus prompting a "coup or assassination attempt."

The Crisis Pre-Planning Group (CPPG) of senior representatives from the State and Defense Departments, the CIA, and the White House met on August 7 at 4:30 p.m. in the White House situation room and endorsed the overall plan outlined in the State Department memo. A meeting of the National Security Planning Group (NSPG) was scheduled for August 14 to consider the next steps the administration would take against Qaddafi. (The NSPG is the key cabinet-level forum in which the president and his top aides discuss and make decisions on the most sensitive policy matters.)

On August 12, President Reagan received a memorandum from his national security affairs advisor, Admiral John Poindexter, summarizing a proposed program of disinformation against Libya. "One of the key elements" of the new strategy, the Poindexter memo said, "is that it combines real and imaginary events through a disinformation program—with the basic goal of making Qaddafi think that there is a high degree of internal opposition to him within Libya, that his long trusted aides are disloyal, that the U.S. is about to move against him militarily." The purpose of taking additional steps against Libya, according to the memo, was to deter terrorism, moderate Libyan policies, and "bring about a change of leadership in Libya."

The president, Poindexter, and nine other key officials met at the White House on August 14 at 11 A.M. The overall plan as outlined by Poindexter was approved by

Reagan and codified in general terms in a formal National Security Decision Directive signed by the president. Details of the plan were left to Poindexter, the State Department, and the CIA. The Reagan directive ordered covert, diplomatic and economic steps designed to deter Libyan sponsored terrorism and to bring about a change of leadership. The principal means outlined in the directive was a campaign of disinformation. Neither the memoranda themselves nor the meetings held to discuss them addressed the details of any strategy on the dissemination of false stories to reporters.

Although Poindexter's memo said that "the current intelligence community assessment is that Qaddafi is temporarily quiescent in his support of terrorism," soon after the meeting, one or two members of the NSC staff told reporters that the United States had new intelligence indicating that Qaddafi was stepping up his terrorist plans.

On August 25, the *Wall Street Journal* on page one reported that "the U.S. and Libya are on a collision course again" and added that "the Reagan administration is preparing to teach the mercurial Libyan leader another lesson. Right now, the Pentagon is completing plans for a new and larger bombing of Libya in case the President orders it." The report quoted a senior U.S. official as saying of Qaddafi, "There are increasing signs that he's renewed planning and preparations for terrorist acts." The article went on to describe the administration's new "three-pronged program of military, covert, and economic actions" intended "to preempt more Libyan-sponsored terrorism, exacerbate growing political and economic tensions in Libya, and remind Col. Qaddafi and his inner circle that promoting terrorism may be hazardous to their health." The program included joint exercises with Egypt in the Mediterranean, possible joint action with France to drive Libyan troops out of Chad, increased support for dissident military officers, businessmen, and technocrats inside Libya and for Libyan exiles who wanted "to oust Col. Qaddafi," and with European cooperation, tightening the economic and political sanctions adopted in the spring of 1985 by the Common Market and by the Tokyo economic summit.

All three network television evening news programs repeated the substance of the *Journal's* report that night, citing unidentified administration officials. The August 26 issues of many major newspapers quoted unidentified and identified officials who seemed to confirm the *Journal's* article, though there was no explicit official confirmation.

On August 25, in Santa Barbara near the ranch where President Reagan was on a three-week vacation, White House spokesman Larry Speakes said, "Our policy toward Libyan-backed terrorism is unequivocal and unchanged. We will employ all appropriate measures to cause Libya to cease its terrorist policies. We certainly have reason to believe that the Libyan state, headed by Col. Qaddafi, has not forsaken its desire to cause—to create—terrorist activities worldwide, and the capability is still there to do so." In an off-the-record statement at a news conference the next day, Speakes described the *Journal's* article as being "highly authoritative but not authorized."

Fearing that reports of impending American military action against Libya might produce more concern in Europe than in Libya, administration officials in Washington sought to soften the public line on August 27. White House, State Department, and Pentagon officials said they had indications of planned new Libyan terrorist activities aimed at Americans. They stressed, however, that they had nothing approximating a "smoking gun" to justify sending American bombers once again to strike Libya. The officials described new American diplomatic efforts to toughen economic and political sanctions against Libya as the main thrust of administration policy. Vernon A. Walters, the U.S. delegate to the United Nations, was expected to travel to Europe the following week to explore widening these sanctions. One key official expressed the fear that "these panic stories will undercut the Walters mission. The Europeans will ask us for the hard evidence, and we won't have any. It will look like we are crying wolf once again."

Bob Woodward in the *Washington Post* on October 2 disclosed the details of the administration's "secret and unusual plan of deception." The *Post* account said that beginning with the *Journal*'s August 25 report, the American news media reported as fact much of the false information generated by the deception plan described in the August memos.

The White House denied that the administration had planted false reports with news organizations in the United States as a means of bringing pressure on Qaddafi. Mr. Speakes said that the information provided to the *Wall Street Journal* "was not a part of any plan or memo drafted by Poindexter and approved by the President and the U.S. Government." Defending the statements he made in August, the White House spokesman reiterated that "the information contained in the *Wall Street Journal* in these various intelligence reports was information from intelligence sources. That was hard, that was firm."

Responding to the *Post*'s article in an interview on October 2 at the White House with select news columnists and broadcast commentators, President Reagan at first said, "I challenge the veracity of that entire story," but acknowledged that "there are memos back and forth. I can't deny that here and there they're going to have something to hang it on."

Secretary of State George Shultz told reporters on the same day in New York that he knew of "no decision to have people go out and tell lies to the media" but that "if there are ways in which we can make Qaddafi nervous, why shouldn't we?" He noted Winston Churchill's statement in World War II that "in time of war the truth is so precious it must be attended by a bodyguard of lies," adding that "insofar as Qaddafi is concerned we don't have a declaration of war but we have something darn close to it."

In a statement issued on October 2 in reference to the August 25 report, *Wall Street Journal* managing editor Norman Pearlstine said, "We remain convinced, as reported in the *Journal*, that the U.S. government in late summer believed Libya had resumed its active support for terrorism and that the U.S. was considering a range of options aimed at deterring such Libyan actions. We reported this based on not one source, but on information provided by a number of sources here and abroad." Pearlstine concluded by saying, "If, indeed, our government conducted such a domestic disinformation campaign, we were among its many victims." Leaving for a weekend retreat at Camp David, Maryland, on October 3, the President insisted for the second consecutive day that the administration had been trying merely to deceive Qaddafi rather than to mislead the press into printing inaccurate reports. "We are not telling lies or doing any of these disinformation things that we are cited with doing."

The Justice Department asked the Federal Bureau of Investigation to conduct an inquiry into the *Post*'s October 2 report and the *Journal*'s August 25 article. The probe was referred to a new unit in the FBI's Washington field office that was set up under a reorganization in the spring of 1985 to assign veteran agents to pursue leaks of classified information.

The Senate Select Committee on Intelligence initiated an inquiry. Bernie McMahon, the committee staff director, told the Associated Press on October 3 that the staff had concluded that the administration had not deliberately attempted to plant false stories in the U.S. news media. In an interview on the same day, the chairman of the Senate Intelligence Committee, Dave Durenberger, said that individual White House aides may have provided false information without the approval of their superiors, leading to inaccurate stories about Libya by major news organizations, but added that it would take "a quantum leap" to assume that the actions of a few White House officials constituted a formal administration policy of lying to American reporters.

The Iran-Contra Affair
David Nacht

The Iran-Contra Affair was a set of American foreign policy initiatives conducted in secret by a small number of executive branch officials, mainly members of the National Security Council Staff, during the Reagan administration between 1984 and 1986. The affair involved two principal parts: (1) the secret sale of arms to Iran in order to gain the release of American hostages held by Iranian allies in Lebanon and (2) the establishment of a covert mechanism to fund and arm the Nicaraguan insurgency, known as the Contras, at a time when the Congress had cut off funds to the Contras.

This case highlights the actions of two main officials in the affair, Admiral John Poindexter, the national security advisor to the president of the United States, and his aide, Lieutenant Colonel Oliver North. After the affair became public knowledge, two committees of Congress held joint hearings for eight months, at which the "star" witnesses were Adm. Poindexter and Lt. Col. North. Testifying under oath, they were granted immunity for their statements under the terms of the Fifth Amendment preventing self-incrimination.[1] North was fired from his post on the NSC staff, and Poindexter was forced to resign.

In order to preserve the secrecy of the Iran and Nicaragua activities, Adm. Poindexter made sure that few individuals knew about them. The secretary of state, for instance, apparently lacked detailed knowledge of almost all of the activities; the same was true for the chairman of the Joint Chiefs and the secretary of defense. In his relentless effort at compartmentalization, Admiral Poindexter even appears to have excluded the president from knowledge of major aspects of the affair. The director of the Central Intelligence Agency, William Casey, knew about—and in fact may have planned—many of the activities, although this may not have been in accord with Poindexter's wishes, but rather because of Casey's special friendship with Lt. Col. North. Selected members of the CIA, Defense Department, State Department, private individuals and members of certain foreign governments, all of whose participation was deemed by Poindexter and North to be necessary for the success of the mission, were also made aware of the initiatives. However, Congress was not told, even though there are legally required procedures for informing congressional leaders of highly secretive covert operations. Moreover, after an investigation began, Casey, North, and Poindexter fabricated cover stories, and the latter two destroyed documents in an effort to deceive the investigators.

THE SETTING

Public disclosure of both the Iran and the Nicaraguan initiatives was bound to cause controversy. The United States and Iran had been on uncomfortable terms since the seizure of the American diplomats in Tehran in 1979 by the Iranian Revolutionary Guards. Moreover, the Reagan administration had been pursuing a vocal antiterrorism campaign waged largely against Iran and Libya. President Reagan had officially designated Iran as a terrorist nation, forbidding it, under the terms of the amended Arms Export Control Act, to receive arms from the United States. Moreover, the president had personally asked the West European allies not to sell arms to Iran.

The diversion of funds to the Contras, although closer in spirit to stated American foreign policy, concerned many because it flouted a congressional ban on such assistance, and Reagan administration officials had falsely testified that the administration was not arming the Contras. The administration had actively opposed the ruling Sandinista regime in Nicaragua by successively condemning the regime, boycotting Nicaraguan goods in the United States, mining Nicaraguan harbors, and organizing and funding the Contras. The administration's efforts to obtain material support for the rebel force had been hampered by congressional resistance. Congress voted down a number of administration requests to arm the Contras. In December 1981, President Reagan authorized a National Intelligence Finding establishing U.S. support for the Contras. A year later on December 21, 1982, Congress passed the first of five Boland Amendments, named after the congressman who wrote the legislation, barring the CIA or the Department of Defense from spending money directed "toward overthrowing the government of Nicaragua or provoking a military exchange between Nicaragua and Honduras." In September 1983, President Reagan signed another finding authorizing "the provision of material support and guidance to the Nicaraguan resistance groups." On December 8, 1983, Congress responded by placing a $24 mil-

lion cap on funds to be used for supporting the Contras directly or indirectly by "DOD or CIA or any other agency involved in intelligence activities." In October 1984, Congress stopped all funding for the Contras "by any agency involved in intelligence activities."[2] It was at this point that Lt. Col. North essentially took over the role which the CIA had been performing as the logistics coordinator for the Contras.

AIDING THE CONTRAS

Lt. Col. North was a marine who had been "detailed" to the NSC staff. His boss, Robert "Bud" McFarlane, the national security advisor, was another marine colonel. North served on a committee on the NSC staff charged with combating terrorism abroad. Although his position was not very senior, North was self-confident and eager to take the initiative in carrying out policies. He formed friendships with McFarlane, with McFarlane's successor, Adm. Poindexter, and with the director of the CIA, William Casey. North used his personal relationships to learn the priorities of the senior policymakers and to build their trust in him. He appears to have had at least tacit approval for most or all of his activities from the successive national security advisors.

North became the NSC liaison to the Contras. He was charged with "keeping them alive, body and soul" in spite of the cutoff in congressional funding. He interpreted the legal limitation as a prohibition on funding the Contras with money appropriated by Congress. Therefore, his strategy was to get money from other sources—foreign governments and private citizens: "I made every effort, counsel, to avoid the use of appropriated funds. And, as I said, that was why the decision was made in 1984, before this proscription ever became law, to set up outside entities, and to raise non-U.S. government monies by which the Nicaraguan freedom fighters could be supported."[3] In December 1984, he initiated the effort to raise foreign funds by asking Secretary

Shultz to solicit funds from the sultan of Brunei for Contra use. (Shultz's meeting with the sultan and the payment that followed actually did not occur until June 1986.) North, State Department officials, and private citizens solicited a total of $34 million for the Contras from foreign sources between June 1984 and the beginning of 1986. An additional $2.7 million was raised from private contributors.[4]

President Reagan authorized the policy to raise funds from foreign sources and private contributors for the Contras; however, he may not have had the legal authority to conduct these activities. (No Court ruling has yet been issued). President Reagan himself took part briefly in the fundraising, meeting with large donors of both the foreign and private domestic variety, and Adm. Poindexter has testified that "I am confident that he [the president] was aware that these people were making contributions to support the Contras."[5] However, this activity was kept from the Congress. Elliot Abrams, the assistant secretary of state, actively misled a congressional committee about administration fundraising efforts. He later acknowledged his distortions, stating that unless members of Congress asked "exactly the right question, using exactly the right words, they weren't going to get the right answers."[6]

Rumors of NSC staff support for the Contras reached Congress and the press by June 1985. In August 1985, representatives Michael Barnes and Lee Hamilton wrote separate letters to National Security Advisor McFarlane asking for information about these rumors. In October, McFarlane received three additional requests. McFarlane responded to these requests with statements that Col. North later described as "false, erroneous, misleading, evasive, and wrong."[7] Col. North maintains that Col. McFarlane authorized him to submit misleading documents to Congressman Barnes. Col. McFarlane has testified in response that he was unaware of the full extent of the

activities of Col. North. Col. McFarlane has admitted, however, that he lied in his letter of response to Congressman Hamilton of October 7, denying NSC participation in third-country fundraising for the Contras. There is also convincing evidence that he lied regarding his knowledge of Col. North's activities in coordinating logistics for the Contras.[8]

Col. McFarlane repeated these false denials in meetings with senators Leahy and Durenberger on September 5, 1985, and with members of the House Intelligence Committee on September 10. He also gave false testimony after he resigned to the Senate Select Committee on Intelligence in December 1986 concerning his knowledge of NSC staff activities. Although he claimed that he relied on press accounts for his information, McFarlane actually received memos from Col. North via computer notes, which turned up after McFarlane testified. McFarlane worked closely with North and Poindexter to cover up the NSC role in the arms sale.[9]

From July 1985 until the operation was discovered in November 1986, North, with the clear approval of Adm. Poindexter, Robert McFarlane's successor as national security advisor, employed a network of private firms, CIA agents, CIA proprietary firms, nonprofit anticommunist organizations, some State Department officials—notably Assistant Secretary of State Elliot Abrams and the U.S. ambassador to Costa Rica, Lewis Tambs—and a few private individuals to aid the Nicaraguan rebels with logistics and fundraising efforts. The bulk of the money was handled by two individuals who controlled a network of firms, known to the congressional committees investigating the Iran-Contra Affair as "The Enterprise." The Enterprise was a partnership between Albert Hakim, an Iranian-born businessman, and ex-U.S. General Richard Secord, in close coordination with Lt. Col. North. The Enterprise served in a covert capacity as an informal contractor to the U.S. government and to the Contras.

The president was not told about The Enterprise because, according to Adm. Poindexter, it was an "unnecessary detail." William Casey was informed, although Poindexter instructed North not to tell Casey because as director of the CIA, he could be called on to testify before Congress. Poindexter also hid the operation from Donald Regan, the president's chief of staff, because "he talked to the press too much. I was afraid he'd make a slip."[10] The Congress and public were not informed of The Enterprise until the Iran-Contra investigation.

At an undetermined point in 1985, Col. North decided, with the approval of Adm. Poindexter, that the residual profits from the Iran arms sale ought to go toward assisting the Contras. Only a small fraction of the total Iran arms profits actually reached the Contras. According to the congressional committees' investigation, about $3.8 million out of the $16.1 million profit from the Iran arms sales went to support the Contras.[11]

Adm. Poindexter has testified that he did not distinguish among funds coming from private donations, the Iranian arms sales, or foreign sources in terms of their ownership. He argues that he had the authority to let Col. North and The Enterprise use the funds as they saw fit. The funds were used to cover expenses for the many operations, for buying arms for the Contras, for public relations in the United States on behalf of the Contras, and as a source of profits for Secord and Hakim. Some were also spent on a security system for the home of Col. North.[12]

Secord and Hakim controlled most of the money raised for the Contras. At one time when North visited Contra forces and wrote that "the picture is, in short, very dismal, unless a source of bridge funding can be found," there were over $4.8 million in funds in accounts controlled by Secord and Hakim of which North did not know.[13] The Enterprise took in total revenues of $4 million from the arms sales to Iran and the Contras, and

private donations from people who thought they were contributing to the Contras.[14]

All of these operations were kept secret from the Congress. Except for some of the fundraising from foreign sources, and the domestic public relations effort, the State Department was also not informed. The president was not told at this time about the diversion of funds from the Iran arms sale to the Contras.

Based on further press accounts, a new congressional inquiry was launched in June 1986. In the House Intelligence Committee's "Resolution of Inquiry," dated July 1, the president was directed to provide the House of Representatives with information and documents on: contacts between NSC staff and private individuals or foreign governments about Contra provisions; the extent to which NSC staff provided military advice to the Contras; and contacts between NSC staff and certain private individuals who were known consultants to the Contras.

Adm. Poindexter replied to the request by referring to McFarlane's response from the previous year and not mentioning any details. Since Poindexter knew that McFarlane's letter had not been accurate, he continued the deception that his predecessor had begun. The House Intelligence Committee also interviewed Col. North as part of their inquiry. Months later, in his testimony to the Iran-Contra committees, North admitted to lying in that interview.[15]

Both Col. North and Adm. Poindexter acknowledge that they misled Congress and both defend their actions. In his testimony North defended the right of the executive to resist informing the Congress about sensitive matters: "[I sent] . . . answers . . . to the Congress that were clearly misleading. . . . I believed then, and I believe now that the executive was fully legitimate in giving no answer to those queries." When Mr. Nields, the House chief counsel, asked Col. North how he could reconcile lying to Congress with a belief in democratic principles, North responded:

. . . I did it because we have had incredible leaks, from discussions with closed committees of the Congress. I . . . was a part of, some people know, the coordination for the mining of the harbors in Nicaragua. When that one leaked, there were American lives at stake, and it leaked from a member of one of the committees, who eventually admitted it. When there was a leak on the sensitive intelligence methods that we used to help capture the Achille Lauro terrorists, it almost wiped out that whole channel of communications. I mean, those kinds of things are devastating. They are devastating to the national security of the United States, and I desperately hope that one of the things that can derive from all of this ordeal is that we can find a better way by which we can communicate those things properly with the Congress.[17]

In a celebrated statement, Col. North concluded that "I think we had to weigh in the balance the difference between lies and lives."[18]

Critics, including the Senate counsel, Arthur Liman, have argued that Col. North could have revealed to Congress the general policy of aiding the Contras without revealing specific information that would have threatened lives. North maintains that a flaw in the oversight mechanism of Congress prevents the executive from feeling confident that Congress can maintain the confidentiality of sensitive matters. Moreover, he argued that a national debate on the subject would inevitably have led to the leaking of sensitive material.

Adm. Poindexter also admits to deceiving Congress, and he expected Col. North to do the same: "I did think he would withhold information and be evasive, frankly, in answering questions. My objective all along was to withhold from the Congress exactly what the NSC staff was doing in carrying out the president's policy."[19] Poindexter justifies this deception on the grounds that had Congress known the truth, it would have acted to stop the NSC activities. Since those activities, did not, in his view, violate the law, they could be conducted in secret:

that what Colonel North was doing in terms of supporting the democratic resistance was within the letter of the law at the time, although obviously very sensitive, very controversial. We wanted to avoid more restrictive legislation, and so any activity that he would have been involved with on Central America we wanted to keep highly compartmented.[20]

THE IRAN INITIATIVE[21]

In spite of strident rhetoric on the part of both countries, Iran and the United States each had interests in reestablishing ties with one another. Iran wanted weapons and diplomatic support in its war against Iraq, and the United States wanted to diminish the likelihood that Iran would turn pro-Soviet. There were discussions underway between Israeli and American officials concerning the possibility of U.S. sale of arms to Iran in 1984 and 1985. The Israelis maintained a secret communications channel with senior Iranian officials, about which the senior officials of the NSC gradually became aware. Throughout 1985, the number of American hostages taken increased dramatically, placing great pressure on the Reagan administration to do something to bring them home, in spite of public commitments not to give in to terrorist demands. The change in attitude within the administration was expressed in the context of broader U.S.-Iranian relations in a memo to McFarlane by two NSC staffers, Howard Teicher and Donald Fortier, dated June 11, 1985. They called for a radical shift in U.S. policy toward Iran in order to advance American and limit Soviet influence in Iran. One of the steps they recommended was the occasional shipment of arms to Iran. In June, the Iranians transmitted their desire to obtain U.S.-made weapons such as the TOW and HAWK missiles. A number of private businessmen including an Israeli, an Iranian, and a Saudi exerted their influence on NSC officials in an effort to broker a deal. National Security Advisor McFarlane circulated a draft memo on June 17 to Secretaries Shultz (State) and

Weinberger (Defense) and the director of central intelligence, Mr. Casey, suggesting that the United States could sell arms via the Israelis to Iran as part of a broader strategy for improving U.S.-Iranian relations and to help bring the hostages home. Both Shultz and Weinberger replied in memos that they opposed the arms sales.

After a briefing by McFarlane, President Reagan approved, on a still undetermined date in August, the shipment of U.S.-manufactured arms by Israel to Iran. On August 30, 1985, the Israelis shipped 100 TOW missiles to Iran. They sent an additional 408 TOWs on September 14. On September 15, a U.S. hostage, the Reverend Benjamin Weir, was released. In November, there was another arms sale. It remains unclear whether the president was informed of this sale; he does not remember. North, McFarlane, and Poindexter were all directly involved in the sale, and Shultz was briefed. Eighteen HAWK missiles were transferred to Iran, but they did not meet Iranian specifications, and the Iranians returned all but one of them to the Israelis. After this sale, a covert action finding was prepared by the CIA for the president to sign, approving the arms sales.

On December 7, the president met with senior officials, including McFarlane, who had just resigned as national security advisor, and Poindexter, concerning arms sales to Iran. As a result of the meeting, McFarlane, now a private citizen acting as an agent of the U.S. government, was sent to London to negotiate with a Mr. Ghorbanifar, an Iranian middleman who had brokered the previous sales.

According to his own accounts, the president was interested in proceeding with the Iran arms sales if the hostages could be freed. He signed another finding on January 17, 1986, authorizing the direct sale of American arms via the CIA to the Iranians. This decision marked a change from the previous policy of agreeing to resupply Israel with arms that they sold to Iran. Neither Secretary Shultz nor Secretary Weinberger

was informed of this shift in policy, which was developed by the president and Adm. Poindexter. At this point the arms sales became coordinated within the NSC staff, as part of a broader policy aimed at the release of the hostages entitled Operation Recovery. Col. North assumed direct control over the operation under the authority of Adm. Poindexter. North brought in The Enterprise to help with the shipments.

Negotiations with the Iranians had been strained since the unsuccessful shipment of the HAWKS in November. North and McFarlane arranged a meeting with the Iranians to attempt to improve relations. Adm. Poindexter briefed the president in May 1986 in the two weeks preceding the trip, but he did not inform Shultz or Weinberger, and neither did the president. Although no U.S. hostages had been taken during the summer, three more were taken in September and October.

The taking of these hostages led North, McFarlane, and Poindexter, and probably Casey, to mistrust Ghorbanifar. Col. North sought to establish a "second channel" to Iran to replace Ghorbanifar. Acting under presidential authorization, North, along with a CIA agent and Secord, met with the second channel, an individual whose identity has not been revealed, in Frankfurt on October 5–7, 1986. They set up a second meeting in Frankfurt, at which, without presidential authorization, but possibly with Adm. Poindexter's approval, Col. North agreed that the United States would ship more TOWs and HAWKS, supply military intelligence, and pressure the Kuwaiti government to release some terrorist prisoners in exchange for the release of one or two American hostages. U.S. officials continued to negotiate with the Iranian officials through December 1986, after the affair had been made public. The talks broke down, however, and U.S. policy turned actively anti-Iran in the summer of 1987.

On November 3, 1986, the Lebanese paper Al-Shiraa disclosed that the United

States had been selling arms to Iran in exchange for the release of hostages held in Lebanon. The White House issued a series of statements the following week denying the reports; the statements had been prepared in large measure by Poindexter.[22] On November 12 and 13 the cover-up continued, as Poindexter spread inaccurate accounts of the affair to the cabinet, members of Congress, and the press. He did not mention the Nicaragua connection, and he did not refer to two of the three findings signed by the president. He also omitted most of the arms shipments to Iran. On November 18, Poindexter withheld information from State Department counsel, Abraham Sofaer. That same day, Poindexter spoke with Casey about preparing false testimony for a congressional appearance.[23]

On November 19, the president held a news conference reiterating the false claims he had made during his televised address.[24] Secretary Shultz confronted the president about his factual errors on the following day. Meanwhile, McFarlane, Poindexter, and North were constructing inaccurate chronologies of the affair. Because they communicated with each other via computer messages which the congressional committees later retrieved, we have a record of their attempt. The record strongly suggests that their intention was to cover up what they could. For example, in some of their accounts, they claimed the HAWK shipments were really oil equipment, when they had been the officials who had devised the oil equipment deception to preserve secrecy in the first place.[25] On November 21, Director Casey made the same false claim in his testimony to the Intelligence Committee.

Under considerable public pressure, the attorney general, Edwin Meese, decided to launch an investigation into the affair because of conflicting stories about what had actually taken place. When he informed Poindexter of this, Poindexter and North began a massive effort to destroy the evidence of their actions. They both shredded documents; North also altered the documents, deleting references to the NSC staff's ties to the Contras.[26]

When testifying, North admitted that he shredded documents for reasons other than to preserve national security:

LIMAN: Do you deny, Colonel, that one of the reasons that you were shredding documents that Saturday, was to avoid the political embarrassment of having those documents be seen by the attorney general's staff?

NORTH: I do not deny that.[27]

Moreover, North lied to Meese during his interview with the attorney general. Meese confronted North with a document, which Bradford Reynolds, the assistant attorney general, had uncovered, mentioning the diversion of funds from Iran to Nicaragua. North claimed that "no one at CIA knew about it," when Casey, in fact, had known. North also lied about the nature of the Contra supply operations.[28]

BUREAUCRATIC IRREGULARITIES

In the Iran-Contra Affair, many normal bureaucratic procedures were ignored in an effort to maintain secrecy. Both initiatives, which could be considered to be major acts of foreign policy, were handled as covert operations and kept secret from as many senior officials in the government as possible. For instance, U.S. officials negotiated with high-level Israeli and Iranian politicians without the knowledge of the secretary of state. To maintain this secrecy, Adm. Poindexter and Director Casey evidently believed that they had to deceive Secretary Shultz, with whom they dealt on a regular basis, about the activities of Lt. Col. North.

The National Security Council staff was not formed with the purpose of undertaking covert operations or foreign policy initiatives, but for easing the presidential decision-making process, yet the NSC staff took over the job of resupplying the Contras when the CIA was expressly barred from doing so by Congress. The answer to the legal question of whether the NSC staff was included in the cut-off remains uncertain: the Boland Amendment cut-off included "DOD, CIA and other agencies engaged in intelligence activities." In general, the NSC is not considered an intelligence agency, but Executive Order 12333 stated that the NSC was "the highest Executive Branch entity that provides review of, guidance for, and direction to the conduct of all national foreign intelligence, counter-intelligence, and special activities, and attendant policies and programs."[29] Moreover, the covert operations conducted by Col. North included CIA and ex-CIA personnel and were of the type which might normally be conducted by the CIA. Poindexter and North, however, received legal advice from the president's Foreign Intelligence Advisory Board to the effect that the NSC was not covered by the Boland Amendment.

JUSTIFIABLE DECEPTION?

In the congressional hearings, Adm. Poindexter and Lt. Col. North acknowledged their attempts to deceive executive branch officials, the Congress, and the public, but they maintained that their acts of deception were justifiable. The House counsel, John Nields, asked Col. North about the covert operations:

MR. NIELDS: And these operations—they were covert operations?
LT. COL. NORTH: Yes they were.
NIELDS: And covert operations are designed to be secret from our enemies?
NORTH: That is correct.
NIELDS: But these operations were designed to be secrets from the American people?
NORTH: Mr. Nields, I'm at a loss as to how we could announce it to the American people and not have the Soviets know about it . . .
NIELDS: Well, in fact, Col. North, you believed that the Soviets were aware of our sale of arms to Iran, weren't you?
NORTH: We came to a point in time when we were concerned about that.

A few minutes later, Col. North elaborated on his statement:

LT. COL. NORTH: I think it is very important for the American people to understand that this is a dangerous world; that we live at risk and that this nation is at risk in a dangerous world. And that they ought not to be led to believe, as a consequence of these hearings, that this nation cannot or should not conduct covert operations. By their very nature, covert operations or special activities are a lie. There is great deceit, deception practiced in the conduct of covert operation[s]. They are at essence a lie. We make every effort to deceive the enemy as to our intent, our conduct and to deny the association of the United States with those activities. The intelligence committees hold hearings on all kinds of activities conducted by our intelligence service. The American people ought not to believe by the way you're asking that question that we intentionally deceived the American people, or had that intent to begin with. The effort to conduct these covert operations was made in such a way that our adversaries would not have knowledge of them or that we could deny American association with it, or the association of this government with those activities. And that is not wrong.[30]

Col. North claimed that he had been granted authority for all of his deceptions: "I sought approval for every one of my actions and it is well documented. I assumed when I had approval to proceed from. . . Bud McFarlane or Adm. Poindexter, that they had indeed solicited and obtained the approval of the President."[31] Colonel North was supported by Poindexter who testified, "I didn't tell Col. North that I was not going to tell the president."[32] North admitted, however, that following orders is insufficient grounds for breaking the law. Both he and Adm. Poindexter have argued, however, that their activities did not break the law because they did not use money appropriated by the Congress.[33]

Adm. Poindexter's deception was, in many respects, similar to that of Col. North. However, North did not withhold information from his immediate superiors. Adm. Poindexter claims that he deliberately, intentionally failed to inform President

Reagan of the diversion of funds to the Contras in an effort to protect the president from responsibility for a politically controversial act. Poindexter argued in his testimony that he was justified in not telling the president for three reasons: the diversion of funds from Iran to the Contras was legal; the diversion was essentially a "detail" of the larger policy of aiding the Contras; and the president would have supported the policy had he known about it:

> My impression was that it was clear to me that these were third country or private-party funds that would result from the arms sale to the Iranians . . . I felt that it was in terms of supporting and implementing the president's policy, that it was entirely consistent. The president never really changed his policy with regard to supporting the Contras since the early decision back in 1981. It seemed that his method of financing was completely consistent with what we had been doing in terms of private parties and third countries. I knew that it would be a controversial issue. I had at that point worked with the president for three of those five-and-a-half years, very directly, meeting with him many times a day, often spending hours every day with him. So I not only clearly understood his policy, but I thought I understood the way he thought about issues. I felt that I had the authority to approve Col. North's request. I also felt that it was, as I said, consistent with the president's policy, and that if I asked him, I felt confident that he would approve it. But because it was controversial, and I obviously knew it would cause a ruckus if it were exposed, I decided to insulate the president from the decision and give him some deniability; and so I decided . . . at that point not to tell the president.[34]

As of May 1988, no court has ruled on the legality of either the arms sale or the diversion of funds. However, a grand jury returned a conspiracy indictment against Adm. Poindexter, Col. North, Richard Secord, and Albert Hakim. Also, Col. McFarlane pleaded guilty to four misdemeanor counts.

Col. McFarlane struck a deal with the independent counsel, Lawrence Walsh, in which McFarlane agreed to testify as a witness for the prosecution against Adm. Poindexter and Col. North and to plead guilty to the misdemeanors in exchange for his freedom from felony indictments. After his court appearance, McFarlane told reporters, "I did indeed withhold information from Congress."[35]

The indictment against Poindexter and North included their coverup attempt as illegal activity:

> From August 1985 through November 1986, in order to conceal and cover up their illegal activities and to perpetrate the scheme, the conspirators, including the defendants JOHN M. POINDEXTER and OLIVER L. NORTH, deceived Congress and committees of Congress by making false, fictitious, fraudulent and misleading statements and representations, concerning, among other things, the involvement of officials of the United States, including members of the NSC staff, in support of the military and paramilitary operations in Nicaragua by the Contras at a time when the Boland Amendment was in effect. . . .[36]

Following his indictment, Lt. Col. North resigned from the Marine Corps in order to be in a position to subpoena "testimony and records from the highest-ranking officials of our government" during his trial.[37] This action furthered speculation that President Reagan would pardon North, and possibly Poindexter as well, on the grounds that they had only been following his orders. The *Wall Street Journal* editorial board previously argued in favor of pardons for North and Poindexter for precisely these reasons on November 30, 1987.[38] As of May 1988, President Reagan has neither pardoned nor ruled out the possibility that he would pardon Poindexter and North, who have both pleaded not guilty, but whose trials have not yet begun.

The majority and minority reports of the congressional committees differ in their judgments of the affair and its participants. Almost no aspect of the affair—legal, policy, or moral—commands complete acceptance by the members of Congress or others who have studied the issue. The public also holds varying and changing views. In August, at the height of the hearings, more than half of the American public thought President Reagan had lied and was continuing to lie about the affair. They did not like the way he had handled Iranian policy. The president's job approval rating was in the forty percent range, down from his usual mid-sixties. Nevertheless, as a result of other factors, his personal popularity had returned to high levels by December.

The public did not like Adm. Poindexter, but many praised Col. North, who was as passionate and inspiring on the witness stand as Poindexter was detached and pedantic. Nevertheless, a month after North's testimony was over, a number of polls indicated that most people did not believe North had been justified in deceiving the Congress. Additionally, while public support for aiding the Contras rose dramatically during North's testimony, it dropped equally dramatically in the next two months.[39]

NOTES

1. In the House of Representatives, the Select Committee to Investigate Covert Arms Transactions with Iran was chaired by Representative Lee Hamilton. In the Senate, the Select Committee on Secret Military Assistance to Iran and the Nicaraguan Opposition was chaired by Senator Daniel Inouye. The transcript of the public sessions of Col. North was sold under the title, *Taking the Stand* (New York: Pocket Books). The president appointed a panel to review the affair, known as the Tower Commission, which released a report. Much of the closed testimony by Adm. Poindexter was released in a sanitized version by the Senate committee. The committees released a final report in November 1987 with two titles, S. Rept. No. 100–216 and H. Rept. No. 100–413. This case is based substantially on these sources.

2. John Tower, Edmund Muskie, and Brent Scowcroft, *The Tower Commission Report* (New York: Bantam Books and Times Books, 1987), pp. 55–59, 450–452.

3. *Taking the Stand*, p. 243.

4. *Report of the Congressional Committees Investigating the Iran-Contra Affair*, p. 4.

5. *Poindexter Closed Testimony to the Committees*, May 1987, p. 203. Also see p. 53.

6. *Report of the Congressional Committees Investigating the Iran-Contra Affair*, p. 20.

7. Cited in ibid., p. 123.

8. Ibid., p. 127.

9. *Tower Report*, pp. 527, 536.

10. Cited in *Report of the Congressional Committees Investigating the Iran-Contra Affair*, p. 139.

11. Ibid., p. 331.

12. Ibid., p. 341.

13. *Taking the Stand*, p. 552.

14. Report of the Congressional Committees, p. 11.

15. Ibid., p. 141.

16. *Taking the Stand*, p. 245.

17. Ibid., p. 253.

18. Ibid., p. 256.

19. Cited in *Report of the Congressional Committees*, p. 142.

20. *Poindexter Closed Testimony to the Committees*, May 1987, p. 47.

21. This section is based substantially on the *Tower Report*.

22. *Report of the Congressional Committees*, p. 294.

23. Ibid., p. 301.

24. Ibid., p. 298.

25. Ibid., p. 298–300.

26. Ibid., p. 306–7.

27. *Taking the Stand*, p. 362.

28. *Report of the Congressional Committees*, p. 312.

29. *The Chronology* (Warner, 1987), p. 67, compiled by the National Security Archive.

30. *Taking the Stand*, pp. 9, 12.

31. Ibid., p. 13.

32. *Poindexter Closed Testimony to the Committees*, May 1987, p. 70.

33. *Taking the Stand*, p. 487.

34. *Poindexter Closed Testimony to the Committees*, May 1987, pp. 70–71.

35. *New York Times*, March 12, 1988, p. 1.

36. As reproduced in the *New York Times*, March 17, 1988, p. D26.

37. *New York Times*, March 19, 1988, p. 1.

38. *Wall Street Journal*, Nov. 30, 1987, p. 20.

39. For opinion poll data, I have relied upon an extensive collection of *New York Times*/CBS, Roper, *LA Times, Newsweek, Time* and other polls collected by the Congressional Research Service of the Library of Congress. This data is computerized at the Library of Congress in the "CRS Survey Poll File" under the title "Iran-Contra Affair Polls, October 1986 to Present."

Comment

Although Colonel Muammar el-Qaddafi was the intended victim of the deception described in the 1986 directive signed by President Reagan, journalists and the public were also deceived by the campaign of disinformation that ensued. Was the deception of the press and the public necessary to carry out the directive? If so, was the deception justified? More generally, are public officials justified in trying to "manage the news" if necessary to achieve an important, widely shared foreign policy objective? Does this case suggest any other conditions that we should place on public officials before agreeing that they may deceive us? Evaluate the defense of deception that is implicit in Secretary of State Shultz's response to reporters. The Senate Select Committee concluded that the administration did not have a formal policy of lying to American reporters. If we accept this conclusion, are there any grounds on which we could still hold the administration morally responsible for deceiving the press and the public?

Unlike most public officials who engage in deception, Admiral John Poindexter and Colonel Oliver North did not deny that they did so. They justified their deception on grounds that their secret actions (1) were necessary to national security, (2) did not violate the letter of the law, and (3) would have been undermined, through leaks and hostile legislation, had they (or anyone else) informed Congress. Consider to what extent their various deceptive statements and actions satisfy their own criteria of justification. What relevant moral considerations are overlooked by their criteria? Does North, in his response to the House chief counsel, succeed in reconciling his approval of lying to Congress with a belief in democratic principles? Are there any conditions under which lying to Congress can be reconciled with democratic principles?

Unlike North, Poindexter deliberately withheld information not only from Congress but also from his immediate superiors, thereby doubly avoiding accountability. Assess Poindexter's justification for concealing information about "The Enterprise" from the president's chief of staff, Donald Regan. Did Poindexter's deliberate failure to inform the president about the diversion of funds to the Contras constitute deception? If so, of whom? Assume that Poindexter was correct in believing that the president would not want to know about the diversion of funds: is Poindexter then justified in not informing the president (or, as some have suggested, perhaps even obligated not to inform him)?

One of the most striking features of the deception chronicled in "The Iran-Contra Affair" is its pervasiveness. The targets of deception included not only journalists and the American public but also many high-level executive branch officials and congressmen who would normally have been informed about foreign policies of this importance. North and Poindexter seem to have been guided by presumptions favoring deception rather than veracity, and secrecy rather than openness in government. Their testimony provides few if any principled reasons to limit deception and secrecy when public officials act in a cause they believe to be just. What principles could establish a strong presumption in favor of veracity and openness? What political institutions or procedures could guard against unjustified deception by public officials who are motivated either by self-interest or by a passionate dedication to the public interest?

The case and comment are based primarily on information revealed during the congressional hearings. Does information disclosed since then or any subsequent events change your moral assessment of the actions of either North or Poindexter?

The Senate Confirmation of Justice Clarence Thomas

Jillian P. Dickert

In the three months after federal appeals court Judge Clarence Thomas was nominated by President George Bush to sit on the Supreme Court in July 1991, his well-organized opposition searched for ammunition that could defeat him. The stakes were high: if confirmed, Thomas would gain a seat on the nation's highest court at the young age of forty-three, making it possible for him to decide cases through the 2030s. Opponents feared the impact that the lifetime appointment of the conservative black jurist would have on a court poised to review so many high-profile, consequential cases in the coming years. In the 1991–92 term alone, the Supreme Court was preparing to decide such politically sensitive issues as the rights of anti-abortion protesters, school prayer, "hate speech," and school desegregation, and many believed that the Court would soon rule on whether to overturn the 1973 *Roe v. Wade* decision that legalized abortion nationwide.

As the vote on Thomas's confirmation approached in late September, allegations

emerged that could cut to the heart of what many had cited as Thomas's strongest qualification for the high court: his personal character. Throughout the summer of 1991, Thomas had captivated the nation with the story of his extraordinary climb from the poverty and racism of the segregated South. Now—as the fourteen members of the Senate Judiciary Committee prepared for their vote on the nomination—a *confidential* statement from Anita Hill, Thomas's former subordinate at the EEOC and the U.S. Department of Education, purported to reveal a different side of the nominee's character. In graphic language, Hill described how Thomas had sexually harassed her over a three-year period in the early 1980s.

But there were complications. Hill had made it clear that she wanted her charges heard by the Senate Judiciary Committee, but not made public. The Judiciary Committee and its staff would ultimately have to decide how to handle a private charge and also deal with their public responsibilities.

THE POLITICS OF SUPREME COURT NOMINATIONS

In Article II, Section 2, the U.S. Constitution states that the president "shall nomi-

Reprinted by permission of the Case Program, Kennedy School of Government, Harvard University. Copyright © 1992 by the President and Fellows of Harvard and by Princeton University.

nate, and by and with the Advice and Consent of the Senate, shall appoint . . . Judges of the Supreme Court.'' As an important check on presidential power, the Senate's power to consent also involves the power to reject: of the 144 Supreme Court nominees prior to Thomas, 27 (nearly one out of five) have been rejected, withdrawn, or not acted on by the Senate. Historically, partisanship has played a decisive role in a nomination's success or failure. When the president and Senate majority have been of the same party, consent has been given to more than 90 percent of the nominations. When they have been of different parties, more than half of the nomninees have not been confirmed.[1]

Between 1950 and 1991, the Senate and the White House were in the hands of the same party less than half the time.[2] In an era of divided government, the Senate's power to consent often meant the exercise of a clearly political judgment. This may have been intended by the framers of the Constitution: in *The Federalist Papers*, Alexander Hamilton argued that the prospect of Senate disapproval would and should inhibit the president from choosing candidates ''in some way or other personally allied to him, or . . . possessing the necessary insignificance and pliancy to render them the obsequious instruments of his pleasure.'' Nonetheless, the highly politicized nature of Supreme Court nominations was a point of contention for both branches of the federal government.

The subject had been particularly sensitive since President Reagan's 1987 nomination of federal appeals court Judge Robert Bork. In a confirmation battle described as bitterly partisan, Bork became the first Supreme Court nominee since 1970 to be rejected by the Senate. Bork's opponents used his extensive ''paper trail'' of articles, books, and judicial opinions to convince senators that his theory of ''original intent'' was sharply at odds with much of recent U.S. constitutional law. After his defeat, Bork predicted: ''A president who wants to avoid a battle like mine, and most presidents would prefer to, is likely to nominate men and women who have not written much, and certainly nothing that could be regarded as controversial by left-leaning senators and groups.''[3] In fact, neither of the two subsequent nominees, Anthony Kennedy and David Souter, were outspoken conservatives, and neither was subjected to broad opposition.

After ten consecutive Republican appointments over twenty-two years, the Democrat-controlled Senate in 1991 began expressing frustration with so-called ''stealth'' nominees who, during their confirmation hearings, endorsed conventional wisdom and claimed to have ''no agenda'' for the Court, only to emerge as staunch conservatives once on the bench. Critics pointed to Justice Souter. During his confirmation hearings, Souter refused to discuss his views on abortion. Later, in his first term on the Court, Souter joined with four other justices to uphold a ban on abortion counseling at federally funded clinics.

With the retirement of Thurgood Marshall, the Court's last consistently liberal justice, Senate Democrats seemed to gain greater resolve to exercise their power to reject. Shortly after Justice Marshall announced his resignation on June 27, 1991, Senator Howard Metzenbaum (D-Ohio) declared, ''I'm through reading tea leaves and voting in the dark. . . . I will not support yet another Reagan-Bush Supreme Court nominee who remains silent on a woman's right to choose [an abortion] and then ascends to the court to weaken that right.''[4]

A BOOTSTRAPS SUCCESS STORY

On July 2, 1991, President Bush announced the nomination of Clarence Thomas to fill Justice Marshall's seat on the Supreme Court. Standing before the president's ocean-front home in Kennebunkport, Maine, Thomas addressed the nation, his voice choked with emotion. "As a child, I could not dare to dream that I would ever see the Supreme Court, not to mention be nominated to it," said Thomas, who rose to his current status from an impoverished early childhood in rural Georgia. "Only in America could this have been possible." The appointment would elevate Thomas from his seat on the U.S. Court of Appeals for the District of Columbia, a court widely regarded as the nation's second highest and a steppingstone to the Supreme Court. Just fifteen months earlier, the Senate Judiciary Committee had approved Thomas for the federal appeals court by a vote of 13–1.[5]

Judge Thomas's written opinions—which, during his fifteen months on the bench, dealt largely with criminal law and regulatory issues—were not considered revealing of his overall constitutional philosophy. However, in speeches, writings and interviews throughout the 1980s, Thomas took positions on various controversial constitutional issues which some people found surprising for an African-American.[6] Thomas was opposed to racial quotas and other forms of preferential treatment for minorities. He believed that no government program could replace the kind of self-discipline that was instilled in him by the grandfather who raised him and reinforced by the Catholic nuns who schooled him. In 1983, Thomas said that only their philosophy of "God, . . . school, discipline, hard work, and 'right from wrong'" saved him from a life like that of his sister, who was raised by other relatives and later supported four children on welfare.[7] Thomas was expressing these views at the same time Republican party activists were hoping to nurture and promote a black elite that could directly challenge the traditional—and highly Democratic—civil rights leadership.[8]

Thomas's road to success was through the Republican party. After graduating from Yale Law School, Thomas rose quickly through the ranks of the Reagan and Bush administrations. In 1981, President Reagan appointed him assistant secretary for civil rights in the Department of Education, and just one year later, Thomas was made chairman of the Equal Employment Opportunity Commission (EEOC). In his eight-year tenure at the EEOC, Thomas redefined how the federal government handled job discrimination complaints. By the time he left the agency in 1990, Thomas had: (1) changed EEOC policy to emphasize individual redress rather than the use of class action lawsuits that relied on statistical evidence to prove widespread job discrimination at large corporations; (2) largely abandoned the use of minority hiring goals and timetables by employers to correct racial and ethnic disparities; and (3) yielded the agency's once dominant role on civil rights issues to the Justice Department.[9]

Thomas's record at the EEOC drew fire from many liberal groups, who charged that Thomas "dismally" failed to enforce anti-discrimination laws. They pointed to thousands of age discrimination complaints that had lapsed for lack of action during his tenure.[10] Some critics nicknamed him "Uncle Thomas," claiming his conservative views were a betrayal for a man who in law school was himself a beneficiary of affirmative action. (Yale Law School actively recruited minority students in the early 1970s.)[11] Thomas responded to this criticism: "I have been extremely fortunate. I have benefited greatly from the civil rights movement, from the justice whom I am nominated to succeed."[12]

THE CAMPAIGN BEGINS

Within days of Bush's announcement, Thomas's nomination to the Supreme Court grew intensely politicized. On July 11, members of the Congressional Black Caucus voted overwhelmingly to oppose Thomas,[13] promising to organize a national campaign by black leaders to fight the selection. Meanwhile, the White House appointed Washington consultant Kenneth

Duberstein, a former chief of staff to President Ronald Reagan, to play the lead role in "handling" Thomas during the confirmation process. (Duberstein had performed the same role for Justice Souter.) Later, the Citizen's Committee to Confirm Clarence Thomas unveiled a national radio and television campaign designed to convince senators that it would be "politically risky" to vote against Thomas.[14]

The anti-Thomas campaign picked up momentum in August when the National Association for the Advancement of Colored People (NAACP) and the AFL-CIO announced their opposition in a dual press conference. The Leadership Conference on Civil Rights, a coalition of 185 organizations instrumental in the drive to defeat Bork, followed suit soon after. The Leadership Conference claimed Thomas "demonstrated a consistent hostility to many of the Supreme Court's most fundamental civil rights decisions." They also argued that "his judicial philosophy is radical and places him well outside of the judicial mainstream." Not all civil rights groups opposed Thomas, however. The National Urban League, more moderate than the NAACP, voted to take no position on Thomas. "I think it is important that we have a racially diverse Supreme Court, even if he is not my candidate," said John Jacob, the league's president at that time.[15]

Civil rights groups engaged in the campaign to defeat Thomas were joined by other liberal-leaning organizations active in the Bork battle, such as the Alliance for Justice and People for the American Way, and several women's groups, including the National Organization for Women, the Women's Legal Defense Fund, and the National Women's Law Center, which claimed that Thomas's record showed "no commitment to core constitutional or statutory protections for women." Abortion rights activists feared that Thomas's expressed view that the Constitution should be interpreted in light of a "higher law" could signal his op-

position to legalized abortion. Thomas had never decided an abortion case or commented directly on the correctness of *Roe v. Wade*, but in a 1987 speech for the conservative Heritage Foundation, he praised an antiabortion article by conservative Lewis E. Lehrman as a "splendid example of applying natural law."[16] (Natural law is a philosophy typically identified with the premise that there are laws given by a higher authority than government that therefore override any governmental authority.)

To counter this opposition, Thomas's backers quickly painted him as a by-the-bootstraps success story with few strongly held views on specific legal issues. Senator John Danforth (R-Mo.), Thomas's most outspoken defender in the Senate, described him as a "conservative but a compassionate kind of conservative, not rigid or ideological in his views. His very motive is that he empathizes with ordinary people, he's one of them."[17] Danforth added, "I honestly do not know how he would vote [on abortion]. . . . In fact, I don't know how he would vote on any issues."[18] Senate Minority Leader Bob Dole (R-Kans.) praised Thomas as a "man whose very life exemplifies the American dream."[19]

Thomas's supporters suggested that in his rise above poverty and racism, Thomas acquired a perspective greater than that provided by legal scholarship. "Does he understand [that] all men, all women are not always treated equally?" asked U.S. Department of Labor Secretary Lynn Martin, who led the newly formed group Women for Judge Thomas. "Clarence Thomas understands. He knows the inequities, the indignities, the insensitivity."[20]

President Bush insisted race played no part in his selection of Thomas to replace Thurgood Marshall, the Supreme Court's first and only black justice. "Judge Thomas's life is a model for all Americans, and he's earned the right to sit on this nation's highest court," Bush said. "The fact that he is black and a minority has nothing to do with this sense that he is the best qualified at this time."[21] Nevertheless, in the campaigns for and against Thomas, both sides targeted the Senate's Southern Democrats, who derive a substantial part of their power base from black voters. Southern Democrats tipped the scales to defeat Bork in 1987, and it was widely believed that they would hesitate to reject a black nominee for the Supreme Court without a clear message of opposition from home.[22]

A QUESTION OF CHARACTER

Thomas's personal story of success in overcoming obstacles appeared to impress his opponents as well as his supporters. The high-profile, influential groups joining in the fight against Thomas had difficulty generating the groundswell of opposition across the country that was vital in the defeat of Judge Bork. This frustrated anti-Thomas lobbying efforts on Capitol Hill. "The basic feeling is that Republicans have the Democrats over a barrel on this one," said Senator Charles Grassley (R-Iowa), one of six Republicans on the fourteen-member Senate Judiciary Committee, which would be holding hearings that September on whether to recommend that Thomas be confirmed by the full Senate. Many liberal senators who had come out strongly against Bork, including Senator Edward Kennedy (D-Mass.), held their fire on Thomas. According to Senator Orrin Hatch (R-Utah), a key factor in Bork's defeat was that Kennedy "worked it to death. He went out and got all of the black ministers and told them this man was bad for civil rights. He mobilized the unions and every liberal group in this country. He's not doing that with this one."[23] A few Senate Democrats even predicted Thomas's confirmation weeks before the Judiciary Committee's September hearings. In early August, Senator Paul Simon (D-Ill.) told the *Washington Post*, "I think the situation is that he is probably going to be approved. He is working very hard at it. He is making the rounds [to an extent that] no one has ever

done before." Thomas, Simon noted, "is a likable person" and "in some ways the personality things are the toughest things that we deal with here. It's easier to say no on an issue than to say no on a person."[24]

Liberal groups also complained that their anti-Thomas campaigns were in part stalled by the reluctance of Judiciary Committee Chair Joseph Biden (D-Del.) to pursue aggressively leads about Thomas. Biden—whose 1988 bid for the presidency faltered over allegations of plagiarism—was determined to avoid making Thomas's character the focus of the Judiciary Committee's probe before and during its hearings on the Thomas nomination. (Senator Metzenbaum later admitted he was concerned about crossing Biden on that point.[25]) For example, Thomas's Yale Law School friends reported in September that he sometimes entertained them at the dining hall with "hilarious descriptions of X-rated movies he liked to watch for relaxation"[26]—this was not investigated by full committee staff, nor would it be mentioned by any senator during the upcoming hearings. The committee under Biden showed little interest in pursuing other matters that had been dug up by interest groups in the summer of 1991, including stories (which were never confirmed) that Thomas's divorce records contained allegations from his first wife that he beat her,[27] and charges that Thomas had maintained close relations with Jay Parker, a so-called "ultraconservative black leader" who had once lobbied for South Africa.[28] Also considered irrelevant was Thomas's admitted college-age marijuana smoking, although in 1987, federal appeals court Judge Douglas Ginsburg withdrew his nomination to the Supreme Court when his marijuana use became public.[29]

Ron Klain, Biden's chief counsel in charge of the committee's handling of the Thomas nomination, believes that Biden's experience with the 1987 Bork nomination colored the chairman's hesitancy to bring up "character" issues. According to Klain, "the only time Bork started to gain public support was when people were running personal arguments against him, and in fact, when he [Biden] made it about issues and substance, they were ultimately able to vanquish Bork." Thus, with Thomas, Klain says, "Biden's sense was that to shoot and miss on that stuff would create a very sympathetic backlash towards Thomas that would overwhelm the substantive case against the man."

The Committee Hearings

By the time the Senate Judiciary Committee hearings opened on September 10, many expected that Thomas would be approved by the panel of eight Democrats and six Republicans. Thomas needed eight of the fourteen committee votes to be favorably recommended to the full Senate, which traditionally follows the lead of the Judiciary Committee. Thomas could count on the support of at least five Republicans. Furthermore, polls taken in early September showed that while most Americans (65 percent of whites, 63 percent of blacks) were still undecided on the nomination, a majority of those holding opinions on Thomas—both blacks and whites—said he should be confirmed.[30] Southern Democrats—who held the balance of power on the nomination—were thus faced with the possibility that a vote against Thomas might alienate more of their constituents than a vote for him. Although he had not yet announced how he would vote on the nomination, Senator Howell Heflin (D-Ala.)—traditionally a Judiciary Committee swing vote—said his initial reaction was that Thomas was qualified.[31] Also undecided on the nomination were Senator Dennis DeConcini (D-Ariz.), who said he began with a presumption that the president's nominee was qualified, and Senator Arlen Specter (R-Pa.)—the only GOP committee member to vote against Bork—who was up for reelection in 1992 and expected a strong challenge from the Republican right wing.[32]

Publicly, Chairman Biden was another question mark. In his opening statement, Biden made it clear that the "single most important task for the committee" was to ascertain how Thomas would apply to the Constitution his philosophy of natural law. By conceding that Bush had "the right to appoint a conservative" and that any Bush appointee would inevitably move the Court to the right, Biden seemed to conclude that only if Thomas espoused an "extreme, activist" agenda, would he be deemed unfit for the high court.

For the most part, the Republicans' mission for the hearings seemed obvious: steer all questioning away from specific substantive issues and focus on Thomas's personal background and character. Senator Alan Simpson (R-Wyo.), for example, talked for most of his allotted thirty minutes of questioning time, while Senator Hank Brown (R-Colo.) questioned Thomas about the computer system and database he had installed as EEOC chairman. Only Specter appeared to have prepared probing questions for Thomas; in Specter's view, Thomas had "shifted" positions several times during his career on the legality of minority preference programs and set-asides.

Unartful Dodges and Sophistry

During his hearings, Thomas described his interest in natural law not as a constitutional philosophy but as an off-hours interest in political theory. He distanced himself from his earlier hard-line conservatism, mainly recapping the status of current court decisions and offering little about his own views. Instead, Thomas referred frequently to his impoverished youth in Pin Point, Georgia. His compelling descriptions of racism and poverty seemed to deter members of the all-white, all-male committee from asking questions about affirmative action—a politically sensitive topic on which Thomas had been outspoken throughout his career.

Democrats were relentless in their efforts

to determine Thomas' position on abortion, however, barraging him with more than thirty questions on the issue. In each instance, Thomas said he could not answer without compromising his impartiality. Finally, Thomas told Senator Patrick Leahy (D-Vt.) that he had no "personal opinion" on the *Roe v. Wade* decision,[33] and in fact, could not "recollect commenting one way or another" on it, not even in a private setting, in the eighteen years since the ruling. (Early in the hearings, Thomas had described the *Roe* decision as "one of the more important, as well as . . . one of the more highly publicized and debated [Supreme Court] cases.") Thomas said that his only experience discussing the case was "in the most general sense that other individuals express concerns one way or the other and you listen and you try to be thoughtful. If you are asking me whether or not I have ever debated the contents of it, the answer is no, senator." Thomas explained that when the landmark case was decided in 1973, he was a married law student who also worked, and, as a result, "did not spend a lot of time around the law school doing what all the other students enjoyed so much, and that is debating all the current cases."

Leahy was incredulous. "With all due respect, judge, I have some difficulty with your answer," he retorted, pointing out that Thomas had been immersed in a wide variety of conservative policy debates over the past eighteen years and had cited *Roe v. Wade* in a footnote to a law review article, mentioned the abortion issue in a reference to an article about natural law and fetal right to life, and discussed black voters' views on abortion in a newspaper article. "I cannot believe all of this was done in a vacuum, absent some very clear considerations of *Roe v. Wade*," said Leahy.

Unable effectively to make issue of Thomas's views, committee Democrats proceeded to focus attention on his professed lack of them. Most expressed varying degrees of concern that the nominee was being purposely vague and backtracking from or contradicting earlier statements in order to win confirmation. Biden accused the nominee of engaging in "sophistry" after trying to draw him out on natural law and called another answer "the most unartful dodge I have heard." Metzenbaum was just as blunt. "I start with the assumption that public officials mean what they say," he said. "It's difficult to accept the notion that the moment you put on that judge's robe, all the positions and views you held prior to going on the bench just magically disappear." Heflin suggested that perhaps Thomas had undergone a "confirmation conversion," indicating that such a strategy could "raise issues that can affect the evaluation that [we] give as to integrity and temperament."

Backed by committee Republicans, Thomas sought to allay the Democrats' concerns. He argued that he had been "consistent on this issue of natural law" and pointed repeatedly to his previous Senate hearings (for the federal appeals court), where he suggested that he would follow a more traditional approach to constitutional interpretation. Thomas claimed to have "no agenda" for the Court, explaining that in the past he had "advocated as an advocate, and now [he] will rule as a judge." He elaborated that "a judge must not bring to his job, to the court, the baggage of preconceived notions, of ideology, and certainly not an agenda. . . . [A] judge must get the decision right."

The eight days of hearing on the Thomas nomination were the third longest set of hearings in history on any Supreme Court nomination.[34] Nevertheless, after five full days of testimony from Thomas,[35] Democrats complained that they knew little more about Clarence Thomas than at the start of the hearings. "I still don't have quite the sense of how you think and what you would be as a justice," said Leahy, exasperated with the elusive Thomas. The disappointment of Senator Herb Kohl (D-Wis.), was plain. "I think Judge Thomas has demonstrated that he can go through an entire hearing process and confront some very difficult questions by not answering them. Who is the real Clarence Thomas?" Kohl asked. "We really don't know." Heflin confessed that he could not tell whether the nominee was "a closet liberal, a conservative, or an opportunist." Other Democrats seemed at least as unhappy with the nomination process as they were with the nominee. "It seems that somehow it has emerged that if you are evasive, you have a better chance of being confirmed, and that seems to me to be a clearly flawed kind of situation," said Simon.[36]

Committee Republicans defended Thomas's candor and willingness to answer many questions, and argued that any shortcomings in the process should be blamed on the Democrats. "They're the ones that have caused it," charged Hatch. "Clarence Thomas gave a lot of answers. He just didn't give answers to everything they wanted, so they're griping and complaining." Presciently, Simpson advised a panel of Thomas's opponents how to deal with nominees like Thomas: "Stop smearing them, stop ridiculing them, stop tearing their past lives to shreds . . . and they'll start talking. Until then, they won't and who would?"[37]

Despite the partisan debate, Thomas had managed to keep hidden what many senators wanted to understand most about a Supreme Court nominee: his vision of the Constitution. With few clues to Thomas's constitutional philosophy, most senators were left without any firm reason to oppose his appointment. Many recognized that his personal story of success over obstacles had struck a chord with Americans. As a result, when the hearings ended on Friday, September 20, several senators stated that—although the vote might be close—it was almost certain that Thomas would be approved by the committee and then win confirmation by a wide margin in the full

Senate, probably in time for the beginning of the Court's next term on October 7.

THE SEXUAL HARASSMENT ALLEGATIONS

Meanwhile, behind the scene of the hearings, a time bomb was ticking on the nomination, threatening to shatter the public image of Thomas's character. As Thomas was testifying before the Judiciary Committee on national television, Anita Hill, a black, tenured law professor at the University of Oklahoma, was privately telling committee staffers that Thomas had sexually harassed her while they worked together at the Department of Education and the EEOC from 1981–83. Hill charged that, during this period, Thomas frequently asked her out and when she refused, spoke to her in vivid detail about sexual acts he had seen in pornographic films. After a brief discussion of work, Thomas would typically "turn the conversation to discussion about his sexual interests," often describing films he had seen depicting group sex and women having sex with animals, Hill said. He made suggestions to her about what kind of sex she engaged in, asking her in detail about different forms of sex, and suggesting sexual activities he would like to pursue with her. Although Thomas had not explicitly threatened her job if she refused to have sex with him, Hill said she felt pressured to submit in order to continue getting good assignments.

Hill said Thomas's misconduct began when she worked as his attorney-advisor at the Education Department in 1981, stopped for a while when he started dating someone else, then resumed when she began working as his special assistant at the EEOC. According to Hill, when she resigned from her post at the EEOC to accept a teaching job at Oral Roberts Law School, Thomas asked her to go out to dinner and warned that she could ruin his career if she revealed his behavior. Hill never filed a formal complaint against Thomas—as chairman of the EEOC, the agency charged with handling sexual harassment claims, Thomas was, in effect, the nation's chief enforcement officer on the subject.[38]

The behavior Hill described would have constituted sexual harassment under the guidelines set forth by the EEOC in 1980, which expanded the definition of sexual harassment and declared it illegal sex discrimination under the federal job discrimination law administered by the EEOC. The EEOC's 1980 definition of sexual harassment—issued while the agency was still under the chairmanship of Eleanor Holmes Norton—included, for the first time, unwelcome sexual advances resulting in a hostile working environment. While the EEOC's standards were supported by many lower courts in the 1980s, the "hostile environment" part remained controversial. "Verbal sexual abuse" was not legally recognized as a form of sexual harassment in a federal court until mid-1983 (when Hill had decided to leave the EEOC), and the EEOC's guidelines were not confirmed by the Supreme Court until 1986.[39] Nevertheless, in 1980, unwelcome sexual advances of any kind were generally considered unacceptable in the American workplace.

HOW THE CHARGES WERE HANDLED

In 1991, the Senate Judiciary Committee had no formal, written rules which specifically addressed the handling of sexual harassment allegations or other confidential information or investigative materials. However, the respect for confidential arrangements had traditionally been investigative materials. However, the respect for confidential arrangements had traditionally been considered crucial, and since the 1970s, the committee often relied on the Federal Bureau of Investigation to conduct interviews and write background reports.[40] Guidelines and practices regarding the treatment of FBI materials—including document control systems and a limited number of staff with FBI clearance—were reportedly well-established and adhered to.[41] In addi-

tion, Thomas was not the first nominee before the Judiciary Committee who had faced a sexual harassment charge. According to Chief Counsel Ron Klain, "the Judiciary Committee deals with this stuff all the time"—although mainly with district court nominees. Typically such charges emerge as committee staffers conduct their routine investigations before a nominee's hearings begin. If a charge is determined to have merit, Klain says, "usually Bien and [Ranking Minority Member Strom] Thurmond [(R-S.C.)] sit down and make a decision that . . . the person's got a problem. That person is confidentially approached, and [usually] that person just withdraws and the public never knows about it—there's no big deal." Klain adds that the "quiet, outside-the-media-spotlight ways" used to deal with such charges are "not available in the context of the Supreme Court nomination due to its highly public nature."

The sexual harassment allegations against Thomas were first uncovered during the summer of 1991 by the Alliance for Justice, a Washington-based public interest group opposed to Thomas. The Alliance received the tip at a dinner party from a Washington lawyer who attended Yale Law School with Hill.[42] In July and August, the Alliance passed on the information—along with other allegations of Thomas's personal misconduct—to several members of Senator Metzenbaum's staff.

During a mid-August meeting of Metzenbaum staffers working on the Thomas nomination, it was decided that Gail Laster, counsel to the Labor Subcommittee chaired by Metzenbaum, should contact Hill. Laster was first able to reach Hill by telephone on Thursday, September 5. During their conversation, Laster referred generally to an allegation that Thomas had harassed female employees. Hill's response was that Laster should investigate the charge. (Laster never asked Hill whether she had been harassed by Thomas, and Hill did not volunteer the information.) Laster then described this interchange to her immediate supervisor, James Brudney, chief counsel to Senator Metzenbaum's Labor subcommittee, who immediately recognized Hill's name from law school.

Meanwhile, Bonnie Goldstein, Senator Metzenbaum's investigator, related the information given to her by the Alliance to Ricki Seidman—chief investigator for the Senate Labor and Human Resources Committee chaired by Senator Kennedy—during a late August meeting where the two compared notes on the Thomas nomination. After some additional research, Seidman proceeded to call Hill on Friday, September 6. They talked at length about Thomas, but when asked about the call from Seidman on September 9, Hill said she had decided to talk about the issue, but had not yet decided how far she wanted the information to go. Seidman suggested that Hill might be more comfortable discussing the matter with Brudney, with whom she had attended Yale Law School.

On Tuesday, September 10—the first day of the committee's hearings on Thomas— Hill detailed her allegations in a telephone conversation with Brudney. Hill told Brudney she did not wish to testify publicly and expressed reservations about making allegations if no other woman made similar charges. Brudney discussed with Hill the law on sexual harassment, some alternative methods of informing the committee of her charges, and how the committee might proceed once informed. Some possible outcomes were also discussed, including the possibility that the nominee might withdraw.[43] When the call ended, Brudney understood that Hill was undecided about whether she wished to report her allegations to the committee.

Brudney immediately advised Metzenbaum and the senator's senior staff about Hill's charges. Metzenbaum responded that the charges were too serious for a single member or staff to deal with and should be referred to Senator Biden as chairman of the Judiciary Committee. Brudney explained this to Hill; Hill replied that she felt a responsibility to go forward and was willing to proceed with Biden's staff as Metzenbaum requested. On the following day, September 11, Brudney relayed Hill's allegations to Harriet Grant, chief counsel for the Judiciary Committee's nominations unit. After some confusion over who would contact whom, Hill called Grant on Thursday, September 12. Grant took charge of handling all subsequent conversations with Hill for Senator Biden and the "full" committee staff.

During her September 12 conversation with Grant, Hill described Thomas's alleged misconduct in detail. Hill repeated her concern that a single complainant would not be believed and again expressed her desire for confidentiality—according to Grant, Hill did not want the nominee to know her name or that she had stated her concerns to the committee. Grant assured Hill that her charges would be kept confidential, but "little could be done" unless Thomas was informed and given the opportunity to respond. Grant's account of the conversation reflects that Hill thought reporting the allegations to the committee would "remove responsibility" and "take it out of [her] hands." Grant did not push Hill to go further.[44] As the conversation ended, Hill mentioned an unnamed friend who could corroborate her charges but was also uncomfortable about coming forward. Grant told Hill that "the next logical step in the process would be to have Hill's friend contact the committee if she so chose." (Grant says that, in dealing with Hill, she followed a "rape crisis center counseling mode," such that "you give the victim every opportunity to come forward, but you don't pressure them, and it ultimately has to be within that person's control and that person's decision" to come forward. Grant says she felt "very concerned about her [Hill], first and foremost, because this place is a rough place.")

The full committee staff under Biden had

no other contact with Hill between Thursday, September 12 and Thursday, September 19—a full week. Senator Biden was briefed on either Friday, September 13, or Monday, September 16. All agreed that nothing further could be done to investigate Hill's allegations unless Hill agreed Thomas could be told of the charges.[45] No committee staffer was sent to Oklahoma to question Hill more thoroughly, and Biden decided at this time not to tell other committee members of her allegations. Biden, according to his staff, felt strongly that he was not going to circulate "some anonymous charge."[46] At this point, Biden, Kennedy, and Metzenbaum were the only senators on the Judiciary Committee who knew of Hill's charges.

In the meantime, Brudney, having heard nothing from Grant, called Hill on September 13 and 15. (Brudney later said he "felt responsible for Hill because he had placed her in a difficult situation" and did not want Hill to feel that he or his colleagues "had deserted her."[47]) Through his conversations with Hill and another Metzenbaum staffer who had spoken with Grant, Brudney gained the impression that Grant had misunderstood the scope of Hill's request for confidentiality and that Hill was upset with the committee's response.[48] (Klain suggests that Hill's reaction may have been in part due to her apparent belief that she had been dealing with the Judiciary Committee all along, when, in fact, she had not connected with a full committee staffer until she spoke with Grant on September 12. Klain claims that no one on the full committee staff under Biden was aware that Hill had been in contact with Seidman, Laster, or any other Senate staff person outside the full committee staff—besides Brudney.)

Whatever Hill may have said to Brudney to convey irritation with the committee's response, Hill did not call Grant immediately, nor did she call her corroborating witness, Susan Hoerchner, until Monday, September 16.[49] Hoerchner, a California worker's

compensation judge who was a Yale classmate of Hill's, telephoned Grant on September 17. Hoerchner told Grant that Hill had complained to her about Thomas's behavior in the spring of 1981 and said that it caused Hill to doubt her own professional abilities, thus appearing to corroborate Hill's charges. Like Hill, Hoerchner expressed a strong desire for confidentiality.

By this time, Kennedy's staff had caught word of Brudney's concerns about a possible misunderstanding between Hill and Grant and proceeded to contact two of Senator Leahy's chief staffers, Ellen Lovell and Ann Harkins. With Leahy's permission, Lovell and Harkins met with Grant and other senior members of Biden's staff on Tuesday, September 17. After discussing Brudney's concerns, Lovell and Harkins suggested that Grant place another call to Hill to determine whether she in fact meant to "cut off all committee activity through her request for total anonymity." Harkins calculated that at least ten people already knew of Hill's allegations and warned that "disclosure could embarrass the committee if nothing more was done." However, Ted Kaufman, Biden's chief of staff, was "adamant" in his belief that it would be wrong to push Hill in any way, given her request for confidentiality. Later that evening, Senator Leahy briefly discussed with Biden the possibility of additional investigative efforts. Biden, too, "believed nothing more should be done."[50]

In any event, Hill called Grant on Thursday, September 19—three days after Thomas had finished testifying and other witnesses were before the committee. Hill told Grant she was afraid that Grant had misunderstood her concerns; Hill, in fact, had wanted all members of the committee to know about her complaint and was willing to use her name if necessary. Hill later said she had become "frustrated" in her efforts to "get the information in the right hands" and demanded of Grant: "What do I have to do in order to get this information in front of all the committee?''[51] Grant says she ''repeated: 'before committee members could be apprised of [her] concerns, the nominee must be afforded an opportunity to respond; that is both committee policy and practice.''' According to Grant's notes of the conversation, Hill said she needed to know her options, wanted to make choices, and did not want to abandon the matter. At this point, Grant felt that clear instructions from her superiors were in order; Grant deferred any further response until she spoke with Jeff Peck, the Judiciary Committee's staff director.[52]

On Friday morning, September 20—the final day of Thomas's hearing—Grant called Hill back and explained that, in order to proceed, Hill's allegations would be given to the Federal Bureau of Investigation, and the bureau would interview Hill, Thomas, and anyone else with relevant information. (Judiciary staffers agree that the committee's limited investigative capacity required the use of the FBI to conduct the field interviews. The FBI, for example, had a field office in Norman, Oklahoma—the Senate Judiciary Committee did not. In this case, Klain explains, there was also hope that Thomas's responses to an FBI investigator's questions would be ''more dispassionate, more honest, more straightforward, and less politically charged than if it was Harriet Grant showing up.'' Klain believed that an FBI investigation would, in the end, be perceived as more credible by Thomas's supporters than would one conducted by the committee itself.[53]) Hill responded that she was unsure of the ''utility'' of an FBI investigation and wanted to discuss the idea with someone she had been using for advice. (Since September 18, Hill had been talking with Georgetown University Law Professor Susan Ross, whom Brudney had proposed as a possible advisor familiar with the law on sex discrimination.) Hill then spoke with Ross and Brudney about her concern that her charges against Thomas would be distorted by FBI inter-

viewers. It was suggested that Hill prepare a written statement in her own words. With Hill's authorization, Ross sought counsel from Judith Lichtman, president of the Women's Legal Defense Fund, who gave similar advice.[54]

On Saturday, September 21, Grant called Hill for a response to the FBI question. According to Grant, Hill told her that ''she did not want to go through with the FBI investigation, because she was not convinced that the information would be communicated to the committee members in a way with which she was comfortable.'' Hill said she did not know if the FBI was experienced in handling matters of this sort, and told Grant she would call back with another option. Hill then spoke with Brudney twice more over the weekend. According to Brudney, Hill had not decided to go forward with an FBI interview as late as Sunday evening but was drafting a statement as her counsel had advised.[55]

Early Monday morning, September 23, Hill called Grant and said that she had prepared a statement outlining her allegations against Thomas and wanted it to be made available to the members of the Judiciary Committee. Then, Hill told Grant, she would submit to an interview with the FBI ''if necessary.''[56] Hill's written statement reaffirmed her desire for confidentiality: ''I make this statement for the benefit of the Committee only,'' Hill wrote. In her statement, Hill added: ''While the procedure available for and the timing of getting this information to the Committee are less than perfect, the sensitivity of the information compelled me to proceed cautiously. I trust that each Members [sic] of the Committee will give due consideration to the statement made.''

At Grant's request, Hill telefaxed her personal statement to Grant that afternoon. A copy of the four-page statement was then delivered to the office of Ranking Minority Member Strom Thurmond, and an FBI investigation was initiated immediately. That evening, the FBI interviewed Hill in Oklahoma and informed the White House of her charges.[57] Thomas was interviewed by the FBI two days later on Wednesday, September 25; he denied Hill's allegations.[58] On the afternoon of the 25th, the FBI completed its report and immediately delivered copies to the Senate and the White House. The FBI report contained background information from interviews and record checks, a synopsis of the investigation, and a supplemental report on sexual harassment allegations.[59] (According to Klain, the FBI had interviewed "approximately ten people in about seven different cities in around forty-eight hours.") Those who saw the report said "it read like a bad wire [service] story, a collection of he-said, she-said quotes that reached no conclusion."[60]

Also on September 25, Hill called Grant to inform her that she would be faxing a corrected copy of her personal statement. (The statement she sent on the 23rd contained typographical errors.) Unbeknownst to the full committee staff under Biden, Hill had also faxed an exact copy of her statement to Brudney earlier that morning. Brudney wanted a written description of Hill's allegations for a memo he was preparing on sexual harassment for possible use by Senator Metzenbaum, and assured Hill that he would hold her statement in confidence. (At the time, Hill believed that her statement would be circulated to all members of the committee as soon as the FBI report was completed.) In a conversation with Grant later that day, Hill asked Grant for an explicit assurance that her statement would be circulated to all members of the Judiciary Committee, as she had previously requested. Grant—unsure about how Biden planned to proceed—assured Hill that the information would be made available to all members, but said she could not guarantee that hard copies of the statement itself would be physically distributed. Hill was upset.[61] (Grant says that the decision to distribute copies of Hill's statement—given the in-

creased risk of its public disclosure—was "beyond the staff level." It remained unclear why the statement was not immediately circulated to all committee members as Hill desired.)

That same day, Chairman Biden—under White House pressure to confirm Thomas before the Supreme Court started its term on October 7—proceeded to schedule the committee vote on the nomination for Friday, September 27 (two days later), even though he knew his colleagues would not be briefed on Hill's charges until just before the vote. Klain says Biden acted out of "the desire to protect Hill's confidentiality"; the press had begun to get suspicious. Committee rules dicate that nominees be voted on seven days after their hearings end, and Biden had already delayed the committee vote for ten days while the investigation was underway. Klain explains that "even with that [three-day] delay, I was getting press calls every day, asking: 'Why are you putting this thing off? What's going on?'" Klain recalls one conversation he had with Ruth Marcus, a reporter covering the Thomas nomination for the *Washington Post*: According to Klain, Marcus telephoned him on September 25 and said, "You guys have delayed longer than ever before in announcing a vote. There's no explanation for this, other than there being additional personal charges about Judge Thomas. What are they?" Klain says he felt forced to "affirmatively lie" to Marcus in order to protect Hill's confidentiality; Klain told Marcus, "Look, Ruth, there's nothing there. What's on the record is there, period."

Immediately after receiving the completed FBI report on September 25, Biden began notifying all Democratic members of the Senate Judiciary Committee on Hill's allegations and Thomas's denial. He also briefed Senate Majority Leader George Mitchell (D-Maine) and Minority Leader Bob Dole (R-Kans.), but the allegations were not shared with the full Senate. A committee aide later told the *New York Times* that "some committee members were briefed [orally] on Wednesday evening and the rest on Thursday [the 26th]," one day before the scheduled committee vote. The aide said that "at these briefings by Biden's staff, the senators were told they could see Ms. Hill's affidavit and the FBI report if they chose, and some took advantage. And some did not."[62] In fact, only senators Simon, DeConcini, and Specter asked for and reviewed the FBI report prior to Friday's scheduled vote.[63] "After receiving a briefing, no committee member requested further investigation or delay of the committee's vote," Biden added later.[64] But on September 26, Senator Heflin—to the surprise of many—announced his opposition to Thomas,[65] virtually assuring a deadlocked committee vote and renewed controversy over the nomination.

Biden left it up to the committee's ranking minority member, as was customary, to advise all Republican committee members about the sexual harassment allegations and the FBI report. Senator Thurmond did not do so.[66] Senator Specter first heard about Hill's charges on Thursday night from DeConcini; he called Senator Danforth and then met with Thomas for thirty minutes the morning of the vote. Senators Hatch and Simpson heard of the allegations and discussed them with Thurmond and Biden before the vote. It was later reported that GOP staffers informed Senator Brown of the FBI report, but said it contained "nothing of significance," while Grassley said he learned of the news "while we were sitting there the day of the final vote"—in passing, a colleague asked, "Did you hear the latest?" Grassley had not.[67]

Meanwhile, on Thursday morning, September 26, Hill called Brudney. She was upset that her statement had not been circulated to all committee members.[68] Hill then enlisted the help of several friends. One of Hill's friends, Sonia Jarvis, called Simon's office and arranged for the senator to speak with Hill that day. During their conversation, Hill expressed concern that her statement would not be considered by the committee before the vote, and asked Simon—who had not yet seen Hill's statement but was generally aware of her allegations—to give her statement out to all senators, with the understanding that the statement and her name be kept confidential. According to Simon, he told Hill "that would be impossible. If I sent it to one hundred senators, it would be in the newspapers and on television the next morning." Simon sensed that Hill was troubled, but told Hill that it was her choice; she "could either make it public and undergo massive media attention, or . . . withhold her name and the document but be troubled by her inaction."[69] Simon says he did not want to advise Hill either way; in the end, Hill decided against the full Senate distribution. Simon was the only senator to speak with Hill prior to the committee vote.

Simon later said he found Hill to be a credible witness that day on the phone. By contrast, DeConcini, who only saw Hill's statements and the FBI report, said he did not find Hill to be very credible: "If you're sexually harassed, you ought to get mad about it, and you ought to do something about it, and you ought to complain instead of hanging around a long time and then all of a sudden calling up anonymously and say, 'Oh, I want to complain.' I mean, where is the gumption?"[70]

Kim Taylor—another friend of Hill's—tried a different route to get to the committee. That day, Taylor contacted Professor Charles Ogletree at Harvard Law School and informed him in very general terms of the sexual harassment allegations, repeating Hill's concern that her statement had not been circulated within the committee. (Hill's name was not mentioned.) Ogletree, in turn, called his Harvard colleague, Professor Lawrence Tribe, and passed on the information. Tribe was able to reach Klain—a former student of Tribe's—at the Judiciary Committee on September 27, the morning of the vote. Tribe told Klain that "a group of women professors on the West Coast" were concerned that an unidentified woman's allegation of sexual harassment had not been circulated to the committee. Klain, who declined to discuss the subject with Tribe, assured him that any allegations had been thoroughly investigated.[71]

Klain immediately reported Tribe's call to Biden early that morning and recommended distribution of Hill's statement to all Democratic members of the Judiciary Committee. Less than an hour before the scheduled 10:00 A.M. vote, Judiciary staff delivered the document to each Democratic senator on the committee in individual envelopes marked "Personal and Confidential, For Senator's Eyes Only." All Democratic members read the statement. The committee hearing concluded at 12:46 P.M., and by 3:15 P.M., every copy of the statement was retrieved in its original envelope by Senator Biden's office and destroyed. A committee aide later said that, in distributing Hill's statement before the vote, Biden acted out of concern about "what it could look like if it would become public."[72] It was not clear why Hill's statement had not been distributed to the committee's Republican members as well.

DEADLOCK

On September 27, the Senate Judiciary Committee failed, by a vote of 7–7, to recommend Thomas's nomination to the full Senate. The vote fell along party lines, except for DeConcini, who voted with Republicans for Thomas. All seven Democrats voting against Thomas cited reasons unrelated to the harassment charges for their "no" votes—primarily his reluctance to give direct answers to questions. No member pushed for postponement of the Committee vote in order to hold a closed-door session with Hill.

DeConcini, the only committee Democrat to support Thomas, referred to the nominee's "remarkable life story" in his speech, stating that he believed Thomas was capable of growing into a fine jurist. In announcing their votes for Thomas, committee Republicans also highlighted his struggle and his career. Specter emphasized the importance of having a black justice on the Court. "Why not rely on his character?" Specter asked, adding, "I pay more attention to his roots than to his writings." However, Senator Brown conceded that Thomas had not been forthcoming on his judicial philosophy. "I just don't have a good feeling of where he's going to come out on all the issues," Brown said, explaining that his support for Thomas was "basically a judgment to his personal character and his qualifications."[73]

In opposing Thomas, Biden cast the last vote needed for the Committee deadlock but said he did so "with a truly heavy heart." "It's a close call for me," Biden said. "I'm not proselytizing." Biden said he found Thomas "to be a man of honor," and voiced his conviction that "there are certain things that are not at issue at all, and that is his character. . . . This is about what he believes, not about who he is. . . . For this senator, there is no question with respect to the nominee's character, competence, credentials or credibility." Perhaps recognizing that the committee deadlock might encourage Thomas's opponents to publicize Hill's charges, Biden then gave what appeared to be a warning to his colleagues: he urged "everyone else to refrain from personalizing this battle, to the extent that it is one on the floor of the Senate. And I don't expect that to happen on the floor of the Senate. I don't expect it to happen off the floor, but I hope it won't happen on the floor in the Senate." Biden apparently considered the matter of the sexual harassment charges closed.

After the deadlock, the panel voted 13–1 to send Thomas's name to the full Senate without recommendation. The lone dissenter was Simon, the only senator who had personally spoken with Hill before the vote. Simon said the committee should not send nominations to the Senate without guidance; the panel had never before done so.[74]

THE CAMPAIGN RE-OPENS

The 7-7 vote against Thomas was far more negative than had been anticipated at the start of the hearings. Not since the 1950s had a Supreme Court nominee been approved by the full Senate without an endorsement from the Judiciary Committee.[75] The surprising split vote sent White House officials scrambling to contain fallout while opponents, seeking to build on the momentum, stepped up lobbying efforts against Thomas. "Today's vote was a dramatic moment," said Ralph Neas, executive director of the Leadership Conference on Civil Rights. "I believe it will have a catalytic effect on the Senate process."[76] Neas, who opposed Thomas, added that "while it will be, of course, difficult to defeat the nomination, the odds have been dramatically reduced."[77]

Senators were also moved by the committee deadlock. "Certainly, if it was much closer to unanimous, with more of the moderate liberals voting with him then [it] would feel much easier to say 'OK, I'll support him,'" said James Jeffords (R-Vt.).[78] Although Terry Sanford (D-N.C.) remained undecided on Thomas, he found Heflin's vote to be significant: "After my initial interview with Thomas, I had concluded that he was considerably unprepared academically and intellectually for the Supreme Court, but that he might just mature into an adequate Constitutional scholar. I thought it was a risk that might be worth taking. Since Senator Heflin's appraisal, there's a new impetus to look at it again." Reminding his colleagues that the confirmation battle was not yet over, Sanford forewarned: "You're always in trouble until the last vote is counted."[79]

Meanwhile, knowledge of Hill's "confidential" allegations (and to some extent the FBI investigation) was beginning to spread among the interested Washington commu-

nity. The sexual harassment allegations were mentioned during at least two dinner parties on Saturday evening, September 28, and made their way back to Judiciary staffers.[80] In addition, two news reporters, Timothy Phelps of *Newsday* and Nina Totenberg of National Public Radio, were going after the story. Phelps had picked up on Senator Biden's speech warning Thomas's opponents to "stay away from personal attacks," and in an article published on September 28, Phelps described Biden's admonition as an apparent reference to what sources said was a reopening of the FBI background investigation on Thomas to check opponents' allegations of personal misconduct."[81]

According to Klain, it was difficult for the Judiciary Committee to gauge how many people actually knew about Hill's charges. "Because it was confidential," Klain explains, "no one was discussing how unconfidential it might have become." (Klain says "probably a hundred is not a bad guess—maybe even more than that.") Nevertheless, Klain, Grant, and others on the Judiciary Committee staff admit they had begun to get a "sense that this was starting to grow exponentially," but "the rush of events and the pressures of time simply overwhelmed [their] ability to stop and take stock of that." Klain now says that "the pressure to maintain Hill's confidentiality was driving a lot of what was, in retrospect, bad decision-making." To Klain: "Probably the better decision would have been to call Hill and tell her, 'Look, I'm sorry, I know you want this to be confidential, but it's just not feasible in this environment. This is just too political, too charged, too visible, and someone's going to leak this anyway. You have to go public on your own, because . . . we're not going to be people who sit on a powder keg waiting for it to explode.'"

FULL SENATE DEBATE

On October 3—with Hill's charges still considered confidential by the Judiciary Committee—the debate on Thomas's confirmation moved to the Senate floor. The first two days of full Senate debate revealed that while Democrats were deeply divided over the nomination, they were united in attacking President Bush for pursuing what they described as racial, political and ideological agenda for the Supreme Court. The harshest criticism came from Senator Bradley (D-NJ). Bradley compared the president's nomination of Thomas to the use of Willie Horton—a black convicted murderer who raped a white woman while on a Massachusetts prison furlough—as a campaign issue against Massachusetts governor Michael Dukakis in the 1988 presidential race. Bush's "tactical use of Clarence Thomas, as with Willie Horton, depends for its effectiveness on the limited ability of all races to see beyond color and, as such, is a stunning example of political opportunism," blasted Bradley, who planned to vote against Thomas. Bradley contended that Thomas's nomination conveyed "many subtle and not so subtle messages," including the suggestion that blacks do not need government intervention, that "white America has no responsibility for the failure of blacks," that "tokenism is the only acceptable form of affirmative action" and that "an administration [which] nominates a black for the U.S. Supreme Court has answered the critics of its racial policies." Bradley was also critical of Thomas's "chameleon-like behavior before the committee," which Bradley said included stressing his personal background "as if he were a modern candidate repeating a sound bite" while disavowing positions he had taken "over a decade of right-wing political activism."

Another Democrat, Joseph Lieberman (Conn.), claimed that the Reagan and Bush administrations had treated "Supreme Court nominees as just one more campaign promise" and had "badly promised voters one kind of Court or another." Yet Lieberman conceded that after Bork's rejection, the administration could not be blamed for

choosing nominees with "thin" written records or coaching those with fuller records to be cautious on some issues. In announcing his support for Thomas, Lieberman said that while he was disappointed with Thomas's testimony, he concluded that his performance was more a reflection of the "shortcomings of the process, of which he was a victim, than an indictment of Judge Thomas's abilities or character."

The full Senate vote on Thomas's confirmation was scheduled for Tuesday, October 8. Thomas's confirmation hinged on fifty-one votes—a bare majority of the one hundred senators. By Friday, October 4, thirteen of the fifty-seven Democrats in the Senate had announced their support for Thomas, and none of the forty-three Republicans had yet voiced opposition; according to Danforth, forty-one Republicans were committed to his confirmation. Even senators like Metzenbaum recognized there was only a "very slim chance" that Thomas would be defeated. However, the vote was likely to be a close one: Thomas's opponents claimed they could muster more than forty votes against him. If so, Thomas would take his seat on the court with the largest number of negative votes ever recorded.[82]

LAST-MINUTE STRATEGIES

As the Senate prepared for a weekend recess on Friday, October 4, Thomas's opponents had only four more days to change the minds of at least six senators. One possible avenue of attack was a filibuster, which could have delayed the nomination until sixty senators voted to shut it down.[83] While Republicans said they feared such a maneuver, Democrats seemed loath to start one.[84] Even Leahy—one of Thomas's strongest critics—declared himself "totally opposed to a filibuster," and Simon stated, "I don't exclude that possibility, but I don't have any such plans."[85] Hatch pointed out that a filibuster had often been used in the past by those opposed to civil rights, and to start one on Thomas would be "just the greatest irony of all. . . . Can you imagine liberals using a filibuster on the second black nominated to the Supreme Court?''[86]

Those who knew about Anita Hill had another option: publicize her sexual harassment charges. Whether the allegations could be proved or not, Thomas's confirmation was likely to be put in grave jeopardy. Charges of sexual harassment involve a violation of the law, and under Thomas's own guidelines for evaluating sexual harassment charges filed at the EEOC, it was plausible to believe that the benefit of the doubt would have been given to Hill.

However, a public disclosure of Hill's charges or her personal statement would have breached her stated desire for confidentiality. It would have violated Senate rules as well: a senator or staff member found to have disclosed such confidential information was subject to expulsion or dismissal.[87] What is more, disclosure of a confidential FBI report would have constituted a federal crime. Yet Senate leak probes rarely led to conclusive outcomes, and for the most part, anonymous leakers escaped detection: only two senators had ever been disciplined by the Senate for breaking secrecy rules, and both cases were a century old.[88] Those who contemplated whether or not to publicize Hill's allegations had little more than a weekend left to decide what to do. . . .

THE LEAK

Sometime between October 1–5, just days before the scheduled Senate vote on the nomination of Clarence Thomas to the Supreme Court, the contents of Anita Hill's confidential statement to the Senate Judiciary Committee were leaked to two reporters[89]: Timothy Phelps of *Newsday* and Nina Totenberg of National Public Radio. Hill's sexual harassment allegations were then reported in *Newsday* on the evening of October 5 and broadcast on NPR the following morning. The story instantly became the lead item on most network news programs.

By Monday, it made front-page headlines of newspapers across the country. Virtually overnight, the Senate Judiciary Committee found itself at the core of a nasty and embarrassing controversy that riveted the nation.

Hill confirmed reports that she told the FBI that Thomas had sexually harassed her in the early 1980s, but declined to discuss the details with Phelps on Saturday since he seemed not to have hard copy of her statement to the committee. However, when Totenberg began reading verbatim from the statement, Hill granted the reporter an interview. (Hill said she wanted to be able to respond to the information before it was made public.) As she detailed her allegations for Totenberg, Hill explained that, initially, she had decided against telling her story, but when Senate staffers approached her in early September, she felt an obligation to provide information about the nominee. ''Here is a person who is in charge of protecting rights of women and other groups in the workplace and he is using his position of power for personal gain for one thing,'' Hill said of Thomas, ''and he did it in a very ugly and intimidating way.''

As word of the allegations spread over the weekend, the White House and Thomas's supporters mounted a swift counterattack. White House Deputy Press Secretary Judy Smith immediately responded that a ''full, thorough and expeditious'' FBI investigation of Hill's charge had been ordered on September 25, and after reviewing the FBI's report, the White House had ''determined that the allegation was unfounded.'' President Bush stressed that he did not believe Hill's charge, while White House spokesman Marlin Fitzwater called her accusation ''absolutely'' untrue, a ''smear'' and reminded reporters that ''this charge was considered by the [Judiciary] committee and dismissed on the basis of the reports of information they had, and it was by us, as well.'' Hatch called the disclosure of Hill's allegations a ''last ditch attempt to smear the judge'' and said one of his colleagues had violated Senate rules by leaking her confidential statement to the media.

Meanwhile, Simon—the only senator to have spoken with Hill prior to the Judiciary Committee's vote on Thomas—called Saturday for the postponement of the full Senate vote scheduled for Tuesday, October 8. "I think it is a serious enough charge that the committee ought to look at it and if necessary the vote ought to be postponed," Simon told reporters, adding that published accounts of Hill's allegations were "basically correct" and that the White House statement "simply isn't supported in fact." On Sunday, Metzenbaum said the allegations were "very disturbing" and suggested the full Senate review them before voting. Leahy agreed: "I can't imagine a senator feeling that he or she can vote on this without reading the [FBI] report."[90]

In a statement released Monday, October 7, Biden rejected the idea that the full Senate vote should now be delayed. "The Senate and [Judiciary] committee leadership and all Democratic members of the committee were briefed regarding Professor Hill's allegations several days before the Senate set a vote on the Thomas nomination. They all had the right to object to a [full Senate] vote on Tuesday at 6 P.M., and none did. At the same time, none believed that the information which we then possessed necessitated a delay in voting. I see no reason why the addition of public disclosure of the allegations—but no new information about the charges themselves—should change the decision." Senate Majority Leader George Mitchell concurred: the members who demanded a delay "knew what was in the FBI report before they scheduled the [full Senate] vote and they went ahead. So why change now? It would be pure politics."

HILL'S PRESS CONFERENCE

Composed and articulate, Hill introduced herself to the public on Monday, October 7, in a nationally televised news conference from Oklahoma. Assailing the Judiciary Committee for seeming to ignore her repeated allegations against the nominee, Hill stated that she had raised her complaint reluctantly but with utmost seriousness. "I made it perfectly clear to the Senate Judiciary Committee through Chairman Biden that I wanted this information to all the members of the committee. And I was willing to use my name in that. But that I was not willing to have this made public." Hill described how she struggled for nearly two weeks in September to put before the committee a confidential account of her harassment: "The control of the timing and release of this information has never been with me," said Hill. "It was not until the 20th of September that an FBI investigation was suggested to me. It was at that time I was told that this is the way to get the information before the committee . . . so to say that I perhaps delayed it is not true." Hill said she "was very surprised" that the committee had not called her to testify: "I felt that they had an obligation to hear what I was saying once I had come forward."

Hill, who had strongly supported Judge Bork's nomination to the Supreme Court in 1987, denied that she was a "political opportunist," as the White House and some committee members sought to portray her.[91] Hill asked that others "look at the fact that this has taken a great toll on me personally and professionally. . . . There is no way that I would do something like this for political purposes." Hill added: "It has never been an issue that I tried to publicize, [nor] something I wanted to grandstand about. . . . I resent the idea that people would blame the messenger for the message rather than looking at the content of the message itself."

Finally, Hill demanded an "official resolution" of the situation:

My integrity has been called into question by people who have never spoken to me, [who] have not considered the facts carefully as far as I know, and I want an official resolution of this because at this point the issue is being deflected. People are talking about this as a political ploy. And all that is, is an attempt not to deal with the issue itself. It is an unpleasant issue. It's an ugly issue, and people don't want to deal with it generally, and in particular in this case. . . . If the members of the Senate carefully consider this and investigate it and make a determination, then I have done what I'm obligated to do. . . . But until that happens, I think that none of us [has] done our jobs.

At the end of her one-hour press conference, Hill expressed her willingness to talk with senators and cooperate with any further investigation.

COMMITTEE ON THE DEFENSIVE

"The Judiciary Committee didn't screw up on anything," Biden snapped at reporters questioning the handling of Hill's charges.[92] Shortly after Hill's press conference, Biden released a chronology of his full committee staff's contacts with Hill in September. His statement emphasized two points. First, the Judiciary Committee's "handling of the investigation was guided by Hill's repeated requests for confidentiality," which "initially precluded the committee from conducting a complete investigation until she chose to have her name released to the FBI for further and full investigation, which (as is customary) includes the nominee's response." Second, "Hill's wishes with respect to the disposition of this matter were honored. The Republican leadership and all *Democratic* members of the committee were fully briefed of her allegations and all were shown a copy of her statement prior to the committee's vote on the Thomas nomination."[93]

Meanwhile, other members of the Judiciary panel fiercely defended Thomas—and their own actions. Before Hill finished her statement to the press, DeConcini called his own news conference to declare that he believed the nominee's denials. Simpson said questions about the Senate's "sensitivity" were "a crude and absurd observation. . . . The committee took the most serious

and effective course it could have taken under the circumstances: it turned the allegations over to the FBI."[94] Hatch took the Senate floor that night to say that, impressive as she may have been, "the facts do not line up on Ms. Hill's side." (When the *New York Times* asked Hatch why he had not read the FBI report before voting on Thomas's nomination, Hatch replied: "Well, I should have. There's no question about it," and added, "I knew what was in it.") Thurmond went further, claiming that "after a complete investigation by the FBI, these allegations have been found to be totally lacking in credibility and are without merit." And Specter—who had questioned Thomas about Hill's charges before the committee vote—told reporters that, given "the lateness of the allegation, the absence of any touching or intimidation, and the fact that she moved with him from one agency to another, . . . I felt I had done my duty and was satisfied with [Thomas's] responses." (When asked later about his comment, Specter, a former prosecutor, said he did not understand that touching was not required in a sexual harassment suit; that verbal harassment was also against the law.[95]) Specter added that he "looked [Thomas] straight in the eye" and asked him bluntly if "he talked about movies with animals and women having sexual relations." Thomas "was aghast," Specter said. "He denied ever having asked her out or talked to her about anything like that. . . . I figured why mince words?"

"THEY JUST DON'T GET IT"

"What disturbs me as much as the allegations themselves is that the United States Senate appears not to take the charge of sexual harassment seriously," declared Senator Barbara Mikulski, a Democrat from Maryland and one of two women in the Senate. Many people in and out of Congress were critical that Biden did not fully discuss Hill's charges with all panel members. They were angry that the committee neither questioned Thomas personally nor brought Hill to Washington to hear her side of the story, yet some Judiciary Committee members seemed automatically to believe Thomas over Hill. Many felt the public reaction of some committee members revealed not only that men did not give the matter much weight but that they did not understand the law on sexual harassment. Critics pointed out that with just two women members—one from each party—and no minority members, the Senate operated like an exclusive club for white men only.[96] Over and over, the question was repeated: were the fourteen members of the Judiciary Committee, all white men over fifty, capable of sensitively evaluating sexual harassment allegations?

Thousands of phone calls from constituents demanding that senators get to the bottom of Hill's charges, intense lobbying by women's groups, and exhaustive newspaper and television coverage underscored the extent of many women's anger. "They just don't get it" became the phrase of the week. "They are men," said Representative Nancy Pelosi, a California Democrat. "They can't possibly know what it's like to receive verbal harassment, harassment that is fleeting to the man, and lasting and demeaning to the woman." Representative Patricia Schroeder (D-Colo.) agreed: "They tried simply to dispense with her [Hill] in short order," adding that "it's a male bonding thing. . . . They all think of themselves as potential victims, thinking, 'We need to stick together or all these women will come out and make allegations setting us up.' "

Many Republican women joined female Democrats in lashing out at the Judiciary Committee's handling of the issue. "It speaks of the lack of integrity and the hypocrisy that has come to control the Senate," declared Representative Nancy Johnson (R-Conn.). "It's an outrage that people's character has been sullied because the Senate did not deal properly with the information." Johnson was joined by Senator Nancy Kas-

sebaum (R-Kans.), who said she found Hill very "credible" in her news conference. "I think it was most unfortunate that the Judiciary Committee didn't assume greater responsibility when they had seen [Hill's] affidavit in the FBI report" and "more thoroughly examined these charges," Kassebaum said. "Would it not have been wise to call Anita Hill to meet with members of the committee? As a group, they could have pointed out that if she continued to remain anonymous, her testimony would be invalid."

On October 8, seven female Democratic members of the House marched over to the Senate, with plans to crash a Democratic senators' policy meeting. Joining the march was Eleanor Holmes Norton, the District of Columbia's nonvoting delegate to Congress. "We had just watched in bewilderment at the apologias on the Senate floor, offered without any sense that the matter could be put to rest by resolving it rather than avoiding it," Norton said. "A lot of people are angry with us" for forcing the issue, added Schroeder, who accompanied Norton and the five other representatives, "but this set off a grassroots firestorm. Maybe the Senate needs to learn what the Supreme Court laws on sexual harassment are." Although the women were barred from the meeting,[97] the image of the seven female House members marching up the Senate stairs came to symbolize many women's determination to end their exclusion from what was seen as the ultimate men's club: the U.S. Senate.

THE SENATE DEBATE CONTINUES

On the Senate floor, some erosion of Thomas's support set in almost immediately, and by early morning Tuesday, the pressure to delay the vote was intense. Many Democrats—including eight senators who had previously supported Thomas—called for a postponement of the Senate vote. One by one, senators took to the floor, agreeing that the matter had "touched a nerve'' with women on Capitol Hill, and any ''rush to judgment,'' as several senators put it, would surely be taken by many to mean that the Senate considered Hill's charges trivial. Simon hammered the message home: ''I think there is, in a body that is ninety-eight males to two women, a lack of sensitivity toward women's concerns and black and Hispanic concerns. . . . If there were twenty women who were members of the Senate we could delay the vote right now.'' Other senators complained that the Judiciary Committee had let them down by not informing them of allegations in the first place.

Meanwhile, Republicans focused on the fact that a breaching of Senate rules had occurred. In his floor speech, Senate Minority Leader Bob Dole demanded an inquiry into the disclosure of Hill's confidential allegations. ''I think many of us felt when the vote was postponed until Tuesday there would be a weekend revelation. We're not totally naive in this body,'' said Dole, a Thomas supporter. ''Somebody on the [Judiciary] committee has been driving this to this result.'' Senator Danforth was clearly incensed: ''Someone violated the rules of the Senate [and turned] this whole confirmation process into the worst kind of sleazy political campaign.'' Thomas, Danforth railed, ''is being crucified. This isn't 'advise and consent.' This is slash and burn.'' In declaring his opposition to a delayed vote, Danforth contended that Hill's charges had come to light in the Senate through an infraction of the rules and therefore were not valid. ''Think about voting down the nomination of Clarence Thomas solely on the basis of a violation of Senate rules. Talk about scandal,'' declared Danforth. ''I guess if we want to defeat somebody, we destroy them—no holds barred. What are the rules of the Senate? Rules are made to be broken.''

Kennedy tried to derail all the talk about rules, remarking that ''it is not a question of having the Senate train run on time, but whether we can stop the Senate train from running off the track.'' Kennedy, who had been silent over the weekend,[98] also asked for a delayed vote, suggesting that Hill's claims ''call into question Judge Thomas's views on women and sex discrimination in the workplace.'' Specter surprised many Republicans by joining in the push for a postponement, stating that ''the Senate is on trial at this point.'' In the end, even Biden said he favored a delay ''in light of the fact that Ms. Hill has lifted all conditions of anonymity,'' while Mitchell worked to persuade swing Democrats to reverse their votes as a protest against going ahead without further investigation of Hill's charges.

Simpson tried another approach. Whoever leaked the information on Hill had destroyed her reputation, Simpson charged, since she would come out of the dispute ''sullied'' and discredited. ''I think it's a cruel thing we're witnessing,'' Simpson said. ''It's a harsh thing, a very sad and harsh thing, and Anita Hill will be sucked right into the . . . very things she wanted to avoid most. She will be injured and destroyed and belittled and hounded and harassed, real harassment, different than the sexual kind.'' Simpson than warned his Senate colleagues: ''When you go for the jugular, the beast comes out.''

THE TURNING POINT

Less than two hours before the floor vote, Danforth took the floor to request a forty-eight-hour delay of the vote. Danforth reported that Thomas was requesting time to ''clear his name.'' Danforth quoted Thomas—who had been publicly silent up to this point—as saying: ''They have taken from me what I have worked forty-three years to build: my reputation.'' Danforth then distributed the following five-sentence statement signed by Thomas:

1. As I told the Federal Bureau of Investigation on September 28, 1991, I totally and unequivocally deny Anita Hill's allegations of misconduct of any kind toward her, sexual

or otherwise.[99] These allegations are untrue.
2. At all times during the period she worked with me, our relationship was strictly professional. During that time and subsequently, the relationship has been wholly cordial.
3. I am terribly saddened and deeply offended by these allegations.

Danforth later told reporters, "If he is telling the truth and he loses the nomination because of this, that to me is an earth-shaking development—to have the nomination of Clarence Thomas for associate justice of the United States Supreme Court lost because of the illegal distribution or leaking of the content of an FBI report,[100] [sic] plus charges which are totally refuted by the nominee."

Although Danforth portrayed Thomas as seeking the delay, most agreed that the postponement was forced on Republicans and the White House; according to Dole, the tide seemed to be running so strongly against Thomas that night that the nominee might have been rejected altogether.[101] "There are some who would have rolled the dice at 6 P.M.," said Dole. "It seemed to me a gamble that shouldn't be taken. . . . I couldn't put together fifty votes at 6 o'clock." Dole said he counted only forty-one firm votes for the nominees, with sixteen to eighteen undecided, "depending who you count."[102]

At 8:11 P.M. on Tuesday, October 8, more than two hours after its originally scheduled vote, the Senate agreed by unanimous consent to put off the vote on Thomas's nomination for one week. According to Mitchell, the Senate had done the best it could: "Whatever the circumstances leading up to this allegation, we are now confronted with it. . . . In the circumstances we find ourselves, it was a reasonable, fair, and common sense" decision to make. "The delay approved," Mitchell added, "is important to the integrity of the Senate, the integrity of the confirmation process, the integrity of the Supreme Court, and the integrity of the individuals involved."

A *Washington Post*/ABC News poll taken that evening found that Americans were sharply divided over the Senate's decision to delay the vote. While 50 percent of those polled approved of the Senate's action, 39 percent disapproved and 11 percent were undecided. Yet in a *New York Times*/CBS News poll taken the following day, 67 percent of those polled said if the sexual harassment charges were true, Thomas should not be confirmed.

NEGOTIATING THE GROUND RULES

With the vote now delayed until Tuesday, October 15, senators began negotiating the ground rules for a new set of Senate Judiciary Committee hearings on the Thomas nomination. The hearing process, Chairman Biden cautioned, "is incredibly difficult in cases where women have been victimized. We must be careful that the victim not be victimized by the system." However, Biden said, the hearings would be public: "We are going to ventilate this subject to give Professor Hill the opportunity to make her case in full and we are going to give the nominee the opportunity to make his defense in full." (According to Ron Klain, chief counsel for the Senate Judiciary Committee, there was "little question" that the hearings would be open to the public: "It was simply untenable to have closed hearings . . . there would just be no credibility." Klain adds that "if you had done them closed, the hearings would have been reconstructed in the newspaper. . . . The story would have been inaccurate, and there would have been tremendous pressures on both sides to leak.")

Determining who would testify first was one of the more hotly debated issues. The Judiciary Committee ultimately agreed that, out of courtesy for the nominee, Thomas would be given the opportunity to testify first if he wanted and again at the hearings' conclusion in order to rebut any charges made against him. At a caucus of the committee, Biden also made a controversial ruling that there would be no questioning about the personal lives of either Thomas or Hill during the hearings, including questions relating to whether Thomas had viewed pornography at home[103] and questions about Hill's sex life.

Biden announced that the Judiciary Committee would subpoena witnesses if necessary but that the scope of the inquiry would be limited to allegations of sexual harassment, either by Hill or any others who might step forward. Danforth wanted the hearings limited to Hill's accusation, but Biden insisted that if any other credible allegations of sexual harassment appeared, they should be covered. Danforth complained that, as a result, "this is going to go on all next week." If the investigation was going to be a "fishing expedition" that would "advertise for people to come forward with anything they have to dump on Clarence Thomas," then "that is not what this senator understands." Biden consoled Danforth, "The senator knows what I told him earlier." Biden did not elaborate on his off-the-floor comment to Danforth, but signaled that "anyone who wants to make charges against Thomas would have to be willing to testify in public session. . . . This is not a star chamber." Both parties agreed that there would be no surprise witnesses, but Biden later admitted he "wouldn't be very surprised if someone doesn't come out of the blue and say something."

MORE CHARGES ARISE

In fact, just two days later, the Senate Judiciary Committee disclosed the name of another woman accusing Thomas of improper sexual advances at the EEOC. Angela Wright—assistant metropolitan editor for the *Charlotte Observer* newspaper in North Carolina—was subpoenaed to testify at the new round of public hearings. Wright told the committee that Thomas had persistently tried to date her, commented on the size of her breasts, and once showed up unannounced at her apartment while she worked as chief spokeswoman for the EEOC from 1984–85. The committee also subpoenaed Rose Jourdain, a former speech writer for Thomas at the EEOC, who said Wright confided in her at the time that Thomas's remarks about "her figure, her body, her breasts" had bothered her. Wright insisted she was not "stating a claim of sexual harassment" against Thomas, and that she found his conduct "at the most . . . annoying and obnoxious." "My desire is not to keep Clarence Thomas off the Supreme Court," stated Wright, a registered Republican. However, Wright said, "I know enough about the man to know he's quite capable of doing what she [Hill] said he did. . . . We are talking about a thing, you know, that pretty much pops out of Clarence Thomas's mouth when he feels like saying this. . . . We are talking about a general mode of operating." Wright, who had never met Hill, said she hesitated at first in coming forward with her story: "I saw Anita Hill on television on Monday night, and my conscience started bothering me. . . . The thrust of my concern was not to watch her become victimized, when I knew of similar situations that I had had with Mr. Thomas." Wright said she was still trying to decide whether to contact the Judiciary Committee when she received a call from a Senate investigator on Wednesday, October 9. Wright was then interviewed by several Judiciary staffers in a two-hour telephone conversation on October 10.

Immediately after Wright's name was disclosed, White House officials questioned her honesty. They described her as "the classic disgruntled employee" and promised to produce a witness to refute her charges. On October 10, the White House also issued a statement criticizing the Judiciary Committee for neglecting what is called the "normal practice" of first seeking an FBI investigation.

The committee also received a sworn affidavit from Sukari Hardnett, a special assistant to Thomas at the EEOC from 1985–86. In her affidavit, Hardnett testified that Thomas's treatment of women at work was more than that of "a mentor to protégés."

"If you were young, black, female, reasonably attractive and worked directly for Clarence Thomas," Hardnett wrote, "you knew full well you were being inspected and auditioned as a female. . . . And you knew when you had ceased to be an object of sexual interest because you were barred from entering his office and treated as an outcast, or worse, a leper." Although Hardnett also said she was not charging Thomas with sexual harassment, she stated that she "found his attention unpleasant, [and] sought a transfer. . . ."

THE THOMAS-HILL HEARINGS

The Senate Judiciary Committee hearings reconvened on Friday, October 11, riveting the nation over the long Columbus Day weekend. The first two days of proceedings were carried live on ABC, NBC, and CBS; on public television; and on CNN and other cable networks. (On Sunday, only public television stations ran the hearings.) Friday morning, Thomas testified first, followed by seven hours of afternoon testimony from Hill. After Hill was finished, Thomas again testified before the committee during "prime time" that evening. Thomas testified a third time all day Saturday. On Sunday, witnesses appearing on behalf of Hill and Thomas began their testimony at noon and continued through the wee hours of the morning. Neither Thomas nor Hill appeared before the committee on Monday. The full Senate vote was scheduled for Tuesday, October 15, at 6:00 P.M. (The Judiciary Committee would not vote again.)

In his opening statement, Biden explained the ground rules of the hearings. The primary responsibility of the committee, was, in Biden's view, fairness. "That means making sure we do not victimize any witness who appears here and that we treat every witness with respect. . . . Fairness means understanding what a victim of sexual harassment goes through, why victims often do not report such crimes, why they often believe that they should not or cannot leave

their jobs. . . . Fairness also means that Judge Thomas must be given a full and fair opportunity to confront these charges against him, to respond fully, to tell us his side of the story, and to be given the benefit of the doubt." Biden then informed all witnesses that "they have the right under Senate Rule 26.5 to ask that the committee go into closed sessions if a question requires an answer that is quote 'a clear invasion of their right to privacy,' end quote."

The Judiciary Committee decided that Biden, Leahy, and Heflin would conduct almost all the questioning for the Democrats while the other members would sit and listen. For the Republicans, Hatch would question Thomas and any witness called to support him, while Specter would interrogate Hill and her supporters. A senator from each party would ask questions for thirty minutes, then give way to a senator from the other party. Biden reminded his colleagues that he, as chairman, had "the power to rule out of order questions . . . not relevant to [the] proceedings, namely private conduct; out-of-the-workplace relationships; and intimate lives and practices of Judge Thomas, Professor Hill, and any other witness that comes before us." Biden emphasized that "this is not a hearing about the extent and nature of sexual harassment in America," and decided not to allow testimony from sexual harassment experts who might explain Hill's behavior. In addition, Biden ruled out the use of polygraph tests to resolve contradictions between Hill and Thomas. (When asked, Hill said she was willing to take such a test.) Biden said polygraph tests were "not the appropriate way to get the truth," stating it would be a "sad day for the civil liberties in this country" if they became the basis for important decisions.[104]

CONFLICTING TESTIMONY

In his three appearances before the committee, Thomas categorically denied all of Hill's charges—including her charge that he attempted to date her.[105] Appearing to be near tears at times and almost shaking with rage at others, Thomas claimed that he was a victim of historical racial stereotypes about the alleged sexual prowess of black men. He assailed the Senate confirmation process as "a circus" and a "national disgrace"—from his standpoint as a black American, it was "a high-tech lynching for uppity blacks who deign to think for themselves." According to Thomas, interest groups opposed to his confirmation "concocted"Hill's story in collusion with liberal Senate staffers. Thomas charged that "unless you kowtow to an old order, this is what will happen to you. You will be lynched, destroyed, caricatured by a committee of the U.S. Senate rather than hung from a tree." Thomas indignantly refused to discuss his private life with the committee. "I will not provide the rope for my own lynching," Thomas said, and declared: "I would have preferred an assassin's bullet to this kind of living hell that they have put me and my family through." Thomas added that he would "rather die than withdraw" his nomination.

In her testimony, Hill directly contradicted her former boss with graphic detail. For seven hours on Friday, Hill meticulously recounted her story of how Thomas had humiliated her with his constant talk of women's breasts, the size of his penis, and accounts of movies of group sex and bestiality. She denied that liberal groups and others opposed to Thomas had prompted her appearance and expressed personal anguish in discussing the alleged sexual harassment on national television. "It is only after a great deal of agonizing consideration that I am able to talk of these unpleasant matters to anyone except my closest friends," Hill said. "Telling the world is the most difficult experience of my life."

Sunday afternoon, a panel of four witnesses appeared to corroborate Hill's story. Testifying on behalf of Hill were Judge Hoerchner; Joel Paul, a law professor at American University; John Carr, a partner in a prominent New York law firm; and Ellen Wells, an official of the American Public Welfare Association in Washington, D.C. All four witnesses—who had never met each other before the hearings—described Hill as an honest, reserved woman who confided in them about her situation in the early 1980s, at the time of the alleged harassment.[106]

After Hill's four corroborating witnesses finished, sixteen character witnesses were presented on Thomas's behalf,[107] many of them women who had worked with Thomas at the EEOC or the Department of Education. During Sunday's long hearing, each described Thomas's character as impeccable and swore they could not imagine Thomas ever doing what Hill described.

PARTISAN STRATEGIES

The hearings were rife with partisan bickering and personal attacks. Committee Republicans initially blamed Democrats for publicizing Hill's charge, demanded an FBI investigation into the leak, and tried to turn the debate to whether Thomas was victimized by the Senate confirmation process. Republicans then launched what many reporters called a "scorched-earth" strategy to discredit Hill. They sought to chip away at Hill's credibility, suggesting that she was mentally unstable and merely fantasizing about the sexual harassment as part of a conspiracy to defeat Thomas. Simpson claimed that letters, faxes, and statements were pouring into his office "over the transom," warning that he "watch out for this woman." Simpson complained that "nobody's got the guts to say that, because it gets all tangled up in this sexual harassment crap."[108] (Simpson went on to say that he takes the issue of sexual harassment seriously.) Specter and Hatch repeatedly questioned why, if Thomas had harassed her as she claimed, Hill did not file complaints about the alleged incidents. Why, they asked, had Hill followed Thomas from one agency to another, and then kept in contact with him over the years? (Republicans submitted into the record telephone logs kept at the EEOC showing that Hill had telephoned Thomas ten or eleven times in the eight years since her departure from the agency.)[109] Specter publicly accused Hill of "flat out perjury" in part of her testimony after she elaborated on her response to an October 9 *USA Today* article reporting that she "was told by Senate staffers that her signed affidavit would be the instrument that 'quietly and behind the scenes,' would force [Thomas] to withdraw" his nomination. (Hill initially said she could not recall if that specific comment had been made. Later, Hill conceded that, during her September 10 meeting with Brudney, Thomas's withdrawal had been mentioned as one possible outcome.)

Democrats on the committee did not move forcefully to rebut the Republican's attack on Hill's character, and for the most part, Hill stood alone against the senators. Hill told the committee she moved with Thomas to the EEOC because, if she quit, she would have been jobless—there was a hiring freeze in the federal government at the time, and she wanted to stay in Civil Rights. Hill said she did not file a complaint against Thomas for fear of retaliation, and later kept cordial, but distant contact with him for professional reasons. Regarding the telephone logs, Hill claimed that, in most cases, she was simply returning Thomas's calls, while some of the other reported phone calls had never been made.

When asked why the Democrats were not more aggressive vis à vis the Republicans, Leahy replied, "I will not smear and lie just because they do." Biden agreed. "I think the Republicans were more partisan in their objective" while "we were trying to find out the truth. We could have gone in there and said we aren't going to listen to what he says, and everything she says will be put in a positive light. I didn't think that was the way to conduct his hearing."

Committee Democrats generally appeared stunned by Thomas's angry charges of racism, and seemed almost apologetic in having to ask Thomas about the issue of sexual harassment. All respected Thomas's repeated refusals to discuss his personal life. Not a single committee member asked Thomas about a statement made by a friend and former Yale Law School classmate of his, Lovida Coleman Jr. (Coleman's statement was issued October 9 in response to stories circulating in the Capitol that Judge Thomas had often been a patron of X-rated movie houses at Yale Law School in the early 1970s.) Coleman said that Thomas "at least once humorously described an X-rated film to [her] and other colleagues," and acknowledged that this had occurred more than once.[110] The subject was not mentioned at all until very late Sunday night—after most viewers had gone to sleep—when Leahy asked a witness testifying for Thomas if he was aware of Coleman's statement. The witness—a former dean at Oral Roberts University—said he could not imagine Thomas ever watching a pornographic film.

Biden later conceded that he "could have brought in the pornography stuff." "I could have decimated him at that," said Biden, "but it would make a lie of everything I fought for."[111] Simon later said he agreed with Biden's decision: "I am not sure there is a direct link between watching pornographic films and sexual harassment," adding that he too "felt uneasy getting into that field."[112]

ANGELA WRIGHT

Before Thomas left the stand on Saturday, Biden reassured him: "The presumption [of innocence] is with you, judge." According to Biden, sexual harassment "doesn't happen in isolated instances—it's a pattern. If there's not a pattern," he told Thomas, "to me, that's probative," or legally meaningful. Late Sunday night, however, Biden announced that Angela Wright and Rose Jourdain—whom Hill's supporters believed might have helped establish Biden's required "pattern"—would not testify publicly as originally planned, despite the fact that Thomas had been given the opportunity on Friday to try to discredit Wright. (Thomas testified that he "aggressively and summarily" fired Wright because of reports that she "referred to another male member of [his] staff as a faggot.")[113] On Sunday night, Biden stated that he would have preferred to have the two women testify in person, but because of the late hour, agreed to enter the unsworn, seventy-page transcript of their telephone interviews with Judiciary staff into the record of the hearings.[114]

It remained unclear why Angela Wright and her corroborating witness did not appear before the committee that night until well after the hearings had concluded. Cynthia Hogan, a Judiciary Committee lawyer who led the committee's questioning of Wright, explains that although she "thought Angela Wright was a very credible witness" and "conveyed that to Senator Biden who accepted that," Biden soon learned that he was the only committee member who wanted Wright to appear. According to Hogan:

Anita Hill's lawyers had lobbied the other Democratic members of the committee to say they don't want Angela Wright called. I think they bought into some of the stuff the Republicans were saying, and they thought that her reputation wasn't maybe as great or she would somehow taint Anita Hill. I think this was terrible advice. . . . At the same time, I was dealing with Angela Wright's lawyers who watched what happened to Anita Hill and said to me, "she doesn't want to testify, but she doesn't want to publicly say [that]."[115] . . . We did not want to put her on without a corroborating witness, and her corroborating witness [Jourdain] was in the hospital until late in the afternoon on Sunday. . . . We had arranged to have an ambulance pick her up and bring her [to the hearings]. . . . Then out of the blue, the Republicans— who were clearly terrified of Angela Wright—said: "We don't want her to testify

and we will accept the transcript of her deposition *unrebutted.*" . . . Which to a lawyer means they're accepting it as basically true, so we thought this was a tremendous victory.

Hogan says she was "horrified" when no major news outlet treated the deposition as significant the following day and concedes that the committee "misjudged the way it would be perceived by the press and other senators." Senator Simon later agreed the committee's decision was "a mistake," observing that Wright's deposition "received little attention, because she did not appear before the committee, and did not reach the television audience."[116]

Later that night, Biden announced that both Hill and Thomas would pass up the chance to address the senators again on Monday. Just after 2:00 A.M., with many questions left unanswered, Biden gaveled the hearings to a close.

THE BENEFIT OF THE DOUBT

On Tuesday, October 15, the Senate confirmed Thomas for the Supreme Court by a vote of 52–48. It was the closest confirmation vote in the twentieth century and a much slimmer victory than had been predicted before the uproar. Voting in favor of Thomas were eleven Democrats and forty-one Republicans; forty-six Democrats and two Republicans voted against Thomas.[117] While three Democrats publicly shifted their positions, both sides estimated that Thomas lost about ten votes that he might have had before the sexual harassment allegations emerged.[118]

Some lawmakers evidently calculated that it was politically safer to vote for Thomas than against him. This was particularly true for Southern Democrats, who need to build coalitions that include conservatives as well as blacks. The Thomas nomination presented them with a rare opportunity to please both groups: according to a CNN-Gallup Poll, black support for Thomas shot up after the hearings, from 54 percent favoring his confirmation before the hearings to 71 percent afterward. Senator John Breaux (D-La.) described his decision-making: "It's important to know that in Louisiana, where we have about 27 percent black population, that the majority, and I think a pretty substantial majority, were in favor of Judge Thomas," Breaux explained. "That's a large chunk of voters as well as a majority of the white voters, so it was not that difficult a decision for me."[119] (On the Senate floor, Breaux said that he was not sure who was telling the truth, but since he could discern no continuing pattern of questionable conduct, he stayed with Thomas.) In the end, eight of seventeen Southern and border-state Democrats voted to confirm Thomas, and four of the eight faced reelection in Deep South states.

The three Democratic senators who switched their votes were Lieberman and Nevada Senators Richard Bryan and Harry Reid. Lieberman said he went "up and down" during the hearings "like everyone else," but ultimately decided to vote against Thomas. "What made up my mind was Professor Hill's testimony and then those four corroborating witnesses. Ultimately it just raised too many doubts in my mind. I decided if I was going to err, it was better to err on the side of caution." Bryan asserted that "the critical factor for me was I found it difficult to ascribe a motive to Ms. Hill in her testimony." Reid, who was up for reelection in 1992, said "from a political standpoint, I badly wanted to vote for Clarence Thomas. However, my conscience wouldn't let me do it. I thought she was telling the truth."

The two women in the Senate ultimately voted in line with their respective parties. Kassebaum continued to support Thomas while Mikulski's vote was an outraged "no." Both, however, assailed the Judiciary Committee for their behavior during the hearings. In Mikulski's view, committee members "approached this not as a hearing, but as an inquisition. And, sadly, there were senators who rushed in to the role of grand inquisitor. . . . The message for women is: your courage in coming forward will be met with suspicion and scorn . . . [and] unproven, unsupported charges of being mentally unbalanced, fantasizers, jealous, or opportunists." In voting for Thomas, Kassebaum said "it would be manifestly unfair for the Senate to destroy a Supreme Court nominee on the basis of evidence that finally boils down to the testimony of one person, however credible, against his flat, unequivocal, and equally credible denial. . . . But let me make clear, I have no intention of being a party to a 'high tech lynching'—a phrase I flatly reject as having any validity here—but I also have no intention of being party to an intellectual witch hunt against Professor Hill."

While no Judiciary Committee members changed their votes after the second round of hearings, members intensely debated whether or not Thomas should have been given the benefit of the doubt. DeConcini said he sympathized with Thomas in his ordeal, saying Thomas "does not deserve to be punished for something that is inconclusive." Hatch insisted that "if you believe both of them, anybody who believes in the system of jurisprudence and our system of fairness will give Clarence Thomas the benefit of the doubt." Kennedy argued the opposite. "There is a very strong likelihood that Professor Hill is telling the truth," Kennedy asserted. "In a case of this vast magnitude, where so much is riding on our decision, the Senate should give the benefit of the doubt to the Supreme Court and to the American people, not to Judge Clarence Thomas." Senator Robert Byrd (D-W.V.) agreed. "This is not a court case; this is a confirmation hearing. . . . A credible charge of the type that has been leveled at Judge Thomas is enough, in my view, to mandate that we ought to look for a more exemplary nominee."

In a statement issued after the roll-call was completed, President Bush came to Thomas's defense. "Judge Thomas has demonstrated to the Congress and to the nation that he is a man of honesty, dedication, and commitment to the Constitution and the rule of law. The nation and the Court benefit from having a man of principle who is sensitive to the problems and opportunities facing all Americans.'' Senator Danforth concurred: ''Clarence Thomas is going to surprise a lot of people. He is going to be a good and competent and decent and fair justice. He is going to be the people's justice on the United States Supreme Court.''

REFORMING THE PROCESS

The day after the confirmation vote, the Senate began a grim reappraisal of the entire process surrounding Supreme Court nominations. While some senators argued that the public hearings exemplified democracy in action, others contended that they illuminated the politicization that has characterized Senate confirmation hearings since the 1987 defeat of Bork's nomination. Sam Nunn (D-Ga.) and others proposed that the Senate refrain in the future from public hearings on confidential allegations, even if they have been leaked to the news media. ''Now we have seen the consequences of fulfilling the momentary desire to accommodate the public's 'right to know' and providing for resolution of allegations in a trial-type public hearing,'' Nunn said. ''The appetites we have struggled to control in the past were not suppressed, and the Senate now faces public revulsion, rather than accolades, for our indulgence.''

President Bush agreed that the Judiciary Committee should have met privately to examine sexual harassment accusations against Thomas rather than broadcast the ''graphic detail'' of the charges around the country. ''I was thinking of my little grandchildren hearing some of the graphic sex allegations,'' Bush complained. Lieberman was skeptical, however. He argued that serious charges could not be kept secret by a committee from the full Senate and questioned whether they could be kept confidential after being disseminated to one hundred people. In this case, Americans would have suspected a ''cover-up'' if public hearings were not held, Lieberman argued.

Nunn proposed that when senators have concerns about a nominee, the president ''must take those concerns seriously, not simply take the position that each nominee warrants unqualified support for political reasons,'' he said. However, if the president wants to rely on confidential information, he ''must be willing to engage in serious discussions when serious, legitimate questions are raised about the qualifications of nominees,'' Nunn argued. ''The president cannot have it both ways.'' Simon put this in the form of a nonbinding resolution asking the president to undertake ''informal, bipartisan consultations with some members of the Senate'' before a nominee's name is submitted for confirmation. The resolution also asserted that the president ''should keep philosophical balance in mind, so that the law is not like a pendulum, swinging back and forth depending on the philosophy of the president.''

For his part, Biden said he regarded the events surrounding the Thomas nomination as a ''terribly ugly chapter on Capitol Hill,''[120] but continued to believe the committee's handling of Hill's charges, prior to their public disclosure, was proper. Still, Biden told the *Washington Post* ''there was no question that this would have to come out'' once the allegations were made to Senate staff and that ''the best thing would have been for [Hill's] allegation to have been made public from the outset.'' Aware that his critics believed that a committee investigator should have gone to Oklahoma in September to interview Hill and try to convince her to come forward, Biden defended his actions: ''It would have been immoral for me to have done that,'' he said. ''Going out and pushing her and cajoling her . . . would be thrusting an incredible burden on someone who is going to go through a difficult decision that is going to have a dramatic impact on her life." "I know others think differently," Biden acknowledged, but "for me to go out there and push her, to do anything but explain to her what" the procedures were, "would be wrong."

In June 1992, as part of a major speech on reforming the confirmation process, Biden submitted several new procedures for handling investigative matters confronting the Senate Judiciary Committee. In his speech, Biden declared: "Conservatives cannot have it both ways: they cannot ask us to refrain from rigorous questioning of judicial philosophy, and instead focus on a nominee's personal background—as they did during the early phase of the Thomas nomination—and then complain loudly when this examination of personal background turns into a bitter exploration of the nominee's conduct and character." Earlier, Biden had suggested that he would continue to play down character issues in upcoming confirmation battles; during the Thomas hearings, Biden said that there had been "more nominees sent up here with the last two administrations that have drug problems that I've never even told these folks [members of the Senate] about because it happened ten, twenty, thirty years ago. . . . So I'll take the heat and I'll take the responsibility and I'll continue to do it as long as I am chairman. . . ."

On October 24, 1991, the Senate passed Resolution 202, which provided for the appointment of a temporary special independent counsel to "conduct an investigation of any unauthorized disclosure of nonpublic, confidential information from Senate documents." In offering the resolution, Senator Mitchell stated:

> Every leak is to be condemned. Every leak is to be deplored. The end does not justify the means. And a leak which harms the opponent is just as wrong as a leak which harms a friend. A leak which injures a cause I oppose is just as wrong as a leak which injures a cause I favor.

On May 4, 1992, the Senate-appointed special counsel, Peter E. Fleming, released a three-inch-thick report on his investigation. After interviewing more than two hundred witnesses and reviewing thousands of pages of documents, Fleming concluded: "We are unable to identify any source of these disclosures. The evidence indicates there were multiple sources." Although reporters Timothy Phelps and Nina Totenberg refused to answer Fleming's questions about the source of their stories, Fleming found that "Phelps's unidentified source was a person who had seen Hill's statement to the Senate" and Totenberg's "source was a person within the Senate, and not Anita Hill." The two reporters said their right to conceal their sources was protected by the Constitution's freedom of the press provisions.

EPILOGUE

More people watched the Thomas confirmation hearings than any act of American governance ever before in history.[121] According to Gallup polls completed the week of the Senate vote, Americans generally approved of the way Biden ran the hearings but were dismayed by the overall confirmation process and the behavior of the Senate. Biden received a favorable response from 63 percent of those polled—the highest rating for a member of the Judiciary Committee.[122] However, 66 percent of those responding to an ABC News poll the same week said they disapproved of the Senate's handling of the confirmation process, and Gallup researchers found that 48 percent of respondents had less confidence in Congress as a result of the hearings, compared with 21 percent who had more.[123] A *New York Times*/CBS News poll taken on October 13 revealed that 58 percent of those polled believed the hearings would result in "nothing good," while 36 percent believed "something good" was accomplished by the hearings. In the same poll, 59 percent believed the committee's questions and testimony went too far for what should be allowed in a public hearing, while 33 percent believed the questions and testimony were appropriate.

In a survey of one hundred state and federal judges conducted by the *National Law Journal* after the hearings, fewer than half the judges said that they would want to be nominated to the nation's highest court.[124] One out of three surveyed believed the process had damaged the credibility of the Supreme Court, while many more believed that Bush and Congress had been harmed. Eighty-five judges rated the Senate Judiciary Committee's skill in examining the witnesses as "fair" or "poor."

Polls taken just after the hearings showed that a plurality of both women and men from every age, income, and educational group said they believed Thomas more than Hill.[126] Nevertheless, feminist activists vowed to mobilize women's anger at the Senate toward helping more women run for office and unseat senators who had supported Thomas. "The Senate has done more in one week to underscore the critical need for women in the Senate than feminists have been able to do in twenty-five years," said Eleanor Smeal, president of the Fund for a Feminist Majority and former president of the National Organization for Women. In fact, a record number of women ran for elective office in the 1992 elections, and the number of women elected to the Senate tripled from two to six. In January 1993, two of the new senators, Dianne Feinstein (D-Calif.) and Carol Moseley Braun (D-Ill.), were named as the first female members of the Senate Judiciary Committee. The selection of Braun, the Senate's only African-American member, gave the Judiciary Committee minority as well as female representation. Both women had, during their campaign, criticized the Senate's handling of Hill's charges.

Some people worried that the hearings would worsen race relations in America. The public airing of Hill's sexual harassment allegations before the all-white Senate committee painfully evoked some of the old-est and ugliest racist sexual stereotypes, and gave resonance to Thomas's denunciation of the hearings as a "high-tech lynching." Others credited Hill's appearance before the Senate with making possible the passage of a bipartisan civil rights bill in October 1991, ending the two-year battle that had been waged over the legislation. Co-sponsored by Danforth and Kennedy, the bill reinstated protections for victims of job bias, and allowed for the first time limited money damages for victims of sexual harassment. Danforth conceded that "the emphasis on sexual harassment and the energizing of women on [getting money damages for harassment] might have created in the mind of the administration the feeling that they should complete action on the bill or they would lose everything."[127]

In the year after the Thomas-Hill hearings, sexual harassment complaints soared nationwide. Judith Lichtman, president of the Women's Legal Defense Fund, told the *Washington Post*: "We worried that other women wouldn't come forward after Anita Hill was treated so badly. The converse has in fact happened."[128] In the first half of fiscal 1992, there was an estimated 60 percent increase in the number of claims filed with the EEOC. Shortly after the Senate hearings, Hill had said she was glad that her story had heightened national awareness of the sexual harassment issue and expressed gratitude that she had been "able to go out and tell what [she] knew." In an interview on NBC's *Today* show one year later, Hill added: "When I think of what has happened in a larger sense, beyond myself, then I would not change anything."

NOTES

1. Stanley Feingold, "Sure It's Politics; When Wasn't It? The Senate's Role in Supreme Court Nominations," *National Law Journal*, Sept. 2, 1991, p. 18.

2. *New York Times*, Oct. 20, 1991, p. D1.

3. Feingold, "Sure It's Politics," p. 18.

4. *Washington Post*, July 2, 1991, p. A1.

5. Senator Metzenbaum dissented.

6. Polls taken at the time showed that conservative

Republicans like Thomas represented only a small proportion of African-American opinion (*Washington Post*, July 4, 1991, p. A1).

7. *Washington Post,* July 2, 1991, p. A1.

8. Ibid., p. A7.

9. Ibid., Sept. 10, 1991, p. A1.

10. During his 1990 judicial confirmation hearings, Thomas admitted this was "the worst event during [his] tenure." Thomas blamed the growing backlog of unaddressed cases on a lack of funds (*Washington Post*, Sept. 10, 1991, p. A1.)

11. *Washington Post National Weekly Edition*, Sept. 16–22, 1991, p. 9.

12. *Congressional Quarterly Weekly Report*, July 13, 1991, p. 1902.

13. The group's lone Republican, freshman Gary Franks of Connecticut, was the only dissenting voice.

14. *National Journal*, Sept. 7, 1991, p. 2154.

15. *Washington Post*, Aug. 1, 1991, p. A1.

16. Lehrman's article described *Roe* as a "coup against the Constitution" leading to a "holocaust" for fetuses (*Congressional Quarterly Weekly Report*, Aug. 3, 1991, p. 2364).

17. *Washington Post*, July 2, 1991, p. Al.

18. *Congressional Quarterly Weekly Report*, Aug. 3, 1991, p. 2170.

19. *Washington Post*, July 2, 1991, p. Al.

20. *Congressional Quarterly Weekly Report*, Aug. 5, 1991, p. 2170.

21. *Washington Post*, July 2, 1991, p. Al.

22. *Congressional Quarterly Weekly Report*, Aug. 31, 1991, p. 2359.

23. *Washington Post*, Aug. 3, 1991, p. Al.

24. Ibid., p. A1.

25. *US News and World Report*, Oct. 21, 1991, p. 34.

26. *US News and World Report*, Sept. 16, 1991, p. 29.

27. *Washington Post*, Oct. 12, 1991, p. A1.

28. Thomas denied that he knew about Parker's ties.

29. A reporter had disclosed that Ginsburg smoked marijuana in his thirties while a professor at Harvard Law School. Thomas revealed his marijuana use to the White House during his 1990 nomination to the federal appeals court, and it was not news to the Senate Judiciary Committee.

30. *New York Times*, Sept. 10, 1991, p. Al.

31. *Congressional Quarterly Weekly Report*, Aug. 31, 1991, p. 2359.

32. Republicans were infuriated with Specter's vote against Bork. At a press conference held shortly after Bork's defeat, angry GOP conservatives held up a dead rubber duck and said, "This is your political career, Arlen." (*Congressional Quarterly Weekly Report*, Aug. 31, 1991, p. 2359.)

33. Like Souter, Thomas did say he believes the right to privacy—the legal underpinning for the Court's recognition of a constitutional guarantee to abortion—is a fundamental constitutional right for married couples. But he declined to say whether or not he believes that right extends beyond the marital setting.

34. Peter Fleming, Jr., *Report of Temporary Special Independent Counsel Pursuant to Senate Resolution 202*, May 4, 1992, p. 22.

35. Thomas completed his testimony on September 16. During the remainder of the week, through September 20, other witnesses testified before the committee on behalf of or against the nominee. These included special interest groups, legal scholars, and individuals who knew or had worked with Thomas.

36. *Washington Post*, Sept. 21, 1991, p. A7.

37. Ibid.

38. Between 1980–1991, fifteen harassment complaints had been filed against EEOC employees. Of those, several were rejected by the agency as unjustifiable, one was settled "with corrective action" and the fate of the others was either pending or unknown (*Boston Globe*, Oct. 10, 1991, p. 31).

39. The EEOC's new guidelines were severely critiqued in a 1980 Reagan transition team report co-authored by Thomas. Complaining that the guidelines would lead "to a barrage of trivial complaints against employers around the nation," and that "the elimination of personal slights and sexual advances which contribute to an 'intimidating, hostile or offensive working environment' is a goal impossible to reach," the report advised that "expenditure of the EEOC's limited resources in pursuit of this goal is unwise" (Timothy M. Phelps and Helen Winternitz, *Capitol Games: Clarence Thomas, Anita Hill, and the Story of a Supreme Court Nomination* [New York: Hyperion, 1992], p. 382).

40. According to Klain, the Senate Judiciary Committee was the only committee of the Congress that received raw FBI reports on nominees.

41. Fleming, *Report*, p. 152.

42. It was later reported that this "tip" may have originated from a conversation held between Hill and her Yale law school friend, Gary Phillips, within days of Bush's July 1 nomination of Thomas. When Phillips asked Hill what she thought about the nomination of her former boss, Hill apparently replied: "I never told you this before, but I was sexually harassed by Clarence Thomas." Over the next few weeks, Phillips reportedly told friends he knew a woman who had been harassed by Thomas, and the story quickly "made the rounds" (*US News & World Report*, Oct. 12, 1992). Phillips said that, at the time, Hill was "struggling personally with whether to say anything," and "wasn't planning to because she thought people wouldn't believe her," among other reasons (*Washington Post*, Oct. 9, 1991, p. A9).

43. This represents Hill's account of her conversations with Brudney, as stated before the Senate Judiciary Committee on Oct. 11, 1991.

44. Fleming, *Report*, p. 32.

45. Ibid., p. 33.

46. Phelps and Winternitz, *Capitol Games*, p. 213.

47. Fleming, *Report*, p. 33. According to Fleming's report, Brudney says that during these conversations, he did not encourage Hill to press her charges. Hill, however, recalls Brudney's stance as more persistent, and says she told Brudney on several occasions that it was her decision to make. "From Hill's perspective, the difference in approach was her own experience that allegations of sexual harassment are often disbelieved, whereas Brudney was confident that Hill's statements, with evidence of a contemporaneous complaint to a friend in 1981, would be credited," the report says.

48. Ibid., pp. 33-34.

49. Ibid., p. 34.

50. Ibid., p. 35.

51. Hill's news conference, Oct. 7, 1991.

52. Fleming, *Report*, p. 36.

53. In retrospect, Klain says, if he had known what Thomas's answers were going to be, he "might well have sent someone who would have been more adversarial and more cross-examination-oriented." Klain says he did not expect Thomas to categorically deny all of Hill's charges, and that his guess that Thomas "was going to admit the facts but dispute the significance of the facts colored how we [committee staff] handled the investigation."

54. Fleming, *Report*, pp. 36-38.

55. Ibid., pp. 38-39.

56. Ibid., p. 88.

57. The FBI regards the White House as its "client agency" in its background investigations of nominees. For that reason, any investigative assignments requested by the Senate must pass through the White House (Ibid., p. 40).

58. Both the *New York Times* and the *Washington Post* later reported, apparently inaccurately, that Thomas told the FBI he had asked Hill out a few times, but eventually dropped all advances after she declined.

59. *Washington Post*, Oct. 8, 1991, p. A7.

60. *Newsweek*, Oct. 21, 1991, p. 28. According to the FBI's Civil Rights and Special Inquiries section head, the bureau serves only as an information-gatherer, and avoids offering conclusions about the validity of allegations as a general rule (*Washington Post*, Oct. 8, 1991).

61. Fleming, *Report*, pp. 41-42.

62. *New York Times*, Oct. 8, 1991, p. A22. To ensure Hill's confidentiality, committee members were required to scan the FBI report in the presence of a committee staffer and then return it when finished.

63. Fleming, *Report*, pp. 42-43.

64. *Washington Post*, Oct. 7, 1991, p. A1.

65. One of the most conservative of the Southern Democrats, Senator Heflin, voted with the Republicans more often than not. Publicly, Heflin said he would vote his "conscience" and oppose Thomas for his "outright disavowals" of past positions (*Congressional Weekly Report*, Sept. 28, 1991, p. 2787).

66. Fleming, *Report*, p. 43.

67. *US News and World Report*, Oct. 21, 1991, p. 36.

68. Fleming, *Report*, p. 45.

69. Senator Paul Simon, *Advice & Consent: Clarence Thomas, Robert Bork and the Intriguing History of the Supreme Court's Nomination Battles* (Washington, D.C.: National Press Books, 1992), pp. 104-5.

70. *Congressional Quarterly Weekly Report*, Oct. 12, 1991, p. 2957.

71. Fleming, *Report*, pp. 45-46.

72. *Washington Post*, Oct. 8, 1991, p. A9. According to *US News and World Report*, Biden told Danforth at one point that he "wouldn't be surprised" if it all became public. The worry, said Danforth, was that "perhaps she [Hill] would hold a press conference" (Oct. 21, 1991, p. 35).

73. *New York Times*, Sept. 29, 1991, p. A24.

74. *Washington Post*, Sept. 28, 1991, p. A1.

75. *Congressional Quarterly Weekly Report*, Oct. 5, 1991, p. 2867.

76. *Washington Post*, Sept. 28, 1991, p. A1.

77. *New York Times*, Sept. 29, 1991, Section 1, p. 24.

78. Ibid.

79. Ibid.

80. Fleming, *Report*, p. 50.

81. *Newsday*, Sept. 28, 1991. At this point, Phelps had learned from others that the FBI was investigating Hill's charges of sexual harassment. However, he did not know what the specific allegations were and did not have enough information for a full story. (See Phelps and Winternitz, *Capitol Games*, p. 228.)

82. The record was held by Chief Justice William Rehnquist, who drew 33 votes against when he was elevated to associate justice in the 1980s (*Washington Post*).

83. A motion to postpone the Senate vote would have required the unanimous consent of the Senate.

84. *Congressional Quarterly Weekly Report*, Sept. 28, 1991, p. 2786.

85. *Washington Post*, Sept 28, 1991, p. A1.

86. Hatch spoke as he was seated next to Thurmond, who held the personal record of 24 hours and 19 minutes for a filibuster against a civil rights bill in 1957 (*Washington Post*, Sept. 28, 1991, p. A1).

87. Rule 29.5, the general Senate rule against disclosure of confidential information, provides: "Any senator who shall disclose the secret or confidential business or proceedings of the Senate shall be liable, if a Senator, to suffer expulsion from the body; and if an officer, to dismissal from the service of the Senate, and to punishment for contempt." (Rule 29.5, Standing Rules of the Senate, reprinted in S. Doc. No. 101-1, at 62.)

88. *Congressional Quarterly Weekly Report*, Oct. 12, 1991, p. 2956.

89. Contrary to the impression created by early press reports, the contents of the FBI report had not been

disseminated outside the Senate in whole or in part (Fleming, *Report*, p. 5).

90. *Washington Post*, Oct. 6, 1991, p. A1.

91. Hill described herself as both a conservative and a Democrat (CBS, *Sixty Minutes*, Feb. 2, 1992).

92. *New York Times*, Oct. 9, 1991, p. A18.

93. Not all Republican members of the Senate Judiciary Committee were fully informed of Hill's charges before the September 27 committee vote.

94. *Washington Post*, Oct. 9, 1991, p. 24.

95. *New York Times*, Oct. 8, 1991, p.A21.

96. Congress exempts itself from most federal labor laws, including those governing sexual harassment.

97. Mitchell suggested instead that the women help lobby the thirteen Democratic senators supporting Thomas in order to delay the vote.

98. Many attributed Kennedy's general low profile throughout the Thomas debate to fallout from rape charges recently brought against his nephew, William Kennedy Smith.

99. Thomas was formally interviewed by the FBI on September 25. It is unclear why his statement said September 28.

100. No portion of the FBI report was leaked.

101. *New York Times*, Oct. 9, 1991, p. A1.

102. Ibid., pp. A1, A18.

103. Two owners of video stores in Washington had indicated to journalists that they had rented pornographic movies to Thomas in recent years (Phelps and Winternitz, *Capitol Games*, p. 393).

104. On Sunday, Hill's lawyers released the results of a polygraph test conducted by Paul K. Minor, former chief polygraph examiner for the FBI. According to Minor, it indicated "no deception" in Hill's answers to questions about her charges. Thomas did not take a polygraph test. (Polygraph tests were generally not admissible in court, and there was no scientific consensus about their reliability. However, Presidents Reagan and Bush vastly expanded the use of polygraphs in the 1980s, routinely administering them in the course of "leak" and national security investigations, while liberal Democrats were traditionally critical of their use.)

105. On Saturday, Thomas said that the FBI agent who interviewed him on September 25 later told him the bureau had incorrectly reported that Thomas admitted asking Hill out on a few dates.

106. Paul said that during Hill's 1987 interview for a teaching position at American University, Hill told him that she had left her job at the EEOC because she had been sexually harassed by her supervisor.

107. According to *Newsweek*, Biden initially tried to shorten the list of witnesses supporting Thomas, but backed down after the Bush administration threatened to hold a press conference to denounce the committee for being unfair (Oct. 21, 1991, p. 26).

108. Simpson did not elaborate on the sources of content of the statements, but after critics demanded he do so, Simpson eventually put some of the material in the *Congressional Record*.

109. It is standard procedure in many federal offices to maintain daily records of office telephone calls for several years. The EEOC phone logs did not indicate whether Hill had initiated the calls or returned previous calls from Thomas.

110. Coleman, a Washington lawyer, also said that neither she nor other students "were offended by his amusing accounts. Indeed, we would have been hypocrites to have been offended since very few of us failed to attend one or more similar films that were shown on the Yale University campus while we were in school." Coleman also described Thomas as "particularly sensitive and caring regarding the professional and personal concerns of the women he knows and with whom he has worked," and said she seriously doubted that he had sexually harassed Hill (*New York Times*, Oct. 10, 1991, p. B14).

111. *Washington Post*, June 19, 1992.

112. Senator Paul Simon, *Advice & Consent: Clarence Thomas, Robert Bork and the Intriguing History of the Supreme Court's Nomination Battles* (Washington, D.C.: National Press Books, 1992), pp. 120–121.

113. The *Charlotte Observer* stated that when they called Thomas for a reference in 1990, Thomas described Wright as "an excellent employee" and told them Wright had resigned her post at the EEOC.

114. Biden later admitted that the committee might have halted the hearings to investigate whether there was a "pattern of behavior" on Thomas's part. However, Biden said, "had we announced we were holding up this hearing . . . he [Thomas] would have been cannibalized" (*Washington Post*, June 19, 1992).

115. Wright later told *US News & World Report* that Biden's staff "is lying"—that Hogan "pressured" her attorney to withdraw his client as a live witness and instead submit her statement for the record. Wright said she finally succumbed when "it became apparent that hardly anyone would be around" to hear her story late that night (*US News & World Report*, Oct. 12, 1992).

116. Simon, *Advice & Consent*, p. 118.

117. Jeffords and Bob Packwood (Ore.) were the only Republican senators to oppose Thomas.

118. *Congressional Quarterly Weekly Report*, Oct. 19, 1991, p. 3030.

119. CBS, *This Morning*, Oct. 16, 1991.

120. *Wall Street Journal*, Oct. 11, 1991, p. A10.

121. Senator Joseph R. Biden, Jr., "Reforming the Confirmation Process: A New Era Must Dawn," June 25, 1992, p. 23.

122. *Boston Globe*, Oct. 16, 1991, p. 6.

123. Ibid.

124. Of the one-hundred judges surveyed, seventy-five were state judges while twenty-five were federal judges. Ninety-four judges were male, with forty-five Democrats and thirty-six Republicans (*National Law Journal*, Oct. 28, 1991, pp. 1, 22).

125. By a 2–1 margin, the judges also said they found Hill's testimony more credible than Thomas's flat-out

denial: 41 percent found Hill more credible, while 22 percent chose Thomas. (Thirty-seven percent were not sure.) If the judges had been voting on his confirmation, Thomas would have been defeated 45–41, with 14 undecided (*National Law Journal*, Oct. 28, 1991, pp. 1, 22).

126. A poll taken almost one year later showed that public opinion had shifted dramatically to a dead heat: 38 percent believed Thomas and 38 percent believed Hill (*US News & World Report*, Oct. 12, 1992).

127. *Congressional Quarterly Weekly Report*, Nov. 2, 1991, pp. 3202–3.

128. *Washington Post*, Oct. 13, 1992.

Comment

Was the Senate Judiciary Committee justified in making Hill's charges public? Anita Hill initially had made her statements on the condition that they be treated as confidential. She said she had come forward only reluctantly, out of a sense of duty, to provide the information and let the Committee investigate. If the chief counsel of the Judiciary Committee reasonably understood Hill to be insisting on a degree of confidentiality that included not telling the nominee about her identity, then the Judiciary Committee had a strong reason to keep her allegations secret. But respecting her request confronted the committee with a dilemma. The committee could ignore the charges, in which case they would fail in their constitutional duty to examine Thomas's qualifications thoroughly. Or they could consider the charges without telling Thomas, in which case they would violate Thomas's right to confront his accusers. (The question that faced some members and staff—whether to leak information about Hill's charges—should be considered in the context of the issues raised in chapter 4, which deals with official disobedience.)

Clarence Thomas also had a claim to privacy. He believed that a public hearing on the allegations would be a humiliating and degrading intrusion into his private life even if he could prove the allegations were false. But the allegations were also relevant to one of the most important questions that Congress decides, who is qualified to sit on the Supreme Court. Thomas did not have a right to this job, and this was not a criminal trial, contrary to what some comments of the chairman of the committee implied. The committee believed that Thomas's rights could be adequately protected if he were given a fair chance to defend himself in the proper kind of forum.

Some argue that public hearings in a case like this tend to reinforce racist and sexist attitudes in this country. Staging a dramatic confrontation between two black citizens in the atmosphere of a "high tech lynching" was not likely to reduce racial prejudice. Nor was the spectacle of the all-male, all-white committee sitting in judgment of Hill and Thomas a positive lesson in equal justice. But others argue that public hearings were desirable precisely to expose these attitudes and inequalities. Furthermore, if we do not publicly confront and collectively discuss issues such as sexual harassment, homosexual rights, or racial justice, we may never learn how to do so responsibly.

Even if we decide that the value of publicity outweighs the claims of privacy in this case, we might not conclude that full public hearings were required. An executive session of the committee, closed to the press and the public, might have been acceptable to Hill, fairer to Thomas, and still consistent with the committee's constitutional responsibilities. In principle, the hearings could have been kept confidential, with full records to be released at a specified future date. But in practice, in this instance, by the time the committee had to decide about the hearings, too many people already knew too much about the case, and too many stood to lose or gain too much by its outcome.

A decision to hold open hearings need not remove all ethical limits on publicity. The committee refused to pursue some lines of investigation that risked even greater exposure of the personal lives of the witnesses. For example, they did not permit Thomas's supporters to introduce testimony about Hill's past relationships with men, and they did not seek records of videos that Thomas rented for his personal use, even though some of this information would have been relevant to the committee's deliberations, at least to assessing the credibility of witnesses. Were they justified in setting these limits on publicity? Should they have set more limits? It could be argued that, if the committee had held closed hearings, it would have been less justified in limiting the inquiry in these ways. The fact that the hearings were public let citizens judge for themselves whether the inquiry into the allegations had been extensive enough.

Recommended Reading

The most comprehensive treatment of the problem of deception is Sissela Bok, *Lying: Moral Choice in Public and Private Life* (New York: Random House, 1979), especially ch. 1, 2, 3, 6 to 8, and 12. The appendix provides substantial excerpts from works by Augustine, Aquinas, Bacon, Grotius, Kant, Sidgwick, Harrod, Bonhoeffer, and Warnock. Also, see Hannah Arendt, "Truth and Politics," in P. Lasett and W.G. Runciman (eds.), *Philosophy, Politics and Society*, third series (Oxford: Blackwell, 1967), pp. 104–33; Charles Fried, *Right and Wrong* (Cambridge, Mass.: Harvard University Press, 1978), chapter 3; Christine M. Korsgaard, "The Right to Lie: Kant on Dealing with Evil," *Philosophy & Public Affairs*, 15 (Fall 1986), pp. 325–49; and Peter Johnson, *Frames of Deceit* (Cambridge, England: University Press, 1993). An insightful discussion of hypocrisy is to be found in Judith Shklar, *Ordinary Vices* (Cambridge, Mass.: Harvard University Press, 1984), ch. 2.

On secrecy, Bok again provides a valuable overview in *Secrets: On the Ethics of Concealment and Revelation* (New York: Pantheon, 1982), especially ch. 8, 12, 14, 17, and 18. The classic contrast between utilitarian and deontological views of publicity can be brought out by comparing Immanuel Kant, "On the Disagreement Between Politics and Morality . . .," *Perpetual Peace*, Appendix II, in *Political Writings*, pp. 125–30: and Jeremy Bentham, "Of Publicity," in *Essay on Political Tactics, Works*, vol. 2, pp. 310–17. For a sample of the various approaches to the value of privacy, see Ferdinand Schoeman (ed.), *Philosophical Dimensions of Pri-*

vacy (Cambridge, England: Cambridge University Press, 1984). The problems of privacy in politics are discussed by Dennis F. Thompson, *Political Ethics and Public Office* (Cambridge, Mass.: Harvard University Press, 1987), pp. 123–47.

For a discussion of the principle of publicity in political ethics, see Amy Gutmann and Dennis Thompson, *Democracy and Disagreement* (Cambridge, Mass.: Harvard University Press, 1996), ch. 3. The most influential contemporary philosophical discussion of the principle is John Rawls, *A Theory of Justice* (Cambridge, Mass.: Harvard University Press, 1970), pp. 130–36, 177–82; and *Political Liberalism* (New York: Columbia University Press, 1993), lecture 6.

3 Corruption

Introduction

George Washington Plunkitt, the less than saintly Tammany Hall boss who dominated New York city politics in the early part of this century, made a point of distinguishing "honest graft" and "dishonest graft." He disapproved of dishonest graft, such as bribery and extortion, because no one makes "big fortunes" that way. But he saw nothing wrong with honest graft—using inside information to make a profit on a sale of land to the city. "I might sum up the whole thing by sayin': 'I seen my opportunities and took 'em'."

Although what Plunkitt called honest graft is illegal in the United States today, the spirit of the distinction between honest graft and dishonest graft, redrawn to fit modern politics, is alive and well. It survives as a distinction between legal and illegal corruption, embodied in the difference between a campaign contribution and an official bribe. A politician's taking money from wealthy contributors who expect him or her to do favors for them looks a lot like accepting a bribe and may have much the same effect. That is why some critics of the American system of campaign finance regard it as a form of corruption. But unlike bribery, the practice of accepting contributions and doing favors is an accepted, even cherished, part of the American political system. Politicians and their supporters see their opportunities and take them.

Political corruption is the improper use of public office for private purposes. The use is improper if it involves an exchange that violates standards that should govern a healthy democratic process. When a member of Congress takes a bribe in return for a political favor, the exchange serves no legitimate political purpose. The personal gain is not part of the salary, and the service is not part of the job. This is straightforward individual corruption, and because it is clearly wrong, it is relatively easy to condemn and to discipline.

But corruption can occur even if nobody acts for personal gain or shows any favoritism. In the case of "The Keating Five," a group of prominent senators were charged with improperly intervening in regulatory proceedings on behalf of a major campaign contributor. The way they pressed this contributor's case with the regulators violated standards that govern such proceedings, and the way they solicited contributions gave rise to reasonable doubts about their motives. Accepting campaign contributions from constituents while helping them with their problems is part of the job, but doing it in ways that damage the democratic process should be seen as institutional corruption.

Corruption is institutional insofar as the gain received is political rather than personal, the service provided is procedurally inappropriate, and the connection between the gain and the service tends to undermine the democratic purposes of the institution. Recognizing and punishing institutional corruption is difficult because it is so closely related to conduct that is a necessary part of institutional roles. The individuals engaging in it may even believe, as the Keating Five evidently did, that they are just doing their job and acting for the benefit of the institution. And it is often hard to pin the responsibility for any harm on particular individuals: it is easier to blame the institution.

But even if the source of the corruption is to be found mainly in defects of an institution, we can still identify individuals who helped cause the defects, took advantage of them, or at least should be held responsible for correcting them. And it is important to do so. The harm that institutional corruption causes is often greater than that produced by individual corruption. Intertwined with the duties of office, institutional corruption by its nature strikes at the core of democratic institutions. It is also more systematic and more pervasive than individual corruption, which typically consists of isolated acts of misconduct, their effects limited in time and scope.

Some of the most important ethical issues of corruption therefore center not simply on those who engage in the corruption, but on those who must decide what to do about it. In "Scandal in Santa Clara," Judy Nadler, a newcomer to the city council, believed that charges of corruption against some city officials warranted an independent investigation. But her colleagues on the council thought that the city's internal investigation, which found no serious violations, was adequate. Appreciating the dilemmas she faced and how she thought about them helps to clarify the complexities in the problem of corruption in contemporary democratic government.

The Keating Five
U.S. Senate Select Committee on Ethics

The senators who are remembered as the "Keating Five" included Democrats Dennis DeConcini (Arizona), Alan Cranston (California), John Glenn (Ohio), and Donald Riegle (Michigan) and Republican John McCain (Arizona). They had never worked together as a group before, and it is safe to assume never will again.

The Five were first brought together by

The text of this case is from the Report of the Select Committee on Ethics of the U.S. Senate, *Investigation of Senator Alan Cranston*, Nov. 20, 1991 (Washington, D.C.: U.S. Government Printing Office). Introduction copyright © 1995 by Dennis Thompson.

Charles Keating, Jr., a successful real estate financier and developer with business interests in several states. As head of a home construction company in Phoenix, Keating bought Lincoln Savings and Loan in California in 1984. Exploiting the newly relaxed regulations for thrift institutions, he shifted Lincoln's assets from home loans to high-risk real estate projects and other speculative investments. He lived lavishly at the company's expense and engaged in questionable foreign trading and stock manipulation, counting on his political connections to keep the federal and state regulators at bay. For more than five years he and his army of lawyers battled state regulators who believed that Lincoln and its parent company were violating a variety of rules governing accounting and investment practices and financial disclosure. In 1989 Lincoln collapsed, wiping out the savings of 23,000 (mostly elderly) uninsured depositors and costing federal taxpayers more than $2 billion. It was the biggest failure in what came to be the most costly financial scandal in American history. Keating himself was eventually convicted on charges of fraud and racketeering and went to prison.

But to many in the financial community during the years before the collapse, Keating was a model of the kind of financial entrepreneur that the Republican administration wished to encourage through its policy of deregulation. Many saw him as a freewheeling businessman, perhaps a little too interested in high living and a little too willing to play fast and loose with the rules, but basically an honest financier whose willingness to take risks had made lots of money for himself and those who worked for him, and provided jobs and investment opportunities for many people in the region.

Keating's most visible political lobbying was directed against a new rule prohibiting direct investment by S&Ls, which many legitimate financial institutions and members of Congress also opposed. Keating's most prominent and persistent target was Edwin Gray, the head of the three-member Federal Home Loan Bank Board that regulated the industry and a supporter of the rule. Gray was himself a controversial figure, widely regarded as an inflexible bureaucrat, well intentioned, perhaps, but unimaginative and hostile toward newcomers to the industry.

The fateful meeting that would forever link the Keating Five took place on April 2, 1987, in the early evening in DeConcini's office. The senators asked why the investigation of Lincoln and their "friend" Keating was taking so long, and they cited a letter from a managing partner of the respected

accounting firm Arthur Young that concluded that federal regulators were harassing Lincoln. (The author of the letter, Jack Atchison, went to work for Keating a year later.)

Gray claimed that the senators proposed a deal: if he would abolish the direct investment rule, Keating would move Lincoln back into traditional home loans. Gray, who was desperately seeking more funds from Congress to take over troubled S&Ls, said he was intimidated by this "show of force." The senators deny that any deal was proposed. Gray suggested that the senators could talk directly to the regulators in San Francisco, which they did a week later. In that meeting, several of the senators, particularly DeConcini, pressed Keating's case vigorously, but as the regulators revealed more and more unfavorable information about Lincoln, the tone of the meeting began to change. The revelation that the examiners were about to make a criminal referral against Lincoln appeared to cause the senators to become more cautious.

After the meeting none of the five had any more contact with Ed Gray or the San Francisco regulators. McCain and Riegle had no further dealings with Keating. McCain had already broken off relations with Keating, who had called him a wimp for refusing to put pressure on the Bank Board. Glenn arranged a brief lunch the following January. Cranston and DeConcini continued to act on Keating's behalf. During a two-month period in early 1989 Cranston approached regulators at least six times (once in an early morning phone call to a Bank Board member at home) to express his interest in the proposed sale of Lincoln. (To satisfy regulators, Keating had agreed to sell Lincoln, but the buyers turned out to be his business associates.) DeConcini, who had lobbied for Keating causes in earlier years, also called state and federal regulators repeatedly about the sale of Lincoln.

The Keating Five, especially DeConcini and Cranston, provided this constituent with good service. What did the senators get in return? $1.3 million in campaign contributions. But this figure obscures some important details, in particular the timing and uses of the funds, that should affect any assessment of corruption. Cranston received the bulk of the contributions (almost $1 million), most of it in 1987 and 1988 while he was actively intervening for Keating. But the money primarily went to voter registration groups, the largest portion to the felicitously named Center for Participation in Democracy, headed by Cranston's son.

McCain and Glenn received the largest totals in campaign and political action committee funds, but all well before (in McCain's case five years before) Keating enlisted their help with his problems at Lincoln. Riegle and DeConcini solicited contributions while intervening for Keating. Riegle received $78,250 and DeConcini $48,000 in direct contributions to their 1988 campaigns. Keating had also given contributions to DeConcini earlier and had committed himself to raise larger amounts in the future. In addition, Keating often acted as a broker for others and sometimes as a "bundler," taking "the separate individual contributions and bundling them together . . . claiming credit for the harvest." All the contributions were technically within legal limits.

In February 1991, the ethics committee rebuked four of the senators. DeConcini and Riegle received a more severe scolding than McCain and Glenn and announced their retirement two and one-half years later. Cranston's conduct was more serious, the committee said, and it warranted further action. (Ironically, it was Cranston who had been one of the earliest and strongest advocates of campaign finance reform in congressional elections.) In November, after much behind-the-scenes negotiation, the committee reported to the full Senate that Cranston had "violated established norms of behavior in the Senate." To avoid a stronger resolution by the committee (which

would have required a Senate vote), Cranston formally accepted the reprimand. In a dramatic speech on the floor he also claimed that he had done nothing worse than most of his Senate colleagues had done.

THE COMMITTEE'S CONCLUSIONS FROM THE PRELIMINARY INQUIRIES

A. CONCLUSIONS GENERALLY APPLICABLE

1. Intervention in the Administration Process

It is a necessary function of a Senator's office to intervene with officials of the executive branch and independent regulatory agencies on behalf of individuals when the facts warrant, and it is a Senator's duty to make decisions on whether to intervene without regard to whether those requesting the assistance have contributed to the Senator's campaigns or causes. Ample evidence was received during the hearings which showed that Senators should and do provide such essential constituent services.

In this case, each of the Senators under inquiry had information that reasonably caused concern about the fairness of the Federal Home Loan Bank's examination of Lincoln Savings and Loan Association (Lincoln), and which was sufficient to justify the Senators contacting Bank Board personnel. In addition, there are many reasons why a Senator may intervene on behalf of an individual including, but not limited to, the fact that the individual is a constituent.

Each of these Senators also had a legitimate interest which justified his involvement on Mr. Keating's behalf. As a resident of Arizona, Mr. Keating was a constituent of Senator DeConcini and Senator McCain. Moreover, Mr. Keating's company, American Continental Corporation [ACC] (parent company of Lincoln), employed approximately 2,000 Arizona residents and was the largest homebuilder in their state. Senator Cranston had an interest as a Member of the Banking Committee and because Lincoln employed hundreds, and held the deposits of thousands, of people in California. Senator Riegle also had an interest as a Member of the Banking Committee. In addition, ACC had invested approximately 37 million dollars in a downtown Detroit hotel and had plans to pursue another significant Detroit development project. Finally, with respect to Senator Glenn, Mr. Keating was an Ohio native and ACC was an Ohio chartered corporation.

The degree of intervention with the regulators varied as to each Senator. The evidence clearly shows that their contacts with federal regulators regarding Lincoln did not cause the eventual failure of Lincoln or the thrift industry in general, nor does the evidence establish that their contacts affected the regulators' treatment of Lincoln.

Prior to April 1987, four of the Senators took actions supported or sought by Mr. Keating. Senators Cranston, DeConcini, Glenn, and McCain officially expressed opposition to or raised question about the adoption of a "Direct Investment Rule," promulgated by the Federal Home Loan Bank Board (FHLBB). This Rule was opposed by many Members of Congress and a large number of thrift organizations. Senators DeConcini and McCain contacted the executive branch regarding the nomination of former IRS Commissioner, Lee Henkel, to the FHLBB. Senator DeConcini also supported Mr. Keating's appointment as ambassador to the Bahamas and complained to the White House about Mr. Edwin Gray's directorship of the Federal Home Loan Bank Board.

The Committee has concluded that, when considered in and of themselves and without regard to any contribution or other benefit, the opposition expressed or the question raised about the Direct Investment Rule, contacts relating to the Henkel nomination, the Keating ambassadorship, and Mr. Gray's directorship did not constitute improper conduct.

There were two meetings between Federal Home Loan Bank officials and groups of Senators. The first was on April 2, 1987 between Federal Home Loan Bank Board Chairman Edwin Gray, and Senators Cranston, DeConcini, Glenn, and McCain and ended when Chairman Gray advised the Senators that he had no knowledge about the Lincoln examination being conducted by the San Francisco Federal Home Loan Bank (FHLB) and suggested that they could obtain the information they sought from the San Francisco FHLB regulators.

One week later, on April 9, 1987, there was a second meeting in Washington between four representatives of the San Francisco Federal Home Loan Bank and Senators DeConcini, Glenn, McCain, and Riegle, with Senator Cranston making a one-minute appearance. The Committee finds that, when considered without regard to any contribution or other benefit, no Senator violated any law or Senate rule or engaged in improper conduct by attending these meetings.

Following these two meetings, neither Senator McCain nor Senator Riegle took any action on behalf of Lincoln.

On January 28, 1988, almost ten months after the April meetings, Senator Glenn was host at a luncheon meeting he arranged for Mr. Charles Keating to meet House Speaker Jim Wright.

Between February and mid-April 1989, Senator DeConcini made telephone calls to FHLBB members and other regulatory officials urging prompt consideration of applications for the sale of Lincoln.

In 1987, following the April meetings, and in 1988, Senator Cranston set up meetings between FHLBB Chairman M. Danny Wall and Mr. Keating, and made several telephone inquiries to Chairman Wall on behalf of Lincoln. In 1989, Senator Cranston made calls to FHLB Board members and other regulatory officials urging consideration of applications for the sale of Lincoln.

The Committee finds that, when considered in and of themselves and without regard to any contribution or other benefit, none of the activities of Senator Cranston, Senator DeConcini, or Senator Glenn concerning Mr. Keating or Lincoln, following the April 1987 meetings, violated any law or Senate rule or were improper.

2. Official Actions and Campaign Contributions

While the Committee has concluded that none of the Senators' actions described above, when considered in and of themselves and without regard to any contribution or other benefit, violated any law or Senate rule, each act must also be examined against more general ethical standards to determine if there was any impropriety because of any relation between those actions and campaign contributions or other benefits provided by Mr. Keating and his associates.

It is a fact of life that candidates for the Senate must solicit and receive assistance in their campaigns, including the raising of campaign funds. Such fund raising is authorized and regulated by law, and contributions and expenditures under the Federal Election Campaign Act are required to be publicly disclosed. Furthermore, contributions under the Federal Election Campaign Act are not personal gifts to candidates.

Based on all the available evidence, the Committee has concluded that in the case of each of the five Senators, all campaign contributions from Mr. Keating and his associates under the Federal Election Campaign Act were within the established legal limits and were properly reported. Similarly, from the available evidence, the Committee concludes that the Senators' solicitation or acceptance of all contributions made in these cases to state party organizations were, standing alone, not illegal or improper; nor did any such contribution constitute a personal gift to any Senator.

Moreover, the Committee concludes that the contributions received by Senators De-

Concini, Glenn, McCain and Riegle were not improperly linked to the actions taken by each Senator. The fact that a Senator has received substantial contributions from an individual does not disqualify that person from receiving assistance.

3. Recommendation for a Bi-partisan Task Force on Constituent Service

As noted earlier in this report, the Senate has no written standards embodied in the Senate Rules specifically respecting contact or intervention with federal executive or independent regulatory agency officials.

The Committee, believing that the Senate should adopt written standards in this area, proposed that a bi-partisan Senate Task Force be created for this purpose. This was done on April 16, 1991.

4. Recommendation for Bi-partisan Campaign Reform

The inquiries in these five cases have shown the obvious ethical dilemmas inherent in the current system by which political activities are financed. The Committee notes that more than 80 percent of the funds at issue were not funds raised by candidates for Senate or House campaigns under the Federal Election Campaign Act. Rather, such funds were undisclosed, unregulated funds raised for private organizations with political activities, political party "soft money" and a non-federal political action committee. Any campaign finance reform measure will have to address these mechanisms for political activities, as well as campaign fund raising and expenditures directly by candidates, in order to deal meaningfully and effectively with the issues presented in these cases.

The Committee urges the leadership and Members of both the Senate and the House to continue their efforts, working together in a bi-partisan manner to address the urgent need for comprehensive campaign finance reform. The reputation and honor of our institutions demand it.

B. THE COMMITTEE'S CONCLUSIONS AS TO
   SENATOR DECONCINI

Mr. Keating, his associates, and his friends contributed $31,000 to Senator De-Concini's 1982 Senatorial Campaign and $54,000 to his 1988 Senatorial Campaign. As noted in Section IIIA(1), and fully explored in the hearing record, from 1981–1989, Senator DeConcini took actions on Mr. Keating's behalf or at his request. The Committee finds that Senator DeConcini had a basis for each of these actions independent of the contributions he received from Mr. Keating, his associates and friends.

Based on the evidence available to it, the Committee has given consideration to Senator DeConcini's actions on behalf of Lincoln. Aggressive conduct by Senators in dealing with regulatory agencies is something appropriate and necessary. However, the Committee concludes that, given that Senator DeConcini knew that Mr. Keating had not been forthcoming with him in the past and that he had accepted substantial campaign contributions from Mr. Keating and his associates, it was inappropriate for Senator DeConcini to be as aggressive as he was in pursuing Lincoln's cause without making a more thorough inquiry into the merits of Mr. Keating's allegations. The Committee further concludes that Senator DeConcini's contacting the Bank Board employees and California regulators after the April 9, 1987 meeting where he learned of the criminal referral, was not improper in and of itself.

While the Committee concludes that Senator DeConcini has violated no law of the United States or specific Rule of the United States Senate, it emphasizes that it does not condone his conduct. The Committee has concluded that the totality of the evidence shows that Senator DeConcini's conduct gave the appearance of being improper and was certainly attended with insensitivity and poor judgment. However, the Committee finds that his conduct did not reach a level requiring institutional action.

The Committee therefore concludes that no further action is warranted with respect to Senator DeConcini on the matters investigated during the preliminary inquiry.

C. THE COMMITTEE'S CONCLUSIONS AS TO
   SENATOR GLENN

Mr. Keating contributed a total of $200,000 in corporate funds to the nonfederal account of Senator Glenn's multicandidate PAC in 1985 and 1986. Mr. Keating, his associates, and his friends contributed $24,000 for Senator Glenn's Senatorial Campaign, and $18,200 for the Presidential Campaign. Senator Glenn received no contribution from or through Mr. Keating after February 1986.

As noted in Section III(A)(1), and fully explored in the hearing record, from 1984–1988, Senator Glenn took actions on Mr. Keating's behalf or at his request. The Committee finds that Senator Glenn had a basis for each of these actions independent of the contributions he received from ACC, Mr. Keating, his associates, and friends.

Based on the evidence available to it, the Committee has given consideration to Senator Glenn's actions on behalf of Lincoln Savings & Loan Association. The Committee concludes that Senator Glenn, although believing that the Lincoln matter was in the process of resolution, exercised poor judgment in arranging a luncheon meeting between Mr. Keating and Speaker Wright on January 2, 1988, almost ten months after Senator Glenn learned of the criminal referral. There is disputed evidence as to whether Lincoln's problems with the Federal Home Loan Bank Board (FHLBB) were discussed at that meeting. The evidence indicates that Senator Glenn's participation did not go beyond serving as host. The Committee further concludes that Senator Glenn's actions were not improper or attended with gross negligence and did not reach the level requiring institutional action against him.

Senator Glenn has violated no law of the United States or specific Rule of the United

States Senate; therefore, the Committee concludes that no further action is warranted with respect to Senator Glenn on the matters investigated during the preliminary inquiry.

D. THE COMMITTEE'S CONCLUSIONS AS TO SENATOR MCCAIN

Mr. Keating, his associates, and his friends contributed $56,000 for Senator McCain's two House races in 1982 and 1984, and $54,000 for his 1986 Senate race. Mr. Keating also provided his corporate plane and/or arranged for payment for the use of commercial or private aircraft on several occasions for travel by Senator McCain and his family, for which Senator McCain ultimately provided reimbursement when called upon to do so. Mr. Keating also allowed Senator McCain and his family to vacation with Mr. Keating and his family, at a home provided by Mr. Keating in the Bahamas, in each of the calendar years 1983 through 1986.

As noted in Section IIIA(1) and fully explored in the hearing record, from 1984 to 1987, Senator McCain took actions on Mr. Keating's behalf or at his request. The Committee finds that Senator McCain has a basis for each of these actions independent of the contributions and benefits he received from Mr. Keating, his associates and friends.

Based on the evidence available to it, the Committee has given consideration to Senator McCain's actions on behalf of Lincoln. The Committee concludes that, given the personal benefits and campaign contributions he had received from Mr. Keating, Senator McCain exercised poor judgment in intervening with the regulators without first inquiring as to the Bank Board's position in the case in a more routine manner. The Committee concludes that Senator McCain's actions were not improper nor attended with gross negligence and did not reach the level of requiring institutional action against him. The Committee finds that Senator McCain took no further action after

the April 9, 1987 meeting when he learned of the criminal referral.

The Committee reaffirms its prior decision that it does not have jurisdiction to determine the issues of disclosure or reimbursement pertaining to flights provided by American Continental Corporation while Senator McCain was a Member of the House of Representatives. The Committee did consider the effect of such on his state of mind and judgment in taking steps to assist Lincoln.

Senator McCain has violated no law of the United States or specific Rule of the United States Senate; therefore, the Committee concludes that no further action is warranted with respect to Senator McCain on the matters investigated during the preliminary inquiry.

E. THE COMMITTEE'S CONCLUSIONS AS TO SENATOR RIEGLE

Mr. Keating organized and hosted a Riegle re-election campaign fund raising event in March 1987 in Detroit at his company's Pontchartrain Hotel. As a result of Mr. Keating's efforts, approximately $78,250 was raised from Keating associates and friends for Senator Riegle's 1988 campaign.

As noted in Section III(A)(1), and fully explored in the hearing record, Senator Riegle took actions on Mr. Keating's behalf in early 1987. The Committee finds that Senator Riegle had a basis for these actions independent of the fund raiser that Mr. Keating held for him.

Based on the evidence available to it, the Committee has given consideration to Senator Riegle's actions on behalf of Lincoln. The Committee finds that Senator Riegle took steps to assist Lincoln with its regulatory problems at a time when Mr. Keating was raising substantial campaign funds for Senator Riegle. During the course of the hearings, possible conflicts arose concerning actions on the part of Senator Riegle that caused the Committee concern, but the

Committee finds that the evidence indicates no deliberate intent to deceive. The evidence shows that Senator Riegle took no further action after the April 9, 1987 meeting where he learned of the criminal referral.

While the Committee concludes that Senator Riegle has violated no law of the United States or specific Rule of the United States Senate, it emphasizes that it does not condone his conduct. The Committee has concluded that the totality of the evidence shows that Senator Riegle's conduct gave the appearance of being improper and was certainly attended with insensitivity and poor judgment. However, the Committee finds that his conduct did not reach a level requiring institutional action.

The Committee concludes that no further action is warranted with respect to Senator Riegle on the matters investigated during the preliminary inquiry.

THE COMMITTEE'S CONCLUSION FROM THE INVESTIGATION OF SENATOR CRANSTON

A. THE COMMITTEE'S FINDINGS

The Committee finds that Senator Cranston engaged in improper conduct that may reflect upon the Senate, pursuant to Section 2(a)(l) of S. Res. 338, 88th Congress. Based on the totality of circumstances including those surrounding four specific incidents in which Senator Cranston solicited or accepted contributions from Mr. Keating's companies, as well as evidence regarding Senator Cranston's fund raising and constituent service practices in general, the Committee finds that Senator Cranston engaged in an impermissible pattern of conduct in which fund raising and official activities were substantially linked. The Committee finds that this conduct was improper.

The Committee finds that from early 1987 through April 1989, Senator Cranston personally, or through staff, contacted the Bank Board on behalf of Lincoln approximately a dozen times, and that during this same period, Senator Cranston solicited or accepted from Mr. Keating's companies contributions totalling $850,000 to voter registration groups with which Senator Cranston was closely affiliated. As discussed in detail below, the Committee has identified four separate occasions when Senator Cranston solicited or accepted contributions from Mr. Keating at times when he knew that Mr. Keating recently had requested or received the Senator's assistance for Lincoln.

The Committee further finds that Senator Cranston's office practices evidenced an impermissible pattern of conduct by substantially linking fund raising and official activities. By condoning and participating in such practices, Senator Cranston engaged in improper conduct.

Although much of this conduct was engaged in by staff, in particular by his chief fund raiser, Joy Jacobson, often the staff acted with Senator Cranston's knowledge and permission, and often at his direction or with his participation. At the time of the events under investigation, Ms. Jacobson was not a member of Senator Cranston's Senate staff, nor did she have any official Senate duties or substantive expertise, other than her fund raising duties. However, as detailed below, she scheduled and attended meetings between Senator Cranston and contributors in which legislative or regulatory issues were discussed, and served as an intermediary for Mr. Keating or Mr. Grogan when they could not reach the Senator or the Senator's aide on the Banking Committee, Carolyn Jordan.

Senator Cranston also received several memoranda from Ms. Jacobson which evidenced her understanding that contributors were entitled to special attention and special access to official services. Senator Cranston never told her that her understanding was incorrect, nor did he inform her that such a connection between contributions and official actions was improper.

B. THE EVIDENCE UNDERLYING THE
COMMITTEE'S FINDINGS

1. Benefits Provided by Mr. Keating

In total, Mr. Keating raised approximately $994,000 for organizations closely affiliated with Senator Cranston. In addition to the contributions discussed below, Mr. Keating provided $49,000 to Senator Cranston's 1984 presidential and 1986 Senate campaigns, $85,000 to the California Democratic Party in the fall of 1986, and made available a $300,000 line of credit which was ultimately never drawn upon.

As noted below and fully explored in the hearing record, from 1984 to 1989 Senator Cranston also took actions on Mr. Keating's behalf or at his request. The Committee finds that Senator Cranston had a basis for each of these actions independent of the contributions he received from ACC, Mr. Keating, his associate, and his friends.

2. Evidence Regarding Senator Cranston's Solicitation and Acceptance of Contributions and Official Actions

The evidence demonstrates that between February 1987 and February 1988, at a time when Senator Cranston was intervening actively with federal regulators at the request of Mr. Keating, Mr. Keating's companies contributed $850,000 to voter registration groups closely affiliated with Senator Cranston. The evidence regarding these contributions, as well as an additional solicitation by Senator Cranston in 1989, reveals a pattern of substantial contributions from Mr. Keating being linked to Senator Cranston's actions on behalf of Lincoln. On each of four separate occasions, Senator Cranston took official action on behalf of Lincoln and solicited or accepted contributions in a manner which demonstrated an impermissible pattern of conduct where official activities and fund raising were substantially linked. In light of the seriousness of the charges against Senator Cranston, the evi-

dence regarding these occasions is reviewed in detail:

a. Early 1987. On January 2, 1987, Joy Jacobson, the Senator's fund raiser, wrote the following memorandum to Senator Cranston:

> Cases/Legislation: Now that we are back in the majority there are a number of individuals who have been very helpful to you who have cases or legislative matters pending with our office who will rightfully expect some kind of resolution.
>
> * * * *
>
> Charlie Keating: Is continuing to have problems with the Bank Board and Ed Gray. Jim Grogan and the company's legal counsel, Bob Kielty, are coming to see you on Friday at 1:00 p.m. to get your advice on how to handle the current problem.

This meeting was rescheduled to January 28, 1987, when Senator Cranston met with Mr. Keating and Mr. Grogan to discuss Lincoln's problems with the Bank Board.

On February 24, 1987, Senator Cranston attended a meeting of members and contributors to America Votes, the predecessor to USA Votes, a partisan voter registration organization of which Senator Cranston was co-chairman. At the meeting, Senator Cranston announced that he had secured a commitment of a $100,000 donation to America Votes. Following the meeting, Senator Cranston told the organization's Executive Director, Robert Stein, that the $100,000 commitment to America Votes came from Mr. Keating. On March 3, 1987, Lincoln contributed $100,000 to America Votes. On April 2, 1987, Senator Cranston and three other Senators met with Chairman Gray on behalf of Lincoln. The following week, he made a brief appearance at the April 9 meeting between four other Senators and the San Francisco regulators.

b. Fall 1987. According to Federal Home Loan Bank Board Chairman Danny Wall, Senator Cranston contacted him about Lincoln in July or August 1987 very soon after he became Chairman of the Bank Board on July 1, 1987. Senator Cranston called to urge that a prompt decision be made on the Lincoln examination.

On September 6, 1987, Ms. Jacobson wrote Senator Cranston a memorandum to prepare him for a meeting with Mr. Keating. She attached a press clipping about new Bank Board Chairman Wall, noting that his views "obviously are good news to Keating." She added, "You should ask Keating for $250,000."

On September 24, 1987, Chairman Wall met with Mr. Keating and told him "that the Bank Board would take a fresh look at the San Francisco examination." Later that same day, at a meeting in his Whip office, Senator Cranston asked Mr. Keating for $250,000 for voter registration groups. A follow-up letter from Senator Cranston, dated October 6, 1987, indicates that at that meeting the two discussed both Senator Cranston's request for $250,000 and Mr. Keating's meeting with Chairman Wall.

On November 6, 1987, Mr. Grogan personally delivered checks totaling $250,000 for voter registration organizations from Mr. Keating's company ACC to Senator Cranston in the Whip's office. Senator Cranston's calendar contains the following notation for that date: "Jim Grogan $250,000—$25 to USA Votes/225 to Forum." Moments after receiving this money, Senator Cranston and Mr. Grogan called Mr. Keating on a speaker telephone. Mr. Grogan testified that Mr. Keating requested that Senator Cranston call Chairman Wall on his behalf to set up a meeting with Chairman Wall and that Senator Cranston said he would be happy to do so. Senator Cranston's notes reflect that he called Chairman Wall six days later, on November 12, 1987, and Chairman Wall told him that there were "personality problems" between Lincoln and the San Francisco regulators. Senator Cranston stated that such problems should not be allowed to cause difficulties. Senator Cranston testified that he made a status inquiry of Chairman Wall but that he does

not believe that he requested that Chairman Wall meet with Mr. Keating.

c. Early 1988. On January 8, 1988, Senator Cranston, his son Kim Cranston, Mr. Keating and Mr. Grogan dined at Jimmy's Restaurant in Los Angeles. Kim Cranston was the unsalaried President and a member of the Board of Directors of the Center for Participation in Democracy, a non-profit California organization whose purpose was to increase voter registration and participation. Kim Cranston attended the dinner to discuss fund raising for voter registration groups, and Mr. Keating volunteered to make additional contributions to voter registration groups. Mr. Keating also complained about the Bank Board and, either at this meeting or shortly thereafter, asked Senator Cranston to call Chairman Wall to arrange a meeting.

At the dinner, Mr. Keating told Senator Cranston that a former Federal Home Loan Bank Board Member, Don Hovde, had told Mr. Keating that Chairman Gray was "out to get him." Senator Cranston asked Mr. Keating for Mr. Hovde's number so that he could call him. Later, Mr. Grogan called Ms. Jacobson to advise her of what had occurred at the dinner and to provide Mr. Hovde's telephone number. On January 18, 1988, Ms. Jacobson wrote Senator Cranston a four page memorandum which included a paragraph reminding Senator Cranston of Mr. Keating's request that he call Chairman Wall. Senator Cranston called Chairman Wall two days later, on January 20, to ask that he meet with Mr. Keating. Chairman Wall agreed to do so. Senator Cranston reported this conversation to Mr. Keating and told Mr. Keating that he could call Chairman Wall. Mr. Keating met with Chairman Wall on January 28, 1988.

Senator Cranston and his son visited ACC's headquarters in Phoenix on February 9 and 10, 1988. While Senator Cranston was visiting ACC, Mr. Keating personally handed him $500,000 in contributions for two voter registration groups affiliated with Senator Cranston.

Senator Cranston called Chairman Wall on February 16, 1988. He testified that he did not believe this telephone call was related to Lincoln. However, Senator Cranston's notes of this conversation reference a three-year business plan that appears to be the plan described in a draft Memorandum of Understanding prepared by Lincoln on February 12, 1988.

On May 5, 1988, the Bank Board voted to enter into a supervisory agreement with Lincoln and directed its staff to negotiate a Memorandum of Understanding with Lincoln. Mr. Grogan contacted Carolyn Jordan. Ms. Jordan then spoke with two high-ranking Bank Board officials. According to her memorandum to Senator Cranston recounting this conversation, she told the officials that Senator Cranston was concerned about the Board's decision to take the "supervisory approach." The Bank Board officials advised her that Senator Cranston should "wait until after the discussions with Mr. Keating and his lawyers next week before taking any action." Bank Board officials also told Ms. Jordan that Mr. Keating would have another opportunity to convince them that action was unnecessary and that the Bank Board's order "is not in writing and is subject to some degree of negotiation." At the end of her memorandum to Senator Cranston, Ms. Jordan noted, "You should call Danny Wall on this."

Senator Cranston met with Chairman Wall on May 16, 1988. Chairman Wall testified that Senator Cranston asked him during this meeting when a decision would be made concerning Lincoln, but did not suggest a course of action. After Chairman Wall's testimony, Senator Cranston submitted an affidavit that stated that he now believed he did "inquire as to the status of the Lincoln matter" but did not urge a particular resolution. On May 20, 1988, Lincoln entered into an agreement with the Bank Board.

Neither Senator Cranston nor Ms. Jacob-

son solicited or received any contributions at the time of the May contacts.

d. The Sale of Lincoln. On December 14, 1988, Senator Cranston, Ms. Jordan, Mr. Grogan, and Mr. Keating met for dinner at the Bel Air Hotel in Los Angeles. According to Mr. Grogan, the meeting was set up so that Mr. Keating could bring Senator Cranston up to date on where he stood with the regulators and inform him that he had decided to sell Lincoln Savings. According to Mr. Grogan, Senator Cranston "came up and patted Mr. Keating on the back, and said 'ah, the mutual aid society.'"

On January 28, 1989, Mr. Grogan, his wife and other ACC officials attended a fund raiser for Senator Cranston's political action committee. ACC contributed $10,000 to the PAC.

On February 7, 1989, Senator Cranston, Ms. Jordan, Laurie Sedlmayr and Gene Harp of Senator DeConcini's staff, and Kevin Gottlieb of the Banking Committee staff attended a briefing by Mr. Grogan which provided details on a proposed sale of Lincoln for which Bank Board approval was required. Mr. Grogan testified that he and Mr. Keating wanted Senators to understand the terms of the deal so "that there wouldn't be opposition to it." Ms. Jordan testified that Mr. Grogan informed them that negotiations with the Bank Board had broken down and requested that the Senators call the Bank Board to get things going again. Ms. Jordan testified that on February 8 she called Darrel Dochow of the FHLBB to clarify what Mr. Grogan had told them at the meeting and to inquire about the sale.

Between February 8 and April 14, 1989, while the sale of Lincoln was pending, Senator Cranston made at least six calls to regulators and met once with Chairman Wall to encourage prompt consideration of Lincoln sale proposals. Senator Cranston reported conversations with Bank Board members to Mr. Keating. The Senator's notes also indicate that in both the calls to the Bank Board and to Mr. Keating, he discussed the terms of the proposed sales and what would be needed to make them work.

On April 8, 1989, Mr. Keating sent a facsimile to Senator Cranston urging him to take action in an effort to get the pending proposed sale approved. Senator Cranston testified that he saw this facsimile at the time it was sent and continued to make calls on Mr. Keating's behalf, but he did not urge approval of the sale.

Chairman Wall testified that he did not consider these calls to be improper. Chairman Wall stated in his affidavit, however, that in his experience it was "unusual for a Senator to place so many telephone calls to me with regard to a single savings and loan institution."

On April 12, 1989, Senator Cranston called Federal Home Loan Bank Board Member Martin between 10 and 11 P.M. at his unlisted home number. According to Mr. Martin, Senator Cranston told him that Mr. John Rousselot, head of the pending buyers group, wanted to meet with the Board because he believed the proposed acquisition was not getting a fair hearing from the Board's Office of Regulatory Affairs. Senator Cranston recalls calling Mr. Martin, but does not recall whether he asked Mr. Martin to meet with Mr. Rousselot.

Mr. Martin testified that Senator Cranston did not state whether he felt the proposed acquisition should be approved or whether the Board should look favorably or unfavorably on the proposal. He also testified that there was nothing improper about the substance of these calls, but he found the calls "highly unusual." Mr. Martin met with Mr. Rousselot for breakfast the following morning.

Senator Cranston testified that there was some urgency to his call to Mr. Martin on April 12, 1989 because the Bank Board was going to meet about the sale on April 13, 1989 and it was "either going to be resolved or there would be a disaster." The Senator's notes of that date indicate that he had been informed by Mr. Keating that bankruptcy

was imminent, and that if ACC declared bankruptcy, 40,000 to 50,000 California citizens would lose $200 million.

On April 13, 1989, Senator Cranston also called Bank Board Member Lawrence White about the Lincoln sale.

During this time, Joy Jacobson or Senator Cranston also spoke with Mr. Keating or Mr. Grogan about making an additional $100,000 contribution to voter registration organizations. Ms. Jacobson wrote Senator Cranston a memorandum on March 1, 1989 which included the statement, "Charlie Keating—Joy is talking with Jim Grogan[.] 100,000 wherever its [sic] needed." According to Ms. Jacobson, Mr. Grogan told her that Lincoln could not consider making such a contribution while the sale of Lincoln was pending. Ms. Jacobson did not inform Senator Cranston of Mr. Grogan's unwillingness to contribute until the sale was resolved. Senator Cranston does not recall any conversation regarding this $100,000 contribution. No contribution was subsequently made.

3. Evidence Regarding Senator Cranston's Fund Raising Practices

The evidence demonstrates that Senator Cranston engaged in a pattern and practice of mixing fund raising and substantive legislative or regulatory issues. Although this practice was largely carried out by staff, Senator Cranston condoned, supervised, or participated in it.

Ms. Jacobson authored memoranda which mixed discussions of fund raising and substantive issues, and revealed an attitude that contributors were entitled to special access to and actions from the Senator. Senator Cranston allowed her to attend meetings between him and contributors, the purpose of which was to discuss the contributor's legislative or regulatory problems. She did so despite having no substantive experience or responsibility and not being a Senate staff member. For example, she recalled being present at a meeting between Senator Cranston, representatives of Lincoln and the economist Alan Greenspan, the purpose of which was to discuss the Direct Investment Rule. Unlike some Senate employees who, in addition to substantive legislative or constituent service duties, are designated to solicit and accept contributions, Ms. Jacobson had no reason to be at these meetings other than as part of her fund raising duties. She attended these meetings, according to Senator Cranston, because she would be more effective in fund raising if she knew what problems constituents or potential contributors have.

Senator Cranston also permitted Ms. Jacobson to act as an intermediary between him and his legislative staff and contributors seeking his office's assistance. Sometimes when Mr. Keating or Mr. Grogan sought an appointment with Senator Cranston, Mr. Grogan would contact Ms. Jacobson at her home office and request an appointment. She then would put Mr. Grogan "on hold," call Senator Cranston's scheduler and schedule the meeting. Similarly, Ms. Jacobson acted as an intermediary for Mr. Keating and Mr. Grogan when they were unable to get through to Senator Cranston or Ms. Jordan, seeking assistance on substantive issues.

An example of Ms. Jacobson's pattern of mixing fund raising and substantive issues occurred in October 1986 when she was the Finance Chairman of Senator Cranston's re-election campaign. At that time, Mr. Grogan tried to reach Ms. Jordan about an amendment being considered on the Senate floor that Lincoln vigorously opposed. Unable to reach Ms. Jordan, he contacted Ms. Jacobson. Ms. Jacobson called Mr. Grogan back to report that she had spoken to Ms. Jordan and alerted her to the amendment. Ms. Jacobson told Mr. Grogan that Ms. Jordan was in touch with another lobbyist who knew the issue. Ms. Jacobson then said that she "want[ed] to switch gears" to a "totally unrelated" subject. She asked Mr. Grogan for a $300,000 loan to Senator Cranston for

his re-election campaign. Ultimately, a $300,000 line of credit at market rate was arranged for the Cranston re-election campaign but was subsequently canceled without being used.

Senator Cranston is directly responsible for Ms. Jacobson's fund raising activities. As the recipient of her memoranda and having attended substantive meetings at which she was present, he was fully aware of her practices. Senator Cranston never informed Ms. Jacobson of any prohibition against the solicitation of funds on Senate property. He never directed Ms. Jacobson not to mix fund raising and substantive issues in memoranda to him, although he said that "perhaps" he should have done so. He never discouraged Ms. Jacobson from attending substantive meetings with contributors. In fact, Senator Cranston participated in discussions in which Mr. Keating's substantive problems were linked with fund raising. Mr. Grogan testified that:

> [w]e would have those substantive discussions, and after those substantive discussions, normally, as we were leaving, either Mr. Keating would say, is there any way I can help you, Senator. I appreciate our relationship. Or at times, Senator Cranston would say could you help in this area, could you help raise money here, could you do that. After these kinds of meetings, Mr. Keating would generally follow up either with Joy Jacobson or with Senator Cranston. So there were meetings where substance and fund raising were discussed in the same meetings.

However, when Mr. Grogan was asked:

> "Was there any suggestion, either by word or by body language, or by raised eyebrow, that Senator Cranston's interest in Lincoln Savings' problems was tied to Mr. Keating's support of the non-profit voter registration efforts?"

Mr. Grogan responded: "Never."

C. THE STANDARDS THAT THE COMMITTEE APPLIED

The Committee has based its determination that Senator Cranston engaged in improper conduct upon its analysis of relevant statutes, resolutions, the history of Senate disciplinary cases, and established norms of Senate behavior, including the standards of individual Senators as reflected in their actual conduct. All of these sources provide notice to Senators of their ethical obligations in conducting their activities. The Committee concludes that certain standards govern the ethical propriety of accepting political contributions and taking official action on behalf of the contributor, and that Senator Cranston's behavior violated these standards.

Senators are obligated to honor the public trust and to respect the laws designed to protect the integrity of the legislative process and maintain the American people's confidence that public officials are acting in the public interest. The bribery statute, for example, prohibits a public official from corruptly accepting anything of value, personally or for anyone else, in exchange for being influenced in the performance of any official act. The Committee has not made a finding that Senator Cranston violated the bribery statute because it requires a corrupt *quid pro quo*, which the Committee did not find. No evidence was presented to the Committee that Senator Cranston ever agreed to help Mr. Keating in return for a contribution. Furthermore, Senator Cranston had a valid reason to be concerned with Lincoln's problems given the numerous California employees and depositors which would be affected by the failure of Lincoln.

However, conduct which does not constitute a violation of criminal law nonetheless can constitute "improper conduct which may reflect upon the Senate" pursuant to S. Res. 338. The evidence before the Committee shows that Senator Cranston impermissibly linked his official activities and fund raising.

In reaching its conclusion that established norms of Senate behavior do not permit linkage between a Senator's official actions and his fund raising activities, the Committee also considered the hearing testimony of several Senators about actions which they have taken to translate general ethical principles into office practices designed to avoid such linkage.

Senator Cranston disregarded these standards of conduct by linking, by time and other circumstance, the solicitation and receipt of contributions from Mr. Keating with official action on behalf of Lincoln.

This Committee recently addressed the linking of campaign contributions and official actions. In Interpretative Ruling 427, this Committee stated that Senators should not offer access to policy discussions or access to Senate services in return for campaign contributions.

This standard does not prohibit a Senator from providing constituent service for a contributor. It does, however, impose a special obligation on that Senator to guard the public trust in that Senator, the Senate, and the governmental processes by ensuring that the service is being provided because the Senator reasonably believes it is in the public interest or the cause of equity or justice to do so, and not because the individual is a contributor. Senators may endeavor to meet this special obligation in a number of ways, for example, by establishing office practices indicating that only constituent cases that they or their staffs reasonably believe have merit will be pursued. Senator Cranston did not meet this special obligation.

D. SENATOR CRANSTON'S DEFENSES

1. Senator Cranston Contends That There Is No Evidence That Mr. Keating's Contributions Caused His Actions on Mr. Keating's Behalf

Senator Cranston contends that his conduct cannot be deemed improper absent a finding that Mr. Keating's contributions caused him to take official action on Mr. Keating's behalf, action that he would not otherwise have taken. Senator Cranston's standard requiring a "causal connection" between a contribution and official action appears to equate impropriety with illegality. This position fails to recognize that conduct that does not constitute illegal behavior may still be improper.

Senator Cranston's view of what constitutes improper conduct is at odds with the plain language of this Committee's authorizing legislation and is contradictory to the history of Senate disciplinary proceedings. Senate Resolution 338 confers on this Committee authority to investigate and recommend disciplinary action to the full Senate for violations of laws, Senate Rules and "improper conduct which may reflect upon the Senate." Moreover, the Committee is not required to find causation in order to find improper conduct.

As discussed above, there is clear and convincing evidence before the Committee showing that Senator Cranston solicited and received contributions from Mr. Keating in a manner which linked the contributions with official action.

2. Senator Cranston Contends That His Fund Raising and Constituent Service Practices Were the Same as Those of Every Senator

Senator Cranston contends that his conduct in this matter and his office practices in fund raising and providing constituent service were no different than the conduct and office practices of every other Member of the United States Senate. Senator Cranston introduced several exhibits to advance this argument. First, he provided a chart listing every Senate staff member designated under Senate Rule XLI to solicit and receive contributions to argue that Ms. Jacobson's role in his office was the norm.

In fact, Senator Cranston's chart of the Senate aides designated to solicit and receive contributions is compelling evidence that Ms. Jacobson's role was unusual. The chart lists Senate staff members. Ms. Jacobson was not a member of Senator Cranston's Senate staff. As Senate staff members, each person listed on Senator Cranston's chart

has responsibilities other than fund raising which could require his or her presence at meetings with constituents regarding legislative and regulatory matters. Ms. Jacobson had no substantive expertise nor responsibility. According to Senator Cranston, she attended substantive meetings with constituents because she would be a more effective fund raiser if she knew what problems the constituents or potential contributors had.

It should be noted that prior to the adoption of Rule XLI in 1977, *any* Senate employee could engage in campaign fund raising activities on his or her own time. Senate Rule XLI restricts such activities by providing that for other than three assistants to a Senator "No officer or employee of the Senate may receive, solicit, be a custodian of, or distribute any funds in connection with any campaign . . . (for federal office)." Thus, the Rule constitutes a restriction on the campaign related activities of Senate employees. It must be understood that, in order to ensure that taxpayer funds are not improperly used for campaign purposes, even these three employees must neither engage in campaign fund raising activities on Senate time nor use Senate facilities in connection with these activities. Other employees may not participate in campaign fund activities in connection with Federal elections even on their own time.

Senator Cranston also argues that his fund raising on behalf of voter registration organizations was not unusual or unethical. He introduced another exhibit that listed various Members' affiliations with nonprofit organizations. Senator Cranston's exhibits highlighting other Members' affiliations with nonprofit organizations and various fund raising events are inapposite. Leaving aside the fact that in two instances Mr. Keating arranged for his companies to make significant contributions at Senator Cranston's request to organizations that did not have tax-exempt status (Lincoln and ACC's contributions to America Votes and USA Votes, which totaled $125,000, were not tax deductible because these organizations were partisan voter registration organizations), an ethical problem arises when there is a linkage between a Senator's official action and his fund raising for an organization, regardless of whether it is a tax exempt organization. In this case, the Committee finds that Senator Cranston engaged in an impermissible pattern of conduct not because he raised money for tax exempt organizations, but because of *the relationship* between his fund raising for voter registration organizations from Mr. Keating and his intervention with the Bank Board on behalf of Lincoln.

3. *Senator Cranston Argues That He Received No Personal Benefit from Mr. Keating's Contributions, and Therefore He Could Not Have Engaged in Improper Conduct*

None of the financial support arranged by Mr. Keating for Senator Cranston's campaigns or organizations closely affiliated with him provided a personal financial benefit to Senator Cranston or any member of his family. This fact, while significant, neither excuses Senator Cranston's conduct nor precludes the Senate from disciplining him.

This Committee is authorized to investigate and recommend discipline for "improper conduct which may reflect upon the Senate," and it is improper conduct to link official actions to charitable and political contributions. The Senate expressly chose to give this Committee jurisdiction that "would take into account all improper conduct of any kind whatsoever." There is no limitation that improper conduct must include personal financial benefit to the Senator.

The Senate has disciplined Members for improper conduct that did not lead to personal financial benefit. The Committee finds that it is improper conduct to link fund raising to official actions.

4. *Senator Cranston Argues That All His Contacts with the Bank Board Were Routine and Proper Constituent Service Status Inquiries*

Senator Cranston contends that every contact he had with the Bank Board was a permissible constituent service "status inquiry" or request for careful consideration of matters involving Lincoln. Although the evidence demonstrates that a number of Senator Cranston's contacts with the Bank Board cannot be characterized fairly as routine status inquiries, the Committee did not find any of Senator Cranston's contacts in and of themselves to be improper. It is the relationship of those interventions to Mr. Keating's contributions that was improper.

Comment

Some of the supporters of the Keating Five argue that the defendants in this case should have been the "Keating 535." Like Senator Cranston, the supporters claim that what the Five did was no different from what most of their congressional colleagues do most of the time. The plea that "everyone does it" is a familiar excuse in political ethics, and it is sometimes even valid. If the action is in fact an unavoidable part of the job (a candidate for office will be unfairly disadvantaged if he or she does not do it, for example), then the excuse should be taken seriously. And what the Keating Five did in this case can be described in a general way that would apply to most other legislators in the current system: they all solicit contributions from constituents for whom they then do favors. What exactly did the Keating Five do and how if at all does it differ from normal congressional politics? In analyzing corruption we need to be as specific as possible in the description of the conduct, but as systematic as possible in our evaluation, as we consider the implications for the institution and the democratic process as a whole.

Constituent service provides a check on the abuse of power by executive agencies in individual cases—in effect, fulfilling the role filled by an ombudsman in some other political systems. Even if the casework done by each individual member is perfectly proper, the collective consequences of casework may not be so beneficial for the system as a whole. One danger is that as constituent service becomes such a prominent part of the job, legislative duties suffer. Voters also pay more attention to personalized service than to legislative records, and political responsibility withers. What standards should govern the conduct of members when they intervene in administrative agencies on behalf of their constituents? Did the Keating Five violate these standards?

The Ethics Committee found the contributions that the Keating Five received and the services they provided to Keating to be "substantially linked" through an "impermissible pattern of conduct," but the committee stopped short of finding "corrupt intent." Why did the committee decline to find criminal corruption here? Since "corrupt intent" is the language of the bribery statutes, the committee did not dare suggest that campaign contributions could be bribes. The line between contributions and bribes must be kept bright. But is the line so bright? "Almost a hair's line difference" separates bribes and contributions, Senator Russell Long once testified. There is no good reason to believe that connections that are proximate and explicit (the criteria for criminal bribery) are any more corrupt than connections that are indirect and implicit. The former may be only the more detectable, not necessarily the more deliberate or damaging, form of corruption. Corruption that works through patterns of conduct, institutional routines, and informal norms may leave fewer footprints but more wreckage in its path.

Are we driven, then, to accept the view of some critics of our political system who regard all contributions as corrupt? This approach does have the virtue of highlighting serious structural flaws in the current system of campaign finance. But it does not encourage the kinds of distinctions necessary in the kind of politics we actually have now and are likely to continue to have in the foreseeable future. This approach provides no basis for judging some forms of corruption worse than others and therefore no guidance in deciding which reforms should have higher priority. Treating corruption as so pervasive obscures important moral differences in the kinds and degrees of wrongdoing in which politicians may engage. It would, for example, have us see an explicit proximate bribe as morally equivalent to a regular $1,000 campaign contribution to one's long-time party favorite. Try to formulate some standards that would draw more nuanced distinctions among the various connections that link service and contributions.

Scandal in Santa Clara

Anna Warrock and Esther Scott

Less than a year after her election to the Santa Clara, California, City Council, Judy Nadler found herself at odds with her fellow council members. At issue was the handling of an incipient scandal that threatened to taint the entire city government. In the summer of 1986, the San Jose *Mercury News* had published a series of articles alleging that local contractor Ray Collishaw had purchased influence through personal favors and fundraising efforts on behalf of some city officials. Among the most potentially compromising favors was a $52,000 loan that Collishaw—whose companies were doing work for the city—had made to the director of Santa Clara's Parks and Recreation Department.

Nadler wanted the city council to authorize an independent investigation of the loan and a survey of city employees to uncover other questionable favors. But both the city manager and the mayor argued that the city's internal investigation, which had not turned up any flagrant violations, was sufficient; and the other city councillors went along with their view.

This was not the first time Nadler had found herself in disagreement with her colleagues on the city council. In the ten months she had held office, she had challenged them on a number of largely procedural issues that, she felt, reflected their failure to conduct their business in full view of the public, without undue influence from development or other special interests. These challenges had won her the resentment, if not the enmity, of the other councillors, who saw her, at best, as a zealous neophyte or, in a darker light, as an ambitious attention-grabber. By August 1986, she was feeling her isolation. "I wasn't feeling the heat as much as the freeze," she says. "When I walked into a room, they would just stop talking."

Now, stymied in her efforts to get the council to launch an inquiry, Nadler had to consider how far to push her point. As she studied her options, it became apparent that continuing to fight for an investigation would mean making an end run around her colleagues and taking her case to an independent arbiter: a state ethics commission or a county grand jury.

THE COLLISHAW CONNECTION

Judy Nadler's crisis of conscience had begun on August 10, 1986, when the San Jose *Mercury News*—the leading newspaper in the Santa Clara valley—printed the first of its four-part series on Ray Collishaw, detailing the contractor's numerous ties to local government officials and the many real estate and contracting deals that had made him one of the wealthiest men in the area.

The *Mercury News* articles appeared against a backdrop of a fifteen-year economic boom that had transformed Santa Clara from a quiet rural community—known as the "valley of heart's delight" for its many fruit orchards—to a bustling city of 90,000 in the heart of Silicon Valley. Along with prosperity had come the usual headaches associated with rapid growth—traffic congestion, loss of open space, spiraling real estate costs. For developers and contractors like Collishaw, however, Santa Clara's newfound popularity was an unalloyed delight. As the *Mercury News* put it, "The story of Collishaw's rise from small-time contractor to wealthy land baron is the

Reprinted by permission of the Case Program, Kennedy School of Government, Harvard University. Copyright © 1989 by the President and Fellows of Harvard.

tale of Silicon Valley in a minor key. Not a whiz kid or a big stakes entrepreneur, Collishaw nonetheless cashed in on the electronics boom at its fringes through a series of lucrative land deals.''

At the heart of the *Mercury News* stories were allegations that Collishaw had been able to profit from Santa Clara's boom at least in part through the judicious use of gifts, campaign donations, and personal favors to local officials, whose decisions on contract awards and land use, the paper claimed, were crucial to his success.[1] Collishaw, the paper reported, had contributed generously to campaigns of both parties and at all levels—from governor to board members of local community colleges; his contributions from 1981 to 1986 reached a total of $82,000, while companies he owned donated a comparable amount and employees from those firms chipped in an additional $44,000 in donations. He helped candidates as well by sponsoring numerous fundraising events to boost their campaigns. So valuable were his efforts, claimed the *Mercury News*, that Collishaw had become ''almost indispensable to the political process in Santa Clara County.''

Collishaw was equally generous at a personal level to a number of officials in Santa Clara and other nearby communities, entertaining them lavishly, providing them with vacations at his resort homes, or helping them out in business deals. In turn, the *Mercury News* suggested, Collishaw had reaped the benefits of some key decisions made by city officials. For instance, the paper reported, the value of a parcel of land owned by Collishaw increased after the Santa Clara Council agreed, without a formal vote, to extend water and sewer services to it; soon after, Collishaw sold the land for about six times what he paid for it. The *Mercury News* also claimed that Collishaw's various landscaping and construction enterprises had had ''great success in securing public jobs,'' landing over $26 million in contracts

from local governments over a ten-year period.

The *Mercury News* articles supplied the names of several Santa Clara officials who had at various times been the beneficiaries of Collishaw's largesse, whether in political donations or personal favors. They included newly appointed City Councillor Vern Deto, current Mayor Everett ''Eddie'' Souza, and Parks and Recreation Director Earl Carmichael. It was the allegations concerning Carmichael that appeared most damaging, at least to the reputation of Santa Clara's city government.[2] According to the *Mercury News*, in 1978 Collishaw had arranged a $52,000 loan for Carmichael, Santa Clara's parks director for twenty-seven years, at favorable interest rates; Carmichael had not, the paper noted, reported the loan in public disclosure statements ''as is required.''[3] Collishaw had also provided all-expenses-paid trips and vacations for Carmichael and his wife and arranged a real-estate investment opportunity that had yielded the parks director roughly $16,000 in tax write-offs. Over the same ten-year period, the paper continued, ''Carmichael took part in decisions that enabled Collishaw to get more out of his financial dealings with Santa Clara—dealings that included $1.2 million worth of parks contracts.'' The article particularly noted Carmichael's authority to recommend change orders to the city council, which had resulted in more money or more time to complete the work under contract.

Carmichael, along with the other government officials named in the article (at least those who would speak to the *Mercury News*), vigorously denied showing any favoritism toward Collishaw either in contract issues or in land use decisions. The parks director insisted, for example, that all the change orders he had recommended were standard and in no way reflected special privileges accorded to Collishaw. Others sprang to Collishaw's defense, noting his even-handedness in political donations and his generosity to philanthropic causes, contributing and raising millions of dollars to a variety of causes, such as the Crippled Children's Society.

While Collishaw refused to talk to the *Mercury News* reporters, he had outlined his reasons for making political contributions in a 1984 press release which the paper quoted. "Basically we donate money to a candidate; we're not buying," Collishaw said. "You're doing it for one thing: when you call, they return your phone call and you can put your position before them." According to Eddie Souza, mayor of Santa Clara since 1985, Collishaw did not abuse even the privilege of calling politicians. The only time Collishaw called him, says Souza, was to ask if he (Collishaw) could help expedite a parking variance for a respite house for crippled children and their parents. "He said, 'Can I help?'" Souza—himself the parent of a disabled child—recalls. "[I said] 'Hey, you don't even have to ask, that's something I strongly see needed.'"[4]

Souza expressed outrage at the *Mercury News* articles, claiming that the paper's presentation distorted the facts and their significance. "It says Eddie Souza, mayor, received $6,000 in contributions and in turn granted numerous contracts and change orders that benefited Collishaw," he says. "I did? When the hell did I do that? There's a difference between putting my hand in your pocket and ripping the money off and somebody giving you money as a campaign contribution which was all legally noted and recorded." Moreover, Souza says, Collishaw contributed the $6,000 over the course of three elections and several years—a fact the newspaper did not point out. Both Souza and City Councillor John Mahan questioned the *Mercury News'* motives in publishing the articles on Collishaw. "I think the *Mercury News* is trying to be the controlling interest in Silicon Valley," says Mahan.

"They're trying to go head to head with the *San Francisco Chronicle*."[5]

But not everyone in Santa Clara city government discerned ulterior motives in the *Mercury News'* reporting. Judy Nadler was disturbed by what she read, by both the particulars of Collishaw's ties to Santa Clara city officials and by the pattern of "cronyism and . . . old-boy network and . . . just taking care of their own" that those ties revealed. It was concern for precisely that pattern of governing that had prompted her to run for office less than a year ago, and it was to fight the very abusers noted in the articles that she believed she had been elected.

RUNNING FOR OFFICE: JUDY NADLER

Nadler had lived in Santa Clara for over a decade before she decided to enter the race for city council. She had come in the area in 1974 after graduating from George Washington University, where she had majored in politics and journalism; in her last year at college, she had worked as an intern for Representative Al Ullman (D-Ore.), chairman of the House Ways and Means Committee. In Santa Clara, she found work as an editor at *Sunset*, a regional magazine that focused on Western living, while her husband Jerry attended Santa Clara Law School and then took a job as a deputy district attorney for Santa Clara County.

At first Nadler was content with volunteer civic duties—she served on the library board and her husband on the civil service commission—but after the birth of her daughter in 1984, her need for involvement in the community deepened. "When Sarah came along," Nadler recalls, "I thought, this is her hometown, and what is she going to say [about it] when she grows up? Is she going to say, 'Santa Clara was such a wonderful place to grow up,' or is she going to say, 'Oh, I grew up in Santa Clara' and sort of not want to talk about it?"

Nadler worried that Sarah might opt for the latter. In her view, those in charge of

Santa Clara's destiny had shown a weak hand at the tiller. She was disturbed by what she saw as the city's failure to cope with development pressures.[6] In the years since she had first come to Santa Clara, she had watched open space give way to highways, traffic congestion, and high rise developments. There were questions in her mind about who was benefiting from the untrammeled growth she saw. She had followed with consternation the city's controversial acquisition of a failing amusement park; the turbulent negotiations to purchase the park—at enormous expense—often took place behind closed doors, heightening her sense of "all this chaos [that] seemed to be going on in the city government."

The combination of these concerns propelled Nadler to toss her hat into the ring in 1985, offering herself to voters as an independent candidate for city council unconnected to any special interests. "Grassroots," she says, "was clearly the way that I wanted to go." Nadler's candidacy bypassed the traditional routes to public office in a couple of ways. Although a member of the library board, Nadler had not served on either the city's civil service or planning commission—the "traditional stepping-stone," she says, to elected office in Santa Clara. She also did not avail herself of the usual sources of financial support. Steering clear of Collishaw and other major contributors, Nadler raised money for her race from friends and family in a door-to-door campaign. "People asked me when I walked door-to-door, 'How much money have you taken from Collishaw or [former mayor Gary] Gillmor?'"[7] Nadler recalls. "And I said truthfully, 'None.' And they said, 'Well, you've got my vote.'"

Just before election day in November, Nadler's candidacy was buoyed by an editorial in the San Jose *Mercury News*. Decrying what it called "dense industrial and commercial development" in Santa Clara, as well as "cronyism, back-room deals and the triumph of special interests" in the city's government, the paper endorsed Nadler as the "outstanding" candidate in the race. Her election, said the editorial, "could mark a turning point in Santa Clara's politics."

Nadler went on to win her seat by just three votes, edging out Vern Deto, a native of the area who had served nine years on the planning commission.[8] "While it's not winning in the traditional sense," says Nadler, "for someone who was young and a woman with a one-year-old, who was not born and raised here, who'd never been on the planning commission, it was quite a statement."

ON THE CITY COUNCIL

When Nadler took her seat on the Santa Clara City Council in November 1986, she was one of four Democrats—the first time Democrats had even made up a majority on the council.[9] In other ways, though, she was in the minority—sometimes of one. She was one of two women councillors, and only the third woman ever to serve on the council. She was not from the Santa Clara valley (Nadler hailed originally from Oregon), and she had been educated in the East. Nadler says that she and fellow council member David Tobkin (who attended Santa Clara University) were "the best, quote, formally educated people on the council."

From the very start, she felt a chill in the air. There was no welcoming party, she says, and in fact, on the first night of business, Councilman James Ash proposed voting on the spot to appoint her opponent, Vern Deto, to fill the seat left vacant by Souza. (The councillors decided not to do this; instead Deto, following the usual procedure, applied for the position and was then appointed in December.)

In the ensuing weeks, the chill intensified perceptibly, as Nadler took unpopular stands on issues that had previously been matters of routine procedure. The first skirmish arose over the issue of late adjournments. The city council held weekly public meetings every Tuesday evening beginning at 7:00; the press of business often kept the sessions going well past midnight. "I think the first night I got on the council," Nadler recalls, "we adjourned at 1:00 A.M. and the next week it was 1:30 A.M. and then it was 2:00 A.M." Since few Santa Clarans stayed for the duration, Nadler felt the situation was akin to meeting behind closed doors. Moreover, she says, it was hard to think straight at that time of night.

Things came to a head in early spring when the city council took up the matter of a change order on the golf course the city was building on part of its landfill, a project that had begun to run seriously over budget. "The killer was," Nadler recalls, "we were handed a change order on the golf course for some horrendous amount of money[10] at one or two in the morning and it had to be signed off on that night. I felt it was irresponsible. I wouldn't refinance my house at two in the morning." It was unreasonable, she felt, to be "handed the papers and told, in three minutes you have to sign this." Accordingly, Nadler abstained. Her colleagues did not, approving the change order by a 6–0 vote. Undaunted, Nadler announced that she would thereafter abstain from voting on any council business after 11:30 P.M.

Nadler's position won her notice in the *Mercury News*, but few friends on the city council. The longer she kept up her policy of abstention after 11:30, the more irritated the other councillors became. Nadler had "a valid point," says Councillor David Tobkin, "but to keep it going for a long period of time like she did wore a little thin on people." Another councillor, Sue Lasher, felt that Nadler had exaggerated the problem. Most meetings did not run past midnight, Lasher says, and most were well attended by the public. "I'm sure Nadler was aware of the length of meetings when she decided to run," she adds. " . . . A lot of things [Nadler] kept bringing up, I said, 'She's new, let's give her time,' " Lasher

recalls. "We're all green when we get on [the city council]. You have to know precedents, you have to know what has been done in the past to solve problems. And until you find out, you don't know what it costs to solve all the problems, and I don't mean just money."

Despite her colleagues' displeasure, Nadler did not back off from challenging their practices. That spring, there was another confrontation, this time over the seemingly innocuous matter of a used conference table and chairs. Ray Collishaw had offered the furniture—valued at $1,200 and $2,000—to the city after, he says, a fire inspector, who was checking out a building Collishaw had just bought, noticed it, and suggested the fire department could use it. The city council was all for accepting the offer—except for Nadler. Especially in view of the sizable change order for the golf course the council had just approved which she felt had given Collishaw "an easy break," Nadler felt uncomfortable about the propriety of the offer. "I kept thinking, why would he give us this table and chairs? He's very involved with the Crippled Children's Society and raises thousands, hundreds of thousands probably, for various charities, and why wouldn't he want to give the table and chairs to one of them? It wasn't on our wish list or anything." She urged her colleagues to refuse the furniture. "I made a statement to the council members at the time that I felt it was inappropriate," Nadler recalls.

Once again, her colleagues did not agree with Nadler. They voted to accept the table and chairs; Nadler cast the lone dissenting vote. "She [wasn't]—at least I don't think— previously aware that we had accepted other things in the community," says Vern Deto, such as an annual donation of $1,000 from wealthy Santa Claran Austin Warburton to a trust fund he had set up "for the benefit of the community." Others, like Mahan and Tobkin, felt it was good common sense to take the furniture. "If the city can get something free that's useful to the city, that's a cost savings as far as I'm concerned," says Tobkin. "You have to ask yourself, does a conference table and chairs influence you? My answer is no."

Tobkin was not without sympathy for Nadler's position. Elected to the city council in 1979 at the age of twenty-seven, Tobkin had been, by his own admission, "a purist." He had had his own tangles with the council over Collishaw—he had opposed the parking variance Collishaw sought for the respite house for families of crippled children and refused transportation (plus drinks) offered by Collishaw to council members for a visit to a real estate development. Over the years, through, Tobkin had mellowed and learned to pick his battles. "You can be a purist all you want to," he says, "but [the other councillors] keep this little file in the back of their heads, and things that they should have supported they shot down on occasion just because I was a purist for so many years."

Others on the council were not so sure Nadler's motives were pure. The favorable notices she continued to receive from the *Mercury News* led some to believe that, because of her connections as a journalist, she was getting special treatment from the paper, not to mention hogging the limelight. Nadler denied any special treatment or self-serving motives. "Having been a journalist," she explains, "I know how to give a good quote and put out press releases."[11] Nevertheless, she acknowledges, her high profile in the *Mercury News* did not help her with her colleagues. "I was hearing from other people in the community," she recalls, "about conversations that were being held about me in restaurants, grocery stores, golf courses, etc., by council members. . . . Some of the stories were incredible, not only about my ties to the *Mercury*, but what I really had in mind—that I didn't care about Santa Clara, it was obvious that I had my eyes on higher things, I'd sell my soul—those kinds of things."

DEALING WITH THE COLLISHAW "SCANDAL"

It was in the context of her worsening relations with her fellow councillors that Nadler read the *Mercury News* series on Ray Collishaw and his ties to Santa Clara city officials. If she found that the articles made for disturbing reading, she was not alone. "When I read it, I couldn't believe it, because I know Ray," says Sue Lasher. "Then I felt someone maybe found out something I didn't know." As she read on, she says, her primary concern became "whether this is fact or not. The first thing I wanted to do is get down to the base yes or no. It sounded like there was some wrongdoing, something I thought was detrimental to the city." Mayor Souza agreed with Lasher on the need to get the facts. On August 12, after the third article had run in the *Mercury News*, he asked his staff to prepare a report on the number of city contracts on which Collishaw had bid from 1981 to 1986, the number he had been awarded, and the number of change orders that had been approved. Souza told his staff he wanted "the record to be clear," and he wanted to be prepared to answer questions from reporters or citizens. The city engineer, who oversaw the bidding process for city contracts, asked for two weeks to complete the report. In the meantime, concerned that the report would be at best a halfway measure, Nadler did some research of her own.

The object of Nadler's study was to find out what resources were available to define and investigate potential conflicts of interest and unethical conduct in government. A lot of her concerns, she discovered, had been, at least in theory, addressed by the California legislature, when it passed the Political Reform Act of 1974. The law established a new watchdog agency, the Fair Political Practices Commission (FPPC), which was authorized to examine campaign practices and questions of ethics and to devise regulations governing conflict of interest issues.

In the regulations it subsequently promulgated, the FPPC set up strict reporting rules and procedures for state and local officials. For example, the FPPC prohibited a public official from participating in a decision that could affect a company or individual who had given the official cash or in-kind gifts, or made a political donation, of more than $250 in the preceding year. It also required elected officials and upper management appointees in state and local government to file financial disclosure statements. Finally, under FPPC rules, donors whose contributions to political campaigns in a single year totaled more than $10,000 (raised from a limit of $5,000 in 1985) were obligated to file a "major donor" statement listing their contributions.

FPPC regulations also required city and state agencies and local governments to create their own policies on gifts, conflicts of interest, and limits on campaign contributions. In fact, Nadler discovered, even before the passage of the Political Reform Act, Santa Clara already had a code of ethics on its books. Written in 1963 and amended in 1974, the code set rules of behavior for city officials and employees. It was not a familiar document in city hall. Mayor Souza for instance, had never heard of it. It was also frequently confused with the conflict of interest code the city put together in 1976 (revised in 1981) in accordance with FPPC regulations. "When I asked for the code of ethics," Nadler recalls, "I got one document from the city attorney and [a different] one from the city manager."

The confusion went deeper than mere titles: in one key area, the two documents contained conflicting language. The older code of ethics prohibited any city council member, official, or employee from accepting gifts valued at over $20 from anyone doing business with the city. The conflict of interest code, following the lead of the FPPC regulations, simply required that all gifts over $25 be reported on the proper financial disclosure forms. To complicate

matters even more, FPPC regulations merely required mayors, city managers, city attorneys, members of planning commissions and city councils, as well as candidates for any of those elected positions, to report any gifts over $50. Most officials in Santa Clara, including the mayor, believed the state code made the local code unnecessary.

It was not clear to Nadler that the FPPC would be helpful in clearing up the confusion in ethical codes. She had concluded from her research that the agency had done little to publicize the requirements of the Political Reform Act or its own regulations. Despite his well-known involvement in politics, for example, Collishaw had never heard of the major donor requirement, much less filed one. He was by no means alone in this. Nor had the FPPC taken an aggressive stance as a watchdog agency, evidently preferring an advisory to an investigative role.

However, the FPPC, Nadler learned, was not the only body authorized to investigate the actions of local governments. Under the provisions of California's state constitution, grand juries were empowered to oversee the operations of county and local government agencies. (Only Nevada's constitution delegated similar power to grand juries.) Grand juries in California could investigate independently and on a regular basis such institutions as a county board of supervisors or a city department without any initiative from the district attorney's office (although the district attorney did act as an advisor to the grand jury) and even in the absence of any direct suspicion or evidence of criminal wrongdoing. Grand juries could decide to investigate an agency simply because it was due for scrutiny or in response to a complaint from a citizen. Typically, the source of a complaint was kept confidential, even after the grand jury released its final report. (Nadler confirmed the details of grand jury operations with her husband, who continued in his role as deputy district attorney for Santa Clara County.)

At the end of her research, Nadler was convinced that something more than the internal investigation that Souza had launched was needed to probe further into the *Mercury News* revelations. However, she had also concluded that the city, not she, should take steps to ensure that something was done. When a reporter from the *Mercury News* telephoned her to ask for city council news, she told him that she was going to request an independent inquiry into the circumstances surrounding the loan to Carmichael.

The story of Nadler's pending request broke on Friday, August 22, a few days before the next scheduled council meeting on August 26. "I don't think we can afford to ignore this," Nadler told the paper. "When any city employee is involved in a situation like the one with which we've been presented, I think it's worth looking into." (The paper made no mention of Souza's inquiry.) Formally, Nadler would ask City Manager Donald Von Raesfeld to recommend an investigator; he could, she told the reporter, go to the FPPC, the grand jury, or "conduct his own review." The *Mercury News* followed up the story a few days later with an editorial that appeared on August 26, the morning of the city council meeting. Entitled "Not Business as Usual," the editorial applauded Nadler for "questioning things that many people in Santa Clara take for granted," but warned that "[a] majority of the council may genuinely wonder why naive little Judy is so upset about Earl Carmichael's taking favors from Ray Collishaw." After detailing campaign contributions Collishaw had made to five of the seven council members in the last five years,[12] the editorial concluded: "Good luck, Councilwoman Nadler."

THE MEETING AND ITS AFTERMATH

When the Santa Clara City Council convened on the evening of August 26 and dispensed with opening formalities, Nadler was the first to speak. Reading from a brief, plainly worded memo, she noted that "[r]ecent reports in the press" had indicated that a city employee had not reported a loan. "In order to clarify the facts surrounding the loan," Nadler requested the city to undertake a number of actions: (1) an investigation "by an appropriate body" into the circumstances of the loan itself, with the results to be made public; (2) a survey of city employees to turn up other unreported gifts; and (3) a clarification of the city's policy on accepting and reporting gifts and loans. Nadler also asked that copies of the city's code of ethics be distributed to all employees.

There was no immediate response to the substance of Nadler's request. When Souza deflected discussion of it on procedural grounds and moved the council on to a consideration of the findings of the internal investigation he had ordered, Nadler offered no resistance.

Donald Von Raesfeld—Santa Clara's city manager for twenty-five years—read the report of the investigation to the assembled councillors. "I find no cause to be concerned with [Carmichael's] job or performance," he told them as prelude. "His administration and handling of money has never been under question." Von Raesfeld went on to report that out of a total of ninety-eight engineering contracts the city had put out for bid between 1981 and 1986, companies owned by Collishaw or a family member had bid on sixteen and, as low bidders, had been awarded nine. One of those nine was a contract with the Parks and Recreation Department and hence under Carmichael's supervision. As was standard practice with public contracts, all bids were sealed and opened publicly at the same time, and, Von Raesfeld reminded the council, change orders were approved by the councillors themselves. In sum, "the ability for an individual department head to play favorites with a contractor is very remote." Von Raesfeld reported that he had spoken with the FPPC, which had advised Carmichael to file an amended disclosure form with the city clerk. Beyond complying with that, the city manager saw no reason to ask more of Carmichael. "I find no basis," he concluded, "[to suspect] favoritism with respect to a specific contract at that time or subsequent to that time."

Nadler stuck by her request for an investigation by an "appropriate body," to be determined by the city manager or city attorney, or even the FPPC. "I feel it would be appropriate for us to clear up questions," she told Souza. She found some support for her position from the audience, when a representative from the ad hoc Citizen's Advisory Committee stood up to urge the council to launch an independent inquiry. "We believe the citizens of Santa Clara have a right to expect arms-length relationships between the officials who run the city and contractors who do business with the city," the committee chairman told the council. "There seems to be some evidence, as far as financial relationships [go, that] there isn't."

But the debate on Nadler's request basically ended there. Souza told the councillors he had been in touch with the city manager, the city attorney, and the FPPC. All had advised that Carmichael should file an amended disclosure form. "The attorney general and the FPPC [can get involved] if there are charges made," he continued. "And this time I haven't heard any charges." If there were a formal investigation, Souza added, "I'm sure the council will make the information [in the report] available." With the report of the internal investigation in hand, he concluded, "basically, I think the action has been taken." With that, Souza called for a motion to "note and file" Nadler's request, and Nadler, ambiguously, responded, "I will move to note and file if that's the action the council wants to take." The motion passed unanimously, with only Lasher abstaining.[13]

Technically, "note and file" means that a piece of council business—a report or a request, for example—is noted in the minutes and then filed away. No action has been taken on the matter and it is shelved, until and unless someone puts it back on the council agenda at a later time. However, a vote to note and file does not necessarily preclude further action by city officials, so that Von Raesfeld, who had oversight of all city employees, was theoretically free to seek an independent inquiry into the loan to Carmichael. Most of the city councillors apparently took the vote to note and file as strictly a shelving action that put the Carmichael matter and the issue of further investigation to rest, essentially for good. Von Raesfeld could have persisted and pursued an inquiry on his own, says Tobkin, but "from a political point of view it would be suicide for him, because he would have had the other six [councillors] beating [on him]."

But the seventh councillor—Nadler—saw it differently. She understood the vote to note and file as a move that gave tacit approval to her request and cleared the way for Souza and Von Raesfeld to seek an investigation. It was not unusual for the council to move to note and file, she contends, and "that doesn't mean that no action is going to be taken." Satisfied that a probe would be launched, she had not wanted to press too hard at the council meeting. "Having seen [the vote to note and file] happen before," she says, "and not wanting to create bad blood—which this was clearly on the verge of doing—I thought we'd all agree to that [i.e., an investigation] and it would be kind of a quiet way not crucify anybody in public."

But when, the day after the council's vote, she met with the city manager to ask "how he was going to proceed on the investigation," she was surprised to hear he was not planning to proceed at all. Von Raesfeld was going with the stricter interpretation of "note and file." "The decision to note and file [Nadler's] request," he says, "was basically a decision to do nothing. That's what the council does when they've decided they don't want to handle something." More-over, he felt he had discharged his own re-sponsibilities as city manager. "As far as I was concerned," he says, "I had conducted an investigation." Carmichael had been cleared of all but a technical financial re-porting error.

This left Nadler in a not unfamiliar quan-dary, where, as far as the city council was concerned, she seemed to stand apart and alone on an issue. "If everyone believed this loan was okay, I thought to myself, my God, what else was out there that people thought was okay and not okay," she re-calls. Moreover, she felt that the residents of Santa Clara didn't necessarily believe the loan was "okay"and she had appealed spe-cifically to the electorate's concerns about ethics in city government in her campaign. "I couldn't accept," she says, "that people all over Santa Clara would accept the lack of action and say, 'Well, this is the way business is, and it goes on every day.' "

In view of her colleagues' decision to let the matter of the Carmichael loan rest where it was, Nadler faced some tough choices. She could go along with them, but that might violate what she regarded as her mandate from voters: to "challenge the thinking as it has been," and not be "intimidated by the political powers, and not be aware of them." She could seek an investigation on her own by going to the FPPC or to the grand jury, which would, if she wanted, keep her request confidential. But any move, confidential or otherwise, was al-most certain to isolate her further from the other councillors. Already her frequent ap-pearances in the press had served, some felt, to diminish her efficacy on the council. "Judy could have been a part of a team that could have made a lot of social changes in Santa Clara," Souza contends, "if she would have cut back on her nitpicking and holding press conferences every two weeks to try to discredit us."

Nadler insisted, however, that she was not out to discredit anyone. "I did not want

to nail Earl Carmichael," she says. "I did not want to nail Ray Collishaw. I wanted to look into the policies and practices sur-rounding the acceptance and reporting of gifts and loans." The fact that none of her colleagues agreed troubled her, but she was not sure that she had to have their backing. "Do you take [a stand]," she asks, "only when you've got your support lined up?"

When Judy Nadler learned that Santa Clara City Manager Donald Von Raesfeld had no intention of pursuing an investigation into the Carmichael loan, she responded first by arguing with him. "[He] said it was not a big deal," she recalls, "and I said, 'Well, I really think it is a big deal. It's a real big deal that we respond, it's really the city that's being criticized in this . . . and we as the city ought to make some kind of statement.'" Von Raesfeld was not moved by Nadler's arguments nor was she by his. When "he told me I was developing scru-ples and I shouldn't worry so much," she says, "something just snapped."

That same day—August 27, 1986—Nadler fired off a letter to the forewoman of the Santa Clara County grand jury asking that the jury look into the circumstances of the Collishaw loan to Carmichael, "[i]n as much as the City of Santa Clara has decided not to pursue its own investigation of the matter, or refer it to an independent body for review." She also asked the grand jury to examine the "policies and practices sur-rounding the acceptance and reporting of gifts and loans by city officials and employ-ees." At the same time—waiving her right to confidentiality—Nadler prepared a press release announcing her decision to go to the grand jury. Recounting her differences with Von Raesfeld over the council's vote to note and file, Nadler wrote: "It has become clear to me that there is no interest on the part of the city manager or the Santa Clara City Council to conduct the type of investigation I think the public demands." The following day, August 28, the story appeared in the

San Jose *Mercury News*. It was from the newspaper that the other city councillors learned for the first time that Nadler had written to the grand jury.

Not surprisingly, Nadler's colleagues expressed shock and disappointment that she had not come to them before resorting to an outside body for support. "All of a sudden, I read in the newspaper that [Nadler's] calling for a grand jury report," Mayor Eddie Souza recalls. "She didn't come to me saying 'Eddie, I really have some misgivings about the vote. I still think there's something wrong here, I want an investigation.' I would have been the first to say, 'Okay, if you want to clear it up, I support it. . . . But . . . we've got to show some proof of what we're going for, so we don't look like a bunch of jerks.' If she had any problems, why didn't she at least talk to me and the rest of the council?"[14] "I was shocked," echoes Vern Deto. "I feel very bad that Judy felt that she couldn't come to me. . . . As intelligent as Judy is—and she's one of the sharpest, if not the sharpest, on the council—I think her manner of handling it was a poor choice."

But Nadler argues that neither Von Raesfeld nor the other councillors were likely to be swayed by a reiteration of her concerns. "There was no point, I felt [in going back to the council]," she says. "The city manager clearly was not wavering, his opinion was quite obvious, and the council supported him and the parks director [Carmichael]." Moreover, she feared that in continuing the debate over the investigation, "we were going to get into a really negative situation. I felt that there was only one alternative, one independent body that was empowered by law to conduct these kinds of investigations, and that was the grand jury."[15] Nadler also defended her decision to make her letter to the grand jury public. An investigation by the grand jury would take months, she says, and if she did not inform her constituents of her action, "people would continue for a year or so to have a crisis [of confidence] with local elected officials."

As it was, the months following her letter to the grand jury posed something of a crisis for Nadler. The freeze she had felt earlier from her colleagues on the council intensified. And while some Santa Clarans supported her action, others attacked her for it. Nadler remembers one city council meeting when one resident stood at the microphone and harangued her for several minutes. He was "screaming at the top of his lungs," she recalls, "saying things that were personal, criticizing my husband, saying I had started this so that I could run for city council and appoint my husband city manager. Granted, it was a little off the wall, [but] still; he said things like, 'If you don't like Santa Clara, then we're better off without you.'" Equally significant to Nadler, Mayor Souza made no move to curtail or control the outburst.

THE GRAND JURY REPORT

On June 31, 1987, nearly a year after Nadler had submitted her request, the grand jury released its report. Its scope turned out to be much broader than an investigation of Collishaw's loan to Carmichael (in fact the grand jury didn't even call Collishaw to testify nor did its report refer specifically to the loan). According to Dolores Wulfhorst, head of the grand jury's government subcommittee at the time, other complaints, which remained anonymous, led the grand jury to examine the overall operation of Santa Clara's city government.

The grand jury's findings lent support to Nadler's concerns about ethical shortcomings in the city's handling of its business. "The City of Santa Clara has placed little emphasis on its Code of Ethics in recent years," the report stated. Moreover, the grand jurors found, "[b]y accepting gifts on behalf of the City from persons doing business with the City, the Santa Clara City Council violated the spirit of its own Code of Ethics." (The report also noted the confusion between the city's code of ethics and its more recent conflict of interest code, written after the state legislature passed the Political Reform Act of 1974.) The grand jury went on to criticize much about the way Santa Clara officials ran their city's affairs, from their failure to conduct performance evaluations of top-level managers to their weak management of a number of major projects, including construction of the municipal golf course. The report also noted that Santa Clara officials' penchant for approving change orders that substantially altered the scope and cost of construction projects was raising "serious concerns" about the city's "fair and open competitive bid practices." Finally, the grand jury report stated that it had referred "numerous possible violations" of the state's Political Reform Act of 1974 to the FPPC, and "possible violations of the anti-trust laws" to the state attorney general. The report did not indicate what those possible violations might be.

The grand jury report got extensive coverage in the press and generated considerable negative publicity. When the *Mercury News* carried the headline, "Santa Clara violates code of ethics," the day after the report was released, Souza recalls, "My God, it looked like we were horrible, politically corrupt politicians, something I had fought against all those years prior to, and while I was on, the council." Souza believes the press had rushed to judgment. No sooner was the grand jury report published, he remembers, than the reporters arrived in droves: "I had started going over some things [in the report] . . . and all of the sudden, the microphone comes into my mouth—not just my face—'Why did you violate your code of ethics?' What? What code of ethics? We had been operating by the 1974 State Political Reform Act," which, according to Souza, superseded the city's earlier ethics code.

Much the same arguments were made in a letter to the *Mercury News* that appeared on July 9. Written in response to an editorial critical of the city council, the letter asserted that the paper "has hung Santa Clara in effigy without benefit of hearing the other side." "You tell us to pay attention to what the grand jury said," the letter continued. "We will! What needs correcting will be corrected. What isn't broken won't be fixed." The letter was signed by Souza and Councillors Ash, Lasher, Tobkin, Deto, and Mahan. Nadler had declined to sign the letter, choosing instead to send her own, which appeared on the same page in the *Mercury News*. Nadler's letter commended the grand jury for its report and detailed a series of reviews and reforms the city council should initiate immediately in response. "We must act swiftly and wisely," the letter concluded, "to respond to valid criticisms about our municipal government."

THE CITY RESPONDS

The city's formal response to the grand jury report, issued in late August, was a disappointment to Nadler. Conceding nothing, the city rebutted the grand jury's findings point by point. In the area of ethics and conflict of interest, it found no confusion among the various codes defining ethical conduct and disclosure. The city's conflict of interest code governed all city employees except the city council, mayor, city manager and a few others, who were governed under another section of the state government code. The city's own ethics code, on the other hand, was "an idealistic guide for wholesome government," with no legal penalties attached for violations. Moreover, the FPPC had recommended that Santa Clara continue its policy of "encouraging and accepting gifts" to the city. In fact, the city asserted in its response, "The City Councillors deserve commendation for adopting a Code of Ethics in a nonrestrictive manner so as not to preclude accepting gifts on behalf of the City which can enure [sic] to the benefit of the taxpayer."

In addition to answering the grand jury's specific findings, the city came up with a few criticisms of its own. In a cover memo to the city council, Jennifer Sparacino, who succeeded Von Raesfeld after he retired from his post as city manager, noted inaccuracies in the grand jury's report. "Although I am sure the Grand Jury worked in good faith," she wrote, "the lack of correct information and a significant number of errors indicate a less than thorough process." The city also criticized the grand jury for its handling of the release of its report. "Santa Clara got bad press," the city claimed, when the grand jury announced its findings without indicating that the city had not had a chance to review and respond to them or making clear that it had been involved in a civil—not a criminal—investigation. Moreover, the city stated in its response, the grand jury "gave fodder to the imagination of [the] San Jose *Mercury News* with its immunity from libel for judicial comment to have a field day slandering the City and its officials."

Beyond its rebuttal and criticisms, the city's response contained few proposed reforms. The thirteen recommendations listed at the end of the document consisted largely of commendations of past actions by the city councillors and other officials, and resolutions to continue, with some modifications, current practices in city government. In fact, the major change proposed by the city concerned the law governing civil investigations by grand juries. "Unless a better suggestion is received from the Presiding Judge of the court with whom this response is filed," the city wrote, "the City Council shall seek state legislation to amend the law to make sure that other local governments do not have to suffer the unwarranted bad press experienced by Santa Clara in connection with this type of Grand Jury reporting."

The response to the grand jury report had been prepared under the supervision of City Manager Sparacino and then discussed in a city council meeting. The council approved the written response in a 6–1 vote, with Nadler again the lone dissenter. She was,

she later told the *Mercury News*, disappointed in the city's response. "It says, 'We're doing everything right. There's no reason for improvement other than silencing the critics,'" Nadler said. "I am not pleased, but I am not surprised," she added. "My only consolation is that it's going without my endorsement."

LOOKING BACK

With time, Nadler's view of events brightened. While she continued to feel isolated from her colleagues in the aftermath of the grand jury report, she found support for her views elsewhere. "There was tremendous pressure [from] being outside the group," Nadler recalls. "I had to draw strength from outside." City councillors and managers in surrounding cities would call her up, she says, "and say, 'Let us take you to lunch. You're not crazy. Any time you want to move here and run for city council, you can.' And that helped me realize that I wasn't crazy—that other city managers had performance reviews and other cities followed their code of ethics."[16]

The grand jury report did not entirely disappear from the scene after the city submitted its response. It was, according to Nadler, "quoted extensively" in one campaign during the 1988 city elections. However, the candidate who did the quoting lost the election—to Sue Lasher, who received, she reports, "the largest number of votes ever of anybody running for office with opposition. The residents in the city of Santa Clara know the story of Chicken Little. I'm glad to say they know the difference between fact and fiction." Still, Nadler came to feel the report would have an enduring effect on the political consciousness of the community. "It has, from my perspective several years down the road, had a positive aspect, opening up the government and [letting people know] what are the proper channels. I'm not saying people were transformed or converted. At least they're definitely more aware."

NOTES

1. Collishaw has filed a multimillion dollar lawsuit against the newspaper, charging that the allegations were false.

2. Another potentially damaging revelation concerned Leo Himmelsbach, district attorney for Santa Clara County. According to the *Mercury News*, Collishaw contributed substantially to Himmelsbach's political campaigns and arranged a real estate investment that generated at least $10,000 in income for the district attorney.

3. Techically, the loan was made to Carmichael's daughter and son-in-law; Carmichael had co-signed the loan.

4. Collishaw helped the cause by calling other city councillors to alert them to the issue. On reflection, though, Souza could recall another request from Collishaw: "[He asked] if I'd write a letter wishing his mother a happy birthday on a certain day. That's the only other thing Collishaw has ever come to lobby me on."

5. Souza and Mahan also suspected that the articles in the *Mercury News* (which, one councillor says, was sometimes referred to as the "Murky News") were printed in retaliation for a libel suit against the paper brought by a local politician; apparently, some at the *Mercury News* believed Collishaw had bankrolled the lawsuit, though Collishaw had denied doing so.

6. Not surprisingly, some in city government did not see their response to Santa Clara's growth as a failure. "We were encouraging development," says City Councillor Sue Lasher, "and increasing our tax base."

7. A real estate broker and close friend of Collishaw, Gillmor was also, according to the *Mercury News*, a "major political donor."

8. According to the *Mercury News*, Collishaw had supported Deto's two previous, unsuccessful runs for city council and helped bail out a local newspaper of which Deto was part-owner. After the election, Deto was appointed to the city council to fill the seat vacated by Eddie Souza, who was elected mayor in the same race.

9. The Santa Clara City Council consists of seven members, including the mayor, who serve staggered four-year terms. The Democrats on the council were James Ash, Vern Deto, Eddie Souza, and Nadler. The Republican members were John Mahan and David Tobkin. The seventh member, Sue Lasher, had registered as "declined to state."

10. The change order was actually an add-on for golf cart paths and two greens, requested by the city staff. The Collishaw Corporation, which had been awarded the landscaping contract for the golf course, was given this work as a change order in the amount of $412,625. City staff recommended that the company doing the landscaping should do this additional work, and did not put out a public bid.

11. Nadler urged a more sophisticated use of the press on other city officials. She suggested, for instance, that the city council follow the lead of other cities and publish its agenda in the newspaper or in a newsletter. City Manager Donald Von Raesfeld rejected the notion, arguing, she recalls, that "there's no place in government for PR." Nadler felt just the opposite. "I said, 'We need to market our company, we need to let people know what services we provide them with, like a utility or the parks and recreation or the library.'"

12. Only Tobkin and Nadler had not received donations from Collishaw.

13. Lasher had argued that the Carmichael affair was personnel business—normally the preserve of the city manager—and should be discussed by the council, if at all, only in closed session.

14. Souza also questioned whether it was appropriate for Nadler to seek an investigation from the grand jury, which works with the district attorney's office; Nadler's husband was a deputy district attorney. Nadler countered that her husband worked in an area—hazardous wastes—that would not involve him in this particular investigation. Santa Clara district attorney Leo Himmelsbach (Nadler's husband's boss), who had been linked to Collishaw in the *Mercury News* articles, formally withdrew from his role as advisor during the grand jury probe.

15. A couple of weeks after she wrote to the grand jury, Nadler also sent a letter to the Fair Political Practices Commission (FPPC), asking it to investigate Collishaw's loan and other gifts to Carmichael "to determine if violations of law have occurred," and to review for "accuracy and completeness" the financial and campaign disclosure forms of "all appointed and elected city officials in Santa Clara" over a ten-year period. The FPPC did not follow up on her request.

16. Nadler says she was also buoyed by her activities in county and state organizations. She was, for example, elected president of the Intercity Council, an association of mayors and council members in Santa Clara County.

Comment

City Manager Von Raesfeld argued that because bids for city contracts were sealed and change orders were approved by the council, individual department heads had almost no opportunity to "play favorites with a contractor." If as a low-bidder Ray Collishaw deserved the contracts he won, what if anything is unethical about his giving gifts to officials or officials' accepting them? Keep in mind that corruption does not necessarily require that citizens receive a benefit they do not deserve. It can occur if the process by which the benefits are allocated is flawed—for example, in ways that unnecessarily create serious doubts about whether the benefit is deserved.

Political scientists generally find that although contributors cannot usually buy votes they often can and do buy access. Collishaw claimed that he was not trying to win special treatment; he was just trying to make sure that his phone calls would be returned. To what extent is unequal access to officials unfair, and to what extent should the city's ethical rules seek to prevent it?

"There's a difference between putting my hand in your pocked and ripping money off, and somebody giving you money as a campaign contribution . . .," Mayor Souza said. What exactly is the difference? Also consider the differences in the potential for corruption in these practices: campaign contributions to one candidate or council member, "even-handed" contributions to all candidates or council members; sponsorships of fundraising events for council members; gifts to the city; unreported loans to city officials at favorable rates; reported loans of the same type; lavish entertainment; resort vacations for officials; and advice on business deals.

Was Judy Nadler, as her colleague David Tobkin implied, too much of a "purist"? Though sympathetic to her cause, Tobkin seemed to suggest that Nadler would have to learn, as he had, to compromise with her colleagues. Nadler might be criticized for some of her choices of issues (e.g., the used conference table and chairs) and for some of her tactics (e.g., calling for a grand jury investigation before telling her colleagues). And the criticism would be based on ethical, not just prudential grounds: the virtues of compromise and cooperation are important in politics. But these virtues turn into vices if they lead to complicity with corruption. Nadler might well argue that only by acting as independently as she did was she able to bring the actual or potential corruption to public attention and to help prevent it from occurring in the future.

Recommended Reading

The most useful collection of readings on political corruption is: Arnold J. Heidenheimer, Michael Johnson, and Victor T. LeVine (eds.), *Political Corruption: A Handbook,* 2d ed. (New Brunswick, N.J.: Transaction, 1989). Much of the literature on corruption emphasizes an individual approach and neglects institutional conceptions; a notable exception is: Peter deLeon, *Thinking about Corruption* (Armonk, N.Y.: M.E. Sharpe, 1993). The definitive work on bribery, presenting a rich history of the practice in its legal, political, and ethical dimensions, is John T. Noonan, *Bribes* (Berkeley: University of California Press, 1984). On a subtler form of official misconduct, see Andrew Stark, "The Appearance of Official Impropriety and the Concept of Political Crime," *Ethics*, 105 (January 1995), pp. 326-51.

Among the most theoretically illuminating works in the large literature on campaign finance are Charles Beitz, *Political Equality* (Princeton, N.J.: Princeton University Press, 1989), pp. 192-213; Daniel H. Lowenstein, "Political Bribery and the Intermediate Theory of Politics," *UCLA Law Review*, 32 (April 1985), pp. 784-851; and "On Campaign Finance Reform: The Root of All Evil Is Deeply Rooted," *Hofstra Law Review*, 18 (Fall 1989), pp. 301-67.

For a classic discussion of corruption that influenced the Founding Fathers, see Baron de Montesquieu, *Spirit of the Laws*, trans. and ed. Ann M. Cohler et al. (Cambridge, England: Cambridge University Press, 1989), Books VIII, XI (ch. 6). For the discussions of Montesquieu and other traditional political theorists' views of corruption, see J. Patrick Dobel, "The Corruption of a State," *American Political Science Review*, 72 (September 1978), pp. 958-73; and J. Peter Euben, "Corruption," in Terrence Ball, James Farr, and Russell L. Hanson (eds.), *Political Innovation and Conceptual Change* (Cambridge, England: Cambridge University Press, 1989), pp. 220-45.

For further analysis of the Keating Five and more generally of legislative ethics and corruption, see Dennis F. Thompson, *Ethics in Congress: From Individual to Institutional Corruption* (Washington, D.C.: Brookings Institution, 1995).

4 Official Disobedience

Introduction

What should public officials do when they disagree with a policy or decision of their government? For officials who have not been elected, this question poses a particularly difficult dilemma. They are bound to carry out the orders of others; yet they should not act contrary to their own moral convictions. Their duty to carry out policy rests in part on the requirements of the democratic process. We do not want officials whom we cannot hold accountable to impose their own views on us, overriding the policies determined by the democratic process. We also usually assume that officials consent to the terms of office. They know in advance what is expected of them, and they should not hold office if they cannot accept a policy once it is formulated. On this view, the moral responsibilities of the nonelected public official are completely captured by the imperative "obey or resign."

Critics of this view argue, first, that it underestimates the discretion that administrators exercise in modern government. Neither the law nor their superiors can determine all decisions that administrators make, and they must use their own judgment on many occasions. Second, if all public officials followed this imperative, public offices would soon be populated only by people who never had any inclination to disagree with anything the government decided to do. Men and women of strong moral conviction would always resign. Third, officials have broader obligations to the public—not merely obligations to their own consciences or to their superiors. "Obey or resign" presents too limited a menu of moral options. Depending on how serious the moral violation is and the good that officials can do by opposing it, officials may be warranted in staying in office and expressing their opposition in other ways. They may, for example, organize internal opposition, issue public protests, refuse to carry out the policy personally, support outside opponents of the policy, or directly obstruct the implementation of a policy.

The methods of disobedience that seem the most difficult to accept are those that are illegal or violate governmental procedures and lawful orders of superiors. The justification for such tactics resembles in part the rationale for civil disobedience by citizens. A democratic society benefits from permitting moral dissent. Extreme measures are sometimes necessary to force democratic majorities and governments to recognize that they have made a serious mistake, and sometimes officials are the only people in a position to bring such a mistake to public attention. But since it

141

is an extreme measure, civil disobedience is generally thought to be justified only under certain conditions. Those who disobey must: (1) act publicly; (2) act nonviolently; (3) appeal to principles shared by other citizens; (4) direct their challenge against a substantial injustice; and (5) exhaust all normal channels of protest.

The cases in this chapter—three instances of disobedience, one of a successful threat to resign, one of quiet and unsuccessful dissent, and another of strong criticism stopping short of disobedience—can help us understand whether official disobedience is justified, if so under what conditions, and whether the alternatives are better. The first case—a protest by attorneys in the Justice Department against their superiors' decision to delay school desegregation—seems the easiest to justify under the traditional criteria of civil disobedience. But some critics of the attorneys believed that their protest went too far, and others suggested that it did not go far enough. The case also raises the question of the moral responsibility not only of lawyers but of all professionals who hold public office—for example, doctors, engineers, journalists, and teachers.

The second and third selections in this chapter invite a comparison of two instances of unauthorized disclosure (otherwise known as leaks). Otto Otepka, a State Department official, passed classified information to a congressional staff member in an effort to undermine the department's policy on security clearance, which he believed endangered national security. Daniel Ellsberg gave the classified Pentagon Papers to the *New York Times* to encourage opposition to the Vietnam War. Unlike the attorneys in "Revolt at Justice," Otepka and Ellsberg acted alone and in secret.

George Shultz did students of political ethics a great service when he made quite different decisions about whether to dissent on two issues he faced at the same time while serving as secretary of state. When the White House issued a directive that required polygraph testing of all federal officials with access to sensitive information, Shultz publicly threatened to resign, and the president rescinded the directive. But when Shultz discovered the scheme to trade arms for hostages in the Iran-Contra affair, he objected privately but made little effort to resist it, and it continued. Because the same official at about the same time took quite different approaches to two difficult moral issues, the cases considered together offer a rare opportunity for comparative ethical analysis.

In the case of the space shuttle *Challenger*, nobody involved in the decision-making process that culminated in its disastrous launching threatened to resign or publicly protested. Yet two senior engineers protested as strongly as they believed possible, short of disobeying or threatening to resign. Evaluating their actions can help clarify both the moral advantages and limitations of lawful dissent in organizations with close connections to government, as well as in government itself.

Revolt at Justice

Gary J. Greenberg

When a lawyer is admitted to the bar, he takes an oath to support the Constitution of the United States. When a lawyer joins the Department of Justice, he takes another oath—the same one that is taken by the Attorney General and, in fact, by all federal employees.

That oath reads:

> I solemnly swear (or affirm) that I will support and defend the Constitution of the United States against all enemies, foreign and domestic, that I will bear true faith and allegiance to the same; that I take this obligation freely, and without any mental reservation or purpose of evasion; and that I will well and faithfully discharge the duties of the office on which I am about to enter. So help me God.

It was largely because of this oath—and the pressures we were under to violate it—that a majority of the attorneys from the Civil Rights Division of the Department of Justice gathered in a Washington apartment in August of 1969. We wanted to ascertain whether, under the Constitution, there was any legal argument that might conceivably support the Nixon Administration's request in a Mississippi courtroom, for a delay in implementing desegregation in thirty-three of that state's school districts. The assembled lawyers concluded that there was not. Thus was born the reluctant movement that the press was to call "the revolt" in the Civil Rights Division.

August 19, 1969, was a historic date in the field of civil rights. It was on that day that Robert H. Finch, the Secretary of Health, Education, and Welfare, in letters to the U.S. District Judges for the Southern District of Mississippi and to the Chief

Reprinted with permission from *The Washington Monthly*. Copyright by The Washington Monthly Company, 1611 Connecticut Ave., N.W., Washington, D.C. 20009.

Judge of the U.S. Fifth Circuit Court of Appeals, sought to withdraw school desegregation plans that his department had filed in the district court a week earlier. It marked the first time—since the Supreme Court's 1954 decision in *Brown v. Board of Education*—that the United States had broken faith with the black children of Mississippi and aligned itself with the forces of delay on the issue of school desegregation.

Less than a week later—on August 25—Attorney General John N. Mitchell placed the Department of Justice imprimatur on Finch's actions when Jerris Leonard, the Assistant Attorney General in charge of the Civil Rights Division, joined local officials in a Mississippi district court to argue for a delay.

The same day, in Washington, some of my colleagues in the Civil Rights Division and I prepared and distributed a memorandum inviting the Division's attorneys to a meeting the next evening to discuss these and other recent events that had, in the words of the memo, cast ominous shadows over "the future course of law enforcement in civil rights." The meeting's purpose was "to determine whether we have a common position and what action, if any, would be appropriate to take."

The forty who attended the meeting that next night first heard detailed factual accounts from those lawyers with firsthand knowledge of the government's actions in school desegregation cases in Mississippi, Louisiana, and South Carolina. We discussed the legal principles at length. We could find, as lawyers, no grounds for these actions that did not run cross-grain to the Constitution. We concluded that the request for delay in Mississippi was not only politically motivated but unsupportable under the law we were sworn to uphold. I then asked whether the attorneys in the Civil Rights

Division should protest the actions of Messrs. Mitchell, Finch, and Leonard. Much to my astonishment, the answer was an unhesitating, unequivocal, and unanimous call for action.

But how? The group's immediate, though probably unattainable, goal was a reversal of the Justice Department's actions in Mississippi. Beyond that, however, we wanted to ensure that future Mississippi-type decisions would not be made; we wanted guarantees that the Administration would, in the future, take the actions that were required by law, without reference to the political exigencies. We hoped that the protest could serve as a deterrent to future political accommodation. We agreed to write a dignified and reasonable statement of protest that would make our views known and demonstrate our unity and resolve. We chose a committee of six to draft the document.

Two evenings later, on August 28, we held another meeting to review the draft submitted by the committee. The fifty attorneys in attendance discussed the draft, modified it somewhat, and then adopted it unanimously. (It was later signed by sixty-five of the seventy-four nonsupervisory attorneys in the Civil Rights Division, some of whom had missed one or both of the meetings because they were out of town.)

The four-paragraph, 400-word document expressed, in painstaking language, the continuing concerns, motivations, and goals of the signatories. The last two paragraphs said:

> It is our fear that a policy which dictates that clear legal mandates are to be sacrificed to other considerations will seriously impair the ability of the Civil Rights Division, and ultimately the Judiciary, to attend to the faithful execution of the federal civil-rights statutes. Such an impairment, by eroding public faith in our Constitutional institutions, is likely to damage the capacity of those institutions to accommodate conflicting interests and ensure the full enjoyment of fundamental rights for all.

> We recognize that, as members of the Department of Justice, we have an obligation to follow the directives of our departmental superiors. However, we are compelled, in conscience, to urge that henceforth the enforcement policies of this Division be predicated solely upon relevant legal principles. We further request that this Department vigorously enforce those laws protecting human dignity and equal rights for all persons and by its actions promptly assure concerned citizens that the objectives of those laws will be pursued.

Why did the consciences of sixty-five federal employees compel them to protest a government law-enforcement decision? Why did sixty-five members of a profession that generally attracts the conservative and circumspect to its ranks—and reinforces those characteristics in three years of academic training—launch the first "revolt" within the federal bureaucracy?

Part of the answer lies in the fact that the new Administration was elected largely by voters who expected—and, from the rhetoric of the campaign, had every reason to expect—a slowdown in federal civil rights enforcement efforts. Those political debts ran counter to the devotion and commitment of the attorneys in the Civil Rights Division. They had labored long and hard in civil rights law enforcement, and had come to realize by experience that only unremitting pressure could bring about compliance with the civil rights statutes and the Fourteenth Amendment. Yet this conflict of commitments did not of itself lead to the revolt. There was no inevitability in the situation.

Certain other irritants played a part in creating an attitude among the attorneys which made "revolt" possible. There was Leonard himself, a politician from Wisconsin with no background in civil rights and, indeed, very little as a lawyer. He was insensitive to the problems of black citizens and other minority-group victims of discrimination. Almost from the beginning, he distrusted the attorneys he found in the Division. He demonstrated that distrust by isolating himself from the line attorneys. Still another element was the shock of his ineptitude as a lawyer. In marked contrast to the distinguished lawyers who had preceded him in his job, Leonard lacked the intellectual equipment to deal with the legal problems that came across his desk.

His handling of the Mississippi case enlarged this mood of irritation and frustration. Secretary Finch's letter—drafted in part, and approved in full, by Leonard—said that the HEW plans were certain to produce "a catastrophic educational setback" for the school children involved. Yet the Office of Education personnel who prepared the plans and Dr. Gregory Anrig, who supervised their work, and the Civil Rights Division attorneys, who were preparing to defend them in court, had found no major flaws. Indeed, Dr. Anrig, in transmitting the plans to the district court on August 11, wrote that in his judgment "each of the enclosed plans is educationally and administratively sound, both in terms of substance and in terms of timing." It was not until the afternoon of August 20, only hours before the attorneys were to defend the plans in court, that Leonard called them in Mississippi to inform them of the Administration's decision. Finally, in justifying the government actions to his own supervisory attorneys and in arranging that they, and not he, would inform the line attorneys of the reasons for the requested delay—Leonard could be no more candid than to say that the chief educator in the country had made an educational decision and that the Department of Justice had to back him up.

But, again, these superficial signs of malaise were not what led to the lawyers' widespread revolt. Discontent only created the atmosphere for it.

The revolt occurred for one paramount reason: the sixty-five attorneys had obligations to their profession and to the public interest. As lawyers, we are bound by the Canons of Professional Ethics and by our oaths upon admission to the bar; as officers of the United States, we were bound by our oaths of office.

Membership in the bar entails much more than a license to practice law. One becomes an officer of the courts, dutybound to support the judiciary and to aid in every way in the administration of justice. The scope of this duty was nicely summarized by U.S. District Judge George M. Bourquin in the case of *In re Kelly* in 1917, when he wrote:

> Counsel must remember that they, too, are officers of the courts, administrators of justice, oath-bound servants of society; that their first duty is not to their clients, as many suppose, but is to the administration of justice; that to this their clients' success is wholly subordinate; that their conduct ought to and must be scrupulously observant of law and ethics; and to the extent that they fail therein, they injure themselves, wrong their brothers at the bar, bring reproach upon an honorable profession, betray the courts, and defeat justice.

The Canons of Ethics command that an attorney "obey his own conscience" (Canon 15) and strive to improve the administration of justice (Canon 29). The Canons go on to echo Judge Bourquin's words:

> No . . . cause, civil or political, however important, is entitled to receive, nor should any lawyer render, any service or advice involving disloyalty to the law whose ministers we are, or disrespect of the judicial office, which we are bound to uphold. . . . When rendering any such improper service . . . the lawyer invites and merits stern and just condemnation. . . . Above all a lawyer will find his highest honor in a deserved reputation for fidelity to . . . public duty, as an honest man and as a patriotic and loyal citizen. [Canon 32]

Bearing these obligations in mind, examine for a moment the situation confronting the attorneys as a result of the decision to seek delay in Mississippi.

In May 1954, the Supreme Court declared that "in the field of public education the doctrine of 'separate but equal' has no place. Separate educational facilities are inherently unequal." One year later, the Court decreed that school officials would be required to make a "prompt and reasonable start" toward achieving the Constitutional goal with "all deliberate speed." Tragically, a decade went by and little was accomplished; that was the era of "massive resistance." In 1964, the Supreme Court ruled that "the time for mere 'deliberate speed' has run out." In 1968, the Court held that school officials were under a Constitutional obligation to come forward with desegregation plans that worked, and to do so *"now."* The Fifth Circuit Court of Appeals interpreted that edict, in the summer of 1968, to mean that the dual school system, with its racially identifiable schools, had to be eliminated in all of the states within its jurisdiction by September, 1969. (Mississippi is one of those states.)

Secretary Finch's letter, besides suggesting the possibility of a catastrophic educational setback if desegregation were effected at once, spoke of the certainty of chaos and confusion in the school districts if delay were not allowed. That allegation was based upon the uncontestable existence of hostility to desegregation within the local communities. While there was a danger of chaos and confusion in the desegregation of public schools in Mississippi, the Supreme Court had ruled again and again that neither opposition to Constitutional rights nor the likelihood of a confrontation with those opposed to the Constitutional imperative may legally stand as a bar to the immediate vindication of those rights.*

Thus, while pledged by our oaths to support and defend the Constitution and bound by duty to follow our consciences and adhere to the law, we faced a situation in which the Administration had proposed to act in violation of the law. We knew that we could not remain silent, for silence, particularly

in this Administration, is interpreted as support or acquiescence. Only through some form of protest could we live up to our obligations as lawyers and as officers of the United States. The form that this protest should take emerged so clearly that it then became a matter of inevitability, rather than a choice made from among several alternatives.

For the duty to serve the law, to promote the administration of justice, to support and defend the Constitution is more than a negative command; it is more than a "thou shalt not." It is an affirmative duty to act in a manner that would best serve and promote those interests. Thus, at the first group meeting, we immediately and unanimously rejected the notion of mass resignation because it would have served no positive purpose. It would only have removed us from association with the supporters of delay, it would not have fulfilled our obligation to act affirmatively to ensure that Constitutional rights would be protected and that the civil rights laws would be vigorously enforced.

Many of the attorneys thought that our obligation could not be met by merely drafting, signing, and delivering a protest statement. If delay for the purpose of mollifying a hostile community did not comport with the Constitution—thus impelling us to raise our voices in protest—then we were likewise duty-bound not to support the Mitchell-Finch-Leonard position through any of our official actions. The bureaucratic concept of "loyalty" notwithstanding, some of us concluded that we could not, for example, defend the government's position in court.

The question arises as to whether the action taken by the group met the burden imposed upon us by our obligations to the law and to the public interest. Did our fidelity to these obligations demand more than the soft and lofty importunings of the protest statement? Should all of the attorneys have explicitly refused to defend in court the action taken in the Mississippi case? Should the attorneys have embarked on a more di-

---

*On October 29, of course, the Supreme Court unanimously rejected the Administration's efforts at delay by enunciating the rule that the Constitution requires desegregation "at once." That ruling is not a part of this narrative except as it demonstrated anew that the position we had taken on the law was unassailable.

rect course of action to block the government's efforts to win a year's delay for school desegregation in Mississippi?

To begin with, we were hard pressed to come up with some appropriate alternative to the protest statement as a vehicle to make the views of sixty-five people known. But beyond that, it was vitally important to preserve the appearance of dignity and professionalism if our protest were not to be dismissed as the puerile rantings of a group of unresurrected idealists who, except for their attire, bore a close resemblance to the "Weathermen" and the "Crazies." To generate the public support we thought vital to the success of the protest, we had to act in a responsible and statesmanlike manner. Furthermore, it seemed to us that the presentation of any statement signed by nearly all of the attorneys in the Division would be a remarkable feat and that a demonstration of commitment was more important than the words actually used. In our view, the soft language implied everything that a blunter statement might have said. It also had the virtue of not putting the Administration up against a wall, which might have forced it to respond with a hard-line position of its own.

Though duty and conscience compelled a protest, reason dictated the nature of that protest. We did not merely seek an opportunity for catharsis; we sought to devise a course of action that had a chance to reap a harvest of practical results. This being the overriding consideration, the attorneys chose the course of a mildly worded group statement. Other overt manifestations of disagreement were left open for individuals to pursue as they saw fit.

The group action we took—that is, the drafting and signing of the statement—was a "protest," if by that we mean a dissent from the actions of one's administrative superiors. The language of the statement did not move into the area of "revolt," if by that we mean an explicit refusal to obey the orders of one's superiors—although the

statement was intended to imply that "revolt" was in the air.

Compelled by what they felt to be their obligations to the law, individual attorneys took a number of actions on their own, most of them in that murky area where there is a confluence of protest and revolt.

Even before the first group meeting, the Division lawyers assigned to Mississippi expressed their disinclination to present the government's case for delay in the district court. As a consequence, Leonard made his first appearance in a federal district court as Assistant Attorney General and argued the motion for delay himself. In mid-September, two Division attorneys (the author being one) appeared in federal courts in other school desegregation cases. When pressed by those courts to reconcile the government's "desegregate-now" position in those cases with Leonard's position in Mississippi, both attorneys said they could not defend the government's action in Mississippi.* Some of the Division's attorneys went a step further; they passed information along to lawyers for the NAACP Legal Defense Fund in order to aid their Mississippi court battle against the delay requested by

---

*In my situation, I was in St. Louis before the Eighth Circuit court of Appeals, sitting *en banc* (i.e., the full seven judges of the court were present), arguing that a delay granted by the district court to an Arkansas school district for the desegregation of its high schools should be reversed. One of the judges asked whether I could assure the court that the Attorney General would not "come along and pull the rug out from under" them if they ordered instant integration. I was pressed to reconcile my request for immediate integration in Arkansas with the position taken in the Mississippi case. After the court listened to my attempts to distinguish between the two cases, one judge said it appeared to the court that the practical effect of the government's posture was that Mississippi was being given special treatment. At this point, a number of judges called upon me to state my personal views on the contradictory positions taken by the government. I responded by saying I assumed that the court knew from the press accounts of the "revolt" what the feelings were in the Division. I indicated that, as a signatory of the protest statement, I could not be expected to defend the government's action in Mississippi.

the Administration. Others spoke with the press to ensure that the public was fully aware of the role political pressures had played in the decision to seek delay.

These actions, while neither authorized nor approved by the group as a whole, were individual responses to the same crisis of conscience that had led to the protest statement itself. One may have reservations as to the propriety of some or all of these acts of defiance. (Indeed, I have doubts as to whether it was proper for a Division attorney to furnish information to the NAACP after the government's action transformed the NAACP into an opposing party.) But it is important to recognize that the demands of conscience compelled more than just the signing of a piece of paper, and, in this sense, the protest was, realistically, a "revolt."

When the storm clouds first began to gather within the Civil Rights Division, the hierarchy of the Department of Justice, including the Attorney General and Leonard, reacted with a professed sense of surprise and even shock. Despite this, however, the Administration's actions were, at the outset, nothing short of accommodating.

The supervisory attorneys in the Division took the position that we had a perfect right, under the First Amendment, to meet and discuss matters of mutual concern. Prior to our second meeting, Leonard Garment, President Nixon's special consultant for youth and minority problems, let it be known through an intermediary that the Administration was likely to respond favorably to a reasonable and responsible protest. Indeed, Garment and the Deputy Attorney General, Richard G. Kleindienst, facilitated the protest by allowing us to hold our second meeting behind closed doors in the Department of Justice.

But later, when the Administration came to a fuller appreciation of the depth and unanimity of the protest, this attitude began to change.

On September 18, Leonard responded to the attorneys' statement for the Administration. We were informed that his reply was a final articulation of policy; in other words, if we did not like what we read, we should resign. The reply was curiously unresponsive. Whereas the attorneys' statement was carefully limited to questions concerning the intrusion of political influences into areas of law enforcement where only considerations of law belong, Leonard's reply outlined how the Administration would go about desegregating public schools. To this extent, the reply completely missed, or avoided, the point of the protests. We had never challenged the discretionary authority of the Attorney General and the President to determine the method by which the Constitutional imperative would be achieved. In matters where discretion is vested in the Attorney General to choose among policy alternatives, the attorneys have no business challenging his right to make the choice. But in the matter of enforcing Constitutionally required school desegregation in Mississippi, the Attorney General had no discretion. He was bound to uphold the dictates of the law, an obligation that could not be squared with the decision to seek delay.

Aside from its nonresponsiveness to the questions we had raised, Leonard's reply was disturbing on two other counts. First, it conceded, with delayed candor, that political pressures had played a role in the Mississippi decision. Second, it announced a new touchstone for civil rights law-enforcement policies: future actions would be taken on the basis of "soundness," rather than on the basis of the law. Thus, when defense appropriations are thrown into the balance, a decision to seek delay of school desegregation in Mississippi in return for the continued support of Senator John Stennis (D-Miss.) on the ABM can presumably be certified as "sound," notwithstanding its inconsistency with clear legal mandates.

The attorneys decided that we would neither accept the response nor resign. But the situation demanded further action, and we chose to reiterate our commitment to the law. On September 25, we delivered a new statement to the Attorney General and Leonard. It expressed our view that Leonard's reply "indicates an intention to continue with the policy of civil rights law enforcement toward which our August 29 statement was directed, a policy which, in our view, is inconsistent with clearly defined legal mandates."

The Attorney General's patience was wearing thin. The next day he told the press that "policy is going to be made by the Justice Department, not by a group of lawyers in the Civil Rights Division." At a news conference three days later, Leonard said that he thought the position taken by the attorneys was wrong. He warned that the revolt would have to end as of that date.

On October 1, Leonard called me to his office. He told me that he considered it to be the obligation of all of his attorneys to defend the government's Mississippi action in court. He asked whether I would be able to do so in the future. I said that I could not and would not. Our obligation was to represent the Attorney General, he said, and John Mitchell had decided that delay was the appropriate course to follow in Mississippi. I countered by explaining that I was obliged to represent the public interest in court and that my responsibility was to enforce the law. Leonard then made his attitude on the meaning of law enforcement very clear. "Around here the Attorney General is the law," he said. The difference of opinion was irreconcilable, and I was told to resign or be fired. I said I would forthwith submit a letter of resignation, and did—effective immediately. Leonard concluded the meeting by heaping effusive praise upon my abilities as a lawyer and offering to write a glowing letter of recommendation if I requested one. I did not.

Later that day, Leonard issued a memorandum that banned any "further unautho-

rized statement . . . regarding our work and our policies." He directed the attorneys to keep all "decisions of our work and policies within this Department."

Thus, the Administration's official attitude boiled down to an absolute ban on any further protest activity. The public was to be kept in the dark as a matter of policy. Law-enforcement decisions were to be made by John Mitchell, and the test for those decisions was to be soundness, including the relevant political considerations. The attorneys' job was to articulate and defend the Attorney General's decisions in court, and this duty would apply without reference to one's individual oath of office and the dictates of conscience.

As attorneys, I and my former colleagues who still remain in the Civil Rights Division cannot accept this point of view. The Justice Department lawyer's primary obligation must be to the Constitution. That should hold true whether the attorney is John Mitchell, Jerris Leonard, or Gary Greenberg. In his role as an officer of the United States, the Justice Department lawyer represents the public interest. While Jerris Leonard equates that obligation with obedience to the President and the Attorney General, I and my former colleagues could not. The Justice Department lawyer is not hired to represent John Mitchell in court. He is hired to represent the United States.

The ban on future protest by attorneys was unreal. Indeed, it would have been self-deception for John Mitchell or Jerris Leonard to assume that the "massive resistance" in the Civil Rights Division was over. The revolt may have been driven underground, but the attorneys remain within the system. They retain their voice and their ability to influence policy from within. They continue to adhere to their view of the law, and they see their obligation to the public, and to their oath of office, as paramount. The attorneys remain a potent and organized deterrent, ready to act should there be another Mississippi.

Whether or not the revolt achieved its long-range objectives, one cannot yet judge. There are indications that in the area of civil rights, as in other matters, the Attorney General is either unaware or contemptuous of the forces that conflict with the politics of the Southern Strategy. The attorneys in the Civil Rights Division continue to take a hard line in individual cases. They assume this posture every day in the pleadings and briefs they present to the Attorney General and Leonard for approval. So long as the Administration is kept in the position of having to say no—an attitude adopted so far only in those few cases in which the political pressures were intense—it is not likely that it can effect the wholesale retreat on enforcement of the civil rights laws which it seems ready to trade for public support. But while it is vital that the revolutionaries remain within the Division, and while their presence within the system may deter future Mississippi-type decisions, there is some question whether their determination will sustain them for the balance of this Administration. If not, the prospects for even the grudging enforcement of civil rights laws are bleak indeed.

A NOTE ON THE LITIGATION*

On July 3, 1969, the Fifth Circuit Court of Appeals ordered desegregation plans submitted and put into effect by that fall in thirty-three Mississippi school districts. The Justice Department and the Mississippi Attorney General asked for a delay, arguing that the time was too short and administrative problems too difficult to accomplish an orderly implementation of the plans before September. Both the District Court and the Court of Appeals accepted this argument, and on August 28, the Court of Appeals suspended its July 3 order and postponed the date for submission of new plans until December 1. Plaintiffs in fourteen of these districts appealed to the U.S. Supreme Court. On September 5, Justice Black, as Circuit Judge, denied their request for an immediate suspension of the postponement even though he personally believed the postponement was unjustified. [*Alexander et al. v. Holmes County Board of Education*, 396 US 19 (1969)]. Black wrote in part:

. . .when an individual justice is asked to grant special relief, such as a stay, he must consider in light of past decisions and other factors what action the entire Court might possibly take. . . . Although Green [*Green v. County School Board of New Kent* 391 US 430 (1968)] reiterated that the time for all deliberate speed had passed, there is language in that opinion which might be interpreted as approving a "transition period" during which federal courts would continue to supervise the passage of the Southern schools from dual to unitary systems. Although I feel there is a strong possibility that the full Court would agree with my views, I cannot say definitely that they would, and therefore I am compelled to consider the factors relied upon in the courts below for postponing the effective date of the original desegregation order. . . . The District Court found as a matter of fact that the time was too short, and the Court of Appeals held that these findings were supported by the evidence. I am unable to say that these findings are not supported. Therefore, deplorable as it is to me, I must uphold the court's order which both sides indicate could have the effect of delaying total desegregation of these schools for as long as a year.

When the full court heard the case on October 23, Assistant Attorney General Leonard and the Solicitor General argued again for delay. Although they insisted that the government was fully dedicated to ending segregated schools, they maintained that the best means of achieving this goal was to follow the Court of Appeals' order so that

---

*Prepared with the assistance of Mike Comiskey.

the school boards would have time to develop reasonable plans for desegregation. They argued that the views of the lower courts should be respected because of their "close familiarity with these cases and distinguished experience in the field." In a *per curiam* opinion decided on October 29, the Supreme Court rejected these arguments and vacated the Court of Appeals' suspension order. A unanimous Supreme Court held that all motions for additional time should have been denied. Continued operation of segregated schools under a standard of allowing "all deliberate speed" was no longer constitutionally permissible, and every school district was obligated to terminate dual school systems at once and to operate only unitary schools.

Comment

Although the initial protest was seen as an exercise of free speech, further opposition became disobedience once Leonard ordered the attorneys to cease their public protest or resign. Was Greenberg right to resign at this point? The attorneys who remained in office (carrying out their duties but still publicly opposing the policy) engaged in a kind of civil disobedience in office. Does their action meet the traditional test of justifiable civil disobedience? In what respect (if any) should that test be revised to deal with disobedience by officials?

Evaluate the actions of the attorneys whose protest went beyond signing the petition by (1) expressing opposition to the government's case in Mississippi while representing the government in another desegregation case in another district; (2) refusing to present the government's case for delay in any district; (3) giving the press inside information that might fuel public opposition to the attorney general's policy; and (4) passing information to lawyers for the opponents of the government's case. Would any other means of protest have been better?

To what extent does the justifiability of disobedience depend on assuming that the attorney general's position was against the law? Suppose (contrary to Greenberg) that the attorney general was acting within his lawful discretion but against the moral rights of some Mississippi citizens. On what basis could you defend the protest or other forms of opposition?

If you accept some part of the "revolt," ask yourself to what extent your acceptance depends on your agreement with the policy the attorneys favored. Reverse some of the facts in the case and see if your conclusions change. Consider, for example, whether (and why or why not) your judgment would change if the protest had been organized by lawyers who opposed an attorney general's effort to speed up school desegregation beyond what was required by law.

The Odd Couple

Taylor Branch

The public reaction to two whistle-blowers, Otto F. Otepka and Daniel Ellsberg, clearly illustrates the disorienting spells cast upon fervent observers by the spectacle and drama of disclosures that involve national security. Otepka violated our national security by slipping classified documents to veteran Red-hunter Julien G. Sourwine, counsel to the Senate Internal Security Subcommittee. He was fired for his transgressions in 1963, lost his position as chief of the State Department's security-evaluation division, became a martyr of the right wing, and is considered by some to be the first whistle-blower in the modern period. Ellsberg violated our national security by slipping classified documents, later to be called the Pentagon Papers, to numerous senators and newspapers. He was indicted for his transgressions in 1971, lost his security clearance at the RAND Corporation, became a martyr of the left wing, and is often considered the capstone whistle-blower of recent years.

While these two men are ideological opposites, there are unmistakable similarities between their respective exploits, viewed on a suitably high plane of reflection after all the human juices and interesting particulars have been drained away to leave the arid generalities in which lawyers earn their keep. Like colliding planets, Ellsberg and Otepka still operate by the same laws of motion in some ways, following their higher instincts regarding the public interest as they see it, exposing treachery in places of power regarding questions of life and death. These similarities suggest that anyone who wants to fight institutional rigor mortis by encouraging people to speak out from within the government is obliged by honesty and consistency to take his Otepkas with his Ellsbergs, and vice versa—to take a man like Otepka, who thought his bosses were ruining the country by being too sweet to communists everywhere, with one like Ellsberg, who thought his former colleagues were ruining the country by killing numerous people and lying about the whole affair. Regardless of who is right on the lofty world-view questions, the comments on the two men by prestigious newspapers and politicians suggest a strange kinship that bears some examination.

Otepka had been in the government for twenty-seven years and in the Office of Security for ten years when he was fired on November 5, 1963, on charges of "conduct unbecoming an officer of the Department of State." President Kennedy, setting a precedent for dealing with criticism from the right, assuaged a Calley-like tide by announcing that "I will examine the matter myself when it comes time," but he was killed before the review process got underway. It seems that Otepka, described by *Reader's Digest* as a "tall, quiet, darkly handsome man," by *Newsweek* as "a sad-eyed, introverted man," and by the *New York Times* only as "stocky," (descriptions indicative of the impact of political position on the eye), had been running afoul of important people in the Kennedy Administration for some time.

In 1955, for example, he had refused to dispense with the formalities of the security clearance with the formalities of the security clearance procedure for Walt W. Rostow, when Secretary of State Dulles wanted Rostow on State's Committee on Operations. Subjecting Rostow to a full-dress examination of his character was considered an affront to his dignity. When President Kennedy wanted Rostow on the team in 1961, Otepka again refused to waive security proceedings, which, some say, is why Rostow ended up in the White House while Otepka was at State, rather than going through the State security mill. (Apparently Otepka was a bit troubled by the internationalist leanings of Rostow's writings on economic development, hesitant to be taken in by possible ruses like Rostow's "non-Communist Manifesto," *The Stages of Economic Growth.* Also, as a professor, Rostow's commitment against communism was suspect a priori. Although subsequent events and the Pentagon Papers were to show that Otepka was dead wrong in his doubts about Rostow, some beneficiaries of hindsight have wished that he had possessed more clout in his efforts to keep Rostow out of the government.)

In addition to the Rostow rebuke, Otepka had nettled the new administration by locating and firing the State Department employee who had leaked a secret survey of U.S. prestige abroad to the Kennedy campaign forces in 1960. The survey, showing a dip in America's international esteem, was used with telling effect by John Kennedy in the campaign to show that the Republicans were blowing things in foreign policy, partly by following what seemed to be a deliberate path toward national weakness. Otepka had also been critical of the lax security procedures for the Cuba desk officers at the State Department, one of whom, William Wieland, was considered by the Republican Party almost single-handedly responsible for delivering Cuba into the enemy camp. Otepka testified before a Senate committee that he had dissented from the decision to clear Wieland without further study of his inner proclivities, and so much stir was created over Wieland that President

Kennedy was forced to defend him publicly in a press conference.

Finally, Otepka had refused to waive security investigations for six men of decorum whom Secretary Rusk wanted in 1962 for the Advisory Committee on Management Improvement to the Assistant Secretary of State for International Organization Affairs. The six, which included Harding Bancroft, Sol Linowitz, and Andrew Cordier, were chosen to that august and rather useless body to study whether or not American employees of international organizations should be required to pass U.S. Security investigations. The issue itself was one of some controversy, spurred on by a letter to the *New York Times* on July 30, 1962, that attacked the security regulations as a dangerous legacy of the McCarthy era. The letter came from Leonard Boudin, who is now the chief attorney for Daniel Ellsberg. In any case Otepka refused to waive security clearances for men who were going to study the need for security clearances, and that kind of zeal to check out the private leanings of prestigious people had long since aggrieved the Kennedy Administration.

John F. Reilly, Assistant Secretary of State for Security, was so intent upon getting rid of his anachronistic subordinate, the John Wayne rough rider on the New Frontier, that he bugged Otepka's telephone and set up an elaborate system of surveillance to catch him in an act of shame that would stand up as evidence for doing him in. Reilly's sleuths scoured Otepka's "burn bag," a receptacle used to mark for instant destruction items like doodle pads and carbon paper and other parts of the afterbirth of state secrets that might leave telltale signs, and finally scored one day when they found classification stamps which Otepka had clipped from classified documents. Thus declassified informally, the documents were being sent by Otto over to old J. G. Sourwine at the Senate Internal Security Subcommittee, where they were used to help surprise and embarrass Otto's bosses regarding how lightly they took the red menace right here at home. The burn bag also contained a used typewriter ribbon, an instant replay of which revealed that Otepka had worked up a primer of questions for Sourwine that he could use to catch State Department officials in factual errors regarding the communist question.

OTTO'S HIGHEST LOYALTY

When the State Department used the burn bag evidence to fire Otepka, the fireworks and orations began. The *Chicago Tribune* skipped over the classified document problem to define the issue as a test of the principle of patriotism: "There can be no doubt that this case reflects an intention by the Kennedy Administration to conduct a purge of patriots." The Charleston, South Carolina, *News & Courier* agreed: "To reprimand a U.S. citizen for doing his duty would be a shame and an outrage." *Reader's Digest* later published an article called "The Ordeal of Otto Otepka," subtitled, "Why have State Department employees been using tactics of a police state to oust a dedicated security officer whose only sin seems to be loyalty to his country?", which pretty well summed up the conservative presentation of the problem. The police state argument reflects the tactical guideline that it is easier to attack the process by which the opponent operates than the substance of what he says. However, it also bore some risk of the "corner problem," by which people paint themselves into a corner through the hasty use of principles whose future application might haunt them. In this case, the *Digest*'s forthright position against a police state was quite risky. It not only made it tougher to argue in subsequent tirades that the State Department was undisciplined and namby-pamby, but it also would require a redefinition of the issues when the wiretapping and surveillance of J. Edgar Hoover came to the fore. Most conservative

journals ignored the classification question and the he-broke-the-rule point of view, except perhaps to note in passing that classification was nonsense in general and that Otepka's leakage of secret material did not hurt the national interest anyway, but rather struck another blow against the pinkos in the State Department.

Meanwhile, in the Senate, members surveyed the Otepka affair and concluded that the main issue at stake was, as is so often the case, the dignity of the U.S. Senate. Conservative Senator Williams of Delaware remarked that, "In this instance, all that Mr. Otepka was guilty of was cooperating with a congressional committee." Senator Dominick of Colorado thanked Senator Dodd for having "pointed out the very difficult position Senate committees would find themselves in if it continued to be held that the executive branch could prevent any of its employees from coming before Senate committees, either by threatening them with dismissal or by verbally preventing them from testifying under that threat." Dodd, a foreign policy buff, defined the question in terms of national survival: "If those forces bent on destroying Otepka and the nononsense security approach he represents are successful, who knows how many more Chinas or Cubas we may lose?" But Dodd, too, was anxious about the powers of himself and his colleagues, and he entered a long discourse with Senators Strom Thurmond and Frank Lausche on November 5, the day Otepka's dismissal was consummated, which Thurmond climaxed by declaring that the Kennedy Administration's action would "nullify our system of government by tending to destroy the constitutional system of checks and balances." There was no commander-in-chief talk on that day, no talk about how the President's powers were essential to survive in a hostile international environment. The conservatives were safe from the corner problem, however, because the war in Vietnam had not yet begun. The doves in the Senate would not really discover the checks and balances principle until about 1968, leaving the conservatives ample time to switch over to the commander-in-chief line without undue embarrassment.

"ORDERLY PROCEDURES ARE ESSENTIAL"

The liberals in the Senate were exceedingly mousy about Otepka as the supporters of the Kennedy Administration sought to ride out the storm in public silence. This does not necessarily mean that they were apathetic, for some Otepka supporters claim that there was great pressure to let the Otepka fervor die out like the groundswell for General MacArthur. Clark Mollenhoff, a straightforward, very conservative reporter for the *Des Moines Register*, made a speech about the obstacles to coverage of the case:

> I realize the broad range of direct and indirect pressures brought to discourage a defense of Otepka, for I met most of them at some stage from my friends in the Kennedy Administration. One put it crudely: "What are you lining up with Otepka and all those far-right nuts for? Do you want to destroy yourself?"
>
> There were also hints that I could be cut off from the White House contacts and other high Administration contacts if I continued to push for the facts in the Otepka case.

Liberal newspapers made slightly more noise in the dispute than their compatriot senators, and their editorial writers swept aside all the chaff about higher loyalty and patriotism and the dignity of Congress to focus on the principles at stake, with a fixity that is born of discipline. The *Washington Post*, for example, zeroed in on the law and order question, following the rule that it is always best to attack on matters of procedure: "For all of Senator Dodd's sputtering, he must know that what Otto Otepka did was not only unlawful but unconscionable as well. Mr. Otepka certainly knew this himself—which is no doubt why he did it covertly instead of candidly. He gave classi-

fied information to someone not authorized to receive it." The *New York Times* took a similar line, with slightly greater emphasis on propriety: "The disturbing aspect of this case is that both Mr. Otepka and members of the Senate subcommittee have defended their actions on ground of 'higher loyalty'. . . . Orderly procedures are essential if the vital division of powers between the legislative and executive branches is not to be undermined. The use of 'underground' methods to obtain classified documents from lower level officials is a dangerous departure from such orderly procedures."

The liberal press also used words like "controversial," "McCarthyism," "tattle," and "infidelity" as often as possible in connection with Otepka's name. This strategy, following from the rule that it is often useful to adopt your opponent's principles and turn them back on him in verbal counter-insurgency, amounted to McCarthyism turned on its head, as Marx did to Hegel, or guilt by association with McCarthy. Thus, when Otepka defended himself by citing the government employees' Code of Ethics (which charges employees to place loyalty to conscience, country, and the "highest moral principles" above "loyalty to persons, party or government department"), the *Washington Post* news story stated that "the last time that issue was raised with public prominence, it was raised by Senator McCarthy in sweeping form. . . ." A *New York Times* story by Neil Sheehan in 1969 continued this theme of the beat-them-at-their-own-game campaign: "The enthusiastic pursuit of 'subversive elements' in the government loosed by the late Senator Joseph McCarthy slowed to a desultory walk in later years, but Mr. Otepka . . . did not change."

"HIS TRAINED JACKAL, JACK ANDERSON"

Otepka returned to the public light in 1969, when President Nixon made good on his campaign promise to review the case "with a view to seeing that justice is accorded this man who served his country so long and well.'' The Subversive Activities Control Board seemed like an appropriate resting spot for a seasoned personnel sniffer, who could spend the rest of his days perusing political groups for loyalty blemishes. Actually, the SACB was a secondary choice for Otepka, who really wanted to go back to the State Department but was frustrated in his desire by Secretary of State Rogers, who did not want him. Senator Dirksen, claiming Otepka as a constituent and an ideological brother, suggested the SACB spot and went to work with the other conservative senators to give the board and its $36,000-a-year members something to do. They knew that Otepka would be an additional burden in the annual battle with the liberals over the fact that the SACB members are so inert that they appear strikingly like welfare recipients, at ten times the poverty standard.

The task of selling Otepka himself was undertaken with the old principles of patriotism and higher loyalty. In the Senate, the four hoariest members of the Judiciary Committee—Eastland, McClellan, Dirksen, and Hruska—assembled for a confirmation hearing to pay homage to the SACB nominee. "You have been punished because you attempted to protect your country," said Chairman Eastland to Otto, and the four senators respectfully declined to ask the witness anything other than his name.

And Senator Dodd, now deceased, led the fight on the floor of the Senate and helped organize Otepka Day, on which patriots around the nation celebrated his resurrection. Every time Senator Dodd took the floor to wax eloquent about Otepka's higher mission against international communism, he represented the largest collection of loyalty contradictions ever assembled in one place—a veritable one-man intersection of passions on the morality of exposure. For since Dodd had first praised Otepka for exposing the State Department with pilfered documents and denounced the State Depart-

ment for firing the higher patriotism of Otepka, Dodd himself had been exposed for pocketing campaign contributions and other financial misdealings. While Dodd praised the patriot who exposed corruption in the State Department, he fired the infidel who exposed corruption in himself—his administrative assistant of twelve years, James Boyd. Boyd's medium of exposure, the Drew Pearson/Jack Anderson column, decided to switch in the Otepka affair— exposing the exposer, Otepka, because of his leanings to the right. In this vortex of half-hero, it was not surprising that Dodd would resort to arguments tinged with the *ad hominem*, "The press campaign against Otto Otepka has been spearheaded by Drew Pearson, the lying character assassin and his trained jackal, Jack Anderson."

In the end, however, Dodd regained the lofty, joined by the honey tongue of Senator Dirksen—who read to the Senate a moving letter from Mrs. Otepka, describing the hardships the family had faced since Otto had been demoted in 1967, while his dismissal was still being appealed, to a $15,000-a-year job that was so "demeaning" that Otto protested by taking a leave without pay and forced her to go to work to support him. What is $36,000 for a patriot, asked Dirksen and Dodd of their fellow senators, and the two crusaders went to their graves knowing that the world would be better with Otepka on the SACB. Otepka, for his part, called the Senate confirmation "my vindication," and a well-deserved one to boot, because as he later wrote, "I have disagreed only with those who quarrel with the truth. I shall continue to disagree."

NAILING DOWN THE CASE

The vindication did not come easily, for during the period when Senate confirmation was pending, the *New York Times* practiced an enthusiastic brand of beat-them-at-their-own-gamism. Reporter Neil Sheehan was dispatched to check up on Otepka's acquaintances, and began his April 4, 1969, story as follows: "A fund with John Birch Society ties has paid about 80 percent of the $26,500 in legal costs incurred by Otto F. Otepka in his four-year fight to win reinstatement as the State Department's chief security evaluator." The story went on to pin down Otepka's "ties" to the Birchers by declaring that "last summer he attended the four-day annual God, Family, and Country rally in Boston, organized by Birch Society leaders." Sheehan also tracked down James M. Stewart, chief fund-raiser of the American Defense Fund, which channeled money to Otepka's lawyers. Stewart looked and acted like a Bircher, although Sheehan wrote triumphantly that he "would neither affirm nor deny whether he was a member of the Birch Society," saying, like Pete Seeger, "I am not answering that question because it is irrelevant." Beyond such waffling on the affiliation question, Stewart further hanged himself with his reading material, because Sheehan found out, after a hard-nosed inquiry, that "he does subscribe to a number of Birch Society publications."

Having established that Otepka's legal defense was being solicited by a man who might as well have been a Bircher, if he were not in fact a bona fide one, and that Otepka himself was hanging around in right wing crowds, the editorial board of the *New York Times* concluded that Otto was ineligible for membership on the SACB. According to the April 8, 1969, editorial, "The disclosure that Otto Otepka received $22,000 from a fund with extreme right-wing associations should be enough to kill his nomination to the Subversive Activities Control Board. After this, senators of conscience cannot vote to confirm Mr. Otepka in a $36,000-a-year job, where his work, if any, will be to judge the loyalty of American citizens and organizations."

Rather than taking the political view that the whole SACB concept is unconstitutional and therefore should not be supported—or the resigned view that the SACB is a useless bit of welfare, doing nothing, but that it was a shame for the President to use his discretion to appoint, in the *Times'* view, a schmuck like Otto—the editorial rested its case on the assertion that Otto was too tainted to do the job right as a subversive-hunter, and that a neutral mainstreamer would be more efficient. The *Times* thus ventured onto the turf of subversive-hunting and declared Otepka ineligible by the very standards the SACB uses to ferret out dangerous organizations.

An average newspaper might have rested its case there, but fortunately the *Times* is not an average newspaper and therefore was possessed of a "wait a minute" person on the board—the long view of responsibility. Apparently, such a person noticed that the Otepka editorial might look like McCarthyism to some readers, and told his colleagues that such an impression, left uncorrected, would be detrimental to the *Times'* historical commitment against Joe McCarthy's methods. So the argument was sealed with the addition of the following mop-up paragraph:

> The far right doubtless will cry "guilt by association," the charge made long ago by civil libertarians against the likes of Mr. Otepka, but there is a crucial difference here. Mr. Otepka's link to Birchites is no youthful indiscretion of many years ago but an activity carried on as recently as last summer.

Thus, the editorial board took the precautionary measure of protecting its flank against charges of McCarthyism by recalling the best case against old Senator Joe—the telling point about the unfairness of using "youthful indiscretions" that the *Times* itself had once made—and beating it down. This done, the *Times* had at least as strong an indictment against Otepka as McCarthy would have had against his victims if he had not ruined it all by rummaging through their old college notebooks.

The fact that Otto's sins did not fall in the "youthful indiscretion" category probably did carry some weight with a liberal readership—with people who remembered going to the verbal barricades for Alger Hiss and others like him over whether their doings on the left were permanent blemishes of character or merely the wanderings of callow youth. Those people who (perhaps for tactical reasons) had said that what was really wrong with Joe McCarthy was his reliance on outdated evidence, his once-a-subversive-always-a-subversive line, would be relieved to learn that Otepka, unlike Hiss, was still at it. "As recently as last summer," concluded the *Times*, in an apparent reference to the God, Family, and Country rally that Sheehan had uncovered. (Some sources suggest that the freshness of Otto's blight could have been established also by the subscription dates on James Stewart's magazines.) Anyone who bought all of McCarthyism except for the Senator's attacks on people for what they did in the past would be sympathetic to disqualifying Otto from the SACB for associations that persisted well into his maturity.

"HIS PECULIAR INFIDELITY"

After Sheehan wrote another story for the Sunday *Times* on April 20, emphasizing Otepka's right-wing associations and his likeness to a bureaucratic version of Joe McCarthy, Senator Strom Thurmond strode to Otto's battlements by declaring on the Senate floor that the *Times* had deliberately smeared Otepka. He charged that *Times* executive editor Harding Bancroft had commissioned the Sheehan investigation in order to get even with Otto for vexation caused back in 1962, when Bancroft was examined for loyalty before going on the Advisory Committee on Management Improvement to the Assistant Secretary of State for International Organization Affairs, or ACMIASSIOA. The *Times* had no comment on this counter-smear, holding to its position that its interest in Otepka sprang from the logical force of the youthful indiscretion editorial.

Whatever the motivation behind the Sheehan articles, their spirit caught on in the Senate, culminating in Senator Stephen Young's speech against the Otepka nomination on June 24, minutes before the vote. Senator Young avowed that James Stewart, who raised money to give to Otepka's lawyer to use in Otepka's defense, had, on June 16, 1969 "attended a fund-raising party at the home of Julius W. Butler . . . an admitted fund-raiser for the John Birch Society and active in several John Birch front organizations. . . .The guests at Mr. Butler's home last week included Robert Welch, founder and head of the John Birch Society, who spoke at length spewing forth the usual John Birch lunatic obsessions. Mr. and Mrs. James Stewart, I am told, were in charge of the refreshments that were served at the meeting and were introduced to the crowd and received with applause."

All this failed, and the Senate confirmed Otepka by a vote of 61 to 28. The *Washington Post* emphasized the fidelity question in its editorial lament: "Otto Otepka's long and unfaithful service to the State Department certainly entitled him to some reward from those on Capitol Hill who were the beneficiaries of his peculiar form of infidelity." The *New York Times*, as is its custom, focused on the who-are-you question to bewail Otto as a "living symbol of some of the worst days of the McCarthy-McCarran era."

THE ELLSBERG REVERSE

Two years after his investigation of Otepka, Neil Sheehan was ensconced in a New York hideaway as head of a *New York Times* writing team that prepared stories based on the top-secret Pentagon Papers— slipped to the *Times*, the *Washington Post*, and other parties by Daniel Ellsberg. Rather than investigating the left wing associations of Ellsberg (such demented pariahs as Noam Chomsky, SDS leaders, the staff of the *Harvard Crimson*, and the editors of the *Washington Monthly*), or noting the glazed-eyed, Martin Lutherish manner in which Ellsberg had been starting speeches by confessing himself as a war criminal, Sheehan stuck to the material at hand and exposed the deceptions perpetrated by Ellsberg's former bosses. It is possible that Sheehan's views on classified material had changed over the two years since 1969, as had his views on the war in Vietnam. As late as 1967 Sheehan had described himself as only half way along the path from war support to war opposition in a *Times* magazine article entitled "No Longer a Hawk, But Not Yet a Dove." By 1971, he had progressed far enough to write a piece in the *Times* speculating on the possible criminality of people behind him on the path, and this progress helped both Sheehan and Ellsberg decide that the classified document issue paled in significance compared with the overriding injustice of the war.

Of course, the decisions regarding publication of the Pentagon Papers were not made by Sheehan, but by the management of the *Times* and the other papers involved. By 1971, the editors of the *Times* had decided that the real issue involved in the exposure of classified documents was not orderly procedures, but the people's right to know as embodied in the freedom of the press. A June 15 editorial in the *Times* stated that the paper felt it had an obligation to publish the Pentagon Papers "once these materials fell into our hands." The *Times*, almost as disposed to see conflicts in light of its own powers as the Senate is likely to see them turning on Senate dignity, defined its position so narrowly that it left Dan Ellsberg out in the cold. Rather than presenting the Pentagon papers as a joint venture between Ellsberg and the newspaper, the *Times* argued that retribution for "declassifying" the Pentagon Papers was a matter between Ellsberg and the government. The *Times* took responsibility for the papers only when they fell on its doorstep out of nowhere, after which their news value required publication. (There is considerable circumstantial evidence that the *Times* was not as passive in the matters as it implies.)

The *Times'* forthright exposition of press duties in matters hot enough to be classified must have convinced Otto Otepka that *he* could in the future slip classified documents to the *New York Times* and expect to see them published. He must have been heartened by the *Times'* objectivity—by the fact that the editors took no overt political or moral positions regarding why the war papers should be read in spite of their classifications, and that there was no editorial at all on the war series until the government stupidly tried to suppress it and introduced the freedom of the press question. The editors then said that the people should have a chance to read the papers, that neither the government nor the press should stand in the way of such fireside enlightenment, and that no one but the people can really tell what they mean. Otto must have reasoned that the people could also decide what his documents meant—that they could supply the political judgment if the press would only give them the chance, as the *Times* said it should.

Of course, Otto is no fool at $36,000-a-year, and he might have concluded that the *Times'* opinion on the war really did have something to do with its willingness to publish the Pentagon Papers, despite appearances and circumstantial evidence to the contrary. He might have guessed that the *Times* would not have published material like the Pentagon Papers in 1961, 1968, or even in 1969 when he joined the SACB. Even so, the newspaper's changing views on the war would also help get Otto exposure. His previous efforts to sully the reputations and political judgment of war criminals like Walt Rostow and McGeorge Bundy had not been appreciated at all, but the *Times* seemed to have come around enough on the war that it would go for a batch of documents on such men now. Both the *Times'* increasing readiness to examine the doings of war criminals and its agnosticism about the actual meaning of the Pentagon Papers should logically work in Otto's favor—and get his documents at least in the back pages. Nevertheless Otepka must fear lest the strictures about orderly procedures reappear, rising ever above the freedom of the press to leave him out in the cold again.

Despite apparent abandonment by the *New York Times*, the need for orderly procedures was identified as the central issue in the Pentagon Papers controversy by such newspapers as the Richmond *Times-Dispatch*. This journal, which had been all courage and patriotism and Paul Revere when Otto was riding, might well have dipped into the *Washington Post*'s clipping file on Otepka for its editorial on Ellsberg: "If each clerk, administrative assistant, or under secretary could ignore departmental policy and decide for himself how information should be classified, nothing would be safe." Senator Gordon Allot, a supporter of Otto, chimed in with his attention similarly focused on the rules, as he felt they should apply to the *New York Times*. "The point is that the *Times* has neither the right nor the duty to decide which classified documents should be classified in which way."

The State Department has been one of the few bastions of consistency in the Otepka and Ellsberg matters, opposing both men on the procedural grounds of loyalty and classification rules. But while the State Department has seen both the Ellsberg and Otepka cases through a monocle, most of the rest of us have been so wall-eyed on the matter that we have seen no parallel between them at all. When columnist Carl Rowan suggested that Otepka, was "a sort of Daniel Ellsberg in reverse," most of his readers were shocked at the connection proposed, even a reverse one. One reader, Otto Otepka, scoffed at such a kinship in an interview with UPI reporter Marguerite Davis, who wrote that "Otepka said he gave no classified documents to newspapers but merely provided senators, at their request, with information to support his own sworn testimony." Thus, even Otto—convicted by the *New York Times* on a technicality—distinguishes himself from Dan Ellsberg on a

technicality, and a misleading one at that since part of the "information" he gave the senators was a batch of classified documents.

FIDDLING OVER RULES

It is highly ironic that the cases of these two men, whose purposes are so far apart ideologically that it is dangerous to suggest a similarity at any level, have been argued on virtually interchangeable principles. None of them—the Senate's right to know, the people's right to know, freedom of the press, orderly procedures, or national security—went to the heart of the matter. Both men made an essentially moral choice, much like the civil rights sit-ins, to take a specifically illegal step in order to dramatize an injustice that they felt transcended the classification system. Otepka thought the classification system was important, but that the Administration's spinelessness in the Cold War was more important. Ellsberg thought the classification system was important (which is why his decision produced such personal anguish), but that the history of the Vietnam war was more important in its lessons about the past and the nature of the war. Both men made their decisions in the midst of ethical conflict, and any evaluation of them demands that you take a position on why that stand is or is not worthy of support. In other words, given that it is possible for something to be important enough to transcend the classification regulations, you have to make a political judgment about the purposes of Otepka and Ellsberg.

It is well for those of us who support what Ellsberg did—because the Pentagon Papers changed some minds on the war—to keep the Otepka episode in mind. Thinking of his arguments and the furor around him should keep people from being opportunists in debate—from latching on to the arbitrary rules that pop up here and there, like prairie dogs, around any such controversy. These rules, and the sonorous platitudes that editorial writers and politicians trumpet in their names, provide ludicrously poor guidance in evaluating as serious and complex a matter as the Pentagon Papers. By themselves, the rules make an ungrounded compass, each one pointing east for Ellsberg and west for Otepka, in a spectacle that is nearly comic in the conviction people work up over principles like orderly procedures.

Arguing in support of Dan Ellsberg on the basis of the obvious weaknesses in the classification system is shaky because it runs headlong into opposite impulses regarding Otepka. But more importantly, such an argument misses the point. It is like speaking out for a sit-in because of impro-

prieties in the disturbing-the-peace laws, when the real issue is race. Whatever positive force there is in what Ellsberg did comes from the nature of the war and what the Pentagon papers say about the war—from political and moral issues that have no simple ground rules. When the debate strays from that central question, it loses both its passion and its logic, leaving a dusty bag of rules that Otto Otepka can use just as well. When the discussion centers on personalities and sideline skirmishes, it makes fewer converts for the antiwar message of the Pentagon Papers and Ellsberg, and thus detracts from what he is trying to accomplish.

Daniel Ellsberg and the Pentagon Papers
David Rudenstine

Daniel Ellsberg was born in 1931 in Chicago. His parents were middle-class Jews who converted to Christian Science and eventually moved to Detroit, where Ellsberg grew up. In 1948 Ellsberg entered Harvard on a scholarship, studied economics, became president of the *Advocate*, an undergraduate literary magazine, and was elected to the editorial board of the *Crimson*, the college daily newspaper. By his junior year he was married to Carol Cummings, a Radcliffe sophomore and the daughter of a Marine colonel.

He graduated summa cum laude and third in his class in 1952. After another year of study as a Woodrow Wilson Fellow at King's College, Cambridge University, Ellsberg entered the Marines in 1954, where he excelled and obtained the distinction of Marksman. He served as a rifle platoon leader, rifle company commander, and operations offi-

cer. Whereas other lieutenants usually had to surrender their command within a few weeks to captains, Lieutenant Ellsberg was not replaced because his company "won more awards than any other in the battalion and was foremost in inspections and on maneuvers." After Egyptian leader Gamal Abdel Nasser seized the Suez Canal in 1956 Ellsberg extended his enlistment for eight months, so that he could accompany his battalion to the Sixth Fleet in the Mediterranean.

In 1957 Ellsberg returned to Harvard as a junior member of its Society of Fellows, "the most illustrious assemblage of young scholars in American academia," to work on his doctorate, which he earned in 1962. In March 1959 Ellsberg delivered the Lowell Institute Lectures at the Boston Public Library on "The Art of Coercion: A Study of Threats in Economic Conflicts and War," an outgrowth of his academic interest in the theory of bargaining, a popular interest among academics during the 1950s. About the same time Henry Kissinger, a Harvard professor, invited Ellsberg to give two lectures at his seminar on "the conscious political use of irrational military threats." . . . Following his honorable discharge from the Marines, Ellsberg worked as a strategic analyst in the Santa Monica office of the RAND Corporation, a civilian research institute as well as "the brain trust" of the Air Force. He helped to perfect plans for nuclear war against the Soviet Union, China, and other communist states. While there he was given clearances beyond top secret—clearances designated by codes so secret that even members of Congress were unaware of them. Ellsberg then gained potential access to the nation's most highly classified secrets." . . .

Ellsberg left RAND in August 1964, immediately after the United States retaliated for alleged North Vietnamese attacks on U.S. vessels in the Gulf of Tonkin. He joined the Defense Department at the highest possible civil service level, the "super-grade" rank of GS-18. He became an assistant to John T. McNaughton, McNamara's assistant secretary of defense for international security affairs, whom Ellsberg had known for a couple years. McNaughton headed the Pentagon's foreign-policy office and played a key role within the Pentagon on Vietnam issues. McNaughton told Ellsberg that he was spending 70 percent of his time on Vietnam and that he wanted Ellsberg to spend 100 percent of his time on it. Ellsberg knew little about Vietnam, but he was eager to learn and anxious to observe the government's decision-making process from the inside. During the spring of 1965 he helped plan for the dispatch in June of U.S. ground troops to Vietnam. He also defended Rolling Thunder, the code name for U.S. air attacks against North Vietnam, to members of Congress and to audiences on college campuses.

The following year Ellsberg's personal life disintegrated when his wife insisted on a divorce. Ellsberg had two children and became despondent. That, combined with a sense of romanticism, a need to prove himself, and a sense of duty that he should be with the soldiers in Vietnam since he helped develop the plans that put them there, led Ellsberg to want to return to Vietnam. McNaughton had become "skittish" about Ellsberg because he boasted about what he knew—a characteristic that became heightened by his divorce. As a result McNaughton let Ellsberg leave the Pentagon without a struggle. Ellsberg volunteered to fight in Vietnam as a Marine company commander but was informed that he ranked too high in the civilian bureaucracy for such "mundane" military duty. He then managed to find another way to return to Vietnam—by becoming a special liaison officer under retired Major General Edward G. Lansdale, "a free-wheeling expert on counterinsurgency." Lansdale was returning to South Vietnam as a member of the State Department, attached to the U.S. embassy in Saigon. Officially, Lansdale and his team were assigned to act as a liaison between the embassy and Saigon's Rural Reconstruction Council, a group that theoretically coordinated the government's pacification programs. In fact Lansdale's operation was trying to reform the Saigon regime and develop an effective pacification program.

During his Vietnam tour as a civilian, Ellsberg studied the pacification program and went out on patrol with Marine units in central Vietnam and accompanied Army units in the Mekong Delta. During these military operations he carried a carbine, was repeatedly caught in combat, and risked his life on several occasions. Years later, Ellsberg vividly recalled these patrols: "a couple of times when I was with the lead squad going through a paddy, Vietcong rose from the paddy we had just walked through and fired at the people behind us.". . .

Ellsberg's Vietnam experiences profoundly affected him. When he arrived in Vietnam in 1965, Ellsberg thought of "the war's tactics morally justified on the assumption that the war itself was necessary." A few years later he himself summed up his views to a *Look* reporter: "I had accepted the official answer, . . . namely that there was a civil war going on, that we had a right to intervene and pick one side or the other if our interests were involved, and our interests were involved. That if the wrong side should win this war, it would be worse for the Vietnamese people, worse for the United States and for world peace. It would mean victory for the people who wished us ill and who would behave more aggressively in other parts of the world, which we would also have to counter." However, by the spring of 1967, when a severe case of hepatitis caused Ellsberg to return to the United States, he had become discouraged by the continuing violence of the war and by the unwillingness of the United States to change its approach. Overwhelmed by the war's futility, he felt a growing sense that "the programs we were pursuing had no chance of succeeding." He was convinced that the programs in Vietnam "were not in any way proceeding as people thought they were back in Washington," and he had essentially concluded that the United States "should get out of the war."

This was Ellsberg's frame of mind when, in the late summer of 1967, Halperin and Gelb asked him to join the staff of the Pentagon Papers project. Ellsberg has stated that Helperin and Gelb "were very anxious to get" him to become one of the so-called Pentagon historians and that he was one of the first people they approached. From a personal point of view Ellsberg thought it was "crucial" for him to become part of the staff, since he viewed the study as a way of rethinking U.S. policy and discussing what had gone wrong. Ellsberg has said that he insisted as "the price . . . [of] participating as a researcher" that he be permitted to read "the whole study," but neither Halperin nor Gelb recall such an understanding.

Ellsberg chose the Kennedy administration's 1961 policy in Vietnam for his assignment, largely because he felt more familiar with this period. He spent roughly four months locating documents and assembling research material. Then, in December 1967,

he wrote approximately 350 pages of a draft report. He wanted to return to the West Coast to finish the draft, but Gelb objected because he worried that Ellsberg would not complete the work if he left Washington. Ellsberg left anyway and has claimed that his essay remained largely intact when the full study was eventually concluded. Leslie Gelb has stated, however, that "very few of Ellsberg's words finally appeared."

Ellsberg's attitudes, perspective, and values continued to shift during 1968. In early April he attended a conference on "America in a Revolutionary World" at Princeton University. For the first time in his life he met "activists" from the antinuclear movement of the 1950s and the civil rights and antiwar movements of the 1960s. At his luncheon table he sat across from a young woman from India who was dressed in a sari and who had a dot of red dust on her forehead. Her name was Janaki. At one point during the conversation Janaki said: "I come from a culture in which there is no concept of 'enemy.'" Ellsberg was confused by the statement and captivated by the woman. He felt that he came from a culture "in which the concept of 'enemy' was central, seemingly indispensable: the culture of RAND, the Marines, the Defense and State Departments, international and domestic politics, game theory and bargaining theory."

Identifying and understanding the enemy had been part of Ellsberg's "daily bread and butter, part of the air I breathed." Now he was "intrigued" by this Indian woman and what he considered her "Gandhian algebra." He talked with her throughout the day and into the evening. He learned about her life and her commitment to nonviolence. He asked what books she thought he should read if he wanted to learn more about Gandhi and his way of thinking. At the end of the day they learned that Martin Luther King had just been killed and that "Washington was burning."

Clearly, Ellsberg was deeply disoriented and in the process of major shifts in thought and belief. Indeed, his deepening rejection of his prior support of the war; his sudden fascination with nonviolence; his apparent willingness to accept that there are cultures with no concept of enemy; and his later recollection that this was the day "when my life started to change": all of these, as well as other factors, suggest a set of beliefs and attitudes that were in the midst of intense and radical change.

Tumultuous public events of the late winter and spring of 1968 fueled Ellsberg's evolution. The Tet offensive, which had occurred shortly before Ellsberg met Janaki, seemed to intensify his conviction that the violence in Vietnam was senseless and immoral. The assassination of Senator Robert F. Kennedy—only a couple months after King's—caused Ellsberg to lose confidence in the efficacy of traditional political processes. After the Democratic party rejected a peace plan at its Chicago national convention Ellsberg felt even less confidence in the political system. Increasingly unanchored and without a political compass, Ellsberg got little work done, dated many women, and began psychoanalysis with Doctor Lewis Fielding in Beverly Hills.

Soon after his election in 1968, Nixon appointed Henry Kissinger as his national security adviser. One of Kissinger's first moves was to telephone Henry Rowen, president of RAND and a former Pentagon official, to ask him to prepare a paper that listed the administration's possible options for the Vietnam War. Rowen asked Ellsberg to take on the assignment and he accepted. On Christmas Day Rowen, Ellsberg, and another RAND official flew to New York and met with Kissinger at Nixon's transition headquarters in the Pierre Hotel. Ellsberg's paper did not include a "win" or a "threat" option, but it did list an option of unilateral withdrawal by the United States. Thomas C. Schelling, a Kissinger colleague from Harvard, commented on the absence of the "win" and "threat" alternatives. Ellsberg told the group that he did not think "there is

a win option in Vietnam" but that he would include a "threat" option even though he did not understand "how threatening bombing is going to influence the enemy because they have experienced four years of bombing." Before the paper was completed Kissinger arranged for the elimination of the "withdrawal" alternative. Shortly thereafter, Kissinger asked Ellsberg to prepare an exhaustive list of questions about Vietnam that could be presented to various parts of the government, including the Defense and State Departments, the CIA, and the American Embassy in Saigon. In February 1969 Kissinger again asked Ellsberg to return to Washington, this time to summarize the answers to the questionnaire. Ellsberg worked on the project through most of March.

It was around this time (and for reasons that are not clear) that Ellsberg decided he wanted to read the entire Pentagon Papers. He was working on a Defense Department project at the RAND Corporation, but he did not need access to the classified study to complete his research. Nor did he seem to have any larger political purpose for reading the report. What seems likely is that, given his own deep involvement with Vietnam and his complete change of viewpoint, he was beginning his own search into the historical records to understand what had happened in Vietnam; to trace his own relation to the war as it had evolved; and perhaps to find a far greater clarification or revelation of the entire experience than had so far been fully grasped by anyone.

Ellsberg asked Henry Rowen to help him gain access to the top secret Pentagon study. Since Morton Halperin and Paul Warnke had stored a copy of the report at RAND, Rowen contacted Halperin, who telephoned Gelb. But Gelb did not trust Ellsberg to protect the confidentiality of the study and would not consent to the request. Shortly afterward, Halperin contacted Gelb again, this time pressing harder, arguing that Ellsberg had worked on the project, that he was doing an assignment for the Pentagon, that access to the classified report would be useful, and that Ellsberg had all the requisite security clearances. He added he did not believe they had any reasonable basis for turning Ellsberg down. All these reasons made it awkward for Gelb to continue his objections. Halperin passed the word along to Rowen, so Ellsberg gained access to the secret history.

Ellsberg's six-month study of the Pentagon history greatly affected his thinking. It was not any one document or any one incident or series of incidents that had such an impact on him. What was most striking was the fact that American policy in 1969 appeared to be a direct descendant of the policy pursued by the Truman administration immediately following World War II. As Ellsberg explained to a reporter in 1971: "The startling thing that came out of them was how the same sets of alternatives began to appear to each President, and ultimately the choice was neither to go for broke and adopt military recommendations, nor negotiate a settlement to get out. The decisions year after year were to continue the war, although all predictions pointed to a continued stalemate with this kind of approach and thus to prolong the war indefinitely." As a consequence of his analysis, Ellsberg came to see the war not as "Kennedy's war or Johnson's War" but as the result of a "pattern of behavior that went far beyond any one" president. "It was a war," Ellsberg concluded, "no American President had . . . the courage to turn down or to stay out of." When Ellsberg applied these insights to the Nixon administration, he concluded that "Nixon was the fifth President in succession to be subjected to the same pressures that had led four other Presidents to maintain involvement; that his assurances that he had no intention of staying in Indochina were no more to be believed than other Presidents' assurances . . . that whatever his feelings were as of '69, the more he got involved, the more sure it was that he would stay involved.

Even before he studied the Pentagon Papers, Ellsberg had already begun to change his view of what Nixon was prepared to do in Vietnam. He wanted to believe Kissinger's representations that the Nixon administration intended to extricate the United States from the war, and he had initially hoped that the conflict would soon begin to wind down. By September 1969, however, Ellsberg had concluded that Nixon and Kissinger intended to escalate hostilities in hopes of coercing North Vietnam to accept a political settlement acceptable to the United States. Specifically, Ellsberg thought Nixon would not go into the 1972 elections without having mined Haiphong harbor. Ellsberg believed this because of information that Halperin, who had by now resigned from the national security staff, had passed on to him.

About the same time Ellsberg attended a conference at Haverford College organized by the War Resisters International. Ellsberg did not think of himself as a pacifist, and indeed he mentioned once that he particularly admired the character played by John Wayne in the *The Sands of Iwo Jima*. Now, however, he noticed that those whom he admired were often women and nonwhite, and he now "wanted to meet people who did see themselves" as pacifist.

Ellsberg was impressed by the draft resisters he met at Haverford. He found them "conscientious, reasonable, and not fanatics. . . . They just seemed to feel that they could not collaborate in the war and were prepared to go to jail." But it was a young man named Randy Kehler who most affected Ellsberg. Kehler had been impressive earlier at the conference. He was one of the organizers of the entire session, and Ellsberg noted that Kehler "listened carefully, responded thoughtfully and with good sense. Of the many younger American activists I had met at the conference, he was the one I most wanted to see more of." Kehler struck Ellsberg as having a "simple and direct manner," as well as "warmth and humor." When Kehler finally spoke on a panel on the last day of the conference, Ellsberg was "surprised" to learn that, like himself, Kehler spoke of friends who had recently gone to prison and of his own impending imprisonment because of draft resistance. He spoke with fervor. Some in the audience stood silently; others applauded.

While listening to Kehler, Ellsberg began to cry. His friend Janaki was to speak next, but he was too upset to stay. He left the amphitheater and made his way down the back corridor to a men's room. Once inside he began "to sob convulsively, uncontrollably." He remained there alone, for over an hour, without getting up, his head sometimes tilted back against the wall, sometimes in his hands.

It was at this moment that Ellsberg began to consider seriously what he might do to change American war policy in Vietnam. He also felt that, if he were going to take a major risk, he wanted to be certain he could have a major impact. Because Ellsberg had been close to power and to people in power, it is most unlikely that he could imagine being an unsung imprisoned war resister or another anonymous body in a protest crowd. What is more likely is that Ellsberg imagined he would be in the center of events, with a central role in whatever drama was to be enacted.

Before long Ellsberg found himself thinking of the 7,000-page top secret report that was in the RAND safe. Reading the report had convinced him that U.S. efforts to maintain or to escalate the war would fail to bring North Vietnam to the bargaining table, and he began to believe that others might be similarly affected if they could see the documents. He also thought he might be able to change the political calculus, so that Nixon would begin to be more fearful of political attacks from the antiwar constituency than from those who would attack him if North Vietnam were to win the war—or at least to hold its own indefinitely. Ellsberg brooded over whether he could actually leak the classified study. He had been a RAND em-

ployee, a Pentagon employee, a White House consultant, and a confidant of high-ranking Pentagon and State Department officials. Could he actually betray his friends, his colleagues, and the trust that had been placed in him by making the top secret report public?

Ellsberg's indecision ended on September 29, when he learned that Secretary of the Army Stanley R. Resor had decided not to file charges against six Special Forces men accused of assassinating an alleged South Vietnamese double agent. Ellsberg thought that in its most immediate sense the army's decision to drop charges meant that military officials could not be trusted to hold soldiers responsible for their conduct. But, more generally, what was left of Ellsberg's faith in the military's willingness to enforce its own rules was undermined by Resor's announcement.

Ellsberg telephoned Anthony Russo, his friend from Vietnam and RAND who was also strongly opposed to the war. Ellsberg asked Russo if he knew of a photocopy machine that could be used to duplicate the Pentagon Papers. Lynda Sinay, Russo's girlfriend, ran her own advertising agency, and she agreed to let the two men use the agency's machine. Ellsberg had no trouble bringing the top secret documents out of RAND or returning them. He would fill his briefcase with parts of the study about 11:30 P.M., carry the briefcase past the security guard, who did not examine his bags; presumably because he knew Ellsberg. Ellsberg would photocopy the documents for several hours, have breakfast at a local restaurant, and return the documents to his RAND safe early in the morning. He followed this pattern for several weeks, sometimes making as many as forty or fifty copies of a particular document. On occasion Russo would help Ellsberg, and at least once Ellsberg's two children helped out.

Ellsberg consulted a few lawyers, whom he has refused to identify, about whether his disclosure of the report would subject him to any criminal liability. Ellsberg's memory of what he was advised is vague and incomplete. But it seems likely, given that Ellsberg came to believe that he ran the risk of long-term imprisonment if he made the Pentagon Papers public, that the lawyers told him he would be liable under existing espionage laws if he gave the documents to anyone not authorized to receive them. Consequently, the best way for Ellsberg to avoid criminal liability was to give the papers to someone who had the proper security clearance. One option that Ellsberg aggressively pursued, for example, was to give the documents to a member of Congress who had the requisite clearances and would be willing to make the papers public in Congress or at a congressional committee hearing so they might be published in the *Congressional Record*. Members of Congress are protected from criminal prosecution by the Constitution in accordance with the speech and debate clause for actions they undertake consistent with official duties and responsibilities. Ellsberg did remember that the lawyers advised him that "the surest way to get myself in prison for a long time" was to give the Pentagon Papers to the press.

In early October Ellsberg met with Senator J. William Fulbright, chairman of the Foreign Relations Committee and the senate's leading dove; he also had the necessary security clearances. Ellsberg told him about the Pentagon Papers, gave him some documents from the study, plus a summary of the entire study and what he thought it revealed. Fulbright had previously scheduled public hearings before the Foreign Relations Committee on Vietnam, with the aim of considering legislation to stop funding for the war. Fulbright invited Ellsberg to be a witness and to make public whatever he wanted. But shortly thereafter, Fulbright backed away from his intention to hold public hearings. He told Ellsberg he had changed his mind,

because "I believe the President's own statement that he is trying to wind down the war in Vietnam." Ellsberg tried to persuade Fulbright to change his mind by convincing him that Johnson had deceived him over the Tonkin Gulf Resolution. But Ellsberg could not budge Fulbright, and eventually Fulbright informed Ellsberg that there was no support in his committee for testimony critical of the war. Fulbright, however, did tell Ellsberg that he would write Secretary of Defense Melvin Laird and request that the classified history be declassified and released to his committee. . . .

Ellsberg eventually concluded that Fulbright was not going to make the documents public. He was frustrated and unsure of what to do next. He spoke with more lawyers about the possibility of a war crimes investigation in which he might appear as a witness and disclose the documents. In this way, particularly if the documents were subpoenaed, he hoped that his criminal liability would be minimized. But the lawyers apparently did not think the proposal was practical and did not follow up his suggestion.

At this point Ellsberg began to explore several alternatives. He became a consultant to Senator Charles Goodell and helped to prepare testimony the senator gave before the Senate Foreign Relations Committee in February 1970. Goodell was testifying in support of a bill that would require the withdrawal of U.S. troops from Vietnam. In the process Ellsberg gave Fulbright more pages from the classified history, including the Joint Chiefs of Staff study of the Tonkin Gulf incident, hoping the senator would make the documents public. He also gave a substantial portion of the study to Marcus G. Raskin and Richard J. Barnet, who were based at the Institute for Policy Studies and were writing a book on the Vietnam War. But as active as Ellsberg was in trying to find an outlet for the Pentagon Papers, he was still unable to do so. . . .

In January 1971 Ellsberg turned to Senator George McGovern for possible help. McGovern was a sponsor of a major end-the-war amendment and the first announced candidate for the 1972 Democratic party presidential nomination. Ellsberg told McGovern that he was in possession of classified documents that would expose the misguided nature of U.S. policy in Vietnam and, if revealed, could hasten the end of the war. McGovern was initially interested in discussing the study with Ellsberg but then abruptly decided against any involvement in an effort to place classified documents in the public domain. He terminated further conversations with Ellsberg, stating he did not trust him. McGovern counseled Ellsberg to turn the papers over to the *Times* or the *Post*. But that makes little sense if McGovern was convinced the documents were authentic, and he seems to have accepted their authenticity. Distrust may well have played some role in McGovern's decision. But McGovern also must have realized that disclosure of the top secret history might strike a large portion of the public as irresponsible and thus undermine his effort to convince the public that he had the stature to be president.

By late January 1971 Ellsberg was so frustrated that he took a step that essentially ended his relationship with Kissinger. At a conference sponsored by MIT Ellsberg took advantage of the question period to ask Kissinger, who had made a presentation, about the administration's estimate of the Asian casualties that would result from Vietnamization. Kissinger hesitated and then characterized Ellsberg's question as "cleverly worded" and stated that "I answer even if I don't answer." Kissinger then tried to avoid the question, but Ellsberg interrupted, repeated the question, and stated: "can't you just give us an answer or tell us that

you don't have such estimates?" Kissinger did not answer the question, and the student moderator, sensing the sudden tension in the room, abruptly ended the panel discussion.

In February Ellsberg began to give more serious consideration to the advice that several political leaders, including McGovern, had given him: to give the classified study to the *New York Times*. Ellsberg had been reluctant to do this, because he feared the possibility of criminal prosecution. But he no longer had any other apparent option. He had asked many prominent members of Congress, including Senator Fulbright, Senator McGovern, Senator Charles Mathias, and Representative Paul N. (Pete) McCloskey, to release the documents, but all had refused. His efforts with Kissinger had also come to naught. The issue Ellsberg had to decide now was which reporter to contact. His most likely prospect was Neil Sheehan of the *New York Times*. . . .

Ellsberg and Sheehan had met in Vietnam and again in Washington. Ellsberg has claimed that he even leaked information to Sheehan during the late 1960s and that he was favorably impressed with how Sheehan had dealt with the information and had protected him. In December 1970 Ellsberg became convinced that Sheehan might be the right reporter to get the Pentagon Papers to the public when he read Sheehan's highly critical book review of Mark Lane's *Conversations with Americans* in the *Times*. In the course of the review Sheehan called for an inquiry into "war crimes and atrocities" committed by the U.S. military in Vietnam, an idea Ellsberg supported. Sheehan wrote that the "country desperately needs a sane and honest inquiry into the question of war crimes and atrocities in Vietnam by a body of knowledgeable and responsible men not beholden to the current military establishment." Sheehan thought the "men who now run the military establishment cannot conduct a credible investigation." Sheehan claimed that the "need" for such an inquiry was "self-evident," since "too large a segment of the citizenry" believed such acts had occurred.

Nevertheless, Ellsberg did not contact Sheehan until mid-February. When they met, Sheehan showed Ellsberg a draft of a long essay, eventually published in the *New York Times* book review section, reviewing thirty-three antiwar books and addressing the question of whether the United States had committed war crimes in Vietnam. Ellsberg was impressed, but he did not give Sheehan the Pentagon Papers. Ellsberg returned to Washington during the last weekend in February. He was scheduled to participate in a panel discussion at the National War College on Vietnam on Monday. He met with Raskin and discussed his frustration with making the Pentagon Papers public. Raskin urged Ellsberg to discuss with Sheehan the possibility of having the *Times* publish the papers. Ellsberg was persuaded. He telephoned Sheehan on the last Sunday in February. They met at Sheehan's Washington home and spent the night discussing the war.

Ellsberg told Sheehan of the study and what it contained. Sheehan already knew of the study; he had probably even discussed it with Raskin, Barnet, and Ralph Stavins, all of the Institute for Policy Studies, when they contacted him after Sheehan's December book review was published. Ellsberg asked Sheehan's advice on what he should do with the history. From the start Sheehan took the position that he could not help Ellsberg unless he read the study. He also told Ellsberg that he could not make any commitments on behalf of the *Times* and that the *Times* would not make any commitments until its editors had read the study.

Ellsberg told Sheehan that he had two conditions that had to be met before he could give the study to the *Times*. One, he wanted the *Times* to devote substantial space so that a great portion of the 7,000 pages were published. Two, he wanted the newspaper to

print documents. It would not be enough to print a report based on the documents. Ellsberg wanted readers to read the documents themselves. Sheehan made it clear to Ellsberg that he and the *Times* editors had to see the documents first. The meeting ended without either man making a commitment of any kind. . . .

After several discussions Ellsberg agreed to make the papers available to Sheehan. On Friday March 19 Sheehan and his wife, Susan, a writer, traveled to Cambridge, Massachusetts, and checked into the Treadway Motor Inn as Mr. And Mrs. Thompson. As previously arranged, Sheehan met with Ellsberg, who took him to an apartment in Cambridge. Ellsberg allowed Sheehan to read the Pentagon Papers, the Joint Chiefs of Staff report on the Tonkin Gulf incident, and early drafts of some historical studies that ultimately became part of the Pentagon Papers. He withheld from Sheehan the four volumes that traced the diplomatic history of the war from 1964 to 1968, so as to minimize any criticism that he had jeopardized peace discussions, and the footnotes, out of fear they might compromise U.S. intelligence interests.

The understanding between Ellsberg and Sheehan remains unclear to this day. What seems likely is that Ellsberg gave Sheehan permission to read the classified material and to make notes on what he read. He did not give Sheehan permission to copy or to duplicate the documents in any way. Sheehan accepted these terms, and Ellsberg gave Sheehan a key to the apartment so he could come and go as he pleased over the weekend.

Ellsberg must have realized he was taking a risk by leaving Sheehan unmonitored with thousands of pages of newsworthy, top secret documents. Sheehan was an able news reporter who had already publicly called for a war crimes investigation. Sheehan might well look upon the secret history not only as evidence of war crimes but as the spark that might prompt an official war crimes inquiry. Indeed, the whole situation suggested that Ellsberg wanted and expected Sheehan to do precisely what he told him not to do: photocopy the documents.

Ellsberg wanted the documents out and the *Times* was the best option he had for making them public. But Ellsberg did not want to give Sheehan the documents, because lawyers had told him he ran the risk of going to prison if he gave the documents to the press. Thus, Ellsberg may have decided that the best way to reduce his risk of criminal prosecution was not to give Sheehan the documents but to place him in a situation in which he could do precisely what Ellsberg told him not to do.

Once alone with the documents, Sheehan apparently swiftly proceeded to photocopy the documents. From a pay phone Sheehan called William Kovach, the *Times*'s Boston correspondent. Sheehan told Kovach he wanted to copy some important documents he had obtained from MIT and that he had to return them by Monday morning. He also told Kovach he needed money to pay for the photocopying. Kovach called the owner of a photocopy shop in Bedford who agreed to hire additional help for the weekend so the job could be completed by Monday morning. Sheehan and his wife loaded the documents into several shopping bags and took a taxi to Bedford. Kovach telephoned the *Times*'s New York office and asked that $1,500 be wired to him, which it was. Al-though the photocopying machines in Bedford broke before the job was completed, a second shop was located, and the job was completed by the end of the weekend. It is not known if Sheehan or Ellsberg saw or spoke to each other at the conclusion of the weekend.

Although Sheehan has not offered a public explanation for his actions, he was likely motivated by several considerations. As did Ellsberg, Sheehan believed that the disclosure of the secret Pentagon history might well shorten the war and force a war crimes investigation. Sheehan was unsatisfied with his reporting assignment, and his prospects at the *Times* seemed limited. Getting his hands on McNamara's secret Vietnam history may have been a way of resuscitating his reporting career and his chances of becoming a *Times* editor. It would also give him a crack at winning a Pulitzer Prize.

Sheehan and Ellsberg stayed in touch with each other during the next several weeks. Apparently Sheehan never told Ellsberg he had photocopied the documents, and Ellsberg never told Sheehan—at least in so many words—that he could do so. What they said to each other is not known, but the conversations served to keep each somewhat informed of the other's actions. Ellsberg, who was still hoping to orchestrate the disclosure of the Pentagon Papers, wanted to stay abreast of Sheehan's activities. Sheehan, worried that Ellsberg might give the papers to another reporter, wanted to stay informed of Ellsberg's movements.

Comment

Do you agree that "anyone who wishes to justify civil disobedience by officials must take his Otepkas with his Ellsbergs"? Both Otepka and Ellsberg broke the law and acted alone in secret and in the service of what they believed to be an important public interest. It is tempting to try to distinguish the two acts of disobedience by saying that one sought the right end and the other did not. But this evades the problem of what means are justifiable when society disagrees about the ends. Consider whether these differences in the means make any moral difference: (1) releasing information to the press or to a congressional staffer; (2) extensive or negligible efforts to appeal to other officials; (3) some or no likelihood that release of information could endanger national security; (4) status as a private citizen or as a public official at the time of the act.

The State Department's view about such disobedience would treat Otepka and Ellsberg alike; both were wrong. Evaluate the best argument you can construct for this view. An alternative position that also treats Otepka and Ellsberg alike would conclude that both were justified. One difficulty with this conclusion is that neither acted publicly, as the traditional theory of civil disobedience requires. Should official disobedience always have to be public to be legitimate? Does the comparison of Ellsberg and Otepka suggest any revisions in the traditional criteria of civil disobedience when they are applied to public officials?

George Shultz and the Polygraph Test
Don Lippincott

On December 19, 1985, Secretary of State George Shultz, widely considered to be a politically discreet team player (unlike his predecessor, Alexander Haig), stung the administration when he publicly threatened to resign. This action was not based on a substantive disagreement over foreign policy. Rather, Shultz was demonstrating—in no uncertain terms—his strong opposition to an administration plan to require polygraph (lie detector) tests for all government officials with access to "highly classified information." Roughly 182,000 government employees—including some agency heads like Shultz—were to be affected by this plan, including about 4,500 members of the State Department. In remarks to reporters in the department,

Shultz proclaimed that his first lie detector test would be his last, adding. "The minute in this government I am told that I'm not trusted is the day I leave."[1]

BACKGROUND: THE REAGAN ADMINISTRATION AND THE POLYGRAPH

From the outset, the Reagan Administration has been strongly interested in crushing espionage activities within the U.S. government. While the problem has plagued governments since time immemorial, a rash of recent revelations about spying in the United States has alarmed many Reagan officials as well as much of the public. Among the recent examples of espionage within the government was the late 1983 arrest of a California engineer accused of selling secret defense papers to the Poles. (The engineer's wife, who worked for a California company doing military research, had security clear-

Reprinted by permission of the Case Program. Kennedy School of Government, Harvard University. Copyright 1986 by the President and Fellows of Harvard College.

ance.) At the end of 1984, an ex-CIA employee was arrested on the charge of spying for Czechoslovakia. Then, in what the *Washington Post* termed "the year of the spy," 1985 witnessed an unprecedented wave of spying accusations within the U.S. government. In June, the FBI nabbed three members of the Arthur Walker family, who had apparently been passing important naval intelligence information to the Soviets for years. According to one administration official, these arrests were only "the tip of the iceberg."[2] This claim was substantiated in late November when arrests of four alleged spies in five days grabbed the nation's attention.

Former Ambassador to the United Nations Jeane Kirkpatrick offered her views of the problem of espionage in an editorial in the *Washington Post*:

> Whether the spy works for money (as the Walker ring apparently did) or for love of another country or ideology (as the Rosenbergs did), spying can seriously damage national security. The Walkers, for example, have apparently compromised our communication system and endangered aspects of our defenses.
>
> That the Soviet Union encourages such betrayals of national security is beyond reasonable doubt. They also rely on spying to promote development. Documents captured when the French government broke a major spy ring two years ago (and expelled 47 Soviet officials) confirmed that the Soviets rely heavily on planned theft and stolen technology and field large networks of spies to steal the desired technology.
>
> Spying is big, serious, dirty business and does us real harm. Recent disclosures suggest, moreover, that it may be increasing.[3]

Whether spying has been increasing or whether there is simply better counterespionage today is a debatable issue. What's clear is that the wave of spying revelations has whetted the appetite of certain administration officials—such as CIA Director William Casey—for tighter security controls. The polygraph has been one of his favorite

tools. The CIA and National Security Agency use the device to screen the backgrounds of all prospective employees, with random examinations given subsequently. The State Department does neither.

On another front, the administration has proposed on more than one occasion that polygraphs be used to help prevent leaks from government employees to the press. Ex-Ambassador Kirkpatrick offers her views of how leaks have affected the Reagan Administration:

> For five years leaks—of information and disinformation—have plagued the Reagan Administration, embarrassing the government, complicating policy-making and creating international problems. Leaks have been used at high, high levels of government to undermine policy rivals and advance personnel ambitions. They have caused real damage to policies and policymakers. They have undermined our government's dignity. They have called into question the president's competence.[4]

Throughout the Reagan years, Congress has been decidedly more hesitant about supporting government use of polygraphs (although it did authorize a pilot Defense Department polygraph clearance program—for 3,500 employees and contractors in 1986 and twice that number in 1987—in the summer of 1985). For instance, when President Reagan sought approval of an order to require government employees to submit to the polygraph during investigations of leaks to the media, Congress blocked the move. Moreover, during the 99th Congress, Congress was also "seriously considering a [bill] to ban the use of polygraphs in the private sector."[5]

While admitting the seriousness of the threat to national security posed by espionage, polygraph opponents argue that the tests are an invasion of privacy as well as a form of harassment. Opponents also contend that the polygraph is hardly an infallible instrument. They have argued that not only do polygraphs often "miss" known spies—

such as Larry Wu-Tai Chin, an ex-CIA employee who spied for China for more than thirty years—but they also intimidate and run the risk of jeopardizing the careers of innocent people, who are not trained to react with the icy calm (or feigned emotion) that CIA and KGB "spooks" utilize to beat the system. They also point out that the results of polygraphs "are not used as evidence in Federal court . . .because of the[ir] notorious unreliability."[6] An article in the *National Journal* entitled "To Tell the Truth," discussed some competing views concerning the reliability of polygraph tests for pre-employment screening:

> Use of the test for [employment] screenings raises the loudest objections from civil libertarians. One objection is that "there is little research or scientific evidence to establish polygraph test validity in screening situations," as the congressional Office of Technology Assessment (OTA) concluded in 1983. The CIA and NSA, though, say that despite its limitations in actually finding liars, the test often compels confessions.[7]

Deja Vu

The Reagan administration had discussed instituting more widespread use of polygraphs, prior to issuing its new directive in late 1985. On at least one occasion, news leaks had been the major impetus for the discussion. The *Washington Post* sketched an interesting vignette of the earlier episode:

> Shortly before noon on Sept. 14, 1983, [White House aide Michael] Deaver entered the Oval Office to find Edwin Meese III (then White House counselor) and William P. Clark (then national security affairs adviser) in an intense and apparently confidential conversation with Reagan about a paper they wanted him to sign. The paper, Deaver discovered, would have authorized the FBI to use polygraphs to investigate top officials who were privy to highly classified decision-making about Lebanon.

Two days earlier, NBC News had reported that Reagan was secretly considering air strikes against Syrian positions in Lebanon where Marines were being shelled heavily. Meese and Clark were furious at the leak and determined to identify the culprit.

Deaver described the Oval Office scene he had encountered to James A. Baker III (then White House chief of staff) while the two were driving to lunch. According to a later account, Baker was so alarmed that he ordered the car back to the White House, where Baker and Deaver barged into a luncheon meeting of Reagan with Shultz and Vice President Bush.

Shultz and Bush were startled to learn of the plan and like Deaver and Baker, they criticized any requirement that top officials submit to polygraphs. If asked to prove his veracity with a polygraph, Shultz declared, "Here's a secretary of state who isn't going to stay."[8]

The Meese-Clark paper ultimately went unsigned by the president.

August 1985: Directive 196

The most recent directive emerged from the administration's National Security Planning Group (NSPG), a small National Security Council (NSC) committee chaired by National Security Adviser Robert McFarlane and including Schultz, CIA Director William Casey and Defense Secretary Casper Weinberger. In an August committee meeting about possible countermeasures of spying, Casey had been the chief advocate of employing the polygraph tests, which were already in wide use at the CIA and National Security Agency. Casey apparently claimed that it was vital for national security to monitor all agency personnel handling highly classified information. According to the *Washington Post*, at this meeting:

> Shultz reportedly expressed his deeply felt view that what he termed "so-called lie detector tests" are misleading and ineffective, and that their imposition on public servants in non-secret jobs carries the message that their loyalty and character is in question."[9]

The meeting apparently produced no decision on the Casey recommendation. A subsequent article reported that the defense secretary had experienced a change of heart after learning of Shultz's position:

> Weinberger was "no big fan" of lie detectors, but when he discovered Shultz's opposition, the defense secretary "fell in love with polygraphs," one involved official sa[id].[10]

THE PRESIDENT SIGNS

On November 1, President Reagan signed National Security Decision Directive 196, affirming the NSC committee recommendation that:

> The U.S. government adopt, in principle, the use of aperiodic non-lifestyle, CI (counterintelligence)-type polygraph examinations for all individuals with access to U.S. government sensitive compartmented information (SCI), communications security information (COMSEC) and other special access program classified information.

Though a member of the committee, Shultz only learned of the decision when the White House mailed him a copy of the five-page directive shortly after it was signed. He was not pleased. According to one aide, who informed the secretary that certain State Department officials would threaten to resign if they were forced to submit to the polygraph, Shultz tersely replied, "And I'm one of them."[11]

GEORGE SHULTZ

An economist by trade, the sixty-five-year-old Shultz left the deanship of the University of Chicago's School of Business to join the ranks of government service as Nixon's secretary of labor in 1969. Subsequently, Shultz served as the budget director (1970–72)* and secretary of the treasury (1972–74). When Shultz returned to government in 1982 to replace the resigning secretary of state, Alexander Haig, he was president of Bechtel, Inc., a San Francisco-

---

*Shultz's deputy at the budget bureau was Caspar Weinberger, a long-time competitor if not adversary.

based engineering firm. He was also teaching part-time at Stanford University.

In addition to having a reputation as a consummate team player, George Shultz is widely regarded as a man of high integrity with a "deep sense of personal rectitude."[12] A significant portion of this assessment is based on Treasury Secretary Shultz's much-publicized refusal to provide President Nixon with information on the tax returns of certain individuals on Nixon's enemies' list.

As far as President Reagan was concerned, the generally even-tempered Shultz was a welcome relief from the combative, ambitious Alexander Haig. Ex-White House aide Michael Deaver described the president's behavior during an Oval Office meeting with Shultz several months before he joined the Reagan team:

> As I watched, the president just visibly relaxed with Shultz. He has a marvelous staff style that appeals to Reagan, and he is a tough guy, a good interlocutor and a consummate government official. It was clear the president was very comfortable with Shultz.[13]

On substantive matters, Shultz's record as Reagan's secretary of state had been relatively smooth up to the end of 1985—the only major foreign policy failure being Lebanon and especially the terrorist killing of 245 U.S. marines there in 1983. At the same time, critics claimed that his tenure had no major foreign policy successes—e.g., no breakthroughs in the Middle East or Latin America or with the Soviet Union. Former Undersecretary for Political Affairs Lawrence Eagleburger compared him to some highly respected predecessors: "There is a bit of the moralism of [John Foster] Dulles in Shultz. And he is solid and steady with a style reminiscent in some ways of [Dean] Rusk. . . . It's possible to say someone was a good secretary of state because he took events and prevented them from making things worse." another government official added: "Shultz is very self-possessed. He likes power, he likes to run things and he likes to have his own way."[14]

REAGAN PLAN REVEALED

Information about the new polygraph requirement was shielded from the public until the *Los Angeles Times* broke the story about the directive on December 11, a week before Shultz's outburst. The *Times* revealed that the president's directive would require thousands of federal employees and contractor personnel with access to highly classified information to submit to lie detector tests on an irregular and random basis. The White House responded to the story the next day through press spokesman Larry Speaks, who announced that the president was attempting to address espionage and unauthorized information disclosures (leaks). While the directive was designed to target "a selective number of individuals who have highest levels of access" to secret information, according to Speaks, he denied that the action was related to recent and highly publicized revelations about spy activity within the U.S. government. Speaks also emphasized that "the new directive would be used mainly for counterespionage rather than for trying to identify officials who help journalists."[15] When asked by reporters for copies of the directive, Speaks claimed he could not provide it because the directive was itself a classified document. As the *New York Times* reported, "[T]his produced a round of laughter . . ., since news of the directive had already appeared in the *Los Angeles Times*."[16]

While these revelations were coming out in the national press, George Shultz was in Europe visiting several heads of state and foreign ministers. When reporters there questioned him about his opinion on the White House directive, Shultz refused to discuss the matter on the grounds that it was a domestic policy issue and should be discussed when he returned to the United States.

SHULTZ RETURNS

Only hours after his return to Washington from Europe on December 18, Shultz requested—and got—a private meeting with President Reagan. Apparently this meeting neither changed the nature of the directive nor mollified Shultz. The next day Shultz went public with what amounted to his ultimatum. After the secretary made clear his "grave reservations," one senior White House official told the *New York Times* that it was nonetheless unlikely that Shultz would resign, adding, however, that, "This is one thing that sends him through the roof. It touches a nerve."[17]

Reacting only hours after Shultz's strong criticism of the polygraph, the CIA issued a statement claiming that "selective, careful use" of polygraph tests was essential for those "branches of government" (i.e., the State Department) that received classified information. (See Exhibit 2.) The CIA spokesman also pointed out that CIA Director "Casey and all his predecessors had voluntarily taken polygraph tests" to set an example for their employees. In an interview on television, Caspar Weinberger said that taking the test "wouldn't bother me a bit."[18]

THE WHITE HOUSE RETREATS

The following afternoon, after another meeting between the secretary and President Reagan, the White House issued a statement which said that the president believed polygraph tests to be "a limited, though sometimes useful tool when used in conjunction with other investigative and security procedures in espionage cases." The statement added that the secretary "fully shares the president's view of the seriousness of espionage cases and agrees with the need to use all legal means in the investigation of such cases."[19] In effect, the White House was backing down from its earlier position, expressed in NSDD 196, that increased and widespread use of polygraphs was necessary and should be implemented. Nonetheless, CIA Director Casey and other secret agency heads could still use the tests as a screening test for employment.

After his meeting with Shultz, the president, when asked if the secretary would have to take a lie detector test, responded, "Neither one of us are going to," adding, "I just explained to him that what he read in the press in Europe was not true."[20] A State Department official told the *New York Times* that the White House statement indicated that the president and Shultz agreed that such "tests should be limited to cases of suspected espionage," adding that the secretary "believed his public comments had helped modify the president's position."[21]

POSTSCRIPT

Three days later, the Christmas Eve edition of the *Washington Post* ran a front-page article under the headline, "President Said to Be Unaware of Sweep of Polygraph Order." In this article, "administration sources" claimed that the president "was not fully aware of the sweeping nature" of the directive in question, nor were several other key administration figures, including Chief White House Counsel Fred Fielding and Treasury Secretary (and ex-Chief of Staff) James Baker.[22] The Christmas edition of the *Post* contained an article in which Larry Speakes denied the claim about Reagan, asserting that the president had been "fully aware of the scope" of the directive.[23]

EXHIBIT I. SECRETARY OF STATE GEORGE SCHULTZ'S REMARKS TO THE PRESS (DECEMBER 19) CONCERNING HIS VIEWS ON POLYGRAPH TESTING

Personally, I have grave reservations about so-called lie detector tests because the experience with them that I have read about—I don't claim to be an expert—it's hardly a scientific instrument.

It tends to identify quite a few people who are innocent as guilty, and it misses at least some fraction of people who are guilty of lying, and it is, I think, pretty well demonstrated that a professional, let us say, a professional spy or a professional leaker, can probably train himself or herself not to be caught by the test.

So the use of it as a broad-gauged condition of employment, you might say, seems to me to be questionable. That's my viewpoint. . . . The minute in this government that I am told that I'm not trusted is the day that I leave.

EXHIBIT 2. CIA WRITTEN STATEMENT (ISSUED DECEMBER 19)

Thousands of people in the intelligence community submit to polygraph examinations in recognition of the need to protect the nation's secrets and because of the proved usefulness of the polygraph as an investigative tool.

They understand that the government, in granting access to the nation's secrets, also bestows a special trust as well as a shared responsibility for protecting those secrets. The number of leaks of sensitive, classified information in recent years makes clear that a growing number of those given special trust have not lived up to their obligations. The reality is that the loss of classified information is severely damaging our foreign policy and our intelligence capabilities.

The use of polygraphing in the intelligence community has proven to be the best deterrent to the misuse of sensitive information. There is an acute need to extend its selective, careful use to branches of government that receive that information.

The director of Central Intelligence and his predecessors voluntarily have been polygraphed, believing in the importance of setting an example in that all those with access must do what they can to protect our secrets and to cooperate in identifying those who do not.

NOTES

1. *New York Times*, Dec. 20, 1985, p. 30.
2. Ibid., June 7, 1985, p. 1.

3. *Washington Post*, Dec. 29, 1985, p. 29.

4. Ibid.

5. *National Journal*, Jan. 18, 1986, p. 184.

6. *New York Times*, Dec 20, 1985, p. 30.

7. *National Journal*, Jan. 18, 1986, p. 184.

8. *Washington Post National Weekly Edition*, Feb. 17, 1986, p. 8.

9. *Washington Post*, Dec. 21, 1985, p. A8.

10. *Washington Post National Weekly Edition*, Feb. 17, 1986, pp. 6–8.

11. Ibid.

12. Ibid.

13. Ibid.

14. *National Journal*, Feb. 15, 1986, p. 377.

15. *New York Times*, Dec. 12, 1985, p. A19.

16. Ibid.

17. *New York Times*, Dec. 20, 1985, p. 1.

18. Ibid.

19. Ibid, Dec. 21, 1985.

20. Ibid.

21. Ibid.

22. *Washington Post*, Dec. 24, 1985, p. 1.

23. Ibid, Dec. 25, p. A16.

George Shultz and the Iran-Contra Affair

Taeku Lee

ARMS FOR HOSTAGES

On June 17, 1985, Robert McFarlane, President Reagan's national security advisor, circulated a draft document (NSDD: National Security Decision Document) to Secretary of State Shultz, Secretary of Defense Weinberger, and Director of Central Intelligence Casey, which set out immediate and long-term objectives for U.S. relations with Iran. This NSDD draft included the recommendations to: "Encourage Western allies and friends to help Iran meet its import requirements so as to reduce the attractiveness of Soviet assistance and trade offers, while demonstrating the value of correct relations with the West. This includes a provision of selected military equipment as determined on a case-by-case basis."[1]

On June 29, 1985, Secretary Shultz re-

This revised and expanded version of a case originally prepared by Taeku Lee was edited by Simone Sandy, copyright © 1996 by the President and Fellows of Harvard College. Reprinted with permission of the Program in Ethics and the Professionals. Except where otherwise indicated in the endnotes, the section "Arms for Hostages" is a compilation based on *The Chronology: The Day by Day Account of the Secret Military Assistance to Iran and the Contras*, copyright © 1987. Text has been modified and is reprinted with the permission of the National Security Archive.

sponded in writing to the NSDD draft, arguing that the proposed policy was "perverse" and that to "permit or encourage a flow of Western arms into Iran is contrary to our interest both in containing Khomeinism and in ending the excess of this regime. We should not alter this aspect of our policy when groups with ties to Iran are holding U.S. hostages in Lebanon." Weinberger's initial response to the draft was simply to write "almost too absurd to comment on" in the margin.[2]

On August 6 and 8, 1985, Shultz and other National Security Council (NSC) principals met with the president to discuss David Kimche's proposal to ship U.S.-made arms via Israel to Iran, with the understanding that four hostages would be released. McFarlane testified that Casey, White House Chief of Staff Regan, and Vice President Bush had been in favor of the transfer of arms and Shultz and Weinberger had been opposed to it. McFarlane's testimony also indicated President Reagan's approval of the arms transfers on the condition that they should not contribute to further terrorism or alter the balance of the Iran-Iraq War.[3]

On November 18, 1985, McFarlane updated Shultz on the details of the arms transfer, which was scheduled to occur on November 21. Shultz testified, "I complained to Mr. McFarlane that I had been informed so late that it was impossible to stop this operation. I nonetheless expressed my hope that the hostages would in fact be released."[4]

The November 1985 arrangement ultimately collapsed. On November 30, McFarlane resigned as national security advisor; Vice Admiral John Poindexter replaced McFarlane on December 4. The same day, Lieutenant Colonel Oliver North brought a new arms-for-hostages deal to Poindexter.[5]

On December 6, 1985, a full-scale White House meeting on the Iran initiative was called at Shultz's insistence. Thus far, only one hostage had been released after three arms shipments to Iran. State Department officials considered this meeting an opportunity for Shultz to protest continuation of the program.[6]

On December 7, 1985, NSC principals met at the White House. Both Shultz and Weinberger left this meeting with the impression that the arms component of negotiations with Iran was finished. Shultz returned to the State Department with news that Weinberger and Regan also strongly opposed further arms initiatives with Iran. After this meeting, Secretary Weinberger believed that he and Shultz had persuaded the president "that it might be a good thing to achieve these objectives, but it wouldn't work, and that this was not a good way to do it."[7]

According to the Tower Commission report, "the initiative seemed to be dying" until January 2, 1986, when Amrinam Nir brought a proposal to Poindexter to exchange 3,000 (U.S. made) Israeli TOW missiles and twenty Hizballah prisoners held by Israeli-supported Lebanese Christian forces for the release of five U.S. hostages in Beirut. The president signed a draft Covert Action Finding approving this plan. (This draft may have been signed by mistake, however, President Reagan did not recall signing this draft.)[8]

On January 7, 1986, President Reagan met with Bush, Shultz, Weinberger, Attorney General Meese, Casey, Regan, Poin-

dexter, and McFarlane. Although the president made no decisions at this meeting, several participants recalled leaving the meeting persuaded that he supported the Nir proposal. During the days following this meeting, Poindexter, Regan, Casey, and North reportedly considered ways to bypass Shultz and Weinberger in pursuit of this effort.[9]

Secretary Shultz on the January 7 meeting:

I recall no specific decision being made in my presence, though I was well aware of the president's preferred course and his strong desire to establish better relations with Iran and to save the hostages. . . .I stated all of the reasons why I felt it was a bad idea, and nobody in retrospect has thought of a reason that I didn't think of. I mean, I think this is all very predictable, including the argument against those who said, well, this is going to be a secret or it is all going to be deniable; that is nonsense. So, all of that was said.

And in that January 7 meeting, I know that I not only stated these things, but I was very concerned about it, and I expressed myself as forcefully as I could. That is, I didn't just sort of rattle these arguments off. I was intense. The president knew that. The president was well aware of my views. I think everybody was well aware of my views. It wasn't just saying oh, Mr. President, this is terrible, don't do it. There were reasons given that were spelled out and which are reasons that you would expect . . .I took the initiative as the person in the room who was opposed to what was being proposed. I cannot give you a full accounting, but it was clear to me by the time we went out that the President, the Vice President, the Director of Central Intelligence, the Attorney General, the Chief of Staff, the National Security Advisor all had one opinion and I had a different one and Cap [Weinberger] shared it. . . .[10]

Don Regan on the January 7 meeting:

The president was told, but by no means was it really teed up for him of what the downside risk would be here as far as American public opinion was concerned. There was no sampling. No one attempted to do this. The NSC certainly didn't in any paper or any discussion say that. I don't believe the State Department in its presentation arguing against this really brought out the sensitivity of this. None of us was aware of that, I regret to say.[11]

Secretary Weinberger on the January 7 meeting:

> The only time that I got the impression the president was for this thing was in January . . . and at that time it became very apparent to me that the cause I was supporting was lost, and that the president was for it.[12]

By January 17, 1986, a revised Covert Action Finding was submitted to the president. The revised draft was almost exactly the same as the previous one, but the cover memorandum proposed a major change, which would establish the United States as a direct arms supplier to Iran. In contrast with the Nir proposal (presented within the Finding), the cover memo suggested that the CIA buy 4,000 TOWs from the Department of Defense and, upon receiving payment, make a direct transfer to Iran (again with Israel making the "necessary arrangements"). Shultz, Weinberger, and Casey were not present at the meeting at which this decision is made. Furthermore, the January 17 Finding was neither given nor shown to certain key NSC principals, including Shultz and Weinberger, who testified that they did not see the signed Finding until after the Iran initiative became public knowledge on November 10, 1986.[13]

On May 3, 1986, Secretary Shultz received a cable from Under Secretary Michael Armacost suggesting that the Iran initiative was still on. This cable contained a report from Ambassador Charles Price in London describing meetings between Iranian representatives Khashoggi, Nir, and Ghorbanifar and British entrepreneur Tiny Rowlands, during which arms shipments to Iran allegedly were discussed. According to the cable, "The scheme, moreover, was okay with the Americans. It had been cleared with the White House. Poindexter allegedly is the point man. Only four people in the U.S. government are knowledgeable

about the plan. The State Department has been cut out."[14]

Unable to find Poindexter, Shultz confronted Don Regan about this matter instead. "I told Mr. Regan, and I showed him this—I said that he should go to the president and get him to end this matter once and for all. I opposed dealing with people such as those identified in the message and said it would harm the president if actively continued. Mr. Regan, I felt, shared my concern, said he was alarmed and would talk to the president. I later learned that Vice Admiral Poindexter reportedly told Ambassador Price that there was no more than a smidgen of reality to the story. . . . Soon thereafter I recall being told by both Vice Admiral Poindexter and Mr. Casey that the operation had ended, and the people involved had been told to 'stand down.'"[15]

On May 6, 1986, the State Department issued a policy statement on terrorism, proclaiming in part: "The U.S. Government will make no concessions to terrorists. It will not pay ransoms, release prisoners, change its policies, or agree to other acts that might encourage additional terrorism. . . . The policy of the U.S. Government is, therefore, to reject categorically demands for ransom, prisoner exchanges, and deals with terrorists in exchange for hostage release." Meanwhile, with Poindexter's approval, Lieutenant Colonel North was busily planning a trip with McFarlane to Tehran to negotiate arms and spare parts shipments in exchange for the release of more hostages.[16]

By November 1986, arms transfers to Iran were proceeding at full throttle. During this time, two additional hostages—Reverend Lawrence Jenco and David Jacobsen—were released. The key operatives had also begun diverting funds from the arms transfers to the Contras. With the release of Jacobsen in November, however, the first public news of the Iran initiative began to spread. The Jihad Islami claimed that the release of Jacobsen was *quid pro quo* for "overtures" from the

U.S. government; on November 3, the Lebanese magazine *Al Shiraa* reported on McFarlane's visits to Tehran and noted U.S. supply of arms to Iran.[17]

Upon learning of the public revelations, Secretary Shultz expressed concern to Poindexter that the arms deal might be viewed as a violation of the existing U.S. counterterrorism policy. Shultz proposed public disclosure of the NSC initiative to clarify "that this was a special one-time operation based on humanitarian grounds and decided by the president within his constitutional responsibility to act in the service of the national interest."[18]

On November 16, 1986, unable to convince President Reagan to declare a cessation of arms deals with Iran and to place the State Department in charge of Iran policy, Shultz appeared on television to state his opposition to any such further deals. Shultz also publicly contradicted the president's earlier claims that Iran had suspended its terrorist acts in recent months, maintaining that "Iran has and continues to pursue a policy of terrorism."[19]

On November 18, 1986, two State Department officials were permitted to view a copy of Director Casey's prepared testimony for his upcoming (November 21) appearance before Congress. This draft stated that all U.S. officials involved "believed that the November 1985 shipment of arms was actually oil drilling equipment." Two days later, Shultz confronted Reagan about the accuracy of Casey's prepared testimony. Casey's testimony—which was coordinated by Poindexter—was altered to reflect Shultz's and other officials' concerns. (However, congressional sources still doubted the full candor of Casey's written remarks.)[20]

On November 22, 1986, the president reportedly relayed a message telling Shultz, "Support me or get off the team." On November 25, the president met with Shultz and Regan, and reportedly put the State Department in charge of Iran policy and asked Shultz to remain in his post.[21]

On December 8, 1986, Secretary Shultz appeared before the House Foreign Affairs Committee. In his testimony, he distanced himself from the NSC actions in Iran-Contra. "I learned not as a result of being involved in the development of the plan, but, so to speak, as a plan was about to be implemented. I learned in various ways of two proposed transfers during 1985, but I was never informed and had the impression that they were not consummated. . . .I did not learn about any transfers of arms during 1986 in a direct way. But, as is always the case, you have bits and pieces of evidence float in. And so I weighed in on the basis of that, restating my views. What I heard was conflicting: at times that there was some sort of deal or signal in the works, and at other times that the operation was closed down. . . . So, again, there was this ambiguity from my standpoint. I would say to you that I did take the position . . . recognizing that if the president's initiative had any chance of success it would have to be a secret initiative for all the reasons that have been developed . . .whenever I would be called upon to do something to carry out those policies, I needed to know, but I didn't need to know things that were not in my sphere to do something about. . . . Now I believe that the conduct, the operational conduct of diplomatic activity, should be lodged in the State Department. And by and large it is. And if there is a lesson out of all of this, insofar as how things operate are concerned, I think that the lesson is that the— that operational activities, and a staff for conducting operational activities out of the National Security Council staff, is very questionable and shouldn't be done except in very rare circumstances.[22]

On March 14, 1987, President Reagan expressed regret for not having listened to Secretary Shultz and Secretary Weinberger's opposition to the Iran initiative in his weekly radio address. "As we now know, it turned out they were right and I was wrong."[23]

THE TOWER COMMISSION REPORT

[In December of 1986, President Reagan established a Special Review Board "to examine the proper role of the National Security Council Staff in national security operations, including the arms transfer to Iran.''[24] Following are excerpts from the *Report of the President's Special Review Board*, more commonly known as *The Tower Commission Report*, released on February 26, 1987.]

Beyond the President, the other NSC principals and the National Security Advisor must share in the responsibility for the NSC system. President Reagan's personal management style places an especially heavy responsibility on his key advisors. Knowing his style, they should have been particularly mindful of the need for special attention to the manner in which this arms sales initiative developed and proceeded. On this score, neither the National Security Advisor nor the other NSC principals deserve high marks. . . . The principal subordinates to the President must not be deterred from urging the President not to proceed on a highly questionable course of action even in the face of his strong conviction to the contrary. . . . It does not appear that any of the NSC principals called for more frequent considerations of the Iran initiative by the NSC principals in the presence of the President. None of the principals called for a serious vetting of the initiative by even a restricted group of disinterested individuals. The intelligence questions do not appear to have been raised, and legal considerations, while raised, were not pressed. No one seemed to have complained about the informality of the process. No one called for a thorough reexamination once the initiative did not meet expectations or the manner of execution changed. While one or another of the NSC principals suspected that something was amiss, none vigorously pursued the issue.[25]

The NSC principals other than the President may be somewhat excused by the insufficient attention on the part of the National Security Advisor to the need to keep all the principals fully informed. Given the importance of the issue and the sharp policy divergences involved, however, Secretary Shultz and Secretary Weinberger in particular distanced themselves from the march of events. Secretary Shultz specifically requested to be informed only as necessary to perform his job. . . . Their obligation was to give the President their full support and continued advice with respect to the program or, if they could not in conscience do that, to so inform the President. Instead, they simply distanced themselves from the program. They protected their record as to their own positions on this issue. They were not energetic in attempting to protect the President from the consequences of his personal commitment to freeing the hostages.[26]

CRITICISM AND DEFENSE

[Following are excerpts from Shultz's testimony in Joint hearings on the Iran-Contra Investigation, July 23–24, 1987.]

REPRESENTATIVE MICHAEL DE-WINE, Republican of Ohio. I think it is clear, that the facts are very plain, that you were right about a lot of this. With regard to the arms sale, you were right about the whole thing. In essence, you were a prophet. Just about everything you said was going to go wrong did go wrong. . . . I think the basic problem, at least in this Congressman's mind, was that neither you nor the President really know the essential facts. You gave Admiral Poindexter complete authority to decide what you needed to know. You took the risk, and it was a risk, that he would give you enough information about the Iran initiative for you to do your job. In essence, you left the fox to guard the chicken coop. . . . I am in basic agreement with what the Tower Commission said . . . in my opinion, you let Admiral Poindexter cut you out. You discussed your resignation on three separate occasions, one of those occasions having to do with a polygraph. But you did not discuss it in regard to what has turned out to be the major foreign policy disaster of this Administration. You stated you did not want to know the operational details. In my opinion you purposefully cut yourself out from the facts. . . . It seems to me, Mr. Secretary, you permitted Admiral Poindexter to get between you and the President, just as he got between the President and the American people.

SECRETARY OF STATE SHULTZ. Well, I will just say that is one man's opinion and I don't share it.[27]

REPRESENTATIVE HENRY J. HYDE, Republican of Illinois. Now, Mr. Secretary, I can't escape the notion that had you opposed this flawed policy and were willing to resign over this . . . you could have stopped it dead in its track. And if you couldn't, you and Secretary Weinberger sure could. . . . I cannot believe, if you had been that forceful and that committed to opposing this flawed initiative, as much as Poindexter and North were committed to advancing it, you couldn't have stopped it dead in its tracks. And I ask you if that is not so?

SHULTZ. I doubt it very much. I will describe to you my own thinking and course of action. As I have thought about . . . what happened, there is a sense in which it falls into . . . three time periods. . . .

The first period was from some time in the middle of 1985 through, say, the middle of December 1985. During that period, I unearthed it; I opposed it; I thought I had taken part in killing it on more than one occasion. . . . [I]t was clear as it went on that the President had a desire to do it, and I didn't just say, "Well, you seem to be leaning against me, I'm going to resign." . . . The President listened to everything and he decided what he decided. . . . [W]ould you have said I should have sat there on December 7 in the White House and said "Mr. President, I see you are wavering, and if you should decide against me, goodbye?" That is not the way to play this game at all. . . .

The second episode goes, as I see it, between early January 1986 and late May, early June. . . . There we had a special proposal made, brought to us by the Israelis, which became the topic of a meeting, and I

took a position in that meeting . . . and while there was no decision made at that meeting that I recall, I certainly did have the sense that Secretary Weinberger and I were on one side of the issue and everybody else, including the President, was on the other side, and that somehow or other this was going to move ahead. So again, I didn't say, "agree with me or goodbye." . . . [T]here is a lot more going on around the world than this particular set of events . . . So always in the question of whether you resign or not is the question of the chance to help the President accomplish some positive things . . . nothing ever gets settled in this town, and you can say, "I will give up and leave," or "I will stay and fight." . . .

And then comes early June . . . when it became known to me . . . that there had been the mission to Tehran and it had fizzled. And Admiral Poindexter told me that the whole thing had been told to stand down. So at this point, I don't have anything to resign about. Subsequently, a couple of other things took place that gave me the feeling . . . that we were going forward with the effort with Iran which I thought was something worth doing . . . in a proper way. So I have no, no problem. . . .

I have never hesitated in my time in the Cabinet to speak up to Presidents, or to resign, if I felt the situation warranted. In this case, I looked at it the way I did.[28]

SENATOR DANIEL K. INOUYE, Democrat from Hawaii. Mr. Secretary, I have another question. And I ask this with great reluctance, because I realize that it is rather personal in nature, but I think it is relevant . . . I've been advised that in August of 1986 you tendered a letter of resignation to the President of the United States. Is that true? And if so, can you tell us something about it?

SHULTZ. . . . That is true. And I have asked the President to let me leave this office on a couple of other occasions, earlier.

INOUYE. Was that in any way related to the Iran-Contra affair?

SHULTZ. Well, in August of 1986 I thought that it was over. . . . [O]n the effort with Iran, I thought it was basically on a proper track.

But it was because I felt a sense of estrangement. I knew the White House was very uncomfortable with me. I was very uncomfortable with what I was getting from the intelligence community, and I knew they were uncomfortable with me, perhaps going back to the lie detector test business. I could feel it.

What I have learned about the various things that were being done, I suppose, explains why I was not in good odor with the NSC staff and some of the others in the White House. I had a terrible time. There was a kind of guerrilla warfare going on, on all kinds of little things. For example, as you know, the Congress doesn't treat the State Department very well when it comes to appropriated funds. And not only have we historically taken a beating but we've been cut brutally . . . and I think in a manner that it is not in the interests of the United States.

But anyway, one of the conventions that's grown up because we have no travel money to speak of . . . [is] the Air Force runs a White House Presidential Wing and when the Secretary of State has a mission, that gets approved, and then I get an airplane and the airplane, it's paid for out of this budget. If I had to pay for that airplane, I couldn't travel. So you have me grounded unless I can be approved.

Now it's not a problem. The system works all right and it's just assumed that that's the way it's supposed to be. But I started having trouble because some people on the White House staff decided that they were going to make my life unhappy and they stopped approving these airplane things. And we fought about this and so on. And finally—I hated to do this—I went to the President and I gave him little memorandums to check off "yes," or "no." That's no business for the Secretary of State to be taking up with the President of the United States. . . .

And so I told the President, "I'd like to leave and here's my letter." And he stuck it in his drawer. He said, "You're tired.

It's about time you go on vacation, and let's talk about it after you get back from vacation." So I said, "OK," and I guess everybody knows what happened. . . .

At an earlier time, in the middle of 1983, I resigned. And that was because I discovered that Bud McFarlane, who was then the Deputy National Security Advisor, was sent on a secret trip to the Middle East . . . without my knowledge, while we were busy negotiating out there. And also, I found some things happened with respect to actions on Central America that I didn't know about beforehand.

So I went to the President and I said, "Mr. President, you don't need a guy like me for Secretary of State if this is the way things are going to be done, because when you send somebody out like that McFarlane trip, I'm done." . . . When the President hangs out his shingle and says, "You don't have to go through the State Department, just come right into the White House," he'll get all the business. That's a big signal to countries out there about how to deal with the U.S. Government. And it may have had something to do with how events transpired, for all I know. But it's wrong. You can't do it that way.

So the other time I resigned was after my big lie detector test flap, and again I could see that I was on the outs with everybody, so I said, "Mr. President, why don't you let me go home. I like it in California." And again, he wouldn't let that happen. That was late in 1985. Mr. McFarlane had resigned, and Mr. McFarlane and I, I think, worked very effectively together in . . . our efforts with the U.S.S.R. and . . . in the end, I didn't feel, with Mr. McFarlane having left, that it was fair to the President of the country for me to leave at the same time, so I didn't.

But I do think that in jobs like the job I have, where it is a real privilege to serve in this kind of job, or the others that you recounted, that you can't do the job well if you want it too much. You have to be willing to say goodbye, and I am.[29]

NOTES

1. The National Security Archive, *The Chronology* (New York: Warner, 1987), 114, 17.

2. Ibid., 118.

3. Ibid., 140–41.

4. Ibid., 177.

5. Ibid., 197, 200.

6. Ibid., 207.

7. Ibid., 208–11.

8. *Report of the President's Special Review Board* (Washington, D.C.: Feb. 26, 1987). III–12.

9. *The Chronology*, 242.

10. Ibid., 247.

11. Ibid., 248.

12. Ibid., 249.

13. Ibid., 261–62.

14. Ibid., 356.

15. Ibid.

16. Ibid., 359.

17. Ibid., 535–37.

18. Ibid., 537.

19. Ibid., 559.

20. Ibid., 561, 574.

21. Ibid., 582, 592–93.

22. *New York Times*, Dec. 9, 1986, A12.

23. *The Chronology*, 654.

24. *Report*, I–1.

25. *Report*, IV–10, IV–11.

26. Ibid., IV–11.

27. *Iran-Contra Investigation*, Joint Hearings before the Senate Select Committee on Secret Military Assistance to Iran and the Nicaraguan Opposition and the House Select Committee to Investigate Covert Arms Transactions with Iran, 100 Cong. 1 Sess., 180–81.

28. Ibid., 131–34.

29. Ibid., 58–60.

Comment

Although the polygraph case and the Iran-Contra affair invite comparative analysis, it is best to begin by considering the polygraph case on its own. Had George Shultz followed the imperative "obey or resign," he would have quietly left office. By publicly threatening to resign, he succeeded in changing governmental policy. Should our judgment of Shultz's actions depend on whether he was acting according to his own conscience, whether his position on polygraph testing was morally correct, or both?

To clarify the moral basis of Shultz's objection, assume that polygraph tests can sometimes be effective for some purposes. (As Richard Nixon said: "I don't know how accurate the tests are, but I know they'll scare the hell out of people.") Shultz's moral objection seems to be expressed in personal terms, as a matter of personal honor: he is offended by the implication that he is not be to trusted. Are there ways of restating the objection that would make it less dependent on an official's own sense of honor? (Some other grounds include: invasion of privacy, deception, self-incrimination, the chilling effect on legitimate dissent, and recruitment for government service.) More generally, consider whether in order to be justifiable the dissent must be based on principles that apply to all public officials, not just those who happen to be offended, as Shultz is. Would Shultz's objection still have been valid if the policy had exempted him? All members of the State Department? All who conscientiously opposed such tests?

In the same month that the polygraph test was proposed, Shultz began objecting to the arms-for-hostages plans. Although he continued to object throughout the fall and early winter, he "distanced [himself] from the march of events" (according to the Tower Commission). Contrast this low-keyed opposition with his angry protest in the polygraph case. Some critics of Shultz might state the contrast even more sharply: when his personal honor was at stake, the secretary threatened to resign; but when national blackmail and violations of democratic procedure occurred, he objected only privately and then mostly tried to disassociate himself from the plan.

What exactly is the difference between the two wrongs that would justify such different responses by Shultz? On the face of it, many of the differences (the seriousness of the consequences, the relevance to role) would seem to favor a stronger reaction against the hostage deal than the polygraph test. (A stronger reaction does not necessarily mean threatening to resign.) Perhaps Shultz really believed that he had stopped the plan ("strangled the baby in the cradle"), but he had plenty of signs that the operation was continuing (for example, the report from Ambassador Price in May). He may have believed that he was more likely to be able to stop the polygraph proposal but that belief would not itself justify his differential response.

It might be argued that Shultz saw the arms-for-hostages plan as a policy difference about which officials could legitimately disagree but viewed the polygraph proposal as a purely moral issue on which one should not compromise. Although this may partially explain Shultz's reactions (only partially, because dealing with terrorists, he seemed to believe, would be wrong even if successful), it does not justify them. A question persists: what is the ethical difference between legitimate policy disagreements and purely moral issues? And it is worth remembering that there may be ethically relevant differences among policy disagreements themselves: in some policy disputes officials may be obligated only to register their objections, but in others they may be required to resist the policy more vigorously.

The Space Shuttle *Challenger*
Nicholas Carter

January 28, 1986. The space shuttle had already successfully flown twenty-four times and would that day attempt its twenty-fifth flight. To the outside observer, it seemed that NASA had, after more than a decade's work, successfully built a "space truck." After so many apparently flawless flights, there was little interest in this

launch. For the first time, none of the networks was planning to show it live, despite the fact that this flight would mark the first time a civilian went to space.

At 11:30 A.M., the final countdown for lift-off had begun. It was a clear, crisp day. For those who had come to Cape Canaveral to watch, it looked like a beautiful day for flying. Many people were present but most conspicuous among the crowd gathered were the astronauts' families surrounded by photographers and NASA escorts. The astronauts' families were excited, yet nervous as well. They knew that, although the shuttle had successfully flown many times before, there were still dangers. After all, this launch had already been delayed three times. The adults had butterflies. The children, however, were full of enthusiasm. They were getting special treatment, and they knew that something very special was about to occur.[1]

In Brigham, Utah, in the shadows of the Wasatch Mountains, the engineers at Morton Thiokol who had designed the solid rocket boosters (SRBs) that lift the *Challenger* into orbit gathered around a monitor to watch the lift-off. Bob Ebeling, one of the engineers, settled into his chair as Roger Boisjoly (pronounced "bo-zho-lay") walked by. Boisjoly was Morton Thiokol Inc.'s (MTI) most senior engineer on the SRB project. Ebeling went after his friend and asked him to come and watch. But Boisjoly had decided earlier he would not watch this launch attempt. In the last two days, it had grown unusually cold at Cape Canaveral. The freezing temperatures had alarmed Boisjoly and Arnie Thompson, one of the other senior Thiokol engineers. They felt that the O-rings might not be able to seal in such cold weather.

The O-rings are the bands designed to prevent pressure, heat, and flames from escaping through the SRB joints. (The SRB—there are two—provides the power to lift the Shuttle into orbit.) Upon ignition, the internal pressure in the SRB forces the walls to balloon out causing "joint rotation," and the gap the O-rings are supposed to fill becomes wider. It only takes a split second for this gap to grow too large for the O-rings to fill. After ignition, therefore, the O-rings must seal instantaneously (within the first three-fifths of a second). Otherwise, the O-rings do not deal properly, creating the likelihood of a shuttle explosion or crash.

Because the O-rings are rubber, the cold makes them less resilient and impairs their ability to move into the joints and fill them.

One temperature test had been undertaken in March 1985 at Morton Thiokol to examine the effects of cold on the O-rings. Boisjoly conducted the tests, which involved compressing the O-rings with a metal plate and then drawing the metal plate away slightly to see how resilient the O-rings were at varying temperatures. At 100 degrees F., the O-rings never lost contact. At 75 degrees F., they lost contact for 2.4 seconds. And at 50 degrees F., the seals never regained contact. During ten minutes at 50 degrees F., the O-rings were unable to retake their original form. For Boisjoly, this was damning evidence that the O-rings were unreliable at low temperatures.[2]

The night before the launch, Boisjoly and Thompson had strenuously argued against launching. They believed it was too risky given the cold weather at the Cape. However, they had failed to convince either NASA or their own management at Thiokol. Angry and concerned, Boisjoly did not want to watch the take-off. But Ebeling was persistent, and Boisjoly finally relented.

Ebeling returned to his chair. Boisjoly found a place on the floor in front of Ebeling. On the screen was the gleaming Space Shuttle Challenger, cocked and ready for flight. Boisjoly hoped the flight would be successful. He hoped that the O-rings would seal. But he also hoped that when NASA recovered the SRB's they would find that the first of the two seals had failed.[3] This had happened before. He also hoped that the secondary seal would show more erosion than ever before. Then perhaps someone with authority would stop the launches until the O-ring problem was solved.[4]

The final seconds elapsed. The engines ignited. The mechanized arms holding the rocket upright moved away. The shuttle rose powerfully. Smoke and dust billowed out from underneath, creating enormous rolling clouds. The shuttle kept driving toward the sky. The critical stage for the O-rings had passed. The engineers breathed a sigh of relief. Ebeling turned to Boisjoly and told him that during the lift-off he had been praying that everything would go all right. The first minute of flight passed and everything looked good. Boisjoly kept watching. Suddenly an eruption of smoke engulfed the *Challenger*. And the rocket came apart. No one, not even NASA officials, knew what had happened. Back at Cape Canaveral, the crowd was bewildered. The families drew together. The children cried uncontrollably. There was no hope that the seven astronauts had survived.

Without a word, Boisjoly got up and went back to his office to be alone. He spent the rest of the day unable to do anything. At one point, two engineers stopped in to see if he was O.K. Boisjoly could not speak. He just nodded that he was all right. After a long moment of silence, they left. Boisjoly knew what had gone wrong. His O-rings.[5]

. . .

The day before the *Challenger* disaster, a cold front had swept down the East Coast. The temperature hovered around 31 degrees F. Through tests NASA had determined that below 31 degrees F. the shuttle would not work.[6] The launch was scheduled for the next morning and a decision had to be made in time to start the twelve hour countdown. The cold weather had not been a factor in the previous launch delays, but the temperature was dropping now and was beginning to cause concerns, especially among Thiokol's engineers in Utah. Temperatures would be below freezing that night, and the engineers estimated that the temperature at the joint where the O-rings operated would be between 27 and 30 degrees F. by late morning the next day. The temperature in the air might be 31 degrees, passable by NASA rules but alarming to the Thiokol engineers. The coldest it had ever been for a launch, in January 1985, was 53 degrees F. During that launch, Flight 41-C, one of the SRB joints experienced the worst case of blow-by in the shuttle's brief history. (Blow-by occurs when the SRB's scalding gases have "blown by" the O-ring before it has sealed,

burning the grease that dresses the O-rings.) Another flight later in 1985 (Flight 41-B) also gave the Thiokol engineers pause. On the day of that flight's launch, the temperature had been in the upper 50s. But the primary O-ring at one of the nozzle joints never sealed. Fortunately, the back-up seal did, but among Thiokol's engineers there was a growing suspicion that cold weather impaired the O-rings' sealing function.

These experiences of blow-by in cold weather led Thiokol to undertake tests to determine whether cold temperatures actually affected the O-rings. The O-rings are "activated" (i.e., pushed into the gap of the joint where they seal) by the initial pressure of the hot gases inside the SRB. When the force of the gas hits the O-ring it is so powerful that the O-ring is squashed. How long it stays squashed depends on its resiliency, its ability to bounce back and resume its original shape. And, in turn, the resiliency of the O-rings depends on the temperature. The tests showed that the O-rings, which are made of hard rubber (Viton), became less resilient when cold. The hot gases blowing past the O-ring will have enough time to burn away so much of it that it will lose its ability to seal altogether.

Tests and experience were revealing that cold definitely slowed the O-rings' sealing speed. Actual launch experience showed only that the O-rings worked at 53 degrees F., and even at that temperature there had been significant blow-by. No one knew how much colder it could be before the O-rings failed. In 1985, Thiokol began running tests on the joint design but they were proceeding slowly. Other than launch experience, there was no data to prove the O-rings' resistance to cold. The one temperature test that had been run showed that cold temperature *slowed* the sealing speed.

Even though the data base was small, it was the only evidence with which to make a decision. The Thiokol engineers did not feel it was safe to fly. On January 27, they communicated their concern to NASA officials at the Marshall Space Flight Center. Marshall was the NASA center responsible for the development of the SRBs; when Thiokol communicated with NASA, it was always through Marshall. They arranged to discuss the problem over a teleconference which they scheduled for that evening at 5:45 P.M. At this first teleconference, Thiokol engineers told Stanley Reinartz, manager of the Shuttle Projects Office at Marshall, and Judson Lovingood, his deputy, that they did not recommend launching until noon or later in the afternoon of the next day, the 28th. In order that Thiokol could "telefax" its data to Marshall officials at Marshall and at the Kennedy Space Center at Cape Canaveral, and in order to include other, responsible officials, they agreed to a second teleconference at 8:45 P.M.

At 8:45 P.M., the second teleconference began. The senior officials and key participants included, at Morton Thiokol, Utah: (1) Jerald Mason, senior vice president, Wasatch Operations; (2) Calvin Wiggins, vice president and general manager, Space Division, Wasatch; (3) Joe Kilminster, vice president, Space Booster Programs, Wasatch; (4) Bob Lund, vice president, Engineering; (5) Roger Boisjoly, member, Seal Task Force; and (6) Arnie Thompson, supervisor, Rocket Motor Cases; at Kennedy, Stanley Reinartz, and Lawrence Mulloy, manager, SRB Project (both Marshall officials); also at Kennedy, Allan McDonald, director of the Solid Rocket Motor (SRM) Project for Morton Thiokol; at Marshall, George Hardy, deputy director, Science and Engineering, and Judson Lovingood.

Essentially, there were three groups participating in the teleconference: NASA, the Thiokol management, and the Thiokol engineers. Reinartz was the senior NASA official at the teleconference. At this meeting, he had the ultimate say about whether or not to launch. He did have his superior at Marshall, the director, Dr. William Lucas. But NASA rules did not require Dr. Lucas to be present at this meeting. At Thiokol, the senior representative was Mason.

The teleconference began with Thiokol engineers explaining why they believed it unsafe to fly the next day. Their argument hinged on the evidence that the functioning of the O-rings was adversely affected by the cold. By the time preparations for the *Challenger* launch were underway, there had been several incidences of blow-by but not one on a launch where the temperature had been 67 degrees F. or higher. Boisjoly and his colleague, Arnie Thompson, presented this data and recommended not launching until the ambient temperature had reached at least 53 degrees F.

However, NASA officials challenged Thiokol's engineers and the connection they were making between O-ring failure and cold weather. Someone at NASA (and it is not known who) brought up Flight 61-A. That flight had experienced blow-by past the primary O-ring and it had been launched at *75 degrees F*. NASA could not square this evidence with that of Thiokol. Here after all was an instance where there had been an O-ring problem when it had been *warm*.

Boisjoly's explanation was that the blow-by on 61-A had been much less serious than on the colder flights. Moreover, although 61-A may have seemed an anomaly, compared to the total shuttle flight history it fit a pattern. Out of twenty flights at 66 degrees F. or higher only three showed evidence of O-ring malfunction. However, all four flights launched at temperatures below 66 degrees F. showed signs of O-ring malfunction.

Nevertheless, NASA's Marshall officials disagreed with the conclusions the Thiokol engineers were drawing. When asked by Stan Reinartz for his reaction to Thiokol's recommendation not to launch, George Hardy said he was "appalled" but that if that were their recommendation, he could not override it. As for Mulloy, NASA's SRB expert at Marshall, he stated that Thiokol's data was "inconclusive" and objected to the suggestion of Thiokol's engineers that all launches be postponed until the ambient temperature reached 53 degrees F. He pointedly asked, "My God, Thiokol, when do you want me to launch, next April?" This pressure on Thiokol to reconsider the engineers' recommendation was due to NASA's preflight review process that required, as a first step, contractor approval of Shuttle readiness.

Since its first days, NASA had had a staff that made safety a priority, and the new willingness to launch at risk to human life surprised many of those who participated in the teleconference. The attitude at NASA had always required proof that it was safe to fly, until January 27, when NASA officials were demanding rock-solid proof that it was *not* safe to fly. NASA's new attitude astounded Boisjoly. It had the same effect on Thiokol's vice president of engineering, Bob Lund, who reported to the presidential commission on the shuttle accident (the Rogers Commission), "I had never heard those kinds of things (i.e., the pressure to launch) come from people at Marshall."[7] Even some NASA officials were taken aback by the unprecedented relaxation of safety standards. Wilbur Riehl, a veteran NASA engineer involved in the teleconference, wrote a note to a colleague, "Did you ever expect to see MSFC [Marshall Space Flight Center] want to fly when MTI-Wasatch didn't?"[8]

After Boisjoly and Thompson had presented their view and Hardy and Mulloy had responded, Joe Kilminster, one of the four Thiokol managers involved in the teleconference, asked for a five minute "caucus" for Thiokol to discuss the situation among themselves. All agreed, and Thiokol went off the line. Mason, the senior vice president who had said nothing up to this point, took charge in the Thiokol-only discussion. Before anyone else spoke, he said in a soft voice, intending only the managers to hear, "We have to make a management decision."[9]

Boisjoly was furious. He and Thompson were sitting at the table with the managers and had overheard Mason's comment. They knew what Mason was driving at. By speaking of "a management decision," he meant overruling the engineers. Boisjoly and Thompson, alarmed, got to their feet and tried once again to show why Thiokol must uphold the recommendation not to launch. The mood was tense as they again presented their arguments and the data. Everyone knew what NASA wanted to hear: they wanted Thiokol to give them the go-ahead. As the two engineers struggled to convince the managers, Mason looked at them threateningly.[10] It did not take long before Boisjoly and Thompson recognized that the other managers were now impervious to their appeals. They sat down. Again, Mason said in a soft voice, "We have to make a management decision," then turned to Lund. Of the four managers present, Lund had the best understanding of the O-ring problem, since he had worked most closely with the engineers in designing and developing the SRB. That afternoon, when the engineers first heard about the projected cold weather for the next day's launch, they had gone to him and explained why they felt it was unsafe to fly. In the end, they had convinced him, and he in turn had supported their conclusion in the teleconference with NASA. Perhaps more than the engineers, the pressure was on him. Now, Mason turned to him and said, in words that became famous during the Rogers Commission hearings, "It's time to take off your engineer's cap and put on your manager's cap."[11] By the end of the managers' discussion, Lund had changed his mind. He would support the managers' conclusion that, though conditions for launching were not desirable, they were acceptable.[12]

Thiokol resumed its teleconference with NASA and told NASA officials of its final decision. As was required, Mulloy asked Kilminster to put in writing this recommendation to launch, sign it, and "telefax" it to NASA.

. . .

In the early 1970s, the Shuttle program was sold to the president and Congress in a way that led inexorably to the arm-twisting in the teleconference and the shuttle disaster the following day. On January 27, only a few individuals, particularly Mulloy at NASA and Mason at Thiokol, were responsible for the reckless decision to launch. However, blame should not be restricted to them. A brief review of NASA's history shows that Nixon's space policy and his NASA administrator, Dr. James Fletcher, were responsible for developing the shuttle despite inadequate funding. It was a disastrous course on which to set NASA for the future.

Under President Kennedy, NASA had the political and financial support to work at a safe pace, never compelled to risk astronauts' lives. Kennedy saw the exploration of space as an important race between the United States and the Soviets. He ordered Vice President Johnson to determine how the United States could beat the Soviets in space. In his report, Johnson captures the Kennedy administration's attitude toward space. He writes, "In the crucial aspects of our Cold War world, in the eyes of the world, first in space is first, period. Second in space is second in everything."[13]

With a feeling that this was perhaps the most important undertaking of his administration, Kennedy poured money and support into space exploration. There would be no cutting corners. Things were going to be done right. Most importantly, safety was made a top priority, even at the expense of losing out to the Soviets in the short run. For example, in 1961, James Webb, NASA's administrator under Kennedy (and Johnson), was under tremendous pressure to attempt to send the first human being into suborbital flight. The Soviets were on the verge of accomplishing the feat themselves, and America was ready. But Webb, like T.

Keith Glennan before him, knew that safety had to come first. There was still more testing necessary to guarantee the safety of the astronaut. Not only were these NASA officials deeply concerned for the safety of the astronauts, but they also realized that NASA's long-term interests would be best served by a safe space program. NASA could survive being beaten by the Soviets but could not if it killed astronauts. The essential tests were carried out, and the Soviets did beat the Americans in the race to launch a man into space, with the flight of Maj. Yuri Alexseyevich Gagarin on April 12, 1961. But the United States followed suit thirteen days later with the launching of Alan Shepard.

The Soviet successes continued, yet NASA officials proceeded only when they knew they were ready. In August 1961, the Soviets successfully completed a manned seventeen-orbit mission. Six months later, John Glenn became the first American to orbit Earth. With Kennedy's wholehearted support, NASA embarked on plans for a manned lunar mission.

With testing and the oversight of contractors' work a top priority, the moon mission proceeded cautiously. On Sunday, July 20, 1969, the lunar race ended when the United States successfully landed Apollo XI on the moon, thereby fulfilling Kennedy's promise of landing a man on the moon within the decade. Though the Apollo program spent more years under Johnson's watchful eye than under Kennedy's and the moon landing actually occurred under President Nixon, everyone knew that NASA belonged to JFK. It had been his leadership and support that had created the lunar attempt.

Nixon, more than anyone else, understood that NASA was still Kennedy's agency. Realizing he would get very little political mileage from another space program and recognizing that after the lunar landing the public's interest in space had at least been temporarily satisfied, Nixon did very little for the space agency.[14]

Three options were presented to his administration concerning America's future in space. Option A was presented by a team of NASA scientists perhaps most responsible for the success of the lunar landing. They wanted to develop (1) an economical shuttle to ferry people to and from (2) a space station from which (3) manned and unmanned flights to Mars would proceed. Option A would have cost about $10 billion a year. The idea of a manned flight to Mars appealed to many, and Spiro Agnew actually predicted that Nixon would opt for it. Option B called for an end to manned spaceflight by 1974 and provided a paltry $3 billion for research into possibilities for future manned or unmanned programs. Option C, presented by NASA Administrator Thomas Paine, was an enormous and totally reusable system. To develop this version of the shuttle would cost about $10-$12 billion. In the end, Nixon chose Option B. It was the least he could get away with politically without killing manned spaceflight completely. Paine resigned when he realized that he would not be able to win from Nixon the kind of financial support he felt NASA should have.[15]

In response to the same budgetary constraints, George Low, acting as NASA administrator until another could be named, forwarded a cheaper plan than Paine's. Because Low cared so strongly about keeping the manned spaceflight programs alive, he went to all lengths to sell the shuttle to the Nixon administration. Though Paine's team had estimated that the cheapest shuttle system that could be developed was $10-$15 billion, Low said it could be done for $8 billion.[16]

Dr. James Fletcher was appointed NASA administrator in 1971. An ambitious man, Fletcher wanted another big, Apollo-like project for NASA to which he could attach his name. Option B did not give Fletcher the funds necessary to develop a manned space shuttle, but he decided to develop the shuttle anyway. Where former NASA ad-

ministrators demanded the best, Fletcher was willing to proceed with whatever he could get. He continued to prune the shuttle budget, cutting costs that eroded safety margins.[17] Because it was less expensive, NASA agreed to use solid fuel rockets, not previously used by NASA in manned flight because, once ignited, they cannot be shut down. Thus in an emergency they leave the astronauts helpless. Another cost compromise was the elimination of an escape system for the astronauts.

In the end, Fletcher pared the shuttle cost projections down from $8 billion to $5.5 billion plus $1 billion for contingencies. The aggressive Office of Management and Budget (OMB), under the leadership of George Schultz, forced Fletcher back down to the $5.5 billion level.

But some former and current NASA officials recognized immediately the impossibility of putting the shuttle together on Fletcher's budget. John Naugle, who had been at NASA under Webb and was there under Fletcher, knew that the shuttle could never be self-financing as Fletcher predicted. He felt Fletcher was deceiving the public, and he believed that Fletcher should have told Nixon that the shuttle should operate as a purely public, R & D program and assume great costs, or that the United States should get out of manned spaceflight altogether.[18] Dr. Seamans, one of the top three NASA officials under Kennedy and secretary of the Air Force under Nixon, knew that NASA needed much more than Fletcher was projecting to develop the shuttle properly. He sensed that Fletcher was distorting the figures because he had a personal stake in the shuttle, wanting to oversee his own great space program.[19]

Fletcher sold the shuttle to Congress based on the idea that it would be "operational," that it would cover its costs by trucking satellites into space for the military and others. The promises he made in the early 70s were so unrealistic that the shuttle never approached being truly "operational.'' Much of Fletcher's sales pitch came from a study by Mathematica, a research firm commissioned by NASA to study the shuttle's cost effectiveness. Fletcher used the study to argue that the shuttle could pay for itself if it flew at least thirty times a year.[20] At that launch rate, Fletcher predicted that a pound of payload would only cost $100 and would be commercially competitive. But cost overruns were tremendous. According to the Congressional Budget Office, the cost per pound of payload, adjusted for inflation, is now $5,264 if all the development costs are included. If only the current per flight operational costs are considered, then the price per pound is $2,849.[21]

According to the General Accounting Office, Dr. Fletcher gave ''misleading'' and ''overly optimistic'' accounts of projected costs. He had predicted that the cost per launch would be $10.45 million. Not including all the construction costs, the cost today (adjusted for inflation) is $151 million ($279 million including construction costs).[22] Launch operations cost almost fifteen times more than originally predicted.

Boosting the launch rate was an ongoing demand at NASA. Officials at NASA understood that only a higher launch rate would quiet their critics in Congress and the Pentagon, and only a higher launch rate would enable the shuttle to compete with the unmanned Ariane, a French rocket able to send commercial satellites into space cheaply. In March 1985, James Beggs, administrator of NASA said, ''The next eighteen months are very critical for the shuttle. If we are going to prove our mettle and demonstrate our capability, we have got to fly out that [flight] manifest.''[23] The goal for 1986 was awesome, if not crazy—twenty-four flights.

The impossible promises that Fletcher made in the early 70s thoroughly affected NASA and the shuttle program. NASA had agreed to let economics be the measure of success. If it could produce a cost-efficient space craft, then and only then would the critics on Capitol Hill be silenced. Technological achievements sending human beings to the moon or building a reusable ''space truck'' were no longer enough to satisfy politicians or the public.

In order to succeed, the shuttle had to stay within budget, which meant that many corners had to be cut. Where money was saved, safety was spent. NASA cut back on the shuttle's design. In awarding contracts, NASA gave first priority to cost, not quality. For example, in choosing among design proposals for the SRB, NASA's Source Evaluation Board passed over the monolithic, unsegmented aerojet design that was judged to be safest. The monolithic SRB avoided the problems of joints where pressure and hot gas might escape, but it was too costly.

Moreover, there were cutbacks in testing and NASA oversight of contractors. Between 1974 and 1977, at least five studies found that NASA was shirking its responsibility to test shuttle parts under construction. One study, conducted by thirty-five aeronautical and space experts, found that testing was being ''highly compressed''—from sixteen months to three—and called for more testing.[24] But NASA said that more testing would not be ''cost effective.'' Over the course of the shuttle's development, more than half a billion dollars were cut from testing. Furthermore, the number of NASA officials responsible for checking the work of the contractors declined precipitously. NASA oversight of contractors practically stopped altogether. During the Apollo era, the Johnson Space Flight Center had twenty-eight contract monitors, whereas in 1980 it only had two.[25] Dangerously flawed parts went unnoticed. At one point, it was discovered that JetAir, a subcontractor of Rockwell had doctored X-rays revealing cracks and faulty welding in the Orbiter.[26] Many hands were involved in putting the shuttle together, and NASA had lost control of them and the quality of their work.

Given the lack of funds, did NASA have any alternative to compromising its safety standards? Yes, NASA could have exited from manned spaceflight altogether or at least not committed to a completely manned space program like the shuttle. Except for the publicity that manned spaceflight receives and, consequently, the financial support that accrues to NASA from that favorable coverage, there is apparently very little that people can do in space that could not be done for much less by unmanned programs. Important groups outside NASA were, in fact, making this argument when the shuttle was still on the drawing board. Dr. Seamans, secretary of the Air Force at the time, did not support the idea of a manned shuttle. In his mind, it was unnecessary to have people aboard with all the requisite life support systems just to put satellites into orbit.[27] Even Mars and deeper space can be explored without human beings. Currently, in fact, the Voyager, an unmanned space vehicle, has far surpassed the shuttle in important discoveries.

But NASA officials, especially Fletcher and Low, wanted manned flight. And there were signs that the public wanted it too. Nixon apparently agreed to the shuttle idea primarily because he did not want to be remembered as the president who killed manned spaceflight. Therefore, it was political obstacles and ambitions among NASA Administrators that brought about the decision to man the shuttle.

. . .

With all the cost overruns and the shuttle delays, the pressure to live up to that "manifest" to which James Beggs had referred became intense. It was this pressure, constantly in the minds of every NASA manager, that led to risk-taking. With the goal set for twenty-four flights in 1986, the pressure had reached a new high. Even if no one talked explicitly about it, everyone felt it. The contractors, like Thiokol, knew that NASA did not want to hear the recommendations that a launch be delayed, especially

if the delay were indefinite as it probably should have been with the O-rings.[28] And NASA managers knew that their superiors did not want to hear that recommendation from them either. In this kind of cover-your-eyes-and-go-for-it setting, loss of life was almost inevitable.

Because Fletcher had accepted an inadequate budget for the shuttle, he deserves much of the blame for risks taken later. However, he is not culpable alone. There were outside observers who were aware of potential dangers but remained silent. The General Accounting Office, a congressional watchdog agency, openly warned of safety compromises that NASA was allowing. But because of the success of the Apollo program, neither Congress nor the press paid much attention.[29] There were also NASA insiders who had access to reports disclosing mechanical flaws in the shuttle. At one time or another, engineers at NASA and at Morton Thiokol urgently warned about weaknesses in the O-rings' design. For several years, NASA engineers at Marshall expressed their concern over the O-ring design. In 1978, John Q. Miller, Marshall's chief of the SRB project, wrote George Hardy that the O-ring design might allow hot gas leaks that could result in "catastrophic failure." But Hardy did not respond to these warnings. He did not question Miller or the other engineers about their concerns, nor did he press Thiokol to address the design problems.[30] By 1981, NASA's engineers had stopped raising concerns about the O-rings even though no design changes were ever made.

And at Morton Thiokol, after flight 41-C where there had been substantial blow-by on one of the primary O-rings, the engineers began seriously to express their fears about the O-ring design. In the year preceding the *Challenger* disaster, the engineers' worries continued to escalate. A task force was established by Thiokol to improve the O-ring design. By midsummer 1985, some of Thiokol's engineers were deeply concerned. The management had been dragging its feet on the redesign effort and not assigning as many people to the task force as were needed. The engineers stopped mincing words. In one memo to the management, Bob Ebeling, one of the task force engineers, expressed how urgent it was that the task force become Thiokol's first priority. He wrote, "HELP! The seal task force is constantly being delayed by every possible means. We wish we could get action by verbal request [they had been frequently going to one of the managers, Joe Kilminster], but such is not the case. This is a red flag."[31]

Roger Boisjoly also wrote a memo: "This letter is written to insure that management is fully aware of the seriousness of the current O-ring erosion problem in the SRM joints from an engineering standpoint. . . . The mistakenly accepted position on the joint problem was to fly without fear of failure and to run a series of design evaluations which would ultimately lead to a solution or at least a significant reduction of the erosion problem. This position is now drastically changed as a result of the SRM 16A nozzle joint erosion [Flight 41-B] which eroded a secondary O-ring with the primary O-ring never sealing. If the same scenario should occur in a field joint (and it could), then it is a jump ball as to the success or failure of the joint because the secondary O-ring cannot respond to the clevis opening rate and may not be capable of pressurization. *The result would be a catastrophe of the highest order—loss of human life.*"[32]

Despite the engineers' appeal to Thiokol's management, the seal redesign effort continued to be neglected. After the accident, the redesign effort was finally made first priority at Thiokol. It went on day and night, and in two and a half months a solution had been found. Before the accident, only eight people out of an employee pool of two thousand had been assigned to the SRB redesign task force. With such a small task force, it would have taken two and a half years to come up with the same solution

they found in two months of aggressive research.[33]

Knowledge of the dangers did exist. Still, the pressures to make the shuttle "operational" were such that both Marshall officials and Thiokol managers continued to recommend launching. Everyone knew that the lives of the astronauts and their families were being jeopardized, but the men in power pressed on willing to take the risks. The end result was a tragedy that could have been avoided.

EPILOGUE

The official Rogers Commission report blamed NASA's system of communication for the shuttle accident. It concluded that sufficient information about the O-ring problem existed before the accident to have prompted an indefinite launch delay.[34] That the launches continued was due, the commission found, to mid-level NASA managers deciding independently that continuing the flights would not endanger the lives of the astronauts. Despite serious questions raised by Thiokol's engineers, these managers (such as Mulloy and Reinartz) never informed their superiors of the gravity of the engineer's concerns. The commission was "troubled by what appears to be a propensity of management at Marshall to contain potentially serious problems and to attempt to resolve them internally rather than communicate them forward."[35] The commission also concluded that NASA had made it clear that they did not welcome shuttle delays, thereby pressuring contractors to override internal dissent and approve flight readiness.[36]

However, due to the candid testimony of two Thiokol employees, Boisjoly and Allan McDonald, certain individuals were blamed, unofficially at least, for the accident. Mulloy seemed particularly responsible, especially after letting Morton Thiokol know how he was unhappy with the engineers' recommendation not to launch. He appeared to have pressured Thiokol into reversing that recommendation. Though

NASA offered to continue his employ, he went into early retirement.[37] At Thiokol, the CEO blamed Mason for having "risked the company."[38] Mason also retired early. Kilminster was transferred out of all space programs but continued his job at Thiokol.

Boisjoly and McDonald were demoted for publicly speaking against the company's pro-launch decision. After Boisjoly testified before the Rogers Commission, a senior Thiokol official chastised him for having aired the company's dirty laundry. Sure, tell the truth, he was told, but put the company in a favorable light too.[39] Boisjoly was kept on the payroll but was stripped of any responsibility in the SRB redesign effort.

After Chairman William Rogers vigorously protested the demotion of the two whistle-blowers, Thiokol quickly responded and promoted McDonald to head the SRB design effort. Boisjoly, however, was so stricken by a sense of responsibility for the lives of the astronauts that he could not continue to work and took a leave of absence. For months following the accident, he could not sleep and began to take medication. Finally, a year after the accident, he was well enough to speak publicly about his experience, which he has been doing now for over a year. He states that for personal reasons he will never be able to work on the shuttle again.

Four out of seven of the astronauts' families settled with the U.S. government for, unofficially, more than $750,000. Two of the families have filed suits against NASA, one for $15 million. A third filed suit against Thiokol. As of August 1987, none of these suits had been settled.

NOTES

1. Malcolm McConnell, *Challenger: A Major Malfunction* (Garden City, N.Y.: Doubleday, 1987), 207–49.

2. Roger Boisjoly, "Company Loyalty and Whistleblowing: Ethical Decisions and the Space Shuttle Disaster" (videotape), Jan. 7, 1987.

3. Each joint had a primary and a secondary seal.

4. Interview with Boisjoly, Fall 1987.

5. Boisjoly video and Boisjoly interview.

6. McConnell, 165.

7. *Report of the Presidential Commission on the Space Shuttle Challenger Accident* (Washington, DC, June 6,1986), Vol. I, p. 94.

8. McConnell, 198.

9. Boisjoly interview, and McConnell, 199.

10. Boisjoly interview.

11. *Report of the Presidential Commission*, Vol. I, 94.

12. *Report of the Presidential Commission*, Vol I, 97; and McConnell, 200.

13. Joseph J. Trento, *A Perspective for Disaster* (New York: Crown, 1987), 36.

14. Trento, 84–87.

15. Ibid., 93–94.

16. Ibid., 102–3.

17. Fletcher's soft stand on safety is a point Trento makes throughout *Prescription for Disaster*.

18. Trento, 118–21.

19. Ibid., 112–13,

20. McConnell, 41.

21. Stuart Diamond, NASA Wasted Billions, Federal Audits Disclose," *New York Times*, 12 April 1987, 1, 1:1

22. Ibid.

23. McConnell, 62.

24. Ibid.

25. Ibid.

26. Ibid.

27. Trento, 112.

28. "The [Rogers] Commission concluded that the Thiokol management reversed its position and recommended the launch of 51-L [the *Challenger*], at the urging of Marshall and contrary to the views of its engineers in order to accommodate a major customer." *Report of the Presidential Commission*, Vol. I, 104.

29. McConnell, Ch. 6, "The Spellbound Press."

30. *Report of the Presidential Commission*, Vol. I, 123–24.

31. McConnell, 180.

32. *Report*, Vol. I, 139 (emphasis added).

33. Boisjoly interview.

34. *Report*, Vol. I, 148.

35. Ibid., 104.

36. Ibid.

37. The Associated Press, "Ex-Shuttle Rocket Chief Quits Space Agency," *New York Times*, 17 July 1986, V, 19:1.

38. Boisjoly interview.

39. Boisjoly video.

Comment

Roger Boisjoly and Arnie Thompson argued long and hard, but failed to convince the managers of Morton Thiokol to recommend against launching the shuttle. We are not told whether Boisjoly and Thompson thought about threatening to resign or publicly protesting in other ways. But if they did, they might understandably have rejected public protest, expecting that it would lead to their dismissal and would leave no high-level defenders of safety standards at Thiokol or NASA. (They enjoyed neither the public prominence nor the career alternatives that George Shultz had.) In judging whether Boisjoly and Thompson should have done more (or less), keep in mind that they had to decide their own course of action when they had only rough estimates of the probabilities of a successful or disastrous launch. Also, by remaining on the job, their subsequent action (including their testimony) in defense of improved safety standards may have been more effective. However, it can be argued that had they publicly protested or threatened to resign before the launch, they might have actually stopped the launch and prevented the disaster.

Many discussions of official disobedience emphasize how much trouble officials get into by publicly protesting, leaking information, or otherwise employing unauthorized tactics in pursuit of a just cause. The *Challenger* case, in contrast, reveals the problems that officials can have simply by doing their jobs well, even if they do not disobey their superiors or violate any procedures. The case also suggests the need to look beyond the immediate decisions and decision makers to those policies and policymakers who create the conditions that lead to bad decisions. What practices at Thiokol and NASA hindered people like Boisjoly and Thompson from doing their jobs well? Who was responsible for those practices? How might the practices be changed so as to make official disobedience less necessary and internal criticism more effective?

Recommended Reading

An excellent statement of the theory of civil disobedience is John Rawls, *A Theory of Justice* (Cambridge, Mass.: Harvard University Press, 1971), pp. 363–91. Ronald Dworkin develops and applies some important distinctions in *A Matter of Principle* (Cambridge, Mass.: Harvard University Press, 1985), pp. 104–16. Still useful though not widely available is Jeffrie Murphy (ed.), *Civil Disobedience and Violence* (Belmont, Calif.: Wadsworth, 1971).

General discussions of the concept of obligation that relate to civil disobedience are Michael Walzer, *Obligations* (New York: Simon and Schuster, 1971), chapters 1 and 2; George Klosko, *The Principle of Fairness and Political Obligation* (Savage, Md.: Rowman and Littlefield, 1991); and A. John Simons, *Moral Principles and*

Political Obligations (Princeton, N.J.: Princeton University Press, 1979). Also, see R. Kent Greenawalt, *Conflicts of Law and Morality* (New York: Oxford University Press, 1987), parts 3 and 4.

Specifically on the obligations of public officials, see the astute analysis by Arthur Applbaum, "Democratic Legitimacy and Official Discretion," *Philosophy & Public Affairs*, 21 (Summer 1992), pp. 240–74. On the ethics of whistleblowing, see Sissela Bok, *Secrets* (New York: Pantheon, 1982), pp. 210–29; and Myron P. Glazer and Penina M. Glazer, *The Whistleblowers: Exposing Corruption in Government and Industry* (New York: Basic Books, 1989). The practical and theoretical aspects of resignation are discussed in Edward Weisband and Thomas Franck, *Resignation in Protest* (New York: Penguin, 1975), and Albert Hirschman, *Exit, Voice and Loyalty* (Cambridge, Mass.: Harvard University Press, 1970). A social psychological approach to the problem of official dissent is Herbert Kelman, *Crimes of Obedience* (New Haven, Conn.: Yale University Press, 1989). For discussion focused on the ethics of engineers like those featured in the *Challenger* case, see Michael Davis, "Thinking Like an Engineer: The Place of a Code of Ethics in the Practice of a Profession," *Philosophy & Public Affairs*, 20 (Spring, 1991), pp. 150–67.

For contending views on the problem of ascribing moral responsibility for government decisions to individual officials, see John Ladd, "Morality and the Ideal of Rationality in Formal Organizations," *Monist*, 54 (October 1970), pp. 488–516; Ronald Dworkin, *Law's Empire* (Cambridge, Mass.: Harvard University Press, 1986), pp. 167–75; and Dennis F. Thompson, *Political Ethics and Public Office* (Cambridge, Mass.: Harvard University Press, 1987), pp. 40–65.

Part Two

The Ethics of Policy

5 Policy Analysis

Introduction

The question of means and ends—the focus of the first part of this book—speaks to only part of the moral world of politics. No less important is the question of the ends themselves: how should we choose among competing goals of policy? The most common framework for answering this question is some version of policy analysis, including cost-benefit, cost-effective, and risk-benefit analysis.

All of these approaches draw on the moral framework of utilitarianism (insofar as they draw on any moral framework at all). They assume (1) that the ends or values of policies can be compared by a common measure of expected utility (also called happiness, satisfaction, or—most commonly—welfare) and (2) that the best policy or set of policies can be compared by a common measure of expected utility. The great appeal of this approach is that it appears to resolve conflicts among competing ends and seems to do so in a neutral way by simply adding up the preferences of all citizens. (Utility or welfare is typically defined as some form of the satisfaction of preferences.) The approach also appears democratic, since it purports to give the most people as much as possible of whatever they want.

Critics of policy analysis attack both of its assumptions. First, they point to problems of aggregation—the way the policy analyst adds preferences to arrive at total utility. Among criticisms of this kind are: (1) that individual utilities cannot be compared (How can we say whether a job for me is worth a slightly higher cancer risk for you? Or whether cheaper electric power for you is worth fewer fishing, hiking, and rafting opportunities for me?); (2) that ultimate values cannot be traded off against other goods (How can we put a price on life itself? Or even on the environment?); and (3) that individual preferences cannot be taken as given (How can we assume that public deliberations about policy will not significantly alter public perceptions of the value of environmental protection and economic development?)

The second set of criticisms concerns problems of distribution. Critics challenge the maximization principle because it ignores how utility is allocated among individuals. They object that for the sake of maximizing general utility, policy analysts will sacrifice (1) the rights of disadvantaged citizens in their own society; (2) the welfare of poorer nations; and (3) the welfare of future generations. Policy analysts try to take account of such groups, but the problem of distributive justice remains a formidable obstacle to the acceptance of their method.

The policy analysis undertaken in "Saving the Tuolumne" poses a classic choice between environmental protection (in California's beautiful Tuolumne Canyon) and economic development (in the form of new dams and reservoirs for more water and hydroelectric power). Many federal and state agencies—like the Federal Energy Regulatory Commission and the California State Water Resources Control Board in this case—operate under a legal mandate to approve new dams and reservoirs if and only if their public benefits are shown to exceed their costs. Critics of such legal mandates claim that policy analysis is biased in favor of economic development and against environmental protection. However, the policy analysis conducted by the Environmental Defense Fund in this case concludes in favor of protecting the Tuolumne Canyon instead of pursuing the Clavey-Wards Ferry Project.

To decide whether to preserve the Tuolumne Canyon or to build the dams and reservoirs, a policy analyst must quantify and compare many different values over time, including the values of water and hydroelectric power, whitewater rafting, fishing, boating, camping, and hiking. The Environmental Defense Fund's analysis uses sophisticated techniques of quantification, but even the most sophisticated techniques are subject to morally significant criticisms and often yield conflicting policy recommendations. Taken together, the Environmental Defense Fund's analysis and the critical review by the engineering consulting firm of R. W. Beck and Associates offer an opportunity to probe the moral strengths and weaknesses of policy analysis.

The aim of policy analysis is to estimate as many costs and benefits over time as are amenable to quantification. The controversy over saving the Tuolumne illustrates the value of quantifying even some of those values—such as hiking and whitewater rafting—that are often assumed to be unquantifiable. The controversy also illustrates the limits of such quantification. Policy analysts rarely if ever claim to have captured all the costs and benefits of alternative policies, but they attempt to capture as many as possible, as accurately as possible. Their quantification, even if completely accurate, is therefore only part of the broader analysis that would be necessary to determine whether the environmental protection in question is—all things considered—more or less valuable than the economic development.

Assigning utility to policy options and systematically assessing the quantifiable costs and benefits can help dispel some uncertainties and confusions regarding the policy decision of whether to preserve the environment or to develop energy resources. But the quantification is typically both controversial and incomplete. Although the controversy over the analysis in the Tuolumne case may seem merely technical, it reflects ethical differences about such questions as the value of noneconomic pursuits (such as hiking) versus economic pursuits (such as generating electrical power) and the obligation to future generations (to preserve natural beauty). Beyond the problem of adding up the costs and benefits, the problem of distributing them within a society and over time plays an important role in the controversy but a less than fully explicit role in the policy analysis. Although neither the report by the Environmental Defense Fund nor the critical review by Beck and Associates claims to deal with all the issues in the conflict between the values of environmental protection versus economic development, we should read them with as much attention to what they omit as to what they include.

William Ruckelshaus, who was responsible for setting emissions standards in the Asarco case, was as sensitive to the weaknesses of policy analysis as he was to its strengths. Ruckelshaus held a series of public meetings with the people who would be most directly affected by his decision to discuss both the technical and moral dimensions of setting emissions standards for the Asarco smelting company. Some observers criticized Ruckelshaus for abdicating his responsibility to make policy on the basis of his own best technical and moral judgment. Others praised him for trying to educate the public about the difficulties of making decisions on the basis of imperfect and incomplete knowledge. The Asarco case does not provide a solution to the philosophical or technical problems of how to aggregate preferences to arrive at total utility and how to distribute risks among people. Instead, it suggests a political process by which the resolution of these problems may be more fairly and fully considered.

Saving the Tuolumne
Linda Kincaid

From its origins high on Mount Lyell and Mount Dana in Yosemite National Park, the Tuolumne river flows 158 miles west to California's San Joaquin Valley. Despite hydroelectric developments at either end of the Tuolumne, the river still runs free in a 30-mile stretch through Tuolumne Canyon, between the O'Shaughnessy Dam in Yosemite and the headwaters of the New Don Pedro Reservoir. Here the Tuolumne hurtles down the western slope of the High Sierra, fed by four major tributaries—the Clavey River, Cherry Creek, and the Middle and South Forks. Only two roads wind into the isolated canyon, where the river courses between sheer granite cliffs and rugged slopes covered with digger pine, incense cedar, and oak. Mink, screech owl, river otter, and the endangered southern bald eagle share the canyon with large deer herds that travel there each winter from Yosemite. The cold water pools of the Tuolumne and Clavey Rivers harbor some of California's finest trout reserves—by one

estimate two to three times more productive than the state's best flatwater fishing areas. Tuolumne Canyon also contains several historic and prehistoric sites, including ruins of abandoned gold mines and sites inhabited by the Miwok Indians, who lived in the canyon until the mid-1800s.

The Tuolumne's continuous succession of rapids and cataracts make it one of the nation's finest and most popular whitewater rafting rivers. Each year between March and October, thousands of rafting enthusiasts travel a single-lane dirt road into Lumsden's Landing to make the 18-mile trip downriver to Wards Ferry. With twenty-five major rapids and a white-knuckle plunge over the eight-foot high Clavey Falls, this stretch of the Tuolumne is considered comparable to the Colorado River in the Grand Canyon or Idaho's Salmon River. More than 15,000 rafters from all over the country made this run in one- to three-day trips in 1982, and a few hundred others braved the more treacherous stretch of the Tuolumne above Lumsden's Bridge. About 9,000 of those boaters ran the rapids on their own, while another 6,000 took trips arranged by one of ten commercial expedition firms. With government studies documenting an increasing demand over time for rafting on the Tuolumne, some expedition operators and environmental groups expect the number of Tuolumne rafters to double within the next decade.

While rafting is the Tuolumne's major attraction, others travel to the area to hunt, fish, hike, and camp. The U.S. Forest Service recorded 22,000 visitor-days at its campgrounds on the Tuolumne in 1983; and total recreational use is estimated at 35,000 user-days annually. Tuolumne River Canyon is also home to three city-run family campgrounds, operated by the cities of Berkeley, San Jose, and San Francisco, which provide low-cost camping and recreation for city residents.

With its steep, narrow canyon walls and large volume of flowing water, the Tuolumne River Canyon is also an ideal site for hydroelectric development. In April 1983, the City and Country of San Francisco and two irrigation districts in Merced and Stanislaus counties commissioned a feasibility study of their longstanding proposal to dam the Tuolumne for power and water. At the same time, a coalition of environmentalists, rafters, fishing enthusiasts and California residents known as the Tuolumne River Preservation Trust was lobbying Congress to protect the river from further development under the federal Wild and Scenic Rivers Act. The dam proponents had already produced several favorable cost-benefit studies of their proposal; in June 1983 the Trust asked economists at the Environmental Defense Fund to respond to those studies with an economic assessment of the proposed dam's environmental costs.

HYDROELECTRIC DEVELOPMENT ON THE TUOLUMNE

By 1983, existing hydroelectric developments on the Tuolumne captured 90 percent of its water and more than 70 percent of its power generating capacity—enough to supply drinking water to nearly 2 million

Californians, irrigate 230,000 acres of farmland in California's Central Valley, and generate electricity to power some 400,000 homes. The City and County of San Francisco drew 300 million gallons of water a day from the Hetch Hetchy Reservoir, located inside Yosemite, and from two additional reservoirs on tributaries of the Tuolumne. The Hetch Hetchy System's three powerhouses provided nearly 300 megawatts of electrical capacity, which the San Francisco Public Utilities Commission sold to municipal departments of the city and to nearby utility districts and industrial customers. Thirty miles downstream, the New Don Pedro Dam and Reservoir provided electricity and irrigation to the Modesto and Turlock Irrigation Districts (MID and TID).

The two irrigation districts distributed irrigation water and power to the city of Modesto, several smaller towns, and 230,000 acres of farmland in Stanislaus and Merced counties.[1] Located less than 100 miles west of San Francisco, in California's Central Valley, the two districts contained some of the richest farmland in the world, as well as a burgeoning population of professionals, industrial workers, and retirees. Electricity consumption in the MID-TID service area had increased more rapidly than in California as a whole from 1965–75, thanks to a dramatic increase in irrigated acreage and an influx of agricultural processors and other industries who had moved their plants from the metropolitan areas to Central Valley towns. A 1975 study by the consulting firm Arthur D. Little predicted that rapid economic growth would continue in the MID-TID service area through the year 2000. In 1979, a study of electricity demand in the MID service area by consultants Hittman and Associates found that the area's industrial growth had slowed somewhat, but predicted that electricity demand would still grow at an annual rate of 4.1 percent.

By 1983, the 150-megawatt (MW) power station at New Don Pedro Dam met only

EXHIBIT 1. COMBINED MID AND TID PROJECTED DEMAND REQUIREMENTS
VERSUS RESOURCES

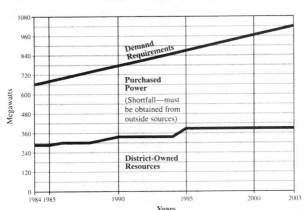

Source: R.W. Beck and Associates, *Clavey-Wards Ferry Projects, FERC Project No. 2774, Phase II Feasibility Evaluation*, for Modesto and Turlock Irrigation Districts.

half the electricity demand in the two irrigation districts, forcing them to purchase additional power from the statewide utility, Pacific Gas and Electric Company (PG&E), and from San Francisco's Hetch Hetchy System. Using Hittman's 4.1 percent annual growth predictions, district planners projected that the gap between demand and generating capacity would continue to grow, to about 500 MW in 1995 and 600 MW in 2000 (Exhibit 1). Historically, MID and TID customers had enjoyed some of the lowest electricity rates in the nation, but rates began to rise in the early eighties as the districts invested in new sources and bought more PG&E power to keep up with rising demand. District planners expected electricity prices to rise further after 1985, when they would have to renegotiate the price for power purchased from Hetch Hetchy.

Faced with rising demand for electricity and rising prices for outside sources, managers of both irrigation districts turned to the last undeveloped stretch of the Tuolumne and to a 1968 engineering study originally done for San Francisco, which recommended construction of two new hydroelectric facilities on the river—one at the mouth of the Clavey River and another

at Wards Ferry, just above the New Don Pedro Dam. In 1976, San Francisco and the two irrigation districts had applied to the Federal Energy Regulatory Commission (FERC) for a preliminary permit to conduct a feasibility study of the so-called Clavey-Wards Ferry (CWF) proposal. But the year before, Congress had asked the U.S. Departments of Agriculture and Interior to study the Tuolumne's eligibility for preservation as a "wild and scenic" river, and FERC was forbidden to act on the permit application until the end of the three-year federal study period. The river study concluded that the entire 83 miles of river that flows through Yosemite National Park and the Stanislaus National Forest possessed "outstandingly remarkable scenic qualities" and should be included in the nation's wild and scenic rivers system. Although Congress never acted on President Carter's 1979 request to preserve the river, his request delayed FERC action on the permit application until 1982. San Francisco and the irrigation districts remained interested in the project, commissioning three updated economic reports on the project during this period. Finally, in April 1983, FERC granted the preliminary permit. MID, TID,

EXHIBIT 2. CLAVEY-WARDS FERRY ALTERNATIVE

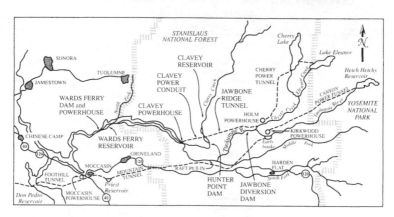

Source: R.W. Beck and Associates, *Clavey-Wards Ferry Project, FERC Project No. 2774, Phase II Feasibility Evaluation*, for Modesto and Turlock Irrigation Districts.

and the City and County of San Francisco promptly hired the engineering consulting firm of R.W. Beck and Associates to perform a detailed three-year feasibility study of the Clavey-Wards Ferry proposal.

THE CLAVEY-WARDS FERRY PROJECT

As described in the FERC preliminary permit application, the CWF development would generate 980 gigawatt-hours (GWh) annually from two separate generating installations, the Clavey unit and the Wards Ferry unit (Exhibit 2). The Clavey unit would include two new dams and reservoirs and a 5.1 mile diversion tunnel. Jawbone Diversion Dam, 175 feet high and 255 feet long, would be located on the Tuolumne River just downstream from its confluence with Cherry Creek. The nearby Jawbone Creek Diversion Dam and Pipeline would divert Jawbone Creek flows into the new Jawbone Reservoir behind the Jawbone Diversion Dam. From Jawbone Reservoir, the Jawbone Ridge Tunnel would carry water to Clavey Reservoir. The Hunter Point Dam and Clavey Reservoir would be located on the Clavey River almost six miles upstream from its confluence with the Tuolumne. A 2.4 mile pressure tunnel would link the

Clavey Reservoir to two 150-MW generating units in the Clavey Powerhouse, to be located underground near the headwaters of the planned Wards Ferry Reservoir.

The Wards Ferry Unit would include a 450-foot high, 1,060 foot-long rockfill Wards Ferry Dam, which would create the Wards Ferry Reservoir. The reservoir would have a usable storage of about 92,300 acre-feet[2]—providing an annual water supply of 12,000 acre-feet—and would store and regulate Tuolumne River flows for power generation and water supply. The Wards Ferry Powerhouse, which would be located underground in the dam's south abutment, would house two 50-MW generating units.

Beck estimated that construction of the CWF project could be completed in 1995, allowing for preparatory studies, FERC licensing, and a four and a half year construction period. Total capital costs were estimated at $860 million in 1995 dollars. The consultants estimated that by constructing CWF, the two irrigation districts would enjoy a net savings of $29 million in the first year of operation over the projected costs of purchasing power from PG&E; the CWF option would cost $18 million less in the first year than constructing or joining other utilities in new fossil-fuel plants.

Both proponents and opponents of the Clavey-Wards proposal agreed that its construction would substantially change existing conditions on the Tuolumne. The planned Wards Ferry Reservoir would inundate approximately 1,200 acres of the Tuolumne River Canyon, including traditional mule deer winter habitats and approximately 12 miles of trout spawning beds and stream habitat on the Tuolumne. Upriver, the Clavey unit was expected to reduce river flows in some 15 miles of the Tuolumne and 6 miles of the Clavey. Dam management would also cause abrupt changes in waterflows in these sections of the two rivers.

THE CASE FOR CLAVEY-WARDS FERRY

Proponents of the Clavey-Wards Ferry argued that the dams would provide a cheap, clean, renewable source of energy to help the districts keep pace with their steadily rising demands. "We needed a source of power," explained Turlock Irrigation District manager Ernest Geddes. "We needed a reliable and economical source. . . . If you look at what are the options, I could build a nuclear plant, or an oil-fired plant or a coal plant, or a hydro plant. . . . [Clavey-Wards Ferry] was the most economical alternative."

For Tuolumne County, which had endorsed the project, Clavey-Wards Ferry would help answer its desperate need for water. Distant communities like San Francisco had long ago appropriated most of the water which flowed through this sparsely populated county in the Sierra foothills, which is dominated by Yosemite National Park and Stanislaus National Forest. In the early eighties, Tuolumne County was one of the fastest growing in the state—its population was expected to grow from 40,000 to 60,000 between 1985 and 2000—and its small water supply was already strained. Under an agreement with MID and TID, the county would get 12,000 acre feet of

water annually from Clavey-Wards Ferry, and a third of the revenue from the project's sales of excess power. (The county planned to dedicate those revenues to developing other water supplies.) The estimated two-hundred-fifty construction jobs and dozens of permanent jobs the project would require were also appealing in the county, where seasonal unemployment had reached 21 percent in the winter of 1983.

The project's proponents argued that the changes Clavey-Wards Ferry would bring to Tuolumne Canyon would increase recreational opportunities in the area (Exhibit 3). The development would bring new roads, opening the wilderness to tourists and permitting the development of more campsites. The new Wards Ferry Reservoir would offer opportunities for flatwater fishing, boating, and swimming. Proponents promised to maintain trout fishing opportunities by setting minimum flood levels at Jawbone Dam and Clavey Dam in consultation with state and federal fisheries agencies. And, they argued, the reduced flows between Jawbone Dam and Lumsden campground might improve fishing conditions, particularly for fly fishing.

Proponents conceded that the dams would reduce the Tuolumne's main whitewater run from 18 miles to 6.6 miles. But Geddes maintained that the dam at Jawbone Creek would increase raftable days by 20–25 percent by holding back the heavy spring runoff that sometimes made the river too wild to navigate in June and early July. (Dam proponents also pointed out that the Lumsden-Wards Ferry run would probably be too wild for rafting without the existing dams at Cherry Creek and Hetch Hetchy.) A more moderate, controlled flow, he said, would allow rafters to make the trip in their own small boats, rather than paying for professional river guides. Besides, they said, flatwater recreation was more popular and allowed a greater density of use than wilderness pursuits like rafting and hiking. "Rafting's a special interest thing," said Jerry

Item	Existing Baseline Conditions	Conditions with Clavey-Wards Ferry Alternative
Lake recreation	• None on affected reach of the Tuolumne between Don Pedro and Hetch-Hetchy Reservoir.	• Create opportunities at Wards Ferry Reservoir.
Whitewater Rafting	• 18-mile long, Class IV run below Lumden campground used by two commercial companies and individuals.	• Reduce Main run to 6.6 miles and reduce number of raftable days. Run will not support commercial operations.
	• Experts-only Cherry Creek run (kayaking and rafting).	• Eliminate Cherry Creek run because of flow diversions.
Fly Fishing	• Concentrated at and above Lumden campground.	• Minimum flow releases would preserve fly-fishing above Lumden campground.
Camping	• Limited to 3 developed campgrounds with 23 campsites; 14 undeveloped sites on Tuolumne used by river boaters.	• Lakeside campsites would be developed at Wards Ferry Reservoir. Some undeveloped sites would be inundated.
Hiking, Hunting, and Other Dispersed Activities	• Hiking and hunting concentrated in hills above Tuolumne Canyon.	• Same as existing conditions but improved access to canyon areas.
River Access	• Very limited.	• Improved.
Visual Character	• Flowing rivers in rugged canyons. Tuolumne flows controlled by releases from Holm with limited evidence of recent human occupation.	• Considerable portions of canyon bottoms converted to lakes. Two dams on Tuolumne, access roads, and transmission line.
Water Supply	• None for Tuolumne County.	• Provide supply from Wards Ferry Reservoir.
Flood Control	• At Don Pedro Reservoir.	• Improve capability.
Cultural Resources	• Area contains known cultural sites.	• Potential for inundation of activity at sites.
Terrestrial Habitat	• Canyons include winter range of mule deer. Habitat of peregrine falcon and bald eagle, and possibly rare snail.	• Inundation causes loss of mule deer winter range and possible interruption of migration routes. Increased human access may make falcon and eagle habitat less favorable.
Aquatic Habitat	• Fish habitat limited by flow variability especially upstream of South Fork. No manmade barriers to fish migration between Don Pedro Reservoir and Early Intake.	• Habitat improvement upstream of South Fork due to more constant flow conditions. Below South Fork, Hunter Point and Wards Ferry dams would convert habitat from riverine to reservoir.

Source: R. W. Berk and Associates, *Clavey-Wards Phase II Feasibility Evalutaion.*

Bellah, a member of the Tuolumne County Board of Supervisors. "I've lived here twenty-three years and I've never rafted the river. Not that many people do it."

THE OPPOSITION

In a sense, the modern environmental protection movement began with an earlier fight over the Tuolumne's future. In the early 1900s, naturalist John Muir led an impassioned campaign to prevent San Francisco from damming the Tuolumne and flooding the Hetch Hetchy Valley, which Muir and his followers felt was as beautiful as the neighboring Yosemite Valley. "Dam Hetch Hetchy!" he wrote, during the first nationwide letter-writing campaign to Congress on an environmental issue. "As well dam for water tanks the people's cathedrals and churches, for no holier temple has ever been consecrated by the heart of man."

Muir lost the battle when Congress passed the Raker Act of 1913, which permitted the City and County of San Francisco to build six dams and reservoirs in the Tuolumne watershed. He died before the dam was completed—of a broken heart, according to conservationist folklore—but from the Hetch Hetchy fight, the Sierra Club emerged as a strong voice for environmental protection.

By the early eighties, the fight to save the remaining 30 wild miles of the Tuolumne took on symbolic importance for environmentalists, who were frustrated by their agonizingly slow progress in protecting the nation's most spectacular rivers from development. When the Wild and Scenic Rivers Act was passed in 1968, conservationists hoped its protective system would include a hundred rivers by 1978 and 200 by 1990. But by 1978, only sixteen rivers had been added to the original eight, and by 1980, only a few more—most of them in Alaska—had won federal protection from Congress. The battle to save Tuolumne Canyon thus seemed to conservationists a test of the nation's commitment to the preservation of wild and sce-

nic rivers. "If we can't win this one," John Amodio of the Tuolumne River Preservation Trust told *California* magazine, "you have to wonder, where can we win?"

THE CASE AGAINST CLAVEY-WARDS FERRY

Opponents of the CWF project believed it would decimate the Tuolumne and Clavey fisheries, eliminate all whitewater boating potential, adversely affect the canyon's wildlife population, and destroy forever the isolated, wilderness character that drew hikers and campers to the area. The Wards Ferry Reservoir would inundate two-thirds of the 18-mile whitewater run between Lumsden and Wards Ferry and virtually dry up the remaining section (minimum project flow releases there were scheduled at 35–75 cubic feet per second [cfs], just a fraction of the 1,000 cfs that professional river guides said were necessary for whitewater rafting). They argued that the Wards Ferry Reservior would inundate 12 miles of prime trout spawning beds and stream habitat, while the Wards Ferry Dam would block spawning runs necessary to perpetuate the trout population downstream in the New Don Pedro Reservoir. The Clavey Reservoir would inundate more than a mile of stream habitat on the Clavey River and block the passage of fish. Average flows in the lower reach of the Clavey and in the Tuolumne below Jawbone Diversion would not meet U.S. Fish and Wildlife Service recommendations for maintaining the fish population. In addition, the fragile nontrout fish population in the lower Clavey would be threatened by flow changes and the encroachment of other species from the Wards Ferry Reservoir. The river fisheries also would be harmed by changes in seasonal flows, changes in water temperature and dissolved oxygen content from water releases from different levels of the reservoirs, and construction-related changes in turbidity and sediment transport. Construction activities, increased human presence in the area, and the erection of electrical transmission lines would destroy the canyon's scenic beauty and threaten several rare species of birds, particularly the endangered southern bald eagle. And a 1982 California Department of Water Resources report warned that the project would block several traditional migration routes used by Yosemite deer.

Opponents also argued that the new recreational opportunities created by Wards Ferry Reservoir would be extremely limited. The project consultants had acknowledged the reservoir would be a long, narrow, and deep lake which would be sunless most of the time. Furthermore, surface water levels would fluctuate by almost 100 feet, and access to the lake would be difficult given the canyon's steep, narrow sides. The fishing opportunities of the reservoir were equally uncertain, opponents argued, citing a former state Department of Fish and Game biologist's estimate that the reservoir would contain less than 10 pounds of fish per acre, compared to the free-flowing Tuolumne's 1,000 pounds of fish per acre. Even the project consultants had acknowledged area fishermen's preference for river fishing, and the federal wild and scenic rivers study had pointed out that "reservoir fisheries are in abundance in the Sierra foothills, whereas river trout fisheries of the quality of the Tuolumne are a rarity in the state."

The opponents complained that neither Beck nor the irrigation districts had adequately considered alternative sources of energy. They pointed out that the irrigation districts would be able to buy surplus off-peak energy from coal-fired power plants in the Southwest and Northwest, and from hydroelectric plants in the Pacific Northwest. They also argued that the districts had not adequately considered ways that conservation and load management could be used to meet the system's capacity needs.

ORGANIZING THE FIGHT

The Tuolumne River Preservation Trust was formed in 1981 to coordinate efforts of conservationists, rafting and fishing enthusiasts, and California residents who opposed further development on the Tuolumne. Led by two Bay-Area Sierra Club members, the Trust helped to make the Tuolumne battle a cause célèbre in California, garnering widespread media coverage, celebrity attention and political support. By the summer of 1983, the campaign to save the Tuolumne had also picked up important support in San Francisco and the state capitol. Both the state Department of Fish and Game and Department of Water Resources opposed further development on the Tuolumne, as did San Francisco Mayor Dianne Feinstein, and the city's Board of Supervisors. (The city's Public Utilities Commission was still a nominal participant in the feasibility study, however.) At the same time, the trust was lobbying hard to persuade California's junior senator, Republican Pete Wilson, to include the Tuolumne River Canyon in his wilderness bill, S. 1515. The trust also hoped to win Wilson's endorsement for S. 142, a bill proposed by California's senior senator, Democrat Alan Cranston, to declare the Tuolumne a wild and scenic river.

In June of 1983, the trust asked economists at the Environmental Defense Fund (EDF) to prepare an economic evaluation of the Clavey-Wards Ferry project, including its environmental costs. The group intended to use the study in its lobbying efforts. But if its run at congressional protection for the Tuolumne failed, a comprehensive quantitative accounting of the project's private and environmental costs could help them fight the project before the Federal Energy Regulatory Commission and the California State Water Resources Control Board. The project proponents would have to obtain a construction license from FERC and a water rights permit from the state board; both agencies operated under legal mandates which allowed them to approve a project only if its benefits to the public exceeded its costs.

EDF had its own, wider interest in the trust's proposal for an economic evaluation of Clavey-Wards Ferry. With 7,000 members in California and nearly 50,000 nationwide, the group focused its research, lobbying and organizing efforts on promoting long-run improvements in natural resource management. EDF had won a reputation for making economic arguments for environmental causes in the early 1970s, when the group had worked to convince utilities that marginal cost pricing would encourage energy conservation and save money. Early in 1983, EDF was searching for a way to deal with an unintended consequence of an earlier environmentalist triumph—the 1978 amendments to the Public Utilities Regulatory Policies Act (PURPA), which required utility companies to buy excess power produced by independent facilities. The new rules had been supported by environmentalists as an incentive for the development of cogeneration energy; in practice they also spawned a new boom in small hydroelectric development. Since 1978, hydro project applications to FERC had increased by 2000 percent, and in the early 1980s, FERC was evaluating hundreds of applications to dam up rivers throughout the Sierras.

EDF felt that FERC's approval of hydro projects in the past had consistently undervalued their environmental costs, because of the agency's practice of weighing a qualitative judgment of environmental losses against the more easily quantified net economic benefits to the project developers. The trust's offer of funding for an economic assessment of the Clavey-Wards Ferry project's environmental costs gave EDF the chance to present FERC—and other environmental advocacy groups—with a method for quantifying the environmental affects of hydroelectric development. As Robert Stavins, the principal author of EDF's Tuolumne study recalled: "Rather than looking at it from a narrow, financial perspective, [we believed] we could look at it from a broader, social perspective by trying to in-ternalize some of the environmental externalities."

While the techniques EDF would use were not new to economists, environmental advocacy groups had traditionally resisted the use of cost-benefit analysis in making decisions about environmental policy—the chairman of the Natural Resources Defense Council, for instance, has called the use of cost-benefit analysis in setting toxic standards "immoral," but most conservation advocates also recognized the power of economic arguments in the political world. "Environmentalists in general will support cost-benefit analysis when it confirms their preconceived position," explained EDF senior economist Zach Willey. "But when it doesn't, it's more controversial. I think, by and large, environmentalists are skeptical of cost-benefit analysis; they've seen how it's been used and will come up with all kinds of arguments about how it's not possible to quantify many environmental values. . . . [But EDF's Tuolumne study] was not inconsistent with the emotional view of many environmentalists that the environment is priceless. In fact, it was consistent in that it added some of the value of the environment to a particular decision."

COUNTING THE COSTS AND BENEFITS

Although Stavins drew much of his raw data from the Beck studies of the Clavey-Wards Ferry project, his analysis differed from theirs in two crucial ways. For one, his cost-benefit model was designed to add the project's environmental, or "external," costs and benefits onto the "internal," or financial, cost-benefit analysis that Beck had prepared. Stavins' estimate of environmental costs and benefits was admittedly incomplete. Although he recognized the project's environmental impacts could range from destruction of historic sites to threatening endangered bird species, he had to rest his calculations on the river's principal (and most easily quantified) existing recreational uses—trout fishing and whitewater rafting.

As the CWF's "external" benefits, Stavins counted the value of the CWF's projected water supply and the flatwater fishing and boating opportunities that would be available at the planned Wards Ferry Reservoir.

Secondly, Stavins took issue with Beck's decision to estimate the project's benefits and costs for only its first year of operation, since such an approach did not account for the uneven streams of benefits and costs which would be spread out over fifty to one-hundred years in such a project. Stavins elected instead to estimate the project's benefit/cost streams over the entire likely life of the project. His analysis produced estimates of the project's levelized annual costs and benefits by finding their present value of fifty years, inflated at 6 percent, discounted at 10.72 percent, and then levelized at 10.72 percent over fifty years. He chose the fifty-year planning period in keeping with FERC guidelines, and assumed the project would come on line in 1994, adding three years to Beck's assumed four-year construction period. (Stavins believed that Beck's assumption was overly optimistic, given the U.S. Army Corps of Engineers estimate that hydroelectric projects even smaller than the Wards Ferry Dam required a six-year construction period.) The 10.72 discount rate was Stavin's estimation of the likely rate at which the districts would be able to float forty-year bonds, based on the Modesto Irrigation District's actual sales in 1983 of tax-exempt energy project revenue bonds. This choice was in keeping with FERC recommendations that for nonfederal projects the overall cost of money to the project developers should be used as the discount rate.

Stavins estimated the project's total levelized annual project benefits at slightly less than $188 million (Exhibit 4). The biggest share of that was the project's $184 million in electricity benefits, which he measured by using the standard industry practice of calculating the avoided cost of the least expensive alternative means of meeting an identical load. Beck, too, had used this method, but had based its analysis of benefits on a mix of coal and combustion turbine capacity and its associated energy. Stavins' least cost mix of alternative energy sources included purchase of coal energy off-peak from southwest and northwest utilities, purchase of off-peak hydro energy from the northwest, with peak energy and capacity provided by the district's own combustion turbines and conservation and load management measures. He also counted the project's expected impact on fishing into the benefit side of the analysis by estimating the project's energy generation at some 295 GWh less than Beck's projections, assuming the project operators preserved enough of the Tuolumne's original flows to protect the river's fish stock.[3]

Other benefits included water yield, which Stavins valued at $1.6 million, based on Beck's estimates that the water would be worth about $105/acre-foot in 1990. And he valued the project's "external" benefits—the 1,600 user-days of flatwater boating and 4,000 user-days of fishing that the Department of Interior had predicted for the Ward's Ferry Reservoir—at $327,000 a year. To place a dollar value on this benefit, Stavins chose the "unit-day" method, which relies on expert opinion to approximate the average willingness-to-pay of users for recreational resources.[4]

Valuing the project's costs was more complicated. Using Beck's 1980 estimate of the project's construction costs, Stavins produced an annual levelized "internal" cost estimate of $134 million. To estimate the project's "external costs," which he defined as the value of Tuolumne River whitewater rafting opportunities to both users and nonusers, Stavins constructed a regional travel cost model. He began by estimating the willingness-to-pay, or consumer surplus, of users, using data on the river's current use to determine per capita visitation rates and costs from various geographic regions (Exhibits 5 and 6).

EXHIBIT 4. SOCIAL BENEFITS, CLAVEY-WARDS FERRY PROJECT

Benefit	Cost (dollars)
1. Levelized Annual Energy Benefit[a] (Table 4: [(2) + (3) + (5) − (4)])[b]	$146,720,000
2. Levelized Annual Capacity Benefit[c] (Table 4: [(1) + (6)])[b]	37,500,000
3. Annual Benefit of Increased Firm, Yield of Water for MID/TID (11,900 AF × $105/AF in 1990, 4 years at 6% to 1994)	1,577,000
4. Levelized Annual Benefit of Increased Firm Yield [(3) × 2.148]	3,388,000
5. Total Internal Levelized Annual Benefits [(1) + (2) + (4)]	187,608,000
6. Annual Flatwater Boating Benefit on Wards Ferry Reservoir (1600 user-days × $20/day, 1994)	32,000
7. Annual Reservoir Fishing Benefit (4,000 user-days × $30/day, 1994)	120,000
8. Total External Levelized Annual Benefits [(6) + (7) × 2.148]	327,000
9. Total Levelized Annual Project Benefits [(5) + (8)]	187,935,000

a. Annual Energy Benefit refers to the avoided cost of running the least expensive alternative to the project.
b. Table 4 not included here.
c. Annual Capacity Benefit refers to the avoided cost of constructing the capacity to provide the least expensive alternative.

Then he econometrically estimated a so-called "participation function," which would be used to derive the net per capita economic value of the river's recreational opportunities for each area. The per capita figures were then converted to regional total values and added together to produce an aggregate economic value. Stavins originally estimated the participation function using three alternative forms: linear, which produced a consumer surplus estimate of $16.6 million; double logarithmic, which estimated the consumer surplus at $2.1 million; and semilogarithmic, which produced an estimate of $3.1 million. In the final analysis, Stavins chose the semilog results, which produced a levelized annual consumer surplus estimate of $3 million. To that he added an estimate of user fees and producer surplus (Exhibit 7).

Stavins then turned to estimating rafting's "option value"—the amount interested nonusers would be willing to pay to insure access to rafting on the river at some future time. Stavins surveyed the economic literature, and found nine studies that had quantified intrinsic recreational values as a positive fraction of user values (Exhibit 8). The nine studies used survey questions to elicit people's willingness to pay to preserve a recreational opportunity; they exhibited ratios of nonuse value to use value ranging from 0.47 to 1.39, with a weighted average of 0.60. Thus, on average, nonuser recreational value per household interested in the project was found to be approximately 60 percent of user recreational value per household. Stavins believed that he could multiply this number by his consumer surplus estimates to estimate the per capita option value for various geographic regions. But then he had to identify the relevant population of

EXHIBIT 5. DATA USED IN TRAVEL COST MODEL (TCM) OF TUOLUMNE RIVER
WHITEWATER RECREATION

Region	Average Travel Costs[a] from Region to Site (dollars)	Per Capita Use from Region $(x10^{-6})$
Humboldt	643.31	70.080
Butte	566.76	11.316
Santa Rosa	441.13	491.137
Yolo	456.09	2059.277
Tahoe-Reno	538.84	752.949
Sacramento	430.22	868.768
El Dorado	401.27	991.147
West Bay	485.56	1510.583
East Bay	470.34	1360.516
South Bay	468.03	716.121
Stockton	384.20	1200.421
Tuolumne	347.48	5315.727
Fresno	474.19	176.380
Los Angeles	629.28	271.885
San Diego	730.78	191.908
Pacific Northwest	1207.16	15.361
Nevada (less Washoe County)	660.27	65.049
West	894.24	33.340
Mountain	1443.66	38.310
Plains	1728.90	1.764
Great Lakes	1991.95	4.690
Atlantic	2065.78	4.492
New England	2102.11	2.752
Southeast	1920.41	0.992

a. Average travel cost for a representative user from a given region, i, consists of three principal
components: actual transportation cost, opportunity cost of time spent traveling to and from the site, and
opportunity cost of time spent on the site: $TC_i = TPC_i + OCT_i + OCS_i$

interested nonusers. Stavins chose to use Sierra Club membership as a proxy for the population of interested nonusers. To be somewhat conservative, he estimated the total California option value as 60 percent of the total California per capita consumer surplus, multiplied by the full California Sierra Club membership; for other regions of the United States, he took 45 percent of the total consumer surplus, multiplied by half the non–California Sierra Club membership (Exhibit 9). All told, he produced an option value estimate of $33.5 million.

In the final analysis, Stavins estimated the annual social costs of the Clavey-Wards

Ferry development at $214 million, outweighing its benefits by some $26 million. The calculations assigned the Clavey-Wards Ferry proposal a cost-benefit ratio of 0.877, indicating that the project would return about $.88 of benefits to society for each $1.00 invested in the project.

Environmentalists won their Tuolumne River protection crusade in September 1984, when Congress passed the California Wilderness Act and granted wild and scenic status to the entire 83 miles of the river above the New Don Pedro Reservoir. Pete Wilson, California's Republican senator,

EXHIBIT 6. COMMERCIAL WHITEWATER RECREATION TUOLUMNE RIVER, 1982

Outfitter	Passenger Use Days
A. A. Wet and Wild	440
Amreican River Touring Association	1,162
Echo: The Wilderness Company	1,077
OARS	576
Outdoor Adventures	783
Outdoors Unlimited	804
Sierra Mac River Trips	377
Wilderness Waterways	585
All Outdoors	83
Sobek Expeditions	327
Zephyr River Expeditions	122
Total	6,336

Source: Environmental Defense Funds: *Tuolumne River: Preservation or Development?*, from Steve Cutwright, of the American River Touring Association.

EXHIBIT 7. SOCIAL COSTS, CLAVEY-WARDS FERRY PROJECT

Item	Cost (dollars)
1. Levelized Annual Internal Costs	$134,224,000
2. 1994 Consumers' Surplus of Users	3,099,000
3. 1994 User Fees (1983 Fee, $3 at 6%/year for 11 years)	128,000
4. 1994 Producers' Surplus (.125 profit × $350 at 6% for 11 years × 6,400)	532,000
5. 1994 Option Value (Consumer surplus/User × option-value × proxy population) CA: $184.14 × 0.60 × 130,836 = $14,455,000 Other: $392.91 × 0.45 × 215,459/2 = $19,048,000	33,503,000
6. 1994 Total Recreational Value [(2) + (3) + (4) + (5)]	37,261,000
7. Levelized Annual Cost of Recreational Value (Present value of 50 years, inflated at 6%, discounted at 10.72%, then levelized at 10.71% over 50 years)	80,039,000
8. Total of Private and Recreational Annual Cost (item 1 + item 7)	214,263,000

had declared his support for protecting the river a half a year earlier after intense lobbying from constituents and environmental groups. (Wilson's aides estimated that he received as many as 2,000 letters a week urging him to protect the Tuolumne.) But the victory wasn't clinched until June 1984, when Wilson and California's Democratic senator, Alan Cranston, agreed on a compromise between their two wilderness bills. In its final form, the act added fourteen new wilderness areas to the nine already designated in the Sierras–1.8 million acres on national forest lands, and another 1.4 mil-

EXHIBIT 8. USE AND INTRINSIC VALUES OF ENVIRONMENTAL RESOURCES FROM PREVIOUS EMPIRICAL STUDIES, 1974–1983

Study	Site	Estimates ($1994/household/yr)[a]		Ratio of Nonuse to Use
		Use	Nonuse	
Meyer 1974	Fraser River, British Columbia	1,943	1,051	0.54
Horvath 1974	Southeastern United States	5,914	3,296	0.56
Dornbusch and Falcke 1974	Communities along seven U.S. bodies of water	—	—	1.39
Meyer 1978	Fraser River, British Columbia	601	754	1.25
Walsh, Greenley Young, McKean and Prato 1978	South Platte River, Colorado	264	138	0.52
Mitchell and Carson 1981	U.S. National	540	253	0.47
Cronin 1982	Potomac River	88	63	0.72
Desvouges, Smith and McGivney 1983	Mononganela River	109	71	0.65
Cronin (forthcoming)	Potomac River	92	73	0.79
	Average Values	1,194	712	0.60[b]

Source: Environmental Defense Fund, *Tuolumne River: Preservation or Development?* From Ann Fisher and Robert Raucher, "Intrinsic Benefits of Improved Water Quality: Conceptual and Empirical Perspectives." *Advances in Applied Microeconomics*, ed. V. Kerry Smith and Ann Dryden White (Greenwich, Conn., 1984), Vol. 3, pp. 37–66.
a. Inflated at CPI to 1982 and at 6%/year to 1994.
b. Does not include results from Dornbusch and Falcke 1974.

lion in Yosemite, Kings Canyon, and Sequoia National Parks.

The Environmental Defense Fund's (EDF) economic assessment of the Clavey-Wards Ferry dam proposal, released in summary form in October 1983, played an important role in the effort to win Wilson over. EDF economist Stavins believes that while politics, not economics, ultimately won Wilson over, the EDF study may have helped reduce his political risks in supporting wild and scenic protection for the Tuolumne. "Wilson wasn't going to read it, or his staff member wasn't going to read it and say, 'oh my God, we're wrong, this project is terrible for the socio-economy, let's change

our vote,'" Stavins said. "What was likely to happen was that Pete Wilson, being the conservative southern California senator, would decide that this was a reasonable trade-off—that he ought to go for the wild and scenic (status) because he does have an environmentalist constituency in California. But he might need some sort of evidence to give to his conservative constituency of why he had done that. He couldn't say 'I did it because I love wild rivers and I don't like electricity,' but he could do it by holding up the study, and saying 'look, I changed my vote for solid economic reasons.'"

After the Tuolumne study was released, Stavins said, local conservation groups in

EXHIBIT 9. ESTIMATING THE OPTION VALUE ASSOCIATED WITH WHITEWATER BOATING ON THE TUOLUMNE RIVER

California	
Consumer surplus per user from TCM model, based upon actual Tuolumne River rafting data	$184.14
Nonuser/user value ratio, based upon previous empirical research summarized by Fisher and Raucher (1983)	× 0.60
Estimated per capita California option value	$110.48
California membership of Sierra Club	× 130,836
Estimated 1994 total California option value	$14,455,000
Other regions of the United States	
Consumer surplus per user from TCM model, based upon actual Tuolumne River rafting data	$392.91
Nonuser/user value ratio, based upon previous empirical research summarized by Fisher and Raucher (1983) and reduced to account for effect of remoteness from site	× 0.45
Estimated per capita non-California option value	$176.81
Non-California membership of Sierra Club, reduced by one-half to account for effect of remoteness from site	× 107,730
Estimated 1994 total non-California option value	$19,048,000
Estimated total U.S. Option Value (1994)	$33,503,000

Maine and New York used its analytic techniques to fight proposed hydroelectric developments in their states. In general, though, the major environmental organizations remained suspicious of the cost-benefit approach, and EDF recognized that the Tuolumne study's success couldn't hope to change that. "I didn't have globe-shaking hopes for the Tuolumne study," said Zach Willey, EDF's chief economist. "What is hoped was that it would influence a couple of senators and it did that."

The dam's proponents were predictably critical of the EDF study's methods and conclusions. R.W. Beck and Associates, the irrigation districts' engineering consultants, challenged Stavins' use of the controversial concept of "option value"—especially since option value accounted for some 90 percent of his estimates of the river's total recreation value.

Beck also maintained that social values could not really be quantified. "In order for a social benefit-cost analysis not to cloud such political decisions, it would have to provide definitive quantification of all externalities, not just a selected few," Beck associate Frank K. Dubar wrote to project manager Lawrence Klein. "The weighing of social values is best served by the political process during the Federal Energy Regulatory Commission licensing and the National Environmental Policy Act procedures for the Environmental Impact Statement using standard federal guidelines for economic determination."

Congress's decision to protect the Tuolumne forced the irrigation districts to look elsewhere for power and water. By 1986 the Turlock Irrigation District was moving ahead with plans to purchase surplus power from Pacific Northwest hydro plants and build more fossil-fuel generators. The district and Tuolumne County also were study-

ing the potential for building a small hydroelectric development on the Clavey River.

NOTES

1. Irrigation districts are governed by five-member
boards elected to staggered four-year terms by the area
residents.

2. An acre-foot equals 325,851 gallons—the amount
of water required to flood one acre of land to a depth
of one foot.

3. Stavins structured a monthly schedule of flows

available for energy generation based on Beck's estimate of Tuolumne river flows minus flow releases recommended by the U.S. Fish and Wildlife Service as
necessary to maintain river fisheries.

4. Stavins said he chose this method based on Water
Resources Council guidelines, which suggest using the
unit-day value method if the project meets the following three conditions: the site does not involve special-
ized highly skilled recreational activities for which opportunities are limited; the number of visits per year
likely to be affected by the proposed project does not
exceed 750,000; and the expected recreation costs do
not exceed 25 percent of total project costs.

Review of EDF Analysis

January 27, 1984

Mr. Lawrence T. Klein
Project Director
Clavey-Wards Ferry Project
P.O. Box 5296
Modesto, California 95352–5296

Dear Larry:

As requested we have reviewed the publication: "The Tuolumne River: Preservation or Development? An Economic Assessment, Summary Report," by Environmental Defense Fund (EDF), October 1983.
Principal author: Robert Stavins. The essence of the Report findings is that the R.
W. Beck and Associates' assessment of the
costs and benefits associated with the
Clavey-Wards Ferry Project, failed to account for identifiable and quantifiable external costs and benefits. Accordingly, had
such external effects been accounted for the
benefit-cost ratio of the project would have
been found to be less than one, and hence
a finding would have been made that the
project is not economically justified. This
conclusion is based on the authors' finding
that the benefits that would be lost (or alternatively costs incurred) in the form of foregone whitewater rafting and fishing, are

sufficiently greater than any benefits gained
as a result of flatwater recreational activities
created. The Report introduces the concept
of "option values" which applies a monetary value to the opportunity for anyone to
go whitewater boating in the future, if they
should decide to utilize that opportunity.
Our comments on the Report follow: . . .
The Report assumes elimination of whitewater boating by project construction. In the
Clavey-Wards Ferry Alternative, the 6-mile
reach upstream of Wards Ferry Reservoir
would still be available for whitewater boating during the spring runoff period in average and wet years. No benefit credit from
whitewater recreation was attached to this
item by the authors. With the Ponderosa Alternative, however, the value of lost
whitewater recreation would be zero; in fact,
an annual benefit over the existing conditions would be attained since seven days of
rafting would be possible during the summer
months, versus five to six days presently.

The Report states that near-total degradation of the trout fishery would occur. This
is not true, since minimum flow releases
for fishery purposes at Jawbone Dam and
Clavey Dam would be set in consultation
with federal and state fisheries agencies.
Further, due to reduced flows between Jawbone Dam and Lumsden campground, it is

considered that fishing conditions will improve, particularly for fly fishing. ·

The Report emphasizes that public policy decisions regarding the use of the nation's scarce natural resources are ultimately political decisions due to the conflicting social concerns. Yet the methodology proposed tries to quantify social values, particularly intrinsic values, which in reality cannot be definitively quantified. In order for a social benefit-cost analysis not to cloud such political decisions it would have to provide definitive quantification of all externalities, not just a selected few. The weighing of social values is best served by the political process during the FERC licensing and the NEPA procedures for the EIS using standard Federal guidelines for economic determination.

The authors have specified the recreation demand function by attempting to establish a casual relationship between number of visits to the recreational site from each of a number of discrete geographical origins and the travel and on-site costs associated with each such visit (this is what the author refers to as the "travel cost model"). The model appears oversimplified in that the demand for visitation to the site is presumed to be almost exclusively determined by price (travel cost), and completely ignores other important ingredients such as income, age, and other factors. The parameter estimates of such a simplified model are almost certain to be biased, which would result in overestimating the magnitude of the consumer surplus (benefits). . . .

Although intrinsic (option) values are not recognized by WRC in its recommended principles and guidelines, the option value shown in the EDF analysis for Clavey-Wards Ferry is some 90 percent of the total recreation value evaluated. If option values were to be quantified and included in an economic analysis, then all possible external social values should be included in order to present an unbiased analysis. For example, the whitewater boating option value could well be balanced by the option value

of having a renewable energy resource to counter the threat of Arab oil embargoes. Clearly, this is outside the scope of an economic analysis. Such varied option values are best evaluated by the NEPA-EIS process. Option values are at best controversial and mask any realistic analysis of recreation user values that might be presented.

In Table 1 of the Report, the total 1994 recreational value is $37,261,000 of which $33,503,000 is the option value (90%). Yet evaluation of the most significant portion of the recreation value is afforded essentially only a footnote stating that the option value is based upon a proportional relationship and that a value of 0.6 for the ratio of nonuse value/household to use-value/household was used. The evaluation of the proxy population, which significantly determines the total option value, is given no discussion in the Report.

On the other hand, the external benefits of flatwater recreational opportunities are based upon the normal unit-day value method in the analysis. This of course provides a substantial bias against the Clavey-Wards Ferry Project, since the option value of flatwater recreation lost if the project is not built has not been considered. For example, the estimated $37 million lost annually by whitewater rafting dwarfs the project recreation benefits (Clavey-Wards Ferry Alternative) of $327,000. Clearly, the cost of travel and value of time of the flatwater recreationists is not included on the same basis as that of the whitewater boaters.

Travel costs are estimated to be all out-of-pocket costs plus the opportunity costs of the travel time and the time spent at the recreational site. The value of such time is likely to be over-stated given that opportunity cost is measured as prevailing wage rates—certainly too high, especially for weekend visitors. Further, the authors seem to treat all whitewater rafters as commercial users, which results in an estimate of lost whitewater benefits of approximately $37 million annually or more than $6,000 per rafter use, a completely unrealistic amount, commercial or not.

On the other hand, income and age are not considered in the evaluation of users' consumer surplus. This is important since rafting is expensive. Differences between weekday and weekend use are also not considered. This could also be significant since rafting flows are somewhat reduced on Saturdays and essentially nonexistent on Sundays under no-project conditions during summer months. The Report also assumes all users take two day trips and neglect the effect of one day trips.

For the whitewater user's opportunity cost of time, a "k" value of 0.6 times the average hourly wage rate of the region considered was used and stated to be conservative. The WRC, however, recommends a "k" value of .25–.33 times the wage rate since most people have free weekends and paid vacations and are not actually choosing between work and play. The analysis also does not consider the numbers of unemployed persons (students and nonworking family members) using the river. A weighted average reflecting the demographic makeup of visitors should be used. . . .

R. W. Beck and Associates conducted several analyses using the EDF method, but based on reasonable assumption for various parameters. Calculations were made to determine the sensitivity of the benefit-cost ratio to variation in the proxy populations used, or to its elimination altogether. With the proxy population reduced by 50 percent (i.e., 50 percent fewer persons would be willing to pay to ensure that whitewater boating would be available in the future *if they should decide* to utilize the opportunity), the total 1994 recreational value is reduced to $20,511,000 rather than $37,261,000, and the benefit-cost ratio becomes 1.054 rather than 0.877, even using the less than satisfactory semi-log method. If the proxy population option value is eliminated, the total 1994 recreational value become $3,759,000 and the benefit-cost ratio 1.32. . . .

In summary the method proposed by the EDF analysis for the environmental economies of hydro power development is not used by the federal regulatory agencies. However, applying reasonable parameters to that method, with appropriate recognition of the environmental benefits of project development, results in substantiation of the benefit-cost ratio of about 1.3 calculated independently by Beck.

Very truly yours,
R. W. Beck and Associates

Comment

The EDF's cost-benefit analysis serves the cause of environmental protection and therefore casts doubt upon the claim that the method of policy analysis is biased against values that are not easily quantifiable. In serving the cause of environmental protection, however, the EDF analysis also diffuses criticisms that are often levied by environmentalists against techniques that quantify environmental values. Interestingly, it is the opponents of environmental protection who call such quantification into question.

Consider the various ways in which the EDF analysis quantifies environmental values and determine the extent to which it successfully establishes a "broader, social perspective by trying to internalize some of the environmental externalities."

Setting aside the possible political advantages of invoking economic arguments to protect the environment, what can one say for and against putting monetary values on the recreational uses of the environment? Evaluate the following criticisms of EDF's analysis: (1) "the methodology proposed tries to quantify social values, particularly intrinsic values, which in reality cannot be definitively quantified"; (2) because it quantifies only some externalities, the analysis obscures the process of political decision making; (3) the analysis overstates the benefits of environmental protection by ignoring other "option values," such as "having a renewable energy resource to counter the threat of Arab oil embargoes" and "the option value of flatwater recreation lost if the project is not built"; and (4) the analysis takes preferences for recreation and energy resources as given even though these preferences typically can change over time.

Suppose that EDF's policy analysis is revised on the basis of new information and the updated analysis yields the opposite conclusion, that the net benefits of proceeding with the Clavey-Wards Ferry project now exceed the costs. Could proponents of environmental protection offer any morally defensible reasons to reject the analysis and to maintain their opposition to the Clavey-Wards Ferry project? Are any considerations omitted from a cost-benefit analysis that are nonetheless relevant to the making of public policy? Are any considerations included in cost-benefit analysis that should be excluded from consideration?

Policy analysis often seems inaccessible to citizens because of its technical vocabulary and quantitative techniques. Yet citizens should be able to evaluate such analyses in general terms by considering whether they address the right questions. Examine the EDF analysis and the Beck review in this spirit by asking: Are the basic assumptions plausible? Are any moral issues misconstrued as merely technical questions? What, if any, morally and politically relevant factors are ignored? If public officials believe that the economic analysis should not completely determine the outcome, can they say more than "I love wild rivers, and I don't like electricity"?

The conventional decision-making rule in policy analysis says "choose the policy that maximizes the total expected utility," where the total expected utility is the sum of the benefits minus the costs, discounting for the uncertainty of each. Some critics of conventional policy analysis suggest that because future generations cannot participate in present decision making and because people generally fear unchosen risk more than they desire unexpected benefits, we should adopt cautious decision-making rules, which minimize the risks to future generations. Assess the moral implications of the following rules: (1) Keep the options open (reject irreversible policies). (2) Protect the vulnerable (give special weight to future generations). (3) Maximize minimum payoff (make sure the worst outcome is as good as possible). (4) Avoid harm (give more weight to causing harms than to failing to produce benefits of the same size). Under what circumstances would these rules lead us to recommend environmental protection over energy development, or vice versa? How would you justify (or criticize) each of the rules?

The Risks of Asarco
Esther Scott

On July 12, 1983, William Ruckelshaus, administrator of the Environmental Protection Agency (EPA), announced in Washington proposed standards that would regulate arsenic emissions from copper smelting and glass manufacturing plants in the United States. Arsenic had increasingly been regarded as a dangerous air pollutant and as such fell within the purview of EPA. Issuing standards for pollutants was nothing new at the agency, but this announcement attracted more than usual interest: Ruckelshaus was proposing to involve the public in helping him decide just how stringent those regulations should be.

The arsenic standards were expected to have their greatest impact on Tacoma, Washington, because of its proximity to a copper smelter owned by the American Smelting and Refining Company (Asarco)—the only smelter in the nation that used ore with high arsenic content and a major source of arsenic emissions. The proposed standards applied the best available technology to reduce emissions; but even so, there would remain a residual risk factor that might, according to EPA calculations, result in roughly one additional cancer death per year among Tacoma area residents. However, imposing further requirements to eliminate that risk could drive up the plant's costs and make it uneconomical to run. The smelter employed more than five hundred people, in a state that was experiencing over 11 percent unemployment. "My view," Ruckelshaus later told a *Los Angeles Times* reporter, "is that these are the kinds of tough, balancing questions that we're involved in here in

this country in trying to regulate all kinds of hazardous substances. I don't like these questions either, but the societal issue is what risks are we willing to take and for what benefits?" To get answers to that question, Ruckelshaus announced EPA's intention of actively soliciting the views and wishes of the people most affected by the proposed regulations: the residents who lived and worked near the Asarco smelter. "For me to sit here in Washington," Ruckelshaus told the assembled press, "and tell the people of Tacoma what is an acceptable risk would be at best arrogant and at worst inexcusable."

RUCKELSHAUS AT EPA

At the time the proposed arsenic regulations were announced, Ruckelshaus had only recently returned to the agency he had first headed in 1970, the year EPA was established. During the brief tenure of his predecessor, Anne Burford (formerly Gorsuch), EPA had become mired in scandal and controversy, and was frequently attacked for failure to enforce environmental laws and to carry out the agency's mission. The appointment of Ruckelshaus, who was highly regarded for his integrity and admired for his work as EPA's first administrator, had done much to restore credibility to the agency, but mistrust of the Reagan administration's commitment to environmental issues lingered in the public mind.

In Ruckelshaus' view, moreover, there were other troubling uncertainties facing his second EPA administration. In the 1980s, scientists were no longer assuming the existence of a threshold of safety from carcinogens: in theory, at least, adverse effects could occur from exposure to even one molecule of a carcinogenic substance. Ruckelshaus, in a June 1983 address to the National Academy of Sciences (NAS), put it this way: "[W]e must assume that life now takes place in a minefield of risks from hundreds, perhaps thousands, of substances. No more can we tell the public: You are home free with an adequate margin of safety." In this starker world, Ruckelshaus told the assembled scientists,

> We need more research on the health effects of the substances we regulate. . . . Given the necessity of acting in the face of enormous scientific uncertainties, it is more important than ever that our scientific analysis be rigorous and the quality of our data be high. We must take great pains not to mislead people regarding the risks to their health. We can help avoid confusion both by the quality of our science and the clarity of our language in exploring the hazards.

THE ASARCO SMELTER

The Asarco copper smelting plant on the edge of Tacoma was a model of the kind of wrenching choices the EPA administrator often faced in proposing regulations. Built in 1890, the Asarco smelter, whose 571-foot smokestack dominated the landscape around it, processed high arsenic content copper ore and produced commercial arsenic as a by-product from its smelter. (Arsenic is present as an impurity in certain ores, such as copper and lead, and can be produced either as a waste or as a by-product in the smelting of these ores. The arsenic was used in the manufacture of glass, herbicides, insecticides, and other products.) The Asarco plant—the only one in the nation that used high arsenic content ore—was also the only domestic producer of industrial arsenic, providing approximately one-third of the U.S. supply of arsenic.

In recent times, the smelter had been in shaky financial condition. World prices for copper had plummeted from $1.45/lb. in 1980 to $.60/lb. in 1982, and U.S. copper processors were facing intense competition from Japan. At the Asarco

plant, the cost of producing copper was $.82/lb. The plant had for awhile been able to make a profit largely due to sales of residual metals—chiefly gold—from the copper smelting process; but as the price of gold dropped, so too did the plant's earnings and, according to Asarco officials, it had been losing money for several years.

For generations, the Asarco smelter had provided a livelihood to the families of Ruston, a small company town (population 636) that had sprung up around the big smokestack, and the surrounding area. In 1983, it employed roughly 575 workers on an annual payroll of about $23 million. (According to company estimates, it could cost the state of Washington as much as $5.5 million in unemployment benefits if the plant shut down.) The smelter also contributed to the economy of the area by spending approximately $12 million locally on supplies, indirectly supporting $13 million of auxiliary business, and paying $3 million in state and local taxes. Seventy-year-old Owen Gallagher, a former mayor of Ruston and an employee of Asarco for forty-three years, spoke for many town residents when he told reporters from the *Chicago Tribune*:

> I've worked in the plant all my life. So have my brothers, and so have my neighbors. We're not sick. This town was built around that plant. People came here looking for fire and smoke in the 1900s to find work. Now the government's complaining about that same smoke and trying to take our children's livelihood away.

But the fact was that Asarco had long been regarded as one of the major polluters in the Northwest, and held what one report called "the dubious distinction of being the worst arsenic polluter in the United States."[1] Commencement Bay, Tacoma's industrial harbor, had been designated a Superfund hazardous waste clean-up site partially because of accumulated arsenic both in the soil around the plant and in the bottom sand of the bay. Asarco was also one of the two major emitters of sulfur dioxide (SO_2, a by-product of burning carbon fuel) in the state of Washington.[2]

Area residents affected by this pollution made no bones about their feelings. Bill Tobin, a lawyer and resident of Vashon Island—a semi-rural, middle-income community two miles offshore from Ruston—pointed out that, because of the high smokestack and prevailing wind directions, "we are the dumping grounds for these pollutants without any benefits such as jobs or Asarco tax payments." Island residents were particularly concerned over high levels of arsenic found in urine samples of their children and in soil from local gardens. "I'm not for the loss of jobs," one homeowner told the *Tacoma News Tribune*; but he added, "Numerous people who staked their life savings on a place and a home are finding they can't enjoy the land because of the emissions of the Asarco plant." Vashon Island was by no means the only reluctant host to emissions from the smelter. Neighboring Tacoma received tons of air pollution from the plant, and little by way of taxes from the smelter to compensate. One member of the Tacoma city council described the effects of the smelter as "somebody standing on the other side of the city line with a thirty-ought-six and firing it into Tacoma."

Over the years, efforts to control pollution from the Asarco smelter came primarily from the regional level.[3] Since 1970, the Puget Sound Air Pollution Control Agency (PSAPCA), a regional air pollution authority, had issued a variety of orders aimed at reducing both SO_2 and arsenic emissions; but Asarco had either failed to comply and paid the relatively small penalties, or delayed action through litigation and variance proceedings.

However, despite the court battles and delays, PSAPCA had made some headway in getting Asarco to comply with its orders. As Asarco officials were quick to point out, the company had spent about $40 million over a ten-year period in equipment and practices designed to reduce pollution; it had also agreed to curtail operations when meteorological conditions would cause high ambient SO_2, levels. In the late 1970s, Asarco and PSAPCA negotiated a compromise agreement covering both SO_2, and arsenic emissions. For the latter, Asarco agreed to install, by 1984, secondary converter hoods, which would reduce "fugitive" arsenic emissions that were not funneled up the smokestack (and were considered more dangerous because they were less likely to disperse before reaching the public).[4] According to later EPA estimates, the cost of the converters would run to roughly $3.5 million in capital outlay (Asarco put the figure at $4.5 million), along with an estimated $1.5 million per year in operating and maintenance expenses. These costs were expected to result in an estimated product price increase of 0.5 to 0.8 percent.

While these local efforts were ongoing, EPA had been, more or less, out of the picture. Under the provisions of the Clean Air Act, the federal agency was required to identify, list, and promulgate National Emission Standards for Hazardous Air Pollutants (NESHAPs) for substances believed to be detrimental to human health. EPA had listed inorganic arsenic as a hazardous air pollutant in June 1980, but had decided the following year not to issue a NESHAP for it. This decision chagrined PSAPCA officials, who felt that a ruling from EPA would give them another tool to use in their dealings with Asarco. But, as it turned out, EPA was soon forced to take a stronger hand in the matter. In late 1982, the state of New York, concerned about arsenic emissions from a Corning Glass manufacturing plant in New Jersey, took EPA to court. The U.S. District Court subsequently ruled that the agency must publish proposed national standards by July 11, 1983, six months later. Thus was the stage set for Ruckelshaus' experiment in risk management.

TAKING IT TO THE PUBLIC

THE RISK ASSESSMENT

On July 12, 1983—the same day that Ruckelshaus announced the proposed regulations on arsenic emissions[5]—Ernesta Barnes, administrator of EPA's northwest regional office, appeared before the press in Tacoma. "We ask the public's help to consider the very difficult issues raised by arsenic air emissions," Barnes told the assembled reporters. "Together we must determine 'What is an "acceptable" or "reasonable" risk to public health from arsenic emissions.'" To aid in that process, she announced public hearings in Tacoma on August 30 and 31, to be preceded by "public workshops and other activities to inform you of the many technical issues involved."

The hearings—wherein the public had an opportunity to present testimony—would have been held anyway, because the proposed standards for the Tacoma smelter were part of a national rulemaking process. What was different, says Ernesta Barnes, was the workshops. The "underlying theory," she explains, was that the decisionmakers had a "moral responsibility" to provide "adequate information" and opportunity for discussion in advance of the hearings, "so that when the actual public hearing was held, those that had chosen to become especially well informed would have not only their own values on which to base their testimony, but also better information about what the facts actually were."

At the press conference, Barnes provided a brief sketch of some of the technical issues the workshops would cover, outlining the risk assessment EPA had performed as part of the standard-setting process. EPA analysts had used a dispersion model to calculate concentrations of arsenic at over one hundred locations within approximately twelve miles of the smelter, and combined those figures with "unit risk numbers"[6] derived from previous epidemiological studies of workers exposed to arsenic. The results of EPA's analyses yielded an estimate of some 310 tons of arsenic emissions spewed out each year by the Asarco smelter, and the risk of up to four related cancer deaths per year within twelve miles of the smelter.

Because EPA considered inorganic arsenic a non-threshold pollutant—i.e., even the most minute trace of it could not definitely be said to be harmless—it determined that the arsenic emissions from the Asarco smelter should be, in the language of the proposed standards, "controlled at least to the level that reflects best available technology (BAT), and to a more stringent level if, in the judgment of the administrator, it is necessary to prevent unreasonable risks." The appropriate BAT, Barnes explained at the press conference, was the converter hoods Asarco had already agreed to (and had in fact begun installing) in its negotiations with PSAPCA.[7] The hoods would, she said, reduce arsenic emissions from the smelter to 189 tons per year. "The number of related cancer cases within a twelve-mile radius of the plant," she added, "would drop from four per year to one a year."

Ruckelshaus was free to impose on his own a "more stringent level" of emission control. He could, for instance, set emissions standards that would require Asarco to use a lower arsenic content ore[8] or to convert to electric smelting. However, Asarco maintained that the added cost of shipping the low arsenic ore would force the company to close the smelter. Similarly, the expense of switching to electric smelting would amount to $150 million in capital outlays, and could also precipitate a shutdown. It was to consider such options and their implications that Ruckelshaus sought public involvement. "Should we interpret the legislative intent of the Clean

Air Act to mandate a total shutdown to produce zero risk to public health?'' Barnes asked at the Tacoma press conference. ''. . . Or is there a level of risk that is acceptable to the community and consistent with the law?''

REACTION

The workshops were not scheduled to start until mid-August, but debate on the issue began as soon as Barnes' press conference was over. Ruckelshaus' proposal to involve the public in the final decisionmaking received, not surprisingly, intense coverage in the local media, but it was widely reported in the national press as well. Many of the headlines depicted Tacomans as facing a stark choice: ''Smelter workers have choice: Keep their jobs or their health'' (*Chicago Tribune*); ''What Cost a Life? EPA Asks Tacoma'' (*Los Angeles Times*); ''Tacoma Gets Choice: Cancer Risk or Lost Jobs'' (*New York Times*). Most articles quoted Tacoma area citizens who stood on opposite sides of the fence on the issue, citing their fears of ill health or unemployment. ''I'm concerned about getting lung cancer,'' one resident told the *New York Times*, while the head of the local union representing the workers at the smelter countered, ''Simply dying from cancer is not different from a man losing his job and then committing suicide.''

Many observers were critical of Ruckelshaus for what one area resident called ''copping out.'' ''It is up to the EPA to protect public health,'' said Ruth Weiner, head of the Cascade Chapter of the Sierra Club, in an interview with the *New York Times*, ''not to ask the public what it is willing to sacrifice not to die from cancer.'' Another local citizen told a *Los Angeles Times* reporter, ''EPA came in recently and found that our drinking water was contaminated and just cleaned it up, saying they'd find out why later. Now, why aren't they just cleaning this mess up instead of asking people how much cancer they would like to have?''

On the day he announced the proposed regulations, Ruckelshaus had told the press that he was not seeking a referendum from the people, only seeing if a consensus emerged from the public meetings; however, he added, in a remark that was widely quoted, ''I don't know what we'll do if there is a 50-50 split.'' Perhaps in part because of that remark, the notion persisted among the public and some of the press that Ruckelshaus was in fact taking a vote. This idea received its harshest expression in a July 16 *New York Times* editorial, titled ''Mr. Ruckelshaus as Caesar,'' that compared the EPA administrator with a Roman emperor ''who would ask the amphitheater crowd to signal with thumbs up or down whether a defeated gladiator should live or die.'' For Ruckelshaus to ''impose such an impossible choice on Tacomans,'' the editorial stated, was ''inexcusable.''

Ruckelshaus responded to the editorial in a July 23 letter to the *Times* insisting that ''no poll of Tacoma's citizens will be taken.'' The people of Tacoma were being asked for their ''informed opinion,'' not a decision, he continued. ''They know that the right to be heard is not the same thing as the right to be heeded. The final decision is mine.'' Ruckelshaus continued to defend his position despite the criticism. ''Listen,'' he told the *Los Angeles Times*, ''I know people don't like these kinds of decisions. Welcome to the world of regulation. People have demanded to be involved and now I have involved them and they say: 'Don't ask that question. What's the alternative? Don't involve them? Then you're accused of doing something nefarious.''

CONTROVERSY OVER NUMBERS

Disagreements with EPA over the proposed arsenic regulations were not limited to how the agency was handling the process. Even before the official round of workshops and hearings began, EPA's risk calculations were being called into question. Just days after Ruckelshaus announced the proposed regulations, Asarco officials noted that their own figures on arsenic concentrations in the vicinity of the smelter—based on routine monitoring on the site—were significantly lower than the estimates —based on a computer model provided by EPA; in a letter to EPA (later published in the *New York Times*), Asarco asserted that the agency had "overpredict[ed] maximum ambient concentrations of arsenic by a factor of 10." It soon turned up that EPA's model had some serious flaws—most notably the assumption that the smelter was on flat land, when in reality it was on the side of a steep hill. EPA quickly announced its intention of revising its estimates; and when they were published, the agency's new figures for overall arsenic emissions were indeed lower: 115 tons per year (instead of 310), to be lowered to 85 tons (instead of 189) with the installation of the converter hoods.[9] However, these new estimates were not available until late October—too late for the workshops but in time for the public hearings; in the meantime, there was uncertainty about what were the right figures and whom to trust. One leaflet distributed by the union at the time of the workshops asserted that the "figures used for the computer model were from 410 percent to 2267 percent higher than the actual figures."

Other questions about EPA's calculations arose around the time the workshops were to begin. Dr. Samuel Milham, Jr., of the Washington State Department of Social and Health Services, told the *Los Angeles Times* that EPA's projections of possible lung cancers were "baloney." Milham, who had conducted studies in the Tacoma area, found elevated lung cancer rates among retired Asarco workers, but, he added, "we have been looking for extra lung cancers in the community (among those who do not work at the smelter) and we haven't found them. Nothing."

THE WORKSHOPS

Against this backdrop of controversy, the northwest EPA office (Region 10) began conducting its workshops, aimed at acquainting residents with the details of the proposed regulations in preparation for the upcoming hearings. The first workshop was held on Vashon Island on August 10, 1983, followed soon after by two more in Tacoma itself. All three workshops (which were covered by local and national TV) were well attended, particularly the two in Tacoma, which drew environmental groups, local citizen organizations, and a large number of smelter workers, who had come at the urging of their union representative. (The importance of stacking the aisles with large numbers of supporters, one observer noted, might have stemmed from a lingering feeling that Ruckelshaus was going to make the decision by counting heads.)

The format of all three workshops was basically the same: after a formal presentation by EPA staff, the audience divided into smaller groups in order to encourage dialogue and permit more individual response to specific questions. EPA national headquarters sent two key policymakers—Robert Ajax, chief of the Standards Development Branch, and Betty Anderson, director of the Office of Health and Environmental Assessment—to assist in the process. They, along with Ernesta Barnes, rotated among the groups, answering questions. Each group had a "facilitator" (hired by EPA for the occasion), a recorder, and three EPA staff from the regional office. "Every comment [from the public] was recorded . . . and [later] typed up," says Barnes. To accompany discussion, staff from the Region 10 office prepared and distributed a number of handouts for the workshop, including illustrations of how hooding helped control emissions, excerpts from Ruckelshaus'

NAS speech, and fact sheets on arsenic controls and risk calculations.

EPA had come prepared to discuss risk assessment figures and dispersion models and present graphs and charts, yet many of the questions they encountered had little to do with verifiable "facts." "The personal nature of the complaints and questions made a striking counterpoint to the presentations of meteorological models and health effect extrapolations," wrote Gilbert Omenn, dean of the School of Public Health at the University of Washington, in a letter to Ernesta Barnes. (Omenn had been hired by EPA to observe and help evaluate the workshops.) People asked about the symptoms of arsenic poisoning, about other health effects from arsenic, about the advisability of eating produce from Vashon Island gardens. One person asked whether it would be necessary to remove a foot of dirt from her garden to make it safe (and who would pay for it); another wanted to know what effect arsenic emissions would have on animals. Ruckelshaus, who had received a personal report on the Vashon Island workshop, later recounted that, after EPA health experts finished their presentation, "A woman got up in the audience and said, 'Last week, my dog ate some spinach and dropped over dead. Did he die of arsenic?'" There were more sobering moments as well, Ruckelshaus noted, as when "another woman got up and said, 'Will my child die of cancer?'"

Nevertheless, technical matters such as the risk figures and epidemiological studies formed the basis for the majority of questions. Several inquiries focused on EPA's dispersion model and the reliability of the proposed control equipment. One resident wanted to know if any studies had been done on birth defects or miscarriages in the area; another asked whether the risk posed by emissions from the smelter was greater than the risk from ambient carbon monoxide from cars. This last question highlighted EPA's difficulties in explaining adequately the risk numbers in a relative context. Although EPA had prepared a table illustrating comparative risk, it was described as "cluttered" and needing fuller explanation. One critic commented, "How can they expect a relatively unsophisticated public to understand what these risk figures mean when the environmental establishment in this state doesn't even understand them?"

Several questions betrayed a lingering hostility toward EPA for not resolving the issue on its own. "Seems like EPA is leaving the interpretation of the law up to the public," one resident commented. "Why has Asarco continued to obtain variances from complying with the law? What authority does EPA have to do this?" Another resident asked, "At this point in time is Asarco in violation of any clean air requirements? If so, why are they allowed to operate? Why is EPA spending taxpayers' money for this process if Asarco is not violating any laws?" "We elected people to run our government, we don't expect them to turn around and ask us to run it for them," said still another. "These issues are very complex and the public is not sophisticated enough to make these decisions. This is not to say that EPA doesn't have an obligation to inform the public, but information is one thing—defaulting its legal mandate is another."

In the end, the workshops got mixed, but generally favorable notices. "Many of the questioners were impressively well informed," Gilbert Omenn wrote. "I expect that some rethinking of elements of the *Federal Register* notice and the presentation of certain assumptions and facts will result from [the workshop]." "We also got educated," agrees Randy Smith, an EPA analyst from Region 10. "The questions raised at the workshops sent some people back to the drawing board."

CLOSING ARGUMENTS: THE HEARINGS

At the conclusion of the workshops, several groups asked EPA to postpone the formal hearing, slated for late August, to allow them more time to prepare the testimony. The agency agreed, and the hearings were rescheduled for early November. In the meantime, EPA participated in a few more workshops run by others—the city of Tacoma and the Steelworkers Union, where the comments and questions bordered on the openly hostile. ("I have seen studies which show that stress is the main source of cancer," one worker told an EPA representative. "The EPA is one main cause of stress.") By the end of the summer, all the interested parties were gearing up to present their arguments at the public hearing.

The hearings began on November 2, 1983. A panel of EPA officials (made up of representatives from the regional office, EPA headquarters, and EPA's research facility in North Carolina) presided over a three-day period, as roughly 150 people representing a variety of groups or just individual concerns offered their views on the proposed arsenic regulations. Their testimony ran the gamut from sophisticated technical arguments for more controls to anxious complaints that EPA was asking Tacoma residents to vote on a death sentence for one of their fellow citizens.[10]

PSAPCA'S TESTIMONY

Harvey Poll, chairman of PSAPCA, was first to speak at the hearings. The PSAPCA board had evaluated EPA's proposed standard, Poll told the hearing panel, and concluded that it had some serious shortcomings. The board's primary objection was that the proposal did not establish arsenic ambient air quality standards. (EPA was, however, constrained by statutory requirements, which directed the administrator to set technology-based, not ambient air, standards in issuing NESHAPS.) PSAPCA was also concerned that because the new hooding would reduce SO_2 emissions, Asarco would be able to operate the smelter more often (instead of curtailing operations during adverse meteorological conditions),

thereby actually increasing the total volume of plant-wide arsenic emissions. PSAPCA wanted EPA to consider requiring Asarco to install a flue gas desulfurization system (at a cost several times higher than the $3.5 million for secondary hooding) or, more drastically, to force the company to convert to a new smelting technology at a projected cost of roughly $130–$150 million. PSAPCA had already issued a compliance order forcing the company to choose one of these options by 1987 in order to reduce SO_2 emissions (and, of necessity, arsenic emissions) by 90 percent.

ASARCO'S TESTIMONY

Next to testify was Asarco, which had hired the public relations firm of Hill and Knowlton to organize and present its case at the hearings. In addition to Armand L. Labbe, an Asarco vice president and former manager of the Tacoma smelter, the company employed five expert witnesses to refute EPA's numbers and modeling assumptions and to assert that "there *now* exists an ample margin of safety" from arsenic emissions from the smelter [emphasis in original]. Most of the experts were affiliated with universities, and each boasted an impressive curriculum vitae with relevant experience.

"Epidemiological studies demonstrate that arsenic emissions from the Asarco Tacoma smelter are not at levels that pose a health risk to the public living in the vicinity of the plant," Labbe flatly stated. Tom Downs, a professor of biology at the University of Texas, disputed EPA's extrapolations of health effects: "[EPA's assumption about exposure to arsenic] is like saying that the effects of taking five aspirin tablets a day for a lifetime are the same as the effects of taking five-hundred aspirin tables per day for 1 percent of a lifetime."

Despite its assertion, that, in the words of Asarco attorney C. John Newlands, "the Tacoma Smelter is now in compliance with Section 112 of the Federal Clean Air Act," the company stated its support for EPA's proposed arsenic standards—and at the same time outlined its opposition to ambient standards or to efforts to reduce emissions further. Asarco also detailed the projects—some of them voluntary—the firm had undertaken over the years to control SO_2 and arsenic pollution. Summing up the firm's position, Labbe reminded his listeners that a prolonged depression in the copper industry had hurt the Tacoma plant's ability to compete, and that the smelter had lost money in recent years. He concluded: "We are unable to commit additional expenditures beyond installation of BAT under present conditions."

ENVIRONMENTAL GROUPS

A host of environmental groups appeared at the hearings—ranging from long-established organizations like the American Lung Association of Washington (which, according to staff member Janet Chalupnick, played a key role in coordinating a coalition of clean air groups) to more recently formed groups like Tacomans for a Healthy Environment.[11] For the most part, the environmentalists' testimony was critical of EPA—arguing that its proposed regulation did not go far enough—and supportive of PSAPCA's more comprehensive recommendations. Several environmental organizations opposed EPA's "best available technology" approach, asserting that it effectively discouraged the development of new technology to improve emissions control. "By allowing a company to only install the available technology it says is affordable, the EPA is creating a situation in which the company is still allowed to emit substantial amounts of toxic substances but may be inclined for financial reasons to resist development of improved control technologies," said Brian Baird of Tacomans for a Healthy Environment. "If BAT standards are regularly used," he continued, "it seems reasonable to anticipate that the pace of technological development of all types of

pollution control will be substantially slowed, because the market for Better Available Technologies will not only have been removed, it will have been significantly undermined."

In its testimony, the National Audubon Society reiterated Baird's point: ". . . If EPA finds zero emissions of a pollutant to be impossible, they should set the standards at the lowest levels possible rather than at the levels achievable through pollution control technologies easily affordable by the polluting industries. In order to protect [the public] health, standards must be used to force technological innovation to pollution control rather than to simply reinforce the status quo." Similarly, Nancy Ellison of the Washington Environmental Council chided EPA for proposing only the "absolute minimum" in regulation; nor did the council agree, she told the panel, "that the only choices available are hood installation or smelter shutdown. This is not a jobs-versus-the-environment issue."

THE SMELTER WORKERS

As Ellison's remark indicated, environmentalists in the area had been making an effort to reverse the longstanding pattern of labor vs. environmental interests, and to find common ground with the workers in resolving arsenic emissions problems. Further evidence of a fragile alliance between the two groups was observable in the testimony of Michael Wright, an industrial hygienist for the United Steelworkers union. "No one has to convince our union that arsenic at high levels is risky," said Wright. "We know what arsenic has done to many of our union brothers and sisters in the Tacoma Smelter and other copper smelters. It was the death of our members which provided the conclusive evidence that arsenic causes lung cancer." Wright went on to urge EPA to encourage the development of technology which would make the plant safer for workers and community residents by reducing pollution.[12] He supported the installation of secondary hooding and research to determine if further controls would be useful and economically feasible.

Not surprisingly, the union spoke out against requiring control equipment that was too costly, and would therefore force the plant to close. Referring to a study which he used to estimate the health risk of forcing the smelter to close, Wright claimed that the stress resulting from unemployment could cause eighty-four deaths in Pierce County over a six year period. "That," he asserted, "is a considerably greater risk of death than what EPA predicts from arsenic after the installation of secondary hooding."

Following Wright's testimony, individual smelter workers spoke before the panel. In what was often emotional testimony, several members of the "twenty-five year club"—people who had worked at the plant for more than a quarter of a century—made their case. "I'm eighty-eight years old and I ain't dead yet. I'm still breathing," said Ross Bridges. The workers reflected on the good life the smelter had made possible for them and their families. If the smelter closed, they maintained, it would leave them jobless. "No high-tech industry moving into Tacoma is going to hire me," one man lamented. "The smelter is all I've got."

VASHON ISLAND RESIDENTS

Residents of Vashon Island (which, except for Tacoma's North End, received the majority of emissions from Asarco) provided equally emotional testimony of the trauma that they had experienced as a result of the arsenic pollution. One man came to the hearing sporting a gas mask, several were clad in hospital patient garb, and some carried young children to the podium to make their point. One woman, who claimed to have been diagnosed by her doctors as ultra-sensitive to arsenic, tearfully told the panel that she and her husband had been forced to sell their small farm for a fraction of its worth—due to depressed real estate

prices on the island—and leave the area. Michael Bradley, chairman of a group named Island Residents Against Toxic Emissions (IRATE), made note of a recent cautionary statement issued by a local health agency warning against eating vegetables grown in the arsenic-laced soil on the island. "If Asarco cannot clean up their act and prevent this kind of pollution then they should be forced to close," he stated angrily.

POSTMORTEMS

After three days of testimony, the hearings came to an end. Ruckelshaus was not expected to make a decision on the final standards for arsenic emissions until February or March of 1984. In the meanwhile, some assessment, at least of the process, had already begun. From an administrative point of view, the brunt of managing the tasks of informing and involving the public had fallen on Ernesta Barnes and EPA's Region 10 office. According to one source, roughly thirty people from the regional office had worked full-time for four months on the Asarco case. Randy Smith of the Region 10 office told one reporter that the "process proved terrifically costly and time-consuming." [13]

But the regional office did feel that there had been an internal payoff for them in a greater appreciation by EPA headquarters of what is meant to be "on the front lines." The regional staff felt that because of their frequent contact with area groups, they were better able to engage the public's participation. "After a while," remarked one regional staff member, "we realized we couldn't let [headquarters staff] do the spiel [in the public workshops]. The people from headquarters were just not enough in touch with the local level. . . . They were too scientific." Another regional office commented:

At headquarters [in Washington, DC] they thought we were a bunch of bozos out here in the region. They could not understand why we were scrambling and bending over backwards to organize the workshops and put out easily digestible information for the public. When they arrived in Tacoma, however, and found themselves face-to-face with a well-informed and often angry public, they began to appreciate our problem a little better.

The process also proved beneficial to the regional office from the standpoint of image and public trust. A number of witnesses and observers agreed with Nancy Ellison of the Washington Environmental Council, who complimented the Region 10 office for its "openness and willingness to share information during this process." The office's cooperation and outreach efforts had, she continued, "gone a long way toward restoring trust and confidence in the agency here in the region."

Even Ruckelshaus' decision to involve the public received gentler treatment at some hands. Ruth Weiner of the Sierra Club, who had earlier criticized the EPA administrator for "copping out," stated at the conclusion of her testimony that the Clean Air Act "requires public involvement." She continued, "Moreover, in becoming involved, the public begins to appreciate the difficulty attendant on making regulatory decisions, the ease with which EPA can be made a scapegoat because the agency's blunders are so readily magnified, and the inadequacy of simply identifying 'heroes' and 'villains' in environmental protection. It may have been hard work and a headache for all of us, but the public involvement is most certainly worth it."

Ruckelshaus himself was largely in agreement with this last sentiment. Back in June, in his speech before the National Academy of Sciences, he had told his audience that, in managing risk, "we must seek new ways to involve the public in the decision-making process." He continued, "It is clear to me that in a society in which democratic principles so dominate, the perceptions of the public must be weighed." Later, as he looked back on the process he

had kicked off when he announced the proposed arsenic regulations for the Asarco smelter, he found validation for these views. Ruckelshaus felt that local citizens had shown they were "capable of understanding [the problem of the smelter] in its complexities and dealing with it and coming back to us with rather sensible suggestions." In fact, he added, "the public—the nontechnical, unschooled public—came back with some very good suggestions as to how they could reduce the emissions of arsenic in the plant [and still keep it open]." But, perhaps, the final proof of the success of the venture would be in the decision that—as he had often repeated—Ruckelshaus alone would make. It was still an open question as to how Asarco might respond to citizens' suggestions, and whether it would feel as sanguine as Ruckelshaus about remaining open. While he pondered his decision on the final standards, the debate on his risk management techniques continued.

NOTES

1. Barnett N. Kalikow, "Environmental Risk: Power to the People," *Technology Review* 87 (October 1984), p. 55. As a result of studies of workers exposed to arsenic in copper smelting and arsenic manufacturing plants, a number of widely respected groups, including the National Academy of Sciences and the National Cancer Institute, concluded that inorganic arsenic was carcinogenic in humans. It has been linked to skin and lung cancer.

2. The other was a coal power plant in western Washington.

3. Under the provisions of the Clean Air Act, EPA routinely delegates many of its powers to regulate and enforce to the states, which in turn can delegate their powers to regional authorities.

4. The actual order from PSAPCA to install the hoods was not issued until 1981.

5. The standards actually comprised three sets of regulations—for copper smelting processing high arsenic content ore, for copper smelters processing low arsenic content ore, and for glass manufacturing plants. The Asarco smelter in Ruston was the only facility in the U.S. that fell into the first category. The risk assessment (and resulting standards) for high arsenic content copper smelters thus applied only to that one plant.

6. In its proposed regulations, EPA defined a unit risk number as its estimate of the lifetime cancer risk

occurring in a hypothetical population which is exposed throughout their lifetime to a concentration of one microgram (1/28 millionths of an ounce) of a pollutant per cubic meter of air.

7. In fact, some critics felt that EPA's (albeit involuntary) entry into the regulatory scene delayed installation of the hoods, while Asarco waited to learn what EPA would propose as best available technology.

8. Asarco-Tacoma used ore that contained 4 percent arsenic; the remaining fourteen smelters in the United States used ores with 0.7 percent or lower arsenic content.

9. In announcing these lower figures on October 20, 1983, Ernesta Barnes did note that the amount of fugitive emissions released near ground level was higher than originally estimated.

10. According to one observer, a number of witnesses at the hearing were confused about the meaning of the term "risk," assuming that the risk of the one additional cancer death meant the certainty of the fatality—not the worst-case probability.

11. Tacoma is the Indian name for Mt. Rainier.

12. The Occupational Safety and Health Administration—not EPA—was responsible for setting safety standards in the workplace itself. According to Ernesta Barnes, OSHA had already issued regulations requiring workers to wear respirators in the smelter.

13. Kalikow, "Environmental Risk," p. 61.

Comment

William Ruckelshaus recognized that even the technically best policy analysis could not yield an answer to the question of what cancer risk should be borne by the residents of Tacoma area, especially when a lower risk was likely to create higher unemployment. As an alternative or supplement to policy analysis, Ruckelshaus solicited the views of the people most affected by the proposed regulations. But he seemed to be uncertain about how best to use the results of this participatory process in making his final decision. In announcing his plan to hold public meetings, Ruckelshaus implied that he would let the people of Tacoma determine his decision: "For me to sit here in Washington and tell the people of Tacoma what is an acceptable risk would be at best arrogant and at worst inexcusable." Yet, in response to the *New York Times*'s charge that to impose such a choice on the citizens of Tacoma would itself be "inexcusable," Ruckelshaus said that he would not simply follow the opinion of the majority of Tacoma's citizens but would make his own decision, presumably on the basis of his own best judgment after taking into account the views expressed by the citizens of Tacoma. Is this a morally consistent position for the head of EPA to take? Is Ruckelshaus abdicating his official responsibility: (1) in giving (or appearing to give) so much weight to current public opinion; (2) in spending public funds on workshops rather than directly on environmental regulations; and (3) in raising levels of social stress among people who do not want to know the environmental risks under which they live?

Evaluate these reasons for involving the public in making regulatory decisions that require technical expertise: participation can (1) help restore (or create) confidence in a regulatory agency; (2) enable the public better "to appreciate the difficulty attendant on making regulatory decisions"; and (3) make the final decision fairer and wiser. Suppose that the workshops generated more criticism of the EPA and left the citizens of Tacoma more dissatisfied with Ruckelshaus's final decision than they otherwise would have been. How (if at all) would this outcome affect your judgment of whether the public should be included in the decision-making process?

Apart from the opinions of the citizens of Tacoma, what should Ruckelshaus take into account in making his final decision, and what importance should he accord to each relevant consideration? Consider how the following factors should be weighed in determining the regulatory standard: Asarco's level of wages and employment; cost to consumers of increased prices of Asarco products as a result of regulation; cost to the EPA of various levels of regulation; scientific uncertainty concerning cancer risk associated with various emission levels; best available technology (BAT); views of citizens who are not residents of the Tacoma area; harms and benefits of future generations; and the imputed value of life.

On the basis of information provided in the case, can you determine what Ruckelshaus' final decision should be? If not, what additional information does Ruckelshaus need in order to decide?

Recommended Reading

An excellent introduction to how advocates of policy analysis intend it to be used is Edith Stokey and Richard Zeckhauser, *A Primer for Policy Analysis* (New York: Norton, 1978). For a flavor of the ethical controversy over policy analysis, see Alasdair MacIntyre, "Utilitarianism and Cost/Benefit Analysis," in Tom Beauchamp and Norman Bowie (eds.), *Ethical Theory and Business* (Englewood Cliffs, N.J.: Prentice-Hall, 1979), pp. 266–76; and Tom Beauchamp, "A Reply to MacIntyre," in Beauchamp and Bowie, pp. 276–82. Also see James T. Campen, *Benefit, Cost, and Beyond. The Political Economy of Benefit-Cost Analysis* (Cambridge, Mass.: Ballinger, 1986), and Rosemary Tong, *Ethics in Policy Analysis* (Englewood Cliffs, N.J.: Prentice-Hall, 1986).

Two contemporary defenses of utilitarianism as a political morality are Russell Hardin, *Morality within the Limits of Reason* (Chicago: University of Chicago Press, 1988); and Robert Goodin, *Utilitarianism as a Public Philosophy* (New York: Cambridge University Press, 1995). Two sophisticated versions of utilitarianism as a foundational moral theory are James Griffin, *Well-Being: Its Meaning, Measurement, and Moral Importance* (Oxford: Oxford University Press, 1986); and Derek Parfit, *Reasons and Persons* (Oxford: Oxford University Press, 1984).

For critiques of utilitarianism as a political morality, see Amy Gutmann and Dennis Thompson, *Democracy and Disagreement* (Cambridge, Mass.: Harvard University Press, 1996), ch. 5; and Will Kymlicka, *Contemporary Political Philosophy* (Oxford: Clarendon Press, 1990), pp. 9–49.

On the issue of justice for further generations, see Peter Laslett and James Fishkin, (eds.), *Justice Between Age Groups and Generations* (New Haven, Conn.: Yale University Press, 1991); and Brian Barry, "Intergenerational Justice in Energy Policy," in Milton Fisk (ed.), *Justice* (Atlantic Highlands, N.J.: Humanities Press, 1993), pp. 223–37. On evaluating risks, see Douglas MacLean (ed.), *Values at*

Risk (Totowa, N.J.: Rowman and Allanheld, 1986), and the review by Elizabeth Anderson, *Value in Ethics and Economics* (Cambridge, Mass.: Harvard University Press, 1993), especially ch.9.

A collection that evaluates the application of utilitarianism to environmental policy is Daniel Swartzman, Richard A. Liroff, Kevin G. Croke (eds.), *Cost-Benefit Analysis and Environmental Regulation: Politics, Ethics, and Methods* (Washington, D.C.: The Conservation Foundation, 1982). For the application, see R. Kerry Turner, David Pearce, and Ian Bateman, *Environmental Economics: An Elementary Introduction* (Baltimore, Md.: Johns Hopkins University Press, 1993). For a philosophical critique of the application, see Mark Sagoff, *The Economic of the Earth: Philosophy, Law, and the Environment* (New York: Cambridge University Press, 1988).

On the question of the value of life in public policy, see Steven Rhoads (ed.), *Valuing Life: Public Policy Dilemmas* (Boulder, Colo.: Westview Press, 1980); and Charles Fried, *Anatomy of Values* (Cambridge, Mass.: Harvard University Press, 1970), ch. 12. More generally on utilitarianism and its problems, see the Recommended Reading in the Introduction.

6 Distributive Justice

Introduction

On what principles should government control the distribution of goods to citizens? Utilitarians and their progeny do not believe that any special theory of justice is necessary. The right distribution is the one that maximizes the total welfare of most citizens, even if this entails sacrificing the liberty and opportunity of the few to the many. While utilitarianism is widely criticized for ignoring claims of individuals that even the welfare of the whole society should not override, critics do not agree on what theory of distributive justice to put in its place.

Libertarians argue that governments should secure only liberty, not distribute goods such as income, health care, or education. Goods, in this view, come into the world attached to specific people who have earned, inherited, or received them by free exchange, and for the state to redistribute their property without their consent is a violation of their fundamental right to liberty. Because "taxation is on a par with forced labor" (Robert Nozick), even a democratic government may not tax the rich to provide welfare for the poor. Nor may it protect the rich from competition by sheltering their industries or licensing their professions. Individual liberty, understood as noninterference, trumps both social welfare and democracy.

Egalitarian critics argue that, just as utilitarianism can be faulted for submerging individuals beneath all social purposes, so libertarianism can be criticized for elevating them above all social responsibility. For egalitarians, our social interdependence creates certain duties of mutual aid or reciprocity.

Most egalitarian theories of distributive justice also give priority to basic liberty over social welfare. But their list of basic liberties differs from that of libertarians. It includes political liberty, freedom of religion, speech, and assembly, and the right to hold personal property. But it does not include an absolute right to commercial property or unqualified freedom of contract. According to egalitarians, although basic liberty has priority, not all liberty is basic, and even basic liberty is not the only good that governments should distribute or safeguard for all individuals. Other primary goods include income and wealth, the distributions of which are just (according to John Rawls' difference principle) only if they maximize the welfare of the least advantaged citizens.

Egalitarians are commonly criticized for subordinating individual liberty to equality. This criticism is compelling only if one accepts the absolute value of the libertarian's expansive understanding of liberty. A more general problem is that

237

the maximization of some primary goods (such as health care, security, and educa-tion) might require an egalitarian government to neglect other primary goods, since there is virtually no limit to the resources that can be spent on making people healthy, secure, and well educated.

Democratic theories of distributive justice build upon this criticism. The people, constituted by democratic majorities at various levels of government, should have the right to determine priorities among goods according to what they deem most important to their collective ways of life. Most democratic theorists recognize that majorities should have the right only when the procedures by which they make decisions are fair. But the requirements of this standard of procedural fairness are controversial. Some democrats argue that it requires governments only to secure certain basic liberties, such as freedom of speech, association, and the right to vote. Others claim that it also requires governments to guarantee the distribution of a basic level of opportunity—in the form of income, education, food, housing, and health care—for all citizens. The first position has been criticized for permitting majority tyranny over disadvantaged minorities, the second, for smuggling egalitar-ian values into democratic theory and thereby encroaching on the rights of democratic majorities who may not favor so much equality.

The political controversies over the distribution of health care and welfare in the United States are instructive problems in distributive justice. Good health care is necessary for pursuing most other things in life. Yet equal access to health care would require the government not only to redistribute resources from the rich and healthy to the poor and infirm but also to restrict the freedom of doctors and other health care providers. Such redistribution and restrictions may be warranted, but on what principles and to what extent? The first case—the Arizona state legislature's decision in 1987 to eliminate funding for most organ transplants—is part of this continuing controversy over whether government has a right or a responsibility to provide citizens with the preconditions of a decent life. The second case, which describes the controversy over AIDS testing by insurance companies in the District of Columbia, highlights the less direct but no less powerful role of government in regulating access to health care. By evaluating these political decisions that in differ-ent ways affect the distribution of medical care, we can redefine our understanding of the relative strengths and weaknesses of competing theories of distributive justice.

The third case—a controversy over welfare reform in California—focuses on an increasingly important set of moral issues that are often neglected by conventional theories of distributive justice. Should a minimal level of economic welfare be guaranteed unconditionally to all citizens? Or should welfare be made conditional on a citizen's willingness to work? If welfare is to be unconditional, how can government justify paying citizens not to work? If welfare is to be conditional, how can a citizen's willingness to work be fairly assessed in an economy where not enough jobs are available? In assessing the controversy over welfare reform in California, we must consider not only the principled relation between the rights of citizens and their responsibilities but also the practical requirements of any welfare policy that seeks to enforce the responsibilities as well as the rights of citizens.

Defunding Organ Transplants in Arizona
Pamela Varley

Dianna Brown, who will be buried this morning in Yuma, was the first person to die under Arizona's newest death penalty law. She was forty-three years old. She had committed no murder. No conspiracy. No theft. No parking violation. No crime. Dianna Brown's only offense was to be poor and sick. Under Arizona law, that's now punishable by death.
> E.J. Montini, *Arizona Republic*
> September 18, 1987

In the spring of 1987, the Arizona state legislature voted to eliminate funding for most organ transplants from the state's health care program for the indigent, the Arizona Health Care Cost Containment System (AHCCCS—pronounced "access"). At the same time, however, the legislature voted to increase other kinds of health coverage provided by AHCCCS. The most controversial item was the extension of basic health service to pregnant women and to children between the ages of six and thirteen[1] in the so-called "notch group"—families that earn too much to qualify for AHCCCS automatically, but still earn less than the federal poverty level.[2]

Although the decision to extend health coverage to these women and children was debated extensively, the decision to defund organ transplants slipped through the legislature with relatively little notice or attention. A few months later, however, the legislators had to confront the effect of their decision in the person of forty-three-year-old Dianna Brown, a Yuma woman suffering from terminal liver disease. In accordance with the new state policy, AHCCCS denied Brown's request for a liver transplant in August 1987. A few weeks later,

she died. In the flurry of news coverage attending her death, several legislators publicly questioned their decision to defund the transplants and called for reconsideration of the matter in the 1988 legislative session.

BACKGROUND

In a brief characterization of Arizona's political landscape, the 1988 *Almanac of American Politics* states, "Arizona citizens face squarely first questions—government or free enterprise, development or environment, regulation or freedom—and tend to come out squarely on one side or the other." More often than not, the Almanac adds, they come out squarely on the conservative side. Arizona is the only state to have voted Republican in every presidential election since 1948, and Republicans heavily dominate both chambers of the state legislature. The Grand Canyon State also prides itself on a certain independent spirit. For instance, Arizona is the only one of the forty-eight contiguous states to have steadfastly resisted the convention of daylight savings time.[3] It was the last state to develop a state park system. And from 1972 to 1981, it was the only state in the country which had not accepted the federal Medicaid program.

Although the Dianna Brown case may have taken the public and even some legislators by surprise, it did not spring from nowhere. It grew out of a several-year struggle within AHCCCS to establish and enforce an organ transplant policy. More broadly, the case arose in the context of longstanding controversy over the type and cost of health care provided to Arizona's poor.

THE BIRTH OF AHCCCS

Medicaid was created at the national level in 1966 as an optional program: if a state met the federal standards established for health care of the poor, the federal government

Reprinted by permission of the Case Program, Kennedy School of Government, Harvard University. Copyright 1988 by the President and Fellows of Harvard College.

would pay a share of the costs (the percentage varied depending on the relative wealth of the state). Many states were quick to sign on, but Arizona legislators steered clear of the program. "State policymakers feared intrusive federal intervention, as well as the potential for fraud and abuse and the uncontrolled cost to the state," according to a June 1987 report on the program prepared by the federal Health Care Financing Administration (HCFA).[4] For the next fifteen years, each county in Arizona continued to provide some measure of health care to the poor with its own dollars. Over time, however, the county system resulted in "unequal eligibility, uneven services [across the state], and, most important, an increasing cost burden on the counties," according to the HCFA report. In the seventies, as elsewhere in the country, health care began escalating dramatically in Arizona—from $49 million in 1974 to $106 million in 1979—until they consumed, on average, a quarter of each county's annual revenues, drawn primarily from property taxes. In 1980, when Arizonans passed a referendum limiting the property tax levy, the counties' budget squeeze became a flat-out crisis: "The counties faced the possibility of a complete fiscal breakdown in 1981," HCFA wrote.

It was under this kind of financial pressure that the state legislature began to talk of ushering in a Medicaid program as a way to tap into federal funds. But many legislators remained reluctant, and during the summer of 1981, they bargained with HCFA to set up a program significantly different from a conventional Medicaid system. The Arizona program would be "experimental," designed "to contain cost by encouraging cost competition among prepaid plans and discouraging overutilization of health care," according to HCFA. In each county, different health maintenance organizations (HMOs) would bid to provide an agreed-upon health care package to AHCCCS-eligible residents in return for a fixed payment per person per month from AHCCCS.[5]

The goal was to create within each HMO an incentive to keep medical costs low for routine health care. Similarly, the federal government would pay a fixed "capitation rate" per month to the state for each Medicaid-eligible person in the program (a departure from the usual method of reimbursement: paying a share of the actual medical costs incurred.[6]) For this reason, the state had an incentive to keep its own costs low and to push for low bids from HMOs.

The set-up of the AHCCCS program was also to be different from conventional Medicaid in several respects. For one thing, the entire program was to be administered by a private firm. For another, AHCCCS would not cover the full array of Medicaid services (the state received a special waiver so that it would not have to provide skilled nursing facilities for long-term care,[7] home health care, family planning, or nurse mid-wife services). Within the state, the program was never even called "Medicaid." In fact, according to AHCCCS Deputy Director David Lowenberg:

> When we submit a budget [to the legislature], or make presentations, or talk about policy issues, it's in terms of "AHCCCS" or—the closest we'll get is "Title IX programs." I've been asked not to put the word "Medicaid" in, because Medicaid brings up all the bad that [the legislators] have either heard personally or read about in other states. There is a high level of concern of the abuse, the fraud. They did not want to be a party to such a system in this state.

The legislature and governor approved the creation of AHCCCS in November of 1981, and the program took effect eleven months later. In retrospect, health care professionals tend to think this speedy implementation allowed too little time for program planning and development. In any event, in its first eighteen months, AHCCCS was "beset with administrative and budgetary problems," according to the HCFA report. The agency was criticized by the public for the lengthy, cumbersome process for determining eligibility. (In some cases, people reportedly died for lack of medical treatment before their eligibility was determined.) Due to financial irregularities, the legislature decided to shift administrative control of AHCCCS from the private firm to the state in March of 1984, and hired Dr. Donald F. Schaller to head the program. Schaller had had extensive administrative experience with health maintenance organizations ever since 1972, when he had left fifteen years of work in private practice to co-found the Arizona Health Plan—one of the oldest HMOs in the state. When he came to AHCCCS, Schaller had also spent a year as senior vice president and medical director of the CIGNA Healthplan, and a year as consultant to a consortium of four HMOs working with AHCCCS.

Although AHCCCS remained controversial within the state under Schaller's leadership, he is widely credited with bringing the agency under fiscal and administrative control. By early 1987, 200,469 people were covered by AHCCCS,[8] and the program had a year-long budget of $294 million. More than two-thirds of Arizona's licensed physicians participated in the program directly or through an HMO, and fourteen different private HMOs were contracted to provide health care for the program.

During its first shaky year and a half of operation, AHCCCS had no policy about funding transplants per se, partly because the agency received few transplant requests. Before his arrival, Schallar says, "I'm not sure how many transplants were paid for or what happened. There may have been one or two."

THE STATE OF THE ART IN
TRANSPLANTATION

The practice of transplanting organs to treat patients began to emerge in the United States in the 1950 and early 1960s—initially with dismal survival rates, which steadily improved. During the 1980s, transplanta-tion became a more viable method of treatment and was used for an increasing number of organs. By 1987, the simplest and most routine transplants available were cornea and bone transplants, followed by kidney transplants. Heart, liver, and bone marrow transplants were increasingly common, and pancreas, heart-and-lung, and other organ combinations, while rarer, were actively being developed.

But there was no question that these organ transplants were costly. According to a 1984 study,[9] the fully-allocated one-year cost of a liver transplant averaged between $230,000 and $340,000, and of a heart transplant, between $170,000 and $200,000. "This is in the range of four to ten times the cost of the other most expensive currently employed medical technologies," the task force reported:

> The costs of doing the transplant operation itself are relatively minor, whether the operation lasts three hours or twenty-three hours. The real costs come from the post-operative hospitalization and the frequent need to rehospitalize transplant patients to treat various complications. These are very common (averaging more than one per case in most reports on the literature). They include rejection episodes, complications from the operation itself, and infections that develop because such patients take drugs to suppress their immune systems to fight organ rejection, making them more vulnerable to other infections. There are also significant costs in pre-operative work-ups, routine post-operative hospitalization, organ procurement, etc.

THE HISTORY OF TRANSPLANT
FUNDING IN ARIZONA

Arizona was home to one of the pioneers of the heart transplant field—a much-celebrated young surgeon named Jack Copeland, who built a nationally recognized heart transplant program at the University of Arizona Medical Center in Tucson. Dr. Timothy Icenogle, a surgeon on Copeland's team, says that progress in the heart transplant arena was swift and dramatic in the 1980s. "Back in 1981, there were very dark days and nights of trying to take care of transplants. Survivorship wasn't very good back then. It was back in the days when there were just a few brave souls venturing into this."

It was also back in the days when transplants were covered by virtually no private insurers. "What happened back in 1981, before anyone was paying for this, [the patients] all had to go out and fundraise. And if they had the money, then they came to the 'active' list." [10] If they couldn't come up with the money, he adds, "they died fundraising." By 1986, however, Icenogle said that "almost all private insurers paid for it and if they didn't want to pay for it, we [encouraged the patient] to sue them, [with] nearly 100 percent success." [11]

> Really, the insurers don't have a choice, because heart transplantation now is not experimental. It is an accepted therapeutic modality, and it is the treatment of choice. It is just as therapeutic as getting penicillin for your pneumonia.

Icenogle adds that some companies—especially HMOs competing for business—have been persuaded that the "public embarrassment" of a protracted battle over payment of a transplant is not worth the fight. "One of them we coerced into paying for a patient, because they realized that the fallout from the lawsuit—and having to go in front of the television cameras and say what schmucks they were—was going to cost them a great deal of money."

"We play a sort of an advocacy role," Icenogle adds. "I think society demands something more from physicians than [to be] just a glob of bureaucrats, and I think we have to take a stand now and then. Our role, essentially, as patient advocate, is to tell them, well, just because the insurance company says they're not going to pay, that is not the end of all the resources. We can help show them other resources that are available."

IN THE CONTEXT OF DEREGULATION

The increasing number of organ transplants, and the growing costs associated with them, coincided with another development in the state's health care system: the deregulation of medical facilities in March 1985. Before deregulation, hospitals were required to seek permission to make capital investments in their facilities. Regulation proponents argued that without such a process, hospitals would begin to perform more and more glamorous high tech, high-dollar medical procedures—like transplants—and that costs would escalate while quality of care would decline. [12] Says Rep. Cindy Resnick (D-Tucson), a member of the House Health Committee, the transplant units "get a great deal of PR and they get a great deal of money."

> It is a money-making system. If it was just pure concern about the [medical] needs out there, we'd have far more burn units than we have transplant units. The reality is they make money on those units. You can bring in anywhere from a million to three million dollars on that service alone to a hospital a year.

"There's also a prestige factor," adds Phil Lopes, a regional director of the regulatory Health Systems Agency before it was dismantled. "You do all these fancy high tech things with somebody's ticker, and there's something sexy about that. Everybody wants to have one of those, wants to have that service. You're in the Big Time."

DON SCHALLER'S VIEW

Right from the start, Schaller was uncomfortable about AHCCCS funding of transplants for several reasons. For one, he questioned whether a program with tight resources should be spending its money on high-dollar, high-risk procedures. After all, AHCCCS was intended as a general health program for the genuinely poor. By contrast, many of AHCCCS' transplant recipients did not start out poor enough to qualify for the program, but—due to their illnesses or to the failure of their private insurance companies to cover their medical expenses—they had "spent down" their assets and become AHCCCS-eligible. Schaller worried that AHCCCS might, *de facto*, be swallowed up by such heavy dollar expenses and turn into a catastrophic health program for the general public. AHCCCS should provide "basic health care to poor people, not just cater to people who have real expensive health problems," he said in an interview aired May 29, 1986, on KAET-TV's "Horizon" program.

Schaller also had several fundamental concerns about the ethics and equity of the complex organ transplant system. For one, he questioned the fairness of the system by which scarce organs were allocated— namely, to those with money, media-appeal, or political support. For another, he objected to the high rates doctors and hospitals were charging for the procedures. When an organ was rejected, for instance, the doctors might re-transplant, substantially increasing the patient's cost: "The way things are set up, when the doctor reoperates, guess what? He gets another fee."

> The charges, I think, are excessive. Most of the funding for these procedures goes to private individuals that charge full bore and excessive fees. I would have less objection if the money went to the University of Arizona, and the University of Arizona had on its staff a physician that got only a salary for performing procedures, not a fee for each service. You could almost say that, since the surgeons charge a fee for service, they might even have a financial incentive to do more and more procedures.

Does Schaller think organ transplants have become a racket? "It's not a racket," he says, "but the financial part of it has come close to that."

Surgeons disagree with Schaller's characterization of the costs. In a September 15, 1987, television interview during KAET-TV's "Horizon" program, Dr. Lawrence Koep, a liver transplant surgeon in Phoenix, said:

> The vast majority of the cost is hospital-incurred cost. Personnel, drugs, beds, those are where we spend the lion's share of the money. Time in the operating room—these are long operations—that's horribly expensive. The kind of technology available, particularly in the OR [operating room] and the intensive care unit, is just mind-boggling.

According to Icenogle, the University of Arizona actually provides one of the least expensive heart transplants in the country, but the basic truth, he says, is that "some health care is just more expensive than other health care."

> If penicillin were more expensive, then the state legislature would not approve penicillin for pneumonias. Outpatient health care is less expensive than inpatient health care. But what it really comes down to is—is the health care proven, effective, and therapeutic?

In a few rare instances, he says, the University Medical Center has waived costs for patients, but he adds,

> I don't think the University Medical Center can make it a policy to absorb the state's responsibility to take on transplantation. Those kind of dollars do not exist. The hospital is a small hospital, it's only three hundred beds. This place does not have money to throw away.

AHCCCS' TRANSPLANT POLICY UNDER SCHALLER

When Schaller came on board, there was an established procedure for handling organ transplant requests. The patient would submit a request to AHCCCS which would eventually end up on the director's desk. The director would make the final decision either to grant or deny the request. Such decisions had been so infrequent before the mid-1980s that they had not caused much consternation within AHCCCS. But when Schaller became director, the number of transplants—and the amount of money spent on them—began to climb.

In 1984, AHCCCS paid for one heart, one liver, and four kidney transplants. In 1985, the program paid for two heart and sixteen liver transplants. The following year, it was one heart, one liver, seven bone marrow, and twelve kidney transplants.[13] Aggregate costs for heart, liver, bone marrow, and kidney transplants rose from $451,012 in 1984 to $1,060,954 in 1985 to $2,141,663 in 1986. In addition, transplant patients' medical expenses after surgery—even when successful—were chronically high as they needed to take immuno-suppressant drugs, at an average cost of $500 per month, for the rest of their lives.

Schaller began to take a hard look at the transplant requests coming to AHCCCS, and to consider the merits of each. Rep. Resnick recalls:

[There was] one instance—perhaps a rumor—that one of our patients, who ultimately had a liver transplant, needed a new liver because they'd used up the last one with alcohol. And they're quickly on the road to using up the second one. That's difficult for physicians in Dr. Schaller's position to see. First, the transplant is imposed on him, and then he's paying for something [and] perhaps—as he said before—the money could have been used much more wisely someplace else.

Schaller soon discovered, however, that he did not always have clear authority to make decisions about transplant requests. "You've got the legislature pushing on one end, the governor says something else, then you've got a judge that says, 'You've got to do this,'" says Schaller. "You know, we tried to have a policy, but it was hard to implement a single policy and apply it the same across every case." The reality was that AHCCCS made its decisions on a case-by-case basis. Before the state legislature took action on the matter—and before the Dianna Brown case surfaced—AHCCCS confronted several controversial transplant cases. Two, in particular, contributed to the development of the legislature's policy.

SHARON BRIERLEY: A CASE OF POLITICAL PRESSURE

Whenever he did deny a transplant request, Schaller found himself engulfed in a whirlwind of political pressure, sometimes from the legislature, sometimes from the governor, and sometimes even from the White House. In 1984, for example, Schaller ran into trouble when he initially refused the request of forty-one-year-old Sharon Brierley for a liver transplant. Brierley had moved to Tucson four years earlier from Vermont after an unhappy marriage, and before she had established a new career, she began to suffer from cirrhosis of the liver, reportedly caused by a previous bout with hepatitis. When Brierley learned she needed a liver transplant, she appealed to AHCCCS. After reviewing the particulars of her case, Schaller refused Brierley's request. (In the interest of patient confidentiality, Schaller declined to talk about any specific transplant decisions.) Two state legislators intervened on Brierley's behalf. At first Schaller stood firm, but in the end, after "much wrangling and political intercession from the State House to the White House," Brierley's transplant costs were shared by the hospital, AHCCCS, and the federal government.[14]

After the Brierley case, Schaller decided to formalize his transplant policy. Following the lead of the Medicare system,[15] Schaller decided that AHCCCS—again, using its own administrative discretion to determine appropriateness—would cover heart and bone marrow transplants, but would cover liver transplants only for patients under the age of eighteen, for whom survival rates were higher. For patients eighteen and older, Schaller argued, liver transplants were still "experimental" procedures, and thus AHCCCS was under no obligation to provide them.

BARBARA BRILLO: A CASE OF JUDICIAL
PRESSURE

This policy soon received a legal challenge, however, Barbara Brillo, a forty-six-year-old woman, requested a liver transplant early in 1986 and was denied by AHCCCS on grounds that she was too old. Brillo's husband, Jerome, frantically tried to reverse the decision—an effort which ended with several state legislators and a White House aide exerting pressure on AHCCCS. At the same time, he tried to fundraise for his wife. By April, still without the requisite $50,000 needed for preliminary tests at the liver transplant center at Phoenix's Good Samaritan Hospital, and with Barbara Brillo's life expectancy down to one or two months, Jerome Brillo arranged for his wife to travel to a Pittsburgh center. "Down deep, I really thought they would come through for us eventually," he told the *Arizona Star* (April 11, 1986). "But, as the weeks went by, my hopes got dimmer. Yes, I'm bitter, because you know what? This could happen to anyone. And believe me, if you don't have the $50,000 (down payment), you're nowhere."

Schaller continued to defend his decision, and to feel the heat for it. In a July 7, 1986, interview on KAET-TV's "Horizon" program, Brillo's attorney, Howard Baldwin, asked, "Why should we pay $110,000 for Don Schaller's salary when we could use that money to provide medical care? Or why should we have a PR man for AHCCCS? It always troubles me to find people fighting for principles over other people's bodies."

After a rancorous court battle, Brillo won her case in the summer of 1986 on grounds that the surgery was medically necessary and was not properly considered experimental. AHCCCS was forced to fund her liver transplant, which had been carried out in Pittsburgh in the interim. Within AHCCCS, "the [Brillo] court decision really precipitated a lot of discussion," says Lowenberg.

I think what that did is showed us how vulnerable we were going to be to make policy on what's covered and not—and just from the real practical standpoint, as an agency—how do you budget that? What you soon learn is that you really don't have control, because [if you deny patients], they're going to take it to court, and you don't know how the judge is going to rule. In this case, we lost.

In fact, as AHCCCS would write in a report to the legislature the following spring:

Although the courts, including the Supreme Court, has stated that the states have wide discretion in determining the scope of benefits that they will provide under Medicaid,[16] several courts have held that a particular organ transplant must be covered, since it was determined to be medically necessary under the circumstances.

The report also stated that although no state policy would be "foolproof in the absence of federal law," AHCCCS's counsel advised that at the least, "a statutory amendment will be required to effectively exclude coverage of organ transplants for medically needy persons, indigent persons, and eligible children." Thus, AHCCCS decided to ask the legislature to enact a state transplant policy into law. The next question: exactly what kind of law did AHCCCS want to recommend to the legislature?

CREATING THE NEW POLICY

During the summer of 1986, Schaller and a group of his top administrators began to discuss various policy options. These discussions were fairly freewheeling, according to Lowenberg, with administrators tossing out a number of possibilities. He recalls:

We started to get into [ideas like], "Well, we'll cover *one* heart transplant, but we won't cover *two* heart transplants"—in other words, if the [first transplant fails and the] person needs another one. [But] what's the rationale for drawing the line [there]?

So early on, the AHCCCS team began to consider a blanket policy: no transplants, period, a position also favored initially by the governor's staff. But, Lowenberg says, the AHCCCS administrators soon convinced themselves that this approach did not really make any sense either:

> Initially it was—either you have transplants or you don't—because when you start making exceptions, then it becomes more and more difficult to draw the line. . . . Then, of course, we began to look at the kidney and say, "Well, wait a minute, that doesn't make sense for the kidney or the cornea."

So Schaller and the AHCCCS team began to consider a policy to fund kidney, cornea, and bone transplants, but no other kind of organ transplants. This, they argued, was easily defensible, because kidney, cornea, and bone transplants were significantly different medically and economically from transplant of heart, liver, and bone marrow. In the case of corneas and bone transplants, the procedures were simple, there was no tissue match, and they could be performed at many health care establishments.

In addition, these procedures seemed to meet the "cost-benefit" test: "For the eye implant, it was [a question:] do we allow the person to be on [the] SSI Disabled [list]? Is that in the best interests of the public, that the person becomes blind and cannot work and must be supported by either the state or the federal government?" says Lowenberg.

Kidneys were different from other major organs in that they did not require the donor's death, and were, in fact, often donated by relatives of the patients. Questions of speed, timing, and tissue match were therefore removed from the equation. What's more, though not cheap, kidney transplants were less expensive over time than the alternative—dialysis treatment. AHCCCS discovered that on average, dialysis cost $2500 per month while the average kidney transplant cost $68,000. Thus, "the 'break-even point' economically justifying kidney transplants may be after two years and three months," AHCCCS wrote in a report to the legislature. Heart, liver, and bone marrow

transplants were in a whole different league, however, in terms of cost and complexity as were new transplant procedures for the pancreas or heart-and-lung.

After some consideration, AHCCCS did recommend, in the form of its budget request, that the legislature fund only kidney, cornea, and bone transplants—but, cautions Lowenberg, "I think it's real important to understand that we didn't present necessarily a 'policy.' We presented [that] this is an issue that you at the legislature and governor's office need to decide."

LEONARD KIRSCHNER'S VIEW

Schaller left AHCCCS to become a private consultant in January of 1987 and was succeeded the following month by Leonard Kirschner, a physician who, most recently, had served as the medical director of an HMO in Phoenix that treated AHCCCS patients.

Although Kirschner came to AHCCCS after the agency had already submitted a recommendation to the legislature, he quickly got behind the proposal: "Philosophically, I was already in agreement with them," he says. Kirschner's reasoning about the issue, however, was somewhat different from Schaller's. To the incoming director, "aggregate costs" were the major concern, and spending dollars where they would do the most good. A physician with twenty-two years of service in the military, Kirschner believed that—like the triage practiced on the battlefield—a public program with limited resources must establish clear priorities for treatment. Thus, he favored broadbased health care for the poor over organ transplant coverage. "You take a high risk population that gets no prenatal care—the teenage pregnancy out of the barrio, doesn't want anybody to know she's pregnant, doesn't take care of herself, is on alcohol, and tobacco, or maybe drugs—the risk of low birth weight is up to about 18 percent," he says.

> What's the cost to society for that bad baby? Neonatal intensive care unit costs for that

baby are probably going to be in the range of $40,000. And to boot, what you are met with on the outside as that child grows up frequently is residual damage from that premature birth: low IQ, low lifetime learning expectancy, won't be able to function, mental retardation, seizures—all the bad things that happen from low birth weight.

So where do you want to spend your money? Do I want to spend my money on doing eight heart transplants at a million and a half dollars? Or go out and get more of these poor people who are not getting prenatal care, and give them some prenatal care? That's about $2000 a case. What's $2000 into a million five? 700 cases? What about 700 deliveries for eight heart transplants?

"This is probably going to make me sound like Attila the Hun," Kirschner adds, but "when I have limited resources, it's women and children first. The *Titanic* concept of medicine."

More broadly, Kirschner believes that the trend toward high-tech medicine is a bad one, not just from a financial point of view but also from a human one. "A young man I was peripherally involved with a year ago had a bone marrow transplant and then went into bone marrow rejection, which is a horrible experience. He died a horrible death," he says. "Obviously spending all those resources and causing him a death far worse than he would have had from the disease makes one sit there and say, 'Well, why in the world did I do that to that person?'

Every time we bring a new person into the world, we accept the fact that that person's going to die, and we're almost reaching the point in society where we want to repeal that biological fact.

Now if there's an individual who does have those resources and wants to purchase that, we live in a capitalist society. So be it. But in a public program, that has the widest range of responsibilities, and limited resources to handle those responsibilities, I think it's unacceptable to use those limited resources in a way that really doesn't further the public good.

LEGISLATIVE ACTION IN THE SPRING OF 1987

The legislature—which meets in regular session for only one hundred days a year in Arizona—confronted major budget difficulties during its 1987 session. Conservative Republican Governor Evan Mecham had just taken office and had come to the legislature with an extremely lean budget. At the same time, the state was dealing with a budget overrun from the preceding year, and the legislature was making some midyear corrections to make up the difference. "So agencies, including ourselves, had to accept serious cutbacks," says AHCCCS's Lowenberg.

What's more, the legislature had to make a number of major budgetary decisions about the AHCCCS program in 1987. The whole program, enacted for five years as a "demonstration," was scheduled to end in October unless the legislature voted to extend it. In addition, the legislature was considering proposals to add services to AHCCCS, including long-term health care, provided at that time by county governments, and service to pregnant women and children between the ages of six and thirteen in the notch group—at that time, not offered at all.

Health care committees in both the House and Senate came up with versions of the omnibus AHCCCS bill. In the Senate discussion, the chair of the Health and Welfare Committee—Senator Greg Lunn (R-Tucson)—played a significant role. Lunn was a moderate young Republican, especially interested in environmental matters, who had come to office in 1981 from a career in broadcast journalism. He was known as an articulate rising young star whose district included the University of Arizona and its Medical Center. Upon learning that the legislature might defund organ transplants, the Medical Center urged its state senator to preserve funding for heart transplants. Lunn found the university's arguments convincing, and, likewise, convinced his colleagues in the Senate to include funding for heart transplants—but not for liver or bone marrow transplants—in the AHCCCS budget. His reason, he says, was "basically twofold":

I thought that relative to the other major categories of transplantation that we were, in essence, precluding payment for in the future—liver transplants and bone marrow transplants—that heart had shown a greater rate of success in terms of the success of the procedure itself, longevity, and the quality of life associated after a successful procedure was done.[17] Additionally, I was certainly persuaded by the fact that I believe we have one of the pre-eminent centers for heart transplantation here in the state at the University of Arizona Medical Center, and I thought it was in the interests of that facility and the research they were doing that AHCCCS continue to be a payer.

When the bill moved to the House Health Committee, the question of organ transplants received little consideration, however, and the committee opted for the recommendation of AHCCCS's administration. The two versions of the AHCCCS bill, with assorted differences, then went to the House-Senate conference committee on health care, also chaired by Lunn, for final negotiations.

THE CONFERENCE COMMITTEE
RESOLUTION

When the AHCCCS bills reached the conference committee, the Senate bill included coverage for heart transplantation and also for psychotropic drugs, another expensive item. The House bill included neither of these items, but did include a significant expansion of coverage for the notch group.[18] "As in any conference committee procedure, you end up assuming that those elements that are consistent are in the bill, and then you argue about the differences," says Lunn. Within the conference committee, therefore, the transplant debate was narrowed to the question of whether or not to fund heart transplants.

Dr. Jack Copeland, the head of the U of A's heart transplant center, weighed in with a letter to the committee. The U of A had performed a total of 125 heart transplants, he wrote. During the past three years, AHCCCS had funded five heart transplants and one artificial heart ("bridge-to-transplant") procedure. "Five of these patients are doing well and living a high quality of life, and the bridge-to-transplant patient has returned to full-time employment. We currently have two AHCCCS patients needing heart transplants who are being evaluated and we project there will be five or six AHCCCS patients per year." Copeland then offered some economic arguments for funding hearts transplants:

For most of our patients (married males, less than fifty years of age with pre-school or teenage children), the major reasons for undergoing cardiac transplantation were to maintain some semblance of family stability and to resume competitive employment. Our patients are generally referred for vocational rehabilitation and one third have returned to work within six months of transplantation.

Copeland argued that even if AHCCCS refused a patient a transplant, it would have to continue to provide some health care to the person while s/he continued to deteriorate and die. Heart transplants were only performed in dire cases—where the patient's life expectancy was less than twelve months—but those health care costs could still run quite high. He wrote that on average, "according to the National Heart Transplant Study, the cost difference between a patient who is transplanted and one who is not is approximately $6,100"—not much money in the scheme of things. Copeland added:

Should the nontransplanted patient die leaving a wife and three children (aged five, ten, and fifteen), the family becomes eligible for monthly social security benefits approximating $1036 which payments continue until the youngest child reaches the age of eighteen or until age twenty-one for all three children should they pursue college educations.

Copeland also included cost estimates for heart transplants ($65,000 to $80,000) in his letter, and mentioned that his center was likely to become one of ten approved transplant centers across the country designated by Medicare and therefore approved treatment facilities for Medicare patients.

These last two points aroused the anger and concern of AHCCCS administrators. For one, they felt Copeland had vastly underestimated the true cost of an average heart transplant (which they calculated to be $165,000).[19] In addition, they saw the emergence of the U of A as a nationally recognized transplant center to be a double-edged sword: in increasing numbers, patients would move to the state to receive medical treatment, and if they established residency and were income eligible, AHCCCS would have to pay for them. Already, two such patients had surfaced, according to Schaller, who appeared before the conference committee as a consultant to the committee:

> We're finding ourselves as a state paying for patients who move in from Idaho and California with no ability to go back to those states and collect from their Medicaid agencies our costs. That's one of the reasons I don't think we ought to pay for this, because if we're going to be attracting people from all over the country who are so impressed with Dr. Copeland's ability, I'm wondering who's gong to pay for 'em. If he wants to be a regional center, let him go out and collect his money from everybody in the region—not AHCCCS.

Furthermore, AHCCCS warned that if the program began to cover each transplant requested, it would not be long before most health insurance carriers would cease to consider transplants as a covered benefit on the theory that AHCCCS (and the taxpayers) is the paying alternative."

AHCCCS also confronted the committee with another problem: The Health Care Financing Administration. While HCFA had been willing in the past to provide extra funding for transplants on a case-by-case basis, the federal agency decided in 1986 that this arrangement was not in keeping with the spirit of the groundrules of the AHCCCS-Medicaid experiment. Thus, HCFA wanted the costs of the transplants to be covered the way any other medical costs were covered—out of the basic capitation rate given to the state. In a letter to AHCCCS dated October 17, 1986, HCFA wrote that "the state will include all organ transplant costs in the base computations used to determine capitation rates for categorically eligible AHCCCS recipients, and HCFA will not provide a regular federal match based on actual organ transplant costs for these procedures on an individual basis." Paul Lichtenstein, federal project officer for AHCCCS under HCFA's Office of Research and Development, says that HCFA would have been more than willing to increase the capitation rate to reflect the cost of transplants for Medicaid-eligible people. But according to Lowenberg, it is not reasonable to try to work such changeable and erratic costs into a standard formula: "It's our viewpoint that with such a low-volume, high price type of incident, i.e., transplant, it doesn't make sense to attempt to include it in a capitation. . . . Capitation is never going to cover all the costs. Never."

This legislative tug-of-war over funding for heart transplants ended with a decision that heart transplants *might* be funded in part, but only if HCFA relented and agreed to share the costs on a case-by-case basis. Says Lunn:

> It ended in a compromise. A lot of people would have just as soon not had [heart transplants] in there at all. I would have just as soon had [them] in there [unconditionally] as an AHCCCS-covered service. So—just tire people out, that's the way—we never finished the bill. When we *abandoned* the bill, that's what it looked like.
>
> Ultimately, everything [in dispute between House and Senate committees] went in the bill, but modified. The way hearts got modified was squirrelly language about "if HCFA

agrees to paying for it the way we would like them to participate, then we'll go ahead and do it." Psychotropics got modified by saying, "subject to legislative appropriation," so it wasn't an entitlement—it was, we'll fight that out when we come to the Appropriations Committee next year. And the notch group stuff was modified by putting it off a year, to a later effective date. It was like trying to fit an elephant through a keyhole. You had to push it in different places to get it to fit.

My recollection is that [the heart transplant compromise] was proposed by AHCCCS itself. I think they probably were much more aware than I at the time of the chances of convincing Health Care Financing Administration to go along on that basis were pretty damned small, because that seems to be the case now. So I think, in retrospect, I may have been snookered.

Another member of the conference committee—Rep. Resnick—characterizes the legislature's negotiations over AHCCCS as "raw politics," primarily focused on the question of funding for pregnant women and children in the notch group. Resnick, who had been in the legislature since 1983, was a liberal Democrat from Tucson who had become active in health policy matters in 1980, when she joined a coalition working to bring Medicaid to Arizona. Like most Democrats, Resnick had initially opposed establishment of AHCCCS in favor of a more comprehensive, conventional Medicaid program. Once the AHCCCS program was in place, however, she and other Democrats had worked to make it as comprehensive as possible. During the 1987 session, the Democrats drew a line in the sand: without the notch group extension, they would vote against extending AHCCCS beyond October. The strategy, says Resnick, ultimately worked; the notch group expansion was included.

The legislative vote on the final omnibus AHCCCS bill—including both the notch group coverage and the transplant policy—was overwhelming: 44 to 6, with 10 not voting in the House; 23 to 2 with 5 not voting in the Senate. But, with so much emphasis

on the notch group coverage and the general extension of AHCCCS, this vote did not reflect legislative opinion on the transplant issue per se, according to Resnick:

There is such a select group in the legislature that actually dealt with the AHCCCS issues— there were probably eight of us at the most, and then probably only three to four of us who were intimately involved with the discussion. I don't think [the others] considered [transplants one way or the other.] In the broad scheme of things, the bill looked okay.

In any event, under the terms of the AHCCCS bill, the new transplant policy took effect August 18, 1987. Within the month, the case of Dianna Brown surfaced.

DIANNA BROWN'S STORY

Dianna Brown, forty-three, was a woman from the city of Yuma with lupoid hepatitis, an ailment which had shrunk her liver so that she could not process liquids properly. She had been nearly incapacitated since January of 1985, when her illness forced her to quit her job as manager of a doughnut shop. "I noticed I couldn't pick up anything from the counters," she told the Arizona Republic.[20] At one point, she remembers, "I nearly fell into the fryer."

"I said, 'I'm going to have to take a leave of absence until I get better.' But then I never got better. I only got worse."

Born in Texas, Brown had quit school at a young age to support her family, and by the summer of 1987, virtually everyone in her immediate family had serious health problems. Her mother was living in a nursing home. Brown had been caring for her niece's two children ever since her niece had suffered brain damage in a car accident. Her sister had recently suffered a heart attack.

"If a transplant isn't necessary, I don't want it," Brown told the Arizona Republic in an interview printed September 7, 1987. "But if it is the only solution, I would like a chance for a chance." She said that she hoped "to work again": "That is a dream off in the future. Surely there is something

I can do. I might not be able to work with my hands like I used to, but I'm sure I still could do something.

"I can understand that you have to look at the overall picture. I always try to understand. I can't say I always do—Lord knows I don't—but I try."

Four days later, the *Republic* reported that the husband of a woman who had undergone a successful liver transplant had started a transplant fund for Brown with $35,000 left over from their family's fundraising effort. A radio talk-show host joined the effort, and within a few days had increased the sum to $37,000. But it was too little too late. On September 11, Brown's kidneys began to fail, preventing her body from eliminating toxins. This led to brain damage, coma, and eventual liver failure. On September 14, she died. "I don't think her death was unreasonably painful or prolonged," her personal physician, Dr. George Burdick, told the *Republic* the next day, "but in my mind it was unnecessary."

Brown's family did not even have enough money for her funeral.

THE AFTERMATH OF DIANNA BROWN'S DEATH

When Dianna Brown died, the press began to reconstruct the legislature's policy decision of the previous spring, and in general, reporters and some legislators characterized it as a conscious "tradeoff" between transplants and the notch group expansion. Some observers and participants, however, believe this represents a rewriting of history. "That argument is just a whitewash," says Icenogle. "What we're talking about here is a legislature that just doesn't want to come up with money, period. And this is their way of trying to defuse the issue."

Rep. Resnick agrees that the legislature was not really trading services. "That's how the press perceived it, and maybe they were not totally wrong, but from my perspective, we weren't making a trade." Instead, she says, dropping funding for transplants was a quick way to respond to Schaller's concern "that the thing was out of control." Other legislators agreed that they relied heavily on AHCCCS's recommendation in making their transplant policy. Says Lunn, "You try to listen to medical experts in terms of what is reasonable and what is cost-effective and what makes sense from a medical standpoint."

"Our legislative session is only one hundred days," adds Resnick, "so it's difficult to say, 'Let's talk about it during the session.' It was easier just to say, 'Let's drop authority for AHCCCS to provide these transplants and then let's re-look at the issue.' No one ever thought that we would just drop it and never deal with transplants."

Resnick saw the transplant debate as part of a larger set of issues. Rather than make an "up" or "down" decision on funding organ transplants under AHCCCS, she believed the legislature should stand back, take a broader view, and "deal with the issue of catastrophic health care."

> We ought to make the health system responsive to those kinds of needs, but it isn't necessarily the AHCCCS system. It isn't necessarily a program for the poor that ought to be responding to that.
>
> What I don't want to see is that we change state policy, allowing more flexibility in the AHCCCS program, without addressing all the other issues related to that decision, without discussing the ramifications of having too many hospitals doing heart transplants, without discussing ramifications related to the insurance industry, which will—if there's somebody out there who's going to pay for these services—back down real quick in providing those for their own clients. So my preference would be that we discuss it all at the same time. Otherwise you get a really bad decision.

Other legislators focused primarily on the financial aspect of the question, and the issue of fairness to individuals in need of transplants. AHCCCS's refusal to fund Brown's transplant was "asinine," "grossly discriminating," and "embarrassing," ac-

EXHIBIT 1. ARIZONA HEALTH CARE COST CONTAINMENT SYSTEM ADMINISTRATION

Human Organ Transplants	Fiscal 1986-1987[a]			Program Change			Fiscal 1987-1988 Request		
	Number	Cost Per	Amount	Number	Cost Per	Amount	Number	Cost Per	Amount
Heart Transplants	0	0	0	8	164,000	1,312,000	8	164,000	1,312,000
Liver Transplants	1	134,000	134,000	5	134,000	670,000	6	268,000	804,000
Bone Marrow Transplants	1	230,000	230,000	7	230,000	1,610,000	8	460,000	1,840,000
Totals	2		364,000	20		3,592,000	22		3,956,000

a. For fiscal 1986-1987, transplants are paid as inpatient hospital in the Fee-for-Service category. Number and costs are estimated as transplant bills have not been submitted at the date of this budget request.

EXHIBIT 2. ARIZONA HEALTH CARE COST CONTAINMENT SYSTEM

MEMORANDUM

TO: Leonard J. Kirchner, M.S., M.P.H.
          Director

FROM: Bill Merrick, Assistant Director
          Division of Financial Management

SUBJECT: Expansion of the Children's Program to Include Age Six (6) through Thirteen (13)

DATE: March 23, 1987

Before going on to the numbers, I calculated the fiscal impact for nine (9) months beginning October 1, 1987, and six (6) months beginning on January 1, 1988. These breaks logically follow our contracting cycle. In my opinion, it would not be cost effective to start the program on July 1, 1987 as AHCCCS would need to bid this population for the period July 1, 1987 to September 30, 1987.

Now the numbers:

	Number of Children	Total	State	Federal
Nine (9) months beginning October 1, 1987	27,000	$10,304,400	$8,449,800	$1,854,600
Six (6) months beginning January 1, 1988	26,200	$ 6,800,500	$5,576,400	$1,224,100

For the purpose of comparison, I also calculated the fiscal impact of just adding the six (6) year olds by the nine (9) and six (6) month breaks.

	Number of Children	Total	State	Federal
Nine (9) months beginning October 1, 1987	4,250	$ 1,708,628	$1,401,075	$307,553
Six (6) months beginning January 1, 1988	4,023	$ 1,078,155	$ 895,009	$183,146

Should you have any questions, just give me a buzz.

---

cording to Rep. Earl Wilcox (D-Phoenix), a member of the House Health Committee. "If we don't make taking care of this problem a priority in our next session, we'll be remiss as legislators."[21]

"It's not a comfortable decision that we had to make," says Senate Minority Leader Alan Stephens (D-Phoenix). "Unfortunately, you have to look at it in the context of Arizona state government."

It's been a battle in this state, in a conservative era, to increase services. And we do it on a piecemeal basis. If you want to look at people's deaths, and the case of Mrs. Brown obviously comes to mind in this situation, but if you went back, I'm sure you could find a lot of people that died in this state as a result of not getting care that's routinely given in other states, because we didn't provide the service that other states provide.

But other legislators stood by their decision. "None of us can live forever," said Sen. Doug Todd (R-Tempe). "I think it was a decision that was made by the legislative body to benefit the most residents of the state of Arizona."[22]

"The public generally is not willing to, say, double the taxes in this state to insure that everyone got the maximum possible health care—the public isn't willing to accept that," stated Rep. Bill English (R-Sierra Vista) in an interview aired September 15, 1987 on KAET-TV's "Horizon" program. While he defended the legislature's decision to defund transplants, however, he left open the possibility of changing the decision in the future:

I'm going to say that next year, the decision may very appropriately be a different decision, with progress in the state of the art [of transplantation]. What is the right decision for today may not be the right decision for tomorrow.

NOTES

1. The legislature had already voted to cover notch group children under age six the year before.

2. In January 1987, AHCCCS's income eligibility cut-off for a family of four was $5,354, while the federal poverty level for a family of four was $13,750. Advocates for the poor estimated that fully two-thirds of Arizona's poor were not eligible for the AHCCCS program.

3. More recently, parts of Indiana have also chosen to exempt themselves from the law.

4. *Evaluation of the Arizona Health Care Cost Containment System*, by Nelda McCall, project director, and Paul Lichtenstein, federal project officer, Office of Research and Demonstrations, HCFA, Department of Health and Human Services, June 1987.

5. HMOs were not expected to finance catastrophic health care, however; thus the relatively exorbitant costs were assumed by AHCCCS. For instance, if any individual's costs exceeded a set amount per year—typically $20,000—then the HMO would be responsible for only a small percentage of the excess; the bulk of the cost would be paid by AHCCCS.

6. This "capitation rate" was to be 95 percent of what HCFA projected it would have paid the state under a conventional Medicaid program (which would have been 60 percent of costs for all Medicaid-eligible residents).

7. Long-term care was still to be provided county-by-county.

8. Of those people, 127,983 were either AFDC or SSI recipients, and thus automatically eligible for federal reimbursement. Another 51,770 were in roughly the same income range, but were not ADFC or SSI recipients; these people were not eligible for federal reimbursement. In addition, 20,716 AHCCCS recipients were children under age six from notch group families.

9. *Report of the Massachusetts Task Force on Organ Transplantation*, presented to the Massachusetts Commissioner of Public Health and the state's Secretary of Human Services in October 1984.

10. Those waiting in line for a suitable donor organ and ready for surgery at any time.

11. AHCCCS did its own informal survey of some twelve HMOs and insurance companies in the state, and found that while many offered some kind of coverage for transplants, they sometimes imposed limits on them as well. For instance, eight of the companies surveyed offered coverage for heart transplants, but one of the eight had a "cap" on the total amount it

would spend and one said its decisions would be based on its own assessment of the individual's case. Thus, in reality, half the companies offered unlimited coverage and half offered limited coverage or none at all.

12. By fall of 1987, no one had traced the impact of deregulation of transplants per se, but a *Phoenix Gazette* reporter, Brad Patten, did a survey of hospitals performing by-pass surgery published on August 26, 1987, and found that: ten hospitals had begun performing by-pass surgery since deregulation; the number of open heart surgeries was up 36 percent from 1983 to 1986, but the number performed per hospital was down 85 percent; hospitals performing a relatively low volume of by-pass operations had a death rate twice that of hospitals performing a high volume of such procedures; and that overall, the death rate for Medicaid patients in by-pass procedures had increased 35 percent in Arizona between 1984 and 1986.

13. Of the forty-five patients to receive these transplants between 1984 and 1986, nine died within a few months of surgery.

14. *Arizona Daily Star*, May 29, 1986.

15. Medicare tends to be a standard-bearer for states in determining which procedures are considered "experimental" and which are regarded as standard medical care. Health care providers and insurers are under no obligation to provide "experimental" care to patients.

16. AHCCCS administrators found that, by 1986, thirty-three states were paying for liver transplants, twenty-four for hearts, thirteen for hearts-and-lungs, and three for pancreases.

17. This view of transplants was not uniformly held. Leonard Kirschner, for instance, argued that on purely medical grounds, he found liver and bone marrow transplants for children to be the most successful and defensible procedures.

18. According to Bill Merrick, assistant director of AHCCCS's Division of Financial Management, health care for some 26,200 notch group children under six between January 1, 1987, and June 30, 1987, was expected to total $6.8 million (with HCFA paying $1.2 million). He estimated that to serve 27,000 children aged six to thirteen from October 1, 1987, to June 30, 1988, would cost $10 million—with HCFA picking up about $1.9 million. (See Exhibit 1.)

19. In fact, the AHCCCS administrators showed the committee that in another context, the university itself had estimated the cost of a heart transplant at $153 million. That cost-estimate included hospitalization as well as twenty-four months of drugs and follow-up care, however.

20. "Patient doomed by policy; AHCCCS refuses to fund transplant," by Martin Van Der Werf, *Arizona Republic*, September 7,1987.

21. *Arizona Republic*, Sept. 16, 1987.

22. Ibid.

AIDS Testing in the D.C.

Leslie Brunetta

In November 1985, District of Columbia councilmember John Ray (D-at large) introduced a bill that would have imposed a five-year moratorium on all kinds of applicant AIDS-testing in the district by health, life, and disability insurers. Ray wrote the bill (entitled the Prohibition of Discrimination in the Provision of Insurance Act) after learning that insurers were testing for antibodies to the AIDS virus in order to predict who would come down with the fatal disease. He believed insurers had panicked, and were using a test whose accuracy and predictive value hadn't yet been properly established—the test had been FDA-approved just the previous March, and exclusively for blood bank screening and research at that. Ray thought that use of such unproven tests constituted civil rights discrimination against applicants because it didn't conform to standard insurance underwriting practices.

Five years, Ray figured, would allow time for the tests to be refined and for solid actuarial data to be collected. At that point, insurers would be able to make reasonable predictions about applicants' future health and to decide fairly whether to charge increased premiums when a test indicated infection with the AIDS virus. In the meantime, insurers would be allowed to deny insurance coverage to applicants actually diagnosed as suffering full-blown AIDS, just as they were allowed to deny coverage to applicants diagnosed as suffering from cancer, heart disease, or diabetes.

If the council passed Ray's bill, the district would become the only jurisdiction in the United States to outlaw all kinds of AIDS-testing by insurers.

THE AIDS EPIDEMIC

Representatives from the district's gay rights groups were the ones first to tell John Ray about AIDS testing by insurance companies in the district. They had reason to be concerned: the burden of the AIDS epidemic had so far fallen heaviest on gay men. Of the 13,611 AIDS cases reported to the United States Centers for Disease Control (CDC) by October 1985, 78 percent had been homosexual or bi-sexual men.

Acquired immune deficiency syndrome (AIDS) was generally believed to be caused by infection with the human immunodeficiency virus (HIV), which had been shown to destroy white blood cells known as T-lymphocytes in laboratory tests. The destruction of these cells severely damaged a person's immune system, making him or her susceptible to infections and cancers normally vanquished by a healthy immune system. These opportunistic infections or neurological disorders caused by HIV were what usually killed AIDS patients, most often within two years of AIDS diagnosis. Although there were treatments that could help some AIDS patients overcome bouts of *Pneumocystis carinii* pneumonia and slow the progress of Kaposi's sarcoma (two of the otherwise-rare diseases commonly attacking AIDS sufferers), there was no cure for AIDS itself.

HIV passed from one person to another via blood or semen—through anal, vaginal, or perhaps oral sex, the sharing of needles by intravenous drug users, or transfusions of contaminated blood or blood products. HIV infection affected different people in different ways. Many people infected with the virus showed no symptoms. Some had

Reprinted by permission of the Case Program, Kennedy School of Government, Harvard University. Copyright 1988 by the President and Fellows of Harvard College.

swollen lymph nodes but felt fine. Others suffered from AIDS-related complex (ARC)—they had fevers, diarrhea, and swollen lymph nodes, but didn't meet the clinical criteria for AIDS diagnosis. Researchers didn't know whether these conditions were just way stations along an ineluctable drive ending in full-blown AIDS, but many suspected that this was true. (In fact, some people died of ARC without ever having met the criteria for AIDS diagnosis.)

As of mid-1986, there were 1 million to 1.5 million people in the United States infected with HIV, according to US Public Health Service (PHS) estimates. How many of those people would eventually be diagnosed as suffering from AIDS was a matter of some uncertainty in 1986: the PHS anticipated that 20 to 30 percent of infected people would go on to develop the syndrome within five years, while the Institute of Medicine and National Academy of Sciences Epidemiology Working Group estimated that 25 to 50 percent would be diagnosed as suffering from AIDS within five to ten years. Other experts made even higher estimates, predicting that in the long run the fatality rate might approach 100 percent.

Further PHS estimates were similarly disheartening. By the end of 1991, less than a decade after the disease was first defined, 270,000 people in the US would have suffered from full-blown AIDS, they predicted. Of that total, 174,000 would be alive and in need of some kind of care during 1991. By the end of that year, the US would have had a cumulative total of more than 179,000 deaths, with 54,000 of those occurring during the year.

By the time John Ray's bill was making its way through council committee hearings, the district had already begun to feel the impact of the AIDS epidemic. The district's Commission of Public Health had counted 349 diagnosed AIDS cases from September 1980 through March 1986, and 191 of those people had died. The CDC calculated that the district, along with California, Florida, New York, and Texas, had one of the five highest rates of HIV infection in the country.

AIDS exacted not only a heavy human toll but also a heavy financial one. Estimates current in 1986 were that total hospital costs for each AIDS patient from diagnosis to death ranged from $50,000 to $150,000. These figures were considered likely to change significantly with the advent of new treatments (which could increase life expectancy and hence costs) and with the institution of lower cost hospice or community care for patients well enough to avoid hospitalization.

The question of who actually paid these costs generated immense speculation. The medical and general press reported various estimates of who was picking up the tab. Some experts said commercial insurers were paying 70 percent of the bill and Medicaid 20 percent, others that commercial insurers were paying 20 percent and Medicaid 70 percent, and others floated every other ratio in between. The true figures were nearly impossible to determine because there was no universal system for either billing or reporting AIDS costs.

TESTING

The AIDS screening tests used by insurers employed relatively new knowledge and techniques gained from the fields of biochemistry and biotechnology. Because the virus itself was difficult to detect, they tested for the presence in the blood of antibody to HIV. The tests involved a series of steps requiring the conscientious attention of lab technicians. And their results were open to divergent interpretation.

The Food and Drug Administration had approved the ELISA (enzyme-linked immunosorbent assay) technique in March 1985 for blood bank screening use. It was relatively easy to use, relatively inexpensive, and quite accurate. But it was not entirely reliable. Blood samples testing positive with the ELISA were therefore routinely retested. If the result was again positive, the blood sample was retested again using the more elaborate Western blot procedure. This test was labor intensive and relatively expensive, and no standard interpretation of its results existed. Scientific opinion on how the test's results should be interpreted shifted with some frequency.

Both the ELISA and the Western blot were often described as being about 99 percent accurate. But in reality, judging their performance was more complicated than pinpointing a single accuracy figure. Medical screening tests were generally evaluated on their "sensitivity" and "specificity." "Sensitivity" was the probability that a test would give a positive result for a person who was actually positive. Test specificity was the probability that a test would give a negative result for a person who was actually negative. Subtracting the specificity rate from 100 percent gave the "false positive rate"—the rate at which people who were truly negative tested positive.

Determining sensitivity and specificity ratings for the ELISA and the Western blot proved a demanding, and often contentious, occupation. The lack of a "gold standard" against which to judge the tests' results presented the greatest obstacle. It was often difficult to isolate actual HIV in AIDS patients, so that it was impossible to independently verify positive ELISAs or Western blots. In practice, sensitivity was calculated by finding the number of positive test results among diagnosed AIDS patients. Specificity was found by counting the number of negative test results among a group of random blood donors who were assumed not to have been infected with HIV. At the time the FDA granted it a license, the most widely used ELISA had a published sensitivity of 93.4 percent and specificity of 99.78 percent. The latter indicated a false positive rate of about two in 1000. (ELISA sensitivity and specificity were found by the accepted protocol of repeating the test on any blood sample initially found positive;

that is, a positive test was one that had tested positive twice.) The Western blot, a technique rather than a packaged device like the ELISA, didn't require an FDA license for use, so it had no published ratings. Trials conducted by the College of American Pathologists found Western blot sensitivity of 90.7 percent and specificity of 95.3 percent.

TESTING CONCERNS

So long as the ELISA and the Western blot were being used just to screen blood donations, not a great deal of controversy about either their employment or accuracy arose. Because false negative results could lead to the use of infected blood, they were all but eliminated by sliding the ELISA cut-point in the direction of heightened sensitivity. The increased false positive rate meant only that some blood donations were needlessly, but prudently, discarded.

But questions surfaced when life and health insurers began to predict which applicants were likely to sustain substantial medical costs or to die before their premiums had paid for their benefits. From the insurance industry's standpoint, testing for the HIV-antibody was no different from testing already done to determine which insurance applicants were prone to heart disease, diabetes, or other life-threatening and expensive disorders.

The district's gay community, and gay rights organizations across the country, reacted strongly. Fearful of increased discrimination, they saw testing as part of a larger social tendency to "blame the victims" of the epidemic, and thereby to isolate and stigmatize them. "A positive test result, if disseminated, is like being branded with a yellow star," Mark Senak, legal director of Gay Men's Health Crisis told the *New York Times*, when asked about his objections to AIDS testing anywhere in the nation. "It not only marks an individual as uninsurable, but can have a devastating impact on that person's ability to obtain housing, employment, and financial services."

Dissemination of results seemed a real possibility to gay advocates. Insurance companies shared information such as medical examination results through the Medical Information Bureau, a central clearinghouse designed to combat applicant fraud. The bureau's records could be subpoenaed by government agencies. Advocates also worried that insurance agents might divulge test results, particularly to employers, who would have an interest in positive results, especially if they shared responsibility for paying employees' medical benefits.

Gay advocates believed that, ever since insurance companies had become aware of the AIDS epidemic, they had been denying insurance coverage to certain kinds of male applicants in some neighborhoods in order to avoid taking on homosexual policy holders. Such practices were called "redlining" after some banks' practice of not issuing mortgages in poor black neighborhoods which had been literally outlined in red on lending officers' maps. In testimony given to the district's council, Steve Smith, a member of the DC Committee on AIDS Issues, said that insurance industry sources had leaked information concerning such practices: "Some companies will attempt specifically to exclude gay men by examining a number of factors, including marital status, relationship to beneficiary, and the observations of sales agents. Some companies propose redlining larger demographic groups in which AIDS cases occur, such as unmarried men aged twenty to fifty living in certain zip code areas."

The insurance industry denied such practices, and argued that, in any case, antibody testing would eliminate even the temptation to redline: testing all applicants offered a much more accurate and fair method of predicting who was at risk. Here, epidemiologists and other medical experts joined the fray. Even though the ELISA and Western blot were very accurate tests, false positive results would always be a possibility. And the proportion of apparent positives who

were false positives would rise when testing a population having a relatively low true positive rate—for instance, the population applying for insurance policies. Some experts calculated that in a population having the same infection prevalence rate as that estimated for American blood donors, as many as 22 percent of confirmed positive results would be false positives. Testing opponents asked whether such a false positive rate—and the loss of insurance coverage and possible fear, loss of security, and discrimination resulting from false positive results—could be justified by insurers' desire to eliminate AIDS from their risk pools.

But testing opponents' primary worries were not with the side effects of testing, but with its intended effect, namely to make an entire group of people uninsurable. Those who tested positive would have no health insurance to cover their costs. And without life insurance, they would not only be unable to provide for their dependents in case of death, but also unable to obtain mortgages or make other long-term financial commitments requiring insurance coverage as security. Furthermore, advocates argued, because many, indeed most, of those who were antibody-positive would not develop AIDS during the period of an insurance contact, healthy people were being unfairly denied coverage. In contrast, they claimed, other tests used by the insurance industry sought to find actual disease—such as the presence of heart disease, diabetes, or cancer. The HIV screens, they argued, showed only that a person might be at risk.

At root, this argument was a debate over who should pay for the costs of AIDS treatment in a system without national health insurance. Gay activists believed that somehow profitable insurance companies could and should bear that burden. In contrast, the industry felt that it was a public responsibility. Further, they argued, companies didn't pay, policy holders did and by not testing you enforced cross subsidy from some policy holders to others. In a competitive market, they continued, that pattern simply could not be sustained.

Some AIDS patients of course did have commercial insurance coverage, usually through their employers, although once sickness forced them to leave work, their coverage usually lapsed after a period of time. For those without commercial coverage, Medicare was little help because few AIDS patients survived the twenty-four month waiting period that program required. The federal government had, however, designated AIDS a "listed impairment" so that qualified AIDS patients could have their costs paid by Medicaid without having to endure a waiting period. But "qualified" meant "poor." Before AIDS patients could receive Medicaid payments, they had to spend down their assets, that is, use all of their savings, other equity, and assets until they reached the qualification limit. In the district, Medicaid patients could own no more than $2500 in assets including all savings, life insurance, policies, stocks and bonds, and possessions and have less than $377 monthly income.

The district government was concerned because, under this system, it wound up bearing a significant share of the costs. Because many private hospitals were reluctant to admit AIDS patients, especially those without commercial insurance coverage, many of these individuals found their way to DC General Hospital, the city hospital funded by the district. As the epidemic grew, it began to batter the hospital's—and therefore the district's—budget. Between 1981 and the beginning of 1986, DC General had spent over $1 million on inpatient AIDS care, very little of which had been reimbursed. It wasn't fair, testing opponents argued, for commercial insurers to take profit from healthy policy holders while forcing AIDS patients to spend themselves into poverty before dumping them on the public health care sector. How large a fraction of the district's AIDS patients (many of whom were drug abusers) would

ever acquire health insurance even if it were available, was a different matter.

THE INSURERS' ARGUMENT

Insurers argued with almost all these points. In fact, insurers asserted, testing opponents had turned the debates concerning the coverage of AIDS costs upside-down. Testing opponents were the ones who were discriminating—by asking other insurance policy holders to subsidize AIDS patients, and by asking that AIDS sufferers be given more favorable access to benefits than those people suffering from cancer, heart disease, diabetes and other maladies disqualifying them from regular coverage.

"Stripping insurance companies of the ability to assess risk literally rips out the foundations of insurance and marks a very dangerous precedent that could ultimately destroy the industry," Karen Clifford, counsel for the industry trade group Health Insurance Association of America, told the *New York Times*. The companies argued that in order to meet their obligations to policy holders (and make a normal rate of profit), incoming premiums had to, over time, amount to more than outgoing claims settlements plus operations costs. Even though some policy holders would turn out to have better luck than others, at the time the policy was written, each one had to be assigned to a "risk pool" of people with equivalent risk. Then those in that pool could be charged a rate so that on average their premiums would cover the payout for which the insurer was liable.

In both the health and the life insurance markets, companies sold both group and individual policies. About 85 percent of the people in the district who had health care insurance had group insurance coverage obtained through their employers. Everybody in the group paid the same premium based upon the last year's health and mortality experience of the group as a whole. So long as an applicant signed on for coverage upon employment or during regular enrollment periods, and had no known preexisting health problems, no physical examination was required. In keeping with this practice, insurers so far had not been testing group applicants for HIV-antibody.

The problem was in the area of individual policies. To assign applicants to the appropriate "risk pool," insurers typically used age, height, weight, occupation, past health experience, personal habits (such as smoking, drinking, drug use, exercise), and the results of a physical examination, including tests for diabetes, cholesterol levels, blood and other disorders. This data was used to calculate expected payouts and hence premium rates. Because groups of employees tended to be in better health than those who applied for individual coverage, group rates were much lower. Indeed, long before AIDS, insurers worried that some who applied for coverage did so because they knew they were sick (adverse selection). Given their inability to predict costs perfectly, insurers rarely gave individual coverage to anyone determined to have five times more than the standard risk of death. For this reason, many applicants suffering from diabetes or heart disease, or having a past history of cancer, were denied coverage.

To insurers, the HIV-antibody tests seemed a natural part of this risk assessment process: If there was a way to find out which otherwise-healthy applicants were at increased risk for coming down with the deadly disease, it was ridiculous to treat them unlike any other group and to assign them to inappropriate risk pools and charge them premiums that did not cover the costs of their health or life policies. Of course, insurers argued, the tests predicted risks imperfectly, but so did all other data companies used. Even if actuarial calculations were based upon the PHS's low mortality estimate (that 20 percent of those testing positive would die of AIDS within seven years) the risks were unacceptable—a thirty-four-year-old man testing positive

was 26.6 times more likely to die within seven years than a thirty-four-year-old man in standard health. The epidemic's demographics only aggravated the situation: men between the ages of twenty and fifty had historically been expected to make least use of health care resources and to pay premiums over many years.

Insurers predicted dire consequences if they were not allowed to test for the HIV-antibody. They already anticipated losses from those AIDS-related health care costs and deaths that they were contractually committed to cover under existing group and individual policies. Based upon PHS estimates that the annual cost of treating AIDS patients could reach $16 billion by 1991, insurance industry estimates were that perhaps more than $10 billion of that sum would fall on insurers' shoulders, not counting death benefits. The only way to stem the tide, and to ensure that the insurance industry could fulfill its obligations to other policy- and stockholders was to make sure that more high-risk policies weren't taken on.

By refusing to allow insurers to test for HIV-antibodies, the District Council would guarantee that the industry would sustain even greater losses than currently predicted, according to industry representatives. Those at high risk would be foolish not to apply for both a health insurance and a large life insurance policy when they knew they would only have to pay artificially low premiums for a short time. This would force up the rates in the individual insurance market, hurting those who could not get into groups or else forcing them out entirely because they couldn't afford premiums. Since the healthiest would be the first to go uninsured, the pool would become sicker, premiums would skyrocket and the cycle would reinforce itself. Without new infusions of cash, insurers would soon be unable to pay out on already contracted policies. Individual life insurance policies and risk pools were structured similarly; the life insurance market would also be destroyed.

Insurance industry representatives said that they sympathized with the plight of AIDS victims. And, they said, they would uphold their commitments to those AIDS patients who already held insurance policies. But AIDS was a societal problem—it was time to ask the nation as a whole to take care of those who were suffering. It was grossly unfair to ask the insurance industry—meaning stockholders and insurance policy holders—to shoulder a large proportion of the financial burden imposed by the epidemic. Many stockholders, after all, were just ordinary citizens who had invested in the company in good faith and were entitled to a return that protected their assets. Indeed since insurance companies are widely viewed as relatively nonspeculative investments, much of their stock is held by small investors and in modest trusts and estates.

JOHN RAY'S BILL

Councilman Ray was not persuaded by these arguments. He believed that use of sound methods of risk assessment by insurers—even if they seemed to affect certain groups of people harshly—was fair business practice. But he also believed that use of sound assessment methods constituted discrimination. As far as he was concerned, use of the ELISA-Western blot protocol as a basis either to deny a person insurance or to charge him or her increased premiums was unsound.

First, Ray argued, FDA-approval of the ELISA specifically stated that the test was inappropriate for any use other than blood bank screening or research. Second, he believed that the test's false positive rate was unacceptable. Third, there had been no time for the development of reliable actuarial studies: the disease, which was believed to have a latency period of perhaps seven years or more, had first been identified only five years before, and the antibody tests had been

in use for less than a year. There were no solid numbers upon which to base morbidity and mortality predictions, a point he presumed the insurance industry conceded, as they hadn't yet produced any actuarial studies.

Ray drafted a bill that he thought would complement existing regulations by ending discrimination against those testing HIV-positive while taking into account the insurance industry's need to assess risk. If enacted, the bill would make it illegal for health, life, and disability insurers to request or require anyone to take any kind of AIDS screening test. If the insurer somehow discovered that an applicant had received a positive test result in the past, it would be illegal either to deny coverage or to charge higher premiums on the basis of that knowledge. Issuing policies having exclusions or reductions of benefits for the treatment of AIDS or any disorders associated with HIV infection (unless the exclusions or reductions applied to other illnesses generally) would be illegal. Redlining of people thought to belong to groups at high risk for HIV infection would also be illegal. But insurers would be allowed to deny coverage to those people already diagnosed as suffering from AIDS, and could order tests for applicants who had other symptoms of AIDS present to the extent that only a test result was needed to complete an AIDS diagnosis consistent with the Centers for Disease Control definition.

Five years after the bill's enactment as law, these restrictions would essentially drop away. At that point, insurers wishing to use any AIDS screening test could apply to the district superintendent of insurance for permission to charge those applicants testing positive increased premiums. If the district commissioner of public health found that the test was "reliable and accurate," and the superintendent of insurance determined that the premium increase was "fair, reasonable, nondiscriminatory, and related to actual experience or based on sound actuarial principles applied to analysis of a substantial amount of scientific data collected over a period of years," permission would be granted and insurers would be free to require the test.

Ray cited several precedents for his bill. During 1985, California, Florida, and Wisconsin had enacted insurance testing bans. (California's law prohibited use of the ELISA but allowed use of another, more general immune response test; Florida's law was ambiguous and the subject of much debate in that state; Wisconsin's law prohibited use of the ELISA until the state medical examiner declared it a worthy test.) At least eight other states prohibited insurance discrimination on the basis of exposure to diethylstilbestrol (DES), which had been linked to vaginal and cervical cancers, or on the basis of genetic traits such as sickle cell anemia (primarily affecting blacks) or Tay-Sachs disease (primarily affecting Jews).

The Bill Gets a Hearing

At the hearing held by the Committee on Consumer and Regulatory Affairs, January 28, 1986, representatives of the DC Committee on AIDS Issues testified that they had evidence of redlining by insurers and knew of cases in which people had been denied coverage on the basis of positive antibody tests. If this practice continued, they argued, those who did develop AIDS would have to rely on publicly financed health care.

Insurance Superintendent Marguerite C. Stokes testified that it was impossible for insurers to carry out usual risk assessment procedures on those testing positive because there was no known actuarial data on their life experiences. However, she also testified that, as usual, insurers should be allowed to discover pre-existing conditions. But this discovery process should be limited to the questions, "Do you have AIDS?" or "Have you ever been medically diagnosed as having AIDS?"

Two representatives from the district health care community also spoke in favor of Ray's bill. The District of Columbia Hospital Association (whose members stood to gain revenue if more patients were covered) supported the bill. Senior Vice President Calbrieth L. Simpson put it this way:

> To allow insurance companies to discriminate against a particular category of patient simply because it requires intensive medical treatment would run counter to the whole purpose of insurance and would establish a terrible precedent of subjecting any group of patients, regardless of disease, to be denied coverage because of a determination that their disease was too costly or socially unacceptable.

The DC General Hospital Ad Hoc Committee on AIDS chairman also spoke in support of the bill, citing principles of equal access to health care and the cost of AIDS treatment already absorbed by the hospital.

Only one insurer testified in favor of Ray's bill—Blue Cross and Blue Shield for the National Capital Area. BC/BS's representatives testified that neither in the district nor anywhere else in the nation did BC/BS demand physical examinations, blood tests, or answers to questions concerning health or "lifestyle" from applicants for group coverage or, during thirty-day annual open enrollment periods, from applicants for non-group coverage. During the rest of the year, applicants for nongroup coverage were asked broad health questions, but none of the questions concerned AIDS or lifestyle.

Two large insurance trade associations sent representatives to speak against Ray's bill. Karen Clifford, counsel for the Health Insurance Association of America, explained the insurers' need to use screening tests when facing the fact that the AIDS epidemic was still spreading. Without use of the tests, she testified, insurers were confronted with the possibility of financial catastrophe. According to Clifford, the bill

> ignored the most basic and traditional principles of insurance and accords both AIDS vic-

tims and those at risk for developing AIDS a position not granted to individuals afflicted with or at risk of developing cancer, heart disease, or any other illness.

Presenting life insurers' arguments to the committee were the legislative director of the American Council of Life Insurance (which represented the 629 companies writing 95 percent of the country's life insurance), Kemper Life Insurance Companies' vice president and medical director, Dr. Gary Graham, and Northwestern Mutual Life Insurance Company's associate medical director, Dr. Robert Gleeson. Gleeson echoed Clifford's position that the bill discriminated against other insurance applicants:

If an insurance company is permitted to obtain information about an applicant suffering from any one of dozens of diseases—heart attacks or anemia, to name just two—why should the carrier of the AIDS virus be given special treatment and a total exemption from relevant tests?

Graham reported that Kemper had been using the antibody tests in all states except California and Wisconsin since October 1985. Use of the test was not discriminatory, he said:

By requiring these tests on all blood samples, we affirm our underwriting practice of not discriminating on the basis of sexual preference. By requiring the test nationwide, we have not redlined any city or locality where there is a known incidence of AIDS.

If Kemper were denied the ability to use the test, he continued, premiums for individual policies would become unreasonable. He predicted that Kemper would pull out of the district if Ray's bill were passed.

Ray asked Clifford, Graham, and Gleeson why the insurers hadn't pulled out of California or Wisconsin, and why the insurers' predictions of large premium surcharges and loss of coverage hadn't come true there. Clifford responded that it was still too early to assess the impact of the testing bans in those

two states, so that premium increases might yet occur. Ray surmised that there had been little impact on the health insurance market for two reasons. First, he said that the per-patient AIDS-care cost estimates of $150,000 publicly quoted by the insurance industry were inflated. He told Clifford that he had obtained minutes from an August 4, 1985, ACLI and HIAA joint meeting citing an HIAA report that estimated per-patient costs of $35,000. Clifford replied that the $35,000 estimate was preliminary and was expected to be increased. Ray secondly predicted that the costs arising from those testing positive who did eventually develop AIDS would have a minuscule effect on premiums because the cost would be spread across a huge pool of people.

Ray also expressed continuing reservations about the adequacy of the test. He brandished a memo attached to the HIAA report that he had obtained, written by the chairman of a drafting group on legislation and supporting documents for the industry position on testing. The memo stated that:

Most aspects of antibody testing are very confused and unsettled at the present time. . . . A person may test positive with Abbott's [one manufacturer's] ELISA and negative with Electro-Nucleonics' [another manufacturer's]. . . . Commercial manufacturers are scrambling for market share by making improvements of one kind or another. Products that we see today will probably not exist tomorrow. Perhaps some persons testing positive today may test negative tomorrow (and vice versa) by virtue of modified or replaced tests.

In all of this, the insurance companies could not argue on free-market principles that they should be left alone. Insurers were exempt from federal anti-trust laws, but subject to a number of regulations, varying from state to state, designed primarily to guarantee that insurers could fulfill their contractual obligations. To conduct business in the district, life and health insurers had to submit records to the superintendent proving that they had sufficient reserves to cover policies and were otherwise financially viable. The superintendent also looked over their actuarial tables and loss experiences each year to ascertain that their premium rates were "fair and reasonable." Furthermore, the district had outlawed premium and benefit differences based on race, and had mandated that treatment for alcohol and drug abuse and mental illness be included in regular health coverage.

John Ray is one of four members of the council elected at-large. Eight others are elected by wards. He is a black with a city-wide base in a predominantly black city. He chairs the Consumer and Regulatory Affairs Committee considering the AIDS/Insurance issue and has a professional background, as an attorney, dealing with insurance firms. In past elections, he has had support from Washington's substantial gay community, though he has not been unusual in attracting such support. His appeal, however, has been broad. There is speculation that he might be a future mayoral candidate. Ray knows that, because of its high incidence among intravenous drug users as well as gays, AIDS is an increasingly prominent issue in the black community. At least one black minister has taken the view that testing should be permitted.

As Ray considers both the policy and the politics, how determined should he be to see that the ban on HIV testing become a part of District of Columbia statutes?

Comment

Did the Arizona legislature make a moral mistake in defunding most organ transplants? To answer this question, we need to consider the practical alternatives open to the legislature: no funding of transplants at all, partial funding (of all transplants), full funding (of some or all transplants), or funding of a more comprehensive health insurance program. We also need to distinguish between the choices available to individual representatives and those available to the legislature as a whole. How should an individual legislator view the alternative suggested by Representative Resnick—extend the funding of AHCCCS with greater "notch group coverage" but postpone the decision to fund organ transplants until the legislature can consider a catastrophic health care policy? How should one assess, from the perspective of the legislature as a whole, Dr. Schaller's worry that a decision to fund transplants might convert AHCCCS from a program for poor people into a catastrophic health program for the general public?

Try to identify the moral principles that underlie the arguments made by various physicians and legislators, and then consider objections to them. What principle, for example, supports Dr. Kirschner's "Titanic" concept of medicine, which favors broad-based health care for the poor over organ transplant coverage? Assess the conception of the public good in Kirschner's argument that it is "unacceptable [for government] to use . . . limited resources in a way that really doesn't further the public good." Can a vote against funding heart transplants be morally defended on grounds that funding will encourage too many heart patients to move to Arizona? Can a vote in favor of funding be defended partly on the grounds that funding will benefit a state medical school that excels in heart transplantation?

Schafer and the AHCCCS team claim that a decision to fund kidney, cornea, and bone transplants but not heart, liver, and bone marrow transplants is "easily defensible" because of the medical and economic differences between the two sets of services. What (if any) is the moral relevance of these differences?

Part of the controversy focused on whether the legislature was deliberately trading off transplant funding for notch group expansion (as the press suggested) or whether they simply did not want to appropriate the funds necessary to fund both (as Dr. Icenogle claimed). How would you decide whether a legislature is trading one health need for another or declining to spend more on total health care? What is the moral difference between these approaches? How should a legislator decide how much money the government should spend on health care? Representative English suggests that the criterion is what the public is willing to pay for health care. Is this a sufficient standard? A necessary one? For what reasons is health care properly considered a more important good than some other goods funded by government? Which others? How much access to health care is enough?

Assess Representative Wilcox's claim that the refusal to fund Dianna Brown's transplant was "grossly discriminating." Is the differential treatment people receive by virtue of their state residence equally troubling, as Senator Stephens suggests? Or are differences in treatment acceptable as long as they "benefit most residents of the state of Arizona," as Senator Todd argues? Explain how we should (and should not) distinguish between those health care services that must be funded and those that need not be funded to satisfy the principle of distributive justice. Compare and contrast the justice of the following: (1) funding treatment for different diseases on the basis of total cost; (2) funding treatment for different diseases on the basis of cost-effectiveness; (3) funding treatment for people suffering from the same disease on the basis of survival rates; (4) funding treatment for people suffering from the same disease on the basis of future productivity; (5) funding basic health care for poor citizens; (6) funding basic health care for all citizens; (7) funding basic and catastrophic health care for all citizens. Before you conclude that only the last avoids injustice, you need to answer the argument that it too is likely to be discriminatory by reducing funds available for other basic human services, such as welfare, education, and police protection.

Should the Arizona legislature be faulted for the process by which it made the decision to defund organ transplants? What might have been gained and lost had the legislative debate (or the committee deliberations) been more extensive and more public?

The AIDS-testing case complicates the distinction between the health services that government should fund and those that people should be free to buy on the market. The issue before the District of Columbia Council concerned the right of the government to regulate the private market in health insurance. When is preventing discrimination a sufficient reason for regulating the private market? What does nondiscrimination require in this case?

Assess the moral force of each of the following arguments for placing a ban on AIDS-testing by insurance companies: (1) the test does not conform to standard insurance underwriting practices; (2) the test's accuracy and predictive value have not as yet been adequately established; (3) the test has an unacceptably high rate of false positives and could therefore make healthy people uninsurable; (4) insurance companies do not yet have reliable actuarial studies on which to base their rates; (5) the test would make an entire group of people uninsurable; (6) the test would shift the costs of treating AIDS patients substantially to the District government; (7) there is precedent for bans on testing and antidiscrimination statutes in other states (though no precedent specifically for a ban on AIDS testing).

Which (if any) of these arguments are essential to the case against AIDS testing? Which are consistent with the policy favored by Council member Ray, who wanted to prohibit AIDS testing but to permit insurers to deny coverage to people already diagnosed as suffering from AIDS? (He would also permit insurers to order tests for applicants who had other symptoms of AIDS.)

Consider the following arguments in defense of the insurance industry's use of AIDS testing: (1) AIDS testing would eliminate the temptation to "redline"; (2) the government rather than private insurance companies should bear the cost of treating AIDS patients; (3) other consumers of health insurance should not be asked to subsidize AIDS patients; (4) a ban on AIDS testing discriminates against people suffering form other diseases (such as cancer and diabetes) that disqualify them from regular coverage; (5) a ban on AIDS testing will eventually destroy the market in health and life insurance; (6) insurance companies avoid discrimination on the basis of sexual preference by requiring nationwide AIDS testing on all blood samples.

Try to formulate the criteria by which to judge when (if ever) it is nondiscriminatory to charge an applicant higher than average rates for insurance. What legislation on this issue should Council member Ray and the District of Council support and why?

California Welfare Reform
David M. Kennedy

In California, 1984 was a year of deep concern about welfare. Conservative Republican Governor George Duekmejian and the Democratic state legislature both felt an urgent need to do something about the spiraling size and cost of the state's Aid to Families with Dependent Children (AFDC)

Reprinted by permission of the Case Program, Kennedy School of Government, Harvard University. Copyright © 1987 by the President and Fellows of Harvard.

program, which paid cash benefits to eligible poor families. California's AFDC benefits, indexed to inflation in the early 1970s, had reached $555 a month for a family of three, the highest of the country's ten largest states. With 11 percent of the nation's population, the state had 15 percent of the entire national caseload, and its annual expenditures accounted for fully 21 percent of the national total. By the end of 1985, the caseload was expected to rise 14 percent over 1977–78 levels to better than 1.6 million.

The caseload expansion and cost-of-living grant increases meant that total AFDC expenditures would increase 94 percent—$1.7 billion—over the same period, to more than $3.5 billion. As elsewhere in the country, eligibility for welfare also conferred access to Medicaid health benefits, which in California were unusually comprehensive and correspondingly expensive.

Governor Deukmejian, first elected in 1982, had come to Sacramento determined to do something about California's AFDC burden. His solution was high-profile "workfare" legislation which would have forced all California welfare recipients to look for jobs under state supervision and, if unsuccessful, to work off their benefits in public service jobs. Deukmejian's bill was carried in the legislature by very conservative members; it was violently opposed by liberal Democrats and welfare rights activits who painted the measure as "slavefare." But by late 1984, the Democrats were themselves feeling pressure to act. An initiative on the ballot that year called for the state's welfare benefits to be cut roughly in half to the average of all other states. Opponents of the measure mounted a campaign focusing on the ill effects passage would have on the very young and very old poor, and it was defeated, but Democrats in Sacramento began to have real fears about facing "soft on welfare" charges in upcoming elections.

It was in this highly charged atmosphere that David Swoap, the conservative secretary of the California Health and Welfare Agency (HWA) and Art Agnos, a liberal assemblyman from San Francisco, began to discuss work and job training programs that might shrink California's welfare rolls and help recipients to self-sufficiency. Swoap and Agnos had strong and opposing views about the nature of welfare recipients and welfare dependency, but they both wanted to break the political deadlock over welfare reform and both felt open, at least potentially, to new ideas.

Agnos and Swoap looked carefully at studies of welfare dynamics and the effectiveness of different work and training programs, and ultimately sat down early in 1985 to design a program for California. As the political significance of Agnos' and Swoap's collaboration became clear, other legislators and welfare rights advocates hastened to join in. The poles of the debate were clear. On the presumption that they would otherwise do little to help themselves, should able-bodied welfare recipients simply be made to work, for the state if necessary? Or, on the presumtion that most recipients would work if only they could, should they be eased off welfare with the help of job training programs, child care, and similar support?

ATTITUDES

David Swoap, who as head of HWA was responsible both for administering California's welfare operations and for developing and pushing Governor Deukmejian's legislation, first sought out Art Agnos, chairman of the Health and Welfare Subcommittee of the Assembly's Ways and Means Committee, in August 1984, after the administration's workfare legislation had died in the legislature for the second time. Agnos was inclined to listen; he was well aware of the political danger welfare was beginning to pose to his party, and he'd dealt with Swoap before on other matters and had found the HWA chief trustworthy and likable.

Still, the two men were almost complete ideological opposites. In an early meeting, Agnos scrawled a few lines on a scrap of paper defining their positions. Swoap and his fellow conservatives, he wrote, believed that "people do not want to work unless intimidated or threatened with sanctions or some forced undesirable alternative." Agnos and his fellow liberals, in contrast, said that "people want to work . . . and will, given opportunity, choice, and training/education." It was a crisp summary of the two-year political deadlock between the administration and the legislature. Liberals had been entirely unwilling to countenance threats and force, and the administration had shown no interest in providing job training or other services.

Swoap had a long history in conservative circles, having held welfare positions under Ronald Reagan both in California and in Washington, as Undersecretary of Health and Human Services, before taking the HWA job in the Deukmejian administration. Swoap believed strongly that it was too easy to get on and stay on welfare, and that it was good for recipients, and just for society, to require them to work. California was still struggling with public services cuts due to a 1978 tax cap, and "particularly in times of fiscal stringency," Swoap said, "there's no reason not to ask able-bodied people to do something in exchange for the support society is giving them." The Deukmejian administration was also convinced that many recipients were working illegally in the underground economy and collecting benefits at the same time, and if forced to report or work elsewhere during the day would simply give up their benefits and continue their illegal work.

Agnos could hardly have agreed less. His responsibilities for welfare at Ways and Means ran more to fiscal matters than to policy, but as a former social worker he tended to believe that most welfare recipients were on the rolls only because they weren't well educated or trained, couldn't afford transportation or day care or manage without Medicaid, or because there was no local work for them to compete for. Workfare, he believed, was little more than punishment for the victims.

Agnos looked instead to a pioneering program in Massachusetts called Employment and Training Choices, which had been brought to his attention by staunch workfare opponent Senator Diane Watson, chair of the Senate Health and Human Services Committee, who represented a very poor Los Angeles district. Participants in the voluntary program were offered a choice of job training programs, given child care and transportation allowances while training, helped to find jobs afterward, and guaranteed an extension of Medicaid benefits if they worked their way off welfare. Mass ET, as the program was invariably called, hadn't been around for very long, but there were early indications that it was both popular and successful.

Agnos' early talks with Swoap simply served to confirm the gulf between them. "On the Democratic side, we were looking at trying to do something for the bulk of people, who will benefit from a positive opportunity if offered education, training, childcare," Agnos recalled later. "There was an obsession on the Republican side with the negative possiblities of every opportunity we talked about. 'They'll cheat here, they'll cheat there.' They wanted simple workfare, where you might end up cleaning bottles or picking up paper in exchange for your welfare check. And that was the programmatic and philosophical impasse that we found ourselves in."

Agnos offered up a new idea. "I said to Swoap, let's do it differently this time," he said later.

> Let's get out of Sacramento, and you take me anyplace in America where you think what you want to do is working. And I'll take you to a place in America where I think what we want to do is working, meaning Massachusetts; because I knew what was going on there. He thought that was a good idea, and I said after the session is over, in a month and a half or so, we'll get together and we'll plan a trip.

As it happened, Swoap threw his back out and the trip was delayed until early 1985. The political situation in Sacramento didn't change to speak of in the interim. The general intellectual climate around welfare reform to some extent did, however. "The debate until 1984, I'd say, was mostly ideological," said Julia Lopez, Agnos' key welfare aide. "You had very strongly held beliefs on both sides, without much solid information to rely on.'' More or less coincidentally, solid information became a little easier to come by just as Agnos and Swoap began their discussions.

THE SAN DIEGO EXPERIMENT

One source was a preliminary evaluation based on the first nine months of a San Diego County pilot workfare program. San Diego had passed a local referendum calling for straight work-for-benefits workfare in 1982. The plan needed state approval, and while the legislature had been skeptical it ultimately gave in to the local sentiment. The resulting "San Diego Job Search and Work Experience Program" got underway in 1983.

The San Diego experiment was an unusual opportunity to take a close empirical look at the kind of program elements often contained in workfare proposals. San-Diego's original scheme was simply to make recipients work in public or private sector nonprofit jobs in exchange for their benefits, but the legislature had insisted, as a price for approving the program, that the county help recipients look for regular jobs before putting them into workfare slots. The experiment as it was finally instituted thus began with a three-week job search workshop in which recipients were instructed in how to prepare a resume, dress for interviews, and the like and then supplied with job listings, yellow pages, and telephones with which to look for work. The next step was an "Experimental Work Experience Program": three months of workfare in a public or private nonprofit agency. This basic pattern, job search followed by workfare, in fact mirrored Deukmejian's statewide welfare reform bill.

The impact the governor's proposal would have if it passed had been hotly debated in Sacramento, with relatively little information to go on. San Diego's experiment was quite consciously intended to help answer such questions. It was designed in conjunction with the Manpower Demon-

stration Research Corporation (MDRC), a New York City-based firm specializing in social science analyses of welfare work experiments, so that the employment and income effects of the job search workshop and of the workshop/workfare combination could be evaluated separately.

In the experimental design that MDRC developed, all new welfare recipients in San Diego were assigned, on pain of denial of benefits, to one of two experimental groups or to a control group (those already on the rolls in San Diego when the program began did not participate in the experiment). Both experimental groups began with the three-week job search workshop. Recipients in one group weren't required to do anything more if they finished the workshop without a job, but still-unemployed recipients in the other moved on to a workfare stint.

EARNINGS AND EMPLOYMENT: MEN AND WOMEN

Probably the most significant of MDRC's findings was that the San Diego program had quite different effects on men and women. AFDC in California was in fact made up of two program elements: AFDC-Family Group (AFDC-FG) supported single mothers and their children (families headed by single men were also eligible, but AFDC-FG was for all practical purposes a single-mother program), while AFDC-Unemployed Parent (AFDC-U)—a much smaller program—for the most part supported families by paying benefits to recently unemployed fathers.

According to MDRC's analysis, AFDC-FG participants, who were almost all women, showed persistent and statistically significant increases in earning—as much as $213.00 over three months—and employment—as much as 10 percent—relative to the control group. Women who went through just the job search component rather than the job search/work experience component seemed to fare somewhat better. AFDC-U participants, almost all men, gained relative to the control group in the short term, in both employment and earnings, from participating in both the job search and the job search/work experience components. Neither of the gains was statistically significant, however, and both declined over the period of the study as the performance of the control group improved.

The California legislative analyst's office had a straightforward interpretation of these findings. "The characteristics of the individuals in each group are very different," it said in a review of the MDRC report.

> In general, services provided to AFDC-U recipients do not translate into increased income and employment because these recipients possess the skills needed to find a job *before they enter the programs.* As a result, the employment services provided by the job search and job search/work experience programs do not significantly increase their chances of finding and keeping a job. On the other hand, AFDC-FG recipients benefit greatly from these services because the services help them increase their chance of finding and keeping a job.

PARTICIPATION AND SANCTIONS

San Diego County had wondered just how successful a workfare program could be at compelling participation. The MDRC's answer was positive, with some qualifications. Half of the recipients assigned to the job search and job search/work experience components actually participated in the job search exercises, compared to perhaps 10–20 percent for "mandatory" programs that had been tried elsewhere (the MDRC defined "participation" as showing up at a workshop for at least one day). Twenty-seven percent of the recipients in the job search/work experience track ended the workshop unemployed and were assigned to work experience jobs; some 17 percent of those assigned actually did such work (meaning, by MDRC standards, that they spent at least an hour in an assigned job). The report was somewhat unclear about

what happened to the majority of nonparticipants who didn't have good cause for their absence. California law governing job search programs required that recipients had to demonstrate a "pattern of noncompliance," and that welfare administrators undertake a "conciliation" process to try to resolve any differences, before penalties ("sanctions," in welfare jargon) could be imposed. Nearly three percent of the recipients who went through the job search workshops were ultimately sanctioned for noncompliance, compared to 0.5 percent in the control group. No such law applied to the special San Diego work experience component, and 17 percent of the recipients in that component were sanctioned.

SANCTIONS AND SAVINGS

San Diego had hoped that its experiment would move people off welfare, save it money, or both, but when the MDRC's report came out little success was evident on either front, and what there was came not through increased employment but through penalties imposed on recipients. For the most part, participants in the experiment simply weren't working their way out of poverty. Even those women whose earnings increased generally didn't make enough money to go off welfare. Nor did women's earnings and employment increases lead to statistically significant welfare payment reductions, since AFDC-FG recipients were allowed to make a number of employment-related deductions (for child care, for instance) which generally kept earnings-related cuts in benefits to a minimum.

Men who went only through the job search component generally didn't have their benefits reduced either. Those who went through the full job search/work experience component did, but not, for the most part, because their earnings went up substantially. Instead, some who went off the rolls into even part-time jobs lost their benefits because of a federal law which forbade AFDC-U recipients from working more than one hundred hours a month. Others lost their benefits for noncompliance. These benefit reductions represented the only verifiable savings from the program.

REACTION

Nobody interested in welfare in Sacramento could afford to ignore the San Diego findings; they were, after all, germane, empirical, and local. None of the parties to the debate shifted very far, however. "People looked at the San Diego data and made anything they wanted out of it," said Joyce Iseri, chief welfare aide to Senate Health and Human Services head Watson. Swoap was especially struck that at least some job search participants had found jobs that weren't advertised or listed with state employment agencies. It reinforced his feeling that it was proper to require recipients to take action for themselves, that there was more work available than his critics would credit. He and those of like mind also saw an AFDC-U sanction rate matching their suspicions about the underground economy. Agnos, Watson, and their allies, on the other hand, saw a program that "hadn't saved a lot of money, put a lot of people in jobs, or cut San Diego's rolls way back," as Iseri put it. The debate continued.

BANE AND ELLWOOD

If the San Diego results seemed to be politically equivocal, Mary Jo Bane and David Ellwood's *The Dynamics of Dependence*, a report released in June 1983, scored unmistakable points for Sacramento's liberals. "It came in very handy in this discussion, because it emphasized that being on AFDC didn't mean that you were handicapped or maimed or somehow not a part of mainstream society," Julia Lopez, Agnos' aide, said.

Bane and Ellwood were both Harvard University welfare and public policy specialists; their study, which was based on an extensive analysis of a large income-history data base at the University of Michigan's

Survey Research Center, broke new ground in its careful empirical examination of how long recipients stay on welfare and why they move on and off the rolls. They asked three main questions: How long do female heads of households with children tend to stay on AFDC? What are the characteristics of those who receive welfare income for relatively long periods of time? How do women escape welfare?

They looked at the data in terms of "spells," or the periods individual women spent on welfare. Their main finding was that, examined this way, the welfare population did not appear homogenous. "The AFDC program seems to serve two purposes for two different groups: short term relief and long term income maintenance," they wrote. According to their analysis half of the women who went on AFDC were off within two years or less, and two-thirds within four years; only 17 percent stayed eight years or more. "Most of the people [AFDC] serves are short-term clients, for whom [long term welfare] dependence is simply not an issue," they argued (although they also reported that a third of all women who ended a spell on welfare returned to the rolls at some time). However, more than half of the people on AFDC at any given time were long-term recipients: the short-term recipients—a majority of those who passed through the program—came and went, while the relatively few long-term recipients accumulated on the rolls. The long-term 17 percent thus ended up receiving over half of all welfare expenditures.

Bane and Ellwood also found that three-fourths of all AFDC spells began with what they called a "relationship change." Nearly half began when a wife became a female head of household, another 30 percent when an unmarried woman "acquired" a child (the authors pointed out that not all single women on AFDC were caring for their own children). Only 12 percent began because the recipient had suffered a fall in income, suggesting, the authors wrote, that "it is not typically the case that a female household head goes on AFDC because she has lost her job, reduced her hours, or experienced a drop in wages." Nearly a third of the women who went *off* welfare did so because their earnings went up, however. A roughly equal proportion went off because they married or rejoined their husbands, and about 14 percent went off because their children turned eighteen or left the household (other, including unexplained, reasons accounted for the other 20-odd percent).

The Dynamics of Dependence served to confirm some of the Sacramento liberals' most basic feelings about welfare and welfare recipients. Art Agnos had in fact held, over the previous several years, a series of hearings around the state to make the point that California's welfare population no longer fit, if it ever had, common stereotypes. "There was a new profile in California of recipients different from the traditional image of low-income women who maybe had been born on welfare, maybe had a child or two on welfare," Agnos said.

> This was what I call the middle-class divorced poor woman: mostly white with a few kids who was there basically as a result of divorce. Very often she'd dropped out of college to put a husband through school or something like that, but there was no need to threaten or start all over with her.

Bane and Ellwood, as far as he was concerned, more than proved that point. "Their study came out and basically said that folks go in and out of the system," said Julia Lopez. "You have a hard core that stays a long time, but it's a system that's very fluid." The study also underscored the liberals' general disagreement with the Deukmejian administration. "They wanted to build a system for the minority, that would prevent them from doing any work in the underground economy," Lopez said. "And we were saying, 'Why develop a system for the few when we really need to help the majority of folks who aren't working for a number of other reasons?'"

LOSING GROUND

Charles Murray's *Losing Ground*, published in 1984, did for conservatives what Bane and Ellwood had done for liberals. A biting critique subtitled *American Social Policy 1950–1980*, the book argued that the last few decades' government policies toward the poor, however well intentioned, had been dangerously counterproductive. Murray focused particularly on welfare policy, his thesis in essence being that welfare caused poverty. Welfare made it easier to avoid working at entry-level jobs, sometimes, he argued, even more profitable not to take such jobs; the result was that the poor never began to move up the job ladder. Welfare made it easier to survive as a single mother, especially as a young single mother; the result was that more such families were formed. Welfare cut away at the causal connection between striving and economic performance; the result was that poor people faced, and responded to, morally perverse incentives.

Murray backed up his arguments with reams of statistics showing deterioration, beginning with the Great Society's federal antipoverty programs, in indicators of poverty, illegitimacy, labor force participation, and the like. "We tried to provide more for the poor and produced more poor instead," he wrote. "We tried to remove the barriers to escape from poverty, and inadvertently built a trap."

Job programs, Murray argued, were no antidote; they simply didn't work. He relied on published studies to make his case. An evaluation of the multibillion dollar Manpower Development and Training Act, a Great Society job training program, found initial earnings increases of $150–500 annually for men, declining to half that, for the same men, as time passed; women did a little better at $300–600. A study of vocational training programs found wage increases attributable to the training of but 1.5 percent. There were other, similar examples. The programs, Murray argued, were thus failures on their own terms: they did not lift participants out of poverty.

Faced with such dismal results, Murray said, liberal advocates historically had turned to two devices to justify job trading programs. A cost-effectiveness case could be made as long as the benefits from training surpassed—eventually—its costs, a condition that usually held if one looked far enough into the trainees' future. "[I]t was to this type of calculation to which the sponsors were reduced," Murray wrote scornfully. "'The average effect [on earnings] for all enrollees is quite large' we find in one evaluation of the Job Corps, then read on to the next sentence, where it is revealed that the 'quite large' effect amounted to $3.30 per week. It was a statistically significant gain."

The other device was the upbeat anecdote: "John Jones, an ex-con who had never held a job in his life, became employed because of program X and is saving money to send his child to college. Such anecdotes, filmed for the evening news, were much more interesting than economic analyses. They were also useful in hearings before congressional appropriations committees." The implication, Murray argued, was that the story was typical, but the fact, he also argued, was that it was rare, "and that depressingly often John Jones would be out of his job and back in jail a few months after his moment in the spotlight."

Murray confirmed and elaborated many of the beliefs senior Deukmejian administration officials already had about welfare, just as Bane and Ellwood had for the administration's opponents. "Everyone seemed to agree with Murray's basic thesis, that there is a serious welfare crisis that is exacerbated by the presence of welfare," said Bruce Wagstaff, a senior HWA analyst.

> That's an underlying assumption of a mandatory work program, that the availability of welfare acts as a disincentive to work, and that you must compel people through the threat of terminating their welfare to engage

in work. That otherwise they wouldn't, because they're too accustomed to just accepting welfare, and they'll continue this long term or generational dependency.

Murray's points about job training programs rang just as true in the administration. "Carl [Williams, Swoap's deputy] gives examples of his previous experiences with these programs, where you'd have a lot—I shouldn't even say a lot, you'd have some—people receiving training, receiving nice certificates, but the training was not directed toward labor market opportunities, so they had these nice certificates but no jobs," Wagstaff said. In fact, it rang true in what might have seemed unexpected quarters as well. Senator Bill Greene, whose district in Los Angeles adjoined Diane Watson's, and who had long advocated training programs for his constituents, had by this time "gotten to the point where he could not support any of this stuff anymore," according to his aide, Allen Davenport.

> People were tired of seeing the programs come and go. It really bugged him that some program would come down the pike from Washington or Sacramento and make all these promises and then would go away and nothing had changed. The only successes in the programs had been their administrators; SRI [the Stanford Research Institute] did a great study on that, showing that the careers that were most enhanced by poverty programs were the careers of poverty program administrators.

THE TRIP

Nobody involved in the California welfare debate, as it turned out, was shifted very fundamentally by any of this analysis; the studies mostly confirmed various participants' original beliefs rather than creating some new common ground. The personal and political inclination to reach some accord remained, however. In March 1985, Agnos, Swoap, and several other legislators and HWA officials embarked for a week's tour of state work and job training programs. Swoap had chosen West Virginia and Pennsylvania, which were running what were to his mind model work-for-benefits workfare programs, essentially the San Diego model without the job search component. Agnos had selected Massachusetts, with its ET program.

Much of the subsequent impact of the trip, the participants later agreed, came simply from the fact that they had taken it together. "It's rare in government for everybody to work from a common basis of experience," Swoap said.

> We'd been talking around this issue in Sacramento for years, and everybody involved knew a lot, but we all had different backgrounds, and often we ended up just talking past each other. The trip was remarkable in that we saw the same things—some very instructive things—talked to the same people, sat up late nights discussing what had happened that day, and while we didn't necessarily agree afterward on what it meant, we *were* all beginning in the same place, which was a very important step forward.

Agnos felt exactly the same way. "The overall thing I learned from this is to get the hell out of the committee and caucus rooms and go into the field," he said.

> Not only is the field a living laboratory where you can put your hands, very often, on the problems that personify one point of view or the other, but when you're done you have the same set of anecdotes to draw on, which is very, very important.

Both sides did, indeed, see things that made lasting impressions. "West Virginia, frankly—now remember that this was sort of the Republican showpiece for workfare—was a disaster," Agnos said. "Or if not a disaster, at least not a great success." While West Virginia's program was for the most part intended simply to ensure that welfare recipients worked, on what amounted to moral grounds, some attention was paid to slotting recipients into jobs that would do them some good in the long run, and recipients were supposed to be reviewed every six months to make sure that they hadn't

hit some kind of unforeseen dead end. The California delegation in fact saw some positive results, as in several recipients who seemed well on their way to learning a trade in the state printing plant. Even this seemed a little sour to Agnos, since the recipients had had no voice in their assignments. "No one had asked them if they wanted to be printers, it just happened, bang, a random kind of thing," he said.

The major lesson, however, came from a visit the Californian's hosts had arranged to a state water treatment facility, where an Appalachian woman named Velda Jenkins—in her mid-thirties, with three children, on welfare because her husband was in prison—was being trained through her workfare job to be a water quality tester. The West Virginian program managers were particularly proud that they were preparing an essentially unskilled woman for such a sophisticated position. In fact, the treatment plant's budget for janitors had been cut and Jenkins had spent her nearly two years on workfare mopping floors. She'd complained politely at her six month reviews, but nothing had changed. "This was our showcase," Agnos said. The delegation, Swoap included, was particularly disturbed that Jenkins had had no effective recourse once she'd been sidelined; the California party started to refer to this as the "Velda factor," something any system for California would absolutely have to address. "We wanted to empower people without the necessity of having a lawyer every time" Agnos said. "We wanted people to be in charge of their own lives."

The group heard some rather unexpectedly positive messages at the same time. "We got a consistent sense from recipients in these jobs, even in jobs that at first glance weren't very interesting, that they were glad to be out doing something," Swoap said. "We saw that repeated all through West Virginia," Agnos said. "People doing things that they didn't necessarily like, saying, 'If they hadn't made me do it I wouldn't have done it, but it's better than doing nothing at home.' That was when my feelings of opposition to the mandatory feature started to change."

The party moved on to Pennsylvania, which had a workfare program much like West Virginia's. The main lesson of that visit came in a National Guard Armory. Agnos had always been inclined to respect California unions' concerns that workfare might cause public sector displacement, while Swoap, according to Sacramento observers, had been inclined to dismiss it, believing that workfare jobs in budget-capped California would at best supplement, rather than supplant, regular workers.

Pennsylvania, according to both men, proved Agnos' case. "This general in the armory," said Agnos,

just blew our minds by saying, "Well, I went up to see the governor to get six more janitors because the place was dirty and he said, 'We don't have the money for it, but have you ever heard of workfare? Get some welfare recipients to do it for you.'" Just coldbloodedly said it. I said to Dave, we don't want to do that; we want to pay for legitimate work like that out of the budget, not end up replacing state workers that we don't want to pay for.

Thus ended the conservatives' portion of the tour. In Massachusetts, as expected, the delegation found a strikingly different approach. The differences began with the state's ambitions for its Employment and Training Choices program. Where West Virginia and Pennsylvania had aimed, at best, to save some money, move some recipients into private sector jobs, and get a return for their welfare dollars Massachusetts claimed that it was making a large improvement in the lives of significant numbers of the poor. "In Massachusetts," said Welfare Commissioner Charles M. Atkins, "we have found a way out of poverty."

As its name implied, choice—exercised by recipients—was central to ET. Recipients chose, first, whether to participate in the program. ET was technically mandatory, but in fact AFDC recipients only had to register for the program, and those not actively interested in pursuing it were placed in an "unassigned pool" with essentially no further obligations. To encourage recipients to enter the program and perhaps ultimately to give up welfare, Massachusetts offered day care and transportation allowances while in ET and if necessary extended the child care allowance and Medicaid benefits for a year after recipients started working.

Participants in ET had four basic options to choose from. They could look for work through a San Diego-style job club, with state assistance in learning job search skills and finding openings. They could undertake "assessment and career counseling," in which state social workers helped recipients figure out what they might want to do and what education and skills they might need to do it. They could select "education and skills training," to learn English as a second language, get a high school equivalent degree, take up to two community college courses, and/or learn a skill. They could choose "supported work" in which recipients' grants were funneled through a private employer who agreed to provide on-the-job training.

They could, finally, put these different options together in almost any order: education and training followed by job search followed by supported work, for instance, or job search—if unsuccessful—followed by assessment followed by a training or supported work stint. Participants' first step in the program was to meet with an ET worker and work out career goals and a plan to meet them, but if they failed to find jobs—or jobs they wanted to stay in—they were, at least in theory, free to cycle through the program indefinitely. They were also free to drop out of the program if they wanted; there were no sanctions for nonparticipation as there were in San Diego, West Virginia, and Pennsylvania.

Mass ET had only gotten off the ground in October 1983, so it had a limited track record when the California delegation came to look it over. The state was nonetheless extremely proud of what it had accomplished. Out of the states' 85,000 AFDC families, 44,000 people had signed up (20,000 of these were on a waiting list; these and the following figures date from May 1985). Fifteen thousand AFDC recipients had been placed in private sector jobs at an average wage of $5.00 an hour, which worked out to annual earnings of $9,700, against the state's typical welfare grant of $6,800 annually. There was no MDRC-style evaluation of Mass ET in the offing, however; Commissioner Atkins had forbidden any scheme involving a control group on the grounds that he would not deny the program to any ambitious recipient.

Swoap, Agnos et al. were struck by several things as they spoke with ET administrators and participants and toured several branch offices. Swoap was impressed that a totally voluntary program was able to generate such participation and by the "palpable" excitement he sensed among both recipients and caseworkers. He wondered, however, whether ET was simply placing the most motivated and job-ready recipients—those most likely to volunteer—thus making the program's performance unrepresentative of what a similar but mandatory scheme might accomplish. He also found Massachusetts' use of an unassigned pool obnoxious: people unwilling to help themselves, he still felt, should be made to do so.

Agnos was enormously taken with the opportunity ET seemed to offer recipients. "In effect it gave a second chance at what many people get earlier in their lives, in high school or in college; it gave them an opportunity to make a choice—with some serious help—about what they wanted to do with the rest of their lives," Agnos said.

Here are people with a couple of kids, on welfare, and ET was stopping the train for

them, letting them get off, and saying here's another crack at it. When you're 30 years old or 40 years old with kids from 5 to 15, how do you stop the train of life and retrain for something that you want to do, now that you're older, a little wiser, a little more mature? ET did that, and that's something you normally don't get.

Somewhat ironically, even though Massachusetts made much of its program being voluntary *and* successful, ET put another dent into Agnos' resistance to mandatory programs. "People had all kinds of options, and it was working for the people they did it with," he said. "I began to wonder, if we believe in a program like that, why shouldn't everybody get the benefit of it?"

THE NEGOTIATIONS

The Californians found their whirlwind tour immensely provocative, but it didn't actually resolve anything about how California might go about a program of its own. "What we accomplished on the trip was simply acquiring a set of common experiences," Agnos said. "Everything substantive was still up in the air when we came back."

Something more was required if there was to be political movement. In April 1985, Agnos convened a series of meetings in an Assembly conference room that was to last, off and on, for almost eight months. Agnos and Julia Lopez attended; Swoap and his top staff attended; Joyce Iseri, Dion Aroner, and Allen Davenport—aides, respectively, to Senator Watson, Assemblyman Tom Bates (Watson's Assembly counterpart), and Senator Greene—attended, as did several other legislators. Agnos and Lopez represented themselves, and Swoap and his deputies represented the administration, but the legislative aides were there on the strict understanding that they did not represent their members. Agnos had invited them believing that their welfare expertise would be useful and that any product they contributed to would be more likely to satisfy their influential legislators, but there was no implication that Bates, Watson, and Greene were in any way committed.

Agnos insisted from the outset that participants put aside, insofar as they could, any preconceptions about what might in fact be politically or fiscally possible and simply think out loud together about what an ideal program might look like. "We sat there, and Art said, 'Let's start talking about creating a system, all the different parts of a system, as we would if we had our druthers.' Dion Aroner said, 'How would you do it?' "

Agnos was simply trying to set a tone: none of the participants felt, or felt their fellows to be, perfectly open-minded, or that a real program would not have to address fiscal and political realities. Agnos had in fact carried back from the trip a one-page handwritten summary, drafted while on a bus in Massachusetts, of the state of play between himself and Swoap.

They were agreed, in principle, that welfare recipients should work, although they still came to that conclusion from different philosophical directions. They disagreed about what components should actually be in a good program—an ET-style menu, for instance, against simple work-for-benefits—about what incentives recipients should be offered to participate, and about what safeguards should be included to placate unions and guard against the "Velda factor." Those issues, Agnos thought, were negotiable. Some issues were not. Swoap clearly would not support a program unless it was mandatory and backed by significant sanctions. Agnos clearly would not support a program unless it offered recipients real choices. And even if Agnos and Swoap could somehow come to terms, there was no guarantee that other influential parties—like Diane Watson and Tom Bates—would go along.

LOBBYING FROM THE LEFT

Agnos made sure that Sacramento's welfare advocates, with whom he generally had

old and close ties, knew about the negotiations, though he swore them to secrecy and told them essentially nothing about the details of the group's discussions. Nonetheless, activists like Casey McKeever, a lawyer at the Western Center on Law and Poverty, and Candace Blase, who worked for the Friends Committee on Legislation of California, knew more than enough about welfare issues and programs to know that they had had a rather different interpretation of the available information.

McKeever and Blase both felt that focusing on recipients and whether a particular program could get them into jobs was a fundamental mistake (although the political appeal in Sacramento of some kind of work legislation was clear enough that they didn't try too hard to change legislative minds on the point). The problem, they thought, was that full-time entry-level jobs often simply didn't pay wages a family could live on. "Look at the San Diego data," McKeever said. "Most who went through both job search and workfare had statistically significant improvements."

But they still weren't getting off welfare, the jobs they were working weren't paying enough to get them off welfare. You can go through the best of programs like that and it's just going to have very marginal impacts. They don't really improve the lot of the participants. So from our perspective, the approach Agnos seemed to be taking just kind of missed the point. You could put all kinds of money in, and require people to do all sorts of things, but you really weren't going to be in any different place than when you started off. It was just making people in Sacramento feel better, like they were doing something, but they weren't addressing what we felt the real problem was.

McKeever and Blase supported higher minimum wages and a program of job creation. "Otherwise," said Blase,

all you're doing with workfare and training programs is increasing the supply of labor in a segment of the labor market which is already underpaid and facing too few jobs. It worsens the condition of those people who are already working in that market, and it doesn't give much bargaining power to the people who are going into it. If you don't deal with the labor market end of it, then you can't improve the condition of large groups you're trying to move into that market.

They also pointed out that in many places around California there didn't seem to be anything like sufficient entry-level jobs anyway. What were the 40 percent of the state's recipients who lived in Los Angeles going to do?

Nonetheless, something, it seemed clear, was going to come out of the continuing—though still largely secret—negotiations. Most of their energies therefore went into supporting the ideas behind Mass ET over those behind San Diego or West Virginia. "We were promoting Massachusetts as the alternative," Blase said. "At that time they were saying they had a certain number of placements and jobs, Agnos was raving about it, everyone was happy with it," McKeever said. "There wasn't much bad to say about it at that point."

BAD NEWS

Such news was not long in coming. As the negotiations continued, Blase received a preliminary analysis of the ET program written by Jean Kluver, a Boston economist, for the New England regional office of the American Friends Service Committee. "The office had been getting a lot of questions from Friends around the country, asking about ET," Kluver said. "'Is this a good program? Is this what we should be pushing for in our states as an alternative to these regressive workfare schemes?'"

The centerpiece of Kluver's analysis was that Commissioner Atkins was wrong, that ET did not in fact represent the way out of poverty. ET graduates in full-time jobs were averaging $5.00 an hour, according to the state. At that wage, Kluver argued, a mother with two children—the most common AFDC family—would lose money moving

from welfare to work. The family's AFDC and food stamp benefits would add up to $555 a month. That was less than the gross monthly income from a $5.00 an hour job— $806.00—but taxes, at $120.00 a month, "work expenses" (clothing, transportation, etc.), at $100.00 a month, and child care, at $105.00 a month, even including the ET subsidy, brought her disposable income down to $546.00. If, after the first year of employment, a working mother had to pay the full cost of medical insurance and child care, the picture was even worse: Kluver's figures suggested that her disposable income could drop as low as $51.00 a month. Moreover, Kluver's information suggested that actual average wages for female ET placements were closer to $4.50. "Thus," she said, "while it is true that the gross income of ET graduates is about 180 percent of their previous AFDC grant, these jobs do not pay enough to provide long-term self-sufficiency for most AFDC families."

Kluver herself was cautious in drawing political implications from her analysis; ET was, in her view, much the best of likely work-program alternatives, and she was more interested in improving it—and perhaps shifting the focus of the debate to wages and job creation—than in killing it. McKeever and Blase, in California, were in fact only slightly disheartened by Kluver's analysis, since they felt generally positive about the voluntary program, they didn't even try to press the report on the negotiators. "We weren't relying on social science data or anything like that," McKeever said, in supporting something like ET in California.

> We were saying that this program makes sense and it's better for recipients because of the way it works. We can see it's better for our people to have a lot of child care; to have the choice of programs, not to have workfare and sanctions.

THE DECISION

Agnos and his colleagues continued to meet regularly, trying to make sense of all they had learned, analytically and impressionistically, about welfare, workfare, and job training. The political desire to come up with a program of some kind remained very strong, but the group was still struggling with some basic questions. Did a program have to be mandatory to be effective? Did voluntary programs misdirect resources to people who would help themselves in any case? How important was it to help participants with child care, transportation, and insurance? Was workfare punishment, or useful preparation for a normal working life?

Should recipients be slotted immediately into minimum-wage jobs, or should California try to educate and train recipients for a better life? "We were working with the political view that everybody in California wanted welfare recipients to go to work," said Allen Davenport. "So we were working along on the data and ideas that we all had. What would a good and effective program look like?"

Comment

Central to the contemporary controversy over welfare reform is the question vividly raised by the San Diego experiment: Should welfare be made conditional on work? Evaluate Swoap's answer: "Particularly in times of fiscal stringency, there's no reason not to ask able-bodied people to do something in exchange for the support society is giving them." First, identify the moral principle implicit in Swoap's argument. Then, consider the practical implications of the principle for welfare reform in San Diego. What difference, if any, would the availability of work make to the claim that able-bodied people should do something in exchange for support by society? If work is unavailable, what demands, if any, may a state make on unemployed citizens? What demands, if any, may unemployed citizens make on the state?

Assess Agnos' argument that most welfare recipients would work if only they could, and the state therefore owes them the education, job training, work opportunities, transportation, child care, and health care that are necessary to enable them to be productive citizens. Is Agnos' argument consistent with the claim that welfare recipients have responsibilities to society as well as rights? If so, what might those responsibilities be? If not, is there a principled argument that would support ascribing welfare rights but not responsibilities to disadvantaged citizens?

To what extent should our assessment of workfare depend on: (1) the data from the San Diego experiment; (2) the analysis in the Bane and Ellwood study; and (3) the analysis in the Murray book? Evaluate the disagreements between supporters and critics of the programs in San Diego, West Virginia, Pennsylvania, and Massachusetts. What additional information would be necessary to evaluate these programs more fully? What features of each program, as described, make it more or less publicly defensible?

Evaluate the moral case for and against these features of a welfare reform program: (1) creating jobs for welfare recipients; (2) assigning welfare recipients to jobs; (3) penalizing welfare recipients who fail to find a job; (4) saving money on welfare in order to lower taxes or reduce the deficit; (5) providing direct income subsidies for poor parents who have child-rearing responsibilities; (6) providing childcare for poor parents with the expectation that they will work outside the home; and (7) raising the minimum wage and/or changing tax policy to make a full-time job pay enough to support a small family.

Although welfare reform proposals and programs continue to be controversial, they are also widely considered an important priority in American politics. Are there any principled grounds on which citizens might mutually agree to support some form of welfare reform? Evaluate the following as possible grounds for a mutually acceptable justification for welfare reforms: (1) the right to work; (2) the right to live a good life; (3) the right to live one's own life, free of responsibilities to unrelated others; (4) the responsibility to work; (5) the responsibility to support one's dependents; and (6) the responsibility to reciprocate social benefits.

Recommended Reading

The most consistent statement of libertarian theory is Robert Nozick's *Anarchy, State and Utopia* (New York: Basic Books, 1974), especially pp. 149–231. For the libertarian case against government subsidies for medical care, see Loren E. Lomasky, "Medical Progress and National Health Care," in Marshall Cohen et al. (eds.), *Medicine and Moral Philosophy* (Princeton, N.J.: Princeton University Press, 1981), pp. 115–38; and Robert Sade, "Medical Care as a Right: A Refutation," *New England Journal of Medicine*, 285 (1971), pp. 1288–92. See also "Letters to the Editor in Response to Sade," *New England Journal of Medicine*, 286 (1972), pp. 488–93.

John Rawls' *A Theory of Justice* (Cambridge, Mass.: Harvard University Press, 1971) is the most systematic statement of egalitarianism. See especially pp. 90–108 and 221–34. See also Brian Barry, *Justice as Impartiality* (Oxford: Clarendon Press, 1995).

The Arizona case is discussed in Amy Gutmann and Dennis Thompson, *Democracy and Disagreement* (Cambridge, Mass.: Harvard University Press, 1996).

For a Rawlsian defense of distributing health care based on need, see Norman Daniels, *Just Health Care* (Cambridge, England: Cambridge University Press, 1985). For a more communitarian perspective on distributing health care, see Ezekiel Emanuel, *The Ends of Human Life: Medical Ethics in a Liberal Polity* (Cambridge, Mass.: Harvard University Press, 1991).

For an assessment of egalitarian principles applied to health-care policy, see Amy Gutmann, "For and Against Equal Access to Health Care," in Ronald Bayer et al. (eds.), *In Search of Equity: Health Care Need and the Health Care System* (New York: Plenum Press, 1983), pp. 43–68. Peter Singer provides a sophisticated utilitarian case for a national health service in "Freedoms and Utilities in the Distribution of Health Care" in G. Dworkin et al. (eds.), *Markets and Morals* (Washington, D.C.: Hemisphere Pub., 1977), pp. 149–73. Ronald Dworkin outlines an egalitarian defense of a national health care plan in "Will Clinton's Plan Be Fair?" *New York Review of Books* (January 13, 1994), pp. 20–25.

On AIDS, see Ronald Bayer, *Private Acts and Social Consequences: AIDS and the Politics of Public Health* (New York: Free Press, 1989), and Christine Pierce and Donald Van De Veer (eds.), *AIDS: Ethics and Public Policy* (Belmont, Calif.: Wadsworth, 1988).

For the role of reciprocity in welfare reform, see Amy Gutmann and Dennis Thompson, *Democracy and Disagreement*, ch. 8. For other philosophical perspectives on welfare, see Robert Goodin, *Reasons for Welfare: The Political Theory of the Welfare State* (Princeton, N.J.: Princeton University Press, 1988); and Philippe Van Parijs (ed.), *Arguing for Basic Income: Ethical Foundations for a Radical Reform* (London: Verso, 1992).

For important contemporary perspectives on welfare policy, see David Ellwood, *Poor Support: Poverty in the American Family* (New York: Basic Books, 1988); William Julius Wilson, *The Truly Disadvantaged: The Inner City, the Underclass, and Public Policy* (Chicago: University of Chicago Press, 1987); and Lawrence Mead, *Beyond Entitlement: The Social Obligations of Citizenship* (New York: Free Press, 1986).

On the importance of employment, see Judith N. Shklar, *American Citizenship: The Quest for Inclusion* (Cambridge, Mass.: Harvard University Press, 1991), ch. 2; Richard J. Arneson, "Is Work Special? Justice and the Distribution of Employment," *American Political Science Review*, 84 (1990), pp. 1127–48; and Jon Elster, "Is There (or Should There Be) a Right to Work?," in Amy Gutmann (ed.), *Democracy and the Welfare State* (Princeton, N.J.: Princeton University Press, 1988), pp. 53–78.

7 Equal Opportunity

Introduction

Imagine a hundred yard dash in which one of the two runners had his legs shackled together. He has progressed ten yards, while the unshackled runner has gone fifty yards. How do they rectify the situation? Do they merely remove the shackles and allow the race to proceed? They could say that equal opportunity now prevailed. But one of the runners would still be forty yards ahead of the other. Would it not be the better part of justice to allow the previously shackled runner to make up the forty-yard gap; or to start the race all over again?—Lyndon B. Johnson

Deciding what is the better part of justice in a footrace is easy. The social problem that President Johnson intended his analogy to address is as difficult as it is enduring: What employment policies does justice require in a society with a history of discrimination that has yet to be overcome? The problem is hard in part because the stakes are so high. Jobs are a means to income, power, prestige, and self-respect. Yet the race for employment cannot be started over again, and employers may not be obliged to help those who have been shackled by discrimination make up the distance in the ongoing race.

The most widely accepted principle governing the allocation of jobs in our society is nondiscrimination. The nondiscrimination principle has two parts. The first stipulates that the qualifications for a job be relevant to its social function. The second specifies that all qualified candidates be given equal consideration for the job.

This simple statement of the principle masks the complexity of its application in particular cases. What qualifications are relevant, for example, to the job of teaching mathematics in a public high school? Knowledge of mathematics clearly is relevant, but the job should not necessarily go to the candidate who knows the most mathematics. Just as relevant to the job but much harder to measure is teaching ability. Certain personality traits—ability to get along with other teachers or to win the respect of students—also predict success on the job. But it would be unfair to refuse to hire blacks or women because other teachers cannot get along with them or because some students have less respect for them. We must therefore add a proviso to the principle of relevance: candidates should not be disqualified on grounds of prejudice.

Equal consideration certainly prohibits employers from refusing to look at a candidate just because the person is a woman or black. But it may also require employers to actively seek applications from women and blacks if they are not applying for jobs because of past discrimination. Equal consideration therefore may require different treatment for different categories of people: more active recruitment for blacks and women than for white males and more active recruitment for blacks than for women.

Proponents of preferential hiring—the selection of basically qualified persons of a disadvantaged group over more-qualified persons of an advantaged group—reject the requirements of relevant qualifications and equal consideration now in order to overcome the effects of past discrimination and to achieve a society of fair opportunity for all in the future. They correctly point out that the requirement of equal consideration does not permit employers to choose less qualified candidates for a job because they are underrepresented in the workforce or have been discriminated against in the past. Although they concede that equal consideration would be justified in a just society, they argue that only preferential treatment can satisfy the principles of fair equality of opportunity in a society still burdened by a history of injustice.

There are three distinct interpretations of how preferential hiring remedies past discrimination. The first is that preferential hiring makes up the distance that women and minorities have lost in the race for employment by giving them the jobs they would have had if they had not been discriminated against. Critics argue that preferential hiring is at best an imperfect means of achieving this goal because the most qualified women and minorities often have suffered the least past discrimination. On the second interpretation, preferential hiring provides compensation or restitution for past injuries. Critics of this view question whether jobs are the most effective or fairest means of compensation. They suggest that the costs of preferential hiring are inequitably distributed and the benefits are rarely directed toward those who have suffered the most. On the third interpretation, preferential hiring breaks down the racial or sexual stereotyping of highly visible social positions—a stereotyping that makes it presently impossible to engage in truly nondiscriminatory hiring practices. Proponents of preferential hiring therefore argue that it establishes the social conditions for nondiscrimination in the future. But critics claim that passing over more-qualified candidates for valuable social positions is too high a price to pay.

The cases in this section illustrate two types of policies intended to promote justice of hiring—policies designed to remedy a private company's particular history of discrimination and policies designed to remedy more broadly based discrimination by providing roughly proportionate representation in the public sector. In judging the AT&T settlement, which affected the jobs of thousands of people, we can draw on statistical generalization about the past employment practices and future goals of the employer. In judging the proposal before the Pasadena City Council, which affects far fewer people, we must rely entirely on statistics showing underrepresentation in the workforce and generalizations about past discrimination not only (or even primarily) by the city government but also by society at large. In both cases, even when we are concerned with justice to individuals, we must attend to the general categories in which policy speaks.

Affirmative Action at AT&T
Robert K. Fullinwider

INTRODUCTION

On January 18, 1973, American Telephone and Telegraph Company (AT&T) entered into an agreement with several agencies of the federal government to implement what was called by the judge who approved it the "largest and most impressive civil rights settlement in the history of this nation."[1] Over a six-year period AT&T spent millions of dollars and undertook extensive overhaul of its personal policies to carry out the terms of the agreement.

Several pieces of litigation flowed directly from the agreement itself. Moreover, the government used its "victory" over AT&T as the springboard for further successes, gaining affirmative action agreements with Delta Airlines later in 1973 and with the Bank of America and several trucking companies in 1974. Also in the same year it won an agreement with nine steel companies, representing 73 percent of the steel industry, which resulted in a backpay settlement of $31,000,000 and extensive changes in the employment practices of the companies.[2]

The case began in late 1970 when AT&T applied to the Federal Communications Commission (FCC) for an increase in long distance rates. In December of 1970, the Equal Employment Opportunity Commission (EEOC) asked to intervene in the proceedings. The EEOC had been created by Title VII of the Civil Rights Act of 1964 to enforce the Title's prohibition of employment discrimination. At the time EEOC sought to intervene in the FCC hearings it had received more than 2,000 individual charges of illegal discrimination against AT&T.[3] Because the FCC's own rules pro-

hibited discrimination in the industries it regulated, the EEOC decided to take advantage of the pending rate hearing to press a case against AT&T on many grounds, accusing it of violating equal pay and antidiscrimination legislation as well as FCC rules.

In January 1971, the FCC decided to establish a separate set of hearings on the employment practices of AT&T and to allow the intervention of EEOC. The hearings were to determine if AT&T's practices violated equal employment opportunity policies and to "determine . . .what order, or requirements, if any, should be adopted by the Commission."[4] During the sixty days of hearings, involving 150 witnesses and hundreds of exhibits, a voluminous record of AT&T employment practices was created.[5]

EEOC charged that AT&T engaged in widespread sex segregation of jobs. Males were consistently channeled away from "female" jobs and females away from "male" jobs; transfers and promotion policies maintained the segregation; most of the lowest paying jobs were "female" jobs; and women were paid less than men when they did comparable work.

Of AT&T's 800,000 employees in 1970 (encompassing those employed by AT&T and its Bell System companies but excluding Western Electric and Bell Labs), more than half were women. Yet women comprised only 1 percent of career management personnel. Those women who held career management positions were generally limited to staff positions, without supervisory functions. Upper management personnel were drawn from two sources. On one hand, they were recruited into management training courses from colleges and universities. Company policy limited or excluded women from these courses. Secondly, management personnel were also recruited from within the Bell companies, primarily from craft positions. These were "male" occupations.[6]

At the nonmanagement level, operator, clerical, and inside sales jobs were considered "female" jobs; craft and outside sales jobs were considered "male." Men and women applicants were given different tests and channeled into different divisions.

> Since women were not allowed to take the tests, they could not qualify for craft jobs in the Plant Department. When openings arose in the Plant Department, women employees with seniority were not permitted to bid on them.[7]

Of the more than 400,000 women employed by AT&T in 1971, 80 percent of them were in three job categories: operator, clerical, and administrative (secretarial). Each of these were overwhelmingly "female" jobs. Sex-segregation of jobs was in fact more extensive within the Bell Companies than within the nation as a whole.[8]

The jobs that women worked in were lower paying than the jobs men worked in even when they did the same work. The inside craft job of "frameman" was a male job in all companies except Michigan Bell, where it was called, "switchroom helper" and was a female job. When it finally concluded its affirmative action agreement with the government, AT&T had to give $500,000 in pay raises to the switchroom helpers at Michigan Bell to bring their wages to the level they would have been paid had they been male framemen.[9]

The EEOC also accused AT&T of discriminating against blacks and other minorities. Of the 72,000 blacks employed in 1970, 80 percent were female. Black males were few and held the lowest-paying "male" nonmanagement jobs. There were extremely few blacks in management positions. Hispanics were likewise poorly represented in the workforce of those Bell companies located in areas of the country with high Hispanic populations.[10]

In 1971, as the EEOC and the company prepared for the hearings, they also began informal negotiations, encouraged by the administrative law judge, to find a basis for settling the case without formal proceedings. The negotiations continued on an intermittent basis throughout 1971 and 1972 as the hearings were conducted. During this period the Department of Labor issued Revised Order #4. This was a set of rules to implement Executive Order 11246, issued by President Johnson in 1965. It required all federal contractors as a condition for retaining or acquiring federal contracts to take "affirmative action" to assure nondiscrimination in employment practices. The Executive Order assigned to the Secretary of Labor the responsibility of designing and enforcing rules to implement the Order. Revised Order #4 contained rules which required contractors to create affirmative action plans containing goals and timetables for the hiring and upgrading of "underutilized" groups—minorities and women. The Department of Labor assigned to Government Services Administration (GSA) the authority to administer Revised Order #4 in the telephone industry.

In the winter of 1972, AT&T submitted an affirmative action plan to GSA. Six months later, without consulting EEOC, GSA approved the plan. EEOC protested to the Solicitor of the Department of Labor, who set aside the GSA approval and joined EEOC in its negotiation with AT&T.[11]

EEOC had by this time filed charges against AT&T in three different federal courts. The hearings before the FCC still held open the possibility it would take regulatory action against AT&T. Moreover, the new participation of the Labor Department meant that AT&T's status as a federal contractor could be jeopardized unless it produced a satisfactory affirmative action plan. Faced with dim prospects of resisting successfully on three fronts, AT&T agreed to a consent decree in January, 1973, which was approved by the federal District Court in Philadelphia, one of the jurisdictions in which EEOC had filed charges. Without formally admitting any wrongdoing, AT&T agreed to undertake to increase the representation of women and minorities in job categories in which they were underrepresented and to compensate through back-pay and wage increases those who were putatively victims of its past discriminatory practices. In return, the government agreed to suspend its legal and administrative actions.

II. The Consent Decree

There were two elements to the agreement embodied in the January, 1973, consent decree. AT&T would first pay $15,000,000 in back-pay to 13,000 women and 2,000 minority men, and would make additional wage adjustments for 36,000 women and minorities.[12] As it worked out, the wage adjustment amounted to $30,000,000 the first year, for a total outlay of $45,000,000. (On March 30, 1974, AT&T and the government signed a second consent decree, which covered management personnel, calling for an additional $30,000,000 in backpay and wage adjustments for 25,000 persons.)

Second, the company formulated a Model Affirmative Action Plan which altered its recruiting, transfer, and promotion policies, and which set hiring and promotion "targets" or "goals" for fifteen job classifications. The ultimate minority goals for each Bell company were set in accordance with the minority ratio in the local labor force. The ultimate female goals were set at 38 percent for most job classifications in which they were underrepresented.[13] Accomplishment of these ultimate goals would result in proportional representation of minorities and women in all the job classifications in which they were underrepresented—that is, would result in minorities and women being employed in the same proportions to their numbers in the relevant labor force. The objective was "statistical parity."

To move toward the ultimate goals, yearly intermediate "targets" were formulated for each Bell company and each job classification by means of an elaborate formula. Based on estimations of yearly hiring and promotion opportunities in a classification, the current percentage of minorities or women in that classification, and the ultimate goal for that classification, yearly goals could be formulated.[14]

For example, suppose in job X at Central Bell 10 percent of the workers were female. Since the ultimate goal for females in X is approximately 40 percent (this is the level of female participation in the nation's workforce), the company was only at 25 percent of "full utilization" (proportional representation). By a special formula, this percentage was to be multiplied by a factor of 2 and the resulting percentage be the goal for female new hires for the year. If, for example, there were ten openings anticipated for the coming year in X, five of those hired would have to be women.

The hiring and promotion goals, consequently, required hiring and promotions at rates proportionately greater than the availability of women and minorities in the relevant labor pools or promotion pools. This was clearly expressed in the Model Affirmative Action Plan:

> The Equal Employment objective for the Bell System is to achieve, within a reasonable period of time, an employee profile, with respect to race and sex in each major job classification, which is an approximate reflection of proper utilization. . . .
>
> This objective calls for achieving full utilization of minorities and women at all levels of management and nonmanagement and by job classification *at a pace beyond that which would occur normally.* . . .[15]

An important feature of the Model Plan, which facilitated this accelerated hiring and upgrading, was provision for an "affirmative action override." In accord with its union contract, the company's promotion criteria called for "selection of the best qualified employee and for consideration of net credited service. . . ."[16]

Where employees were equally qualified, length of service was supposed to be decisive. The "affirmative action override" permitted (and required) both criteria—"best qualifications" and "longest service"—to be defeated whenever adhering to them did not allow the company to meet its goals (targets). In a supplemental order signed in 1976, the obligation of AT&T in regard to its affirmative action goals was expressed thus:

> . . . to the extent any Bell System operating company is unable to meet its intermediate targets in [non-management] job classification 5–15 using these criteria [i.e., best qualified, most senior], the Decree requires that . . . selections be made from any at least basically qualified candidates for promotion and hiring of the group or groups for which the target is not being met . . . .[17]

Thus, the consent decree and the Model Plan quite clearly envisaged the use of racial and sexual preferences. The intermediate targets or goals of the operating companies in the Bell System were mandatory; and the companies could and must hire or promote less qualified and less senior persons over more qualified and more senior persons if this was what it took to achieve the intermediate targets.

Since the consent decree applied to 800,000 employees for six years, it is not hard to imagine that there were numerous instances in which employees or applicants were preferred over others because of their race or sex. It is difficult to establish exactly how frequently AT&T resorted to racial or sexual preferences. The company changed the way it defined "affirmative action overrides" during the duration of the decree, it avoided careful counting, and it never classified as overrides any preferences given in management jobs (classification 1–4).[18]

Two observers report 28,850 overrides in 1973–74, although they differ on how many there were in 1975–76. The first claims there were about 12,000, the second

that there were approximately 6,600.[19] A third observer reports 70,000 overrides during the four-year period.[20] It would probably be a reasonably conservative conjecture that over the full 1973–79 life of the consent decree, and counting both nonmanagement and management jobs, at least 50,000 times AT&T gave a racial or sexual preference in hiring or promoting someone. AT&T acheived 90 percent of its intermediate goals in 1974, 97 percent in 1975, and 99 percent thereafter.[21]

In January 1979, the consent decree expired. AT&T retained most features of its program, aiming in the future to continue efforts toward the long-range goal of approximate proportional representation. It did, however, drop the affirmative action override form its repertoire of affirmative action tools.

III. RESULTS

As a consequence of the implementation of the Model Plan, considerable progress was made in increasing the representation of women and minorities in jobs from which they had been largely excluded in the past. For example, between 1973 and 1979 there was a 38 percent increase in the number of women employed in the top three job classifications (officials and mangers), while there was only a 5.3 percent increase in the number of men. Women made significant strides in sales positions, increasing in numbers by 53 percent (a growth rate seven times faster than that of white males), and in inside crafts, increasing by 68 percent (white males were decreasing by 10 percent).[22] In the outside crafts, the number of women grew by 5,300 while the number of men declined by 6,700. Only in clerical positions did the number of women grow at a lesser rate than men.[23]

Black and Hispanic males also made gains in management and sales positions and inside crafts. In each case their growth rate exceeded the rate of total growth in these jobs.

Although women made important strides in

status and mobility at AT&T, the total number of women employed actually declined between 1973 and 1979. At the end of 1972, AT&T employed 415,725 women (52.4 percent of all employees); at the beginning of 1979, it employed 408,671 women (50.8 percent of all employees). This overall decline was not inconsistent with the consent decree. The decree had two aims in regard to women. One was to move women in significant numbers into previously "male" jobs. The other was related: to break down the stereotype of "male" and "female" jobs at AT&T. Both aims were promoted by acting to increase the number of men in the administrative (i.e., secretarial), clerical, and operator jobs. This both worked against the stereotyping and allowed the company to significantly increase the share of women in other job categories without at the same time raising even higher their share of the total workforce.[24]

Two examples illustrate the steps AT&T took to break down the sex-segregation of earlier years. For one thing, the company made clerical positions entry level jobs for men. In 1973, 17 percent of men hired in the Bell companies entered through clerical positions, while 83 percent entered through craft positions. In 1979, 43.7 percent of men hired entered through clerical positions, while only 56.3 percent entered through crafts. Overall, the percentage of men in clerical roles grew from 5.9 percent to 11.1 percent.[25]

Secondly, the company made valiant efforts to increase the number of women in outside crafts. As a result of its efforts, by 1979 4.7 percent of outside craft workers were women, a 550 percent increase from 1973. This achievement was not without its difficulties or costs. The company inaugurated new pole-climbing courses, instituted new safety procedures, modified equipment for use by women, and recruited aggressively. Even so, the company was never faced with a superfluity of female applicants for outside jobs. There were high rates of female failure in the pole-climbing course, and high rates of attrition among those females who worked in the outside jobs. Accident rates for women were two to three times those of men.[26] In its new affirmative action program after the consent decree expired in 1979, AT&T decided to slow its integration of women into outside crafts.

IV. Costs and Benefits

The affirmative action program with its override provision generated unhappiness and lowered morale among white male employees, who viewed themselves as victims of "reverse discrimination and blocked opportunity." One survey indicated most white male employees were antagonistic toward the program.[27] It is easy enough to understand how perceptions of "reverse discrimination" could occur. In 1976, for example, fully two-thirds of all promotions went to women.[28] Instances in which the override resulted in very qualified and senior men being passed over in favor of inexperienced women doubtlessly occurred often enough to provide ample gripe material on the male grapevine. Thousands of grievances were filed within the copy and there were two dozen reverse discrimination law suits.[29]

The most important law suits were by the major Bell union, the Communications Workers of America (CWA), which attempted without success to overthrow the affirmative action override.[30] In an unusual case, one AT&T worker, Daniel McAleer, did manage to win $7,500 in damages from the company as a result of his being passed over for promotion in favor of a woman. The court, which upheld his claim of reverse discrimination, explained:

> This is a sex discrimination case. Plaintiff . . .was denied promotion by American Telephone & Telegraph Co. (AT&T). He was entitled to promotion under the provisions of a collective bargaining agreement but the job was given to a less qualified, less senior female solely because of her sex.[31]

The disgruntlement of male employees was not the only negative effect of the affirmative action program. One observer reported in *Fortune* that "two different telephone consultants . . .believe the consent decree had done some damage to AT&T's efficiency."[32] The decree resulted in some promotions of inexperienced and inadequately trained persons. There was some lowering of quality standards and the development of "double standards of discipline and performance."[33] Minorities and women were able to air grievances outside of regular channels, and supervisors were more reluctant to discipline or complain about women and minority workers. The supervisors' authority and power were eroded in other ways too, especially by the centralization of personnel decisions in the personnel offices. Previously, supervisors had considerable say about who got promoted.

The policy of forcing men to enter through clerical positions resulted in increased turnover, as did the efforts to increase the number of women in the outside crafts. There, the high attrition and accident rate of women probably resulted in some general decline in performance. However, overall turnover for all employees at AT&T appeared to have actually declined between 1973–1979.[34]

The affirmative action override, requiring the use of racial and sexual preferences, certainly contained the potential of pitting white against black, male against female. Racial and sexual hostility could have been inflamed. However, despite the widespread disgruntlement of white males with the affirmative action program, there appears to have been little adverse impact on employee relations.[35]

On the other hand, AT&T has reaped benefits from the consent decree. A company that employs 800,000 people has a voracious need for labor; and by virtually doubling its pool from which to fill its crafts, sales, and management jobs, the company has a richer source of talent to draw upon than before. Large numbers of qualified and ambitious minorities and women are now able to compete with white males for jobs, often with a resulting increase in the quality of those who win the competition.

Personnel departments, as a result of the need to monitor and manage the achievement of the affirmative action goals, have taken over much of the role in promoting and upgrading workers. Although a negative effect of this is erosion of the authority of supervisors, a positive effect is the greater objectivity and rationality that has been brought to the promotion process. The affirmative action plan and its goals have forced AT&T to be very much clearer about qualification and training standards for career advancement, and this has benefitted both company and workers.[36]

V. THE ISSUE POSED

That white male employees suffered lowered morale under the AT&T affirmative action program is not by itself morally significant. People can be disgruntled by changes which are perfectly legitimate or even morally mandatory. Whites, for example, might resist being supervised by blacks out of prejudice and hatred; or males might resent being bossed by perfectly qualified females. The disgruntlement of employees is more than just a management problem if it is based on *legitimate* grievances. In the case of the AT&T affirmative action program, there is no question that direct and explicit sexual and racial preferences were given in order to fill hiring and promotion goals. The representational aims of the affirmative action program could not otherwise have been accomplished. As a result, the expectations of achievement and advancement were frustrated for many persons because they turned out to be the wrong color or sex.

Is it reasonable or permissible to advance such representational aims by policies which select by race or sex? Aren't such policies unfair to some individuals? In an attitudinal survey taken in 1978, one AT&T worker offered this lament:

One thing that really bothers me is moving up in the company. I am white, male, twenty-five. I am not a brain, but average. I have a lot of drive and want to get ahead. I have just been notified there is some kind of freeze which will last three or four months. [Note: frequently, when a goal couldn't be met, all promotions would be frozen until a person of the right sex or race could be found for the next slot.] In that time, if I am passed over, the company will go to the street. *This is not fair. I work for the company but my chances are less than someone on the street.*"[37]

One irony of the AT&T program was that this "unfairness" was not always confined to white males. As we have noted, a central feature of the consent decree was the aim that male participation in "female" jobs would increase just as female participation in "male" jobs increased. Thus, the Model Plan called for male hiring quotas in clerical jobs, with the ultimate goal of having 25 percent males in this category of jobs. (An informal goal called for 10 percent male operators.)[38] Affirmative action override thus was not applied only against white males; it was actually on occasion applied against women as well.

One AT&T employee, Bertha Biel, went to court when she was passed over for advancement so that a man could be selected. The court record tells the story:

The employee, a female records clerk, on March 29, 1973 applied for a promotion to the position of operations clerk, a higher-paid job, when it became available. In January of 1973, however, the Company had conducted a work force analysis, required by the terms of the Title VII decree, and determined that males were underutilized in clerical positions. Under the decree the position of operations clerk falls into job class 11, a clerical job title which had traditionally been filled by females. The decree required the establishment of male hiring goals for this job class. In October 1973 the Company had one job class 11 opening to be filled for the remainder of the year. It had not met its intermediate goals for that year since no males had sought the opening. Accordingly, it filled its last opening for the year by hiring a male not previously employed by the Company.[39]

The court held against Bertha Biel and for the company. Thus, Bertha Biel could join the twenty-five-year-old male worker's lament: "This is not fair. I work for the company but my chances are less than someone on the street."

On one level, it may seem a legal puzzle that a program like AT&T's which used sexual preferences against both men and women, as the occasion dictated, could be held by courts to be an appropriate expression of a law which says that it is an unlawful practice for an employer "to discriminate against any individual with respect to his compensation, term, conditions, or privileges of employment, because of such individual's race, color, sex, or national origin . . ." (Title VII, Civil Rights Act of 1964, 42 U.S.C. 20002[2]). On another level, we are confronted with the question whether—judicial approval aside—the AT&T program was morally acceptable and an expression of a just social policy. Questions of fairness and justice were central to many of the complaints by AT&T workers and to the litigation by the unions. Likewise, decisions about the moral rightness (or at least moral tolerability) of the affirmative action program were made by management, judges, and government officials involved in its implementation. Moreover, the AT&T consent decree occurred in the midst of an ongoing public debate about the morality of "reverse discrimination."

Notes

1. *EEOC v. AT&T*, 365 F. Supp. 1105 (1973), at 1108.

2. See *United States v. Allegheny-Ludlum Industries*, 11 FEP Cases 167 (1975); Phyllis A. Wallace, "What Did We Learn?" in Phyllis A. Wallace, ed., *Equal Employment Opportunity and the AT&T Case* (Cambridge, Mass.: MIT Press, 1976), p. 278.

3. Phyllis A. Wallace and Jack E. Nelson, "Legal Processes and Strategies of Intervention," in Wallace, ed., *Equal Employment Opportunity*, p. 243.

4. Ibid., p. 246.

5. 365 F. Supp. at 1109.

6. Wallace, *Equal Employment Opportunity*, p. 4; Judith Long Laws, "The Bell Telephone System: A Case Study," in Wallace, ed., *Equal Employment Opportunity*, pp. 160–61.

7. Laws, "Bell System," p. 154

8. Ibid., p. 157.

9. Wallace and Nelson, "Legal Processes," p. 252; and Wallace, "The Consent Decree," in Wallace, ed., *Equal Employment Opportunity*, pp. 273–74.

10. Wallace, "Equal Employment Opportunity," in Wallace, ed., *Equal Employment Opportunity*, p. 258; Herbert R. Northrup and John A. Larson, *The Impact of the AT&T-EEO Consent Decree* (Philadelphia: The Wharton School, University of Pennsylvania, 1979), pp. 6–7 and tables pp. 41–65.

11. Wallace and Nelson, "Legal Processes," pp. 243–51.

12. Wallace, "Consent Decree," p. 272. The text of the decree is given on pp. 283–96.

13. Carol Loomis, "AT&T in the Throes of 'Equal Employment,'" *Fortune* 99 (Jan. 15, 1979), p. 47. The ultimate female goal for the outside crafts was set at 19 percent.

14. For details, see Northrup and Larson, "Impact," pp. 19–22.

15. FEP 431: 82. Emphasis added.

16. *EEOC v. AT&T*, 13 FEP Cases 392 (1976), at 402.

17. 13 FEP Cases at 402.

18. Loomis, "AT&T," p. 54. "All personnel executives interviewed testified that it [giving preference] has been both regular and often has been the only way the targets could be met." Northrup and Larson, "Impact," p. 57.

19. Loomis, "AT&T," p. 54; Northrup and Larson, "Impact," p. 14.

20. Jerry Flint, "In Bell System's Minority Plan, Women Get Better Jobs, But Total Number of Female Workers Drops," *New York Times*, July 5, 1977, C13.

21. Loomis, "AT&T," p. 50; Northrup and Larson, "Impact," p. 12.

22. Northrup and Larson, "Impact," pp. 25, 53, 55, 65.

23. Ibid., pp. 59, 61.

24. Since women compose about 40 percent of the U.S. labor force, they were already overrepresented—in gross numbers—at AT&T. The problem was not the lack of women employees, but the segregating of them.

25. Northrup and Larson, "Impact," pp. 59, 64.

26. Ibid., pp. 60–62; Loomis, "AT&T," p. 50.

27. Northrup and Larson, "Impact," p. 78.

28. Ibid., p. 80; Loomis, "AT&T," p. 54; Flint, "Bell System's Plan," p. C13.

29. 13 FEP Cases at 418; Loomis, "AT&T," p. 54.

30. See *EEOC v. AT&T*, 365 F. Supp. 1105 (1973); *EEOC v. AT&T*, 506 F. 2d 735 (1974); *EEOC v. AT&T*, 13 FEP Cases 392 (1976).

31. McAleer v. AT&T, 416 F. Supp. 435 (1976), at 436.

32. Loomis, "AT&T," p. 57.

33. Northrup and Larson, "Impact," p. 76.

34. Loomis, "AT&T," p. 57; Northrup and Larson, "Impact," p. 68.

35. Northrup and Larson, "Impact," p. 79.

36. Ibid., pp. 68, 232; Loomis, "AT&T," p. 57.

37. Northrup and Larson, "Impact," p. 78. Emphasis added.

38. Loomis, "AT&T," p. 47; Northrup and Larson, "Impact," p. 58.

39. *Telephone Workers Union v. N.J. Bell Tel.*, 584 F. 2d 31 (1978), at 32.

Comment

Consider the evidence that critics of AT&T could present when they first made their charges of discrimination by the company. The statistics on the numbers of women and blacks in various job categories are an important part of the evidence, but they prove nothing by themselves. What additional information makes, or would make, the charge of discrimination against AT&T morally compelling?

Consider separately the justification for the two elements of the consent decree of January 1973: (1) back-pay and wage adjustments and (2) the Model Affirmative Action Plan. Was the government right to require both elements, or would only one have been preferable?

An advocate of nondiscrimination might criticize the consent decree for requiring AT&T to institute preferential hiring rather than to pursue a policy of nondiscrimination in the future. What would a policy of nondiscrimination require of AT&T? Try to specify in as much detail as possible nondiscriminatory qualifications for the various job categories. Consider, for example, whether length of service with the company is a discriminatory standard. Also, try to specify what a nondiscriminatory policy of recruitment would be.

What are the best reasons for rejecting a policy of hiring the most qualified candidates? Would the fact that such a policy takes a long time to break sexual and racial stereotypes and to achieve a balanced workforce be a good reason? How do we decide how long is too long?

Next consider what is morally questionable about the affirmative action override instituted by AT&T. Which, if any, of the following effects of the override can you justify: (1) bypassing more qualified men from outside the company; (2) bypassing more qualified men for promotion from the inside; (3) discriminating against women for clerical jobs; or (4) decreasing efficiency of service and increasing prices to consumers?

Some critics of preferential hiring argue that justice permits using affirmative action goals (employment targets based on predictions of how many women and minorities will be hired if practices are nondiscriminatory) but prohibits using quotas (places reserved for women and minorities regardless of their relative qualifications). Is there a clear distinction between goals and quotas in the AT&T plan? Is the use of either, or both, morally justifiable?

Affirmative Action in Pasadena
Pamela Varley

Early in 1985, the Pasadena city council (formally called the Board of Directors) was asked to extend the city's affirmative action protections to Armenian Americans. At the time, the Southern California city of 130,000 had an Armenian population of 13,000—the most rapidly growing community of Armenians anywhere in the country. If they approved the proposal, the councillors would be

Reprinted by permission of the Case Program, Kennedy School of Government, Harvard University. Copyright © 1988 by the President and Fellows of Harvard College.

setting a national precedent. No other city had ever before named Armenians a "protected class" under affirmative action law. In the past, Pasadena's Affirmative Action Office had designated women, blacks, Hispanics, Asians, native Americans, Pacific Islanders, and the handicapped as the classes to be protected—the same groups covered by federal law.

The city council sent the proposal to its Human Relations Committee for review in January. In early March, the committee returned the question to the council with a recommendation. The matter was scheduled for a vote on March 19.

THE ORDINANCE

Pasadena's affirmative action ordinance, enacted in 1980, required city administrators to take positive action "the goal of which is to see that protected classes are represented in the work force to the same extent that they are represented in the relevant labor market." (The "relevant labor market" means those able and willing to perform the duties of any given job.) The Affirmative Action Office was to work actively with city administrators to establish hiring goals and timetables, to arrange for training and upgrading of protected class members, and to monitor and report on the city's progress. (See Exhibit 1.) When contracting for supplies or services, city administrators were to recruit bids from minority- and women-owned firms and to require that any city contractor be an equal opportunity or affirmative action employer. (See Exhibit 2.) There was some talk of strengthening this part of the law by giving minority- and women-owned businesses a percentage differential in bidding competitions. Local businesses were already given such a differential. Thus, if enacted, all minority- and women-owned businesses would receive some advantage, and local minority- and women-owned firms would enjoy an even greater advantage.

PROFILE OF PASADENA

In spring of 1985, about 25 percent of Pasadena's population was black, 22 percent was Hispanic, (and that number was growing), 10 percent was Armenian, 6 percent was Asian, and 37 percent was white. (Throughout this case, we use "white" to mean "white and not belonging to a designated ethnic minority.") The white population was mostly middle class to wealthy and wielded disproportionate control over city affairs. Of the seven members of the

city council, for instance, six were white—five men and one woman. The other councillor was a black woman. In addition, top management positions in the city were held predominantly by white men, although a few inroads had been made; the Police Chief was a black man; the Deputy City manager, an Armenian man; and both the Finance Director and Assistant City Manager were white women.

On the whole, black and Hispanic residents were the city's most economically disadvantaged population groups. The Asian population was economically mixed. (Newly arrived Southeast Asian refugees were in the worst straits, although their economic status tended to improve quickly.)

The Armenian community, too, was mixed—culturally and politically as well as economically. About half the Armenians in Pasadena were immigrants or descendants of immigrants who arrived in the United States between 1895 and 1925. On the whole, they had assimilated, were economically well off, and tended to be moderate to conservative politically. The others had immigrated within the last five to ten years from Beirut and other Middle Eastern cities, and were struggling economically, some living in low income enclaves. Many had held professional jobs in the Middle East, but encountered difficulty finding similar work in Pasadena due in part to language and cultural barriers. Fighting to retain their identity as Armenians, these newcomers had not assimilated and in fact, felt ambivalent or negative about assimilation. In addition, they were polarized on the question of their lost Armenian homeland. One Armenian city administrator estimated that about 10 percent felt allegiance to Soviet Armenia despite its domination by the U.S.S.R. Another 50 percent strongly supported an independent Armenia and were allied with the Pasadena chapter of the Armenian National Committee (ANC). And roughly

40 percent were neutral or quiet on the question.

PROPONENTS OF THE PROPOSAL

The idea of extending affirmative action protection to Armenians grew out of several incidents in which Armenians had either applied for city jobs or contracts and had been turned down, or had been fired from city jobs. Some Armenian candidates for city positions claimed that they had been weeded out of the complex multi-interview process for city jobs because they "talked with an accent."

The case that received the most attention was a competition among tow companies for the right to remove illegally parked cars from city streets. This contract was quite lucrative: when a vehicle owner could not pay off his/her tickets or towing charges, the tow company could take possession of the car. According to one city councillor, the city's Police Department had never gone through a formal competitive bidding process to award the contract in the past, instead granting it as a matter of tradition to a company called S.M. Ward & Son, owned by a prominent, well-connected white businessman. Under pressure from the city council, the Police Department put the service out to bid in 1985. The criteria for judging the competitors were the amount of the tow charge, the ability to provide prompt, round-the-clock service, and the capacity to store impounded cars. Two Armenian firms competed with Ward's for the contract. The largest of the two, Johnnie's Tow Service, had already won towing contracts with the local sheriff and highway patrol, and offered to charge less than Ward's for its tow jobs. The Police Department, however, awarded its towing contract to Ward's, reasoning that there was no compelling reason to make a change and that Johnnie's already had its hands full with its other towing obligations.

This incident spurred two local activists to action: Bill Paparian, an Armenian-American lawyer and member of the city council's Human Relations Committee, and Rick Cole, a white progressive city councillor. Although his family had lived in the United States for several generations, Paparian had formed an alliance with Armenian newcomers in the ANC and frequently represented them as an attorney. Thus the ANC, with Paparian as its spokesperson, began pushing for "protected" status for Armenians under the city's affirmative action ordinance. Paparian noted that Armenians made up 10 percent of the city population, yet less than one percent of the city work force: only three of the city's 1470 employees were Armenian. Other minority or protected groups tended to be underrepresented as well—particularly at top management levels—but not as underrepresented as the Armenians: 25 percent of the city work force was black, 16 percent Hispanic, 5 percent was Asian, and 31 percent was female. (See Exhibit 3.)

Paparian's proposal was actively supported by Cole, who was working to break up what he saw as a well-entrenched "old boy network" in Pasadena. By extending affirmative action to Armenians, Cole believed that—in addition to opening job opportunities to a broader group—the council would increase the base of support for affirmative action, draw the Armenian newcomers into progressive politics, and ultimately strengthen the city's progressive coalition of young liberals and minority groups.

THE QUIET OPPOSITION

There was little public opposition to Paparian's proposal, but behind the scenes, a number of people were upset about it—among them, established Armenian-Americans who were embarrassed at the suggestion that Armenians required preferential treatment under law. Many of them had fought long and hard to convince their neighbors that they were not inferior or "different," and they worried that being designated a "minority group" would set them back. In addition, the defenders of Soviet Armenia—while they did not play a major role in the debate—opposed the proposal sponsored by their ANC rival.

Some black and feminist activists also opposed the move, fearing that—by increasing the pool of individuals protected by affirmative action—the city would dilute the impact of the program. Already, roughly 75 percent of the city's population was officially covered by affirmative action. The affirmative action law had only been in effect for five years, and blacks in particular felt they were just beginning to win some hard-fought battles in the city. According to John Kennedy, president of the Pasadena chapter of the NAACP (National Association for the Advancement of Colored People), only in the early 1980s were blacks finally able to secure jobs in the Police and Fire Departments. At about the same time, the city narrowly voted to change election laws to allow for greater minority representation on the city council, "but the City of Pasadena has not given up anything without a fight," Kennedy added.

In addition, Kennedy and other activists felt that affirmative action was intended to redress longstanding, deep-rooted discrimination in the United States. "Never was affirmative action intended to right the wrongs of atrocities that occurred in Turkey," he argued, referring to the Turkish government's bloody 1915 genocide of 1.5 million Armenians. By casting too wide a net, the activists feared, the city council would "trivialize" its affirmative action policy. Already the idea of treating Armenians as a protected class had generated some snickering about town. After all, people wondered, why should Armenians be singled out for protection when a number of Armenians in Pasadena were well off if not affluent?

THE RECOMMENDATION OF THE HUMAN RELATIONS COMMITTEE

When the Human Relations Committee considered Paparian's proposal in early March, Paparian—a member of the committee—gave a strong pitch for it. In the end, the committee members concluded that in fact, recent Armenian immigrants were encountering discrimination within the city. In addition, they argued, most recent immigrants confronted prejudice and employment problems. Thus, on March 4, the committee recommended that the city council extend affirmative action protection not only to Armenians, but to any immigrant who had been living in the United States fewer than fifteen years. Two weeks later, with this recommendation in hand, the city council was scheduled to make its decision.

EPILOGUE

On March 19, 1985, the Pasadena city council voted 6 to 0 with one abstention to extend affirmative action protection to Armenian-Americans. (The councillors did not seriously consider the recommendation of the Human Relations Committee to extend affirmative action protection to any recent immigrant.) If anything, however, the question became more controversial during the intervening two years, particularly in the area of city service contracts. A Pasadena citizen's task force on affirmative action began to consider a proposal to give women- and minority-owned firms a 3 to 5 percent differential in bidding for city contracts, but some minority activists did not believe the differential should be given to Armenian-owned firms. Thus, even two years later, the matter was still not fully resolved.

Meanwhile, however, in the next round of contract awards, the Police Department split the city's towing contract between

Ward's and Johnnie's. And in May 1987, attorney Bill Paparian made a successful run for a city council seat in a district with a high concentration of Armenian residents, unseating a three-term incumbent.

EXHIBIT I. PASADENA'S AFFIRMATIVE ACTION ORDINANCE: AFFIRMATIVE ACTION IN CITY EMPLOYMENT, CHAPTER 2.39

2.39.010 Short title.

This chapter shall be known as the "affirmative action in city employment ordinance" (Ord. 5483 § 1 (part), 1980)

2.39.020 Scope.

The principles of equal opportunity in employment are applicable to all city employment, through Section 802 of the city Charter. In addition, the following equal opportunity employment laws apply, by their terms, from time to time, to city employment:

A. California Fair Employment Practices Act, as amended, Labor Code Section 1410 et seq.;

B. Title VII, Equal Employment Opportunity, of the Civil Rights Act of 1964, as amended, 42 U.S.C. Section 2000e et seq.;

C. Age discrimination in Employment Act of 1967, as amended, 29 U.S.C. Section 621 et seq.;

D. Section 504 of the Vocational Rehabilitation Act of 1973, as amended, 29 U.S.C. Section 701 et seq.

This chapter sets forth specific procedure for all city employment and employees. In addition, this chapter provides a specific mandate for the development of affirmative action plans to cover all city employment. (Ord. 5483 § 1 (part), 1980)

2.39.030 Policy statement of city.

This chapter together with the rules and regulations promulgated thereunder and the affirmative action plans generated pursuant to the provisions of this chapter and the rules and regulations promulgated thereunder is a restatement of and supersedes the Affirmative Action Program of the city, dated May 1973,

and adopted by Resolution No. 1812 on June 19, 1973, and reaffirmed by the board by oral motion on October 10, 1978.

The policy of the city shall be to provide equal opportunity employment to all persons and not to discriminate against any applicant or employee because of race, religious creed, color, national origin, ancestry, handicap, sex, or age. In the awareness that the intent of this policy is not necessarily fulfilled with the mere prohibition of discriminatory practices, the city will continue to take affirmative action to review all of its employment practices to assure the fulfillment of its stated commitment. (Ord. 5483 § 1 (part), 1980)

2.39.040 Definitions.

Whenever used in this chapter the following words shall have the meanings indicated:

A. "Affirmative action" means the taking of a positive action by an employer, the goal of which is to see that protected classes are represented in its work force to the same extent that they are represented in the relevant labor market. It is an extension of the concept of equal opportunity employment.

B. "Affirmative action employer" means an employer that practices affirmative action.

C. "Affirmative action officer" means a person designated by the city manager to administer, monitor and enforce the provisions of this chapter and to oversee the city's affirmative action activities.

D. "Affirmative action plan" means a written plan documenting an employer's affirmative action program.

E. "Affirmative action program" means the aggregate of the actions taken by an employer to achieve affirmative action.

F. "Age" means over the age of forty.

G. "Discrimination" means disparate treatment, policies or practices which perpetuate in the present the effects of past discrimination, policies or practices having disparate impact not justified by business necessity or bona fide occupational qualifications, and failure to make reasonable accommodation to an applicant's or employee's religious observances or practices.

H. "Employer" means the city.

I. "Employment practices" means any solicitation of, or advertisement for employees or employment; any action resulting in changes in grade or work assignment in the place or location of work; any determination affecting the layoff, suspension or termination of employees, the rate of pay or other form of compensation including vacation, sick leave and compensatory time; any decision affecting the selection for training including apprenticeship programs, the grant of employee benefits and participatory activities and promotions; any actions taken to discipline employees for infractions of work rules or employer requirements; functional reorganization; and any other actions which affect the terms and conditions of employment. The term "functional reorganization" includes the employment decisions with respect to increases or decreases in staff brought about by changes in management organization but shall not include the actions or consideration giving rise to such changes or the alteration or modification of the duties, responsibilities, or authority of existing staff.

J. "Equal Opportunity Employer" means an employer who practices equal opportunity employment.

K. "Equal Opportunity Employment" means the utilization of employment practices by an employer that do not discriminate against any protected class.

L. "Goals" means numerical objectives established by an employer with respect to the employer's hiring and promotion goals, the purpose of which is to correct any statistically significant underutilization of a protected class as identified by the employer's utilization analyses.

M. "Handicapped individual" means a person who (1) has a physical or mental impairment which substantially limits one or more of such person's major life activities, (2) has a record of such impairment or (3) is regarded as having such an impairment.

N. "Medical condition" means any health impairment for which a person has been rehabilitated or cured, based on competent medical evidence.

O. "Protected class" means a group of persons which is identified with respect to the race, religious creed, color, national origin, ancestry, handicap, medical condition, sex or age of its members.

P. "Relevant labor market" means that pool of workers, for each position that an employer maintains, that is ready, willing, and possesses the requisite skills to perform the tasks, functions, and duties of the position. The relevant labor market varies as a function of the skills required for the positions and the salary and benefits associated with the position.

Q. "Timetables" means the scheduled times for implementing goals. (Ord. 5483 § 1 (part), 1980)

2.39.045 Exemption.

The transition of employees of the Pasadena community development commission into city employment shall be exempt from the provisions of this chapter if the director of employee and community services agency finds and documents that the city position to be filled:

A. Was caused by the transfer of a redevelopment function from the Pasadena community development commission to the city and the duties of the position will remain essentially the same as the prior Pasadena community development commission position:

B. Is identical to the current Pasadena community development commission position; i.e., the job description is the same and the compensation is the same or shall be made so within a one-year period. (Ord. 5533 § 1, 1981)

2.39.050 Affirmative action plans.

A. The affirmative action officer, in conjunction with all department and agency heads, shall develop an affirmative action plan covering all city employment in accordance with the provisions of this chapter and the rules and regulations promulgated thereunder.

B. The ability and success of management personnel, in meeting their affirmative action and equal employment commitments shall be an important factor in determining the amount of their management merit benefit which is provided for in the salary resolution. For department and agency heads, the affirmative action and equal employment commitments include the goals and timetables established under Section 2.39.090 for that portion of the city's work force under their control. The city manager may provide for further sanctions under the personnel rules and regulations the city manager establishes under Section 2.39.050. Failure to achieve the goals and timetables shall be determinative unless a good-faith effort to achieve the goals and timetable has been documented. (Ord. 5495 § 1, 1980: Ord. 5483 § 1 (part), 1980)

2.39.060 Elements of the plan.

The affirmative action plans developed pursuant to this chapter shall contain the following elements:
A. Policy statement;
B. Utilization analyses;
C. Goals and timetables;
D. Employment practices;
E. Internal and external dissemination and reporting;
F. Internal auditing and monitoring. (Ord. 5483 § 1 (part), 1980)

2.39.070 Policy statement.

The policy statement shall be the second paragraph of Section 2.39.030. (Ord. 5483 § 1 (part), 1980)

2.39.080 Utilization analyses.

Utilization analyses of the work force of the city shall be conducted annually by the affirmative action officer in accordance with rules and regulations promulgated by the affirmative action officer but shall, in general include the following for each analysis:
A. An analysis of the work force in question by job classification groupings using the EEO-4 or similar categories, to determine the extent to which those protected classes identified by race, color, national origin, or sex are represented therein.
B. A comparison of the work force statistics developed in subsection A of this section with the equivalent statistics for the relevant labor market for the same job classification groupings to determine any statistical significant under-utilization. (Ord. 5483 § 1 (part), 1980)

2.39.090 Goals and timetables.

A. Goals and timetables for the work force of the city shall be established annually by the affirmative action officer, in conjunction with each department or agency head with respect to that portion of the city's work force under their control, to correct any statistically significant under-utilizations identified by the utilization analysis described in Section 2.39.080.
B. Goals and timetables shall be established in accordance with rules and regulations promulgated by the affirmative action officer and shall be based on projected turnover rate, evidence of which is historical turnover rate. (Ord. 5483 § 1 (part), 1980)

2.39.100 Employment practices.

A. The director of personnel and employee relations, in conjunction with each department and agency head with respect to that portion of the city's work force under their control, shall continually review the city's employment practices to assure the practices do not discriminate against any protected class.
B. The director of personnel and employee relations shall take positive action to assure that vacant positions which will be opened to the public are advertised in media directed towards protected classes. Affirmative action principles, upward mobility, career service concepts, and morale of current city employees shall be considered when deciding whether to open a position to the public.
C. The director of personnel and employee relations, in conjunction with each department and agency head with respect to that portion of the city's work force under their control, shall take positive action to assure that the selection process for filling vacant positions does not have an adverse impact on a protected class, except to the extent that the limiting criteria are job-related. Oral examination boards should include persons who are members of protected classes.
D. The director of personnel and employee relations, in conjunction with each department and agency head with respect to that portion of the city's work force under their control, shall take positive action to assure discipline is uniformly applied to employees without respect to the employee's membership in a protected class. The affirmative action officer or the officer's designee shall participate in the disciplinary process, except for advisory arbitration to the city manager, of any employee who requests such participation and who alleges by way of defense that the disciplinary action proposed is a result of or is excessive because of the employee's membership in a protected class; the management person imposing discipline shall, in such cases, confer with the affirmative action officer or the officer's designee prior to making a final decision.
E. The director of personnel and employee relations and the affirmative action officer, in conjunction with each department and agency head with respect to that portion of the city's work force under their control, shall, to the extent that funds have been budgeted therefor, provide such training for city employees as is necessary to upgrade the employees' potential for promotion. Such training

should emphasize the needs of the various protected classes. (Ord. 5483 § 1 (part), 1980)

2.39.110 Internal and external dissemination and reporting.

A. The affirmative action officer and the director of personnel and employee relations, in conjunction with each department and agency head with respect to that portion of the city's work force under their control, shall take positive action to assure that applicants to and employees of the city are fully informed on the city's commitment to affirmative action and equal opportunity employment and the city's affirmative action plan.

B. All management personnel shall be instructed in the principles and practices of affirmative action and equal opportunity employment and their responsibilities thereunder.

C. All solicitations or advertisements for applicants for employment placed by or on behalf of the city shall include the following statement:

Equal Opportunity — Affirmative Action
Employer

D. The affirmative action officer shall prepare an annual report on the progress achieved under the city's affirmative action plan which shall be presented to the board of directors at one of its regular meetings; the presentation shall include a provision for public comment. Such report shall include the utilization analyses, the goals and timetables, the progress made in achieving the goals and timetables, and suggested corrective actions, if any. (Ord. 5483 § 1 (part), 1980)

2.39.120 Internal auditing and monitoring.

The affirmative action officer shall establish internal auditing and monitoring mechanisms to assure that the city's affirmative action plan meets the requirements of this chapter and the rules and regulations promulgated thereunder and to assure that the commitments set forth in the plan are met. (Ord. 5483 § 1 (part), 1980)

2.39.130 Enforcement.

This chapter creates no private cause of action within the public and may only be enforced by the city. (Ord. 5483 § 1 (part), 1980)

2.39.140 Rules and regulations.

The affirmative action officer shall promulgate rules and regulations to carry out the provisions of this chapter and shall generate or collect statistics on the representation of those protected classes identified by race, color, national origin, or sex within the relevant labor market for various job classification groupings using the EEO-4 or similar categories. Such rules and regulations shall be reviewed by the director of personnel and employee relations, the city attorney and the city manager, prior to submission to the board of directors, to assure that they are compatible with the city's personnel practices, the rules and regulations established by the city manager pursuant to Section 2.26.050, and applicable local, state and federal law. Such rules and regulations shall be submitted to the board of directors, within ninety days after the adoption of the ordinance, codified in this chapter, and shall not become effective until approved and ordered filed by the board. (Ord. 5483 § 1 (part), 1980)

EXHIBIT 2. PASADENA'S AFFIRMATIVE ACTION ORDINANCE: AFFIRMATIVE ACTION IN CONTRACTING, CHAPTER 4.09

4.09.100 Rules and regulations.

4.09.010 Short title.

This chapter shall be known as the "affirmative action in contracting ordinance." (Ord. 5482 § 1 (part), 1980)

4.09.020 Policy.

The policy of the city is to promote the principles of equal opportunity employment and affirmative action in its contracting and to recruit vigorously and encourage persons, and businesses owned by persons, who are members of a protected class to make proposals and bids for its contracts. In addition, the following equal opportunity employment laws apply, by their terms, from time to time, to city contracting:

A. California Fair Employment Practices Act, as amended, Labor Code Section 1410 et seq.;

B. Title VII, Equal Employment Opportunity, of the Civil Rights Act of 1964, as amended, 42 U.S.C. Section 2000e et seq.;

C. Age Discrimination in Employment Act of 1967, as amended, 29 U.S.C. Section 61 et seq.;

D. Section 503 of the Vocational Rehabilitation Act of 1973, as amended, 29 U.S.C. Section 701 et seq;

E. Executive Order 11246, issued September 24, 1965, Equal Employment Opportunity;

F. Executive Order 11375, issued October 17, 1967. Amended Executive Order 11246 to cover sex discrimination. (Ord. 5482 § 1 (part), 1980)

4.09.030 Definitions.

Whenever used in this chapter the words "affirmative action," "affirmative action employer," "affirmative action officer," "affirmative action plan," "affirmative action program," "age," "discrimination," "employment practices," "equal opportunity employment," "equal opportunity employer," "goals," "handicapped individual," "medical condition," "protected class," "relevant labor market," and "time tables" shall have the meanings indicated in Chapter 2.39.

In addition to the definitions incorporated from Chapter 2.39, the following words, when used in this chapter, shall have the meanings indicated:

A. "Awarding authority" means the board of directors or any city employee who is authorized to award a contract on behalf of the city.

B. "Contract" means any contract for labor, material, supplies, or services entered into by the city.

C. "Contractor" means any person who submits a bid or proposal to the city or who has entered into a contract with the city.

D. "Employer" means a contractor or subcontractor, as the context requires.

E. "Nondiscrimination requirements" means those contract requirements set forth in Sections 4.09.060, 4.09.070, and 4.09.080.

F. "Subcontract" means a written subcontract on a contract with the city, regardless of tier.

G. "Subcontractor" means a person who enters into a subcontract. (Ord. 5482 § 1 (part), 1980)

4.09.040 Exemptions.

A. The following contracts are exempt from the provisions of this chapter.

1. Contracts for labor or services rendered by any city officer or employee;

2. Contracts for labor, material, supplies or services furnished by one city department to another city department.

3. Contracts with other governmental entities for labor, material, supplies, or services.

B. The following contracts may be exempted, in whole or in part, from the provisions of this chapter by the awarding authority:

1. Contracts for material and supplies available from one person.

2. Contracts for labor, material, or supplies for actual emergency work;

3. Contracts relating to the acquisition, disposal, or lease of real property.

C. Contracts or subcontracts for which the city's interests are best served by exemption may be exempted in whole or in part. Such determination may be made as follows:

1. By the affirmative action officer for contracts or subcontracts up to $2,500;

2. By the affirmative action officer, with the approval of the city manager for contracts or subcontracts up to $10,000;

3. By the board of directors for any contract or subcontract or class of controls or subcontracts.

Any determination which results in a total exemption must be made prior to the release of the request for proposals or invitation for bids and the exemption shall be noted therein.

This "best interests" exemption process shall only be used to exempt contracts or subcontracts for which the affirmative action and equal opportunity employment results attainable are substantially outweighed by the cost of achieving compliance or to exempt contracts or subcontracts where the policy to further affirmative action and equal opportunity employment is substantially outweighed by another city policy which benefits city residents.

D. Whenever a contract or subcontract is exempted, in whole or in part, from the provisions of this chapter by subsection B or C of this section, the highest authority approving such exemptions shall document the basis for the exemption and that the exemption is bona fide in view of the city's policy set fort in Section 4.09.020. (Ord. 5482 § 1 (part), 1980)

4.09.050 Nondiscrimination certificate.

A. Every contractor submitting a bid or proposal to the city, which, if accepted, would result in a contract subject to competitive bidding, shall submit a nondiscrimination certification with its bid or proposal unless it has an approved nondiscrimination certification on file with the city. Failure to do so will cause the bid or proposal to be deemed nonresponsive. This requirement shall not be waived by the city.

B. No contract shall be awarded until the contractor has submitted to the city or has on file with the city a nondiscrimination certification acceptable to the city.

C. All nondiscrimination certifications shall be subject to the approval of the affirmative action officer or the officer's designee. Such approval shall be effective for one year from the date of approval provided the contractor or subcontractor does not breach its stated nondiscrimination commitment.

D. Nondiscrimination certifications shall be submitted for all subcontractors prior to the award of the subcontract. (Ord. 5546 § 1, 1981: Ord. 5482 § 1, 1980)

4.09.060 Nondiscrimination clause.

A. Every contract, regardless of the amount of consideration, shall contain a nondiscrimination clause whereby the contractor agrees that it shall not discriminate against protected classes in its employment practices during the term of the contract.

B. Every contract, regardless of the amount of consideration shall require the contractor to include such a nondiscrimination clause in each of its subcontracts.

C. The preferred wording of the nondiscrimination clauses is set forth in subsection A of Section 4.09.070. (Ord. 5482 § 1 (part), 1980)

4.09.070 Requirements for contracts or subcontracts in excess of $1,000.

Every contract and subcontract for which the consideration is in excess of $1,000 shall contain the following provisions, which shall be designated as the "Equal Opportunity Employment Practices Provisions" of such contracts and subcontracts.

A. Contractor certifies and represents that, during the performance of this contract, the contractor and each subcontractor will adhere to equal opportunity employment practices to assure that applicants and employees are treated equally and are not discriminated against because of their race, religious creed, color, national origin, ancestry, handicap, sex, or age.

B. Contractor agrees that it will, in all solicitations or advertisements for applicants for employment placed by or on behalf of the contractor, state that it is an "Equal Opportunity—Affirmative Action Employer" or that all qualified applicants will receive consideration for employment without regard to their race, religious creed, color, national origin, ancestry, handicap, sex or age.

C. Contractor agrees that it will, if requested to do so by the city, certify that is has not, in the performance of this contract, discriminated against applicants or employees because of their membership in a protected class.

D. Contractor agrees to provide the city with access to and, if requested to do so by the city, through its awarding authority or affirmative action officer, provide copies of all of its records pertaining or relating to its employment practices, to the extent such records are not confidential or privileged under state or federal law.

E. Contractor agrees to recruit vigorously and encourage business owned by persons who are members of a protected class to bid on its subcontracts.

F. Nothing contained in this contract shall be construed in any manner so as to require or permit any act which is prohibited by law.

No contract or subcontract shall be divided into parts for the purpose of avoiding the requirements of this section. (Ord. 5482 § 1 (part), 1980)

4.09.080 Requirements for contracts or subcontracts in excess of $10,000.

In addition to the requirement of Section 4.09.050:

A. No contract or subcontract, in excess of $10,000, whose performance requires labor and services shall be awarded until the contractor or subcontractor has submitted an affirmative action plan acceptable to the city. The affirmative action officer or the officer's designee shall be responsible for the approval of affirmative action plans submitted pursuant to this section. Such approval shall be effective for one year from the date of approval provided the contractor does not breach its stated affirmative action commitment.

This section shall not apply to contracts or subcontracts which will be accomplished by 3 persons or less.

B. The required affirmative action plan shall, as a minimum, contain the following:

1. A utilization analysis which shall include the following:

a. An analysis of the contractor's or subcontractor's work force, by job classification groupings using the EEO-1 or similar categories, to determine the extent to which those protected classes identified by race, color, national origin, or sex are represented therein.

b. A comparison of the work force statistics developed in paragraph a of this subdivision with the equivalent statistics for the relevant labor market for the same job classification groupings to determine any statistically significant underutilizations. This requirement shall not apply to affirmative action plans for contracts or subcontracts performed outside the Los Angeles-Long Beach Standard Metropolitan Statistical Area.

2. Goals and timetables to correct any underutilizations shown by the analysis. This requirement shall not apply to affirmative action plans for contracts or subcontracts performed outside the Los Angeles-Long Beach Standard Metropolitan Statistical Area.

3. The methods by which the contractor or subcontractor will disseminate the affirmative action plan within its company and to its employment applicants, its subcontractors, and the public.

4. The methods the contractor or subcontractor will use to assure that protected classes are represented in its applicant flow to the same extent that they are represented in the relevant labor market.

5. The methods the contractor or subcontractor will use to assure that its hiring, promotion, training, discipline and other employment practices do not discriminate against protected classes.

6. A statement by the contractor's or subcontractor's highest management person that it will adhere to the letter and spirit of all federal, state and local equal employment laws.

C. Every contractor submitting a bid or proposal to the city, which if accepted would result in a contract with the city subject to this section, shall submit its affirmative action plan with its bid or proposal unless it has an approved affirmative action plan on file with the city. Failure to do so will cause the bid or proposal to be deemed nonresponsive. This requirement will not be waived by the city in awarding any contract.

D. Contractors may, with the prior approval of the affirmative action officer or the officer's designee, submit a copy of its affirmative action plan as prepared for another governmental entity in lieu of the plan required by this section.

E. Contractor agrees to recruit Pasadena residents initially and to give them preference, if all other factors are equal, for any new positions which result from the performance of this contract and which are performed within the city. (Ord. 5546 § 1, 1981: Ord. 5482 § 1 (part), 1980)

4.09.090 Penalties for noncompliance with the nondiscrimination requirements of a contract.

A. The failure of an contractor to comply with the nondiscrimination requirements of its contract shall be a breach of its contract and shall be deemed to be a material breach. Such failure shall only be established upon a finding to that effect by the awarding authority, on the basis of its own investigation or that of the affirmative action officer or the officer's designee. No such finding shall be made except after notice of the alleged violation and an opportunity to be heard has been give to the contractor. The contractor may be given an opportunity to cure such breach.

B. A contractor aggrieved by the finding of the awarding authority may appeal such finding to binding arbitration in accordance with rules and regulations promulgated by the affirmative action officer. No penalties shall be imposed pending deposition of such appeal.

C. Upon a finding duly made that the contractor has failed to comply with the nondiscrimination requirements of its contract, its contract may be canceled, terminated or suspended, in whole or in part, by the awarding authority, and all moneys due or to become due under the contract may be retained by the city. Further, the city may sue to recover any moneys paid to a noncomplying contractor by the city and shall be entitled to court costs and attorneys' fees if it is the prevailing party.

In addition, thereto, such breach may be the basis for a determination by the awarding authority that the contractor is an irresponsible bidder. In the event of such determination, such contractor shall be disqualified from being awarded a contract with the city for a period of two years, or until it shall establish that it is ready, willing, and able to comply with the provisions of this chapter.

D. This chapter creates no private cause of action within the public and may only be enforced by the city. (Ord. 5482 § 1 (part), 1980)

4.09.100 Rules and regulations.

The affirmative action officer shall promulgate rules and regulations to carry out the provisions of this chapter and shall generate or collect statistics on the representation of those protected classes identified by race, color, national origin, or sex within the relevant labor market for various job classification groupings using the EEO-1 or similar categories. Such rules and regulations shall, so far as practicable, be similar to those adopted in applicable federal executive orders. Such rules and regulations shall be reviewed and approved by the city attorney and city manager, prior to submission to the board of directors, to assure that they are compatible with the city's contracting practices and local, state and federal law. Such rules and regulations shall be submitted to the board of directors within 90 days after the adopting of the ordinance codified in this chapter and shall not become operative or effective until approved and ordered filed by the board. (Ord. 5482 § 1 (part), 1980)

EXHIBIT 3. ETHNIC COMPOSITION OF THE PASADENA CITY WORK FORCE IN 1980 & 1985*

1980 Work Force

	Number	Percent
White male	644	41%
White female	272	17%
Black male	259	17%
Black female	126	8%
Hispanic male	131	8%
Hispanic female	64	4%
Asian male	37	2%
Asian female	17	1%
Other	5	—
Total	1,555	100%

1985 Work Force

	Number	Percent
White male	546	37%
White female	243	17%
Black male	245	17%
Black female	116	8%
Hispanic male	160	11%
Hispanic female	80	5%
Asian male	51	3%
Asian female	20	1%
Indian male	5	—
Indian female	1	—
Other	3	—
Total	1,470	100%

*Full-time employees only.

Comment

Although originally intended to overcome past discrimination primarily toward blacks and women, many affirmative action policies have been extended to other social groups. The immediate issue before the Pasadena City Council was whether to extend affirmative action protection to Armenian-Americans. But the case also invites an assessment of the city's general policy of offering affirmative action protection to specific groups.

Begin by assuming that the city council will not consider changing its general policy of affirmative action for "protected" groups of city residents. What is the strongest argument for extending "protected" status to Armenian-Americans? Assess the relevance of the following considerations offered by proponents of the extension: (1) Armenians make up 10 percent of the city population but less than 1 percent of the city work force; (2) Armenians are more underrepresented than any other minority or protected group; (3) Johnnie's Tow Service offered to charge less for its tow jobs but was not awarded the police department's contract; (4) Extending protection to Armenian-Americans would increase support for affirmative action and strengthen the city's progressive coalition of young liberals and minority groups.

John Kennedy resisted the extension, arguing that affirmative action was originally intended to redress deep-rooted discrimination in the United States. Is there a principled reason for an affirmative action policy to redress the effects of past discrimination suffered in the United States but to ignore discrimination suffered elsewhere? Or is the most defensible purpose of Pasadena's affirmative action policy something other than redressing past discrimination?

To answer these questions, we have to examine Pasadena's general policy of affirmative action. The explicit rationale for the policy is "to provide equal opportunity employment to all persons and not to discriminate against any applicant or employee because of race, religious creed, color, national origin, ancestry, handicap, sex, or age." The ordinance also affirms an "awareness that the intent of this policy is not necessarily fulfilled with the mere prohibition of discriminatory practices." Why does equal opportunity employment demand more from the government than mere prohibition of discriminatory practices? How much more? To justify the city's policy of equal opportunity employment, must one show that the city itself engaged in or encouraged discrimination in the past? That businesses in the city did so? The rules governing contracts and subcontracts in excess of $1,000 and those in excess of $10,000 both do more than merely prohibit discriminatory practices, and yet they impose different requirements. Can the differences be justified?

Can the percentage differential that the city offers in bidding competitions to local businesses be justified on grounds of equal employment opportunity? On any other moral grounds? Consider how the percentage differential in favor of minority and women-owned firms might best be defended. Formulate and then assess the strongest critique of this part of Pasadena's affirmative action policy.

Should the city councillors have seriously considered the recommendation to extend affirmative action protection to any recent immigrant? To any poor resident of Pasadena? What policy would you have recommended to the city council had you been on the Human Relations Committee?

Recommended Reading

Only a few contemporary theories of justice specifically discuss the principles governing distribution of jobs. They include Michael Walzer, *Spheres of Justice* (New York: Basic Books, 1983), pp. 129–64; Ronald Dworkin, *A Matter of Principle*

(Cambridge, Mass.: Harvard University Press, 1985), Part 5; and Amy Gutmann and Dennis Thompson, *Democracy and Disagreement* (Cambridge, Mass.: Harvard University Press, 1996), ch.9.

Judith Jarvis Thomson defends preferential hiring when candidates are equally qualified in "Preferential Hiring," in Marshall Cohen et al. (eds.), *Equality and Preferential Treatment* (Princeton, N.J.: Princeton University Press, 1977), pp. 19–39. Robert Simon criticizes Thomson's limited defense in "Preferential Hiring: A Reply to Judith Jarvis Thomson," in *Equality and Preferential Treatment*, pp. 40–48. George Sher considers whether preference may be given to a candidate who is less than the best qualified person for a job in "Justifying Reverse Discrimination in Employment," in *Equality and Preferential Treatment*, pp. 49–60. See also Glenn C. Loury, "Why Should We Care about Group Inequality?" *Social Philosophy and Policy*, 5 (1987), pp. 253–63; Alan Goldman, "Affirmative Action," in *Equality and Preferential Treatment*, pp. 192–209; and Robert Amdur, "Compensatory Justice: The Question of Costs," *Political Theory*, 7 (May 1979), pp. 229–44. Robert Fullinwider provides a clear summary of the principal arguments on both sides of the controversy in *The Reverse Discrimination Controversy* (Totowa, N.J.: Rowman and Littlefield, 1980). Michael Rosenfeld provides another perspective in *Affirmative Action and Justice: A Philosophical and Constitutional Inquiry* (New Haven, Conn.: Yale University Press, 1991).

There are many wide-range collections of essays on affirmative action and preferential treatment. Three of the most useful are Russell Nieli, *Racial Preference and Racial Justice: The New Affirmative Action Controversy* (Washington, D.C.: Ethics and Public Policy Center, 1991); Robert K. Fullinwider and Claudia Mills (eds.), *The Moral Foundations of Civil Rights* (Totowa, N.J.: Rowman and Littlefield, 1986); and Steven M. Cahn (ed.), *The Affirmative Action Debate* (New York: Routledge, 1995).

8 Liberty and Morality

Introduction

"Over himself, over his own body and mind, the individual is sovereign," concludes John Stuart Mill in a classic statement of the principle of individual liberty. Yet a vast number of public policies apparently violate this principle, some for paternalistic and others for moralistic reasons. Paternalism is interference with a person's liberty with the aim of promoting his or her own good. Moralism is interference with a person's liberty with the aim of enforcing social morality (or preventing immorality). John Stuart Mill rejected paternalism and moralism absolutely: "because it will be better for him to do so" or "because it will make him happier" or because it violates social morality (but does not cause harm) never justifies restricting the liberty of a sane adult.

Yet there is much morally to be said about both paternalism and moralism. Most people value other goods, such as health and happiness, along with liberty. And sometimes they can secure these goods, or their future liberty, only if society restricts their present freedom of choice. When Mill considers specific examples where important interests other than liberty are at stake, he abandons his absolutist prohibition against paternalism. He defends preventing someone from crossing an unsafe bridge and approves outlawing slavery based on voluntary contract.

Recognizing that some people always and all people sometimes are incapable of exercising liberty, many contemporary political theorists accept an even broader range of paternalistic restrictions on adult behavior than Mill did. They would favor, for example, banning the use of harmful drugs and requiring the use of seat belts and motorcycle helmets. Others, condemning the rapidly growing intrusion of government into the lives of citizens, defend Mill's explicit absolutism. The controversy in political theory parallels the challenge of paternalism in contemporary politics: can government protect the welfare of its citizens without denying their claims to freedom?

We might begin to meet this challenge by justifying paternalistic intervention only if it satisfies these criteria: (1) the decisions it restricts are already unfree; (2) the intervention is minimally restrictive in time and effect; and (3) the person whose freedom is restricted could accept the goal of the intervention were his or her decisions unimpaired. But to state these criteria is not to solve the problem of paternalism, especially as it arises in public policies that affect many people and have uncertain consequences. When are the decisions of a group of people unfree? How limited must an intervention be (and how limited can it be while still being effective)? In what sense must the affected individuals accept its purposes? Must they all accept it or only a majority?

"Legalizing Laetrile" illustrates each of these problems in deciding whether a paternalistic policy is justifiable. New Jersey legislators and public health officials disagreed about whether cancer patients exercise free choice in deciding to use Laetrile. They differed over what is the least restrictive yet effective means of protecting patients against medical fraud. And they offered competing accounts of what people who use Laetrile really want: an effective cure for cancer, psychic comfort, or both. Many of the same issues posed by Laetrile continue to arise in more recent controversies over the regulation of other new and potentially dangerous drugs that offer hope for victims of diseases such as AIDS.

The debate over the "Do-It-Yourself Kit for AIDS Testing" centers neither on what potential consumers of the kit really want (an accurate and private test for the AIDS virus) nor on whether their decisions (in choosing between professional and do-it-yourself testing) would be unfree. In contrast to the consent-based criteria for justifying paternalism that we suggested earlier, the FDA's rationale for proposing a ban on the kits is welfare-based: people should be protected from an unnecessary risk of false testing and from the psychic trauma of the truth. The question of whether to permit AIDS-testing kits, which the FDA had not finally decided by the spring of 1989, invites an evaluation of two contrasting approaches to justifying paternalism.

At issue in the practice of dwarf-tossing is moralism, which unlike paternalism does not rest on a showing of harm but rather on a claim that an action or practice is morally wrong, independently of any harm it may cause. All the people who participate in dwarf-tossing consent to the practice, and there is no showing of harm to the dwarfs other than the claim that the immorality of the practice itself—the indignity or degradation inherent in this use of human beings— constitutes the harm. Although strict liberals claim that morality should never be enforced and that it is a conservative doctrine of the moral majority, most liberals along with conservatives support some moralistic laws, such as those against public nudity. When, if ever, can government enforce morality without violating legitimate claims to liberty?

Consider three criteria for justified moralism: (1) the action or practice is wrong, independent of any harm it causes; (2) the wrong is of sufficient relevance to public purposes to warrant the enactment of a public policy; and (3) the legal regulation or prohibition is not itself likely to cause greater harms or wrongs than those it is seeking to prevent. Each of these criteria is open to revision or rejection in the course of evaluating whether the ban on dwarf-tossing in bars is justified.

The "Controversial Curriculum" centers on the religious objections of some fundamentalist Christian parents to exposing their children to the reading curriculum prescribed by the school board of Hawkins County, Tennessee. Although nobody in the case challenges the sincerity of the parents' religious claims, many people disagree about the extent to which the religious claims of parents should be given weight within the curriculum in the public school, even when the claims are made only on behalf of the parents' own children. At stake in such disputes are the morality and liberty of parents, the future liberty and democratic citizenship of children, and the legitimacy of parental authority versus that of a democratically elected school board to determine the curriculum of a public school.

Both paternalism and moralism in public policy raise not only the problem of a hard choice among competing goods but also a dilemma of process: who has the authority to make paternalistic or moralistic decisions and by what procedures should they make them? We may agree that the policy is correct but criticize the way it was made. In the "Controversial Curriculum," a democratically elected school board discussed the parents' objection but not publicly and in the end rejected their request to exempt their children from reading the textbooks. The quality of the process by which public policies are made—for example, whether there are adequate and open deliberations—may be relevant to judging the legitimacy of the outcome.

In the Laetrile case, answering the question of whether citizens should be free to use Laetrile also still leaves open a series of other questions concerning the process by which the decisions about Laetrile were made. Did the legislators who voted for legalization in the hope and expectation that the Department of Health would delay effective passage of the bill act ethically? Once the Laetrile law was passed, did Department of Health officials act correctly in interpreting the law as they did and in enforcing the guidelines for testing and manufacturing the drug as strictly as the law permitted? In the case of the AIDS-testing kit, was the FDA right to hold public meetings before rendering its final decision? What should be discussed at the meetings? To what extent (if at all) should the FDA's final decision depend on the opinions expressed in those meetings?

To answer these questions, we must consider the moral duties of legislators and bureaucrats in a democracy. In one theory of democracy, attributed to Joseph Schumpeter, the only moral duty of politicians is to preserve the institutional arrangements that make possible the ongoing competitive struggle for the people's vote. A second democratic theory, associated with Mill, offers a more demanding ideal of representation, which would hold legislators and bureaucrats who have broad discretion accountable for particular policies. Because legislators and high-level bureaucrats wield so much power over so many people, we can insist that they give citizens sufficient information to assess their decisions, especially on salient and controversial issues such as legalizing Laetrile, marketing a test kit for AIDS, and instituting a controversial curriculum.

Legalizing Laetrile

Marion Smiley

Laetrile (also known as vitamin B-17, or Amygdalin) is a derivative of the apricot pit and has been promoted during the last twenty-five years as a cure, treatment, or prophylaxis for cancer. It has also been promoted as a treatment for red blood cell deficiencies, for sickle-cell anemia, for various parasitic diseases, and for arthritis. In 1963 the FDA banned the use of Laetrile on the grounds that Laetrile is not *effective* in the treatment of either cancer or other health problems. Despite the ban, public support for Laetrile grew. In 1977 the FDA conducted further tests on Laetrile and reaffirmed its ban. Although the Supreme Court in 1979 sanctioned in certain respects the FDA's authority to ban Laetrile, the controversy has not been finally resolved. Moreover, the issues raised in the controversy go beyond the matter of Laetrile and are likely to arise in other instances of government regulation in the future. This case study describes the history of the FDA's involvement in the regulation of Laetrile; summarizes the scientific and ethical arguments that have been offered by the proponents and opponents of the drug; and provides an account of the controversy as it evolved in the state of New Jersey.

LAETRILE AND THE FDA

Dr. Ernest Krebs, Sr., who discovered Laetrile in 1920, at first considered it to be too toxic for use in the treatment of cancer. In 1937, Dr. Krebs' son, Ernest Krebs, Jr., "purified" the drug to meet his father's standards of toxic safety, and shortly thereafter, father and son went into the Laetrile business together.

According to Krebs, Jr., cancer cells contain a large amount of an enzyme that releases cyanide from Laetrile. Once released, this cyanide supposedly kills the cancer cells. Laetrile would not kill the normal cells as well, Krebs claimed, because normal cells do not contain nearly so much of the cyanide-releasing enzymes as do cancer cells.

Although the FDA never shared Krebs' view of apricot pits, the agency took no legal measure against the proponents of Laetrile until 1962. The FDA in that year charged Krebs, Jr., with violating the new drug provisions of the Federal Food, Drug and Cosmetic Act; the law provided for the first time that all drugs approved by the FDA must be effective, as well as safe. After many unsuccessful attempts to obtain FDA approval of Laetrile as a drug, Mr. Krebs, Jr., claimed that Laetrile was not really a *drug* but instead was a vitamin. He argued that Laetrile was vitamin B-17, the very vitamin needed to prevent and treat cancer (cancer itself now being conceived of as a disease of vitamin deficiency). The advantage of promoting Laetrile as a vitamin was that in this form it would be exempt from the FDA's drug laws.

In early 1974, the FDA took legal action against two vitamin B-17 products, Aprikern and Bee-Seventeen; the FDA maintained that even if Laetrile were a vitamin, it would also still be a drug and therefore susceptible to FDA drug regulation. In 1975 a federal court judge in California held that vitamin B-17 was not even a vitamin, and he placed the manufacturers of Aprikern and Bee-Seventeen under permanent injunction. In 1976 a federal court judge in New Jersey went a step further and concluded that the promotion of vitamin B-17 products constituted a "fraud on the public" and was therefore to be prohibited.

In response to these legal actions, the proponents of Laetrile changed their account of the nature of Laetrile, or vitamin B-17. Proponents of Laetrile for the most part no longer advertise vitamin B-17 as an independent cure for cancer. Instead, they offer vitamin B-17 as part of a more general regimen that often includes large doses of vitamin C, enzymes of various sorts, and sometimes even transcendental meditation. Furthermore, the proponents of Laetrile do not currently claim that it can cure cancer. Instead, they argue that it can prevent cancer or control it.

On April 8, 1977, Laetrile proponents were successful in a case involving *Mr. Glen L. Rutherford et al. v. The United States of America et al.* in the U.S. District Court for Western Oklahoma. Judge Luther Bohanon ruled that any cancer patient certified by affidavit to be terminally ill should be allowed to use Laetrile. On May 10, 1977, Judge Bohanon issued a subsequent order specifying both the format of the affidavit to be used and the amount of Laetrile that each patient may import.

In opposition to Judge Bohanon's orders, the FDA on August 5, 1977, ruled once again against the use of Laetrile. Donald Kennedy, Commissioner of the FDA, based his decision to keep Laetrile off the market on both scientific and ethical arguments. First, he argued, qualified experts still do not recognize Laetrile as a safe and effective drug. He further argued that doctors who deal with cancer patients find that the patients turn to legitimate therapy too late, having delayed while trying Laetrile. Furthermore, he observed, another substantial group of cancer victims avoids effective treatment altogether and uses Laetrile instead.

Addressing himself to the "freedom of choice" issue, the Commissioner argued that "the very act of forming a government necessarily involves the yielding of some freedoms in order to obtain others." Applying this principle to the Laetrile issue, he wrote:

. . . in passing the 1962 amendments to the Food and Drug Act—the amendments that require a drug be proved effective before it may be marketed—Congress indicated its conclusions that the absolute freedom to choose an effective drug was properly surrendered in exchange for the freedom from danger to each person's health and well-being from the sale and use of worthless drugs.[1]

In response to the FDA ruling, Judge Bohanon in December of 1977 permanently enjoined the FDA from interfering with the use of Laetrile. The FDA appealed to the Supreme Court and, on June 18, 1979, the Supreme Court overturned Judge Bohanon's decision. The Court argued that Congress had included the safety and effectiveness clauses in the federal Food, Drug, and Cosmetic Act in order to protect all citizens—including the terminally ill. The concept of safety, it maintained, is not without meaning for terminal patients: "a drug is unsafe for the terminally ill, as for anyone else, if its potential for inflicting death or physical injury is not offset by the possibility of therapeutic benefit." Furthermore, "the effectiveness of a drug does not necessarily denote capacity to cure; in the treatment of any illness, terminal or otherwise, a drug is effective if it fulfills, by objective indices, its sponsors' claim of prolonged life, improved physical condition or reduced pain."[2]

LAETRILE AND THE SCIENTIFIC ARGUMENTS

Several major studies have tested Laetrile's effectiveness, and virtually all of them have concluded that Laetrile is useless in the treatment of cancer. In 1953, the Cancer Commission of the California Medical Association found Laetrile to be completely ineffective as a cancer cure. Ten years later, when the California Department of Health reported to the public that Laetrile was ineffective in the treatment of cancer, California banned the drug. That same year, the *Canadian Medical Association Journal* reported that two formulations of Laetrile—one an American product, the other produced in Canada—were completely ineffective in the cure of cancer. The Canadian study itself inspired further testing of Laetrile. Between 1957 and 1975, the National Cancer Institute tested Laetrile on five different occasions and concluded on each occasion that Laetrile was useless in the treatment of cancer. Likewise, between 1972 and 1976, the Sloan-Kettering Institute in New York City reached similar conclusions in thirty-seven separate tests of Laetrile.

Whereas these earlier studies generally showed only that Laetrile is ineffective, more recent work has suggested that the drug may be unsafe as well. Recent animal experiments have shown Laetrile to be potentially toxic because of its cyanide content. Furthermore, at least thirty-seven cases of poisoning and seventeen deaths have resulted from the use of Laetrile by humans. Dr. Joseph F. Ross, Professor of Medicine at the UCLA School of Medicine, testified at the July 12, 1977 Senate Hearing on Laetrile that when released in the gastrointestinal tract, the cyanide content of Laetrile interferes with the body's ability to use oxygen, and hence can produce cyanosis, dizziness, stupor, coma, nausea, vomiting, shock, or death. Dr. Robert C. Eyerly, Chairman of the Committee on Unproven Methods of Cancer Management, maintains that the presence of Laetrile in American society poses a danger for children. According to Dr. Eyerly, the ingestion of five capsules of Aprikern or two packets of Bee-Seventeen can be fatal to a child.

Scientific evidence in *support* of Laetrile's safety and effectiveness has been rare. Two scientific papers are sometimes cited in support of the drug. The first paper, however, has been criticized by a committee of university biochemists, who found in the paper twenty-five statements based on erroneous facts or false assumptions. The second paper has had a better reception in scientific circles. But its author, Dr. Harold Manner of Chicago's Loyola University, cautioned

the Senate Committee against accepting his conclusions until the results upon which he based those conclusions could be replicated.

LAETRILE AND THE ARGUMENT FROM FREE CHOICE

Many proponents of the drug in recent years have chosen to defend the use of Laetrile on ethical or political grounds. They argue that to restrict the use of Laetrile is to violate the individual's right to free choice in medical treatment. The group that has become the most powerful supporter of this position is itself called the Committee for Freedom of Choice in Cancer Therapy. In 1978, it claimed to have 450 chapters and 23,000 members. Other groups which have come to the support of Laetrile include the International Association of Cancer Victims and Friends, the Cancer Control Society, and the National Health Federation—all alleged to be right wing organizations, some with the backing of the John Birch Society.

While the position of these groups is essentially that individuals should have the right to choose their own medical treatment, the groups differ on how extensive such a right to choose should be. Some believe that individuals should be able to obtain any drug that they themselves wish to use—regardless of whether that drug may have been deemed unsafe or ineffective. Other more moderate proponents of Laetrile agree that the safety clause should be retained in its present form, but argue that instead of banning drugs found to be ineffective, the FDA should require manufacturers to print a "statement of ineffectiveness" on the label of, say, every bottle of Laetrile tablets sold over the counter or by prescription. Still other Laetrile supporters think that the drug should be dispensed by prescription only. Finally, some supporters maintain merely that Laetrile should be prescribed only to patients who have been certified "terminally ill."

The supporters of the legalization of Laetrile do not all favor the use of Laetrile itself.

Many believe that Laetrile is a fraud but that it should still be legalized. Laetrile should be legalized, they argue, because its prohibition constitutes a violation of an individual's right to free choice. Representative Steven Symms, Republican from Idaho, expresses some of the anti-paternalist perspective that underlies this view:

> Freedom is the issue. The American people should be allowed to make their own decisions. They shouldn't have the bureaucrats in Washington, D.C. trying to decide for them about what is good and what is bad, as long as it is safe. . . .
>
> The FDA is typical of what you get in regulatory agencies—a very protective mentality by bureaucrats who want to protect their own jobs and their own positions. It's easier for them to say "No" to a product—Laetrile or anything else—than it is to say "Yes." The FDA is simply not faced with the urgencies of patient care. . . .
>
> Stringent drug regulation for society as a whole limits therapeutic choice by the individual physician, who is better able to judge risks and benefits for the individual patient.[3]

Similarly, Robert Bradford, president of the Committee for Freedom of Choice in Cancer Therapy, testified:

> The FDA must get off the backs of physicians, cancer patients, and ourselves. What, in the name of humanity, is the agency doing? Whom does it represent? Surely, not the people. . . .
>
> Rest assured, gentlemen, that the people demand Laetrile, and they are going to have it, whether Big Brother likes it or not.[4]

What do "the people" think about drug regulation and Laetrile? Cambridge Reports, Inc., surveyed consumer attitudes concerning drug regulation. One of the questions asked was:

> Some people say companies should tell us in plain English what the possible dangers are in a product, as they do on cigarette packages, and then leave it to us, as individual consumers, to decide whether or not we want to use the product. Would you agree or disagree?[5]

Eighty-two percent of the respondents agreed, 9 percent answered that they were unsure, and 9 percent disagreed. In a study more directly related to Laetrile, a Harris Poll indicated that Americans oppose the ban on Laetrile by a 53 to 23 percent margin.[6]

The proponents of Laetrile repeatedly invoke the individual's right to free choice in medical treatment, including the right to choose foolishly. As one individual in favor of legalizing Laetrile wrote:

> If the people want to use unapproved or home remedies it is their right to do so. If they want to delay conventional and possibly life-saving treatment then it is their right to do so, foolish and tragic as it might be.[7]

The FDA and most of the medical profession disagree with this position. They argue that the legalization of Laetrile will actually *decrease* the opportunities for free choice. In the first place, they maintain that the choice of a product (medical or otherwise) is not a *free* choice if the product in question is a fraud. In the words of one high-ranking FDA official:

> Laetrile is the most unattractive kind of fraud. It is making some people very rich on the basis of promises that, according to all available evidence, are false, and are known by many of the proponents of Laetrile to be false. The major promoter has a very seamy record and there are hints of ties to right-wing paramilitary groups in the case of the Wisconsin operation.[8]

In the second place, they argue that choices made under extreme emotional stress are not really free. Cancer patients and their families are often forced to make choices when they are under such emotional stress, and these choices, therefore, cannot be considered wholly free. Moreover, they argue that choices made under emotional stress—if unwise—can in effect decrease the possibilities for free choice in the future.

The opponents of Laetrile further insist that, whether toxic or not, Laetrile is unsafe simply because it is ineffective. As Dr. Daniel S. Martin, research associate of the Institute of Cancer Research of Columbia University, has stated:

> [N]o worthless drug is without harm; a patient's choice of Laetrile, to the extent that such a choice delays or interferes with swift diagnosis and prompt effective treatment, is potentially fatal.[9]

Dr. Martin cites a number of cases (documented by the American Cancer Society) in which patients with treatable cancer abandoned conventional therapy for Laetrile. By the time these patients realized that Laetrile was not working, their chances for recovery were either poor or nil. Summarizing and broadening the position of the opponents of the legalization of Laetrile, Arthur A. Checchi writes:

> It is in the public interest for legislators to leave basic decisions concerning the safety and efficacy of specific procedures to experts who are qualified to make such judgments rather than to laymen who are not. . . .
>
> In debating special legislation for products such as Laetrile, we must consider who are the likely purchasers and users of the questionable products: it is the desperate with serious diseases not entirely treatable by recognized procedures; and unfortunately, there is a growing group of people in our society which distrusts the government, big industry and our scientific institutions. . . .
>
> There can be Freedom of Informed choice only where the persons making the judgment have the basic training and understanding of the issues to make that choice. That person must be qualified. Unfortunately, the average person is not. . . .
>
> The gullible, like children, should be protected from those who exploit them.[10]

LAETRILE IN NEW JERSEY

While the interstate manufacture of drugs comes under the jurisdiction of the FDA, the control of the intrastate manufacture of drugs falls to the regulatory agencies of each state. Hence, when a New Jersey company announced its plans to manufacture Laetrile in the state of New Jersey, the New Jersey

Commissioner of Health became responsible for deciding whether these plans could be carried out. The responsibility was an unusual one for the Commissioner since drugs are rarely manufactured on an intrastate basis. Furthermore, since the New Jersey State Department of Health never had to review new drugs before, the state never bothered to revise the New Jersey drug law in accordance with the changes the federal drug law made in 1962. Unlike its federal counterpart, the New Jersey drug law requires that a new drug be examined only for its safety, not for its efficacy.

The situation posed a dilemma for the Commissioner, Dr. Joan E. Finley. On the one hand, she strongly believed that Laetrile should not be allowed on the market (agreeing with the FDA that if a drug were to be allowed to be sold, it should first be proved effective as well as safe). On the other hand, she was forced by New Jersey law to examine Laetrile only for its safety.

Without waiting for the Commissioner's decision on Laetrile, three New Jersey State Assemblymen on May 2, 1977, introduced a bill to legalize Laetrile. The bill, A-3295, introduced by Assemblymen Gregario, Deverin, and Karcher, read:

> 1. No duly licensed physician shall be subject to any penalty or disciplinary action by any state agency or private professional organization solely for prescribing, administering or dispensing amygdalin, also known as Laetrile or Vitamin B-17, to a patient who has made a written request for such substance. . . .[The form on which the request is made must include the statement] "Amygdalin has not been approved as a treatment or cure for cancer by the United States Food and Drug Administration. . . . Neither the American Cancer Society, the American Medical Association, nor the Medical Society of New Jersey recommends use of Amygdalin (Laetrile) in the treatment of any malignancy, disease, illness or physical conditon. . . . There are alternative recognized treatments for the malignancy, disease, illness or physical condition from which I suffer which he [my doctor] has offered to provide. . . .''

2. No duly recognized pharmacist shall be subject to any penalty or disciplinary action . . . . for dispensing amygdalin . . . labeled with the following statement: "Amygdalin has not been approved as a treatment or cure of any malignancy, disease, illness or physical condition by the United States Food and Drug Administration."

3. No health care facility or employee thereof may restrict or forbid the use of, refuse to administer, or dispense amygdalin, when prescribed by a physician. . . .

4. No person shall be held liable to any civil or criminal penalty solely for the manufacture . . . in this state of amygdalin. . . .

5. The State Department of Health shall maintain records concerning the use of the substance amygdalin . . . and shall make periodic studies concerning the efficacy of such substances in the treatment of cancer.[11]

Debate on the bill lasted only two days. Arguing against the bill, the Commissioner insisted that the New Jersey drug law is "archaic" and that it should be changed to include some requirements for effectiveness; this change would prohibit drugs such as Laetrile from making their way onto the market.[12] Also testifying against Laetrile were representatives of the FDA and the Public Health Council of the State of New Jersey.

Most of those testifying, however, supported the legislation of Laetrile. One group testified on behalf of friends and relatives who had cancer and who had allegedly been helped by Laetrile or who now sought the "right to hope" that it supposedly provides. Assemblyman Gregario himself fell into this category; he described at length his father's bout with cancer and his own decision to take Laetrile as a preventative treatment for cancer. Then there were representatives from the Committee for Freedom of Choice and Options, Inc. Both of these representatives stressed the individual's right to freedom of choice in medical treatment and the ever-increasing intrusion of government into the lives of citizens.[13]

Outside the hearing room, several members of the federal and state health agencies argued that only they were capable of deciding whether individuals should be allowed to use Laetrile. Many state legislators and assemblymen maintained, on the contrary, that only individuals by themselves or through their legislators were competent to make such decisions.

Donald Foley, Deputy Commissioner of Health for the State of New Jersey and the department official chiefly responsible for drug regulation in the state, argued that his department should have the authority for decisions concerning the legislation of Laetrile. First of all, he argued, "drugs differ from mere commodities; they are lifesaving and life-endangering; and therefore decisions concerning them should be made by those who can best judge them." Second, "the public isn't as informed as they think they are. They're not dumb, but when they read the label they don't understand what they read. They don't know chemistry." Third, individuals with cancer are under emotional stress and therefore cannot always act in a rational manner when choosing their medical treatment. According to Foley, "some of them are in such an emotional state that if you told them that they would be cured if they jumped off the Brooklyn Bridge, they would jump. This is what we want to stop."[14]

Many of the scientists and pharmacists in the Health Department favored giving individuals more free choice than Foley's position permitted. But even they agreed with Foley that the department itself should regulate the use of Laetrile.[15] Thomas Culkin, a department pharmacist concerned with the Laetrile issue, articulated a typical middle position between free choice and government regulation. While he agreed that "individuals must be allowed free choice if they are to be considered adults," he argued that "to talk about freedom without also talking about the regulation of those who might take advantage of that freedom is foolish. . . . This is one reason why the safety clause of our regulations is so important." He continued, "If Laetrile is proven safe, individuals should be able to use it if they want to." In this instance, the "state's job should be one of educator and not father."[16]

Many state legislators went further than Culkin in their commitment to free choice: "only the individual can know what is good for himself" and "while the Health Department is certainly necessary up to a point [to ensure safety], beyond that point it starts to get in the way of the individual's ability to function."[17] Legislators also warned of the general tendency of bureaucracies to stifle medical innovation. As one assemblyman commented on the FDA, "It is not their fault, they just have so much to deal with that it takes them twenty years to get to a drug which could have saved thousands of lives by then. . . . If the drug is safe, why not let people use it and then we'll find out whether it's effective or not."[18]

On January 10, 1978, the bill to legalize Laetrile passed by a wide margin in both houses. Governor Byrne signed the bill one day later, stating that:

> I recognize that the drug Laetrile is not a proven cure for cancer. Clearly, it is no more than a source of psychic comfort to cancer patients. . . . Yet I do not believe that people should be deprived of its use; and I have faith in the medical profession that it will not be abused and that cancer patients will be advised of proven and recognized cancer treatment methods.[19]

Asked why the Laetrile bill passed so easily, health officials and legislators cited, in addition to the ideological and emotional factors discussed above, several more purely political factors. First, the bill came up for a vote at the very end of the legislative session, when almost everyone was fatigued and eager to go home. Second, political bargaining had taken place; some legislators voted for the Laetrile bill only to ensure support for their own bills that would be voted on later.

A third reason for the bill's relatively easy passage, also revealed by interviews, is that several legislators knew all along that, regardless of whether or not the bill were enacted, Laetrile almost certainly could not be manufactured in New Jersey for at least seven or eight years. The legislators knew that the New Jersey Department of Health had the intention and the authority to prolong the procedure for testing the safety of Laetrile. For at least a few legislators, the prospect of an eight-year period during which Laetrile would not be allowed on the market was sufficient to overcome any qualms they had about voting for the Laetrile bill.

Laetrile in New Jersey, according to Deputy Commissioner Foley, is "on hold, and will be for at least seven or eight more years to come . . . until we can prove it is safe enough for the people of New Jersey." Some people contend that the Department of Health is merely stalling. Foley disagrees, but adds that "although we are not stalling (it's simply that testing takes a long time and we have a backload), I think that the seven or eight years it will take to complete the Laetrile tests may be enough time for people to come to their senses. . . . Hopefully by then they will have taken it upon themselves to vote down Laetrile."[20]

IMPLEMENTING THE LAETRILE LAW

The state Health Department delegated to its Bureau of Drugs the responsibility for implementing and enforcing the Laetrile Act.

The state official who is the Director of the Bureau of Drugs is a nationally recognized scientist and administrator. He has published many professional articles concerning drugs, and has recently been elected president of a multistate health association. Because of his professional stature, any Laetrile actions he takes may be followed by other officials in states that have Laetrile laws.

The Director, on the basis of the available scientific evidence, emphatically believes that "Laetrile is not only worthless in the treatment of cancer, but that it is a health fraud; and worse still, citizens in the state are foregoing conventional cancer treatment in favor of Laetrile with fatal results."

The Laetrile Act did not change any existing drug laws in the state. The old state drug law does have a safety requirement for intrastate "new drugs." However, this part of the law has not been enforced in over twenty years because the FDA safety regulations were applied in the state. These regulations require an extensive animal work-up on the toxicity and toxicology of all new drugs prior to distribution in interstate commerce. The extent of *just* intrastate use of a drug is illustrated by the Director's comment that "he can only remember during the past twenty years, only two requests for state approval of a new drug . . .and in both cases he convinced the applicant not to apply."

However, two applications have recently been received by the Division of Drugs for approval to manufacture Laetrile in the state. One application is from a chemical company which has found a method to synthesize Laetrile. The other application is from a company in Mexico which is currently manufacturing the drug and wishes to set up a subsidiary plant in the state. Both companies have followed up their initial requests with phone calls and letters.

Prior to any definitive response to the two manufacturers, the state Director of the Bureau of Drugs has, with the *concurrence* of the Health Commissioner, promulgated, *without public hearings*, regulations under the existing "old" state drug laws pertaining to the safety of intrastate new drugs. In essence, the state has adopted by reference the FDA regulations pertaining to safety requirements of new drugs.

In order to satisfy the very strict "safety tests" regulations, a sponsor would have to initiate a complete animal study which could take several years and cost several hundred thousand dollars. "In effect," the Director said, "even if a company were to do this, the approval and legal use of Laetrile in the state could be delayed from three to eleven years. The FDA experience is that it takes an average of seven to eight years for a 'new drug' to be approved."*

The Director, under the quality control authority of the Laetrile Act, has also, with the concurrence of the Health Commission and without public hearings, adopted by reference the Good Manufacturing Practices (GMPs) regulations of the FDA.

These regulations require that Laetrile manufacturers have *adequately* equipped facilities, *adequately* trained technical and professional personnel, the *necessary* analytical controls and *adequate* record keeping methods. Laetrile not manufactured under conforming methods or in conforming facilities is considered adulterated and will be seized and destroyed by the state.

These GMP regulations rigidly interpreted could also further delay the distribution of Laetrile in the state.

The Director has said that the Health Department interprets the legislative intent as requiring safety testing. He commented, "The legislature is aware of both of these new regulations but, as of yet, is not cognizant of the FDA experience in terms of granting 'new drug' approval (the average of seven to eight years it takes) or the state intention 'literally' to enforce GMPs on Laetrile manufacturers if and whenever necessary."

The Department's actions, the Director has stated, have been taken in effect "so that the state will have time to realize that Laetrile is a most dangerous hoax and health fraud and will repeal the law." In the meantime, he believes that "lives will be saved by conventional cancer treatments rather than lost because of Laetrile."[21]

---

*This time frame also includes satisfying the efficacy requirements for new drugs which may require two to three years of testing.

NOTES

1. HEW Release, Aug. 4, 1977.

2. *U.S. v. Rutherford*, 61LEd 2d 68, 99 S Ct (1979).

3. Representative Steven Symms, quoted in *U.S. News and World Report*, June 13, 1977, p. 51.

4. Arthur A. Checchi, "The Return to the Medicine Man: The Laetrile Story and the Dilemma for State Legislators," *Association of Food and Drug Officials Quarterly Bulletin*, April 1978, p. 94.

5. Cambridge Reports, Inc., 1978.

6. Lewis Harris, *The Harris Survey* (New York: Chicago Tribune-New York News Syndicate, 1977).

7. Editorial, *Buffalo Courier Express*, June 15, 1977.

8. Interview with anonymous official.

9. Dr. Daniel S. Martin, *Philadelphia Inquirer*, Feb. 12, 1978.

10. Checchi, "Medicine Man."

11. Assembly bill No. 3295 introduced May 2, 1977, with Senate Committee amendments adopted on Jan. 10, 1978.

12. New Jersey State Assembly Hearing on A3295, New Jersey State Document 974.90 N222, 1977, p. 3.

13. Ibid., pp. 6–40.

14. Interviews with Donald Foley, Dec. 7, 1978, and Jan. 11, 1979.

15. Interviews with New Jersey Department of Health administrators, scientists, and pharmacists, Jan. 8 through Jan. 16, 1979.

16. Interview with Thomas Culkin, Jan. 10. 1979.

17. Interviews with New Jersey state legislators, Jan. 8 through Jan. 16, 1979.

18. Ibid.

19. Governor Brendan Byrne, quoted in the *Trenton Times*, Jan. 11, 1977, p. 2.

20. Interview with Donald Foley, Jan. 11, 1979.

21. The preparation of this case benefited greatly from the work of Robert Rich.

AIDS Testing at Home

Ted Aaberg

During 1986 and 1987, more than a dozen individuals or companies expressed their intention to market a do-it-yourself kit for testing for the HIV virus associated with AIDS. For less than $40, anyone would be able to purchase the kit by mail order or at a drug store without prescription, and use it in the privacy of his or her own home. The typical kit would consist of a lancet to prick a finger, a vial to contain the blood sample, and a pre-addressed package in which to send the sample to an authorized laboratory, which would report the results by return mail or by phone. This procedure, its promoters say, offers a significantly less expensive and much more convenient method than the usual alternatives—a trip to the doctor's office or a visit to the hospital. It also would be more likely to preserve confidentiality.

In March 1988, the Food and Drug Ad-ministration announced that it was "limiting the marketing of blood collection kits [known as "AIDS home test kits"] at this time to those intended for professional use only."[1] Under the agency's policy, kits would be approved only if they meet these criteria:

1. Kits are labeled and marketed for professional use only within a health care environment (e.g., hospitals, medical clinics, doctor's offices, sexually transmitted disease clinics, HIV-1 counseling and testing centers, and mental health clinics;

2. Kits provide for the collection of a venipuncture or other appropriately validated sample by one who is recognized by a State or local authority to perform such procedures;

3. The testing sequence for all samples collected with the kits includes use of a licensed screening test for HIV-1 antibody and, for those samples testing positive by the screening test, the use of an additional more specific test (i.e., Western blot or comparable test). It is recommended that a licensed test which is more specific for HIV-1 antibody be utilized. However, the agency may accept

a properly validated unlicensed test until licensed tests are more widely available;

4. The instructions for sample collection, storage, shipping, and testing conform with, or are validated as the equivalent to the package insert instructions for the specific licensed HIV-1 antibody test kit used to test samples; and

5. All results of testing are reported directly to a professional health care provider for reporting and interpretation of the result to the person requesting the test, as well as for counseling of the individual.[2]

Although many press accounts interpreted the FDA's action as effectively banning the kits,[3] FDA officials insist that the decision is not a ban but concerns only "what type of kit we will consider for approval."[4] Furthermore, the criteria are intended to be only temporary until public hearings can be held.

One of the FDA's major objections to the kits appears to be that they do not ensure that individuals who test "positive" will receive the personal counseling that they will need to cope with the extreme psychological stress such results usually cause. The FDA also believes that the risk of incorrect diagnoses is too great if trained technicians do not take the blood samples.

The FDA is not alone in its opposition to the kits. Officials at the Centers for Disease Control also emphasize the potential harm to the individual taking the test. Dr. Richard George, responsible for part of the CDC's AIDS program, argues that counseling is necessary to explain the meaning of a positive test result. The result should not be interpreted as necessarily implying that one is "ill" or that "death is around the corner." He also questions the accuracy of a home test, not only because the test taker may "botch the test," but also because the laboratory will not usually have the individual's medical history that should be part of any adequate diagnosis.[5] Another CDC official, Dr. Peter Drotman, doubts that the kits are necessary: hundreds of free public health clinics across the country are now providing high quality testing, along with professional counseling. The clinics, furthermore, have had long experience with sexually transmitted diseases, and can point to an excellent record of maintaining confidentiality.[6]

The CDC also believes that counseling can help prevent the spread of the disease:

> Counseling and treating persons who are infected or at risk for acquired HIV infection is an important component of prevention strategy. Most of the estimated 1 to 1.5 million infected persons in the United States are unaware that they are infected with HIV. The primary public health purposes of counseling and treating are to help uninfected individuals initiate and sustain behavioral changes that reduce their risk of becoming infected and to assist infected individuals in avoiding infecting others.[7]

Outside the government, opinion is divided. The American Medical Association in 1985 praised "home-use in vitro devices" as having "great potential for broadening the base of knowledge and understanding of the American people about their own health."[8] But the AMA also expresses concern about such tests, stating that they should be carefully scrutinized before being permitted on the market. They should be subjected to strict criteria based on this premise: " . . .as the potential harm both to the individual and to society would increase upon occurrence of inaccurate test results, misinterpretation of test results or failure to follow up properly and in a timely fashion on such results, the requirements for demonstration of safety and efficacy should increase commensurately."[9]

The FDA's position has been criticized for undermining the Public Health Service's goal of encouraging more extensive testing throughout the population. One of the manufacturers who wishes to market the kit comments: "We don't understand the FDA's position at all. We were under the impression that the federal government was *for* mass, anonymous testing."[10] Other critics see the FDA's decision as part of a government "plan to remain in complete control of testing and of knowledge of the results."[11]

Critics of the FDA decision also argue that banning the kits would take away the individual's right to have confidential knowledge about their own health. The kits virtually guarantee privacy, while the current health system cannot, as even FDA officials admit.[12] The CDC notes that "disclosures of HIV-testing information [can be] deliberate, inadvertent or simply unavoidable" in the current system. Confidentiality may be breached because of the wide scope of "need-to-know situations, because of the possibility of inappropriate disclosures, and because of established authorization procedures for releasing records. . . ."[13]

The most general objections to the FDA policy invoke the specter of an authoritarian bureaucracy forcing citizens to conform to its view of what is good for them. "In essence, the Federal Government is enunciating the right to ban for general use a simple medical test because the public cannot be trusted with the results . . . the agency had never before used a potential psychic trauma as a justification for restricting sales of a medical product."[14]

In response to these and other public criticisms of its policy, the FDA announced that it would hold a public meeting in the spring of 1989 to "provide an opportunity for all interested persons to make their view known to the FDA and to allow thorough discussion of the issues." The views expressed at the meeting will be considered "in the development of final policy and regulatory decisions" concerning the kits.[15] The meeting was to cover these topics:

A. Topic 1: Blood Collection Kits

1. *Collection and shipping of blood samples by laypersons.* Improper sample collection, preparation, and shipment could adversely affect the accuracy of HIV-1 antibody test results. In addition, it is possible, although most unlikely, that improper sample collection and transport might result in transmission of infection or injury. Therefore, comments are solicited on the ability of laypersons to safely and adequately collect and package these samples for shipment.

2. *Return of test results directly to the person from whom the sample was collected.* Some manufacturers have proposed systems in which the HIV-1 antibody test results would be returned directly to the person from whom the sample was collected. The results of in vitro diagnostic tests often require interpretation (e.g., under what circumstances false-negative or false-positive results might occur) and must be integrated into an overall assessment of a person's medical status. Before returning the results of testing for evidence of infection with HIV-1 to any person other than a health professional, adequate instructions for interpretation of the test results would have to be developed. Comments are solicited on whether such information could be adequately provided.

3. *Counseling outside of a medical health care environment.* This topic is related to the issue of proper interpretation of and follow-up on test results. There is agreement among medical experts that adequate counseling regarding the test results should be part of HIV-1 testing. Comments are solicited regarding the ability to provide effective pre- and post-test counseling in a setting outside the health care environment.

4. *Availability of blood collection systems.* The availability of blood collection systems as over-the-counter (OTC) devices could increase the number of samples tested by making systems more readily available. Comments are solicited on whether blood collection systems should be available as OTC devices.

B. Topic 2: Kits for Collection and Home Testing of Blood for Evidence of HIV-1 Infection

Some have discussed the possibility of developing test kits with which laypersons could not only obtain their own specimen at home, but also perform testing for evidence of HIV-1 infection. The FDA invites comments on issues related to these types of kits. Such issues would include whether the kits should be made available OTC, whether laypersons can reliably and safely perform the test, whether laypersons can adequately interpret the test results, and whether that interpretation in the absence of a medical professional is appropriate.[16]

NOTES

1. "Blood Collection Kits Labeled for Human Immunodeficiency Virus Type 1 (HIV-1) Antibody Testing; Home Test Kits Designed to Detect HIV-1 Antibody; Open Meeting," [Docket No. 88N-0319] *Federal Register* Feb. 17, 1980, p. 7280.

2. Ibid.

3. "Banned at Home: An FDA Ruling on AIDS Tests," *Time* (April 18, 1988), p. 26, and "Home Kits for AIDS Virus Testing Virtually Ruled Out by the F.D.A.," *New York Times* (April 8, 1988), p. A15.

4. Telephone interview with Debra Henderson, special assistant to the director of the Center for Biologics, Research and Evaluation, FDA, Feb. 1, 1989.

5. Telephone interview with Richard George, chief of Developmental Technology Section, AIDS Program, CDC, Feb. 17, 1989.

6. Telephone interview with Peter Drotman, assistant to the director of AIDS Program, CDC, Feb. 17, 1989.

7. Centers for Disease Control, U.S. Department of Health and Human Services/Public Health Service, "Public Health Service Guidelines for Counseling and Antibody Testing to Prevent HIV Infection and AIDS," *Morbidity and Mortality Weekly Report* (Boston, Mass.: Massachusetts Medical Society) Aug. 14, 1987, p. 509.

8. Letter from James H. Sammons, Executive Vice President, American Medical Association, to Jerome A. Donlon, FDA, Oct. 14, 1985.

9. Ibid.

10. "AIDS Tests for Home Use Prohibited: Accuracy, Trauma Worry Officials," *Washington Post* (April 8, 1988), p. A1.

11. Ibid.

12. Telephone interview with Debra Henderson, Jan. 4, 1989.

13. Centers for Disease Control, p. 514.

14. "Banned at Home," p. 26.

15. "Blood Collection Kits," *Federal Register*, pp. 7280–81.

16. Ibid.

Comment

The Laetrile case is best analyzed, first by deciding whether the legislators voted for the best policy and, second, by judging the process by which they and Department of Health officials legalized Laetrile but delayed its approval.

The first step in judging the content of the decision to legalize Laetrile is to decide whether the legislature's explicit policy was paternalistic. Avoid the common tendency to describe all cases of justified paternalism as nonpaternalistic. Mill, for example, denies that intervention in the case of the person crossing the unsafe bridge is paternalistic, "for liberty consists in doing what one desires, and he does not desire to fall into the river." But if the person wants to cross the bridge and if we thwart his desire in order to save his life, then our intervention is paternalistic. Determining whether a restriction on freedom is paternalistic, therefore, must be separated from the question of whether the restriction is justified.

Also, be careful not to conflate the problems of paternalism and democracy by labeling any democratic decision paternalistic simply because its effect is to limit the freedom and protect the interests of a minority. A law devised to satisfy the preferences of a democratic majority may not be paternalistic if, for example, its purpose is to restrict the majority's freedom. Was the ban on Laetrile such an instance?

Was the decision to make Laetrile available only by prescription the best one?

Consider the major alternatives available to the legislature: permitting the sale of Laetrile over the counter, with or without mandatory labeling, and banning its production and sale, with or without exceptions for the terminally ill.

What policy should someone support who, like Representative Symms, believes that "freedom is the only issue"? What restrictions on the availability of Laetrile are necessary and sufficient to create free choice?

If you have doubts about the absolute value of freedom, even of informed choice, you will consider paternalistic alternatives to the free market. The policy explicitly endorsed by the legislature does not leave the choice up to the market: doctors stand between buyers and sellers. May we assume, as Symms seems to, that by permitting doctors to prescribe Laetrile patients are free to choose among therapies by choosing among doctors?

Are claims that cancer patients cannot understand the choice among the therapies and suffer from severe emotional stress sufficient to justify a complete ban on Laetrile? Is it plausible to maintain that those whose freedom is restricted by a ban nevertheless accept the goal of governmental intervention or would accept it if their decision-making faculties were not impaired?

In judging the process by which the Laetrile policy was enacted and implemented, keep in mind the distinction between content (was the right policy adopted?) and method (was it adopted rightly?). The legislators had democratic authority to determine the policy on Laetrile. Are there any grounds for criticizing how they made their decision? Consider whether citizens who supported (or opposed) the legalization of Laetrile had sufficient means for holding their representatives accountable.

Suppose a legislator reasoned as follows: "I will vote for legalizing Laetrile because I am reasonably sure that even if the law is passed, Laetrile will not be marketed for at least seven years. If I vote against legalization, I will probably lose the next election to Joe Smith, whom I know to be incompetent and corrupt. Therefore, it is in the public interest, as well as my own, to concede to my opponents on this issue, despite the fact that I firmly believe that their position is wrong." The legislator votes for legalization. and it passes by one vote. Evaluate his action.

Bureaucratic discretion in the Laetrile case, as in the AIDS-testing case and many others, is great. In the Laetrile case, it gave officials of the Department of Health and the Bureau of Drugs scope to act on their own moral judgments about the value of Laetrile. If the Bureau of Drugs could have tested Laetrile for safety in less than seven or eight years, should it have acted as quickly as possible, or should it have drawn the testing period out as long as was legally possible in deference to the intent of those legislators with whom the director morally agreed? To what extent should Foley have looked at his duties from the perspective of a legislator when he was making (rather than merely implementing) policy? If Foley had a duty of accountability like that of a legislator, what did that duty require of him in this case?

In the AIDS-testing case, the nonelected officials at the FDA recognized that they were making policy and had assumed some of the duties of legislators. They decided, for example, to consult broadly and hold public meetings before they rendered a final decision. What other duties, if any, does this kind of policy-making role require of FDA officials? Should the FDA be making policy at all? Assess the alternatives.

The rationale behind the FDA's proposed policy to ban the marketing of AIDS-testing kits is clearly paternalistic. Is the paternalism justified? To answer this question, we should attend to the two different welfare-based arguments offered by FDA officials: (1) people should be protected from an unnecessarily high risk of false testing; and (2) people should be protected from the trauma of learning a dreadful truth without the aid of psychological counseling. Is there a morally significant difference between protecting people from paying for tests that are excessively unreliable and protecting them from the psychic trauma accompanying accurate (as well as inaccurate) information? Should FDA officials consider whether the people who are likely to seek AIDS tests would consent to both kinds of protections? If actual or hypothetical consent were a factor, how should the FDA go about determining whether people consent? If consent is inappropriate, according to what criteria should the FDA draw the line between justified and unjustified paternalism? Develop a set of criteria based on individual welfare that could guide a paternalistic policy; then evaluate the relative merits of welfare-based and consent-based criteria for justifying paternalism.

Use your evaluation to assess the strongest arguments for and against the FDA's decision to ban the do-it-yourself kits. Then assess the alternatives to the blanket approval of the do-it-yourself kits defended by the commercial laboratories and the absolute ban proposed by the FDA.

If you were testifying at the public meeting set by the FDA, what would you say on each of the topics on the agenda? On other topics not on the agenda? If you were an FDA official, what would you expect to learn from such a meeting?

Tossing Dwarfs in Illinois

Simone Sandy

Deja Vu, a nightclub in Springfield, Illinois, which routinely featured seminude dancing, planned more novel entertainment for August 16, 1989. The club had booked a four-foot, eight-inch, 120-pound man known as "Danger Dwarf" to appear in what was billed as a dwarf-tossing competition. Offering a prize of $100 for the person able to throw Danger Dwarf the farthest and highest, Deja Vu intended

to charge patrons $5 each to watch or participate in the tournament.[1]

The Springfield City Council, the Illinois District Attorney's Office, Springfield members of the Little People of America (LPA), and other concerned residents expressed their opposition to the upcoming event. Bob Church, executive director of Springfield Mayor Ossie Langfelder's office, regretted that the city was "unable through a licensing process to do anything about it."[2] In similar cases elsewhere, city and state officials had prevented dwarf-

tossing competitions by threatening to re-
voke the liquor licenses of offending tav-
erns. Deja Vu, however, did not have a
liquor license. Although Springfield could
do nothing, legally, to prevent the contest,
the city council passed a resolution de-
nouncing events "such as dwarf tossing,
which represent conduct that is both demeaning and insensitive to human values."[3] Deja Vu management canceled the
competition without explanation.[4]

A month later, the city council passed
an ordinance that imposed a series of fees
and restrictions upon dwarf-tossing events,
including the requirement for special permits. According to one critic of the ordinance, "Springfield, Illinois, did not ban
the practice outright, but made dwarf tossing such a burdensome activity that promoters no longer find Springfield an attractive place to toss dwarfs. . . . The
cumulative effect of all these requirements
is to wipe out whatever profit margin a
promoter otherwise would have."[5]

The managers of Deja Vu were neither the
only nor the first club owners to promote a
dwarf-tossing event. During the mid to
late 1980s, tavern owners in several states,
eager to attract more business, held competitions in the event, which originated in
Australia as a contest among bouncers.
Typically, several contestants vie to throw
a dwarf the farthest, and the winner is
awarded a cash prize. The dwarfs wear
protective gear, including padding, neck
braces, and helmets, and are usually
thrown into piles of mattresses. They also
wear harnesses with handles for the convenience of the tossers. In one variation of
dwarf-tossing, commonly known as
"dwarf bowling," a dwarf is strapped to
a skateboard and rolled head-first toward
plastic bowling pins.

Many of the dwarfs who are tossed
apparently find the work easy, lucrative,
and even enjoyable, especially compared
to their former jobs or their daytime em-

ployment. Israel Torres, a dwarf who tours
bars and clubs as "Little Mr. T," earns
up to $2,000 a night being tossed in various
contests. Torres states, "I've never been
hurt. . . . Before this I was a professional
wrestler for seventeen years. Here I make
better money and it's a lot easier. . . . I
like doing it."[6] "Lenny the Giant," a
dwarf who was thrown a winning distance
of eleven feet, five inches in British Dwarf-
Throwing Championships, comments, "I
used to work on an assembly line at an
electronics factory—that's where I really
felt degraded."[7] David "Midge" Wilson,
a dwarf who tours Florida bars, asserts,
"I like what I'm doing. I know what I'm
doing. And it pays."[8]

Like the Springfield City Council and
LPA, many officials and citizens object
that the practice is dangerous for the dwarfs
who are tossed, offensive and demeaning
for all dwarfs, and degrading for our society as a whole. They point out that dwarfs
have more fragile skeletal systems and
extremely sensitive spinal cords, the injury
of which could easily cause paralysis or
death.[9] After he learned of an upcoming
dwarf toss in his city, Mayor Harold Washington of Chicago responded, "This alleged contest is degrading and mean-
spirited, endangers its participants, and is
repugnant to everyone truly committed to
eliminating prejudice against any group."[10]

For many critics of dwarf-tossing, the
most important issue is human dignity.
Paul Steven Miller, a dwarf who is on
the board of directors of the Billy Barty
Foundation (a national dwarf advocacy organization), wrote:

> Dwarf-tossing is not a joke. It ridicules and
> demeans dwarfs. It causes people to view
> dwarfs as objects and freaks to gawk at.
> Dwarf-tossing affects not just the dwarfs
> who are thrown, but such exploitation hurts
> all dwarfs by eroding our self-esteem and
> by perpetuating stereotypes and misconcep-
> tions. Very few dwarfs work in circuses or
> as actors. Dwarfs are successfully employed
> in almost every possible occupation, for

example, as teachers, engineers, lawyers, accountants, medical technicians.[11]

Some public officials have also denounced dwarf-tossing as a practice that debases not only dwarfs but all citizens of the cities and states where such contests are held. After signing legislation penalizing New York bars that sponsor the sport by revoking their liquor licenses, Governor Mario Cuomo said, "Any activity that dehumanizes and humiliates these people is degrading to us all."[12]

Many others, including the dwarfs who are tossed, defend the rights of consenting adults to make a living by being thrown in dwarf-tossing competitions. They say that policies banning such competitions infringe upon dwarfs' rights. Wilson asserts that his decision to earn his livelihood this way doesn't hurt anyone,[13] and that he doesn't think that others, particularly the Little People of America, ought to prescribe how he should handle his dwarfism.[14] Another defender of the activity argues, "The groups and individuals who claim to be harmed . . . do not have any rights violated. Dwarfs who do not get tossed, do-gooders, and a large segment of the general public may find the practice offensive, but that does not mean they have any right to do anything about it, just like no one has a right to prevent Jane from burning an American flag (if she owns it)."[15]

Defenders of the practice also emphasize the safety precautions that the promoters and dwarfs take. They point out that "dwarfs who wish to be tossed assume the risks of their activity," and that many take out insurance.[16] Some of those who believe it wrong to ban dwarf-tossing argue that many widely accepted sports are much more dangerous. "Midge" Wilson comments, "I think it's much milder than two people being in a ring beating each other. They don't protest that."[17]

Florida and New York have enacted

laws that make it impossible for bars to sponsor dwarf-tossing but do not directly prohibit the practice in all cases. In both states, tavern owners can lose their alcoholic beverage licenses if they sponsor dwarf-tossing events. In Florida, they may also be compelled to pay fines up to $1,000. There are no penalties for participation in the competitions. Nor are there penalties for taking part in dwarf-tossing outside of bars.[18]

NOTES

1. Rick Pearson, "Dwarf-Tossing Game Sounds Sour Note for Springfield Officials," *Chicago Tribune*, Aug. 16, 1989; Daniel Egler, "'Dwarf Tossing' Contests Goes Out the Window," *Chicago Tribune*, Aug. 17, 1989.

2. Pearson, "Dwarf-Tossing Game."

3. Egler, "'Dwarf Tossing' Contest."

4. Ibid.

5. Robert W. McGee, "If Dwarf Tossing Is Outlawed, Only Outlaws Will Toss Dwarfs: Is Dwarf Tossing a Victimless Crime?" *American Journal of Jurisprudence*, 38, 335–58.

6. Ibid.

7. Ibid.

8. Amy Wilson, "Short Story: It's a Tall Order Being the Only Dwarf Tossed These Days, But 'Midge' Wilson Fills It Well," *Chicago Tribune*, Jan. 11, 1989.

9. Letta Tayler, "Latest Bar Sport Called Dehumanizing to Dwarfs," *Newsday*, June 27, 1989; Ann Landers, "We Haven't Scraped the Barrel's Bottom Yet," *Chicago Tribune*, July 9, 1989.

10. Mike Royko, "Dwarf-Tossing Thrown for a Loss," *Chicago Tribune*, Nov. 18, 1985.

11. "On Being Little But Not Belittled," *New York Times*, Dec. 10, 1989.

12. Associated Press, "New York Dwarf-Tossing Ban Signed by Cuomo," *Chicago Tribune*, July 25, 1990.

13. Wilson, "Short Story."

14. Anne V. Hull, "Dwarf-Tossing a Controversial Sport," *St. Petersburg Times*, Sept. 16, 1988.

15. McGee, "If Dwarf Tossing Is Outlawed."

16. Ibid.

17. Hull, "Dwarf-Tossing a Controversial Sport."

18. McGee, "If Dwarf Tossing Is Outlawed"; Associated Press, "New York Dwarf-Tossing Ban."

Comment

Evaluate the strongest case for banning the practice of dwarf-tossing in bars and the strongest case for permitting it, considering all the reasons that were given by dwarfs and public officials for and against the practice, and any other reasons that are relevant to resolving the controversy. First, identify the paternalistic reasons and consider the extent to which they are relevant to the case against dwarf-tossing. Is the danger of physical injury to dwarfs, for example, a necessary or sufficient reason for banning the activity? Second, examine the reasons that are based on moral considerations independent of the harm that the practice may cause dwarfs. Third, assess the nature and moral force of the argument that the activity "hurts all dwarfs by . . . perpetuating stereotypes and misconceptions"? Is this a paternalistic argument or a moralistic argument, or neither?

To what extent is empirical evidence relevant to assessing the following criticisms of dwarf-tossing: (1) the activity is demeaning to dwarfs; (2) the activity is harmful to the self-esteem of dwarfs; (3) the activity perpetuates prejudicial stereotypes of dwarfs; and (4) the activity exploits dwarfs? What weight, if any, should we give to the fact that the major organized associations of dwarfs oppose the activity for all the reasons stated above? Does the consent of individual dwarfs to the activity make any difference in whether any of these critical claims should lead to banning or discouraging the practice?

Are there any significant moral differences between (1) banning the practice entirely in any public place; (2) banning bars from engaging in the practice by denying them liquor licenses; (3) levying a fine against bars if they engage in the practice; and (4) passing a public resolution that opposes events "such as dwarf tossing, which represent conduct that is both demeaning and insensitive to human values?" Which, if any, of these responses to dwarf-tossing are justified, and why? What additional information about dwarf-tossing, if any, do you need to answer this question?

What are the implications of your evaluation of dwarf-tossing for any other restrictions on individual liberty that aim to enforce social morality? Consider the ways in which regulating one or more of the following activities would differ in morally relevant ways from regulating dwarf-tossing: (1) public nudity, (2) sodomy, (3) incest, (4) pornography, (5) desecration of shrines and sacred symbols, (6) cruelty to animals, (7) mistreatment of corpses, and (8) commercial sale of bodily organs.

The Controversial Curriculum
Gregory M. Stankiewicz

In January 1983, the Hawkins County school district appointed a textbook selection committee in accordance with Tennessee state law to consider what textbooks should be purchased for the following school year. After examining several basic reading series, the committee recommended the Holt, Rinehart, and Winston series for students from kindergarten to the eighth grade.[1] The Holt series was used by approximately 15,000 school districts in all fifty states.[2]

On May 12, 1983, during a regularly scheduled meeting, the elected members of the Hawkins County Board of Education unanimously approved the committee's recommendation.[3] The books were selected as a means of teaching reading skill as well as citizenship. According to Tennessee state law, education must:

> help each student develop positive values and . . . improve student conduct as students learn to act in harmony with their positive values and learn to become good citizens in their school, community, and society.[4]

The board hoped that the new Holt series would do just that.

MRS. FROST'S DISCOVERY

Vicki Frost vividly remembers the day when she opened her sixth-grade daughter's reading textbook. The textbook was brand new, one in the series of readers that the Hawkins County School Board had just purchased for the 1983–84 school year. What Frost read shocked and dismayed her.

The fictional story her daughter was assigned, "A Visit to Mars," tells about children communicating with aliens through thought transfer, or telepathy. Frost was immediately troubled. She considers herself a

born-again Christian, and her belief is that supernatural powers can be the prerogative only of God. She sincerely believes it to be against her faith for her children to read stories like "A Visit to Mars."[5]

Frost continued reading, discovering that the problem was not limited to just one, or even a few, of the stories in the basic readers. She also examined her second-grade daughter's textbook and found that textbook no less offensive. In all, she discovered seventeen categories of offensive material, including issues of evolution, "secular humanism," "futuristic supernaturalism," pacifism, feminism, the occult, and false views of death. After more than two hundred hours of reading, Frost concluded that the entire Holt series was filled with statements and topics that were incompatible with her religious beliefs.[6]

Frost criticized the series for promoting a belief in the importance of mankind that eclipses the glory of God, a belief that she associates with "secular humanism,"[7] Frost therefore objected to the claim made by one textbook in discussing the Renaissance that "a central idea of the renaissance was a belief in the dignity and worth of human beings."[8] Since Frost defines "futuristic supernaturalism" as the teaching of "man as God," she was offended by the description of Leonardo da Vinci as having a creative mind that "came closest to the divine touch." She also objected to a passage from a story, "Seeing Beneath the Surface," that describes using one's imagination to see things not visible to one's eyes. According to Frost, it is an occult practice for children to imagine beyond the bounds of scriptural authority. And, although the textbooks that discuss evolution contain a disclaimer that evolution is a theory, not a proven fact, Frost also objected to the factual manner in which the theory is nevertheless presented, as well as the pervasive number of times the topic is mentioned.[9]

Moreover, the Holt series portrays situations that Frost associated with feminism and role reversal, points of view offensive to her religious beliefs. One Holt textbook, for example, shows a young boy cooking alongside a young girl who is reading to him from a cookbook. The objectionable passage reads: "Pat reads to Jim. Jim cooks. The big book helps Jim. Jim has fun."[10]

Frost was troubled by the way other of these stories encourage children to make moral judgments, such as whether it is right or wrong to kill animals. Her view is that these textbooks should teach reading, good English, and grammar and not secular humanism or any other moral values.[11]

Frost also objected to stories dealing with the beliefs of other religions. The story "Hunchback Madonna," for example, includes this passage:

> They came to see and pray before the stoop-shouldered Virgin, people from as far south as Belen who from some accident or some spinal or heart affliction are shoulder-bent and want to walk straight again. Others, whose faith is not so simple or who have no faith at all, have come from many parts of the country and asked the way to El Tordo, not only to see the curiously painted Madonna in which the natives put so much faith, but to visit a single grave in a corner of the *campo santo* that, they have heard, is covered in spring with a profusion of wild flowers, whereas the other sunken ones are bare altogether, or at the most sprinkled only with sagebrush and tumbleweed.[12]

Frost could not condone exposure of her children to other religious perspectives (such as the one portrayed by the "Hunchback Madonna") or to values that conflict with her beliefs without a statement that her religious beliefs are correct and the others are incorrect.[13]

The Hawkins County Board of Education had selected the new Holt textbooks partly because the materials *would* expose children

to diverse cultural and religious views. For Frost, however, "Jesus Christ being the only means of salvation, . . . we cannot be tolerant of religious views on the basis of accepting other religious views as equal to our own."[14] Frost believes that her religion requires that she shield her children from the many ideas conveyed in the new readers. Nothing short of complete exemption for her children from reading the Holt series would do.

Organized Protest

On September 1, 1983, Frost and Jennie Wilson, the grandmother of two elementary school children, organized a parents' meeting in the middle school to discuss ways of protesting the textbooks. As a result of the meeting, a small group of Hawkins County residents formed a new group, called Citizens Organized for Better Schools (COBS).[15]

The members of COBS, along with some other protesting parents who never joined the organization, were all fundamentalist Christians from various denominations. The group never gained the support of the majority of Hawkins County residents.[16] Some of the leaders and other members of the various fundamentalist congregations disagreed with Frost's view of the requirements of their religion.[17] The mayor of Frost's town would comment "I think the people support their teachers and school officials, that [the Holt series] is good material, that it is not extreme, that it is not brainwashing the children."[18] A nationwide poll of adult Americans found that 75 percent agreed that students should be exposed to religious beliefs which differ from those of their parents.[19]

Although COBS represented only a small minority of Hawkins county residents, they made themselves heard. Members of COBS attended the September and October meetings of the Board of Education, protesting the Holt series and petitioning the board to remove the series from the schools and return to the older textbooks. At the same time, Frost and seven other families individually approached their childrens' principals, asking that some alternative arrangement be worked out so that their children would not have to read the Holt textbooks. The principal of one elementary school refused; the principals of the middle school and the other two elementary schools decided to allow alternative arrangements. These arrangements consisted mostly in excusing the individual students from class during reading periods and allowing them to read instead from older textbooks in other rooms or offices. The exempted children seemed to be doing well academically under these arrangements. All of them continued to receive above-average grades.[20]

THE BOARD OF EDUCATION VOTES

In its November meeting, the Hawkins County Board of Education was once more confronted by angry COBS members. The board felt it was time to clarify the situation regarding the new Holt series. With no public discussion, the board members unanimously approved a resolution requiring teachers to "use only textbooks adopted by the Board of Education as regular classroom textbooks."[21] The board vote reversed the decision of those principals who had authorized alternative arrangements. All students now would be required to attend regular reading classes.

Shortly after the board's decision, several middle school students who continued to refuse to read the new Holt series were suspended for three days. Upon their return, the students again refused to attend reading classes and/or read the Holt textbooks and were suspended an additional ten days.[22] After this second suspension, most of the protesting families removed their children from the Hawkins County public schools and enrolled them in religious or other area public schools, or taught them at home. Two of the students who did remain, however, were eventually given some accommodation: individual teachers, apparently against the board's ruling, quietly excused these

students from reading the Holt series or noted on the students' worksheets that the students were not required to believe the stories that they read.[23]

THE SCHOOL BOARD'S VIEW

Board members and their supporters acknowledge that COBS members' religious beliefs are genuine, but they argued that the board's decision was necessary to ensure that all public school children be exposed to different cultural and religious ideas. The elected superintendent of the Hawkins County School District pointed out that "while it is true that these textbooks expose the student to varying values and religious backgrounds, neither the textbooks nor the teachers teach, indoctrinate, oppose, or promote any particular value or religion."[24] According to their critics, COBS and the protesting parents were attempting to impose censorship on the public school curriculum. The People for the American Way, a nationwide civil liberties group, would argue that the parents and their supporters were attempting to establish "a right to a sectarian education in the public schools."[25] A lawyer for the Board of Education noted, "There is no way [Vicki Frost] could attend public schools and not be offended," given all of her objections to the textbooks.[26]

Other supporters of the school board's decision emphasized that replacing the Holt series would have been a very expensive option. If the board had chosen the option of allowing some schools to continue providing alternative services, these individual exemptions also would be costly, especially of teachers' time and effort. The exemption could prove disruptive for the other students, leading them to believe that they too could be exempt from their required classes if only they and their parents protested. The Tennessee commissioner of education would argue that:

> [Permitting] individual teachers, students, parents or ministers to choose the textbook of their liking would inescapably result in

widespread chaos not only within the Hawkins County School System but also every public school system within the State of Tennessee.[27]

Alternatively, to avoid disruption, schools would teach from materials so bland as not to offend anybody. Such a response, according to a lawyer for the school board, would lead to the "formation of lowest common denominator education."[28]

THE PROTESTORS' VIEWS

COBS and its supporters denied that they were defending censorship. They argued that they were only trying to protect their right to the free exercise of their religion. The parents had given up on their early attempts to have the Board of Education withdraw the textbooks and now wanted only to exempt their children from reading material that they considered incompatible with their religious convictions.[29]

Concerned Women for America, a national group, would characterize COBS's aim as the establishment of "the right of Christians to refuse to read material which offends their religious convictions."[30] Requiring the children to read the Holt textbooks, the group would argue, is similar to requiring Jewish children to sing Christmas carols or black children to read racially offensive literature.[31]

Others defending COBS also argued that the case revolved around the rights of *any* minority not to be forced by the state to act against its religious beliefs. If protesting parents would not allow their children to read the Holt textbooks, the only alternative the school board left open to them would be to pull their children out of the Hawkins County school system. The school board's actions thereby denied children of the protesting parents a public school education. Michael Farris, a lawyer who would defend the parents, likened this situation to the one faced by black children before the Supreme Court's *Brown v. Board of Education* decision that outlawed "separate but equal"

black schools: "What the state is trying to do is force Christian kids out of public schools. Black kids didn't use to have any choice, either. In this case it's doubly discriminatory because black schools were paid for by the Government."[32] Many of the Hawkins County parents, Farris argued, would have to pay tuition to send their children to private religious schools that did not assign offensive material.

Some observers viewed the conflict as one over who should control the public school curriculum—the state, the county school board, the local community, or parents of enrolled children. Defenders of the protesting parents argued that they—not the state of Tennessee, the county school board, or the local community—should determine their children's education.

NOTES

1. See *Mozert v. Hawkins County Public Schools*, 647 F. Supp. 1194 (E.D. Tenn. 1986), at 1196.

2. Alain L. Sanders, "Tilting at 'Secular Humanism': In Tennessee, A Modern Replay of the Celebrated 'Monkey Trial,'" *Time*, July 28, 1986, p. 68.

3. 647 F. Supp. at 1196. On the school board being elected, see Stephen Bates, *Battleground: One Mother's Crusade, the Religious Right, and the Struggle for Our Schools* (Las Cruces, N.M.: Poseidon, 1993), pp. 163–64.

4. Tennessee Code Annotated (TCA) 49-6-1007 (1986 Supp.), cited in *Mozert v. Hawkins County Board of Eduation*, 827 F. 2d 1058 (6th Cir. 1987), at 1060.

5. Dudley Clendinen, "Fundamentalist Parents Put Textbooks on Trial," *New York Times*, July 15, 1986, p. A14.

6. 827 F. 2d at 1061–62.

7. Sanders, "Tilting at 'Secular Humanism.'"

8. Clendinen, "Fundamentalist Parents," p. A14.

9. This description is taken from the summary of Vicki Frost's testimony, in 827 F. 2d at 1062.

10. The passage and illustration is reprinted in Sanders, "Tilting at 'Secular Humanism.'"

11. 827 F. 2d at 1062.

12. Fray Angelico Chavez, "The Hunchback Madonna," in *Great Waves Breaking* (New York: Holt, Rinehart, and Winston, 1983). Reprinted in the *New York Times*, "2 Examples of Textbook Material Called Objectionable in Suit," Oct. 25, 1986, p. 8.

13. 827 F. 2d at 1062.

14. Vicki Frost's testimony, as quoted in Clendinen "Fundamentalist Parents," p. A14.

15. 647 F. Supp. at 1196.

16. See Bates, *Battleground*, pp. 136–37.

17. 827 F. 2d at 1061.

18. Randall Housewright, mayor of Church Hill, Tennessee, quoted in Clendinen, "Fundamentalist Parents," p. A14.

19. Poll results are from a nationwide Media General/ Associated Press poll of 1,464 adult Americans, who were interviewed by telephone, September 8–17, 1986. The results have a margin of error of plus-or-minus 3 percentage points. Quoted in Associated Press, "Textbook Pool Finds Diversity Is Favored in Treating Religion," *New York Times*, Oct. 22, 1986, p. A23.

20. 647 F. Supp. at 1196, at 1201.

21. Ibid., at 1196.

22. Ibid., at 1196–97, at 1201–02 (fn. 13).

23. 827 F. 2d at 1060.

24. Superintendent Bill Snodgrass, quoted in 827 F.

2d at 1063; on the superintendent being elected, see Bates, *Battleground*, 163–64.

25. Anthony Podesta, president of People for the American Way, quoted in Sanders, "Tilting at 'Secular Humanism.'"

26. Timothy Dyk, quoted in Sanders "Tilting at 'Secular Humanism.'"

27. Robert McElrath, Commissioner of Education of the State of Tennessee, quoted in 647 F. Supp. at 1202.

28. Timothy Dyk, quoted in Dudley Clendinen, "Fundamentalists Win a Federal Suit over Schoolbooks," *New York Times*, Oct. 25, 1986, p. 1.

29. 647 F. Supp. at 1195.

30. Beverly LaHaye, founder of Concerned Women for America, writing in a fundraising letter, quoted in Sanders "Tilting at 'Secular Humanism.'"

31. LaHaye, quoted in Stuart Taylor, Jr., "Supreme Court Roundup; Justices Refuse to Hear Tennessee Case on Bible and Textbooks," *New York Times*, Feb. 23, 1988, p. D29.

32. Michael Farris, quoted in Associated Press, "7 Tennessee Families and Schools Nearing End of Battle over Books," *New York Times*, July 28, 1986, p. A10.

Comment

Citizens disagree about what morality should guide the education of children, yet education cannot be morally neutral. Tennessee state law mandates that schools help children "develop positive values" and "learn to become good citizens in their school, community, and society." Even if the citizens of Tennessee can agree that teaching positive values and educating good citizens are justifiable ends of public education, they disagree about what constitutes positive values, good citizenship, and an education adequate for these ends. May a public school try to educate all its students "to become good citizens" even if some parents object to the kind of citizenship education mandated by the school? If there are multiple ways of educating good citizens, what are the strongest arguments for authorizing an elected school board rather than individual parents to decide which way to educate for citizenship in public schools? Would your answer differ if a controversy like this took place in a private school?

Is respect for the religious freedom of parents a compelling reason to exempt children from a prescribed curriculum in public schools? What about respect for the religious convictions of the students themselves? Assess the analogies suggested by Concerned Women for America: exempting Jewish children from singing Christmas carols and exempting black children from reading racially offensive literature.

Does the existence of the option of sending their children to private schools provide a response to the objections of the dissenting parents? Evaluate the argument that it is doubly discriminatory to require the dissenting parents to pay for a private education for their children. Is this a fair price to ask parents to pay if they disagree with the public school curriculum? Is accommodating the religious convictions of parents a fair price to ask public schools to pay? To what extent do answers to these questions depend on the content of the religious convictions of parents and their compatibility with the aims of education in a democracy? Which of the following claims about the curriculum, if correct, would support the position of the parents or that of the school board: the curriculum (1) indoctrinates children; (2) promotes feminism; (3) promotes a belief in the dignity and worth of human beings; (4) encourages children to make their own moral judgments; (5) offends the religious convictions of some parents; (6) exposes children to cultural and religious ideas that are unacceptable to their parents; (7) increases the chances that children will question their parents' religious convictions.

Consider which of the religious convictions expressed by Vicki Frost and COBS are compatible, first, with citizenship education in general and, second, with the reading curriculum of the Hawkins County school in particular. What kind of education for citizenship would be compatible with the religious convictions of dissenting parents?

What should the Hawkins County School Board have decided in the face of the parental protest? Evaluate the various arguments presented for and against the position of the protesting parents and any others that should carry moral weight in this case. Consider the options open to the Hawkins County School Board, including (1) altering their reading curriculum for all children, (2) not altering it for any children, and (3) altering it only for the children of dissenting parents. Should the school board have any moral discretion in deciding what to do?

Also central to this controversy is the question of who should have the authority to determine the content of education for citizenship in Tennessee. Consider the alternative sources of authority over education in Tennessee and their legitimate claims to influence the outcome of this controversy: parents, teachers, principals, textbook selection committees, school boards, legislatures, and courts. Are there moral limits to the legitimate authority of any or all of these educational agents?

Finally, evaluate the process by which the Hawkins County School Board resolved to require teachers to use only textbooks adopted by the board and to deny any exemption to children of the dissenting parents. Can you recommend a more defensible process by which such controversies should be resolved?

Recommended Reading

The classic source on paternalism and moralism is Mills *On Liberty*, Introductory, chapters 4 and 5. For modern discussions of paternalism, see Gerald Dworkin, "Paternalism," *Monist* 56 (1972), pp. 64–84, reprinted in R. Wasserstrom (ed.), *Morality and the Law* (Belmont, Calif.: Wadsworth, 1971); Joel Feinberg, *The Moral Limits of the Criminal Law*, vol. 3, *Harm to Self* (New York: Oxford University Press, 1986); John Kleinig, *Paternalism* (Totowa, N.J.: Littlefield and Adams,

1984); Dennis F. Thompson, "Paternalistic Power," in *Political Ethics and Public Office* (Cambridge, Mass.: Harvard University Press, 1987), ch. 6; and Donald VanDeVeer, *Paternalistic Intervention: The Moral Bounds of Benevolence* (Princeton, N.J.: Princeton University Press, 1986).

For contemporary discussions of moralism, see Gerald Dworkin (ed.), *Morality, Harm, and the Law* (Boulder, Colo.: Westview Press, 1994); Joel Feinberg, *The Moral Limits of the Criminal Law*, vol. 4, *Harmless Wrongdoing* (New York: Oxford University Press, 1988); Elizabeth Anderson, *Value in Ethics and Economics* (Cambridge, Mass.: Harvard University Press, 1993); and Peter de Marneffe, "Contractualism, Liberty, and Democracy," *Ethics*, 104 (July 1994), pp. 764–83.

More generally on liberty, moralism, and paternalism, see Amy Gutmann and Dennis Thompson, *Democracy and Disagreement* (Cambridge, Mass.: Harvard University Press, 1996), ch. 7; and Gerald Dworkin, *The Theory and Practice of Autonomy* (New York: Cambridge University Press, 1988).

On the ethics of democratic representation, Mill is, once again, a good place to start. See his *Considerations on Representative Government* (Indianapolis, Ind.: Bobbs Merrill, 1958), ch. 5–8, 12, and 15. Compare Joseph Schumpeter, *Capitalism, Socialism and Democracy* (New York: Harper and Row, 1975), pp. 240–83. A useful commentary is Hanna Fenichel Pitkin, *The Concept of Representation* (Berkeley: University of California Press, 1972), ch. 7–10.

On AIDS, see the Recommended Reading in chapter 6.

On the political morality of education, see Amy Gutmann, *Democratic Education* (Princeton, N.J.: Princeton University Press, 1987); "Symposium on Citizenship, Democracy, and Education," *Ethics*, 105 (April 1995); Amy Gutmann, "Undemocratic Education," in Nancy L. Rosenblum, *Liberalism and the Moral Life* (Cambridge, Mass.: Harvard University Press, 1989), pp. 71–88; and William Galston, "Civic Education in the Liberal State," in *Liberalism and the Moral Life*, pp. 89–102.

9   Liberty and Life

Introduction

The idea that all persons have a right to life as well as liberty commands widespread support in this country. But what beings possess the right to life is one of the most divisive questions of our recent political history. The "pro-life" movement defends the fetus's right to life, while "pro-choice" groups defend a woman's right to abortion. They disagree on questions of both personal morality (whether having an abortion is moral) and political morality (whether abortion should be legal and the right to an abortion constitutionally protected).
The structure of the pro-life argument is:

> The fetus is a person in the generic sense.
> It is wrong to kill a person (except in self-defense).
> Abortion is therefore wrong (unless a mother's life is at stake).
> It should therefore be illegal.

The typical pro-choice argument has a parallel logic supporting the opposite conclusion:

> The fetus is not a person in the generic sense but part of a woman's body that significantly affects her life.
> A woman has a right to control her own body and life.
> Abortion therefore is a woman's right.
> It should therefore be legal.

The two sides are divided by fundamentally different perceptions of what a fetus is, perceptions that seem impervious to change by rational argument. Many people on each side view the perception of the other side as "not simply false, but wildly, madly false—nonsense, totally unintelligible, and literally unbelievable" (Roger Wertheimer). While philosophers may not even in principle succeed in resolving this controversy, they have made more modest contributions that are morally and politically significant. They have shown that the premises of each side support less extreme conclusions on the level of both personal and political morality. And they have offered reasons for both sides to recognize and respect some degree of genuine moral disagreement in the abortion debate without forsaking their own fundamental premises.

Some philosophers have argued that even if the fetus is a person, its death may be justifiable. Self-defense is not the only justification for letting an innocent person die. One is not obligated to save an innocent person at great personal sacrifice if one is not otherwise responsible for the person's situation. On this view, the basic premise of the pro-life position leads to a less absolutist stance against abortion:

abortion is permissible in cases of rape and incest. Other writers have suggested that even if abortion is arguably wrong at the level of personal morality, it may still be right for a liberal state to legalize it when the public is so divided about its morality, and its wrongness depends on sustaining a rationally contestable claim about the constitutional personhood of the fetus.

Philosophers also have criticized the logic of the extreme pro-choice position. They have argued that the right of a woman to control her body is not absolute: it does not include the right to destroy for trivial reasons what is admittedly a potential life. And the pro-choice position is not, as some proponents assume, neutral as a political morality. Giving all women a choice between having or not having an abortion is still, for those who believe that the fetus is a person, giving women the right to kill innocent people. To those who believe in the personhood of the fetus, this choice is immoral, just as for those who do not believe that the fetus is a person, outlawing abortion is immoral because it restricts a woman's right to control her own body and her freedom more generally.

The political morality of abortion is complex because no policy can be morally neutral, and neither side has reasons adequate to convince the other of the moral superiority of its position. Political philosophers have suggested several ways of dealing with situations of this kind. One is to consider a compromise that is fair to both sides, though not fully satisfying the moral claims of either. Another is to find a method of decision making that is procedurally fair, even if its results favor one side of the moral controversy. Yet a third is to accommodate the moral convictions of one side to the extent possible without ceding any ground from the side that— all things considered—has the best reasons on its side. Despite the vast literature on abortion, none of these alternatives has yet to be exhaustively examined.

The cases on abortion in this chapter add moral complications to an already difficult political issue and political complications to an already difficult moral issue. Given that abortion is now legal in this country under most circumstances, should the government subsidize abortions for poor women? Most people who believe that abortion is a woman's right also argue that the government should subsidize it for poor women. But critics point out that having a right to free speech, for example, does not obligate the state to provide anyone with a subvention for publication. Most pro-life advocates argue that, even if the law permits some women to obtain abortions, there is no reason for the government to subsidize the taking of innocent lives. Yet some who believe that abortion is morally wrong dissent from this view on grounds that the exercise of legal rights should not be effectively withheld from the poor. In the congressional debate over funding, excerpted in "Funding Abortion," these and other moral positions are passionately represented.

Joseph Califano's account of his position while he was secretary of the Department of Health, Education and Welfare raises yet another issue in political ethics: what should a public official do when the policy he may be instructed to enforce violates his own moral principles?

The conflict faced by Senator Scott Heidepriem in South Dakota concerned his dual responsibility as a state representative: on the one hand, to ensure a fair legislative hearing for a potentially popular antiabortion bill, and on the other hand, to act consistently with his strong convictions regarding a woman's legal right to abortion. Although Heidepriem prided himself on following fair procedures, the question of what constitutes procedural fairness in such a case is almost as controversial as the legalization of abortion itself.

The conflict between life and liberty has taken on unforeseen dimensions in the newly expanding commercial practice of surrogate parenting, leaving state governments without standards for resolving the conflict in one of its poignant forms— dispute over who are the rightful parents of a newly born child. Any legislation that settles this conflict will also have a profound effect on the more fundamental issue of whether government should sanction the commercial (or noncommercial) practice of surrogate parenting in the first place. The first proposal for legislative reform reprinted here recommends legalizing and enforcing contracts for surrogate parenting. Prepared by the staff of the New York State Senate Judiciary Committee, the recommendation is based on the view that enforcement of suitably designed surrogate contracts will both secure the welfare of children born under such contracts and satisfy standards of informed consent required for valid private contracts. The second proposal, presented by the New York State Task Force on Life and the Law, rejects this view. The Task Force concluded that the commercialization of human reproduction is against the best interests of children, degrades women, and (more generally) conflicts with the public good. The task force therefore recommended that the legislature declare surrogate contracts void and unenforceable. Understanding the conflict between the value of life and liberty presented by the practice of commercial surrogacy requires coming to terms with the differing moral perspectives represented by these two proposals.

Administering Abortion Policy
Joseph A. Califano, Jr.

The abortion issue marked my initiation by public controversy as Secretary of Health, Education, and Welfare.

It was certainly not the issue I would have chosen to confront first. The abortion dispute was sure to make enemies at the beginning of my tenure when I particularly needed friends; guaranteed to divide supporters of social programs when it was espe-

cially important to unite them; and likely to spark latent and perhaps lasting suspicions about my ability to separate my private beliefs as a Roman Catholic from my public duties as the nation's chief health, education, and social service official.

The issue whether Medicaid should fund abortions for poor women was more searing than many I faced, but it was quintessentially characteristic of the problems confronting HEW. The abortion dispute summoned taproot convictions and religious beliefs, sincerely held and strenuously put forth by each side, about the rights of poor people, the use of tax dollars, the role of government in the most intimate personal decisions. The pro- and anti-abortion forces each claimed that the Constitution and the American people were on its side, and each truly believed that it was protecting human life. Wherever those forces struggled to prevail—in the courts, the Congress, the executive regulatory process, the state legislatures, and city councils—there were HEW and its Medicaid program. And there was no neutral ground on which HEW or its Secretary could comfortably stand, for any decision—to fund all, or none, or some abortions—would disappoint and enrage millions of Americans who were convinced that theirs was the only humane position.

The controversy exposed me to the world of difference between being a White House staffer—however powerful—and being a Cabinet officer, out front, responsible not only to the President as an advisor but also to the Congress and the American people. It was one thing to be Lyndon Johnson's top domestic policy advisor crafting Great Society programs, but not accountable to the Congress and not ultimately responsible. It was quite another to be the public point man on an issue as controversial as federal financing of abortions for poor people.

Lyndon Johnson had held his White House staff on a particularly short leash. We spoke only in his name—explaining what he thought, how he felt, what his hopes and objectives for America were. "The only reason Hugh Sidey [of *Time*] talks to you is to find out about me, what I think, what I want. He doesn't give a damn about you," Johnson so often told us, "so make sure you know what I think before you tell him what you think I think." Indeed, during my lengthy press briefings on new legislative programs, as Johnson read early pages of the instantly typed transcript in his office, he sometimes sent messages to me to correct statements or misimpressions before the briefing ended.

Cabinet officers, of necessity, function with less detailed and immediate presidential guidance. It goes with the territory for a Cabinet officer to put a little distance between himself and the President, particularly on such controversial issues as abortion. Presidents expect, as they should, that their Cabinet officers will shield them from as much controversy as possible so that precious presidential capital can be spent only for overriding national objectives the President selects.

Jimmy Carter first talked to me about abortion when we lunched alone in Manchester, New Hampshire, in early August 1976. He expressed his unyielding opposition to abortion and his determination to stop federal funding of abortions. He asked me to work with Fritz Mondale to make his views known to the Catholic hierarchy and influential lay Catholics. Mondale was using his Minnesota friend Bishop James Rausch, who was then the general secretary of the National Conference of Catholic Bishops, to get Carter's view across, and Charlie Kirbo would be quietly communicating with Terence Cardinal Cooke in New York, but Carter said he wanted a "good Catholic" to spread the word of his strong opposition to abortion. I was impressed by the sincerity and depth of Carter's views on abortion and I found his determination to get credit for those views politically prudent in view of the inevitable opposition his position would incite. It later struck me that Carter never asked my views on the subject, and I never expressed them. Our conversation simply assumed complete agreement.

The assumption was well grounded. I consider abortion morally wrong unless the life of the mother would be at stake if the fetus were carried to term. Under such tragic and wrenching circumstances, no human being could be faulted for making either choice, between the life of the mother and the life of the unborn child. Those are the only circumstances under which I considered federal financing of abortion appropriate.

During the 1976 presidential campaign, I never had to reconcile my beliefs as a Catholic about abortion with any potential duty to obey and execute the law as a public servant. In promulgating Carter's view, like any proponent of a presidential candidate, I took as a given his ability to translate that view into law or public policy. Since my conversations were with those who opposed abortion, no one asked me what Carter would do if the Congress enacted a different position into law.

In talks with Monsignors George Higgins and Francis Lally, and others at the Catholic Conference, I sought to convince them that Carter shared their view. Higgins was an old friend from the Johnson years and he helped get Carter's position better known in the Catholic community. But Higgins confided that nothing short of a firm commitment to a constitutional amendment outlawing abortion would satisfy the conservative elements of the Catholic hierarchy. When I reported this to Mondale, he expressed doubt that Carter would—or should—go that far, particularly since in January 1976 he had said he did "not favor a constitutional amendment abolishing abortion." I agreed.

Eventually, in response to the numerous questions on abortion during the campaign and after a meeting with Catholic bishops in Washington on August 31, 1976, Carter said that he had not yet seen any constitutional amendment he would support, but he "would never try to block . . . an amendment" prohibiting abortions. He added pointedly that any citizen had the right to seek an amendment to overturn the Supreme Court's 1973 *Roe v. Wade* decision, which established a woman's constitutional right to have an abortion, at least in the first trimester of pregnancy.

In November 1976, after the election, as Mondale, Tip O'Neill, and other friends reported conversations in which Carter or his close advisors such as Jordan and Kirbo were checking on my qualifications, it became clear that I was a leading candidate for the HEW post. Then, for the first time, I had to focus on the depth of my personal religious belief about abortion: As Secretary of Health, Education, and Welfare, would I be able, in good conscience, to carry out the law of the land, even if that law provided for federal funding of all abortions? I asked myself that question many times before others began asking it of me.

Both my parents are devoutly religious Catholics. Their influence and my education at St. Gregory's elementary school in Brooklyn, at the Jesuit high school Brooklyn Prep, and at the College of the Holy Cross had provided me not only with some intellectual sextants but with a moral compass as well. Like many Catholic students and young lawyers in the 1950s, I had read the works of John Courtney Murray, a leading Jesuit scholar and philosopher. His writings on the rights and duties of American Catholics in a pluralistic society and the need to accommodate private belief and public policy were guides for liberal Catholics of my generation. But even with this background, it was an exacting task in modern America to get clarity and peace in my private conscience while satisfying the legitimate demands of public service and leadership.

The abortion issue never came up in the Johnson administration. But family planning, even the aggressive promotion of the use of contraceptives to prevent pregnancy as a government policy, was an issue I had confronted in those years. President Johnson was an ardent proponent of birth control at home and abroad. He repeatedly rejected the unanimous pleas of his advisors from Secretary of State Dean Rusk to National Security Advisor Walt Rostow to ship wheat to the starving Indians during their 1966 famine. He demanded that the Indian government first agree to mount a massive birth control program. The Indians finally moved and Johnson released the wheat over a sufficiently extended period to make certain the birth control program was off the ground.

Johnson spoke so often and forcefully about birth control that the Catholic bishops denounced him publicly. He sent me to try to cool them off. Working discreetly with Monsignor Frank Hurley, then the chief lobbyist for the Catholic Conference in Washington, we reached an uneasy off-the-record truce: If LBJ would stop using the term "birth control" and refer instead to the "population problem," which allowed increased food production as a possible solution, the bishops would refrain from public attacks on him. Johnson agreed, and spoke thereafter of "the population problem"—but with equal if not greater vigor.

During my years with Lyndon Johnson, and the legislative fights to fund family planning services through the Public Health Service and the War on Poverty, I had to relate my private conscience to public policy on family planning. The alternatives of teenage pregnancy, abortion, mental retardation, poverty, and the like were far worse than providing access to contraceptives; to expect all citizens to practice premarital celibacy or all married couples to use the rhythm method was unrealistic in America's increasingly sexually permissive society. I was able to reconcile my private conscience with public policy. I concluded that it made sense for government to fund family planning programs that offered and even encouraged artificial birth control. I had no moral qualms about such a policy in a pluralistic society so long as it respected individual dignity and religious belief. The Catholic bishops disagreed with Johnson. But among theologians there was a great diversity of opinion about the moral propriety of birth control in various personal situations; I inclined to the more liberal position.

Abortion was a far more difficult issue. Here I faced my own conviction that abortion was morally wrong except to save the life of the mother, that medically unnecessary abortions offended fundamental stan-

dards of respect for human life. It is one thing temporarily to prevent the creation of a human life; quite another level of moral values is involved in discarding a human life once created. With abortion, I had to face direct conflict between personal religious conviction and public responsibility.

I was to learn how difficult it would be to preserve the precious distinction between public duty and private belief. Setting forth my own and the President's view of appropriate public policy on federal funding of abortion, putting the issue in perspective, relating it to considerations of fairness, and striving to separate my own personal views from my responsibilities as a public official once the Congress decisively acted on the legislation were to be matters of enormous complexity and lonely personal strain. Whatever inner strength I mustered from my own religious faith, the public anguish would not be eased by the fact that I was the only Catholic in the Carter Cabinet.

The anti-abortion, right to life groups and the pro-abortion, freedom of choice organizations had turned the annual HEW appropriations bill into the national battleground over abortion. The issue was whether, and under what circumstances, HEW's Medicaid program to finance health care for poor people should pay for abortions. It would be debated and resolved in the language of the HEW appropriations law, and the regulations implementing the law. This made the Secretary of HEW an especially imposing and exposed figure on the abortion battlefield.

With the Supreme Court's *Roe v. Wade* decision in 1973, HEW's Medicaid program promptly began funding abortions for poor women as routinely as any other medical procedure. By 1976, estimates of the number of HEW-funded abortions ranged as high as 300,000 per year. The furies that the *Roe* decision and its impact on HEW's Medicaid program set loose turned abortion into a legal and political controversy that the courts and the Congress would toss at each other for years. The federal financing of an estimated 300,000 abortions set off an emotional stampede in the House of Representatives in 1976, led by Republican Representative Henry Hyde of Illinois, and reluctantly followed by the Senate, to attach a restriction to the 1977 HEW appropriations bill prohibiting the use of HEW funds "to perform abortions except where the life of the mother would be endangered if the fetus were carried to term."

Before the restriction took effect, pro-abortion groups obtained an injunction from Federal District Judge John F. Dooling in Brooklyn, blocking its enforcement until he could decide whether the Supreme Court decision in *Roe v. Wade* established an obligation of the federal government to fund abortions, as a corollary to the right to have them performed.

Whatever the courts ultimately ruled, the abortion issue would continue to be a volatile inhabitant of the political arena. Sincerely held as I believe it was, Carter's stand was also a critical part of his election victory. Betty Ford's strong pro-abortion views and Gerald Ford's ambivalence were thought by Carter to have hurt the Republican candidate.

But Carter's appointment of pro-abortionist Midge Costanza as a senior White House aide and his strong support of the Equal Rights Amendment and other feminist causes gave women's groups some hope that his position would be softened. The pro-lifers were suspicious because Carter's colors blurred on the litmus test of supporting a constitutional amendment outlawing abortion. With pro-and anti-abortion advocates poised to battle for the mind of the administration, I prepared for my confirmation hearings on January 13, 1977.

From my religious and moral convictions, I knew my conscience. From my training at Harvard Law School and my life as a lawyer and public servant, I knew my obligation to enforce the law. But on the eve of becoming a public spokesman for myself and the administration, I sought the reassurance of double-checking my moral and intellectual foundation. I consulted an extraordinary Jesuit priest, James English, my pastor at Holy Trinity Church in Georgetown. He came by my law office on the Saturday morning before the confirmation hearing. He sat on the couch against the wall; I sat across the coffee table from him. I told him I wanted to make one final assessment of my ability to deal with the abortion issue before going forward with the nomination. If I could not enforce whatever law the Congress passes, then I should not become Secretary of Health, Education, and Welfare.

Father English spoke softly about the pluralistic society and the democratic system, in which each of us has an opportunity to express his views. Most statutory law codifies morality, he noted, whether prohibiting stealing or assault, or promoting equal rights, and the arguments of citizens over what the law should be are founded in individual moral values. He said that my obligation to my personal conscience was satisfied if I expressed those views forcefully.

I postulated a law that any abortion could be funded by the federal government, simply upon the request of the woman. He said that so long as I tried to pursue the public policy I believed correct, then I was free—indeed, obliged if I stayed in the job—to enforce that permissive law. I was relieved, comforted by his quiet assurance. As I thanked him for coming by, he mentioned an expert in this field, Father Richard McCormick, a Jesuit at the Kennedy Institute of Bioethics at Georgetown, whose advice I might find helpful.

On the following Monday evening, January 10, representatives of the National Women's Political Caucus sat on the same red couch Father English had occupied. It was the most intense of a series of meetings with various special interest groups.

As the women filed through the door to my office, I shook hands with each one.

Their eyes seemed cold and skeptical, and reflected deep concern, even when they smiled. The warm welcome with which I greeted them masked my own foreboding about the imminence of the clash on abortion.

The discussion began on common ground: the failure of the Nixon and Ford administrations to enforce laws prohibiting sex discrimination. One after another, the representatives of each group in the women's political caucus attacked the enemy: discrimination in the Social Security system (in terms far more forceful than Jimmy Carter's quaint accusation that the benefit structure encouraged senior citizens to "live in sin"), in the federal income tax system, and on the nation's campuses. Most mentioned female appointments at HEW, but since they knew I was searching for qualified women, they did not linger on the personnel issue. Margot Polivy, a tough and talented attorney litigating to eliminate discrimination in women's athletics, pressed her case for HEW enforcement of Title IX, the law prohibiting sex discrimination at educational institutions that receive federal funds.

I shared most of the views the women expressed on these subjects and they knew it. When are they going to stop circling their prey, I thought, and ask about abortion?

Dorothy Ross, a committed feminist who had been helping me recruit for HEW jobs, was seated at my left. She had told me abortion would be the key topic and I wanted to get it over with. Then one of the women put the question: "What's your view on abortion?"

I had decided to make my view unmistakably clear. It was important to state my position on abortion before the Senate confirmation hearings. No senator should be able to claim that his vote was cast for my confirmation without knowing my view on this subject. But in the tension of the moment, it was not easy or pleasant to get the words out.

"I believe abortion is morally wrong," I said softly and firmly. "That is my personal belief."

There was a brief moment of breathtaking at the depth of conviction in my voice. Then the women responded.

"Would you deny federal funds for abortion?" one woman angrily asked.

"I oppose federal funding for abortion." The circling was over. The questions were accusations called out like counts in an indictment.

"The Supreme Court gives a woman a right to an abortion. You would deny that right to poor women?"

"You'd deny a woman her constitutional right?"

"How can you be a liberal and hold such a view?"

"Suppose the woman's life is at stake?"

"What about rape or incest?"

"Suppose the child would be retarded, a vegetable?"

"Are you going to impose your religious views on HEW?"

The questions came with such furious vehemence that I had to interrupt to respond.

"Look," I said, "I have no intention of imposing my personal view on anybody. I am prepared to enforce the law, whatever it is."

"But how could you possibly," one of the women asked, "when you have such strong personal views, such religious commitment?"

"There's nothing wrong with religious commitment," I fired back, "and nothing about it prevents me from enforcing the law."

The women made no attempt to disguise their anger or their suspicion. I wanted to end the meeting before it further deteriorated. The subject was even more volatile than I had anticipated. I was shaken by the obvious depth and genuineness of their emotional and intellectual conviction, and the difficulty of some of the questions they had raised. But there was nothing to be gained by heated exchanges. If there were no other matters on their minds, I suggested we conclude the meeting. They were just as anxious as I to cut off discussion: they, out of a desire to report to their colleagues and plan strategy; I, out of relief.

The parting was superficially amicable, but the battle lines had been drawn. Washington's feminist network buzzed with reports of the meeting throughout that evening and the next day. Late that Tuesday afternoon I was told that the women's groups would attack my nomination on the basis of my stand on abortion.

By Wednesday, the day before my confirmation hearing, the National Abortion Rights Action League had asked to appear, on behalf of fourteen groups which supported federal funds for abortion, before both Senate committees scheduled to hear me testify on my nomination.

As I drove to my office early on Thursday morning, the radio news broadcasts were announcing that Senator Robert Packwood of Oregon, a staunch proponent of Medicaid-funded abortions and member of the Finance Committee which had jurisdiction over my nomination, would question me closely on abortion and might well oppose my nomination unless I changed my reported views.

I needed a much more sophisticated grasp of the political code words on abortion. I knew my own position, but the Senate hearing rooms of Washington were paneled and carpeted with good intentions and clear views ineptly expressed by well-meaning witnesses. I wanted to be sure I could maneuver through the verbal and emotional minefield of pro- and anti-abortionists. It was imperative for those in the abortion controversy, from Cardinal Cooke to National Abortion Rights Action League Executive Director Karen Mulhauser, to understand the words I spoke as I meant them, and I wanted to be confident that I knew what they would hear when I spoke. Far more careers have been shattered in Washington because of what people say than because of what

they do—and far more often through words spoken by inadvertence or ignorance than by design.

As I parked my car, I recalled Father English's recommendation of Father Richard McCormick as an ethicist well versed in the abortion controversy. I called him as soon as I got to the office. I told him I had only a few minutes before leaving for the Senate hearing. I quickly reviewed the old ground with him, the obligation to enforce a law contrary to my personal view. Then I moved to some of the harder questions, about pursuing a public policy for our pluralistic country that differed from my personal beliefs.

"What about rape and incest? In terms of public policy, it seems to me that when a woman has been the victim of rape or incest, a case can be made to permit an immediate abortion."

"First of all," McCormick responded, "the woman may be able to solve the problem if she acts fast enough without even getting to an abortion. Even after fertilization but before implantation in the uterus, there are things like twinning and possible recombination of fertilized eggs. These things create doubt about how we ought to evaluate life at this stage. It may take as long as fourteen days for the implantation process to end."

"Do you mean that from an ethical point of view, you don't see any abortion problem for up to two weeks?" I asked.

"I mean there are sufficient doubts at this stage to lead me to believe it may not be wrong to do a dilation and curettage after rape. It's very doubtful that we ought to call this interruption an abortion. Absolutist right to life groups will still complain. But serious studies support this. The pro-abortionists feel very strongly about rape and incest."

"Suppose the doctor says the child will be retarded, or severely handicapped physically?"

"That is a much more difficult question.

The Church would not permit an abortion, and the right to life and pro-abortion groups feel deeply here," McCormick replied.

"And what about some severe or permanent damage to the mother's health short of death?"

"That's another tough question in public policy terms. The Church would oppose abortion."

"Well, it's going to be an interesting morning," I mused aloud.

McCormick summed up rapidly. "You should always keep in mind three levels of distinction here. First, there is the personal conscience and belief thing. Second, there is what the appropriate public policy should be in a pluralistic democracy, which could be more liberal on funding abortions than one would personally approve as a matter of conscience or religious conviction. Actual abortion for rape and incest victims might be an example here. And third, there is the obligation of the public official to carry out the law the nation enacts."

"So I could pursue a policy for the country that funded abortion for rape and incest victims even though the Church—and I as a matter of personal and religious conviction—opposed abortion under those circumstances."

"Yes, you could."

I thanked him and rushed out of the office to my confirmation hearing.

I had to walk past a long line of people waiting to get into the standing-room-only Senate Finance Committee room in the Dirksen Building. Inside the door I had to weave through spectators and climb over legs to get to the witness table. The lights of all three networks were on me, sporadically augmented by clicking cameras and flashing bulbs from photographers sitting and kneeling on the floor in front of me. Seated behind their elevated and curved paneled rostrum, the committee members and staff looked down at me.

The hearing began promptly at 10:00 A.M. After fifteen minutes in which I made a brief opening statement and received some generous praise from Chairman Russell Long, Senator Packwood began:

"Mr. Califano, you know I have some strong feelings about abortion. . . . What is your personal view on abortion?"

The cameras turned on me.

I began by expressing my recognition of the difficulty of the abortion issue and the sincerity and depth of feeling on all sides. I noted that Carter and I shared identical views on the subject, although we came from quite different religious, cultural, and social backgrounds. I then set forth my views:

"First, I personally believe that abortion is wrong.

"Second, I believe that federal funds should not be used for the purpose of providing abortions.

Third, I believe that it is imperative that the alternatives to abortion be made available as widely as possible. Those alternatives include everything from foster care to day care, family planning programs to sex education, and especially measures to reduce teen-age pregnancies.

"Finally, we live in a democratic society where every citizen is free to make his views known, to the Congress or to the courts. If the courts decide that there is a constitutional right in this country to have an abortion with federal funds, I will enforce that court order. If the Congress changes its mind and amends the statute which it has passed, or passes other laws which direct that funds be provided for abortion, I will enforce those laws. I will enforce those laws as vigorously as I intend to enforce the other laws that I am charged with enforcing if I am confirmed, including laws against discrimination against women on the basis of sex in Title IX, the Title VI laws."

Packwood pressed: "You are opposed and would be opposed to federal funds for abortions under any circumstances . . . if the life of the woman is jeopardized, if the fetus is carrying a genetic disease?" I testified I did not oppose federal funding of abortion where carrying the fetus to term endangered the life of the mother. That was not as far as Packwood wanted me to go.

Packwood continued: "What I am really interested in, Mr. Califano, what I would hope is that your feelings as a person would not interfere with the law, the enforcement of the laws." I assured him that my personal views would not interfere with my enforcement of the law.

Packwood asked what my recommendation would be for legislation in the future. The same as Carter's, I responded. "We would recommend that federal funds not be used to provide abortions" in Medicaid or any other program.

Packwood's first-round time was up. The tension in the room eased a little as other senators asked questions on Social Security, balancing the budget, eliminating paperwork, busing, race discrimination, a separate department of education, Medicare and Medicaid management, handicapped rehabilitation programs, fraud and abuse in the welfare program, older Americans, alcoholism, and other matters prompted by special interest constituencies and the concerns of Americans that HEW intruded too deeply in their lives. The ever-present staffers whispered in senators' ears and passed their slips of paper from which senators read questions.

Texas Senator Lloyd Bentsen tried to lighten the atmosphere as he began: "Mr. Chairman, I am very pleased to see Mr. Califano here. I have known him for many years and have a great respect for his ability, intelligence, integrity, and judgment—until he took this job." The room burst into laughter.

At about noon, it was Packwood's turn again. When our eyes engaged, it was a signal for all the buzzing and rustling in the room to stop. As I expected, he went right to abortion, asking how I would change the law if I had the power to do so. I told him that President Carter and I would support the ban on the use of federal funds for abortions except where the mother's life was at stake. "That is the position . . . of the Carter administration," I concluded, quoting from one of the President-elect's campaign statements.

Packwood felt so strongly about the issue his face went florid with anger.

I thought for an instant about raising the issue of rape and incest, but immediately decided against it. This abortion controversy would be with me and the President for a long time and I didn't want to go any further than absolutely necessary without careful thought.

With his blue eyes blinking in disbelief, Packwood's voice rose: "If you had a choice . . . your recommendation would be that no federal funds will be used for those two hundred and fifty or three hundred thousand poor women, medically indigent, mostly minorities, who could not otherwise afford abortions?"

I reiterated: that would be my recommendation and the position of the administration. When I expressed the need to provide alternatives to abortion, Packwood interrupted: "How do you deal with teen-age pregnancies once the teen-ager is pregnant?" I said we needed more sensitive, decent human alternatives, treating the pregnant teen-ager as a person, letting her remain in school or continue her education in a home. I also recognized the need for better sex education and more effective family planning programs.

Packwood expressed support for all such programs. Then, his voice again rising, he said, "What we are saying, as far as the Carter program goes, with all the planned parenthood facilities, all the homes for unwed mothers, all the decent facilities to take care of them, if that woman wants to have an abortion and is poor and cannot afford it, tough luck." The last two words came out in angry disgust.

I could hear the whir of the television cameras.

"Senator, what I am saying is that we should reduce these cases to the greatest extent possible."

Packwood repeated for the television evening news: "Still, tough luck, as far as federal help is concerned."

I noted that "the federal government is not the only source of all funds," and private organizations were free to finance abortions. I then reminded Packwood that the administration position "is what the Congress has said in the Hyde amendment. The Senate and the House . . . voted for that amendment last year."

He asked whether the administration would oppose funding abortions in a national health insurance program. I said it would.

Packwood shook his head in apparent despair. We come to this issue from such different premises, I thought. To him, it is unfair for the government not to fund abortions for poor women when the Supreme Court has established a constitutional right to an abortion in the first trimester. To me, there is no question of equity. I thought abortion was wrong for women who could afford it unless the life of the mother was at stake, so I had no misgivings on grounds of equity in opposing the use of public funds to pay for abortions for poor women, as a matter of statutory law. Where the life of the mother was endangered, I favored public funding of abortions for the poor. The constitutional right to an abortion in the first trimester did not, in my mind, carry with it the right to public funding. The Constitution guarantees many precious rights—to speak and publish, to travel, to worship—but it does not require that the exercise of those rights be publicly funded.

Packwood cited Carter's hedging during the campaign and asked about a constitutional amendment to reverse the Supreme Court decision striking down state abortion laws. I responded that I opposed any constitutional amendment on abortion. "We run to the Constitution to stop busing, we run there on prayers in schools. We have to stop running to the Constitution to solve all of our problems." Packwood, still unsatisfied, had no further questions.

As the television crews disassembled their cameras, Senator Harry Byrd launched an attack on HEW's interference in local schools with excessively detailed civil rights questionnaires, and asked me about my support for voluntary charitable organizations.

The hearing before the Senate Finance Committee lasted so long that I had less than an hour before the Senate Committee on Labor and Public Welfare session began early in the same afternoon. Within fifteen minutes of its start, Senator Jacob Javits of New York asked about my ability to carry out the law, in view of my personal beliefs. I told Javits I had no qualms of conscience about my ability to enforce the law, "whatever the law is."

After a two-and-one-half-hour interlude of questions on civil rights enforcement, the isolation of HEW from the rest of the nation, welfare reform, busing, museums, education funding, biomedical research, national health insurance, conflicts of interest, animal testing of drugs, lack of coordination among Cabinet departments, and HEW's unresponsiveness to state and local government, Maine Democratic Senator William Hathaway returned to abortion. He characterized my position as being "morally and unalterably opposed to abortion," and then asked: "Does this mean that your convictions are so strong that if Congress should enact a law, whether it is national health insurance or whatever, that did provide federal funds for abortion, that you would recommend to President Carter that he veto such legislation?"

I hedged to get time to answer this unexpected question. I had never discussed this situation with Carter and I did not want to box the President in by simply saying I would or would not recommend a veto. "I do not think President Carter, in terms of his own views, needs my advice on whether to veto that legislation.''

As Hathaway pressed, asking what I would recommend if Carter sought my advice and how active a role I would take, I decided to finesse the question. "I cannot answer that question. Laws come over with lots . . . of provisions in them, and whether one provision is of such overriding importance in terms of the national administration's policy that the bill ought to be vetoed . . . is something very difficult to judge in the abstract.'' There was no way I would judge this issue now.

Hathaway sensed what I was thinking and helped out by noting the difference between a national health insurance program that the administration wanted with abortion funding being the only unwelcome provision and a bill that simply provided federal funds for abortion.

He then asked whether I would lobby the Congress against legislation which permitted federal funds to be spent for abortion. I told him that the administration would lobby against such legislation.

Hathaway expressed concern about anyone forcing his religious or other beliefs on the public, citing as examples a Christian Scientist HEW Secretary who did not believe in modern medicine, or a vegetarian Secretary of Agriculture who did not believe food stamps should be spent for meat. I responded firmly that if I had the slightest hesitation about enforcing whatever law the Congress passed, I would not be sitting in front of him.

Hathaway didn't question that. His concern was that no individual "should enforce his particular religious or moral beliefs into the policy-making area." I responded that "the Congress had made a judgment last year that restricting federal funds for abortions was a matter appropriate for legislation." As to my personal views, I was expressing them so every senator who had to vote on my confirmation would know them.

Unlike the exchange with Packwood, the exchange with Hathaway ended on a conciliatory note. He appreciated my candor and hoped that I would maintain an open mind during the course of the debate on abortion.

But neither the press nor the American public was prepared for any conciliation on this issue. Before I had departed the hearing room the first of some 6,473 letters and telegrams and hundreds of phone calls, unyielding on one side or the other, began arriving at my office. That evening, the *Washington Star*'s front page headlined: ANGRY SENATOR BLASTS CALIFANO ON ABORTION. The story featured Packwood's questioning and his "tough luck" comment. It did report my commitment to enforce the law vigorously, and it questioned an assumption that Packwood and Hathaway had made—that the woman's right to an abortion established in *Roe v. Wade* implied a right to federal funds to pay for the procedure. Earlier in the week, during oral arguments before the Supreme Court on pending abortion cases, several Justices had questioned any such right to funds. There were indications that the Court would throw the scalding issue back into the legislative-executive political process. That possibility only enhanced the significance of my views—and President Carter's.

That evening Carter telephoned me: "How did the testimony go today?"

"All right, I think, Mr. President," I responded hesitantly. "I hope I didn't create any problems for you."

"What did they ask you about?"

"Most of the questions were on your campaign promises, like welfare reform and national health insurance, and then typical special interest questions about HEW's constituencies and busing. I testified for seven hours. But the fireworks came in the thirty minutes of questioning about abortion."

"I saw what you said in the paper and on television. You hang tough. You're saying the right things."

"Thank you, Mr. President."

In public comments outside the hearing,

Packwood expressed deep concern and anger. Javits predicted a long and contentious struggle over the issue. And Karen Mulhauser of the National Abortion Rights Action League said it was "unthinkable" that a leading civil rights attorney "would openly discriminate" against indigent women. "We really didn't know until this week how extreme Califano's views were," she added. The lead editorial in the *Washington Post*, my former law client, was headed "Mr. Califano on Abortion," and took after me and my new boss: "The fact that each man reached this conclusion as a matter of personal conviction makes the conclusion itself no less troubling. For, personal or not, the effect of their common position would be to deny the poor what is available to the rich and not-so-rich. To argue as they do, that the emphasis should be on other medical services and/or pregnancy services does not address this inequity."

On Inauguration Day, January 20, 1977, the new President sent the nominations of the nine Cabinet members-designate whose hearings were completed to the Senate for confirmation. Eight were swiftly confirmed. Senator Packwood denied the Senate the necessary unanimous consent to consider my nomination that day.

Majority Leader Bob Byrd called my nomination to the Senate floor on January 24. Packwood was vehement. He said I held my views so passionately, so vigorously, that "I think it is impossible that Mr. Califano will be able to fairly administer the laws involving abortion, assuming that the Supreme Court says women . . . continue to have a right to an abortion, and that they continue to have a right to federal funds to help them."

Javits shared Packwood's view favoring federal funds for abortion, but he felt my qualifications in other areas merited my being confirmed. Other Republicans, from Senate Minority Leader Howard Baker to arch-conservative Carl Curtis, the ranking minority member of the Finance Commit-

tee, supported the nomination. The debate was brief, the vote 95 to Packwood's 1. Strom Thurmond was the first to phone to tell me of the Senate confirmation and congratulate me.

I called to thank each senator who had spoken on my behalf. Then I thought about Packwood. I felt that he had been petty in holding my nomination up four days, and that there had been an element of grandstanding in it. However, I had to accept the fact that his beliefs on abortion were as sincerely held as mine. From his point of view, putting that extra spotlight on me may have provided a little insurance that I would be careful to enforce a law that funded abortions more widely than I considered appropriate. I had been confirmed overwhelmingly, and I had to deal with him as a member of the Senate Finance Committee that had jurisdiction over such key HEW programs as Social Security, Medicare, Medicaid, and welfare. I swallowed a little hard and called him: "Bob, I understand your view on abortion. But I'm now Secretary and you and I agree on virtually every other social issue. I hope our differences on abortion won't prevent us from working together." Packwood, clearly surprised, thanked me for the call.

In a *New York Times* editorial on January 31 condemning my position on abortion, one element struck me as amusing: "Mr. Califano's statement in one sense represents his personal opposition to abortion. In another sense, it is a free political ride, earning credit for the administration from abortion foes without his having any real decision to make. It was Congress, though sharply split, which last fall decreed the ban on Medicaid funds for abortions. It is the courts, now scrutinizing that ban, which will decide. And Mr. Califano has pledged, as he must, to carry out the orders of the courts." I could understand the point of the editorial, but I hardly considered my experience before the Senate committees a free ride.

The abortion issue would track me for most of my term as HEW Secretary. I shortly discovered that, like Champion and Shanahan, few, if any, of my colleagues at HEW shared my view or the President's on abortion. Everyone in the top HEW management who expressed his opinion disagreed with mine. Only at the Christmas open house, when they streamed through my office to shake hands and have a picture taken, would HEW employees—mostly the blacks or Catholics—whisper, "Don't let them kill those black babies," or "God bless you for your stand against abortion."

The same was true at the White House. A few staff members, such as Midge Costanza, were publicly outspoken in favor of federal funding for abortion. Shanahan called me on July 15, 1977, and said she was going to a meeting at the White House, set up by Midge Costanza to organize the women in the administration to urge Carter to change his position on abortion. Shanahan said they might draft a petition asking to see Carter and setting forth their views. I was incredulous that a White House staffer would organize such a meeting. I had no question about Shanahan's loyalty, but was appalled at Costanza's judgment and seriously questioned her loyalty to Carter. Two of the other top appointees at HEW, Assistant Secretary for Human Development Services Arabella Martinez and Assistant Secretary for Education Mary Berry, also went to the meeting.

A story was in the *Washington Post* on the morning following the Friday afternoon meeting. Jody Powell called Shanahan at about 11:00 A.M.. "I just wanted to find out what right you all think you had to have a meeting like that in the White House?" Before Shanahan could respond, he answered, "No right, none at all."

"We have a right to express our views," Shanahan began.

Powell snapped, "At least General Singlaub [who disagreed with the President's policy in Korea] resigned. I can respect him."

"I did not give up my First Amendment rights when I joined the administration," Shanahan shot back.

Powell was incensed. "Most of these turkeys wouldn't have a job if it weren't for the President."

Shanahan spoke firmly, in the tense, modulated tone her voice often assumed when all her energy was devoted to maintaining her composure: "These women left damn good jobs to join the administration. Most are better qualified than men who got jobs of the same rank."

"Not you, Eileen, I don't include you," Powell responded defensively to the former economic correspondent for the *New York Times*, "but these turkeys would not have jobs if the President hadn't given them one."

When Shanahan told me about this conversation later that afternoon, she was still trembling with indignation and rage. Fortunately, she found great satisfaction in her work and she and I had developed a relationship of sufficient respect that she decided not to resign.

I assumed Carter would be enraged when he heard about the women's meeting—and he was, privately, and at the Cabinet meeting on Monday, July 18: "I don't mind vigorous debate in the administration. As a matter of fact, I welcome it," Carter said, "but I do not want leaks to the press or attacks on positions we've already established. If the forty women had listened to my campaign statements, they should know my position." Carter then contrasted Commerce Secretary Juanita Kreps and HUD Secretary Pat Harris with the group of women who met with Midge Costanza. Kreps raised her hand to speak. The President recognized her. In her soft-spoken, polite, and respectful manner, she said: "Mr. President, I appreciate the intent of your comment about me and I, of course, am loyal to you as we all are." What well-chosen words, I thought. "But"—Kreps paused to make certain we were all appropriately postured on the edge of our Cabinet chairs—"you should not take my absence from the meeting of the women as an indication of support for the administration's position on abortion."

Carter seemed somewhat surprised, not at Kreps's position, but at the quiet firmness with which she expressed her view in front of the Cabinet and the "barber shop" patrons (as I sometimes thought of the crew of aides and note-takers that sat against the wall in the Cabinet Room). From across the Cabinet table, Pat Harris promptly agreed with Kreps, but promised to keep her views within the official family. The President, so uncomfortable that he almost sounded defensive, indicated he was of course not talking about "Juanita and Pat," and reiterated his desire for "full debate," but he insisted on "complete loyalty" once an administration decision was made.

When the President walked in to begin the Cabinet meeting two weeks later, on August 1, the first Costanza had attended after her women's meeting, he put his arm around her, kissed her, and said, "Nice to see ya, darlin'."

Whatever distance the President wanted from me on other policies, like school integration, the anti-smoking campaign, or Social Security cuts, he held me at his side whenever he spoke of abortion: during a March 1977 Clinton, Massachusetts, town meeting and on a Los Angeles television show in May 1977 ("Joe Califano, who is Secretary of HEW, feels the same way I do against abortions'); in Yazoo City, Mississippi, in July 1977 (" . . . the Secretary of HEW agrees with me completely on this issue . . ."); at a Bangor, Maine, town meeting in February 1978 ("Joe Califano, who is head of HEW, is a very devout Catholic. . . . I happen to be a Baptist, and his views on abortion are the same as mine"); with college and regional editors and at general press conferences.

There were demonstrations, first in front of the building where my law office was located, then at the corner of Independence Avenue and Third Street, S.W., where the HEW headquarters and my offices were. The demonstrations, always peaceful but with increasingly sensational placards during 1977, were, as I looked out my window, a constant reminder of the potential of this issue to consume my energies to the detriment of other programs. A week after my confirmation, on January 31, 1977, Karen Mulhauser led a contingent of marchers from the National Abortion Rights Action League, carrying signs ("Califano Will Enslave Poor Women") that, however overdrawn they seemed to me, conveyed how many Americans felt. Coupled with the personal turmoil the issue stirred in several key managers I had recruited, both men and women, I decided it was imperative to set an overall tone and strategy from the beginning.

I was a bureaucratic child of the 1960s, acutely sensitive to the potential of an issue that touches on human life to kindle a consuming movement—as the military draft fueled the anti-Vietnam War movement. On abortion, the issue was life itself. If we all believed that life began at the same time, there would be no debate on abortion. If all citizens believed life begins at the moment of conception, then they would consider it intolerable for their national government to permit, much less fund, abortion because it involves the elimination of life. If, however, the body politic unanimously believed that life does not begin until the second or third trimester, or that there is no life until the fetus can be viable separate from the mother's body, then it would offend social justice for the government of such a single-minded people not to fund abortions for the poor when rich and middle-class women could easily obtain them to avoid serious illness or the later creation of retarded or physically handicapped life. However, the American people are far from unanimous in their view of when life begins; indeed, disagreement on that issue has been so strong it spawned as bitter a social and political dispute as the 1970s produced.

I concluded that it was not sufficient simply to express my view clearly and consistently, but that it was also essential to communicate the certainty with which I held it. Any hedging would only encourage those who disagreed to hope for a change that would not be forthcoming, and those who agreed to take steps to stiffen my resolve. By repeatedly and clearly setting forth my position, I could perhaps deflect the resources of some of the pro- and anti-abortion partisans to other targets they felt they had the opportunity to influence or the need to bolster.

My second conclusion was that I must do all I could to avoid unnecessary provocation. My obligation was to keep some measure of political decorum in this emotional debate. I did not have the luxury of an outside antagonist to be flip or hyperbolic. I refused to see or speak before pro-life groups who wanted to give me awards or roses, and I tried (not always with success) to avoid crossing picket lines or confronting demonstrators directly. In 1977, this involved going to a lot of places through the back door.

I had to display a calm and reasoned approach because of my obligation to enforce whatever law the Congress ultimately passed or the courts eventually declared constitutional. On this issue, above all, it was not enough for me to be fair; it was critical for the interested people to perceive they were being fairly treated.

Maintaining a sense of integrity was important not only to the public, but to the professionals in the department. HEW's Center for Disease Control was charged with the surveillance of communicable diseases. Most commonly identified with monitoring and reporting on influenza or other communicable diseases, the center was also responsible for surveillance of abortions

and abortion-related deaths in the United States. In October 1977, at the peak of the legislative debate over Medicaid funding for abortion, there were reports that an Hispanic-American woman had checked into a McAllen, Texas, hospital with complications from an abortion improperly performed in Mexico. There were allegations that the woman was covered by Medicaid and had been told by a Texas doctor that if she had only come a few weeks earlier, she would have been eligible for Medicaid funding for an abortion, but now the law prohibited it. The woman died within a few days of being admitted to the hospital.

I called Bill Foege, whom I had recently appointed director of the center, and asked him to check out the reports. He came to Washington and nervously told me that while it was difficult to establish the facts because the woman might have gone to Mexico to keep the abortion secret, she had received two Medicaid-funded abortions before the Hyde amendment took effect. "So we may have a confirmed death from an abortion improperly performed on an otherwise Medicaid-eligible woman," Foege said, resting his paper on his lap as though trying to produce relief from a tension that still persisted.

I studied him silently for a moment and then realized that he was concerned about my view of the center's role in keeping abortion statistics.

"Look," I said, "You must understand this: I want you to keep statistics as accurately as you can, to investigate as meticulously as you can. Our obligation—whatever my views—is to set the facts before the Congress and the people. Particularly on an issue like this, we must maintain the integrity of HEWs data. The only way to deal with an issue this hot is to be accurate."

His face brightened in relief. "That's just the way I feel," he said.

While I could not predict the route or timetable, I sensed that the abortion issue was inexorably headed for my desk. On

June 20,1977, the Supreme Court decided in *Beal v. Doe* and *Maher v. Roe* that the federal government had no constitutional obligation to fund discretionary abortions that were not medically necessary. Like so many ardently awaited Supreme Court decisions, this one created as much controversy as it resolved. The Court had cleared the way to having the Hyde amendment go into effect, thus restricting Medicaid funding to abortions where the life of the mother would be endangered if the fetus were carried to term. The Court had also moved the debate back into the political arena, to the floors of the House and Senate and the HEW regulatory process.

I asked my staff to prepare a guideline to implement the Hyde amendment. Judge Dooling in Brooklyn would now have to withdraw his order blocking enforcement of that amendment and I wanted to be ready to issue the necessary instructions the same day the judge acted. Any delay would only give the pro- and anti-abortionists more time to demonstrate. If I could act immediately, there would be only one day of newspaper and television coverage.

As we planned to move as quickly and quietly as possible, the President was hit with a question about the Supreme Court decision at his July 12 press conference. I was signing routine mail, casually watching the televised conference, when Judy Woodruff of NBC News caught my attention with a question asking how "comfortable" the President was with the recent Supreme Court decision "which said the federal government was not obligated to provide money for abortions for women who cannot afford to pay for them." The President reiterated his view that "I would like to prevent the federal government financing abortion."

Woodruff followed up: "Mr. President, how fair do you believe it is then that women who can afford to get an abortion can go ahead and have one and women who cannot afford to are precluded?"

In an echo of a statement by John Ken-nedy, the President answered, "Well, as you know, there are many things in life that are not fair, that wealthy people can afford and poor people can't. But I don't believe that the federal government should act to try to make these opportunities exactly equal, particularly when there is a moral factor involved."

I had been leaning back in my chair and almost went over backward. I was stunned at the President's response. It was clear to me that he had no idea of the bitter reaction his comment would incite. It couldn't have been deliberate. At worst, it was an on-the-spot, clumsy attempt to appeal to fiscal conservatives and right-to-lifers; at best it was an inept, off-the-top-of-his-head answer to a question for which he was not prepared. Within an hour Eileen Shanahan was in my office, tears of anger welling in her eyes, to tell me that the press wanted my comment on the President's "life is unfair" remark. "None, none, none," I said.

The only person who told me she agreed with the comment of the President was Eunice Kennedy Shriver, who wrote me on July 15: "In terms of the equity argument, I think the President's answer is satisfactory." It was one of the few times I can recall disagreeing with the political judgment of this extraordinary woman. She had become and remained a dedicated and politically persistent participant in the abortion controversy, an energetic opponent of federal funding.

In July, unknown to the public, to most of the antagonists prowling the halls of Congress with roses and hangers and, indeed, to most congressmen and senators, a secret compromise remarkably close to the agreement the House and Senate would reach in December was beginning to take shape in the mind of Eunice Kennedy Shriver. She called me, as she was undoubtedly calling others, in the middle of the month, three weeks after the Supreme Court tossed the issue back to the Congress. She had "some language that might be acceptable to both the House and Senate" and end the widespread access to abortion. "We've got to face the rape and incest argument, don't you think?" And, spraying words in her staccato Massachusetts accent, she added: "We also have to deal with serious damage to the mother—physical damage, not this fuzzy psychological stuff."

Eunice read me some language and concluded, "I'm sending this over to you, personally and confidentially, and you can use it as your own."

Just as I was about to hang up, she added, "And Joseph, when we get over this, we need a teen-age pregnancy bill. I'm getting Teddy to introduce it and I want the two of you to work together on it." Eunice was working on a bill to fund centers to help teen-agers who were pregnant (she was so well connected within HEW that I got her revision of my draft testimony in support of the bill before I even received the draft from the departmental staff). Impressed by a Johns Hopkins program that helped teen-agers deal with their babies and avoid having more, she wanted to duplicate it around the nation. But even there she stood firmly on abortion. When the teen-age pregnancy bill was being considered in 1978 and HEW Deputy Assistant Secretary Peter Schuck was quoted as saying states might give funds to clinics providing abortions if they were providing services to pregnant teen-agers, Eunice sent me a strong letter: "I certainly have not worked on this bill for three years under the assumption that abortion services would be provided under the bill. . . . I will not continue, quite frankly, if abortion services are permitted under this legislation." Due in large measure to her lobbying on the Hill, when the bill was eventually enacted, no abortion services were funded under it.

The confidential proposal Eunice Shriver sent me suggested modifying the Hyde amendment to prohibit the use of funds to perform an abortion, except in cases of rape and incest, where necessary to save the life of the mother, or where the mother has

an organic disease that would cause grave damage to her body if the pregnancy were continued to term. Under her proposal, she estimated that only a thousand to fifteen hundred abortions per year would be performed under Medicaid, mainly involving mothers with severe heart or kidney disease or severe diabetic conditions. "I am told," her letter concluded, "that 80 percent of the abortions performed under Medicaid would be eliminated by this language."

There were few takers for the Shriver compromise in July, but before the abortion legislation saga ended in December 1977, the House and Senate would agree on language reflecting her influence and access to key members.

On August 4, 1977, Judge Dooling reluctantly lifted his injunction against enforcing the Hyde amendment. Within hours, I announced that HEW would no longer fund abortions as a matter of course, but would provide funds "only where the attending physician, on the basis of his or her professional judgment, had certified that the abortion was necessary because the life of the mother would be endangered if the fetus were carried to term."

The House and Senate Conferees' report on the Hyde amendment approved funding for termination of an ectopic (fallopian tube) pregnancy, for drugs or devices to prevent implantation of the fertilized ovum on the uterus wall, and for "medical procedures for the treatment of rape or incest victims." I had asked Attorney General Griffin Bell to interpret that language. His opinion concluded that the Hyde amendment and the quoted language prohibited funding abortion for rape or incest (unless the life of the mother was threatened), but permitted funding for prompt treatment before the fact of pregnancy was established.

On the same day Judge Dooling lifted his injunction and I issued my guidelines under the Hyde amendment to the 1977 HEW Appropriations Act, the Senate voted by a lopsided 60 to 33 to permit payment for abortions under a broad "medically necessary" standard in 1978. Earlier that week the House had voted 238 to 182 to retain the strict Hyde amendment language.

And on the same August 4th day, the Defense Department revealed that it had funded 12,687 abortions at military hospitals between September 1, 1975, and August 31, 1976. The Pentagon policy was to fund abortions for members and dependents for reasons of physical and mental health. The *Washington Post* story reporting military abortion statistics also noted that federal employees were entitled to abortions under the general health plans, but no records were kept of the number of abortions performed for them and their dependents.

In this state of chaos and division, the House and Senate left Washington for their August recess. When the Congress reconvened in September, high on its agenda was the House and Senate Conference on the Labor-HEW appropriations bill.

There are two ways to block federal funding of a particular activity otherwise authorized. One is to pass a statute that prohibits the federal government from acting. Such legislation must be referred to the authorizing committees of the Senate and the House; normally those committees would be required to hold hearings and report the legislation before it was eligible for consideration on the floor. That can be a long and tedious process—with no certainty that the legislation will ever get to the floor of both Houses for a vote. The authorizing committee can block consideration by simply holding the bill.

The other way to block federal funding for a specific purpose is through the appropriations process, either by not providing funds, or by attaching a rider to an appropriations bill, stating that none of the appropriated funds can be spent for the proscribed activity. The appropriations rider has the same practical force as authorizing legislation, and it offers a significant advantage to legislators: Each year the appropriations

bills for the executive departments must be reported by the appropriations committees and acted on by the Congress if government is to continue functioning. The disadvantage is that, unlike substantive, authorizing legislation, the appropriations rider comes up for review each year.

Until the mid-1960s, there were few such riders. By and large, House and Senate parliamentarians ruled them out of order because "substantive legislation" was not permitted on appropriations bills. But as the government funded more activities, the lines between substantive legislation and limits on the uses of federal funds became increasingly hard to draw. The more controversial the activities funded by the appropriations bill, the more frequent the attempt to restrict spending by riders.

No bill attracted more politically aggressive, true-believing interest groups than the annual HEW appropriations bill. It had become honey for a host of political bees: riders prohibiting loans or grants to students who crossed state lines to incite to riot (a hangover from the Vietnam War), forbidding the use of funds for busing, limiting the use of funds to obtain civil rights enforcement information from schools. Senator Warren Magnuson, Chairman of the Senate Appropriations Committee, told me during my first month in office, "Joe, you won't recognize the appropriations hearing for HEW. It has attracted the Goddamnedest collection of kooks you ever saw. We've got to stop all these riders. Make them go to the authorizing committees." But Magnuson's outburst was to prove nothing more than exasperated hope. For during the fall of 1977, he would be involved in the bare-knuckled, prolonged fight over the abortion rider on the HEW appropriations bill.

Some facts about abortions also helped inflame the issue. In 1975, the nation's capital had become the first city in America where abortions outnumbered births. As the congressional recess ended in September 1977, the District of Columbia government revealed that in 1976, legal abortions obtained by District residents totaled 12,945—an unprecedented one-third more than the city's 9,635 births. And 57 percent of the abortions—7,400—were paid for by the Medicaid program before the Hyde amendment went into effect on August 4. The high abortion rate in Washington, D.C., reflected the nationwide abortion rate among blacks, which was double that among whites.

With the Congress returning to Washington, the pro-abortionists moved to counter the right to life roses. On September 7, pro-abortion leader Karen Mulhauser announced a campaign to mail coat hangers to Representative Daniel Flood, the Pennsylvania Democrat who chaired the HEW appropriations subcommittee, and other anti-abortion members.

The first meeting of the House and Senate all-male cast of conferees on September 12 broke up almost as soon as it started. Magnuson and Massachusetts Republican Senator Edward Brooke (who, like Packwood, strenuously fought to fund abortions under Medicaid) vowed that they would not return to the conference table until the House voted on the Senate version of the abortion rider. House Committee Chairman Flood initially refused. But, under pressure from his colleagues who feared that funds for important HEW programs and paychecks for federal employees would be interrupted if no appropriations agreement were reached, Flood took the Senate proposal to fund abortions where "medically necessary," to the House floor. On September 27, the House overwhelmingly rejected the Senate language, 252 to 164.

Then Flood took Magnuson up on his earlier commitment to compromise if the House would first vote on the Senate language. But Magnuson was not prepared to give much and House conferees ridiculed his attempt to cover genetic disease, with statements that his suggestion would permit abortions where the child had a blue and brown eye. At one point Magnuson proposed limiting funding to situations where the life of the mother was at stake, cases of rape or incest, and situations involving "serious permanent health damage." When I heard about his proposal, I suspected the fine hand of Eunice Shriver. But Flood's initial reaction was scathing. "You could get an abortion with an ingrown toenail with that Senate language," and it went nowhere.

After House Speaker Tip O'Neill complained that only pro-abortionist Magnuson and Brooke attended the conference for the Senate, thus making compromise near-impossible with the dozen House members usually present, more Senate conferees went to the meetings. The conversation became more civil, but the conferees were no closer to agreement as September 30, the end of the fiscal year and the end of HEW's authority to spend money, arrived.

Up to that point I had decided to stay out of the congressional fight over abortion. The administration view was well known. The President did not want to be part of any compromise that was more permissive than his anti-abortion campaign statements. It was one thing to carry out whatever law the Congress passed, quite another to take an active role in easing the restriction. Carter was committed to the former; he wanted no part of the latter.

Popular sentiment, reflected in the polls, was with the strict House view, and many pro-abortionists realized that. On October 6, for example, Norman Dorsen, head of the American Civil Liberties Union, in opposing a constitutional convention, cited his concern that a nationwide convention might be used to outlaw abortion completely. With that kind of popular support, the House was likely to hold to the strict limits on federal funding for abortions that Carter favored.

Moreover, my conversations with members of Congress had led me to the conclusion that I could be of little, if any, help in drafting the substance of an eventual compromise. Abortion was such a profoundly personal issue that neither I nor a President who, during his first nine months of office, had already lost a good deal of respect on the Hill, would have much influence with individual members.

Only once had I come close publicly to entering the debate during this time. I understood the depth of conviction and humane values that motivated most abortion advocates, but I was deeply offended by the cost-control, money-saving argument pushed by the staunchly pro-abortion Alan Guttmacher Institute, the research arm of the Planned Parenthood Federation of America. In late September, the Institute published a report claiming that the Hyde amendment would cost the public at least $200 million, for the first year of their life, to take care of children who could have been aborted under Medicaid. I wanted to denounce this kind of argument in severe terms: it was appallingly materialistic and represented a selfish failure to confront moral issues as such. But in the interests of being firm yet not provocative I waited until I was asked about it at a press conference to express my views, and then did so in muted tones.

Now, however, I had to get into the congressional fight. On October 1, I was compelled to eliminate all hiring and overtime and virtually all out-of-town travel by HEW's 150,000 employees. I also warned that they might receive only half their pay in mid-October unless the House and Senate resolved the appropriations fight over abortion. It was, so far as we could tell, unprecedented at the time for a department to have no authority to operate or spend money after the first of the new fiscal year.

Despite the situation, the conferees again failed to reach agreement on October 3, and postponed any further action until October 12, after the Columbus Day recess. That postponement jeopardized beneficiaries of HEW programs and the pay of Department employees. Across the nation, state rehabil-itation agencies for the handicapped were running out of money to process claims for Social Security disability benefits; New York State would be unable to meet its payroll for employees to process disability determinations; Texas intended to furlough 612 employees on October 12; Idaho would have no money for its nutrition and community services program for the aged.

I called Tip O'Neill and Bob Byrd on October 10th, and asked them to try to break the abortion deadlock in order to avoid severe human suffering. The next day I sent them a letter and made it public. It was, the letter charged, "grossly unfair to hold the vulnerable people of our nation and thousands of federal and state employees hostage" in the congressional dispute over the use of federal funds for abortions. If the Congress could not agree on abortion language, I urged them to pass a Continuing Resolution to give me authority to spend in early 1978 at the end-of-1977 level in order to continue HEW programs that people depend on each day. The Senate opposed a Continuing Resolution because it would also keep the Hyde amendment in effect.

I sent telegrams to the state governors alerting them to imminent funding terminations so they would press their congressmen and senators to act. I asked Labor Secretary Ray Marshall to tell the Congress and the public of the dangers of continuing to hold up 1978 funding, since his department's appropriations were tied to the HEW bill. Marshall announced that further delay could force many states to stop processing unemployment insurance claims and halt federally funded job and health safety programs. At my suggestion, President Carter told the congressional leadership on the morning of October 12 that, while we all recognized what an emotional issue abortion was, the paychecks of federal employees should not be held up while Congress tried to resolve it. House Appropriations Committee Chairman George Mahon warned of "chaos in some parts of our government." By October

13, after wrangling with each other and some spirited debate on the House floor, both legislative bodies passed a Continuing Resolution to provide funds for fifteen days until the end of the month.

On Sunday, October 16, I was scheduled to appear on the ABC-TV program *Issues and Answers*. On the Saturday morning preceding the program, I called the President to review the administration's position on abortion. The President said that his position had not changed since the campaign.

"One issue in sharp dispute is how to handle victims of rape or incest," I said, asking whether he objected to funding abortions for rape or incest victims and referring to his July 12, 1977, press conference. There Carter had said that the federal government "should not finance abortions except when the woman's life is threatened or when the pregnancy was the result of rape or incest. I think it ought to be interpreted very strictly."

I asked the President whether his "very strictly" interpretation was related to the dispute between House and Senate conferees over medical procedures short of abortion for rape or incest performed shortly after the act, as distinguished from outright abortion. Carter said he was unaware of the dispute, but wanted to stay out of it. I said that it might not be possible for me to do that. Then leave the administration position ambiguous on this issue, he suggested. "Above all I want people to understand I oppose federal funding for abortion in keeping with my campaign promise."

The words had the texture of the three dimensions that came into play when Carter discussed abortion with me: his deep personal belief, his sense (particularly in the first year) that he would violate some sacred trust if he did not adhere to his campaign statements, and his insistence on getting the political plusses out of issues that had such significant political minuses as well.

ABC White House correspondent Sam Donaldson asked the first question on the program the next day: What was the administration's position on abortion? I recited the administration position opposing federal funds for abortions "except where the life of the mother is endangered if the fetus were carried to term, or for treatment as a result of rape or incest."

After Bettina Gregory asked about teenage pregnancy, Donaldson pressed for precision on the issue of rape or incest. "The House position . . . would not even allow abortions to be financed in the case of rape or incest, unless someone comes forward and it can be established that there is not yet a pregnancy that has been medically found. Is that reasonable?"

Trying to satisfy the President's desires, I responded: "In the case of rape or incest, you would assume that the individual would come promptly for treatment and that is a matter of several days. Doctors and experts disagree on it. It can be days or a couple of weeks."

Donaldson noted that the House would allow a dilation and curettage only where an abortion was not involved, and asked if I agreed. I hesitated, then in pursuit of the President's overriding objective to be anti-abortion, responded: "Yes, that is the way I feel; that is the way the President feels. He made that clear during the campaign repeatedly, as you are well aware, covering him during the campaign."

I then recalled my own desire to cool the debate, and added: "This is a very difficult issue; it is a very complex issue; it is a very emotional issue. There are strong feelings on all sides. I think in terms of the nation as a whole what is important is that this issue is being debated in every state in the union . . . in city after city. The way to reach a consensus in a democracy is to have people talk about it, where they live; and that is happening now in this country . . . the issue should be debated in more places than in the House and Senate."

When the Continuing Resolution ran out on October 31, House and Senate conferees agreed to language which would permit federal funding for abortion in cases of rape, including statutory rape of minors, or incest, where a prompt report was made to appropriate authorities. They were still split over Senate language which would permit abortions "where grave physical health damage to the mother would result if the pregnancy were carried to term." By the next day, however, the House conferees wanted only forced rape covered. The Senate conferees were furious, and the conference broke up in acrid charges of bad faith. This skirmish marked the first time the House conferees had agreed on abortion, as distinguished from treatment before the fact of pregnancy was established, in any rape situation. Nevertheless, with their conferees unable to agree, the House and Senate voted another Continuing Resolution, giving members a three week respite from the issue until December 1.

But there was no respite from the demonstrations. Without fail, during the week pickets marched outside HEW. The signs got more vivid; the crude printing crueler. There were the color pictures from *Life* magazine and the roses and hangers, which had become calling cards for the protagonists. The rhetoric was increasingly sprinkled with harsh accusations of "murder" by each side—of killing unborn children by Medicaid abortion, or poor mothers by back-alley abortion. Some placards accused me of being a "murderer of poor women."

Wherever I went, pickets greeted me. When I spoke in Oregon at a Democratic political fundraiser, several hundred demonstrators from both sides paraded outside the Hilton Hotel. The Oregon Legislative Emergency Board was scheduled to decide in ten days whether to replace lost federal abortion funds with state money. The pro-abortionists angrily accused me of trying to inject my own views into the Oregon fight, which I had not heard of until arriving in Portland.

The sincerity of the Oregon demonstra-tors and others like them took its toll on me: earnest pleas of both sides were moving. None of the lighthearted sidebars that accompanied most demonstrations—even some during the Vietnam War—were present during pro- and anti-abortion rallies. When I avoided demonstrators by going out a side entrance, as I did that evening in Oregon, I felt like a thief in the night, denying these committed marchers even the chance to know they had been at least heard, if not heeded.

The most vehement demonstration took place in New York City's Greenwich Village on Saturday afternoon, November 12. It was my most draining emotional experience over the abortion issue.

New York University President John Sawhill invited me to receive NYU's University Medal. The award ceremony was to consist of a brief talk and an extended question and answer period. As the day approached I was told that pro-abortionists planned a major demonstration. When I arrived at the NYU Law School in Washington Square, there were several thousand demonstrators. They were overwhelmingly pro-abortion; the handful of right-to-lifers there said they had heard of the demonstration only the evening before and had no chance to mobilize their supporters. Bella Abzug reviled the "white-male dominated White House." Speaker after speaker attacked me for "imposing my Roman Catholic beliefs on poor women." "Our bodies, ourselves" protesters chanted to the beat of a big drum. "Not Califano's."

The crowd was so large and noisy, I could hear it clearly when I entered the law school around the block from the demonstrators. As I reached the back entrance, ACLU Chairman Norman Dorsen, a friend of twenty-five years, greeted me with a broad smile on his face. "It took Califano to bring the sixties back to NYU," he cracked. We all chuckled at that welcome, which broke the tension for the next few minutes.

When Dorsen, who was to moderate the

question and answer period, Sawhill, and I entered the auditorium, my right arm and hand were in a cast, held by a sling, due to an operation on my thumb the week before. The auditorium was crushingly over-crowded. Every seat was taken; every inch of wall space lined with standees. The antagonism of the audience was so penetrating I could physically feel it as I sat on the elevated stage. Even the cast on my arm will evoke no sympathy here, I thought.

Sawhill spoke first about me. He then turned to give me the medal. As I rose to receive it, the last row of the audience unfurled a huge pro-abortion banner across the back of the auditorium. Fully half the audience stood and held up hangers, many with ends that had been dipped in red nail polish. When the medal was presented, at least a hundred people in the audience turned their backs to me. Many of them remained in that position throughout the entire ninety minutes of my speech and the question and answer session that followed.

The question period was largely devoted to abortion, with many emotional statements and speeches. None, however, struck me more forcefully than that of an intense woman who picked up on a comment I had made earlier that year. On the Sunday, March 20, NBC program *Meet the Press*, Carol Simpson had queried me at length on abortion and the adequacy of the administration program for alternatives to abortion. In the course of one extended response, I observed: "I have never known a woman who wanted an abortion or who was happy about having an abortion. I think it is our role to provide for those women the best we can in terms of family planning services, of day care centers for their children, of health, and prenatal services to make sure children are born healthy, and all the decent things in life that every child in this country deserves, whether it is health care or a clean home or a decent schooling, and we will do our best to do that."

To my left, about halfway down the aisle

in the NYU auditorium, a woman rose to the microphone. Her head was tilted sideways, her eyes spilled over with anger, even hatred. "Look at me, Mr. Califano," she shouted with defiant emotion. "I want you to see a woman who wanted an abortion. I want you to see a woman who was happy at having an abortion. I want you to see a woman who had an abortion two weeks ago and who intends to have another abortion."

The room fell into total silence as the tone of her voice became that kind of gripping whisper everyone can hear even when they don't want to: "I want you to go back to Washington knowing that there are women who are happy to have had abortions, knowing that there are women who want abortions. I don't ever want you to make a statement like the one you made saying that you have never known a woman that wanted to have an abortion or never known a woman who was happy about having an abortion. You have now met one."

So draining was the emotional experience at NYU, that afterward, when I got into the car to Kennedy Airport to depart for England, Germany, and Italy to look at national health programs—my first trip abroad as Secretary of HEW—I instantly fell asleep and did not wake up until the driver shook me to say we had arrived at Kennedy.

The abortion issue followed me to Europe. There were questions in England and the Italians were in the midst of their own volatile parliamentary debate on the issue. The latent suspicion of my Catholicism again surfaced in Rome. Immediately after my audience with Pope Paul VI, several reporters called at the Hassler Hotel to see if the Pope talked to me about abortion. He had not mentioned the issue. His focus was on the failure of the food-rich nations such as the United States to feed the world.

I returned to Washington on Thanksgiving eve. I knew the abortion issue would erupt again when the latest Continuing Resolution expired. But I was not prepared for the news the *Washington Post* brought me on the Sunday after Thanksgiving. Connie Downey, chairperson of an HEW group on alternatives to abortion, had written a memo expressing her views to her boss, Assistant Secretary of Planning and Evaluation Henry Aaron. The *Post* headlined the most sensational portion of an otherwise typical HEW memo: TASK FORCE HEAD LISTS SUICIDE, MOTHERHOOD, AND MADNESS: ABORTION ALTERNATIVES CITED IN HEW MEMO.

The memo, written more than four months earlier on July 18, contained this paragraph: "Abortion is but one alternative solution to many of the problems . . . which may make a pregnancy unwise or unwanted. . . . It is an option, uniquely, which is exercised between conception and live birth. As such, the literal alternatives to it are suicide, motherhood, and, some would add, madness. . . ."

The memo had never reached me, but its leak provided a dramatic reminder of the potential for turmoil within HEW and raised the curtain on the final act between the House and the Senate on the fiscal 1978 HEW appropriations bill.

Returning from Thanksgiving recess, the House leadership was determined to press for a compromise. They did not want the Christmas checks of federal employees to be short. Appropriations Committee Chairman Mahon called me on November 29 to say he had decided to take the leadership completely away from Flood, who ardently opposed federal funds for abortion. "He's just implacable on the subject," Mahon said, distraught. "I'm retiring, but this kind of conduct is a disgrace to the House. We all look asinine."

In secret negotiations with Senator Brooke, Mahon eventually produced the compromise on December 7. The House voted twice within less than four hours. The first time members rejected a Mahon proposal and voted 178 to 171 to stand by their strict position against all funding for abortions except those needed to save the mother's life. Minutes later Mahon, dejected but

determined, won speedy approval of new language from the Rules Committee and rushed back to the House floor. The House reversed direction and adopted the new and relaxed standard, 181 to 167. Within two hours, with only three of its hundred members on the floor, the Senate acceded to the House language and sent the measure to President Carter for his signature.

Under the measure, no HEW funds could be used to perform abortions, "except when the life of the mother would be endangered if the fetus were carried to term, or except for such medical procedures necessary for the victims of rape or incest, when such rape or incest has been reported promptly to a law enforcement agency or public health service; or except in those instances where severe and long-lasting physical health damage to the mother would result if the pregnancy were carried to term when so determined by two physicians."

Senator Brooke described the outcome as "not really acceptable to either side, but it makes some progress." Representative Hyde said that the measure "provides for the extermination of thousands of unborn lives." Senator Javits called the action "a major victory for women's rights." ACLU Chairman Dorsen characterized it as "a brutal treatment of women with medical needs for abortion." Any relief I felt at seeing at least some resolution was lost in the knowledge that the protagonists would rearm to battle over the regulations I had to issue.

As soon as President Carter signed the $60 billion appropriations bill on December 9, it landed on my desk, for the final provision of the compromise language stated: "The Secretary shall promptly issue regulations and establish procedures to ensure that the provisions of this section are rigorously enforced."

The antagonists turned their attention to me. Magnuson and Brooke wrote and called with their permissive interpretation. Robert Michel, ranking Republican on the Appro-

priations Committee, wrote with his strict
view. Dan Flood called and other members—and their even more aggressive
staffs—pressed for their interpretation of
words such as "medical procedures,"
"promptly reported," "severe and long-
lasting physical health damage," and "two
physicians."

There was no way in which I could avoid
becoming intimately involved in making
key decisions on the regulations. I decided
personally to read the entire 237 pages of
self-serving and often confused congressional debate and to study the ten different
versions of this legislation that were passed
by either the House or the Senate.

To assure objectivity, to balance any un-
conscious bias I might harbor, and to reduce
my vulnerability to charges of personal prejudice, I assigned the actual regulation writing to individuals who did not share my
strong views about abortion and, more importantly, who stood up for their own views
and did not hesitate to tell me when they
thought I was wrong. The bulk of the work
was done by Richard Beattie, the Deputy
General Counsel of HEW, and HEW attorneys June Zeitlin and David Becker, all of
whom opposed any restrictions on federal
funding of abortions. I also asked the Attorney General to review independently the
regulations we drafted at HEW. Once they
were in effect, I would establish a detailed
auditing system to assure compliance and
fulfill the congressional mandate "to ensure
that the provisions of this section are rigor-
ously enforced."

Finally, I decided not to consult the President about the regulations. Carter had
enough controversial problems on his desk
without adding this one. My responsibility
under the Constitution and under our system
of government was to reflect accurately the
law passed by the Congress. Neither Carter's personal views nor mine were of any
relevance to my legal duty to ascertain what
Congress intended and write regulations
that embodied that intent.

In pursuit of my overall goal of cooling
the temperature of the debate, I wanted to
issue the regulations more "promptly" than
anyone might expect. Not relying solely on
my own reading of the congressional debates, I asked the lawyers for a thorough
analysis of the legislative history. We then
spent hours discussing and debating what
the Congress intended on several issues,
frustrated by the conflicting statements in
the congressional record. We determined
that for rape and incest victims, the term
the "medical procedures" as used in this
new law now clearly included abortions;
that a "public health service" had to be a
governmental, politically accountable institution; that short of fraud we should accept
physicians' judgments as to what constituted "severe and long-lasting physical
health damage"; that the two physicians
whose certification was required must be
financially independent of each other; and
that the rape or incest victim need not personally make the required report to public
authorities. We resolved a host of other issues as best we could against the backdrop
of the heated and confusing congressional
debate. They were wearing days, because
I felt the law was too permissive, and its
provisions were in conflict with my own
position. I revisited many decisions several
times, concerned, on overnight reflection,
that I had bent too far to compensate for my
personal views and approved inappropri-
ately loose regulations, or that I was letting
my personal views override congressional
intent.

By far my most controversial determination was to define "reported promptly" in
the context of rape and incest to cover a
sixty-day period from the date of the incident. Even though the Attorney General
found the judgment "within the permissible
meaning of the words within the Secretary's
discretion," there was a storm of controversy over this decision.

There were widely varying interpretations on the floor of the House and the Sen-

ate. Most of the legislative history on the Senate floor was made by pro-abortion Senators Magnuson and Brooke. They spoke of "months" and "ninety days" to make the period as long as possible. On the House side, Mahon and other proponents of the compromise spoke of "weeks" and "thirty days" as they cautiously maneuvered this difficult piece of legislation to passage. On the floor of Congress, pro- and anti-abortionists could express their views and protect their constituencies. But I had to select a number of days and be as certain as possible that it would stick.

After extensive internal discussion and spirited argument within the department, I concluded that a sixty-day reporting period was within the middle range of the various time limits mentioned in the debates. The dominant issues during debate were access to abortions and prevention of fraud. The sixty-day period was long enough for a frightened young girl or an embarrassed woman who might not want to report a rape or incest, or one in shock who psychologically could not, to learn whether she might be pregnant and to make the report to public authorities. Sixty days was also prompt enough to permit effective enforcement of the law.

I was ready to issue the regulations during the third week of January 1978. On Monday, January 23, the annual March for Life to protest the 1973 Supreme Court abortion decision was scheduled to file past HEW en route from the White House to the Capitol. I decided to delay issuing the regulations until later in the week. The participants were outraged at the House-Senate compromise. As march leader Nellie Gray saw it, "The life issue is not one for compromise and negotiation. Either you're for killing babies or you're against killing babies."

I issued the regulations on January 26. Attorney General Bell concluded that they were "reasonable and consistent with the language and intent of the law." The *New York Times* editorialized that I had "done

[my] duty. . . . He has interpreted the nation's unfair abortion law fairly. . . . On several controversial issues Mr. Califano and his lawyers have performed admirably, hacking their way through a thicket of ambiguities in the law that passed a bitter and divided Congress in December after months of heated debate."

The right to life lobby disagreed. Thea Rossi Barron, legislative counsel for the National Right to Life Committee, called the regulations an example of "a rather blatant carrying out of a loophole to allow abortion on demand." The pro-life groups were particularly disturbed about the sixty-day reporting period for victims of rape or incest. But the most severe critic of that provision was Jimmy Carter.

In testifying before the House Appropriations Committee on the morning of February 21, 1978, less than a month after issuing the regulations, Chairman Flood and Republican Robert Michel pressed me to provide an administration position on tightening the restrictions on abortion.

I called the President during the luncheon break. The President wanted the reporting period for rape or incest shortened. He was "not happy" with the sixty-day time period in the regulations. "I believe such instances are reported promptly," he said coolly.

I told him that the sixty-day period was my best judgment of what Congress intended in the law. Carter "personally" believed sixty days permitted "too much opportunity for fraud and would encourage women to lie."

"But what counts is what the congressional intent is," I argued.

The President then said he thought the regulations did not require enough information. He particularly wanted the doctor to report to Medicaid the names and addresses of rape and incest victims. The President was also inclined to require reporting of any available information on the identity of the individual who committed the rape or incest. Carter said, "Maybe some women wake up in the morning and find their maidenhead lost, but they are damn few. That actually happened in the Bible, you know.''

"Perhaps we can tighten the reporting requirement" I responded, somewhat surprised at his Biblical reference. "Do you have any strong feelings on the legislation itself?"

Carter expressed some strong feelings: "I am against permitting abortions where long-lasting and severe physical health damage might result. I think that might permit too much of a chance for abuse and fraud. I want to end the Medicaid mills and stop these doctors who do nothing but perform abortions on demand all day."

When I testified that afternoon, I gave the House Appropriations Subcommittee some indication of the administration's views and agreed to submit a letter with the administration's position the next day.

After preparing a draft, I called the President and reviewed my proposed letter for the committee word by word. The letter set the administration position as stricter than the December compromise of the Congress. The administration opposed funding abortions in situations involving "severe and long-lasting physical health damage to the mother." The President and I compromised on the rape and incest paragraph: "In the case of rape or incest, we believe that present law requires the sixty days specified in the regulation as the period Congress intended for prompt reporting. In order to reduce the potential for fraud and abuse, it may be advisable to reduce that period to a shorter period of time."

Just as he was hanging up the phone, Carter again directed me to tighten the reporting provisions on rape and incest. "I want rules that will prevent abortion mills from simply filling out forms and encouraging women to lie."

I changed the regulations to require that the names and addresses of both the victim and the person reporting the rape or incest, and the dates of both the report and the inci-

dent, be included in the documentation for Medicaid funding. This change drew immediate fire from the National Organization for Women's National Rape Task Force, but it was well within my discretion under the law and consistent with the congressional intent.

Yet the President was still not satisfied. He wanted the sixty-day reporting period shortened, regardless of congressional intent. He raised the issue again two months later at the Camp David Cabinet summit of April 17, 1978, sharply criticizing "the regulations HEW issued on abortion" among a series of actions by Cabinet officers with which he disagreed.

The concern of the President and others that the regulations were too loosely drawn in the rape and incest area has not turned out to be justified. During the first sixteen months under the law and regulation until shortly before I left HEW, only 92 Medicaid abortions were funded for victims of rape or incest. The overwhelming majority of Medicaid-funded abortions—84 percent of 3,158 performed—were to save the life of the mother; 522 were to avoid severe and long lasting health damage to the mother. Eunice Shriver's estimate of 1,000 to 1,500 Medicaid-funded abortions each year was not too far off, particularly when compared with the 250,000 to 300,000 abortions estimated to have been performed annually under Medicaid in the absence of any funding restrictions.

I came away from the abortion controversy with profound concern about the capacity of national government, in the first instance, to resolve issues so personal and so laced with individual, moral, and ethical values. The most secure way to develop a consensus in our federal system is from the bottom up. But once the Supreme Court established a woman's constitutional right to an abortion against the backdrop of federally funded health care programs, the issue was instantly nationalized. As each branch acted—the Congress with the Hyde amendment, the executive with its regulations, and the Supreme Court in its opinions—the mandates from the top down generated as much resentment as agreement. This is true even though, by 1978, many states had more restrictive provisions on abortion funding than the national government.

In 1978, the Congress extended abortion funding restrictions to the Defense Department budget. In 1979, it applied an even stricter standard to both HEW and Defense appropriations, by eliminating funding in cases of long-lasting physical health damage to the mother, thus funding abortions only when the life of the mother is at stake or in cases of rape or incest, as Carter and I proposed for HEW in February 1978. The Supreme Court in the *McRae* case upheld the constitutionality of the Hyde amendment in June of 1980, concluding that the right to an abortion did not require the government to provide the resources to exercise it and that the Congress could restrict the circumstances under which it would pay for abortions. Months later, the Senate and House agreed to place tighter restrictions on Medicaid funding of abortions. Under the 1981 appropriations legislation, such funding is permitted only where the mother's life is at stake, in cases of rape reported within 72 hours and in cases of incest. That legislation permits the states to be even more restrictive; they are "free not to fund abortions to the extent that they in their sole discretion deem appropriate." Similar language was attached to the Defense appropriations bill.

Conforming the Defense and HEW appropriations bills provides the same standards for most of the federal funding arena. So long as the Congress acts through the appropriations for each department, however, rather than by way of across-the-board authorizing legislation, there will be inconsistencies. Even within HEW, the abortion funding policy has been a quilted one. The restrictions do not apply to disabled citizens whose health bills are paid by Medicare, because that program is financed out of Social Security trust funds, not through the HEW appropriations bill. Nor do the funding limits apply to the Indian Health Service; though administered by HEW, funds for the Indian Health Service are provided in the Interior Department appropriations bill. The Congress has begun to move to prohibit the use of federal funds to pay for abortion through federal employee health insurance. The inevitable challenges in court to new restrictions and the recurrent debate in the Congress assure continuing turmoil and controversy over the abortion issue.

In personal terms, I was struck by how infinitely more complex it was to confront the abortion issue in the broader sphere of politics and public policy in our pluralistic society than it had been to face it only as a matter of private conscience. I found no automatic answers in Christian theology and the teachings of my church to the vexing questions of public policy it raised, even though I felt secure in my personal philosophical grounding.

I was offended by the constant references to me as "Secretary Califano, a Roman Catholic" in the secular press when it wrote about the abortion issue. No such reference appeared next to my name in the stories reporting my opposition to tuition tax credits favored by the Catholic Church or my disputes with the Catholic hierarchy on that issue.

I was dismayed by the number of Catholics and diocesan papers that attacked me for the regulations I issued on abortion. Their attack so concerned Notre Dame president, Father Theodore Hesburgh, that he urged me to speak about the conscience and duty of a Catholic as a public official at the commencement in South Bend in 1979. The assumption of many bishops that I could impose my views on the law passed by Congress reflected a misunderstanding of my constitutional role at that stage of the democratic process. As it turned out, like the President's, their assumption that the sixty-day reporting period for rape or incest constituted a legal loophole was as ill-founded in fact as it was in law.

Throughout the abortion debate, I did—as I believe I should have—espouse a position I deeply held. I tried to recognize that to have and be guided by convictions of conscience is not a license to impose them indiscriminately on others by one-dimensionally translating them into public policy. Public policy, if it is to serve the common good of a fundamentally just and free pluralistic society, must balance competing values, such as freedom, order, equity, and justice. If I failed to weigh those competing values—or to fulfill my public obligations to be firm without being provocative, or to recognize my public duty once the Congress acted—I would have served neither my private conscience nor the public morality. I tried to do credit to both. Whether I succeeded is a judgment others must make.

Funding Abortion
U. S. House of Representatives

[The debate excerpted here took place on the floor of the House of Representatives on September 9, 1988, on a motion to reject a Senate amendment (proposed by Senator J. James Exon, Democrat, Nebraska) that permitted the use of federal funds in state-run Medicaid programs for abortions in cases of rape or incest. The relevant part of the Senate amendment specified that funding would be permitted "for such medical procedures necessary for the victims of rape or incest, when such rape or incest has been reported promptly to a law enforcement agency or public health service." It also stated: "nor are payments prohibited for drugs to prevent implantation of the fertilized ovum, or for medical procedures necessary for the termination of ectopic pregnancy; provided, however, that the several states are and shall remain free not to fund abortions to the extent that they in their sole discretion deem appropriate, except where the life of the mother would be endangered if the fetus were carried to term."]

Mr. OBERSTAR [Democrat, Minnesota].

Mr. Speaker, a few weeks ago while driving

Reprinted from *Congressional Record*, Sept. 9, 1988, pp. H 7350–H 7359.

along I saw a bumper sticker on a car that said, "A fetus is a little human." I think that goes to the essence of this debate. Mr. Speaker, what we are talking about is a human being.

America has come to be known as the disposable society, but that should not include people, the elderly in their sunset years; it should not include the retarded, nor the handicapped, and we certainly should not discard children before they are born.

Dr. Bernard Nathanson, a New York obstetrician-gynecologist, was a founder of the National Abortion Rights League. He was a militant abortion rights supporter before the U.S. Supreme Court decision. Nathanson founded and served as director of the first and largest abortion clinic in the United States. A year and a half and 60,000 abortions later, he resigned as head of that clinic. He wrote:

I am deeply troubled by my own increasing certainty that I have in fact presided over 60,000 deaths. There is no longer serious doubt in my mind that human life exists within the womb from the very onset of pregnancy.

The infinitely agonizing truth is that in an abortion we are taking life.

Mr. Speaker, a few years ago I conducted a hearing in which a doctor recounted the story of a patient who in his words was poor, raped, black, pregnant, and teenaged.

"As I talked with her," he said, "she made it very clear that abortion was not ever a consideration."

She said, "I couldn't do that to something that is half of me."

What public policy question could be more vital to the well-being of society than whether a fetus is human. It is an established biological fact that the existence of a human being begins at conception and that the individual so created remains a human being throughout every stage of biological development thereafter.

But there are some forms of life that people are concerned about enough to protect, to change the law so that vulnerable life can be protected. In Arizona a person can be fined $300 for destroying a Gila monster egg. In that same State, there is no fine for destroying a 28-week-old unborn human being.

The focus of this debate, however, is language to provide for Federal funding of abortion in cases of rape or incest. This issue must be addressed with dignity, with sensitivity and respect for the victims, both mother and potentially unborn child.

Rape is a violent crime against a woman, an innocent victim, a defenseless woman. Abortion is also a violent destruction of equally innocent human life, the unborn, including the unborn resulting from rape, but it is also a fact that prompt medical treatment following rape prevents pregnancy. In correspondence with the former chairman of the subcommittee on then HEW, Mr. Flood, a physician wrote: "As an emergency room physician, I would like to share with you my knowledge about treatment of rape and incest victims, rape treated in the emergency room of hospitals. No competent doctor would expose a woman to the hazards of an abortion when a simple medical curettage is available to prevent pregnancy in rape. The patient is given estrogen

for 5 days, which makes it impossible for the woman to conceive."

Life must not become a privilege reserved for the strong and denied to the old, to the retarded, to the handicapped or to the voiceless and the voteless among us, the unborn.

In this throwaway society of ours, what we ought to throw away is the junk ethic that dismisses the unborn simply as a mass of cells, simply a collection of tissue that can be discarded without remorse, as a hindrance or as a nuisance. That ethic and the legal framework provided by the Supreme Court decision in *Roe versus Wade* does more than destroy unborn human life. It literally has a corrosive effect upon the very fabric of society and demoralizes society itself.

We should resolve to show a strength of principle that will restore meaning to life, the right to life of the unborn, including those who may be the progeny of a pregnancy that results tragically from rape or incest.

Taking innocent unborn life will not ease the abuse of rape, ease the abuse created when an innocent female victim is brutalized. It will not apprehend the rapist. It will not heal the emotional scars of that violent crime.

Mr. Speaker, we should stay with the House position and reject the position of the other body.

Mr. GREEN [Republican, New York]. . . . Let me at the outset say that I understand the depth of feeling of those who support the motion and who feel that abortion should be permitted only when the life of the mother is in danger. I understand the sincerity with which those who advocate that position come to the floor.

I wish they would understand that there are some of us who feel with equal fervor that to force a woman who has been raped to carry to term the fetus that is the product of that rape is an act of horrible cruelty second only to the rape itself.

Now, I know that obviously that position is one that morally is inconsistent with the position of those who are supporting the motion, but I suggest to you it is certainly an understandable, defensible position, and one which I would hope those who do not like abortion would nonetheless understand.

So recognizing the terrible dilemma that we face when a woman is raped and a pregnancy results from that, I would hope that they would at least acknowledge that there is enough moral controversy, that that is a decision as to what should happen to the product of that rape that is best left to the woman's own conscience, the woman's own relationship to God. If you believe that, as I do, I would only hope that you would vote no, so that we can sustain the Senate position.

Mr. HOYER [Democrat, Maryland]. . . . Mr. Speaker, this is an issue on which the opinions of Members are deeply held and on which the consequences to individuals are very substantial. Those on both sides of this issue will talk about the consequences to other human beings.

First of all, let me take a brief time to explain what this is. The other body added an amendment overwhelmingly to their bill which said in the instances—the sole instances—where a pregnancy results as the result of the rape of a woman, or where a pregnancy results from an incestuous attack, in that instance and in the other instances which are presently in the law where the life of the mother is in the balance, in those instances alone, poor women will, like other women who do not need public assistance, [be] allowed to use public funds for abortion services.

There was an additional provision in that bill, interestingly, and language that we have adopted some four times between 1980 and 1982, which says that a State will have the option still to opt out to say no not even in these instances of vicious sexual attack will we exempt a woman from carrying the child of her attacker however psychologi-cally damaging that may be, however permanently damaging that may be.

This amendment simply makes those sole exceptions, and no broader.

I think, Mr. Speaker, this is the appropriate and sensitive and humane step for us to take. We disagree, we understand. I would ask, therefore, that the motion be defeated.

Mr. SMITH [Republican, New Jersey]. . . . Mr. Speaker, clearly rape and incest are unconscionable assaults on women and children. While abortion likewise is a violent assault on an innocent unborn child, I believe that the Federal Government should not be paying for any person to be assaulted, whether he or she is born or unborn.

Mr. Speaker, as I have listened to this debate, and especially as it has proceeded over the years on rape and incest, I am always struck by how the abortion proponents have attempted to frame the debate. We have, of course, in America, abortion on demand, a million and a half children killed each and every year, a staggering and overwhelming number.

It is deeply regrettable that not one of these little persons are to the abortion proponents worth legally protecting. Clearly, this position of supporting abortion on demand from fertilization throughout the total 9 months of pregnancy has scant support in our Nation. So the abortion proponents are not focusing on their extreme position of destroying unborn children for any reason any time prior to birth. No, they are focusing on advocating abortion where pregnancy results from rape or incest. They focus on a situation which rarely occurs, but which is so emotionally laden that they appear to have a reasonable position, while their opponents are painted as being unreasonable.

The fact of the matter is, Mr. Speaker, the proabortion position, notwithstanding its surface appeal, is the unreasonable position and is also the unjust position.

Since 1973, those who promote the violence of abortion have had their season of child deaths, a staggering 22 million have perished. I believe this is a national scandal.

Mr. Speaker, I am encouraged that in the last few years and months that the truth seems to be penetrating society. There seems to be a growing recognition of what abortion is and what it does to the woman, as well as what it does to the baby.

Mr. Speaker, those of us who support life care and we care deeply for both the women and their children. We care, regardless of the circumstances of a person's beginning or his race or creed or whether or not that child is handicapped or suffers some other anomaly, because all human life is so precious.

Mr. Speaker, is it not odd that when we talk about human rights so often in this Chamber that the most basic and most fundamental of all human rights, the right to life, is the one that this country does not respect?

Mr. Speaker, to be sure, we care, those of us in the prolife movement, and we are absolutely repelled by the fact that each day in America some 4,000 unborn children are killed. They are torn apart. They are cut apart. They are poisoned and they are asphyxiated by abortion procedures. This is indeed a national scandal.

We care, Mr. Speaker, and publicly stand for the unborn child, not only when it is convenient to do so, like when the child is wanted or when the child is planned or when the child is perfect, but we also stand for the child when it is most difficult to do so. Clearly, a child is a child and his or her worth is not diminished one iota by the circumstances of that beginning. That again is the truest definition of human rights.

Mr. Speaker, finally, if Members vote to reverse the current Hyde language, children will surely die. I urge a ''yes'' vote, sustain the House position, sustain the Hyde amendment.

Mr. MOLLOHAN [Democrat, West Virginia]. . . .

Mr. Speaker, one of the frustrations of debating the larger issue of abortion is that the two opposing sides are not usually divided over questions of logic. After many years of debate over the general issue of abortion, only a few still question the existence of life before birth. Life begins at conception.

The opposing sides reach their respective positions on abortion based on what value they place on human life at any particular stage of development. Debate over this fundamental question can be difficult, because we do not always agree on the logical framework we should use to answer the question.

The more narrow question before us today, however, is different; whether to allow Medicaid funding of abortion in cases of rape and incest can, regardless of one's view on abortion, be logically answered in only one way, in the negative. It is not a difficult analysis.

Mr. Speaker, those of us who vote on the prolife side have determined that life is worth protecting at every stage of development. Abortion is wrong. It is the taking of human life, life that the sovereign, the Government, has an interest in protecting. The majority of Members of both Houses share this view, as evidenced by repeated adoption of the Hyde amendment. We believe abortion is wrong, and consequently we believe that Federal money should not be used to support it. If you adopt our premise that unborn life is valuable, and therefore abortion is fundamentally wrong, there is no logical reason for allowing exceptions in cases of rape and incest.

Regardless of the tragic circumstances of conception, exceptions in cases of rape and incest.

Regardless of the tragic circumstances of conception, abortion remains the taking of human life. Concede us that point and you must reject an effort to carve out a rape and incest exception.

As an individual Member you may disagree with our premise, but Congress as a whole by adopting the Hyde amendment adopts our premise as its starting point. A prolife Member and a Member who supports abortion should agree logically on this point. There is no basis for compromising the integrity of the Hyde amendment. You either vote for the Hyde amendment or you vote against it. You do not, however, search for some middle ground that logically cannot exist, and you do not vote for the Exon amendment.

Mrs. BOXER [Democrat, California]. Mr. Speaker, will the gentleman yield?

Mr. MOLLOHAN. I yield to the gentlewoman from California.

Mrs. BOXER. Mr. Speaker, I thank the gentleman for yielding to me.

Does the gentleman feel there ought to be an exception for life of the mother if the life of the mother is endangered, then it is permissible to grant an abortion to the woman?

Mr. MOLLOHAN. Indeed, and that is implicit—explicit in the Hyde amendment, because, if the gentlewoman will allow me to finish my answer, when we have two competing lives in being, it is logical to opt for the mature life in being.

Mrs. BOXER. There are two competing lives, and the gentleman comes down on the side of the life of the mother rather than the life of the fetus?

Mr. MOLLOHAN. Indeed, as the Hyde amendment does, and the Congress has affirmed numerous times.

Mrs. BOXER. Let me ask my friend this question. Let us take a situation where a husband and a wife are in the privacy of their own home. An intruder comes in, a rapist, rapes the woman, almost kills her, murders the husband. The woman survived and is pregnant, and this gentleman is saying that that woman should be forced to have that child of the murderer; is that correct?

Mr. MOLLOHAN. We have equally tragic situations that the gentlewoman is describing presenting extremely tough choices, the tragic situation of destroying by

dismembering the unborn life and shattering the life of the mother who has been raped by that person. What I am simply saying is that I am answering the question and that is the proposition that the gentlewoman is proposing creates these tremendously difficult choices. Just to make one point which can be answered based upon what premise the gentlewoman starts with, and that is if we have a life and how much value we place on that life.

Mrs. BOXER. Mr. Speaker, I respect the gentleman, and I respect his opinion, I honestly do.

Mr. MOLLOHAN. We express our opinions on this very difficult issue.

Mrs. BOXER. But I just want to make the point so that there is no misunderstanding that a woman who is raped by the murderer of her husband will be forced to have that child, and I just want to make that the point for the record. . . .

Mr. OBEY [Democrat, Wisconsin]. Mr. Speaker, I have voted on this issue about 60 times, and I have to say that I have come to accept and agree with the legitimacy of the argument that in almost all circumstances Federal dollars should not be used to finance abortions.

The question is what happens to a woman who is raped or who is the victim of incest. This amendment deals only with the question of rape or incest. It does not endorse or recommend in any way abortions in those circumstances. If it did, I could not personally support it.

My wife and I lost two babies, and I do not believe that abortion in the case of rape or incest is the answer. But as a man that is easy for me to say.

All this amendment says is that when a woman is raped or is the victim of incest, she, not I or you, should be able to make the choice in accordance with her own conscience without regard to whether she is rich or poor, if the State in which she resides allows the choice. That is all this amendment does, and reasonable people ought to be able to agree on that.

Mr. WEBER [Republican, Minnesota]. . . . Mr. Speaker, the National Right to Life Committee has called this vote the most important prolife vote of the 100th Congress. We should ask ourselves why that is, because we have cast other votes on this important and emotional issue. I suggest there are a few reasons why this vote, of all of those votes that we have cast in this Congress, is considered the most important prolife vote.

First of all , because it would make a shift in a longstanding existing policy. Particularly Members who have not had to vote on this in the past, and there are many, should understand that fact. The Hyde amendment has been the law of the land since it was passed in 1977. We have not had to vote on it in about 5 years.

We are talking about upsetting a long, well-established, and, in my judgment, proven policy.

The second reason why it is the most important prolife vote of this Congress is because the Hyde amendment is, indeed, working as planned. We used to pay, in this country, for over 300,000 abortions per year. Taxpayers, many of whom were deeply opposed to abortion for moral reasons, were forced to use their taxpayer dollars to pay for abortions. That is not happening anymore.

Furthermore, the terrible effects that were predicted by many on the initial passage of the Hyde amendment have not come to pass. Large numbers of women have not been forced to seek back-alley abortions or lose their lives because of the passage of the Hyde amendment as was predicted on its initial passage in 1977. Those problems simply did not arise.

Third, the same problems that were foreseen by many at the attempt to pass the exceptions for rape and incest back in 1977 would arise if those exceptions were written into law today.

Law enforcement officials from many parts of the country opposed the insertion of a rape-and-incest exception in 1977, and since then, because they believe it would cause large numbers of people to report false rapes, false cases of incest, in order to have the Government pay for their abortions. Even Gloria Steinem on the other side of the issue obviously said that a rape-and-incest exception alone would make many women liars. We do not want to complicate that situation, as the Congress wisely decided not to complicate it back in 1977.

Finally, this is the most important prolife vote of the year because the issue is not really rape and incest, and the issue is not really even tax dollars. The issue is life itself. After all, we do not really expect to see a large number of cases paid for under this particular provision that are genuinely the result of rape and incest.

Medical procedures are available, legal in every State, to prevent the woman recently raped or the victim of incest from conceiving a child. That is the answer to the question of the gentlewoman from California who was just involved in the debate.

All in all, it is expected that perhaps the number of abortions resulting from rape and incest may well be in the hundreds, not even in the thousands every year, and certainly not all of those wish to abort. We are talking about a very small number of cases.

The larger issue, here again, is simply the issue of life, the issue of availability of abortion, and the issue of forcing taxpayers to pay for abortions. It is against the standard of taking of a human life that all other actions, even actions as horrible as cases of rape and incest, must be judged, so we urge support for the chairman's position. We urge maintaining a standard that has been established in this country for over 10 years that says that the taxpayers are not going to be forced to pay for abortions against their will. . . .

Mr. VOLKMER [Democrat, Missouri]. Mr. Speaker, I wish to commend the gentleman for his remarks, especially in regard to the question on law enforcement.

What we have here is a potential of making law enforcement look at people, ladies, when they come in, and/or girls when they come in and complain of a rape, the question of whether there actually was rape, whether they should go out and investigate, or is this just for the purposes of getting an abortion funded, that has been something that law enforcement has been very concerned about, and I think everyone should be concerned about, because I think rape is one of the most heinous crimes there is. Yet to then turn around and say that we should relegate that to the fact that is a way to get an abortion because that is what is going to happen, as the gentleman said, even Gloria Steinem has commented what we are trying to do basically with the opposition is to make liars out of women so that they can get an abortion funded by the Government.

I commend the gentleman, and I, too, urge the Members of the House to vote "aye" on the motion of the gentleman from Kentucky. . . .

Mrs. MORELLA [Republican, Maryland]. Mr. Speaker, I rise in support of the Exon amendment, to allow Medicaid funding for abortion services in cases of rape and incest. This amendment would allow Federal funding of abortions only in *promptly reported* cases of rape and incest and contains a State's rights provision to allow each State to determine whether it will fund abortions in cases of sexual assault.

The justice campaign, a national campaign to secure public funding for abortion for the victims of rape and incest, is made up of representatives of a number of religions, including Hebrew, Episcopal, Baptist, Methodist, Unitarian, and Presbyterian congregations. The vast majority of the American public supports this coverage— even many who support the Roe versus Wade decision. Polls taken over the last 15 years indicate that 8 in 10 Americans believe abortion should be an available option for women who have been the victims of sexual assault.

Poor women who are pregnant as a result of rape or incest—victims of brutal acts— should have access to the same health care options as more affluent women. I urge my colleagues to join the justice campaign to preserve the Senate language in supporting the Exon amendment to H.R. 4783. . . .

Mr. EDWARDS [Democrat, California]. . . . Mr. Speaker, I rise in support of the Senate's position.

Mr. Speaker, earlier this summer, our colleagues in the other body did a courageous thing.

By voting to provide Federal funding for abortions in promptly reported cases of rape and incest, the other body was only trying to put into law the views of the vast majority of Americans. The time has come for the House of Representatives to do the same thing.

Recent surveys show that 81 percent of Americans believe abortion services should be available to women who become pregnant as a result of sexual assault. . . .

Mr. Speaker, for the first time since 1979, we have the opportunity to do the decent and humane thing.

I urge a "no" vote. . . .

Mr. DORNAN [Republican, California]. Mr. Speaker, I want to congratulate all of my colleagues for the high tone of this debate. We do not seem to be talking past one another any longer on this issue. We seem to be reaching out to understand one another's position.

One of the most incredible acts of political courage I have ever seen was on America's most-watched television show "60 Minutes." Our current President, Ronald Reagan, was pressed forcefully but politely by one of the star interviewers of our era, Mike Wallace, on this issue of rape/incest and abortion. It was not a direct question. Mike Wallace simply was probing for one of those confessions from a politician. He said: "Mr. President, what is the biggest mistake you have ever made in political life?'' I immediately, as a politician, like a baseball player will anticipate a move, I answered in my mind: "Oh, that is for my opponents to tell you, I would rather talk about some of the good things I have done.'' The President did not say that. He said, and this is almost verbatim: "Mike, that is easy. The biggest mistake I ever made was my first year as Governor of California when I did not really understand in depth the issue of abortion.'' President Reagan was referring to a bill that bore the name of one of our distinguished colleagues here, Mr. BEILENSON, a good friend of mine who is on the opposite side of the issue. Mr. BEILENSON was in the State senate in California at that time. President Reagan went on and said: "The Beilenson bill came up in California. I signed it to allow abortion for rape and incest.

"And I didn't realize what I was doing. I opened a Pandora's box.'' And he said: "And what's happened ever since has been a national scandal.'' He said it was used as an excuse for unlimited abortion on demand for every cause, and that is the problem that faces this House today.

The rape problem is as tough as we can get on this issue. I happen to have a personal friend whose daughter was raped at noon on a college campus. I believe it was at the instigation of one of America's slimiest pornographers, who offered $400 the night before the rape to anybody who could get a story on my friend's daughter. She was pulled off of the parking lot and into the bushes, and she was raped by three or four students, she cannot remember exactly. The next night her father, who is a nationally known official, held a press conference and said that we have done everything that we can to avoid this pregnancy that our church will allow. He said that: "If my daughter ends up pregnant, she told me from the hospital that she wants to have the baby. She will not commit an act of violence when

there is no capital punishment for the men who raped her in an act of violence.''

I applaud the cause of Joan Andrews, who I think is a martyr. She is taking her legal punishment for unplugging one of these suction pieces of equipment in modern American life that tears a living child from its mother's womb, and spins the aborted baby into a gel in one of these whirling, razor blade machines. . . .

Ms. SNOWE [Republican, Maine]. . . .

Mr. Speaker, I rise in opposition to the motion to insist on the House position.

And I do so, Mr. Speaker, as a Member who has opposed Federal funding of abortion on demand. I subscribed to the notion that the Federal Government should not bear the responsibility to fund abortions for women who choose—who chose—not to take proper precautions.

Rather, it is a question of a woman taking responsibility for her own actions, no matter what income level.

But instances occur, tragic instances, when the choice is taken out of the woman's hands—more accurately, when it is violently and brutally taken from her. A woman who has been raped, or who is the victim of incest, faces enormous physical and emotional consequences. And these are consequences that simply are not of her own making.

Yet women of economic means who have thus suffered have options which we currently deny to low-income women. They have choices in this hideous circumstance that are now withheld. We have made income and economic status the basis by which women contend with the aftermath of rape or incest—as if falling victim to those crimes were not degrading enough.

In this debate, Mr. Speaker, we have spoken in the dispassionate terminology of legislatures as to what lower-income women are being forced to do and contend with. Yet the cruel and agonizing reality of their fate is far removed from such debate.

Further, there is a great deal of talk about

"rights," about who has what kind and what take precedence. I would suggest, rather, that we should speak not of rights but of obligations. And there is an obligation in our society toward a rape victim, toward the victim of incest, to provide the basic array of choices in these horrifying circumstances regardless of income.

To preclude women, in the wake of the crudest and most degrading of crimes, from recovering from those crimes simply on the basis of economics goes from the realm of unfairness toward base cruelty.

I urge my colleagues to defeat the motion to insist on the House position. . . .

Mr. FAZIO [Democrat, California]. Mr. Speaker, I rise in strong support of the centrist Senate compromise on this matter, and it is important for Members to realize that the 19 opponents in the Senate were made up of Members on both sides of this issue who could not compromise.

This is really an opportunity to add a small element of compassion to the Hyde amendment, and I mean a small one. Statistics show us that in 1986, 90,000 cases of rape occurred in the United States, and over 100,000 cases of child abuse, some of which were incest. Yet in 1979, the last year in which we were able to gather data on this prior to the enactment of the Hyde amendment, only 72 people qualified for this form of Federal assistance. So we are not talking about an awful lot of people.

But we are talking about a very important principle, and that is why I think the demeanor of this debate is so important.

As the gentlewoman from Maryland [Mrs. MORELLA] said, we are requiring prompt reporting of the crime. This is not a new loophole that people will be able to use to violate the broader Hyde amendment. We are giving the States local control to make decisions about whether they wish to use their State Medicaid funds for this purpose.

But I think we have overlooked one fundamental issue, and that is the question of economic justice. We all know that under the law currently in this country women who wish to have an abortion can have one. I do not think very many of us who are in the affluent element of our society realize what a burden this can be to poor people. An abortion today could cost half the family's monthly income for people who qualify for AFDC, the people we are talking about here today, that 20 percent of our society or less who will fall into the lower-income bracket.

We are talking about economic justice. If the Constitution says that is one of our purposes of being here, if we have said in adherence to the Supreme Court rulings like Roe versus Wade that this abortion concept can exist in our society, we cannot allow this disparity to continue. I ask my colleagues to support the Senate compromise. . . .

Mr. FRENZEL [Republican, Minnesota]. Mr. Speaker, it has been mentioned a number of times on the floor that this is a very narrow kind of compromise. It applies in a very limited number of cases, only on two occasions, after reporting, and the States can undo everything that we might do here today.

I would like to suggest that this is not abortion on demand. It has nothing to do with abortion rights. That matter is determined elsewhere. What we are talking about is whether a poor woman has the same opportunity in the United States as a rich woman. All we are talking about is whether there is an opportunity for the poor to be treated the same way as the rich.

It seems to me that if we have any dedication to equality in this House that we have no other course than to support the Senate amendment. . . .

Ms. PELOSI [Democrat, California]. . . . I rise today in support of Senate language providing Medicaid funded abortions for women whose pregnancy results from rape or incest.

It is ironic and tragic that Medicaid, the very program which was created to provide necessary medical care to poor women, has been transformed into a program that denies poor women who are pregnant access to all available medical options. Poor women who are victims of the brutal crimes of rape or incest should have access to the same legal rights to abortion as other women in our society. Denying them access to these services is nothing but a policy of discrimination against the poor.

In 36 States in this country, no public funds are available to help women whose pregnancies are the result of violence and assault. In an ideal world, abortions would not be necessary. Unfortunately, in the real world, the brutal realities of crimes of aggression such as rape and incest occur with alarming frequency. We have the opportunity today to assist some women on the long road to regaining control of their lives. It is unfair, unreasonable and inhumane to deny them this assistance. I urge my colleagues to oppose any measures to weaken the Senate language restoring Medicaid funding for abortions for women victimized by rape and incest.

Mr. Speaker, I come from a culture as an Italian American, Roman Catholic mother of 5 children of my own who worships children. This has nothing to do, as the gentleman from Minnesota [Mr. FRENZEL] said, with the question of abortion, but it is a question of fairness, and a question of not denying people their rights.

I ask every Member of this body to examine his or her conscience and say if any one of our children or spouses of male Members were confronted with this circumstance of rape or incest, would they deny that member of their family the opportunity to every medical option. I do not think the time is now for hypocrisy, but it is a time to really face the reality and truth of the situation, and not deny to women, just because they lack the financial resources, the same medical options we reserve for our own families and our own spouses. . . .

Mrs. JOHNSON [Republican, Connecticut]. Mr. Speaker, I thank my colleagues from both sides of the aisle for this opportunity to speak on what I consider to be a very, very important matter. Preceding speakers have spoken eloquently to the fact that this is not abortion on demand that we are talking about. This is rather an issue of equity and a deeply human right, which at times life demands that we be allowed to exercise from the deepest reservoirs of our own individual being.

This amendment does not offer abortion on demand. It talks only about incest and rape. It is narrowly drawn. It is thoughtfully drawn with the States rights provisions and the other sections that have been mentioned today.

But what it talks about is not narrow. Rape is not a narrow experience.

Rape is being in fear for your life. Rape is being violently subdued.

Picture your daughter, picture your own wife, picture the terror, picture the pain. I ask Members to take unto yourselves the full responsibility for this vote. I ask Members to know that with a knife at your throat, with fear in your heart, maybe an hour, maybe over an hour, an experience of such extraordinary brutality, and under those circumstances to be penetrated. Yes, we are not talking about assault and battery. Rape is not assault and battery. It is penetration.

Men and women experience this situation very differently. Penetration is different than penetrating.

And that is part of what this is all about. I will tell you that if your 13-year-old daughter—I have three daughters—but picture your sobbing 13-year-old daughter in your arms convulsed in terror and anguish, are you going to ask her day after day to relive that experience? Are you going to make that decision for her? Can every man in the House of Representatives take upon themselves at this moment the right and responsibility to make this kind of decision for every poor woman and child—yes, child—in America?

This bill is about incest. Now, who com-mits incest? Who is the victim of incest? Female children.

I appreciate the time allotted to me, because I do think this is no ordinary matter. I think—I hope that I have made that plain. We are only asking that under extraordinary, brutal, deeply human situations that that woman, that child, be allowed the same choice as your wife, or your child, because you can pay for it, and because you have the power to choose.

Believe me, rape is not something that is over when it is finished. It is not done when it is done. It is with you the rest of your life. These choices are not choices that can be taken on in the well of the House. . . .

Mr. SCHEUER [Democrat, New York]. Mr. Speaker, the last 4 minutes during which we heard the statement of the lady from Connecticut [Mrs. JOHNSON] constitutes the 4 most deeply moving minutes that I have spent in this Congress in the last 20 years. I must say that all of the debate from both sides of this issue has been thoughtful, has been deeply felt and has dignified this Congress.

Mr. Speaker, I only have a minute. We have heard that abortion is an assault on an innocent unborn life, we have heard that abortion is the taking of a human life, that the issue of life itself is what we are talking about, and that the fetus is a human being.

We have heard that abortion has a corrosive effect on the fabric of society, it takes an innocent life.

However, there is another view to consider. There is the view that I adhere to, the view that abortion is not the taking of human life but a sublime humanitarian act that, in this case, will ease the suffering of human beings.

This does not mean that I am anti-life. I and my colleagues who support a woman's right to choose also support life-sustaining legislation. My colleagues, when you are asked if you are prolife, give them the record of life-sustaining legislation you have supported this year.

Tell them what you are doing to lower the abysmally high infant mortality rate in this country. Point to the health care programs you have supported to curb fatal diseases among the Nation's 37 million citizens without basic health services.

The Children's Defense Fund cited 10 House votes this year as being critical to the physical, mental, and spiritual health of the Nation's children. The bills provided for food, clothing, shelter, education, and health care for children. These are true life-sustaining bills.

Many religious organizations, including the U.S. Presbyterian Church, the Union of American Hebrew Congregations, and the United Church of Christ, support the Exon amendment. Seventy percent of Americans in a Lou Harris poll, commissioned by Planned Parenthood, believe that abortion in this circumstance is acceptable. Our colleagues in the Senate passed the amendment by an overwhelming vote of 73 to 19.

Furthermore, in every single developed nation in the world, with the exception of Ireland, abortion for rape and incest victims is legal. This includes Spain, Italy, and France, three of the most Catholic countries in the world. Not only is abortion legal in this instance, but it has been since the early 1930's.

If a victim of sexual assault wants to terminate her pregnancy she should have that right—regardless of her financial circumstances. Congress should not stand between a woman and her body, especially in cases of rape and incest. . . .

Mr. AuCOIN [Democrat, Oregon]. Mr. Speaker, for the last 15 years in virtually every public opinion poll in this country, the overwhelming majority of Americans have supported the right of rape and incest victims to choose to end the pregnancy that results from that rape or that incest. That is what the polls say.

But today the law of the land is not in step with nor does it represent the mainstream thinking of the American public. The law that this Congress has mistakenly created says that a victim of criminal rape must bear the rapist's child. I think, Mr. Speaker, that not only a majority of Americans, but a majority of the Members of this House honestly, in the bottom of their hearts, believe that is a gross denial of justice.

Rape and incest cases are increasing across this country. Many of those victims of violent sexual assault are young women who are poor and who depend on the Federal Government for their well-being and their health care.

Now some of my colleagues have said that a woman who has been victimized once by conceiving against her will should be also victimized again by her own government and be forced to deliver against her will. Mr. Speaker, I ask, and my colleagues on our side ask for simple compassion. Surely Members of this body think that women are more than incubators for rapists and criminals and perpetrators of incest. If you do believe as we do, you will accept the Senate revision. It exempts rape and incest victims and it requires cases of rape and incest to be promptly reported and that states agree to accept the funds.

These provisions assure that claims of rape and incest are legitimate and that the opportunity for fraud is minimized. These provisions give State governments the option to participate in the policy decisions. And most importantly, it leaves to a violently impregnated woman the moral right to choose for herself whether or not she will deliver the criminal rapist's child.

In the name of compassion, in the name of justice for women who have suffered enough, I urge my colleagues to vote "no" on the motion and to accept the Senate provision. . . .

Mr. HYDE [Republican, Illinois]. Mr. Speaker, I just want to say parenthetically something that the last speaker said about bearing the child of a criminal rapist, that strikes me as the Scarlet Letter, as though the innocent child, the second victim of the rape, somehow must bear the stigma of the criminal act of the father. I have difficulty following the logic of that.

Now we have heard in some painful detail the emotional trauma of what a rape can mean. Let me also say that incest is a form of rape, only it is within the family. Let me say also abortion does not cure that family's situation. Something more has to be done to get the poor victim of the incest away from the perpetrator of the incest and abortion does not go to that at all.

But I think to understand fully this soul-wrenching issue, let us focus for a moment away from the woman, just for a moment, and look at the other victim, the unborn child, and let us try to figure out what an abortion does to that child.

Now it is not a tonsillectomy, it is not an appendectomy; by definition, by intention it is the killing, the killing of an innocent, an innocent human life.

Thomas More when he was beheaded by Henry VIII is noted for a famous line. He said to the axman, "Be careful of my beard, it hath committed no treason." So as his head was cut off, he wanted his beard to maintain its dignity; "it hath committed no treason."

The little baby has not committed a crime, a rape, the little baby is an innocently inconvenient victim along with the victimized woman.

The law protected the rapist. The Supreme Court has said, "You may not impose capital punishment on a rapist." This is cruel and unusual punishment. But you are saying to exterminate, not terminate, a pregnancy—every pregnancy terminates at the end of nine months—exterminate this innocently inconvenient residual of the rape, the product of the rape, the consequence of the rape. Visit on that innocent child the penalty the law will not visit on the rapist. This is really, really what you are saying.

Now let us stipulate on compassion. Let us stipulate—I will, I stipulate that Mr.

HOYER, NANCY JOHNSON, VIC FAZIO, everybody has an abundance of compassion. How can you not? We are talking about one of the most traumatic situations in literature, in life. But stipulate, please, that we have compassion too. We have what we like to think is more than a one-dimensional compassion, a compassion that extends beyond sympathy and bleeding for and with and weeping with the victim of the rape, but extends to the innocently inconvenient consequence of that rape.

We want to enlarge the circle of persons for whom society will be responsible, to include within that circle of protection the little stranger, the little intruder who through no fault of his or her own has been made a party to this terribly criminal act. Rape is not over when it is finished, that is right, oh, that is right. But neither is abortion.

Abortion is terminal, abortion is killing.

Now no one, not even a woman who has been raped, God bless her and help her, and we help her and bless her, but nobody has the right to kill another innocent life, nobody. And no circumstances give that God-like power to anybody.

I have heard "picture your own wife or daughter." OK, fair enough. Now I am going to give you a picture, a little newborn baby that you are holding in your arms, think of that when you vote on this issue and ask yourself if you can be an accessory to exterminating that little child because his father committed a crime.

That is as real a picture for you to form in your mind as anything else. It is a matter of focus, of emphasis.

I ask you to extend your compassion to that abstraction that you cannot see, you cannot touch it because it is in the mother's womb, that tiny child of transcendent human value surrounded by a woman who has been victimized but who indeed is a mother.

In the fullest sense of the term, this is a human rights issue and you have in all of these situations conflicting rights, conflicting rights. You have the right of the first victim to have her body free from the consequences of a criminal act of rape. That is over here.

And over here you have the very right to life, itself, the right to live of the second victim, the unborn.

Now when rape and incest occur, a great injustice occurs, an enormous, monstrous, inhumane, humiliating, brutal injustice occurs. In all honesty I cannot say other than that forcing a woman to carry to term the child of the rapist is anything but a terrible injustice.

But that having been said, must we visit another injustice on top of that? Must we superimpose that on this crime of rape by destroying in the womb an innocent preborn child? It is not a tumor, it is not a bad tooth or swollen tonsils. That little microscopic entity is a tiny member of the human family that has committed no treason, has committed no crime, and we must perform an act of virtue, some act of will to transfer due process and the equal protection of the law to the second victim, because that is the second victim. But it is a far greater injustice to kill the child, superimposing that injustice on the injustice of the rape.

We cannot avoid injustice in a rape situation. We cannot avoid injustice in an incest situation. We can ameliorate, we can mitigate, we can help, we can nurture, we can alleviate, but we cannot escape injustice. But why must we compound the injustice by adding to it the extermination of an innocent human life, one that cannot rise up on the street, cannot speak out, cannot defend himself or herself, and cannot escape?

The injustice of rape lasts at least nine months. It is a terrible injustice, but it can be helped psychologically, financially, and spiritually. But abortion is the second injustice. There is the taking of a life, and there is no help for that. There is no remedy for that.

Interestingly enough, we have heard very few statistics on this. We have heard some from the gentleman from Oregon, ambiguous, I must say, and the reason is that there are not any. It is very hard to find out from anybody how many pregnancies result from rape and incest. The answer is that there are very, very few.

Now, on the economic argument that a poor woman should have the advantages of a rich woman, may I suggest that Planned Parenthood gets millions of taxpayer dollars from this Government. Let them pick up the cost for the very few who insist on exterminating their young. They should not make us accessories. They should not make us a part of that double tragedy of rape and exterminating an unborn child.

There are very, very few such pregnancies in this country. We cannot get the statistics. There are studies I can quote for the Members that say it almost never happens. But I must suggest to Members that we should let Planned Parenthood pay for those who insist on punishing the child for the crime of the father. Why must the Federal Government supply the only answer and be an accessory in the extermination of an innocent life?

These are poor women, yes. But there are poor babies. They are defenseless, defenseless babies.

Ethel Waters was a great black actress who passed away a few years ago. She played a famous role in "Cabin in the Sky." I do not know whether many remember it; perhaps only I do, but perhaps some who are a little older will remember it also. She was a great lady, a great person, and she wrote a book about her life that she called "His Eye is on the Sparrow." She said, "My father raped my mother when she was 12, and now they are dedicating a park to me in Chester, Pennsylvania."

Out of great, great tragedy some good can come.

Let me just leave the Members with something that was said by Sam Levinson, the comedian, some years ago. Levinson said, "I believe that each newborn child arrives on Earth with a message to deliver to mankind.

Clenched in his little fist is some particle of yet unrevealed truth, some missing clue which may solve the enigma of man's destiny." He has a limited amount of time to fulfill his mission, and he will never get a second chance. Nor will we. He may be our last hope. He must be treated as top sacred.

So as the Members vote on this—and it is not easy—let us not accuse anybody of lacking compassion. Let us consider focusing our compassion beyond what we see and touch and hear and take into consideration the abstract, this little atom of humanity, defenseless and innocent, and let us know that while rape is a terrible thing, an abortion is worse, because rape, with all of its horror, is not killing. Where there is life surely there is hope. But abortion terminates a life, and one of those little lives might have found the secret to cancer, to multiple sclerosis, to world peace; one of those little lives that is now thrown out like a crushed empty beer can.

Mr. Speaker, it is a tough vote. But I plead with the Members to support the gentleman from Kentucky [Mr. NATCHER] and support the gentleman from Massachusetts [Mr. CONTE], who have been like Gibraltars on this issue for years. They are responsible for saving many babies. Yes, the unborn of the rich are at risk. We cannot save them if their mothers want an abortion, because they can go out and buy one. But if we can save the unborn of the poor, occasionally, that is no small achievement.

Mr. DeFAZIO [Democrat, Oregon]. Mr. Speaker, I want to commend the Senate for adopting the Exon amendment which allows Medicaid funding to terminate a pregnancy that is the result of rape or incest in cases that are promptly reported to a law enforcement agency or public health service.

It is an outrage that the victims of brutal physical and mental assault have to carry an unwanted pregnancy to term because they are dependent upon the Federal Government for their health care. For most economically disadvantaged women health care options and choices about abortion are available only if they are financed through programs such as Medicaid.

While the Exon amendment would be a step forward in what has been a backward approach to this issue, the "promptly" reported language in the amendment is a disservice to a majority of women it's supposed to benefit. We are just beginning to realize the alarmingly high incidence of incest. These cases are rarely "promptly" reported. The young victims live in a daily environment of fear, confusion, anger and helplessness. They are unable to defend themselves from the perpetrator and are often led to believe that the situation is their fault. We cannot expect these young women to come forward seeking assistance when we send a message, "don't come knocking on the door of the Federal Government for help if you're poor."

The overwhelming majority of public opinion polls over the past 15 years have found that eight in 10 Americans support availability of abortions for sexually assaulted women. In 1978, my home state of Oregon was the first State to vote on a ballot initiative that would have prohibited the use of public funds for abortions. That measure was defeated. In 1986, the question again appeared on the ballot and the voters again opposed it. Clearly, restricting the availability of abortions for these victims is not the policy that most Americans want.

Mr. Speaker, I urge my colleagues to reconsider this discriminatory policy and, at the very least, allow the use of Federal funds to provide abortion services to poor women who are the victims of sexual assault. I urge my colleagues to vote no on the House language.

Mr. WEISS [Democrat, New York]. Mr. Speaker, I want to express my strong support of the motion to agree to the Senate provision on abortion funding to the Labor, Health and Human Services, Education appropriations conference report for fiscal year 1989. By restoring Federal funding to abortion in the cases of rape and incest, this provision would begin to redress the gross injustices of our current abortion laws.

In 1973, the Supreme Court affirmed that it is a woman's constitutional right to end a pregnancy in its early stages. Yet over the 15 years since then, the Congress has enacted a series of measures that have denied poor women this constitutional right. We cannot continue a policy that condemns women to the trauma of bringing an unwanted child into the world, or to a back alley abortionist, simply because she does not have enough money for a safe abortion.

Mr. Speaker, a woman should have the freedom to make her own decision about a pregnancy that is the result of violence and assault. The highest court in our land has affirmed that right. But the issue before us today is a question of resources and rights. Our Government is straddled with an abortion policy that discriminates against the poor, and we are now presented with the opportunity to remedy this travesty.

Congress has an obligation to assure equality of health care to all our citizens, and I urge my colleagues to join in supporting the motion to restore Federal funding for abortion in the case of rape and incest.

[The House voted 216 to 166 in favor of the motion, thus rejecting the Senate amendment to permit exceptions for rape and incest. The deadlock between the two bodies was overcome when the Senate four days later reversed itself and accepted the House position. The Senate amendment had been attached to a major spending bill for health, education, and labor programs, and many Senators who switched their vote said they wished to insure that federal spending for the programs in the bill, including research for AIDS and other diseases, could begin when the fiscal year started on October 1. The federal abortion law remained as it had been since 1981, allowing Medicaid financing of abortions only to save the life of the woman.]

Abortion in South Dakota
Jillian P. Dickert

In the two years after the United States Supreme Court handed down its 1989 decision on the Missouri abortion case, *Webster v. Reproductive Services*, the national battle over abortion rights raged on at the state level. By permitting greater regulation of abortion by states that could show a "compelling state interest" in the life of a fetus—including standards relating to where, how, and under what circumstances abortions could be performed—*Webster* opened a floodgate of state legislative activity on the abortion issue. Several states—such as Pennsylvania, Utah, Louisiana, and the territory of Guam—strove to tighten their abortion statutes under the new standards. Meanwhile, other states—including Maryland, Connecticut, and Washington—took *Webster* to mean that a state would be free not only to regulate abortion but also to permit it. These states sought to adopt statutes securing abortion rights independent of Supreme Court direction.

A highly restrictive abortion bill introduced in the South Dakota legislature in January 1991 pushed the midwestern state to the front lines of the national abortion conflict. A test case, House Bill 1126, was designed by the antiabortion National Right to Life Committee to ultimately be heard by the Supreme Court in an effort to chip away and possibly overturn the landmark *Roe v. Wade* decision, which ruled that states could not interfere with the fundamental right of a woman to obtain an abortion. In South Dakota, the bill—which aimed to outlaw most abortions in the state—ignited a political firestorm, that burned throughout the

Reprinted by permission of the Case Program, Kennedy School of Government, Harvard University. Copyright © 1993 by the President and Fellows of Harvard.

1991 legislative session. Lobbying activity by citizens and activists reached unprecedented levels, particularly among antiabortion advocates, as state legislators prepared to go on record on an emotionally and politically volatile issue.

Bearing the brunt of the lobbying pressure was Republican senator Scott Heidepriem of Miller, South Dakota. Heidepriem's influential position as chairman of the Senate Judiciary Committee—which would hold hearings and vote on the abortion legislation in February—placed the thirty-four-year-old lawyer under the political microscope. As chairman, Heidepriem was charged with handling as fairly as possible a bill he staunchly opposed—on legal as well as moral grounds—but that enjoyed widespread support within his district and throughout the state.

BACKGROUND: A POLITICAL LIFE

Politics had always played an important part in Scott Heidepriem's life—indeed, one could say politics was in his blood. Heidepriem grew up in the South Dakota legislature; his father, Herbert A. Heidepriem, served in the Senate for the first twelve years of Scott's life. The young Heidepriem's political career was marked by a rapid succession of campaign victories in his home state. In 1980, shortly after graduating from the University of South Dakota Law School, Heidepriem ran as an Independent and was elected state attorney for Jerauld County. Running as a Republican just two years later, Heidepriem was elected to the South Dakota House of Representatives. Heidepriem was then reelected to the House in 1984, and after an unsuccessful bid for U.S. Congress in 1986, he again sought and won a seat in the South Dakota House of Representatives in 1988.

In 1989, South Dakota Senator Mary McClure resigned her post to accept a position as White House special assistant for President George Bush. Heidepriem was appointed to take her place in the Senate. Upon his appointment, Heidepriem—then the youngest member of the Senate—was made chairman of the small but powerful Senate Judiciary Committee. (Heidepriem had given up the vice chairmanship of the legislature's Executive Board to move to the Senate.[1]) Then, in 1990, Heidepriem won election to the South Dakota Senate, retaining his post as Judiciary Committee chair for the 1991 session. At age thirty-four, Heidepriem was already considered by many a soon-to-be gubernatorial or congressional candidate.

As Judiciary chairman, Senator Heidepriem—a moderate Republican—sought to downplay partisan politics within the seven-member committee. "My view is that most of the things that state legislatures deal with really shouldn't be partisan. I felt like the Republican party tended to reject the Democrats' agenda automatically and *in toto* without thinking. My view was that we could pick and choose a number of their ideas that were actually good, blend them with our own, get Democrat votes, and actually have some unifying elements in the process instead of the sort of acrimony that I think tends to make the public sick" of politics. As chairman, Heidepriem tried to develop a leadership style that emphasized fairness and gave room to minority (in this case, Democrat) initiatives and concerns: "It was important to me that minority members of the committee did not feel that their bills were getting shot down just because they were in the minority."

HEIDEPRIEM ON ABORTION

Throughout his political career, Heidepriem's position on the abortion issue was no secret: he considered himself "pro-choice." "I believe there are circumstances where to abort or not should be left to a woman, her physician, and her God," he told the *Pierre Capitol Journal* in 1991. "My view is that there is no perfect answer," Heidepriem explains, "but I've read *Roe v. Wade* a number of times and I'm amazed at how close [Justice Harry] Blackmun gets it right." Heidepriem's views on abortion reflected those of his father—another Republican in favor of abortion rights—and his sister, Nikki Heidepriem, a Washington political consultant of liberal-feminist leanings actively involved in the work of the National Abortion Rights Action League (NARAL). "Nikki was a Republican until the party abandoned women in the 1980 platform," adds Heidepriem.

Heidepriem says he felt anchored in the "pro-choice" position, but as a legislator, he—unlike his sister—never stressed the abortion issue. "I've tried to avoid it," Heidepriem admits. "I've probably done everything I could to get out of the way of it. The only time I address it is when the question's put to me squarely, and then I'll answer it. But I would just as soon not talk about it; I don't like to think about it."

Over time, Senator Heidepriem learned that that wasn't always possible. His large, rural district, which spanned the four central counties of South Dakota's James River Valley—an area Heidepriem describes as "about five times the size of Rhode Island but with less than 20,000 people—contained the highest concentration of antiabortion organizations in the state: eight in 1991. Heidepriem believed that many, if not most, of his constituents opposed abortion as did a large number of South Dakota residents. A series of statewide polls taken for Democratic candidates in the 1990 election showed that, on average, approximately 50 percent of South Dakotans believed abortion should never be permitted or permitted only in cases of rape, incest, or "danger to the mother's life."

From the start of his legislative career, Heidepriem felt pressure from his colleagues to take a stand against abortion. Heidepriem recalls an incident in 1984 where the lieutenant governor, the majority leader, and another prominent member of the South Dakota House of Representatives called him into the House chamber after a debate on an abortion bill sponsored by the majority leader. According to Heidepriem, the three men—considered the pillars of the South Dakota Republican establishment—warned him: "Look, we think you have a very promising future in politics. But we want you to know that abortion is one issue you can't straddle the fence on, and we hope we can count on you to be in the pro-life category."

Abortion was "very much an issue" in Heidepriem's 1986 campaign for the Republican nomination for U.S. Congress.[2] (Heidepriem was just twenty-nine years old at the time.) That year, the controversy surrounding President Reagan's enthusiastic support for a "Human Life Amendment" to the U.S. Constitution stating that "life begins at conception" trickled down to the South Dakota Republican primary. Heidepriem found himself the only candidate in the primary field opposed to the amendment. "It ended up being sort of a pivotal issue in the campaign," Heidepriem reflects. "I ran a very aggressive, knock-on-doors type of campaign, and I had only two people express to me their hope that I was pro-choice, and many on the other side." According to Heidepriem, one of his anti-abortion opponents, Dale Bell, "spent about forty thousand dollars in the last two weeks [of the primary] telling the state that I was the only one who didn't [support the Human Life Amendment]. Seventeen days out and we were dead even, and his ads just demolished us." Bell won the Republican primary with 46 percent of the vote, versus 29 percent for Heidepriem.

During Heidepriem's four campaigns for the state legislature, however, abortion rarely became a dominant issue. "Aside from questions at forums and occasional letters to the editor urging my retirement," Heidepriem explains, "no great waves of opposition had been generated"—an outcome Heidepriem attributes to "the lack of a legislative vehicle to serve as a focus for the emotion generated by the issue."

ABORTION IN SOUTH DAKOTA

At the time of Heidepriem's tenure in the Senate, South Dakota was one of an increasing number of states where an abortion, although legal, was extremely difficult to obtain. In the years after the Supreme Court handed down its landmark *Roe v. Wade* decision legalizing abortion nationwide in 1973, just two physicians dared to acknowledge that they performed abortions in the state: Dr. Ben Munson provided services in Rapid City, a town on the west side of the state with a population of about 55,000; and Dr. Buck Williams practiced in Sioux Falls, South Dakota's largest city—approximate population 100,000—located in the state's southeastern corner. In 1990, Munson retired, leaving Williams as the sole physician providing abortion services in a state with a total population of almost 700,000.

In the early 1980s, when both Munson and Williams were in practice, the number of abortions performed in South Dakota peaked at an average of 1,150 to 1,250 abortions per year. The number of abortions declined annually in the 1980s—while increasing in the United States as a whole—and dropped off significantly when Munson retired in 1990. From 1980 to 1987, South Dakota experienced a greater decline in the number of abortions performed than any other state in the country: 38.9 percent versus the national average decline of 8.2 percent.[3] By 1991, with only Dr. Williams performing abortions (Williams limited his practice to the first three months, or trimester, of pregnancy), the number dwindled to 900[4]—the lowest per capita number of abortions performed in any state in the United States.

The paucity of abortion services in South Dakota may have been related to the state's long-standing antiabortion stance. Abortion was outlawed in South Dakota in 1890, and the state had only legalized abortion when compelled to by federal statute under *Roe v. Wade*. Furthermore, although the 1973 South Dakota Codified Laws enacted *Roe*'s provisions in Section 34-23A, "Performance of Abortions," the following "trigger" clause was added: "this chapter is repealed on that specific date upon which the states are given exclusive authority to regulate abortion." Only nine other states included this kind of antiabortion language within their laws legalizing abortion after *Roe*.[5]

During his three terms in the South Dakota House of Representatives, Heidepriem witnessed a few attempts—each one unsuccessful—to alter the state's law on abortion. In the mid-to-late 1980s, two House bills were filed: one would have made it possible for a court to create a "guardian" of the fetus, where the guardian—someone other than the pregnant woman—would have the right to exercise judgment about whether to terminate the pregnancy; the other would have required parental consent for a minor seeking an abortion.[6] Heidepriem opposed both bills. Neither bill made it through the legislature.

In 1990, South Dakota Right to Life (RTL), a state chapter of the antiabortion National Right to Life Committee, introduced a bill that would recriminalize abortion in South Dakota in the event that the Supreme Court chose to return to the states the authority to regulate abortion. South Dakota RTL feared that the state's existing "trigger law" contained loopholes and needed stiffening. During the 1990 state legislative session, high-powered South Dakota lobbyist Jeremiah Murphy met with Senator Heidepriem on behalf of RTL to discuss the bill. Heidepriem was able to con-

vince Murphy that the provisions of the RTL bill were already covered by the state's existing trigger law. Ultimately, RTL elected to pull the bill, but it was not the last time Heidepriem would face the powerful antiabortion lobby.

A TEST CASE

In 1990 and 1991, the National Right to Life Committee continued its efforts to enact antiabortion statutes at the state level, hoping to design a bill that would present a desirable vehicle for overturning *Roe v. Wade*, as many anticipated the Supreme Court would soon do. By 1990, the RTL antiabortion bill of choice was a highly restrictive measure that aimed to ban abortion "as a means of birth control." In 1990 and 1991, this bill was introduced in several states, including Minnesota, Utah, Alabama, Mississippi, Idaho, and Louisiana. The bill was able to make it through the Idaho legislature in 1990 but was vetoed by Governor Andrus. In early 1991, both Louisiana and Utah passed the RTL bill.[7] By August of that year, Louisiana's statute had been declared unconstitutional at the district court level, and the state showed no shyness in continuing its appeals through the court system until the statute could be heard by the Supreme Court. Utah's legislative leaders and governor, on the other hand, prevented their antiabortion law from taking effect in 1991 until the Supreme Court ruled on the constitutionality of Louisiana's statute.

Inspired by November 1990 election surveys showing that a majority of the South Dakota House of Representatives opposed abortion, RTL viewed the state as fertile territory for its antiabortion campaign. By December, 1990, RTL was ready to introduce its model statute prohibiting abortion "as a means of birth control" in South Dakota. RTL had clearly been encouraged by the *Webster* decision: Section 5 of the RTL bill stated its intent to "reasonably and constitutionally . . . regulate abortion in accor-

dance with the current abortion jurisprudence of the majority of justices of the
United States Supreme Court,'' adding that
''the state's compelling interest in unborn
life throughout pregnancy justifies preventing the use of abortion as another means
of birth control.'' The bill defined abortion
as the ''use or prescription of any instrument, medicine, drug, or any other substance or device to terminate the pregnancy
of a woman known to be pregnant with an
intention other than to increase the probability of a live birth, to preserve the life or
health of the child after live birth, or to remove a dead, unborn child.''[8]

If made law, RTL's bill would outlaw all
abortions in South Dakota except where a
mother's health was endangered by her
pregnancy; when a ''medical judgment was
made that the child, if allowed to be born,
would have profound and irremediable
physical or mental disabilities''; or in cases
of rape or incest,[9] if the event had been reported within one week of its occurrence.
Under the proposed legislation, persons
performing or attempting to perform an
abortion would be subject to civil fines of
$10,000 for a first ''offense,'' $50,000 for
a second, $100,000 for a third, and in excess
of $100,000 for the fourth or more. No fine
would be assessed against the woman seeking the abortion, nor against persons assisting in the abortion, such as nurses and
office staff. The state attorney general,
county prosecutors, the pregnant woman,
parents of a minor, and the father of the
unborn child would all be able to bring legal
action under the proposal.

With the freshly-drafted antiabortion bill
in hand, Washington-based lawyer Burke
Balch, state legislative director of National
RTL, flew to South Dakota in late 1990 to
meet with several legislators to garner sup-
port for the measure. On December 27,
Balch, accompanied by South Dakota RTL
lobbyist Lori Engel, sought out Scott
Heidepriem at his law office in Miller,
South Dakota. Heidepriem recalls that

Balch and Engel were very excited about
the possibilities for their new bill and for a
few hours put on ''quite a road show'' to
obtain his endorsement. ''Regardless of
how you felt in the past,'' the RTL representatives told Heidepriem, ''we don't think
you support abortion as a means of birth
control.'' Heidepriem read the proposed
legislation on the spot, noting to Balch that
it was unconstitutional according to current
Supreme Court jurisprudence. Balch agreed
and added that it would be declared unconstitutional at both the district and circuit levels on its way up to the Supreme Court.
However, Balch explained that, when drafting the bill, he felt encouraged by the recent
writings of Supreme Court Justice Sandra
Day O'Connor, whose opinions after *Webster* seemed to reaffirm her belief that the
state's ''compelling interest'' in the life of
a fetus extended from conception to birth.
Balch took it as a sign that Justice O'Connor—whom many considered a swing vote
on the abortion issue—would vote to sustain
the South Dakota antiabortion bill as a
proper expression of a state's compelling
interest. Heidepriem was unconvinced. In
response, Heidepriem informed both RTL
representatives that he was ''not supporting
legal experimentation with taxpayer's dollars.'' The meeting ended cordially, but
without Heidepriem's endorsement of the
bill.

Evidently, Balch and Engel had better
luck with other lawmakers. When the 1991
legislative session opened on January 16,
1991, Rep. Harvey Krautschun (R-Spearfish) introduced RTL's antiabortion bill in
the seventy member South Dakota House
of Representatives with twenty-five House
co-sponsors, and twelve of the state's thirty-
five senators were already on board. Given
the large, bipartisan group of sponsors, passage of the bill in the House was virtually
assured. As Heidepriem puts it, ''the question was not whether it would pass [the
House], but by how wide a margin.''

CONTROVERSY

House Speaker Jim Hood (R-Spearfish) assigned the bill—now known as HB 1126—to the House Judiciary Committee for its first hearing on January 31, 1991. Supporters of HB 1126 saw it as a compromise bill, a reasonable and moderate alternative to a complete ban on abortions. "This bill is designed to pass constitutional muster," declared Rep. Krautschun. Senator Richard Bellatti (R-Sioux Falls), the prime Senate sponsor of the bill, agreed. "We've got to be realistic," said Bellatti. "It's unreal to assume that we're going to have a 'human life' amendment."[10]

Several opponents of HB 1126, including Senate Majority Leader George Shanard (R-Mitchell), contended that the bill was a costly and unconstitutional violation of a woman's right to privacy. "I question some of the provisions and practicality of enforcing the law," Shanard stated.[11] Supporters of the bill agreed that it would test the Constitution, but argued, "it's worth the price." "The time has come to do what you think is right, and I think it's right," said Senator Bellatti. "I'm ready to take the consequences."[12]

Given the explosive potential of a bill that would outlaw most abortions, legislators braced themselves for a political firestorm. State Rep. Mary Edelin (R-Vermillion) lamented that the bill would split legislators for the rest of the session: "It's just too bad. . . . People will be divided all session over this, and it will carry over to almost every other proposal. . . . You can't keep it from becoming emotional, and you can't keep it from dividing all of us."[13] House Majority Leader Jerry Lammers (R-Madison) concurred. "It's a hot one," Rep. Lammers said. "You have to put on your flak jacket, because people come at you from both sides. I'm sure it will be very divisive and the debate will be intense." In response, Rep. Marie Ingalls (R-Mud Butte)—a co-sponsor of the bill—sought to portray the issue as a straightforward one.

"It's an issue we vote our constituency, we vote the way people back home want us to vote," Ingalls said.[14]

A POSITION OF POWER

As chairman of the Senate judiciary Committee and the Senate's only lawyer, Heidepriem was poised to play an influential role in the success or failure of HB 1126. One of just ten Senate committees, the Judiciary Committee was charged with handling the second largest number of bills in the legislature, and it was likely to be the next stop for the antiabortion bill if it passed the House as expected. As judiciary chair, Heidepriem would have complete power over the committee hearings on the bill, including the authority to schedule the hearings, determine their length and content, and decide when to call for a vote on the bill.

Heidepriem's power over the fate of the bill was restrained somewhat by South Dakota's "smokeout" rule, which enabled lawmakers to force a floor vote on a bill in the full Senate (or House) if the committee voted to table it. In the Senate, twelve of the thirty-five senators (one-third of the chamber) would be required to vote for the smokeout in order to get the bill out of committee. Then, eighteen senators—a simple majority—would have to vote to place the bill on the calendar for floor debate. The smokeout procedure was frequently used for bills dealing with highly partisan issues since both parties claimed at least one-third of the seats in both chambers. At the same time, legislative rules in South Dakota mandated that the session end in no more than forty days, and the entire smokeout procedure could take up to six days. Thus, Chairman Heidepriem would always have the option to hold off a committee vote long enough to make it impossible for senators to use the smokeout rule without a suspension of the rules, which would require a tough-to-obtain two-thirds majority vote in the full Senate.

Although state legislative rules required that a bill be posted before its hearing, there was no rule requiring the committee to post the date and time of its vote. As a result, says Heidepriem, "committee chairs tend to hold controversial bills until the hottest-tempered adversaries have left town, and then they dispose of them." However, Heidepriem adds, "the chairs generally try to gauge the amount of public interest in any question and then attempt to accommodate that interest, regardless of how they feel about the bill." For his part, Chairman Heidepriem says, "I'd usually wait until we had collected a number of [bills]—say, when ten or fifteen had been assigned to us—then, depending on time and the number of hearings I had, I would try to group the bills by subject matter so that people would not have to come twice. We tried hard to accommodate everyone."

TAKING A STAND

Just two days after the HB 1126 was introduced in the House, Heidepriem came out publicly against the bill. "I applaud the Right to Life movement for what they're trying to accomplish," Heidepriem told the *Aberdeen American News*, "but there is no question about the constitutionality of this proposal. The idea as I understand it would be unconstitutional." "If this bill passes," Heidepriem warned, "it will embroil South Dakota in legal turmoil for years to come." Heidepriem speculated that the law would inevitably be challenged by a woman seeking a legal abortion, and the ensuing court battles would in all likelihood continue until the law could be heard by the U.S. Supreme Court. In the process, Heidepriem estimated, the state would amass court fees from $700,000 to $1 million—even more if the state was required to pay for the woman's legal expenses. "There are plenty of states wealthier than South Dakota able to spread the cost of that legal creativity upon their taxpayers in a way that's less burdensome," argued Heidepriem, noting that

South Dakota typically generated less than $500 million dollars in taxes each year, and the state legislature was required by law to balance the budget annually with a mandated reserve.[15]

Heidepriem's position on the bill was bolstered by state attorney general Mark Barnett, who privately agreed that his office probably could not absorb the costs of a Supreme Court challenge in its $7 million budget.[16] But Rep. Lammers contended that it was premature to worry about the legal costs. "I rather suspect there are all kinds of experts who would come to the rescue of South Dakota and offer their service for free. . . . What we do here may be very important in the history of not only the state but the land."[17] Besides, Lammers maintained, a "lawsuit won't cost anything unless the state loses."[18] Meanwhile, supporters of the bill argued that it was not intended to become a test case in the federal courts. "We strongly believe this is a South Dakota issue, and we'll do everything we can to keep it that way," said lobbyist Lori Engel, apparently hoping to blunt the national attention the issue would receive from NARAL, the National Organization for Women, Republicans for Choice, and other national abortion rights organizations.[19]

In an opinion piece published in the *Faulk County Record* on January 30—one day before the scheduled House Judiciary Committee hearing on HB 1126—Heidepriem made it clear to his constituents that he opposed the bill. "I believe this bill is a serious mistake," Heidepriem wrote. "I cannot justify expending nearly one million dollars for a lawsuit that is an exercise in legal creativity." Heidepriem pointed to the antiabortion bill in Utah, which the governor had signed just five days earlier. "Opponents have pledged to challenge it [the Utah law] all the way to the U.S. Supreme Court. South Dakotans, both for and against legal abortion, should wait for the outcome."

WHAT HAPPENED IN THE HOUSE

On Thursday, January 31, the thirteen-member House Judiciary Committee began its deliberations on HB 1126. Almost two hundred spectators packed the committee room to witness and participate in the hearing. Although it was expected that the panel would easily approve the bill, committee discussion was nonetheless charged with emotion. Throughout the hour-long debate, committee members wrangled over the extent to which *Webster* allowed states the right to regulate abortion. Abortion opponents argued that *Webster* had given states "the right to limit abortion and a compelling interest in the life of the unborn," while abortion rights supporters countered that no majority in *Webster* had stated that there was a compelling interest in fetal viability throughout the pregnancy.[20] On February 5, the House Judiciary Committee approved HB 1126 by a vote of 8–5 and sent it to the full House with minor amendments, setting the stage for what promised to be a heated debate on the House floor.

Two days later—February 7—the mass of spectators returned to the House gallery to witness the floor debates on HB 1126. Hundreds of antiabortion activists wearing 'I'm for Life' buttons packed the room as a coalition of five abortion rights groups lobbied representatives behind the scenes. Most expected that the Republican-dominated House would vote to advance the measure to the Senate. (Republicans controlled the House forty-five to twenty-five and men outnumbered women fifty-five to fifteen.)

The spirited House debate lasted about ninety minutes. During the hearing, several amendments to HB 1126 were proposed on the House floor, including a requirement that the South Dakota Department of Health give out free contraceptives at a cost of $807,000; a clause that would abolish the state's death penalty; a plan that would have referred the bill to a public referendum; and a move to set aside $1 million to finance the legal costs involved in defending the bill's constitutionality.[21] None of the amendments was successful.

The House hearing on HB 1126 culminated in a larger-than-predicted margin of victory for the antiabortion bill: 52–18 in favor of the legislation. The overwhelming support in the House was a surprise, with seventeen of the fifty-two "yes" votes coming from representatives who had responded in the 1990 preelection survey that the current law on abortion in South Dakota should not be changed.

One day after the House vote (February 8), Lieutenant Governor Walter Dale Miller assigned HB 1126 to the Senate Judiciary Committee, where Chairman Heidepriem would preside over the bill's next hearing on the bill.[22] Senator Bellatti, the prime Senate sponsor of HB 1126, wasted no time in seeking out Heidepriem on the Senate floor. According to Heidepriem, Bellatti said, "Look, I hope the day will come that I can support you for governor. I consider you a good friend. All I ask is that you be fair with us in scheduling the hearing." Heidepriem pledged his fairness, promising not to manipulate the rule to impede the bill's chance to pass.

Meanwhile, Republican Governor George Mickelson issued a public statement declaring that he "favor[ed] the basic philosophy" of the antiabortion bill and signaled his intention to sign the measure into law if it passed the legislature.[23] Coupled with the bill's overwhelming success in the House, the governor's statement sent shock waves through the ranks of abortion rights activists across the state while adding momentum to an already well-organized antiabortion lobby. The phone calls and letters that had been trickling into senators' offices just one week earlier multiplied in numbers with each passing day as constituents came to grasp the enhanced possibility that abortion could become illegal in South Dakota.

In light of the 52–18 victory in the House, Alcester Democrat and Senate Minority

Leader Roger McKellips—who had once predicted that a strong antiabortion proposal would be defeated in the Senate—stated: "Now I think it's going to be close. It may pass."[24] In 1991, Republicans held a one vote advantage in the Senate (18–17) and men outnumbered women twenty-four to eleven. Abortion opponents believed they had at least the minimum eighteen votes for Senate passage and possibly as many as twenty-one. Rick Hauffe, the South Dakota Democratic party's legislative director, predicted that the bill would be decided by one vote in the Senate.

PUTTING ON THE BRAKES

Senator Heidepriem was alarmed by the speed with which the bill barreled through the House. "It was just rolling," Heidepriem recalls. "It was just going and it was going to pass, I thought, unless some people just tried to slow it down a little and get people to think about it." When his office began receiving twenty letters and forty phone messages each day—most in favor of the bill—Heidepriem decided "it was time for me to do what I could to slow the train down a little."

Shortly after the bill passed the House, Heidepriem made public remarks—run widely in the South Dakota press—reiterating his opposition to the bill. "I'm against the bill because it is certain to cost huge amounts of money for no useful purpose," Heidepriem stated. "Once Utah passed their law, they took away any possible reasons for passing an unconstitutional law. Utah's law will be heard before ours. What South Dakota is allowed on abortions will not be determined by our legislation but Utah's legislation."

Several Republican senators were noticeably cool to Heidepriem after reading his comments in the *Pierre Capitol Journal*. Heidepriem was approached by Senator Harold Halverson (R-Milbank), vice chairman in the Judiciary Committee and Senate president pro tempore. "I saw your picture in the paper," Halverson said, with pointed understatement. To Heidepriem, it was a clear indication that his Republican colleagues were less than pleased that he was actively trying to stop the antiabortion bill. But, Heidepriem recalls, "I didn't think that I could help but announce my feelings about the issue and about the bill. . . . It was one of those things where, going in, we had to get every single undecided vote, and we knew that."

The bill came over to the Senate Judiciary Committee on February 8. Now Chairman Heidepriem was in a position to control when and how the bill would be reviewed. First, Heidepriem wanted the hearing delayed to avert what he described as a "steamroller effect." "I routinely did that with emotional issues," Heidepriem explains. "I didn't want the Senate to make a decision in this crazed atmosphere. I think that's not the proper temperament in which to legislate."

In setting the date of the hearing on HB 1126, Heidepriem sought advice from both supporters and opponents of the bill. "Both [sides] indicated that they might have national people coming in [for the hearing], and I felt that it was necessary to set the day early so that people could make their plans," explains Heidepriem. "I wanted to let both sides contact whomever they wanted to bring in plenty enough time so that no one said, 'I didn't have notice. I couldn't get in.'" According to Heidepriem, opponents of HB 1126 wanted the hearing to be held "as late as possible": "Pro-choice people who were organizing against the bill felt that the longer they had, the better, because they thought that it was a senseless move that would sink in, that people would respond." "They would have been happy if I had tried to use the rules to thwart it," Heidepriem adds.

On the supporting side, Heidepriem consulted with Bellatti, Engel, and former legislator Ed Glasgow, chief lobbyist for the antiabortion Family Values Coalition.

Heidepriem requested that the three agree upon a date for the hearing, but according to Heidepriem, they were unable to.[25] Ultimately, Heidepriem chose to schedule the hearing for Friday, February 22—exactly two weeks after the bill arrived on his desk. For Heidepriem, that date was "later than Lori wanted it and before Ed wanted it, but in plenty of time for them to exhaust their supply of maneuvers." Heidepriem adds that, at the time the decision was made, neither side showed "even a slight expression of disappointment at the scheduling of the hearing."

As judiciary chair, Heidepriem also had the option of setting the committee vote late enough in the session to make a smokeout—which would force a floor vote in the full Senate if the bill were to fail in committee—virtually impossible.[26] However, Heidepriem chose to require that committee members vote immediately after testimony was completed on the day of the committee hearing. "The Right to Lifers were up against it in terms of time," Heidepriem recalls, "so I said to them, 'I will insist that the committee act in such a way that you aren't denied the chance to use those [smokeout] procedures.'" By setting the vote for the day of the committee hearing—February 22, a full seven business days prior to the mandated last day of the legislative session—Heidepriem allowed supporters of HB 1126 ample time to smoke out the bill if it failed in committee. At the time, Heidepriem felt the committee had a "duty"—given the intense interest in the bill—to decide its vote at that time. "I thought it was important to make the decision in front of the people who care about the question," Heidepriem explains.

PRESSURE BUILDS

As the Senate Judiciary Committee hearing on HB 1126 approached, lobbying activity intensified on all sides. By mid-February, abortion rights groups, including Planned Parenthood and NARAL, were spending thousands of dollars on a barrage of newspaper and broadcast advertisements, hoping to gain ground lost in the House to the well-organized RTL lobby. Meanwhile, South Dakota RTL sought to continue its efforts to mobilize citizens on an even larger scale in the state. Republican and Democratic senators alike were deluged with calls, letters, photographs of aborted fetuses, baby rattles, and plastic fetuses wrapped in pink and blue baby blankets. Several lawmakers reported receiving abusive telephone calls and obscenities written in black crayon on their front doors. The home of one Judiciary Committee member, Senate Majority Leader George Shanard, was vandalized with "baby killer" spray painted in large black letters.

Heidepriem's influential position as chairman of the Senate Judiciary Committee ensured that he would bear the brunt of the pressure. "I don't remember any issue where the lobbying has been this intense during my time in politics," says Heidepriem. By mid-February—a week prior to his committee hearing—Heidepriem's Senate office was receiving up to one thousand letters and phone calls per day, many from within his district but most from outside his district and outside the state. Death threats were leveled against Heidepriem and his family. (At the time, Heidepriem had one three-year-old son, and his wife, Susan, was eight months pregnant.) "Particularly memorable," recalls Heidepriem, "was one full-color, bloodbath photo bearing a Rapid City postmark with this inscription: 'Senator, since you like killing so much, take a look at this, and show it to your pregnant wife.'" The pressure led Heidepriem's family to decide, in consultation with law enforcement officials, to send Heidepriem's wife and son to an undisclosed out-of-state location until the matter was concluded. "I felt better knowing that they were somewhere safe," Heidepriem explains. "My wife is a very strong person, but I would have worried a lot more, and it would have added a whole layer of anxiety.''

After an initial antiabortion lead, Heidepriem's mail was split evenly between those for and against the bill. While many of the messages for the senator insinuated that his political future could be in doubt if he took the "wrong" stance on the abortion bill, Heidepriem told the *Pierre Capitol Journal* that the pressure would not change his mind: "There isn't a higher office I want badly enough to cause me to act inconsistently with what I believe is right."[27] Nevertheless, Heidepriem conceded that both the pressure and the emotional intensity of the abortion issue were draining. "People have lost the willingness to respect an opposing point of view. That's what's missing here," said Heidepriem. "It's so frustrating because this process is something I care deeply about. It's an issue that accomplishes nothing positive and has the potential of removing myself and other worthy, thoughtful people from the process. And for what, for what?"

Meanwhile, Heidepriem was lobbied to kill the bill in committee by state representatives who had voted earlier for the measure in the House. It may have been politically safer, Heidepriem told the *Sioux Falls Argus Leader*, for some House members who were "pro-choice" but from antiabortion districts to vote "yes" on the bill and then lobby against its passage in the Senate. "Sure there's politics involved," Heidepriem admitted candidly. "There's a temptation to say, 'Why not?' That temptation is greater in the house of origin."[28]

HEIDEPRIEM'S STRATEGY

As both sides of the abortion debate anxiously awaited the Senate Judiciary Committee hearing on HB 1126, Heidepriem did some lobbying of his own within the committee. Heidepriem approached individually each of his six colleagues—three Republicans and three Democrats—on the Judiciary Committee in order to feel out their positions on the bill and explain his objections to it. As the Senate's only lawyer in 1991, Heidepriem says he "felt a duty to give them [his] best legal read on the question in an objective way."

Heidepriem sought out committee members on the Senate floor and at the hospitality rooms at the Ramkota River Centre, where senators would discuss informally the issues surrounding the 1991 legislative session— namely, the abortion bill. One-on-one, Heidepriem explained to his colleagues that he believed HB 1126 was unconstitutional and would be held so by the federal district court in Pierre, South Dakota's capital. Heidepriem was confident that, on appeal, the district court decision would be sustained by the eighth circuit court in St. Paul. Thus, Heidepriem contended, the state would need to go all the way up to the Supreme Court and ask it to change its mind on *Roe v. Wade*. Heidepriem explained that, even if that route were taken, a decision would come no quicker for South Dakota than for Utah or Louisiana, which had presented similar questions to the Court. "There was absolutely no sense in doing this," Heidepriem told his colleagues, "unless you wanted to potentially pay a million dollars for a symbolic statement and a secondary opinion from the Supreme Court. But you aren't going to change the policy by doing this. It's not possible."

Given the nature of the bill, Heidepriem endeavored to involve in these discussions key women in the lives of his male colleagues. (Two women, Senate Minority Whip Karen Muenster [D-Sioux Falls] and Freshman Senator Roberta Rasmussen [D-Hurley], also sat on the Senate Judiciary Committee.) For example, Heidepriem spoke frequently with Senators George Shanard and Jim Emery (R-Custer), two potential swing votes on the committee. "When Neva and George Shanard were together, I would begin the conversation with Neva," Heidepriem explains. (Heidepriem learned that Neva Shanard did not like the bill.) "When Elaine and Jim Emery were together, I would begin the conversation with Elaine, and I would engage her on the [abortion] question. I would try to steer the conversation [to the abortion] by saying: 'Isn't it interesting that, here we are, never having to face this question, but we're deciding it for people like Elaine, or you Neva, or my wife Susan?'"

If Heidepriem was unable to ascertain a male committee member's position on the bill, he sought out the position of his colleague's wife. For example, Senator Emery took Heidepriem up on his offer to discuss the bill with him. During what turned out to be a long, private conversation, Emery never revealed his position on the bill. Later, on the floor of the Senate, Heidepriem approached Emery and asked him if he had any questions about their previous conversation. Emery did not, so Heidepriem asked how his wife, Elaine Emery, felt about the bill. Emery responded that Elaine did not like the bill. Feeling hopeful, Heidepriem left it at that: "I think that Elaine Emery, aside from being a very impressive person, has a very good relationship with her husband. I thought to myself: 'We are in good shape there.'"

By the time of the hearing, only three members of the Senate Judiciary Committee had publicly stated a clear position on HB 1126. Heidepriem and Shanard[29] had openly opposed the bill, while Halverson had pledged his wholehearted support.[30] On February 21, Roberta Rasmussen—a first-term legislator from a predominantly anti-abortion district—suggested that she was leaning against the bill for constitutional reasons. Jim Emery and Democrats Karen Muenster and Paul Symens (Amherst) refused to say how they would vote. Muenster had answered the preelection abortion survey by stating that in most cases a woman should have the right to an abortion. Although a poll commissioned by Muenster in 1990 showed that 70 percent of her constituents supported abortion rights, Muenster said she feared reprisals against her family if she talked about her vote.[31] Sy-

mens—like the majority of his constituents—was known to oppose abortion, but he had expressed reservations about the bill in its current form.[32] However, Symens told the *Aberdeen American News*, "I don't know how it will come out in the Senate. It will be close. I haven't counted votes, but my gut feeling is it will pass."[33]

Publicly, Heidepriem said he was uncertain how his committee would vote on the bill: "I think most legislators are undecided about most bills until they hear the testimony," Heidepriem told the *Pierre Capital Journal* on February 11. Privately, Heidepriem guessed that Muenster and Rasmussen would join Shanard and him in voting against the bill, thus defeating the measure 4-3. Heidepriem says he believed that Symens—a Baptist fundamentalist—would vote for the bill because of his strong religious convictions and the pressure he was receiving from his church.

While Heidepriem's vote on HB 1126 was certain to be "no," politically, it would not be an easy vote for him to make. In an interview published in the *Sioux Falls Argus Leader* the day before the Senate Judiciary Committee hearing, Heidepriem described his situation: "Every now and then these things pop up, and you stare into your open political grave. Then you vote." "That's exactly how I felt," Heidepriem recalls. "I had to say, 'Well, if it all ends here, is this still what you want to do?'" In deciding how to vote on the bill, Heidepriem recalls, "I ultimately had just to ask myself what I thought the proper policy was for the state, and then having decided that issue in the negative on the bill, I had to decide whether I had any business taking that view in light of what I perceived to be overwhelming support for the bill in my rural district. It was never even a close question for me."

THE SENATE JUDICIARY COMMITTEE HEARING

At 10 A.M. on Friday, February 22, Heidepriem called the Senate Judiciary

Committee to order as three hundred spectators squeezed into Room 412 of the capital building. Most attendees were abortion opponents with large "South Dakotans For Life" signs strapped to their bodies. A smaller group of abortion rights advocates donned purple ribbons to express their opposition to the bill.

Heidepriem opened the hearings with a warning that he would not tolerate any disruption of the proceedings, noting that he had ordered a full contingent of the South Dakota National Guard and capitol police to clear the room if necessary. Heidepriem then offered both sides of the abortion debate an expanded, but fixed, format for the hearing. Both proponents and opponents of HB 1126 would be granted one hour of testimony and ten minutes of rebuttal time, followed by ten minutes from general commentators, including a law expert chosen by Heidepriem to address constitutionality issues. Heidepriem would then close the discussion and call for a vote in the committee. Throughout the hearing, committee members would be permitted to ask brief questions.

Heidepriem arranged for Professor David Day of the University of South Dakota Law School to appear as a commentator at the hearing to address the constitutionality issues surrounding the bill. Initially, Heidepriem had requested that Attorney General Mark Barnett address the hearing, but Barnett felt it was inappropriate for him to testify, since he would have to defend the bill in court if it passed the legislature. Long-time South Dakota lobbyist Jeremiah Murphy—considered by many the most influential lobbyist in the state—was highly critical of the decision to invite Day, since Heidepriem was aware that the law professor was not favorably disposed to the bill.

Heidepriem also decided to allow the proponents of the bill to show a film that would provide viewers with a picture of a fetus prior to an abortion. Opponents of the bill begged Heidepriem—who had not seen the film—not to let it to be shown during the hearing. However, Lori Engel assured Heidepriem that the presentation would be in good taste (no bloody fetuses). Although Heidepriem believed that the film was not "directly on point about the bill," he thought it was fair to let the proponents screen it. "A judge clearly wouldn't have allowed it as relevant evidence, but this wasn't a courtroom," Heidepriem explains. "I made a calculation that you should always err on the side of allowing stuff like that because the price you pay for denying them access is oftentimes greater. And I frankly wanted opportunities to show them that I wanted to be fair about it."

Proponents of HB 1126 testified first, opening with the RTL film. Dr. Calvin Anderson of Sioux Falls screened the video, which depicted what he said was an eight-week-old fetus[34] moving and gesturing in response to external stimulation. "Ladies and gentlemen, that fetus is a prime candidate for an abortion," Anderson said. "I rest my case." Two other physicians testified as well, including the bills' Senate sponsor, Dr. Richard Bellatti—a Sioux Falls anesthesiologist. Bellatti argued that the state had the power to prevent the killing of an unborn child: "You may not choose to kill your child. That makes a farce of choice. . . . Please remember that a life is a life, and abortion kills." Bellatti also addressed directly Heidepriem's stated objection to HB 1126: that the antiabortion legislation was unnecessary in South Dakota since similar bills from Utah and Louisiana would make it to the Supreme Court beforehand. "The Supreme Court has more discretion over its docket and may not accept the pending cases," Bellatti contended. "Thus it would be beneficial for a number of states to pass substantive prohibitions on abortions."

Lori Engel also took the stand to present abortion statistics in defense of the bill. Engel argued that from 1989–90, 1,846 abortions were performed and 100 percent of those were performed as a form of birth control.[35] The committee also heard from two lawyers, both of whom agreed—while conceding that bill would be held unconstitutional at the district and circuit court levels—that there was "a reasonable likelihood that HB 1126 would be held constitutional by the United States Supreme Court should it ever be presented to it for a decision." Both lawyers volunteered to argue the case for the state at no cost. The proponents' final witness, Jeremiah Murphy, asked the committee: "Which side of this fight would Jesus Christ be on if he were here today?" Murphy bet that Christ would vote "on the side of life."

Opponents of the bill were up next. Simon Heller, a lawyer for the American Civil Liberties Union in New York, testified that the bill would fail a constitutional test, which he said would prove expensive for the state. "The local district court in South Dakota will surely find it unconstitutional," said Heller. "You will be certain to lose this case not only in circuit court but in district court as well." Dr. Dean Madison, an obstetrician-gynecologist of Sioux Falls, told committee members of his experience treating women who had had illegal abortions before the 1973 *Roe v. Wade* decision. "There were unbelievable low-life scum out there who would abort these ladies," Madison recalled. "I wish you could pass a law that make abortions go away completely, but ladies and gentlemen, they will be done." Choking back tears, Tilly Black Bear—a Lakota woman from the Rose Bud Indian reservation—reminded the committee that "Indian women cannot access services as readily as privileged women, who are white women. We don't oftentimes have the means to make that trip to Minneapolis."

Several others testified about their personal and tragic experiences at the hands of illegal abortionists. NARAL's start witness was Emmy Award-winning actress Polly Bergen, who was made sterile by a pre-1973 illegal abortion that almost killed her. Bergen described how, as a young struggling actress, she had to borrow $300 to pay for an illegal abortion performed—without anesthesia—by a stranger on the kitchen table of a dark California apartment. Three days after her abortion, Bergen was found dying from loss of blood. "Because of that abortion," Bergen testified, "I was unable to do that which I wanted to do so badly, which was to deliver a child. That could happen to other women—that is, if they don't die." Bergen added: "I don't believe that anyone has the right to tell a woman that she must have an abortion, and I don't think it's right to tell a woman that she cannot have one. . . . No one should be able to make a law that would infringe on the freedom of men and women as to when they will have a family and how large that family will be. That is between them and their God."

Throughout the hearing, the committee remained somber and quiet, asking few questions as several witnesses broke into tears. Hours of wrenching testimony and the presence of hundreds of people demanding a specific result rendered the committee clearly uncomfortable.

After both sides had used up their allotted rebuttal time, Heidepriem closed the hearing and, as promised, called for committee action on the bill. First, Senator Halverson made a motion that the committee approve HB 1126. Several hundred disbelieving eyes stared in awe as Halverson's motion met with silence, failing for lack of a second. Not to be denied, Halverson made a second motion, this time requesting that the committee send the bill to the full Senate without recommendation. Once again, his motion failed for lack of a second. Senator Shanard then moved that the bill be laid on the table. That motion carried 6–1. Halverson was the only senator on the committee to vote against tabling the bill.

After nearly four hours of testimony, the committee took just five minutes, without discussion between members, to reject the bill. Few—Heidepriem included—had anticipated such a lop-sided result. "I was really surprised," recall Heidepriem. "I thought Symens would probably second it. I even thought Shanard would second it as a matter of courtesy. . . . I guess the hearing hardened everyone's position.

When asked later about their votes on the bill, all committee members except Symens acknowledge that their individual minds had been made up on the abortion issue well before the bill was introduced in the legislature. Even Emery—whose position on HB 1126 was unknown to the public before the committee vote—conceded that he simply "voted [his] belief" on the issue. "I don't think I sat and listened to the debate and went back and forth or anything like that," Emery reflects. "I think my mind was probably set before the session."

Symens, on the other hand, told Heidepriem after the vote that it was the toughest one he had cast in his time in politics. Symens says he was convinced that the bill had been poorly written and was basically unfair. "I couldn't see passing a law that would punish a doctor for an action that was asked of him by someone else who had made a decision." At the same time, adds Symens, "I did not necessarily like to have to vote that way because I . . . don't believe in abortion."

THE SMOKEOUT

Immediately after Friday's vote, supporters of HB 1126 began working to force the bill out of committee so that it could be debated in the full Senate before the 1991 legislative session ended seven business days later. A smokeout attempt was planned for the following Monday: "We want to wait until the committee testimony has aired on public TV so some more of the senators can see it," explained Engel. One-third of the Senate chamber, or twelve votes, would be required for the smokeout, and a majority of senators—eighteen votes, the same amount needed to pass the bill—would have to agree

to put the bill on the Senate calendar. Several senators, including Shanard—who voted against the bill in committee—speculated that even some senators opposing HB 1126 might still vote to place the bill on the calendar, just to give it a fair hearing.

Heidepriem, meanwhile, agonized over whether or not he should acquiesce to the pressure to bring the bill to a floor vote in the full Senate or use his influence as chairman to try to prevent the bill from being placed on the Senate calendar: "As chairman of the committee, I felt like I had to be fair to both sides even though I didn't have much respect for the theory behind the other side." However, Heidepriem adds, "I considered it an affront by the credibility of the Judiciary Committee that this bill would come out to the Senate floor after suffering a 6–1 defeat. I took the work of the committee very seriously, and thought the committee did an exceptional job in wading through it and thinking about it and withstood tremendous pressure to do what each of us thought was the right thing. So why go on with it?" Moreover, Heidepriem was firmly opposed to the bill: "It was just completely the wrong idea—the wrong way to go at a difficult problem. I thought it was demeaning." "I felt so strongly about it being a mistake for the state," Heidepriem adds, "that I think if everyone in my district had written me, urging me to vote for it, I still would have voted against it."

Several of Heidepriem's colleagues in the Senate informed him that they were being accused of using the process to defeat the bill. "They're just kicking the hell out of us at home," one senator told Heidepriem. "They're saying that we're afraid of the merits of this bill." Others told Heidepriem they felt a need in their districts to give the bill a public hearing. "That made some sense to me: the credibility of the legislature in allowing a broader forum and more discussion," says Heidepriem. Yet, Heidepriem recalls, "I was afraid it might pass. I thought it was dead even. It's not uncommon for people to vote one way on the committee and another on the floor.'' On the other hand, Heidepriem says, ''I was afraid if I tried to prevent it [the bill] from coming out and I failed, it had a better chance of passing.''

On Monday, February 25, supporters of the bill were able to smoke the bill out of Heidepriem's committee. Eighteen senators—thirteen Republican and five Democrats—stood up to be tallied in favor of the procedure. The number of senators supporting the smokeout was comfortably higher than the twelve votes needed for the procedure and identical to the eighteen votes necessary for the bill to pass the thirty-five-member Senate. Senator Heidepriem—who did not vote for the smokeout—downplayed the effect the eighteen Senate votes might have on the outcome of the bill. ''That means nothing positive or negative,'' Heidepriem said, pointing to Senator Emery, who voted against the bill at Friday's committee hearing but nonetheless stood in support of the smokeout. In order to get the bill on the calendar, Heidepriem noted, those eighteen senators would need to vote yet again. Still, Heidepriem realized, ''If they decide to cast a vote in favor of calendaring the bill, there is nothing I can do about it. And I feared that if—after having gone to them and asked, 'Please don't vote to put this thing on the calendar'—if I were to lose that procedural vote, I'd be weaker for the final vote on the bill.''

At that point, Heidepriem made a political calculation. ''I believed that the perception that the abortion bill was kept from the Senate floor by a procedural technicality was more damaging than to address it head on.'' Heidepriem thus decided to stand on the floor of the Senate and ask his colleagues to ''strike the not,'' thereby permitting a full Senate debate on HB 1126. The motion was carried 34–1 on Tuesday, February 26, and the bill was placed on the Senate calendar for further action that day.

Heidepriem says that he made this decision after Senator Shanard—who voted against the bill in the Judiciary Committee—urged him to bring the bill to the floor:

> I think probably the thing that tipped it for me was when the majority leader—who had hung in there and sat on the committee; never wins by very much; moderate Republican; strong supporter of mine; cares about the process—came to me and said, ''You know, I think you ought to do it. Otherwise, we're all going to look like we snuffed out democracy. It's not going to end unless we do this thing.'' Sort of like closure, I thought. We needed to achieve closure, and we wouldn't if we just let it stay there in the committee.

Having made that decision, Heidepriem admits he was not very happy with it. ''It sort of felt like a defeat. I wanted to run the committee in such a scrupulously fair way that both sides would rejoice at the end and say, 'Well, it's just really fair.' It wasn't to be; they were in this game to win.''

ON THE SENATE FLOOR

That afternoon—February 26—hundreds of spectators returned to the state capitol for a Senate hearing on HB 1126, jam-packing the gallery that overlooked the Senate chamber. No one was certain how the bill would fare in the full Senate, but most agreed the vote would be close—perhaps even decided by a one-vote margin. As a result, lobbying activity picked up tremendously. Even White House chief of Staff John Sunnunu lobbied Senators Emery and Symens—two potential swing votes—by telephone from Washington, D.C. According to Heidepriem, ''the mood in the Senate that day was that we had the power to decide once and for all whether abortion would be legal in South Dakota.''

The Senate debate was aired on television across the state. Senator Bellatti, the prime Senate sponsor of HB 1126, began the proceedings with an introduction that was later described by the *Sioux Falls Argus Leader* as ''The speech of his life.'' ''Abortion is a matter of life and death,'' Bellatti reminded his colleagues. "Current abortion laws sanction legalized murder. When a woman is pregnant, her rights are further limited by the life of the baby." In his floor speech, Bellatti also gave the first hint that some supporters of HB 1126 were annoyed at Heidepriem's scheduling of the hearings on the bill. "I'd like to apologize for any discomfort you might have had waiting for the hearing to take place," said Bellatti. "We introduced the bill on the first day of the session, and here we are on the thirty-fifth day."

When Bellatti finished, several other senators took to the floor to argue for and against HB 1126. One senator, Doris Miner [D-Gregory]—an ardent opponent of abortion—directed her floor remarks to Senator Symens, a potential swing vote on the bill. In a move that Heidepriem describes as "the low point in the debate," Miner read a note she claimed to have been handed to her by Symens' daughter, Stephanie, a legislative intern and a member of South Dakota Right to Life. According to Miner, Stephanie Symens was outraged that a penalty existed for the destruction of an eagle's egg but not for the termination of a human embryo. In her memo, Miner said, Symens "begged" Miner and other senators to "vote for those who can't" vote for the bill.[36]

When it was his turn on the floor, Heidepriem reiterated his position that the other antiabortion bills pending in states such as Utah and Louisiana would provide an abortion test in the Supreme Court, reminding the committee that "abortion will continue legally until and unless the U.S. Supreme Court changes its mind." Heidepriem pointed out that the bill "was drafted in Washington, D.C. It is part of the National Right to Life organization's national agenda." Thus, Heidepriem argued, "the whole question is whether this state wants to be a pawn in the national struggle between these forces." On a more personal level, Heidepriem explained that the birth of his first son three years before reaffirmed

his belief in reproductive rights for women. "I have a vivid memory of that day and that is of the incredible physical strength of a woman," Heidepriem said. "That made me think that decisions women make about reproduction are decisions some of us cannot understand." In closing Heidepriem emphasized, "I mean it when I tell you I stand here for life, for life, but not for this bill."

THE SENATE VOTE

Late in the day on February 26, the moment many had awaited since the session began had finally arrived: the Senate roll call on HB 1126. The roomful of onlookers was silent as, one by one, each of the thirty-five senators stated their votes. It was not until the very last senator voted that the fate of the HB 1126 became known. With seventeen in favor and eighteen opposed, HB 1126 failed on the Senate floor that day.

The vote cut across party lines. Of the seventeen "yes" votes, twelve were Republican and five were Democrat. Of the eighteen "no" votes, twelve were Democrat and six were Republican. Nine of the eleven women in the South Dakota Senate voted against the bill,[37] eight of the nine women voting against the bill were Democrats. Only one Democratic woman, Doris Miner, voted for the bill. Both Senate party leaders, Democrat Roger McKelliops and Republican George Shanard, opposed the bill. In addition, three senators—Democrats Red Allen and Roland Chicoine and Republican William Johnson—had said before the session that the current abortion law in South Dakota should not be changed but voted to change it under HB 1126.

According to Heidepriem, "no member of the Senate suggested that their vote on the bill was determined by anything other than their view of whether abortion should be regulated entirely by the state or the woman." Heidepriem attributes this to the work of Right to Life, which he argues "so successfully dominated the debate that anything short of a declaration of feeling on the issue would have been perceived all around as a dodge. The mail every senator received demanded not just an absence of equivocation, but the willingness to ignore the very significant cost and constitutional issues on the way to vote.'' In Heidepriem's view, ''arguments stating the fact that the state already had in place a statute which repealed legal abortion when the state was given the exclusive rights to regulate abortion met with puzzlement and were passed over quickly.''

Senator Bellatti had a different take on the Senate vote. Noting that two week earlier, it appeared he would have enough votes to pass the antiabortion measure, Bellatti attributed the eroded support for the bill to stepped-up lobbying of abortion rights advocates late in the session. Bellatti conceded that some lawmakers had become fed up with the overwhelming number of phone calls, letters, baby rattles, and pictures of fetuses sent by antiabortion activists. ''I think people plain just got tired.''[38] Still, the experience made Bellatti feel hopeful about the future. ''It demonstrated that there is a tremendous grass-roots pro-life effort'' in South Dakota, Bellatti explained, adding: ''I have no doubt that *Roe v. Wade* will be overturned. Eventually, more and more states are going to fall into line.''[39]

Shortly after HB 1126 went down, Senator Elmer Bietz (R-Tripp) signaled his intention to force another Senate vote on the bill. Senator Bellatti firmly rejected the idea. Since senators had made up their minds and were unlikely to change their votes, Bellatti said, ''I think there's nothing to be gained by working it over again.''[40] Supporters of the bill chose to leave it at that. ''Dr. Bellatti just wants it done,'' said Lori Engel. ''In fairness to him, we'll honor his request.''[41]

REACTION

Immediately after the Senate vote, Katie Michelman, executive director of NARAL, issued a public statement from Washington hailing the decision. ''Today's vote not only

safeguards the lives and health of South Dakota women, it also prevents another case from entering the crowded judicial pipeline to the U.S. Supreme Court and threatening *Roe v. Wade*.'' Meanwhile, Nancy Myers, spokeswoman for the National Right to Life Committee, called the vote ''a betrayal by one or two people who were voted into office as pro-life legislators.''

Some supporters of the bill blamed Senator Heidepriem for the loss, accusing him of delay tactics resulting in what they viewed as a poor timing of the vote. ''It was the delay in committee that killed it,'' Engel contended. ''I think Senator Heidepriem had his agenda set and that was it. . . . Heidepriem wanted it killed.''[42] Engel's remarks clearly stung Heidepriem, who prided himself as a true believer in the sanctity of the political process. ''I gave them every break in the world,'' defended Heidepriem, noting that he did not offer any amendments to try to cripple or kill the bill in committee. ''I think I was just scrupulously fair about the testimony, about witnesses. I let both sides run their show within certain limits. We gave it a fair hearing.''

Although Heidepriem was relieved that the antiabortion bill ultimately failed, he felt no joy in the outcome. ''There's a level of disappointment about it all,'' Heidepriem told the *Argus Leader*. ''I believe that the Senate succeeded in preventing a bad law from taking effect, but none of us runs for office to stop bad things from happening. I think we all run because we're motivated by positive desires to do good things.''

EPILOGUE

When the 1991 legislative session ended in early March, Heidepriem—heeding the advice of his sister—raised $5,000 to conduct a telephone survey of every household in his district to assess the level of political damage that may have resulted from his position on HB 1126. The survey found that 40 percent of Heidepriem's constituents believed the bill should have passed and that

Heidepriem should have voted for it. Twenty-eight percent believed the bill should not have passed and the Heidepriem should not have voted for it. A full 32 percent were undecided.

Meanwhile, the South Dakota RTL reported that hundreds of people had signed up to help defeat Heidepriem in the upcoming November Senate race. Ninety-five people volunteered to help Heidepriem win that fall. In the end, however, Heidepriem decided against running for reelection. "Eight years in that process was probably enough," explains Heidepriem, who said his primary reason for not running was to be able to spend more time with his family. Still, Heidepriem admits, his experience with HB 1126 also played a role in his decision: "the events around this bill were so completely out of proportion to any other legislative experience I had had . . . that it made no sense to just go back. It was so enormously taxing—personally, emotionally, politically—that to continue on in the legislature somehow seemed almost secondary." Heidepriem adds:

> I really felt this experience marked me and changed me. This process had meant so much to me; I watched this from my father's lap for the first twelve years of my life, and he had made me feel that this was a noble human experience. Some of that came loose for me in '91. . . . A lot of people go into the legislature and they're fired up about being in the process, excited about having won an election, and you take the oath and sit down in a beautiful chamber and hope someday you'll do something good or big for your state. And I certainly wanted that, too. And so the time comes, and it was high profile and a lot of attention, but somehow, it wasn't what I had in mind.

With no concrete plans to reenter public life in 1993 or 1994, Heidepriem returned to his law practice in Sioux Falls. Nevertheless, he remained active as a political commentator for some local television shows and would not rule out a future run for political office. "It would be silly to say that I'm not going to do it again," Heidepriem says. "It's been a central theme since birth. . . . I grew up with it, and I'm really enjoying not being in it now, but I don't know how long I'll feel that way."

All other members of the Senate Judiciary Committee—with the exception of Karen Muenster, who suffered a back injury that took her out of politics—sought reelection in November 1992. Emery, Halverson, and Rasmussen won handily, though Rasmussen was targeted by antiabortion forces.[43] Shanard was defeated by Democrat Mel Olsen, who did not reveal his position on abortion prior to the election. According to Shanard, "the abortion issue was used against [him] rather substantially" during the campaign, and there was "no question that [his vote on HB 1126] hurt" him.[44] Senator Symens meanwhile, was reelected by a very narrow margin: three hundred out of approximately six thousand votes. Symens' vote on the 1991 antiabortion bill dominated the campaign.

The November 1992 elections shifted the balance of power on the abortion issue in the South Dakota Senate. At least eighteen antiabortion candidates were elected to the Senate—just enough for a majority vote. Few were surprised, then, that the abortion issue resurfaced in the 1993 legislative session. Although, this time, no bill sought to outlaw abortion in South Dakota,[45] a package of House bills seeking abortion restrictions was able to pass the legislature and was signed into law by Governor Mickelson in March 1993. The new abortion restrictions included: (1) a mandatory twenty-four-hour waiting period before any abortion could be performed; (2) one-parent notification (the bill did not include a judicial bypass provision); and (3) a ban on the use of fetal tissue for research and medical treatment in South Dakota. Two of the restrictions—parental notification and the twenty-four-hour wait—were to be challenged in court by Planned Parenthood in 1993.

NOTES

1. According to Heidepriem, Senator Mike Dietrich, then vice chairman of the Judiciary committee, "was understandably put out" that Heidepriem was given the Judiciary chairmanship. But in the end, Heidepriem says, Dietrich "understood what [Heidepriem] was giving up in the House to come over to the Senate."

2. Heidepriem ran for the U.S. House seat left vacant by Democrat Tom Daschle, an abortion rights supporter. Daschle ran successfully for the U.S. Senate that year.

3. Alan Guttmacher Institute, 1987.

4. 700 of the 900 abortions were performed for South Dakota residents.

5. The other states were Idaho, Illinois, Kentucky, Louisiana, Missouri, Montana, Nebraska, North Dakota, and Pennsylvania.

6. South Dakota adopted a parental consent statute in the late 1970s, but its enforcement was immediately restricted by the federal district court. The law remained unenforced in 1991 despite recent Supreme Court rulings that had permitted this type of requirement in other states.

7. Both the Louisiana and Utah laws would prohibit abortion except in cases of rape, incest, protecting the mother's health, or removing a severely damaged unborn child. The doctor performing the abortion would face a felony charge punishable by up to five years in prison, but there would be no penalties for the woman seeking the abortion. The Utah legislature also passed a resolution creating an abortion law task force, promising that the state would help other states fight to overturn *Roe* if Utah's bill failed.

8. Critics of the bill noted that this definition would probably outlaw the intrauterine device (IUD), the "morning after" pill, and certainly the French abortion pill, RU-486. Proponents of the bill suggested that the IUD would not be outlawed, as the woman would not be "known" to be pregnant at the time.

9. In the case of incest, the victim would have to be a minor in order to have an abortion.

10. *Sioux Falls Argus Leader*, Feb. 17, 1991.

11. *Aberdeen American News*, Jan. 19, 1991.

12. Ibid.

13. *Sioux Falls Argus Leader*, Jan. 16, 1991.

14. *Aberdeen American News*, Jan. 19, 1991.

15. Ibid.

16. Ibid., Jan. 17, 1991.

17. Ibid.

18. *Sioux Falls Argus Leader*, Feb. 1, 1991.

19. Ibid., Jan. 16, 1991.

20. Ibid., Feb. 1, 1991.

21. HB 1126 would have been more difficult to pass if any of the proposed appropriations were included.

In South Dakota, any measure that included spending authority would require a two-thirds majority, rather than a simple majority, to pass.

22. Miller was asked by Senate Majority Leader George Shanard to direct the bill to the Senate Judiciary Committee. Heidepriem believed that Miller "tried very hard to get the bill sent somewhere other than the Judiciary Committee because he sensed that it would get a more favorable hearing somewhere else."

23. In January, Mickelson had said he held reservations about the constitutionality of the bill.

24. *Sioux Falls Argus Leader*, Feb. 11, 1991.

25. Engel wanted it to be held on Monday, February 18, while Glasgow wanted it to coincide with a Family Values Coalition rally that he was planning for Monday, February 25.

26. For example, Heidepriem could schedule the committee vote for the morning of the last—fortieth—day of the legislative session. (State legislative rules required that the session end in no more than forty days.) Since the required steps of a smokeout could take six days to complete, supporters of the bill would have to suspend the rules—which required a two-thirds majority in the Senate—in order to complete all of the smokeout procedures in just one day.

27. Feb. 11, 1991.

28. *Sioux Falls Argus Leader*, Feb. 21, 1991.

29. Shanard believed that 60 percent of the voters in his district opposed abortion.

30. When Heidepriem ran for Congress in 1986, Halverson supported his opponent because of the abortion issue.

31. Muenster's husband Ted planned to run for governor in 1994.

32. *Sioux Falls Argus Leader*, Feb. 21, 1991.

33. Feb. 17, 1991.

34. After the hearing, Heidepriem was approached by several doctors who believed that the fetus looked more like it was twelve weeks old.

35. South Dakota mandated that a reason be given for every abortion performed in the state. In most cases, the physician performing the abortion would check off the "other" box on the mandatory multiple choice questionnaire for the state. Engel interpreted each questionnaire stating "other" reasons for the abortion as evidence that the abortion was performed for birth control purposes.

36. According to Heidepriem, Stephanie Symens later told her father that she had not written a note to Miner.

37. At the time, the South Dakota Democratic caucus was the only caucus in the United States with a female majority; in 1991, nine out of seventeen Democratic senators in South Dakota were women.

38. *Associated Press*, Feb. 26, 1991.

39. *Sioux Falls Argus Leader*, March 3, 1991.

40. *Associated Press*, Feb. 26, 1991.

41. *Sioux Falls Argus Leader*, March 3, 1991.

42. Ibid., Feb. 27, 1991.

43. Emery's challenger did not actively oppose abortion, and the abortion issue did not figure prominently in his campaign. Rasmussen's campaign benefited from legislative redistricting, which in 1992 put her in a district with fewer antiabortion constituents than in 1991. "If my district had stayed the way it was, I'm afraid I wouldn't have gotten reelected," Rasmussen speculates.

44. However, some of Shanard's Senate colleagues believed that unrelated allegations of impropriety dealt the decisive blow to Shanard's campaign.

45. On March 8, 1993, the United States Supreme Court let stand an appeals court ruling that struck down Louisiana's 1991 antiabortion law, which, like the bill that failed in South Dakota in 1991, sought to ban abortions in most situations and stipulated prison terms for physicians performing abortions.

Comment

In the Califano case, Father McCormick helpfully identifies three levels of moral questions about abortion: (1) the personal morality of having an abortion; (2) the political morality of legalizing and funding abortion; and (3) the obligations of public officials in shaping and carrying out the law. We cannot ignore the first level of personal morality in considering our positions on public policy and the obligations of public officials, but these cases focus on the second and third levels.

Begin with the issue of public policy—whether the government should fund abortions for poor women. Note Califano's responses to a representative from the National Women's Political Caucus: "I believe abortion is morally wrong," and "I oppose federal funding for abortion." Must the second position necessarily follow from the first? Senator Packwood, Judy Woodruff, Congressman Fazio, and Congresswomen Pelosi and Morella all suggest that it would be unfair for the government not to fund abortions for the poor as long as they are legal. They thereby attempt to separate the question of whether abortion should be legal from the question of whether the government should subsidize abortion for poor women once it is legal. Assess the responses of Califano, Carter, and Congressman Hyde to the defense of federal funding on grounds of fairness. Is there any principle other than fairness that would favor funding?

On what moral grounds (if any) can one distinguish between the funding of all legal abortions for poor pregnant women and the funding of only those abortions that terminate pregnancies resulting from rape and incest? Congresswoman Morella argues that "poor women who are pregnant as a result of rape or incest—victims of brutal acts—should have access to the same health care options as more affluent women." Congressman Mollohan argues against the moral relevance of any such distinction: "If you adopt our premise that unborn life is valuable and therefore abortion is fundamentally wrong, there is no logical reason for allowing exceptions in cases of rape and incest." Are members of Congress who share Mollohan's premise logically bound to accept his conclusion? Assess Congresswoman Pelosi's defense of funding abortions in cases of rape and incest. Must members of Congress who approve of legalized abortion also approve of funding all legal abortions under Medicaid, not just those that result from incest and rape?

One philosopher has suggested that legalizing abortion but not subsidizing it is a fair compromise between the pro-life and pro-choice positions, although it completely satisfies the moral claims of neither. If a compromise is the best solution to the public policy question, are these the right terms? Should the terms of a fair compromise be more or less generous to poor women? Is a compromise the best way to resolve the public policy question?

Consider the question of whether Califano was correct in thinking that he could act responsibly in public office while personally opposing abortion. Did he use the correct standard—willingness to enforce whatever law Congress passes—in deciding to accept the position? Having accepted the position, did Califano act properly in office? Consider the ways in which his opposition to abortion might have affected his conduct in office, including his public statements. Was he justified in interpreting the intent of Congress as he did in writing HEW regulations on funding abortion? Should he have compromised with the president on the paragraph concerning rape and incest?

The moral conflicts Califano faced might have been even more difficult had Congress instructed HEW to fund abortions through Medicaid. Would Califano then have been justified in doing anything to oppose such a policy? Had Califano been committed to the position that poor women have a right to subsidized abortion, what should he have done in the face of congressional action to the contrary? If both the president and Congress are determined to preserve the Hyde amendment unrevised, are there any circumstances under which someone committed to subsidizing abortions for poor women should accept the office of secretary of Health and Human Services?

As chairman of South Dakota's Senate Judiciary Committee, Heidepriem had the responsibility of overseeing a fair process for considering an antiabortion bill that he opposed on moral as well as legal grounds. Are there any political circumstances under which Heidepriem would have been justified in subordinating procedural fairness to abortion rights, or vice versa? Suppose that Heidepriem had reason to believe that the antiabortion bill had a better chance of passing if it reached the floor for discussion. Would he have been justified in doing his best—within the law and rules of the Senate—to prevent the bill from reaching the floor? Or suppose that everyone in his district had written the senator urging him to vote for the bill. Are there any reasons that his constituents might have offered for their opposition to abortion that would have obligated Heidepriem to vote for the bill?

In light of his support for *Roe v. Wade*, which took the issue of legalizing abortion out of legislatures and into the judicial arena, Heidepriem's critics might question the consistency of his commitment to "make the decision [concerning the antiabortion bill] in front of the people who care about the question." How might Heidepriem defend this commitment and the practical implications for open legislative discussion that he associated with it? Is such a commitment consistent with giving the judiciary authority over the issue of legalizing abortion? Suppose that an open legislative debate led to the passage of the antiabortion bill and its support by the overwhelming majority of Heidepriem's constituents. Would Heidepriem then be obligated to defend the law?

Consider whether Heidepriem's reliance on legal arguments to oppose the bill strengthened his case. What weight, if any, should his colleagues and constituents have placed on Heidepriem's prediction that South Dakota would be embroiled in expensive legal struggles for years to come if the legislature passed the antiabortion bill? If you agree with Heidepriem's pro-choice position, consider what moral weight you would place on the risk of expensive litigation to defend a South Dakota law legalizing abortion in the face of a Supreme Court that had overturned *Roe v. Wade*. Did Heidepriem and his colleagues on either side of the issue overlook any legal or moral arguments that should have been central to public consideration of the bill?

Surrogate Parenting in New York—I
New York State Senate Judiciary Committee

[The report excerpted below supported legislation introduced February 3, 1987, by John R. Dunne, deputy majority leader of the New York Senate, and Mary B. Goodhue, chairman of the Senate Child Care Committee. The legislation would have recognized surrogate motherhood contracts as legal and irrevocable in New York. Although initially there was support for the proposal, the sponsors withdrew it later in the session as opposition grew. The legislature then suspended all hearings on the question of surrogacy until the governor's task force could issue its report (see "Surrogacy in New York-II").]

EXECUTIVE SUMMARY

Many American couples, experiencing the problem of infertility, are turning to surrogate parenting to help them create families. It is estimated that over five hundred surrogate births have occurred in the United States, most of them in the last few years. The purpose of this report is to examine the questions presented by surrogate parenting and to determine the appropriate public policy response.

Generally, surrogate parenting involves an agreement between a married couple who cannot have a child and a fertile woman who agrees to be artificially inseminated with the sperm of the husband of the couple, to carry the child to term, and then to surrender all parental rights. The biological father establishes paternity, and his infertile wife legally adopts the child. A fee, as well as all necessarily incurred costs, is paid to the surrogate, and often a fee is paid to an infertility center or other third-party intermediary for making the arrangements.

This process, by itself, involves little or no state involvement. However, the development of surrogate parenting has outpaced the development of law. Consequently, when the courts are called upon to interpret and enforce these agreements, they must decide issues, such as the status of the child, without the guidance of statutes or caselaw.

National attention has focused on cases

From *Surrogate Parenting in New York: A Proposal for Legislative Reform,* prepared by the staff of the New York State Senate Judiciary Committee, John R. Dunne (chairman), and Roberta Glaros (project director), December 1986.

involving breaches of surrogate parenting agreements. In 1983, a child conceived as the result of a surrogate parenting agreement was born defective, and neither party wanted to accept parental responsibility. More recently, the case of "Baby M," now pending in the New Jersey superior court, involves a surrogate mother's refusal to relinquish parental rights to the child.

In July 1986, Nassau County Surrogate Court Judge C. Raymond Radigan, in the course of an adoption proceeding, ruled on the legality of a surrogate parenting agreement. The major issue was whether the agreement violated state law which prohibits payment of compensation other than medical expenses in adoptions. Judge Radigan concluded that New York State's current laws are ambiguous and provide little guidance to the courts in deciding cases involving surrogate parenting arrangements. In a letter to the chairmen of the judiciary committees of both the Senate and the Assembly, he urged that the legislature examine this issue.

In response to Judge Radigan's request, the Senate and Assembly judiciary committees held a joint hearing in October 1986 to determine what action, if any, the legislature should take in regard to the practice of surrogate parenting. Nineteen witnesses, including legal experts, ethicists, and representatives of religious and feminist groups, provided extremely valuable testimony on the moral, ethical, and legal implications of surrogate parenting. In addition, several witnesses recounted their personal experiences with the practice.

Following the hearing, the Senate Judiciary Committee chairman instructed the committee staff to review hearing testimony, to conduct further research on the subject and to make recommendations regarding legislation to carry out the appropriate public policy. This report outlines the findings of the committee staff and makes recommendations to the legislature with regard to determining a public policy response to the practice of surrogate parenting in New York State.

FINDINGS AND RECOMMENDATIONS

After a careful analysis of the testimony presented to the committee at its hearing and after a careful review of the literature and research into the practice of surrogate parenting, the committee staff recommends that the state recognize surrogate parenting contracts as legal and enforceable. The first and foremost concern of the legislature must be to ensure that the child, born in fulfillment of a surrogate parenting agreement, has a secure and permanent home and settled rights of inheritance. The prospects for achieving this goal will be enhanced if there is informed consent on the part of all parties to the agreement. In addition, legislation should be designed to prevent exploitation of the parties and excessive commercialization of the practice.

The foregoing recommendations are based on the following findings:

1. Surrogate parenting is perceived as a viable solution to the increasingly common problem of female infertility. Thus, the practice is likely to continue in the foreseeable future.

2. In fashioning a response, the legislature must consider the implications of the practice for the parties and for society as a whole. Specifically, the challenge to accepted societal values, the possible physical and psychological harm to participants, and the potential for fraud, manipulation, and coercion of the parties by entrepreneurs must be examined.

3. Clearly, surrogate parenting presents the legislature with the problem of adapting the law to social and technological change. Contract law, adoption law, and constitutional law obliquely touch upon the subject and provide some basis for legal analysis, but no existing body of law fully or adequately addresses the legal issues raised by the practice of surrogate parenting. The gaps and deficiencies of the law result in

the uncertain status of the child born of a surrogate parenting arrangement.

4. In light of the state's interest in ensuring the status of children born under surrogate parenting arrangements, recognition and regulation of the practice is the most appropriate legislative response.

LEGISLATIVE ACTION

The following recommendations are submitted as a framework for correcting the imbalance between the current state of the law and the developing practice of surrogate parenting.

The Role of the Courts

The keystone to any legislation relating to surrogate parenting must be judicial approval of the surrogate parenting contract prior to insemination of the surrogate mother. The purpose of the court proceeding should be to ensure that the parties are fully aware of their rights and obligations under the agreement. In order to achieve informed consent, the legislation should require that the parties have the benefit of independent legal representation and the availability of counseling by a licensed mental health professional.

Legislation regulating surrogate parenting should also provide for judicial approval of the fees paid to the surrogate mother, attorneys, and the infertility center. In reviewing surrogate parenting contracts, the court should apply a standard of "just and reasonable compensation" to determine that all fees and compensation are equitable, appropriate to the services rendered, and without coercive effect.

Provisional Approval

The health and safety of the child and of the surrogate mother require that insemination be performed by a physician licensed by the state and that tests for sexually transmitted diseases be completed before each insemination. For this reason, the court's approval of the contract should be provisional until it receives notice from a licensed physician that he or she has tested the natural father and the surrogate mother for sexually transmitted diseases, that the surrogate has been inseminated with the semen of the intended father, and that conception has occurred. The court's approval of the contract should then become final.

Effect of Court Approval

Any proposed legislation should make explicitly clear that a child born to a surrogate mother, in fulfillment of a contract approved by the court prior to insemination, shall be deemed the legitimate, natural child of the biological father and his wife. This would supplant any requirement that the wife of the biological father adopt the child. The statutory determination of parenthood may be rebutted by the intended father if paternity tests show conclusively that he is not biologically related to the child.

Remedies for Breach

The surrogate mother's agreement to waive parental rights should be irrevocable and enforced at the birth of the child. Prior to delivery, the surrogate mother should be deemed to have full control of the decisions relating to her pregnancy. Surrender of the child should be enforceable through the remedy of specific performance.

Parental obligations, such as support, should be enforceable against the intended parents from the time of conception. Breach of contract, e.g., refusal to accept parental responsibilities, should result in a judgment of support against the intended parents, since they, by operation of the statute, will be the legal parents of the child.

Eligibility

Given the scarcity of empirical evidence about how the surrogacy process affects those involved, it is recommended that the courts recognize as enforceable only those contracts concluded between a surrogate mother and a couple, the female of whom is medically certified as infertile. Legislation should provide for a measure of proof by which medical necessity can be demonstrated to the court. The petition for court review of the contract should be accompanied by the written statement of a licensed physician that the intended mother has a condition which makes conception or birth of a child unlikely or which creates a likelihood that a child of the intended mother will have a mental or physical impairment or disability.

CONCLUSION

These recommendations provide a framework for an effective legislative response to the legal void surrounding the practice of surrogate parenting. Enforcement of the surrogate contract by the state will secure the welfare of children born under surrogate parenting arrangements. Regulation, based on the principle of informed consent, will address the risks associated with the practice. Judicial review and approval of the surrogate parenting contract prior to insemination is crucial to enforcement, regulation, and informed consent and should be considered the keystone of any proposed legislation. . . .

THE DEVELOPMENT OF SURROGATE PARENTING

Surrogate parenting developed as a response to the desire of infertile couples to have a child with a genetic link to one parent. Its growing popularity is due to recent increases in the incidence of female infertility and to the development of infertility centers which facilitate the process. An examination of the phenomenon of increasing infertility supports the conclusion that, because surrogate parenting meets a perceived need, it will continue to gain in popularity in the foreseeable future.

INFERTILITY AND ITS CAUSES

According to recent studies, infertility is currently on the rise. A 1976 study found that "one in ten couples failed to conceive after at least one year of marriage during which no contraceptives were used."[1] By 1983, however, "one in eight American married couples failed to conceive after one year of trying."[2] Statistical studies generally set the infertility rate at from 12 to 15 percent of the couples wishing to conceive. These figures may be conservative since they generally include only those couples who seek clinical assistance for infertility. They do not include cases in which the couple chooses not to conceive for genetic reasons, the female can conceive but habitually miscarries, the female has had an early hysterectomy, or the female can conceive but would experience a high risk pregnancy.[3]

Medical experts attribute the rising rate of female infertility to a combination of factors. Changing work roles and the availability of contraception have led many women to postpone childbearing. Delaying childbearing allows age-related biological factors to increase the rate of infertility. In addition, the widespread use of intrauterine devices for the purposes of birth control and changing sexual practices have increased the incidence of pelvic inflammatory disease, a leading cause of female infertility.[4]

Increases in infertility in the United States have occurred at a time of moral emphasis on the family. There is some indication that the values of the pro-family movement have "reinforced the social image of infertility as a major health problem."[5] Mental health experts agree that the inability to beget, bear, and raise children has grave psychological and emotional implications for many infertile men and women.[6] As one scholar put it, "infertility often implicates the most fundamental feelings about one's self and one's relationship to the familial unit, and may leave persons feeling handicapped or defective in an area that is central to personal identity and fulfillment."[7] Infertile couples often experience isolation, guilt, marital strife, and a loss of confidence and self-worth.

THE OPTIONS OF THE INFERTILE COUPLE

Infertile couples wishing to create families are faced with a limited number of choices. Conventional medical treatments, including hormonal drug therapies and surgical procedures, cure a certain percentage of infertility. Yet, in 1983, it was estimated that some 500,000 American women had either an absence or blockage of the fallopian tubes or oviducts.[8] Surgical procedures to correct this condition are sometimes recommended, but in a significant number of cases, surgery is unsuccessful.[9]

When conventional medical treatment fails, the infertile couple is faced with two options: adoption or the less conventional medical treatments of artificial conception. Traditionally, adoption has been the primary means of relieving childlessness. For many couples, however, adoption is no longer a satisfactory alternative. Professionals involved in child welfare and adoption attribute this to a decreasing supply of healthy infants available for adoption. According to the National Committee for Adoption,[10] several factors may have contributed to the decrease: (1) the accessibility of birth control, (2) the legislation of abortion, (3) the closure of many comprehensive maternity homes, and (4) greater social acceptance of single mothers and greater willingness of single mothers to rear their own children. Due largely to social acceptance of single mothers, the number of adoptions decreased by 32.4 percent between 1972 and 1982, despite a 13 percent increase in the number of live births and a 77.4 percent increase in out-of-wedlock births.[11]

Reduced availability has resulted in longer waiting periods and more stringent applicant requirements. According to Nassau County Surrogate Judge C. Raymond Radigan, waiting periods in New York State can be as long as seven years.[12] Such waits are typical nationwide.[13]

The combined factors of increasing infertility and decreasing availability of healthy infants for adoption are causing more and more couples to seek nonconventional medical treatment of infertility. Nonconventional or alternative reproductive technologies offer the infertile couple the hope of having a child with a genetic link to one or both partners. The two most common techniques, artificial insemination and *in vitro* fertilization, involve the transfer of the sperm or egg out of the body which produced it to another body or medium in order to facilitate fertilization.

Artificial insemination is the introduction of sperm into an ovulating woman for the purposes of fertilization. The technology is simple; it requires only the mechanical introduction of the sperm into the uterus. For this reason, artificial insemination has a relatively high rate of success and has been common practice for several decades.

In vitro fertilization involves the capture of a mature egg before ovulation and the transfer of that egg to an external medium, such as a petri dish or test tube, where it can be exposed to sperm. If fertilization occurs, the fertilized egg is placed in an incubator until it is developed enough to be implanted in the mother. *In vitro* fertilization is the indicated treatment in cases where scarring of the fallopian tubes prevents natural conception. It has severe disadvantages, however. The overall success rate is about 10 percent, a relatively low figure when compared to artificial insemination. In addition, the procedure can be physically and emotionally stressful for the infertile woman. Cost estimates range from $38,000 to $50,000.[14]

SURROGATE MOTHERHOOD—A VIABLE ALTERNATIVE

Surrogate parenting is not a distinct type of artificial conception technology. Rather, it involves a different application of artificial insemination in order to produce a child when the female of the couple is infertile. The distinguishing feature of surrogate parenting is the involvement of the surrogate mother as the third person.[15]

The use of a surrogate mother is indicated when the wife has a condition which makes the conception or birth of a child unlikely or which creates a likelihood that the child will have a serious mental or physical impairment. In most cases, infertile couples resort to the use of a surrogate only after they have exhausted all other medical options and have been discouraged from adopting by long waiting periods and increasingly stringent requirements.

For some couples, a surrogate mother provides the only means to have a child genetically related to one of them. The waiting period is much shorter than in traditional adoptions, and the infertile wife can participate with her husband in choosing a surrogate agreeable to both. The child born of a surrogate arrangement is reared by a couple who so wanted him that they were willing to participate in a novel process with potential legal and other risks.[16]

The process offers potential benefits for the surrogates as well. A recent study[17] found that the motivations of women applying to become surrogate mothers are complex. Approximately 85 percent indicated that they would not participate without compensation but that money was not their sole motivation. Other factors influencing their decisions included the enjoyment of being pregnant, the desire to give the gift of a baby to an infertile couple, and an emotional need to work through the previous loss of a child by abortion or adoption. A significant number of those studied were sympathetic to the problems of infertility, and some had, themselves, been adopted as children by infertile couples. For many, surrogacy represents an alternative income option. For example, some divorced women with young children have chosen to be surrogates in order to support their children and to remain at home to care for them.[18]

THE ROLE OF THE ENTREPRENEUR

For the couple wishing to create a family through surrogate parenting, the most diffi-cult and important step is finding a suitable surrogate mother. In some cases, the surrogate is a close friend or relative of the couple, and the agreement is private and informal. In other cases, the couple advertises for a surrogate, usually in suburban and university campus newspapers. But, increasingly, childless couples are turning to infertility centers to help them make their surrogate parenting arrangements.

The first infertility center was opened in the 1970s in Los Angeles by an obstetrician, two lawyers, and a psychologist. Over the past ten years, entrepreneurs have responded rapidly to the market opportunity presented by increased infertility. Major centers have opened in Detroit, Philadelphia, Louisville, Columbus, Topeka, and suburban Washington, D.C. Two infertility centers are currently operating in New York City, and one recently opened in Buffalo. A Long Island center, opened in 1983 and managed by a photographer, is apparently no longer in business.[19] Since the practice is not recognized or regulated by any state, there is no reliable information on the number of centers in existence at any one time, the qualifications of the entrepreneurs, or the number of surrogate births arranged by each center.

The couple's first contact with a center is likely to involve a preliminary interview, during which they may discuss their particular problem and receive information and counseling regarding infertility. If they decide to proceed with surrogate parenting, they sign a contract with the center and gain access to its files on available surrogate mothers. When the couple becomes interested in an individual surrogate, the center coordinates an interview, arranges for medical and psychiatric evaluation of the surrogate, and provides legal representation for the couple in contract negotiations. When a contract is concluded, the center arranges a schedule for the insemination of the surrogate. If conception occurs, the center coordinates the legal steps necessary to establish the natural father's paternity and to finalize adoption of the child by the infertile wife.

The most important service provided by the center is recruitment of potential surrogate mothers. Selection and screening practices vary widely from center to center. Some centers carefully interview applicants and require a waiting period of several months between the time the surrogate is interviewed and the signing of a contract with an infertile couple. Other centers keep files on prospective surrogates but regard them as independent agents. In these cases, medical and psychological testing are included as part of the surrogate parenting agreement and are paid for by the infertile couple.

A surrogate parenting contract generally contains three major provisions: (1) the surrogate agrees to bear the child and surrender parental rights at birth; (2) the natural father agrees to accept responsibility for the child; and (3) the natural father agrees to pay all medical expenses incurred and the fees of both the surrogate and the infertility center.[20] Secondary provisions may include agreements regarding counseling; medical, psychiatric and genetic screening; amniocentesis or other tests to detect genetic defects in the fetus; restrictions on such behavior as smoking, drinking, or drug use by the surrogate; and provision for changes in the fee structure in the event of miscarriage or stillbirth. Despite the fact that the contracts may not be enforceable, they make provision for legal remedies in case of breach.[21]

After the surrogate gives birth, the wife of the natural father adopts the child, often traveling to a jurisdiction which has an accommodating step-parent adoption statute. For example, the Florida Step-Parent Adoption Act[22] does not include a residency requirement or a requirement for disclosure of any fee or expense involved in the adoption. Taking the baby out of state for adoption is often viewed as necessary because twenty-four states prohibit the payment of any consideration other than medical expenses in adoptions.[23] Recently, however, contracts developed by infertility centers are signed only by the natural father, the surrogate mother, and her husband, if any. One center operator argues that under this arrangement, the wife of the natural father is not responsible for any of the payments made to the surrogate. Therefore, she can petition to adopt in the state of her residence regardless of any prohibition against compensation in adoptions.[24] . . .

OPTIONS FOR GOVERNMENTAL RESPONSE

There are three possible legislative responses to the practice of surrogate parenting: inaction, prohibition, and regulation. This section will examine the public policy and constitutional aspects of each option.

LAISSEZ FAIRE: "LET WELL ENOUGH ALONE"

As discussed in the previous section, New York law does not address the issues raised by surrogate parenting. Although certain aspects of existing law may apply to such arrangements and, to some extent, may serve to resolve the question of the status of the child and to define the rights and duties of the parties, there is no certainty.

Some argue that an absence of settled law regarding surrogate parenting does not require immediate remedial action. They argue that in issues where there are deep-seated controversies or unknown factors, it is best to allow the law to develop without legislative intrusion.[56]

The laissez faire approach ignores the fact that without legislative action, the rights of the child, including the right to a permanent and stable home environment, are at risk. Breaches of an agreement may result in familial upheaval and protracted custody battles. Therefore, the question of contract enforceability should not be left to the "uncertainties of evolutionary legal development."[57]

Hearing testimony and published articles make it clear that legal experts, ethicists, and mental health professionals, whether they oppose or support surrogate parenting, agree that the legislature should fill the legal void that surrounds the practice.

PROHIBITION

In deciding whether the practice of surrogate parenting should be prohibited, the state must first determine whether such a prohibition would deny a fundamental constitutional right. If a fundamental right is involved, any attempt to impair this right will likely be struck down as unconstitutional, absent any compelling state interests.

Neither the United States nor the New York constitution contains language explicitly stating that a person has a right to have a child. Decisions relating to procreation and self autonomy, however, have been discussed within the context of the "right to privacy,"[58] which has been defined as containing ". . . only personal rights that can be deemed 'fundamental' or 'implicit in the concept of ordered liberty.' "[59]

It is arguable that the desire to have a child falls within this concept of "ordered liberty." The Supreme Court, *in dicta*, has repeatedly discussed the right of procreation in the same context as marriage and marital intimacy.[60] In *Skinner v. Oklahoma*,[61] the Supreme Court struck down Oklahoma's Habitual Criminal Sterilization Act, which provided for the sterilization of criminals convicted of two or more crimes involving moral turpitude. The Court ruled that the statute denied equal protection in that the phrase, "crimes of moral turpitude," was too vague. In its decision, the Court stated that, "[t]his case touches a sensitive and important area of human rights. Oklahoma deprives certain individuals of a right which is basic to the perpetuation of a race—the right to have offspring."[62] Furthermore, "[t]he right of procreation without state interference has long been recognized as 'one of the basic civil rights of man . . . funda-

mental to the very existence and survival of the race.' "[63] In a later case, *Eisenstadt v. Baird*,[64] the Court stated: "[i]f the right of privacy means anything, it is the right of the individual, married or single, to be free from unwarranted governmental intrusion into matters so fundamentally affecting a person as the decision whether to bear or beget a child."[65] In 1977, the Supreme Court in *Carey v. Population Services, Inc.*,[66] found unconstitutional a statute which prohibited the sale or advertising of contraception because, "[t]he decision whether or not to bear or beget a child is at the very heart of this cluster of constitutionally protected choices. That decision holds a particularly important place in the history of the right of privacy. . . ."[67] Most recently, the Court has even hinted that the promotion of childbirth, rather than abortion may, in fact, be a legitimate state interest.[68]

From the foregoing, there appears to be ample precedent that the right to have a child is a fundamental right protected by the constitutional right of privacy and that attempts to outlaw surrogate parenting would be construed as unconstitutional interference with that right. The question still remains, however, whether this right of privacy extends to the use of surrogate parenting as a means of procreation. The right of privacy has not yet been interpreted to include a third party,[69] but to prohibit an infertile couple from using a viable alternative such as surrogate parenting may, in fact, preclude those persons from the only reproductive mechanism possible, and, thereby, indirectly deny those persons the right to have a child.

While it is not suggested that the state should encourage the practice of surrogate parenting, it should not prohibit the practice *in toto*, since such a prohibition would perpetuate the legal vacuum which now exists to the detriment of children born of these arrangements.

REGULATION

If it is accepted that the use of surrogate parenting falls within the protections of the right of privacy, then surrogate parenting may only be restricted or denied if there exists a compelling state interest which necessitates such a restriction or denial. "Compelling is, of course, the key word; where a decision as fundamental as . . . whether to bear or beget a child is involved, regulations imposing a burden on it must be narrowly drawn to express only those interests."[70]

The Supreme Court has noted, however, that the right of privacy "is not absolute, and certain state interests may, at some point, become sufficiently compelling to sustain regulation of factors that govern the right. . . ."[71] Surrogate parenting, if accepted as a part of the fundamental right of privacy, involves the interests of several different parties, all of whom may present the state with compelling interests to protect.

IDENTIFYING THE INTERESTS

The state's principal interest, once it decides to allow surrogate parenting, is to ensure the status of the child who is born of the arrangement. The state's interest in protecting the child would be best met if the status and legitimacy of the child were secured upon birth, thus avoiding the possibility of a protracted custody battle.

Aside from the infertile couple's decision whether to have a child, the surrogate mother's benefits and potential risks should also be assessed. Under the *Roe v. Wade* analysis, the surrogate mother has the right to decide whether or not she will give birth to a child. Under current law, the state does not limit her decision concerning who should inseminate her, nor does it prevent her from giving the child up for adoption. The state has traditionally refrained from interfering with these personal decisions.

The state does, however, have an interest in the health, safety, and welfare of the mother because of a mortality rate involved with bearing a child, a risk of transmission of disease, and the psychological and emotional ramifications of giving up a child.

Finally, the state has an interest in preventing the potential abuses which may accompany the commercialization of childbearing. The abuses of this technique would most likely be associated with the use of surrogate parenting by couples who are biologically capable of producing their own offspring but wish their children to have superior genetic traits or wish to avoid the inconvenience of pregnancy and childbirth.

The state may, in addition to other regulations, justifiably limit the use of surrogacy to couples where the female is infertile. A "medically necessary" standard has been employed before and has constitutional precedence. In the case of *Maher v. Roe*,[72] the Court upheld a Connecticut statute which limited Medicaid reimbursement for abortions to those which were "medically necessary." The Court considered whether the medically necessary distinction resulted in a denial of equal protection under the constitution, in that indigent women who wanted to have a medically unnecessary abortion might be precluded from doing so. The Court upheld the Connecticut regulation because it "placed no obstacles—absolute or otherwise—in the pregnant woman's path to an abortion. An indigent woman who desires an abortion suffers no disadvantage as a consequence of Connecticut's decision to fund childbirth; she continues as before to be dependent on private services she desired."[73]

Similarly, a requirement that the couples using surrogate parenting demonstrate medical necessity does not infringe upon the right of fertile couples to have children, since they may do so naturally. Additionally, couples who wish to use surrogate parenting outside of the recommended statutory framework will not have the benefit of court enforcement of their contracts.

In summary, it is the committee staff's

decided conclusion that surrogate parenting is a logical extension of the right to procreate, and accordingly, a part of the constitutional right of privacy. There are state interests and parties to be protected within the surrogate parenting arrangement, which necessitates state regulation of the surrogate parenting process. These restrictions, however, must be narrowly drawn to address the specific concerns of the state.

RECOMMENDATIONS

The fundamental issue considered in this report is whether the state should recognize the surrogate parenting contract as legal and enforceable and, thereby, ensure the legal status of the child. Based on the foregoing findings and analysis, the committee staff recommends that the legislature grant enforceability to surrogate parenting contracts and regulate the practice as set forth below.

THE ROLE OF THE COURTS

Judicial approval of the surrogate parenting agreement prior to insemination of the surrogate mother is the keystone of any legislation relating to the practice of surrogate parenting. For a contract to be enforceable, the parties should be required to apply to the Surrogate or Family Court, prior to insemination, to have the terms of the agreement reviewed and approved by the court.

Promoting the Interests of the Child

Recognition of the contract as legal and enforceable will ensure the legal status of the child born of a surrogate parenting arrangement for the purposes of determining parental responsibilities and rights of inheritance. If the state grants enforceability to the contract, it has an interest in determining before the agreement is concluded that the child will have a stable and suitable home. For this reason, legislation should authorize the court, at its discretion, to order an independent investigation prior to approval of

the agreement. This investigation may include the following information:

(a) the marital and family status, as well as the history, of the intended parents;

(b) the physical and mental health of the intended parents;

(c) the property owned by and the income of the intended parents;

(d) whether either parent has ever been respondent in any proceedings concerning allegedly neglected, abandoned or delinquent children; and

(e) any other facts relating to the familial, social, emotional and financial circumstances of the intended parents which may be relevant to the judge's decision.

Ensuring Informed Consent

Parties to a surrogate parenting contract agree to acts that have irrevocable consequences and involve physical and psychological risks. Accordingly, the state has an interest in ensuring that the parties are fully aware of their rights and responsibilities under the agreement and have sufficient information to intelligently weigh the risks against the benefits. Informed consent will help to assure that the transfer of parental rights at birth does not produce disruptions in the home environment of the child.

Before approving the surrogate parenting contract, the court should determine the following:

(1) that a physician licensed by the state has examined the surrogate mother and advised her of the physical risks she may assume in the course of insemination, pregnancy, and delivery;

(2) that a licensed mental health professional[74] has determined that the surrogate and her husband, if any, are capable of consenting to the termination of their parental rights and have been counseled about the potential psychological consequences of their consent;

(3) that the surrogate's husband consents to the artificial insemination of the surrogate;

(4) that the surrogate mother and her husband agree to assume parental rights if it is later determined, on the basis of paternity tests, that the intended father named in the agreement is not the true biological father of the child;

(5) that a licensed mental health professional has counseled the intended parents and determined that they fully understand the consequences and responsibilities of surrogate parenting and are prepared to assume parental responsibilities for the child born to the surrogate, regardless of the condition of that child;

(6) that each of the parties has had the advice of independent legal counsel in negotiating the terms of the agreement.

Preventing Exploitation

Legislation should allow payment of a reasonable fee to the surrogate mother. A prohibition of compensation would, as a practical matter, be a *de facto* prohibition of the practice itself. According to both hearing testimony and recent studies, most surrogate mothers would not participate in the arrangement without compensation.''[75]

Payment of a fee to the surrogate mother does not fall within the scope of Section 374 of the Social Services Law. The prohibition is intended to prevent the coercion of women who are already pregnant or who have already given birth to the child. The surrogate mother arrangement is distinguishable, since the surrogate mother's agreement to relinquish her parental rights occurs prior to conception. In addition, payment is made, not by some third party, but by the biological father who then gains custody of the child. Since the surrogate parenting contract is an agreement between the natural parents of a child, it should be exempted from statutory prohibitions against payment of compensation in adoptions.

Fees paid to the surrogate mother, attorneys, and infertility centers should be subject to judicial approval. In reviewing surrogate parenting contracts, the court should apply a standard of "just and reasonable compensation" to determine that all fees and compensation are equitable, appropriate to the services rendered, and without coercive effect.

Provisional Approval

The health and safety of both the child and the surrogate mother require that insemination be performed by a licensed physician and that tests for sexually transmitted diseases be completed before each insemination. For this reason, the court's approval of the contract should be provisional until the court receives a physician's certification that the natural father and the surrogate mother have been tested for sexually transmitted diseases, that the surrogate has been inseminated with the semen of the intended father, and that conception has occurred. The court's approval of the contract would then become final.

EFFECT OF COURT APPROVAL

The legislation should provide that any child born to a surrogate mother, in fulfillment of a contract approved by the court prior to insemination, shall be deemed the legitimate, natural child of the biological father and his wife. This statutory determination of parenthood would supplant any requirement that the wife of the natural father adopt the child. The intended father, named in the agreement, may rebut the statutory determination if paternity tests show conclusively that he is not biologically related to the child.

If either the natural father or his wife dies before the birth of the child, the terms of the contract should not be altered and the statutory determination of legal parenthood should remain in effect as to the survivor. If both intended parents die, the surrogate's consent to relinquish parental rights should be voidable at her option. If she elects to claim parental rights, the child would have inheritance rights from the natural father, but not from his wife. The intended parents should be encouraged to nominate a guardian for the child in the event they both die and the surrogate chooses not to claim parental rights.

CONTRACT ENFORCEMENT AND REMEDIES FOR BREACH

The surrogate mother's agreement to waive parental rights must be irrevocable and enforced at the birth of the child. Prior to delivery, the surrogate mother is deemed to have full control of the decisions relating to her pregnancy. Surrender of the child should be enforceable through the remedy of specific performance.

Parental obligations, such as support, should be enforceable against the intended parents from the time of conception. Breach of contract, e.g., refusal to accept parental responsibilities, should result in a judgment of support against the parents, since they will be the legal parents of the child by operation of the statute.

Breach of other provisions of the contract may be handled as the parties see fit in the terms of the contract. It is very important, however, that the monetary damages for breach of these provisions be limited to the amounts contained in the contract. No cause of action should be created for emotional distress or mental anguish due to the conduct of the parties during the contract period.

ELIGIBILITY

Surrogate parenting is the only solution to infertility for a couple when the woman cannot conceive or carry a child to term or would pass on a genetic defect. The same cannot be said for the use of a surrogate mother when the female of the couple is fertile. Although there are no documented cases of surrogacy for nonmedical reasons, the possibility exists that a couple may choose to employ a surrogate as a matter of convenience.

Given the scarcity of empirical evidence about how the surrogacy process affects those involved, it is recommended that the courts recognize only those contracts concluded between a surrogate mother and a couple, the female of whom is medically certified as infertile. Legislation should provide for a measure of proof by which medical necessity can be demonstrated to the court. The petition for court review of the contract should be accompanied by a statement signed by a licensed physician that the intended mother has a condition which makes conception or birth of a child unlikely or which creates a likelihood that a child of the intended mother will have a mental or physical impairment or disability.

CONCLUSION

Any surrogate parenting law must recognize the benefits the practice provides for infertile couples and resolve the present uncertainties regarding the legal status of the child. In order to ensure the smooth and peaceful transition of parental rights at birth, the law must ensure that all parties know, in advance, their rights and obligations under the agreement so that they may give informed consent to its provisions. In addition, the law must attempt to limit the possible abuses of the practice while preserving, to the greatest extent possible, the right of privacy in reproductive matters. It is submitted that the foregoing statutory recommendations meet these requirements.

NOTES

1. Aral and Cates, *The Increasing Concern with Infertility*, 250 J.A.M.A. 2327, 2327 (1986).

2. Center for Disease Control, *Infertility, United States 1983*, 34 *Morbidity and Mortality Weekly Report* 197 (1985).

3. Ontario Law Reform Commission, *Report on Human Artificial Reproduction and Related Matters* 10–11 (1985).

4. Aral, *supra* note 1, at 2329.

5. *Id.* at 2330.

6. Menning, *The Emotional Needs of Infertile Couples*, 34 Fertility and Sterility 313, 314–315 (1980).

7. Robertson, *Embryos, Families and Procreative Liberty; The Legal Structure of the New Reproduction*, 59 S. Cal. L. Rev. 939, 945 (1986).

8. Grobstein, Flower, Mendeloff, *External Human Fertilization: An Evaluation of Policy*, 222 Sci. 121, 127 (1983).

9. *Id.*

10. National Committee for Adoption, Adoption Factbook—United States Data; Issues Regulations and Resources 18–19 (1985).

11. *Id.* at 18.

12. *In Re Baby Girl L.J.* 123 Misc. 2d 972 (1986).

13. There is some indication that such long waiting periods can be shortened to as little as three to nine months when the adoption is arranged individually rather than through a public or private agency. According to the National Committee for Adoption, individually arranged adoptions are more likely now than they have been in the past fifteen to twenty years. Groups, such as the National Committee for Adoption, are concerned that quicker placements may be achieved by eliminating the safeguard procedures used by public and private agencies.

14. Grobstein, *supra* note 8, at 130.

15. Another form of surrogacy involves the surrogate gestational mother, who provides the gestational, but not the genetic, component of reproduction. The wife's egg is fertilized with her husband's sperm through *in vitro* fertilization, and the resulting pre-embryo is transferred to another woman who gestates and gives birth to the infant for the infertile couple. In these cases, the child is biologically related to both the husband and the wife, but not to the surrogate. This application of technology is indicated in cases where the wife has certain uterine problems, implantation difficulties, chronic miscarriage, or health problems that would make pregnancy harmful or lethal.

16. American Fertility Society, Ethics Committee, *Ethical Considerations of the New Reproductive Technologies;*, 46 Fertility and Sterility, Supplement 1. ls, 64s (1986).

17. Parker, *Motivation of Surrogate Mothers: Initial Findings*, 140 Am. J. Psychiatry 117, 118 (1983).

18. American Fertility Society, *supra* note 16, at 64s.

19. *New York Times*, Nov. 20, 1983, at 18.

20. The following fee structure is common: $6,500 to $10,000 for the infertility center, $10,000 for the surrogate mother, all medical expenses not covered by a surrogate's health insurance, $300 for psychiatric evaluation of the surrogate, travel expenses for the surrogate, term life insurance for the surrogate, $400 for an attorney for the surrogate, $400 for maternity clothes, $500 for paternity tests, and $500 in attorney's fees for the adoption.

21. Brophy, *A Surrogate Mother Contracts to Bear a Child*, 20 J. Fam. L. 263, 264 (1981–82).

22. Florida Step-Parent Adoption Act, F.S. Sec. 63.04 (2) (d).

23. Katz, *Surrogate Motherhood and the Baby-Selling Laws*, 20 Colum. J. L. & Soc. Prob. 1, 8 (1986).

24. Brophy, *supra* note 21, at 264.

56. Graham, *Surrogate Gestation and the Protection of Choice*, 22 Santa Clara L. Rev. 291, 318 (1982).

57. Ontario Law Reform Commission, *supra* note 3 at 103.

58. *Griswold v. Connecticut*, 381 U.S. 479 (1965), in which the court struck down a statute making it a crime for a married couple to use contraceptives.

59. *Roe v. Wade*, 410 U.S. 113, 152 (1973). (A Texas statute which outlawed abortions was found unconstitutional as it related to abortions performed throughout the entire term of pregnancy.)

60. *Ibid.*, at 159.

61. 316 US. 535 (1942).

62. *Ibid.*, 536.

63. *Maher v. Roe*, 432 U.S. 464, 472 (1977), citing *Skinner v. Oklahoma*, at 541.

64. 405 U.S. 438 (1972).

65. *Ibid.*, at 453.

66. 431 U.S. 678 (1977).

67. *Ibid.*, at 678.

68. *Harris v. McRae*, 448 U.S. 297 325 (1980).

69. *Griswold v. Connecticut Roe v. Wade, supra.*

70. *Carey v. Population Services, Inc, Id.* at 683.

71. *Carey, Id.* at 683.

72. *Supra* 432 U.S. 464.

73. *Ibid.*, at 474.

74. A mental health professional may be a psychiatrist, psychologist, clinical social worker, or a marriage, family, and child counselor.

75. Parker, *supra* note 17, at 118.

Surrogate Parenting in New York—II
New York State Task Force on Life and the Law

[The report excerpted below was released on May 28, 1988 by a twenty-nine-member task force appointed by Governor Mario M. Cuomo. During the same week, Assemblywoman Helene Weinstein introduced legislation to enact most of the task force's recommendations. The recommendations were still under consideration in the legislature in the spring of 1989.]

EXECUTIVE SUMMARY

PART I: THE MEDICAL, LEGAL AND SOCIAL CONTEXT

Surrogate parenting is not a technology, but a social arrangement that uses reproductive technology (usually artificial insemination) to enable one woman to produce a child for a man and, if he is married, for his wife. Surrogate parenting is characterized by the intention to separate the genetic and/or gestational aspects of child bearing from parental rights and responsibilities through an agreement to transfer the infant and all maternal rights at birth.

The well-publicized Baby M case has given surrogate parenting a prominent place on the public agenda. Nonetheless, the reproductive technologies used in the arrangements—artificial insemination and, increasingly, in vitro fertilization—also pose profound questions about the ethical, social, and biological bases of parenthood. In addition the procedures to screen donors raise important public health concerns. The Task Force will address these issues in its ongoing deliberations and recognizes that they form part of the context within which surrogate parenting must be considered.

Legal questions about surrogate parent-

From *Surrogate Parenting: Analysis and Recommendations for Public Policy*, by the New York State Task Force on Life and the Law, May 1988.

ing, although novel in many respects, arise within the framework of a well-developed body of New York family law. In particular, policies about surrogate parenting will necessarily focus upon two basic concerns in all matters involving the care and custody of children—the protection of the fundamental right of a parent to rear his or her child and the promotion of the child's best interests.

The Supreme Court of New Jersey has ruled that paying a surrogate violates state laws against baby selling. Surrogacy agreements may also be found invalid because they conflict with comprehensive statutory schemes that govern private adoption and the termination of parental rights.

In New York, it is uncertain whether surrogate parenting contracts are barred by the statute that prohibits payments for adoption. If not, it is probable that the surrogate could transfer the child to the intended parents by following private adoption procedures. If a dispute about parental rights arises before the surrogate consents to the child's adoption, custody would probably be determined based on the child's best interests. Regardless of the outcome, the court ordinarily will have no basis for terminating the parental status of either the surrogate or the intended father.

The right to enter into and enforce surrogate parenting arrangements is not protected as part of the constitutional right to privacy. Surrogate parenting involves social and contractual—rather than individual—decisions and arrangements that may place the rights and interests of several individuals in direct conflict. The commercial aspects of surrogate parenting also distinguish the practice from other constitutionally protected private acts. Constitutional protection for the right to privacy is diminished when the conduct involved assumes a commercial character.

The social and moral issues posed by surrogate parenting touch upon five central concerns: (i) individual access and social responsibility in the face of new reproductive possibilities; (ii) the interests of children; (iii) the impact of the practice on family life and relationships; (iv) attitudes about reproduction and women; and (v) application of the informed consent doctrine.

Surrogate parenting has been the subject of extensive scrutiny by public and private groups, including governmental bodies in the United States and abroad, religious communities, professional organizations, women's rights organizations and groups that advocate on behalf of children and infertile couples. Of the governmental commissions that have studied the issue, many concluded that surrogate parenting is unacceptable. In this country, six states have enacted laws on surrogate parenting, four of which declare surrogate contracts void and unenforceable as against public policy.

PART II: DELIBERATIONS AND RECOMMENDATIONS OF THE TASK FORCE

As evidenced by the large body of statutory law on custody and adoption, society has a basic interest in protecting the best interests of children and in shielding gestation and reproduction from the flow of commerce.

When surrogate parenting involves the payment of fees and a contractual obligation to relinquish the child at birth, it places children at risk and is not in their best interests. The practice also has the potential to undermine the dignity of women, children and human reproduction.

Surrogate parenting alters deep-rooted social and moral assumptions about the relationship between parents and their children. The practice involves unprecedented rules and standards for terminating parental obligations and rights, including the right to a relationship with one's own child. The assumption that ''a deal is a deal,'' relied upon to justify this drastic change in public policy, fails to respect the significance of the relationships and rights at stake.

Advances in genetic engineering and the cloning and freezing of gametes may soon offer an array of new social options and potential commercial opportunities. An arrangement that transforms human reproductive capacity into a commodity is therefore especially problematic at the present time.

Public policy should discourage surrogate parenting. This goal should be achieved through legislation that declares the contracts void as against public policy. In addition, legislation should prohibit fees for surrogates and bar surrogate brokers from operating in New York State. These measures are designed to eliminate commercial surrogacy and the growth of a business community or industry devoted to making money from human reproduction and the birth of children.

The legislation proposed by the Task Force would not prohibit surrogate parenting arrangements when they are not commercial and remain undisputed. Existing law permits each stage of the arrangement under these circumstances: a decision by a woman to be artificially inseminated or to have an embryo implanted; her voluntary decision after the child's birth to relinquish the child for adoption; and the child's adoption by the intended parents.

Under existing law on adoption, the intended parents would be permitted to pay reasonable expenses associated with pregnancy and childbirth to a mother who relinquishes her child for adoption. All such expenses must be approved by a court as part of an adoption proceeding.

In custody disputes arising from surrogate parenting arrangements, the birth mother and her husband, if any, should be awarded custody unless the court finds, based on clear and convincing evidence, that the child's best interests would be served by an award of custody to the father and/or genetic mother. The court should award visitation and support obligations as it would under existing law in proceedings on these matters.

To date, few programs have been conducted by the public or the private sector to prevent infertility. Programs to educate the public and health care professionals about the causes of infertility and the measures available for early detection and treatment could spare many couples from facing the problem. Both the government and the medical community should establish educational and other programs to prevent infertility. Resources should also be devoted to research about the causes and nature of infertility. . . .

DEVISING PUBLIC POLICY ON SURROGATE PARENTING

THE FRAMEWORK FOR PUBLIC POLICY

Contemporary American society is characterized by its pluralism. That pluralism embraces the rich and varied threads of different religious, moral and ethnic traditions. It requires a continued effort to express one's own world view and to understand those of others.

One hallmark of a pluralistic society is its commitment to individual freedom and to the right of individuals to choose their own path among the many different traditions and values that make up our social fabric. In particular, certain freedoms considered basic to the expression of personal identity and selfhood are accorded special deference. In the framework of our Constitution, this deference is shown by requiring government neutrality or non-interference with rights deemed fundamental, unless government can show a compelling interest.

Our social policies and law, however, reflect more than the celebration of individual liberty. A broad if seldom articulated consensus of shared values shapes and enriches our common experience. We therefore acknowledge society's interest in protecting and promoting those social values and institutions it deems primary to its collective life. The issue of surrogate parenting confronts

society with the need to weigh the competing claims of individuals involved in the arrangements and to strike an appropriate balance between the individual's freedom to make reproductive choices and other social and moral values.

Decisions about family life and reproduction are intensely private. The rights of adults to make reproductive choices have therefore been granted special protection and status.

Proponents of surrogate parenting assert that the right to enter into such an arrangement is part of the fundamental right to reproduce. They maintain that there is no conclusive or compelling evidence that surrogacy causes tangible harm to individuals. They argue that, without such evidence, society lacks any legitimate basis for intervention. In assessing what constitutes "tangible" harm, proponents dismiss appeals to shared norms and values as vague or symbolic, and hence inappropriate as the basis for public policy. Finally, proponents suggest that pluralism is best promoted by safeguarding and extending the rights of individuals.

The Task Force does not accept these assumptions as the basis for public policy for surrogate parenting. The surrogate contract is not part of a fundamental right supported on constitutional grounds or defensible as a basic moral entitlement. The claims of surrogates and intended parents to reproductive freedom in the context of surrogate arrangements are attenuated in several ways: by the commercial nature of the arrangements; by the potential conflicts between the rights of parties to the surrogate contract; and by the risks of harm to other individuals.

Many individual rights, like freedom of speech or the right of consenting adults to engage in sexual relations, are constrained when they enter the stream of commerce. They lose their strictly private or privileged stature and the claim they exert on society to non-interference and deference. The same holds true for the decision to conceive and bear a child. Society protects that choice when made privately and without financial incentives. Consistent with that protection, society is free to deny women the opportunity to make money from their gestational capacity and to deny others the right to pay someone else to reproduce.

Unlike privacy protections guaranteed to single individuals, surrogate parenting contracts involve potentially conflicting claims between individuals. These potential conflicts may place the surrogate's right to bodily integrity in conflict with a contractual obligation to submit to invasive medical procedures. Most obviously, the surrogate and the intended parents may have competing and irreconcilable claims to parental status and rights. The Task Force concluded that surrogate parenting arrangements also carry the risk of harm to others. Most serious are the potential risks to the children born from such arrangements. Members of the surrogate's family, including the surrogate's other children, might also be harmed.

Once it is recognized that surrogacy is outside the scope of the basic right to reproduce, the arguments by the proponents of surrogacy lose much of their force. Since the right to enter into a surrogate contract is not a fundamental right, society has no obligation to marshal evidence of tangible harm before devising policy on surrogate parenting arrangements. Proponents of surrogacy correctly point out that the risks to children or to the surrogates are unproven—no empirical data exists to confirm these predictions because the practice is so novel. Nonetheless, society can conclude that the potential or likely risks of a practice outweigh the benefits conferred without awaiting broad-scale social experimentation.

Moreover, surrogate parenting touches upon basic values and relationships in our private and collective lives: the interests of children, the role of the family, attitudes about women, and the potential commercialization of human reproduction. Society need not cast aside widely held norms or values about these issues in formulating public policy on surrogate parenting. As long as fundamental rights are not infringed, society can promote and protect a broadly shared vision of the public good. Indeed, our existing laws relating to such areas as the family, medical treatment and criminal sanctions, embody shared social values. Through these laws, society establishes a widely accepted framework within which individuals pursue a more particularized vision of the goods of life.

When no fundamental right exists, the possibilities for government intervention are broad. However, the possibility of such intervention does not render it desirable. Indeed, some strongly favor governmental neutrality on all issues when harm to individuals cannot be demonstrated. Under liberal political theory, this neutrality is viewed as the best assurance that individuals will be unhindered in pursuing their own moral choices.

Yet, even if society wished to adopt a neutral stance with regard to all social policies, it is clear that "neutral" alternatives for policy on surrogate parenting cannot be fashioned. Legislation that upholds the contracts lends the authority of both the courts and the legislature to enforce the agreements. Alternatively, legislation to void the contracts and withdraw the state's active involvement from the arrangements also cannot be considered neutral. Finally, government inaction, while neutral in theory, is not neutral in practice. When disputes arise, the parties will seek relief from the courts, forcing the articulation of public policy on a case-by-case basis. More significantly, however, the practice will proliferate through the existing commercial channels that have sprung up to promote it. The vacuum left by the absence of publicly articulated goals and values will be filled by the practices and mores of the marketplace. The result will not be neutral in any sense nor will the impact be limited to the commercial sector. Instead, the attitudes and practices that guide our most private relationships will be refashioned by commercial standards.

Society has a basic interest in protecting the best interests of children and in shielding gestation and reproduction from the flow of commerce, as evidenced by the large body of statutory law on custody and adoption. A "neutrality" that would leave such fundamental goods vulnerable to the dictates of the marketplace is contrary to the public interest.

AN ASSESSMENT: THE SOCIAL AND MORAL DIMENSIONS OF SURROGACY

The Task Force deliberated at length about the social, moral and legal issues posed by surrogate parenting. Its members began the deliberations with a wide diversity of opinion.

Ultimately, they reached a unanimous decision that public policy should discourage surrogate parenting. Divergent and sometimes competing visions form the basis for this conclusion. Their judgments are informed by different values, concerns and beliefs. The unanimous support for the conclusion reached is no less remarkable because of the diversity of opinion that underlies it.

The Task Force members share several basic conclusions about surrogate parenting. First, when surrogate parenting involves the payment of fees and a contractual obligation to relinquish the child at birth, it places children at risk and is not in their best interests. Second, the practice has the potential to undermine the dignity of women, children and human reproduction. Many Task Force members also believe that commercial surrogate parenting arrangements will erode the integrity of the family unit and values fundamental to the bond between parents and children.

The Task Force concluded that state enforcement of the contracts and the commercial aspects of surrogate parenting pose the greatest potential for harm to individuals and to social attitudes and practices. The conclusions and concerns expressed below relate primarily to these two aspects of surrogacy.

The Interests of Children

The Sale of Babies. Many Task Force members view surrogate parenting as indistinguishable from the sale of children. They reject the practice as morally and socially unacceptable because it violates the dignity of children and the societal prohibition against the purchase and sale of human beings. That prohibition rests on basic premises about the nature and meaning of being human and the moral dictates of our shared humanity. One such premise is respect for the inherent dignity and equality of all persons. Allowing one person to purchase another contravenes this premise and should be rejected regardless of the intentions or motivations of those involved.

The fact that it is the child's father who purchases the child from the child's mother (or, at the least, purchases her right to have a relationship with her child) does not change the character of the arrangement. Euphemisms like "womb rental" or "the provision of services," developed in part as marketing techniques, disserve the public by seeking to obscure the nature of the transaction. The intended parents do not seek a pregnancy or services as the ultimate object of the arrangement; they seek the product of those "services"—the child.

The surrogacy contracts themselves make this intent unmistakably clear. For example, the contract between Mary Beth Whitehead and the Sterns specified that the Infertility Center would hold $10,000 in escrow for Mary Beth Whitehead. If Mary Beth Whitehead had suffered a miscarriage prior to the fifth month of pregnancy, she would not have received any money under the contract. If she had a miscarriage subsequent to the fourth month of pregnancy or if the child died or was stillborn, her compensation would have been $1,000, an amount completely unrelated to the "services" performed. Likewise, if testing indicated that the fetus had genetic or congenital anomalies and Mary Beth Whitehead had refused to have an abortion and had carried the child to term, she would have received little or no compensation. Finally, all doubt about the nature of the contract is removed by virtue of the fact that Mary Beth Whitehead was not entitled to any compensation for her "services" alone; she was only entitled to compensation if she surrendered the product of those services—the child.

The Risks Posed. The Task Force concluded that surrogate parenting presents unacceptable risks to children. First, the fact that the practice condones the sale of children has severe long-term implications for the way society thinks about and values children. This shift in attitudes will inevitably influence behavior towards children and will create the potential for serious harm.

Surrogacy also poses more immediate risks to children. Under the arrangement, children are born into situations where their genetic, gestational and social relationships to their parents are irrevocably fractured. A child may have as many as five parents, or, frequently, will have at least four—the mother and her husband and the father and his wife. Where the birth mother has no genetic link to the child, the child has two mothers.

In contemporary family life, many children are denied the benefit of an ongoing relationship with both their biological parents. High divorce rates and the growing number of unwed mothers leave many children with a close connection to only one parent. When remarriage occurs, children are raised in a reconstituted family unit that does not share the bonds of genetic relationship. The same has always been true for children relinquished at birth or thereafter and raised by adoptive parents. Although some children thrive in these situations, others face greater risk of emotional harm or loss.

Unlike divorce or adoption, however, surrogate parenting is based on a deliberate decision to fracture the family relationship prior to the child's conception. Once parenthood is fragmented among persons who are strangers to one another, there is no basis to reconstruct the family unit or even to cope with alternative arrangements in the event conflict arises.

A child may be caught in the cross-fire of a fractious and lengthy court battle between his or her parents during the early years of the child's life, when stability and constant nurturing are vital. Alternatively, where the bonds of kinship are attenuated, children who are born with physical or mental anomalies are far more likely to be abandoned by both parents. Potentially, neither parent will have a bond with the child at birth; the mother because she successfully preserved her emotional distance and the father because he has not shared the pregnancy and has no relationship to the child's mother. While legislation or contractual agreements can apportion financial responsibility, they cannot compensate for the high risk of emotional and physical abandonment these children might face. Other potential dangers for children include the harm from knowing their mothers gave them away and the impact on brothers and sisters of seeing a sibling sold or surrendered.

Advocates of surrogate parenting suggest that any risks to children are outweighed by the opportunity for life itself—they point out that the children always benefit since they would not have been born without the practice. But this argument assumes the very factor under deliberation—the child's conception and birth. The assessment for public policy occurs prior to conception when the surrogate arrangements are made. The issue then is not whether a particular child should be denied life, but whether children should be conceived in circumstances that would place them at risk. The notion that children have an interest in being born prior to their conception and birth is not embraced in other public policies and should not be assumed in the debate on surrogate parenting.

The Dignity of Women and Human Reproduction

The gestation of children as a service for others in exchange for a fee is a radical departure from the way in which society understands and values pregnancy. It substitutes commercial values for the web of social, affective and moral meanings associated with human reproduction and gestation. This transformation has profound implications for childbearing, for women, and for the relationship between parents and the children they bring into the world.

The characterization of gestation as a "service" depersonalizes women and their role in human reproduction. It treats women's ability to carry children like any other service in the marketplace—available at a market rate, based on negotiation between the parties about issues such as price, prenatal care, medical testing, the decision to abort and the circumstances of delivery. All those decisions and the right to control them as well as the process of gestation itself are given a price tag—not just for women who serve as surrogates, but for all women.

The Task Force concluded that this assignment of market values should not be celebrated as an exaltation of "rights," but rejected as a derogation of the values and meanings associated with human reproduction. Those meanings are derived from the relationship between the mother and father of a child and the child's creation as an expression of their mutual love. Likewise, the meaning of gestation is inextricably bound up with the love and commitment a woman feels for the child she will bring into the world.

In a surrogate arrangement, the intended parents seek a child as a way to deepen their own relationship and to establish a loving bond with another human being. In the process, however, the birth mother uses the child as a source of income and, in turn, is used by the intended parents as a vehicle to serve their own ends. They seek the biological components of gestation from her while denying the personal, emotional and psychological dimensions of her experience and self. If she succeeds in denying her emotional responses during this profound experience, she is dehumanized in the process. If she fails, her attachment to the child produces a conflict that cannot be resolved without anguish for all involved.

Proponents of surrogate parenting urge that neither the surrogate nor the intended parents should be denied their right to choose the arrangement as an extension of their claim to reproductive freedom. Yet protection for the right to reproduce has always been grounded in society's notions of bodily integrity and privacy. Those notions are strained beyond credibility when the intimate use of a third person's body in exchange for monetary compensation is involved.

Women who wish to serve as surrogates would not be limited in their private choices to conceive and bear children—they would only be denied the opportunity to make money from their gestational capacity. Some Task Force members believe that this limitation is justified by the possibility of exploitation, especially in relation to poor women inside and outside of this country. They fear the creation of a class of women who will become breeders for those who are wealthier.

Other Task Force members concluded that the risk of exploitation could be minimized, but remained concerned about the potential loss to society. They believe that societal attitudes will shift as gestation joins other services in the commercial sphere; the contribution and role of women in the reproductive process will be devalued. Abstracted from the family relationships, obligations and caring that infuse them with meaning, gestation and human reproduction will be seen as commodities. Advances in genetic engineering and the cloning and freezing of gametes may soon offer an array of new social options and potential commercial opportunities. An arrangement that transforms human reproductive capacity into a commodity is therefore especially problematic at the present time.

The Family

The Family Unit. The family has long been one of the most basic units of our society—a repository of social and moral tradition, identity and personality. It provides the structure and continuity around which many of our most profound and important relationships are established and flourish.

Social and economic forces have challenged the traditional family unit. At the same time, high divorce rates and the incidence of unwed parents have changed the permanence of the family in the lives of many. Yet, these trends do not alter the importance of the family in our personal and communal lives.

Surrogate parenting allows the genetic, gestational and social components of parenthood to be fragmented, creating unprecedented relationships among people bound together by contractual obligation rather than by the bonds of kinship and caring. In this regard, surrogate parenting, like prenuptial agreements, has been viewed as an extension of a more general social movement from status (or kinship) to contract as a basis for ordering family relationships and the reproductive process.

Although some individuals now choose to shape aspects of their personal relationships with the principles and tools of contract law, society should not embrace this trend as a prescriptive standard. It embodies a deeply pessimistic vision of the potential for human relationships and intimacy in contemporary society. It promotes legal obligations as the touchstone for our most private relationships instead of fostering commitments forged by caring and trust. Rather than accept this contractual model as a basis for family life and other close personal relationships, society should discourage the commercialization of our private lives and create the conditions under which the human dimensions of our most intimate relationships can thrive.

The Relationship of Parent and Child. Surrogate parenting alters deep-rooted social and moral assumptions about the relationship between parents and children. Parents have a profound moral obligation to care for their offspring. Our legal and social norms affirm this obligation by requiring parents to care for their children's physical and emotional well-being.

Surrogate parenting is premised on the ability and willingness of women to abrogate this responsibility without moral compunction or regret. It makes the obligations that accompany parenthood alienable and negotiable.

Many of the Task Force members concluded that society should not promote this parental abdication or the ability of some women to overcome the impulse to nurture their children. Some Task Force members reject all third party donation to the reproductive process because it encourages adults to relinquish responsibility for biological offspring. Other Task Force members distinguish surrogacy from gamete donation because of the surrogate's direct and prolonged relationship to the child she bears.

Surrogate parenting also severs the second prong of the legal relationship that binds parents and children—parental rights. In fact, the practice involves unprecedented rules and standards for terminating both parental status and rights, including the right to a relationship with one's own child. Under existing law, parental rights cannot be denied without a showing of parental unfitness. This high standard embodies society's respect for the rights that flow from parenthood and the relationship those rights seek to protect.

Surrogate parenting rejects that standard in favor of a contract model for determining parental rights. Many Task Force members view this shift as morally and socially unacceptable. The assumption that "a deal is a deal," relied upon to justify this drastic change in public policy, fails to recognize and respect the significance of the relationships and rights at stake.

The Relationship Between the Spouses. Some Task Force members reject surrogate parenting and all third party donation to the reproductive process because they violate the unity and exclusivity of the relationship and commitment between the spouses. According to this view, procreation reflects the spiritual and biological union of two people; children born of that union manifest the uniqueness of the marital relationship. The involvement of a third person as surrogate or as gamete donor contravenes the spiritual and human values expressed in marriage and in the procreative process.

Some Task Force members also believe that an imbalance may be created in the marital relationship when only one parent is genetically related to the child. This imbalance may generate tension in the family unit rather than enrich the relationship between the spouses.

The Waiver of Fundamental Rights

Under the laws of New York and other states, parental rights and status cannot be irrevocably waived in advance of the time the rights will be exercised. By placing these rights as well as others beyond the reach of an advance agreement that is legally enforceable, society seeks to preserve those rights and the values they embody.

Many Task Force members believe that parental rights, including the right to a relationship with one's own child, deserve this special status. They do not view this as a limitation of individual freedom, but as a societal judgment about how that freedom is best protected.

The Task Force's proposal is consistent with existing adoption laws, which provide that a woman cannot consent to her child's adoption until after the child is born. Surro-

gate parenting should not be allowed to dislodge this long-standing public policy.

Informed Consent

Many of the Task Force members support the nonenforceability of surrogate contracts, in part because they believe that it is not possible for women to give informed consent to the surrender of a child prior to the child's conception and birth. Some commentators have argued that this conclusion diminishes women's stature as autonomous adults. The Task Force members reject that assertion.

The debate on surrogate parenting focuses on the ability of women to make informed choices—not because women differ from men in making important life decisions, but because women alone can bear children. The inability to predict and project a response to profound experiences that have not yet unfolded is shared by men and women alike. This inability often stems from the capacity for growth and an openness to experience in our relationships with others. These qualities are a positive and dynamic part of our humanness.

Denying women the opportunity to change their minds does not accord them respect; it limits their options and freedoms. Other avenues exist to inform or influence social attitudes about women. These avenues can be explored without penalizing women by demanding a degree of certainty and irrevocability we do not demand of men or women in making other vital life choices.

Many Task Force members believe that enforced removal of a child from the child's birth mother under a surrogate contract involves severe consequences for the birth mother. Studies have shown that many women who voluntarily relinquish children for adoption face a lingering and deep sense of loss. The harsh consequences of a poorly informed decision to relinquish one's child require a rigorous standard for consent before consent should be considered truly informed. This is why the adoption laws do not permit an expectant mother to surrender her child for adoption and insist that she await the child's birth before making such a decision. While some women have been able to anticipate their response in advance of the child's conception, the long gestational process and the child's birth, others have not. Our policies must recognize that many women may not be able to give informed consent in these circumstances.

RECOMMENDATIONS FOR PUBLIC POLICY

At the outset of its discussion about surrogate parenting, the Task Force recognized that society could choose any one of five broad directions for public policy, subject to constitutional constraints that might apply. Essentially, society could seek to prohibit, discourage, regulate or promote the practice or could take no action.

The Task Force proposes that society should discourage the practice of surrogate parenting. This policy goal should be achieved by legislation that declares the contracts void as against public policy and prohibits the payment of fees to surrogates. Legislation should also bar surrogate brokers from operating in New York State. These measures are designed to eliminate commercial surrogacy and the growth of a business community or industry devoted to making money from human reproduction and the birth of children. They are consistent with existing family law principles on parental rights and reproduction.

The Task Force proposes that surrogate parenting should not be prohibited when the arrangement is not commercial and remains undisputed. The Task Force concluded that society should not interfere with the voluntary, non-coerced choices of adults in these circumstances. Existing law permits each stage of these voluntary arrangements: a decision by a woman to be artificially inseminated or to have an embryo implanted; her decision after the child's birth to relinquish the child for adoption; and the child's adoption by the intended parents. The proposed

legislation would also not bar the payment of reasonable medical and other expenses to surrogates, if the payment is made as part of an adoption and is permitted by existing law.

The Task Force evaluated and rejected the option of upholding the contracts under the regulatory models proposed in many states. This regulatory approach squarely places the state's imprimatur on the surrogate arrangement. It employs the authority of both the legislature and the courts to uphold the contracts. Through these two powerful branches of government, society would be enmeshed in a long series of dilemmas and problems posed by the practice.

The regulatory approach has been justified and supported as the only way to protect the children born of surrogate parenting. The practice is seen as a trend that cannot be inhibited given the existence of the underlying technologies and the intense desire of infertile couples to have children, a desire that now fuels a growing black market in the sale of children. According to this view, regulation does not facilitate surrogacy, but merely accepts and guides its inevitable proliferation.

The Task Force found this justification for regulating and upholding the practice unpersuasive. The difficulty of discouraging a practice does not dictate social acceptance and assistance. Society has not legalized the purchase and sale of babies to establish a better marketplace for that activity despite the fact that both the children and intended parents might be better protected. The laws against baby selling embody fundamental societal values and doubtlessly minimize the practice even if they do not eliminate it.

Public policy on surrogate parenting should also reflect basic social and moral values about the interests of children, the role of the family, women and reproduction. A commitment by society to uphold the contracts removes the single greatest barrier to those considering the practice. In contrast,